Other books by JOEL E. COHEN

A MODEL OF SIMPLE COMPETITION

CASUAL GROUPS OF MONKEYS AND MEN:
STOCHASTIC MODELS OF ELEMENTAL SOCIAL SYSTEMS

FOOD WEBS AND NICHE SPACE

RANDOM MATRICES AND THEIR APPLICATIONS
(edited with Harry Kesten and Charles M. Newman)

COMMUNITY FOOD WEBS: DATA AND THEORY
(with Frédéric Briand and Charles M. Newman)

ABSOLUTE ZERO GRAVITY
(with Betsy Devine)

MUTUALISM AND COMMUNITY ORGANIZATION:
BEHAVIORAL, THEORETICAL AND FOOD WEB APPROACHES
(edited with Hiroya Kawanabe and Keiji Iwasaki)

How Many People Can the Earth Support?

JOEL E. COHEN

W · W · NORTON & COMPANY
New York · London

The text of this book is composed in Bembo
with the display set in Bembo
Composition and manufacturing by The Maple-Vail Book Manufacturing Group.
Book design by Jacques Chazaud

Library of Congress Cataloging-in-Publication Data

Cohen, Joel E.
How many people can the earth support? / Joel E. Cohen.
p.   cm.
Includes bibliographical references (p. 481) and index.
1. Population density.   2. Population—Economic aspects.
3. Population forecasting.   I. Title.
HB1953.C64   1995
304.6'1—dc20   95-6133

ISBN 0-393-03862-9

W. W. Norton & Company, Inc., 500 Fifth Avenue, New York, N.Y. 10110
W. W. Norton & Company Ltd., 10 Coptic Street, London WC1A 1PU

2 3 4 5 6 7 8 9 0

To my wife Audrey,
to our children Zoe and Adam,
and to our children's godfather
William T. Golden

Contents

HOW MANY PEOPLE
CAN THE EARTH SUPPORT?

PART 1

INTRODUCTION

1

Between Choices and Constraints

In the Beginning

SHORTLY BEFORE 1600 B.C., a junior scribe in what is now Iraq transcribed on three clay tablets a Babylonian history of humankind. This poem of 1,245 lines was already old at that time. In the poem, the Babylonian gods created humans on the Earth to do the onerous work of the lesser gods. The gods soon faced a problem:

> *Twelve hundred years had not yet passed*
> *When the land extended and the people multiplied.*
> *The land was bellowing like a bull,*
> *The god got disturbed with their uproar.*
> *Enlil heard their noise*
> *And addressed the great gods:*
> *"The noise of mankind has become too much for me,*
> *With their noise I am deprived of sleep.*
> *Let there be a pestilence (upon mankind)."*[1]

In Tablet II, the gods inflicted plagues to rid the Earth of the excess of humans. When all else failed, they flooded the Earth with the mightiest rainstorm ever. Only Atrahasis, the hero of the epic, survived. Then the gods repented and allowed humans to flourish again. However, to prevent their peace and tranquillity from being disturbed by too many people in the future, the gods imposed religious obligations of infertility on priestesses and created a demon to destroy infants and children.

Furthermore, let there be a third group of people. (Let there be) fertile women and barren women. Let there be the "Eradicator" (a name of *Lamashtu*) among the people and let her snatch the child from the lap of the mother. Establish *ugbabtu*-women, *entu*-women, and *igisitu*-women and let them be taboo and cut off [from] childbearing.[2]

This Babylonian epic, known to today's scholars as the Atrahasis epic, is perhaps the earliest extant account of human overpopulation and the earliest interpretation of catastrophes as a response to overpopulation.

Overpopulation appeared again as a problem for the gods in the lost post-Homeric epic *Cypria,* attributed to Stasinos. The *Cypria* is part of the Epic Cycle written in the period 776–580 B.C. Zeus's first response to overpopulation was to send the Theban War, which destroyed many people. But the problem persisted. After considering universal destruction of humans by flood or thunderbolts, Zeus was persuaded to engineer the birth of the beautiful Helen to provoke a war between the Greeks and the Barbarians.

There was a time when the countless tribes of men, though wide-dispersed, oppressed the surface of the deep-bosomed earth, and Zeus saw it and had pity and in his wise heart resolved to relieve the all-nurturing earth of men by causing the great struggle of the Ilian war, that the load of death might empty the world. And so the heroes were slain in Troy, and the plan of Zeus came to pass.[3]

The notion that gods impose war and plague to prevent the Earth from becoming too full of people persisted at least another two millennia, and survives in the thinking of some people even today.

Around 500 B.C. on the other side of the Earth from Iraq, Han Fei-Tzu complained:

People at present think that five sons are not too many and each son has five sons also, and before the death of the grandfather there are already 25 descendants. Therefore people are more and wealth is less; they work hard and receive little.[4]

Around A.D. 200, Quintus Septimus Florens Tertullianus wrote in *De Anima:*

Indeed it is certain, it is clear to see, that the earth itself is currently more culti-vated and developed than in early times. Now all places are accessible, all are documented, all are full of business. . . . everywhere there is a dwelling, every-where a multitude, everywhere a government, everywhere there is life. The greatest evidence of the large numbers of people: we are burdensome to the world, the resources are scarcely adequate to us; and our needs straiten us and complaints are everywhere while already nature does not sustain us. Truly, pesti-lence and hunger and war and flood must be considered as a remedy for nations, like a pruning back of the human race becoming excessive in numbers.[5]

In 1688, an anonymous author published in London a 24-page booklet of six "Curious enquiries." The fifth enquiry is entitled "Of Europes being too full of people." The author commented on massive unemployment: "how many miserable people lie up and down, begging and starving; and I am not so uncharitable to think, that all do it out of idleness, some there are, no doubt on't, that would work, and cannot get it."[6] The author advised emigration to America.

In 1758, 40 years before the English Reverend Thomas Robert Malthus (1766–1834) wrote his famous short essay on population, the Reverend Otto Diederich Lütken, rector of a parish on the island of Fyn, Denmark, published an article in *Danmarks og Norges Oeconomiske Magazin (Danish-Norwegian Economic Magazine)* entitled "An enquiry into the proposition that the number of people is the happiness of the realm, or the greater the number of subjects, the more flourishing the state." The article began:

> Since the circumference of the globe is given and does not expand with the increased number of its inhabitants, and as travel to other planets thought to be inhabitable has not yet been invented; since the earth's fertility cannot be extended beyond a given point, and since human nature will presumably remain unchanged, so that a given number will hereafter require the same quantity of the fruits of the earth for their support as now, and as their rations cannot be arbitrarily reduced, it follows that the proposition "that the world's inhabitants will be happier, the greater their number" cannot be maintained, for as soon as the number exceeds that which our planet with all its wealth of land and water can support, they must needs starve one another out, not to mention other necessarily attendant inconveniences, to wit, a lack of the other comforts of life, wool, flax, timber, fuel, and so on. But the wise Creator who commanded men in the beginning to be fruitful and multiply, did not intend, since He set limits to their habitation and sustenance, that multiplication should continue without limit.[7]

Concerns that the world has more people than it can accommodate, and that increasing human numbers will lead to painful corrective disasters, continue to this day. Here is a moderate expression of this point of view. In 1992, Walter J. Karplus, an even-tempered engineer at the University of California, Los Angeles, summarized what he called "The Scientific Prediction of Catastrophes in Our Time" and offered "a personal view":

> Overpopulation is the fountainhead of most of the other catastrophes discussed in this book. If only the world population were to become stable at, say, 50% or 75% of its present level, most environmental and public health problems would become more easy to manage. . . . if the world population continues to grow at its present rate, a plethora of catastrophes, including those represented by the Four Horsemen of the Apocalypse, will be certain to overtake us sooner or later. Ironically, these catastrophes will serve as feedback mechanisms to limit the population, albeit at a terrible cost in human suffering. For this reason, I believe that overpopulation is the most crucial global problem that we face today.[8]

Whether or not the Babylonian and Greek gods rightly judged the Earth to be too crowded, whether or not Karplus rightly judged that "Overpopulation is the fountainhead of most of the other catastrophes," it is clear that people of all times and many places have worried about having "too many" people.

In 1000 B.C., roughly 50 million people lived on the Earth.[9] Today's human population is at least 100 times larger, approximately 5.7 billion. It is tempting to laugh at the concerns of the Babylonians and Greeks and, by extension, to question the seriousness of today's concerns about human numbers. To take such concerns lightly might be a mistake for both past and present.

In the past, between 2200 B.C. and 1900 B.C., the Habur Plains of northern Mesopotamia turned to desert. The major cities were abandoned. The Akkadian empire abruptly collapsed. Climates changed and civilizations fell in the Aegean, Egypt, Palestine and the Indus.[10] At present, many people worry that today's societies, both industrial and technologically backward, are also vulnerable to ecological changes and to economic and social collapse.[11]

PROBLEMS

Problems of want and problems of wealth generate tremendous emotions. Those emotions are a sure sign that the causes and solutions of the problems are not thoroughly understood. Here are three anecdotal examples to show why some people are worried about population.

Calcutta, India

In February 1966, in the plaza in front of a train station in Calcutta, I saw dozens of people lying motionless on the ground in broad daylight. Each person was covered with a thin cloth from head to toe. Here and there a skeletal brown arm or foot spilled out from under its dust-gray cloth. Sometimes half a face, eyes shut, was bared to the sun. Passengers with trailing clouds of beggars, porters, hawkers and taxi drivers streamed past without concern, stepping over or around the motionless bodies. I asked my Bengali host whether the people lying on the plaza were dead or sleeping. He answered that Calcutta had perhaps half a million people whose only homes were the city's streets and sidewalks. As for these people, he tried to reassure me, "If a person does not move for three days, the stationmaster has him carted away."

Rural Kenya

A few months later, I stepped out of a Land Rover along a dusty track in Kenya, far from the capital, Nairobi, and far from the nearest paved road. A white foreigner getting out of a private vehicle immediately attracted curious children. What struck me first was not their stunted stature, not even the distended bellies of some of them. It was their eyes. As the children stared up at me, large, black flies walked around on the exposed whites and corneas of the children's eyes. The children did not blink or try to brush the flies away. The flies, I knew, could transmit trachoma, a common disease in the area. Infection, left untreated, could be expected to progress to blindness within months or years. Treatment with sulfa drugs or antibiotics was easy, if you had the drugs. The children and I had no drugs. Treatment would not prevent reinfection. As of 1990, half a billion people were at risk of trachoma and six to nine million people were blinded by it.[12]

New York City, United States

September 1992. My guest, Dr. Michiko Shimoda, a botanist from Hiroshima, Japan, came to see how America manages its wetlands. A bus tour of the wetlands of New Jersey departed at 8:30 A.M. from the American Museum of Natural History on a cool weekend morning. Dr. Shimoda and I walked across mid-Manhattan and through Central Park to reach the museum. In front of an expensive shoe shop on Madison Avenue, a homeless man loaded into a shopping cart the cardboard box in which he spent the night. In Central Park, other homeless men and women still slept on the green park benches or began to awaken. Joggers, bikers and roller-skaters zipped by.

On the tour, we stopped at a restored wetland area of the Hackensack River Meadowlands in New Jersey.[13] The hills that constituted the horizon behind us were immense garbage dumps—dumps that filled these wetlands and now looked down on them. The garbage hills were covered with a plastic membrane, then with several meters of soil, then with grasses, forbs and bushes.[14] Scattered among the garbage hills, white pumping stations sent down pipes to capture and collect the methane generated by the slow decay. Our tour group followed a floating walkway through what had been a swamp. To our right and to our left, towering over us, we saw a nearly pure stand of common reed, *Phragmites australis*. *Phragmites* (rhymes with "bag-MY-teas") tolerates disturbance and pollution, we were told. Inside the Nature Center next to the swamp, we saw an exhibit of the enormous diversity of plant species that inhabited these swamps before *Phragmites* took over.

Returning from New Jersey to Manhattan in the evening, our bus had to pass through one of the two traffic tunnels under the Hudson River. We waited in the congested traffic for our turn to enter the tunnel. Around us, powerful cars imported from around the world alternated between idling and slowly moving their occupants, mostly single individuals, forward a few meters.

What Do These Stories Mean?

For most people with normal human sympathies, stories such as these generate some emotional reaction. Often the emotional reaction leads to a strongly held conviction about who or what is to blame for the evident human suffering and waste. To some eyes, for example, the crowds and cadaverous bodies in front of the Calcutta train station have one cause, pure and simple: overpopulation.[15] To other eyes, Calcutta's crowded poverty is the legacy of forces that have little or nothing to do with overpopulation.[16] Other forces that have been cited include the alleged rapacity of the rich and the alleged indolence of the poor; India's traditional caste system, which allegedly keeps the poor from escaping their poverty; British colonialism, which allegedly extracted wealth from India instead of investing it there; allegedly misguided policies of foreign aid donors or of the Indian government, which catered to industrialization and the urban masses at the. expense of agrarian development and the rural poor, thereby attracting marginal peasants to the cities; Indian militarists who allegedly think that the only way to gain parity with China is for India's population to grow larger than China's, or who allegedly invest India's scarce resources in building atomic bombs to hold Pakistan and China at bay; Marxists who allegedly argue to the Indian government that large numbers of people can be a problem only under capitalism, or who oppose capitalism and free markets in the Indian economy; and the multinational running dogs of capitalist imperialism, who allegedly milk India for profits and interest even after the departure of British colonists.

This round-up of the usual suspects, from overpopulation to multinational corporations, should include at least one culprit to which your gut response is: "Yes, that's it!" and at least one hapless innocent to which your gut response is: "No, that has nothing to do with it!" My purpose is not to declare anybody right or wrong. I want only to shake any assumption that everyone agrees on an obvious cause or causes for the problems in India and Africa and New York.

THEMES OF THE BOOK

What is the scientific basis for concerns that the world has, or will soon have, more people than the world's economies, environments and societies can accommodate in acceptable ways? How many people can the Earth support? For the last several years, I have been trying to understand these questions and the answers to them. This book summarizes what I've learned. The remainder of this chapter outlines themes that will be developed throughout the book and explains how the later chapters are organized.

My first discovery was that I was not alone in not knowing how many people the Earth could support. Numerical estimates produced over the past century have ranged widely—so widely that they could not all be close to right—from less than 1 billion to more than 1,000 billion. More than half of the estimates fell between 4 billion and 16 billion people.

I also learned that the question "How many people can the Earth support?" is not a question like "How old are you?" which has exactly one answer at any given time. The Earth's capacity to support people is determined partly by processes that the human and natural sciences have yet to understand, and partly by choices that we and our descendants have yet to make. A numerical estimate of how many people the Earth can support may be a useful index of present human activities and of present understanding of how to live on the Earth; it cannot predict the constraints or possibilities that lie in the future.

Though the future is hazy, much that is very clear can be known about the present. First, the size and speed of growth of the human population today have no precedent in all the Earth's history before the last half of the twentieth century. Human numbers currently exceed 5.7 billion and increase by roughly an additional 90 million people per year. Second, the resources of every kind (physical, chemical and biological; technological, institutional and cultural; economic, political and behavioral) available to people are finite today both in their present capacity and in their possible speed of expansion. Today's rapid relative and absolute increase in population stretches the productive, absorptive and recuperative capacities of the Earth as humans are now able to manage those capacities. It also stretches human capacities for technological and social invention, adaptation and compassion.

The unprecedented growth in human numbers and in human power to alter the Earth requires, and will require, unprecedented human agility in adapting to environmental, economic and social problems, sometimes all at once. The Earth's human population has entered and rapidly moves deeper into a poorly charted zone where limits on human population size or well-being have been anticipated and may be encountered. Slower population growth, along with many other improvements in human institutions and behaviors, would make it easier for people to retain control of their fate and to turn their attention from the numbers to the qualities of humankind.

These themes have consequences for action. Stopping a heavy truck and turning a large ocean liner both take time. Stopping population growth in noncoercive ways takes decades under the best of circumstances. Ordinary people—including professionals and politicians—still have time to end population growth voluntarily and gradually by means that they find acceptable. Doing so will require the support of the best available leadership and institutions of politics, economics and technology to avoid physical, chemical and biological constraints beyond human control. Migration can ameliorate or exacerbate local problems, but at the global level, if birth rates do not fall, death rates must rise.

If most people would prefer a decline in birth rates to a rise in death rates, then they should take actions to support a decline in fertility[17] while time remains to realize that choice. In choosing how to encourage a global decline in fertility, people should be mindful of a major lesson of the twentieth century: tyranny by governments does not work in the long run. The focus of action should be to create conditions in which people voluntarily regulate their fertility to levels low enough not to require a rise in death rates. Though there is much more to learn about the best ways to do this, certain clearly useful options are already in hand and will be described.

This book is neither an alarmist tract nor a cornucopian lullaby. I personally am very concerned by the vast, inequitable and largely avoidable burdens of hunger, disease, violence, ignorance and poverty borne by too many billions of people. But I will not try to persuade you that the world will end in the next ten years unless everybody changes to a diet of soybeans and contraceptive pills, or that a universal diet of soybeans and contraceptive pills would eliminate hunger, disease, violence, ignorance and poverty. I am also very impressed by the worldwide dramatic improvements this century has seen in the expectation of life (the average number of years a newborn infant would live according to current death rates), in preventive and curative medicine, and in every area of technology, including food production, manufacturing, transportation, communication and information handling. But I will not try to persuade you that the world can easily and comfortably accommodate an unlimited number of additional people at any desirable level of material, mental and civic well-being.

I will describe some proposals for action offered by others and some of my own proposals at the end of the book. My proposals concern infrastructure for problem-solving. But my goal in writing this book is not to sell any specific actions. I aim rather to give a view of the Earth's human carrying capacity that recognizes the interactions among populations, economies, environments and cultures. I believe that if these interactions were better understood, and if more people were aware of these interactions, people could choose better actions themselves.

I write for those who seek factual information about where the human species and its companion species on the Earth are headed. I have in mind a bright, curious reader who takes an interest in important human issues, rejects oversimplification and understands that numbers can be helpful and illuminating. Just as I enjoy reading nontechnical but accurate accounts of current science in fields other than my own, I hope that scientists, scholars and students from other fields will turn to this book for a reliable account of what is known and for a frank confession about theories that are controversial.

This book omits much that is taught in conventional courses in demography. I have minimized the use of technical demographic concepts. You will not find here life tables, net rates of reproduction or intrinsic rates of natural increase, for example. On the other hand, the book includes much that most conventional courses in demography omit. Curiously, technical demography says very little about the absolute size of a human population. Apart from descriptive census totals, demographers generally avoid questions of scale, such as: what determines whether a population is large or small? and what are the consequences of large or small population size? The scale of the human population, though little treated in conventional demography, is a central topic of this book.

How the Book Is Organized

Rapid Population Change: No Precedent

Part 2 is a history of human population growth since the last ice age. While global population growth rates never exceeded 0.5 percent per year until 1750 or later, and never exceeded 1 percent per year until 1930 or so, growth rates since 1950 have never fallen below their present level of about 1.6 percent per year. With 5.7 billion people, a growth rate of 1.6 percent translates to more than 90 million additional people a year, or (allowing for compounding) roughly a billion additional people (five-sixths of the population of China) per decade. In absolute numbers, never before 1950 were so many people added to the Earth's population each year as now.

The percentage growth rate of world population was at its all-time peak of 2.1 percent per year around 1965–70. However, the smaller population size of 3.3 billion to 3.5 billion at that time meant that the annual absolute increment, roughly 70 million people per year, was smaller then than now.

In addition to the global population size and growth rate, the present differs radically from the past with respect to aging, energy, cities and contact of cultures.

The number and fraction of older people in the population now exceed any historical experience. For example, the fraction of population aged 65 years or more increased by more than half (from 7.6 percent to 12.1 percent) between 1950 and 1990 in countries where fertility began to fall significantly before 1950.

The human command of inanimate energy grew from 0.9 megawatt-hour per year per person in 1860 to nearly 19 megawatt-hours per year per person in 1990—in human terms, from the energetic equivalent of less than one to almost 19 full-time slaves per person. The energy gave people unprecedented power to alter, for better and for worse, their biological, chemical and physical environment. The environment provides the food people eat, the water they drink, the air they breathe, the energy they command, the plagues and pests they combat and the mountains, seas, lakes, streams, plants and animals that they enjoy and depend on. The environment is the theater in which political, social and economic institutions are the stage and scenery, and in which people are the actors and audience. While the size of the troupe and audience has grown faster than ever before, their power to furnish the theater gorgeously or to burn the place down has grown still faster.

The estimated fraction of people who lived in cities and towns with at least 20,000 people rose from 2 percent in 1800 to perhaps 45 percent in 1995. By 1995, more than 17 percent of the Earth's population lived in cities with at least three-quarters of a million people.

The cultural implosion of recent decades is the change that is most difficult to quantify. It is also the change that is potentially most explosive. Migrations within countries from rural to urban regions, migrations between countries from one poor country to another and, less frequently, from poor to rich countries, business travel, tourism, radio, television, telephone, fax, Internet, cassettes, newspapers and magazines—all have shrunk the world stage.

The Foggy Future:
Conditional Predictions and Sensitivity Analysis

Part 3 sketches how and what demographers know about the future of the human population. Part 3 is not the end of the book, because more can be known about the future of the human population than can be learned from demography.

For more than two centuries, scholars have devised mathematical methods for peering into the demographic future. With the recent rise of computers and systems analysis for war have come elaborate computer-based models, sometimes called "system dynamics" models. All of these methods have failed to predict events more than a decade or two in the future with quantitative accuracy.

From this bitter experience, demographers have learned to distinguish two kinds of predictions about the future: conditional predictions and unconditional predictions. Here is an example of a conditional prediction: "*If* I hit my thumb with a hammer, *then* it will hurt." This conditional prediction asserts that my thumb feels pain whenever I smash it with a hammer, but offers no assurance that I am about to smash it. Here is an unconditional prediction: "I am *going* to hit my thumb with a hammer and it *will* hurt." According to this unconditional prediction, I am going to hammer my thumb and pain will follow.

In the old days, before demographers learned the modesty born of egregious failure, demographic predictions were usually unconditional, or were at least not explicitly conditional. Those predictions frequently turned out to be wrong. The response of the profession was to retreat to conditional predictions. Most contemporary professional demographers are careful to emphasize that their predictions are the numerical consequences of assumptions that may or may not prove correct in the future. They try to lay out the assumptions as clearly and completely as possible. Usually the assumptions are formulated in terms of the demographic parameters that enter directly into the numerical calculations. *If* rates of birth, death and migration (by age, by sex, by location, by marital status and so on) are such-and-such, *then* population size and distribution will be so-and-so. Demographers call such conditional predictions "projections" to distinguish them from unconditional predictions of population size. If the arithmetic is done correctly, there is no arguing with projections.

Unfortunately, too often economists, politicians, planners, journalists and the general public forget that most demographic projections are really conditional predictions: "*If* fertility rates decline as expected, and *if* survival rates improve as expected, *then* population size will change like this." The assumptions (about rates of fertility and survival) and the outputs (regarding population size and structure) of demographic projections are rarely examined to see what they suppose about the biological, chemical and physical environment in which the projected population would live.

Conditional predictions may seem a weak tool, but in fact can be very powerful. Projections prepared by the United Nations show dramatically that *if* human populations continued to grow, in each major region of the world, at the rate presently observed in each, *then* the population would increase more than 130–fold in 160 years, from about 5.3 billion in 1990 to about 694 billion in 2150. The food required to feed 694 billion people cannot be grown by conventional agriculture on this Earth; the water required to grow the grain to feed that many people exceeds the water that falls from the skies. A clear conclusion from the United Nations' conditional prediction is that population growth rates must decline very substantially in some parts of the world within the next century and a half, or people must learn to eat without growing plants that transpire water back to the skies. If people do not live by bread alone, but also require water for domestic use, and desire clothing, space and other amenities, then some regional population growth rates must decline very substantially long before a century and a half from now.

Another powerful use of conditional predictions is to reveal when outcomes are very sensitive to small differences in assumptions or inputs. This use of conditional predictions is called sensitivity analysis.[18] A simple example of a sensitivity analysis goes like this: A population that grows constantly by only 1 / 1,000th of a percent per year will eventually exceed any fixed size you can name.[19] If the population decreases constantly by only 1 /1,000th of a percent per year, the population will eventually go extinct. If the population growth rate is exactly zero, obviously the population will neither explode nor disappear. The long–run fate of a population with a constant relative growth rate depends "sensitively" on whether the relative growth rate is slightly above zero, exactly equal to zero or slightly below zero.

A much more realistic (but substantially equivalent) sensitivity analysis by the United Nations[20] showed that future global population size is very sensitive to the future level of average fertility. If, hypothetically, from 1990 onward the average couple gradually approached a level of fertility that was just one-tenth of a child *more* than required to replace the parents, then world population would grow from 5.3 billion in 1990 to 12.5 billion in 2050 and 20.8 billion in 2150. By contrast, if, hypothetically, from 1990 onward the average couple gradually approached a level of fertility that was just one-tenth of a child *less* than required to replace the parents, then world population would grow from 5.3 billion in 1990 to an all-time peak of 7.8 billion in 2050 and would drop to 5.6 billion in 2150. If, hypothetically, starting in 1990 and ever after the average couple had exactly as many children as required to replace the parents, then world population would grow from 5.3 billion in 1990 to 7.7 billion in 2050 and would level off around 8.4 billion by 2150.

The Earth's Finite Limits: Where Are They?

No matter what any human law says about individual liberties, parents cannot long continue to have, on the average, more children than required to replace themselves. The finiteness of the Earth guarantees that there are ceilings on human numbers. The levels of these ceilings are tremendously uncertain. They depend on human choices (the behavior of individuals and institutions) and on natural constraints. Some people believe that any ceiling on human numbers is so remote that its existence is irrelevant to present human concerns. Others assert strongly that the present human population of the Earth has already exceeded what the Earth can support in the long run (the meaning of "the long run" is usually left unspecified); they argue that a gradual decline, if not an abrupt crash, in human numbers is inevitable. Still others concede that limits in the short run may exist, given present technologies, institutions and values, but argue that technologies, institutions and values will adapt to changed conditions in ways that are impossible to predict, with the effect of pushing ceilings higher and higher. They would conclude that, like my hairline, the limits may recede forever.

In 1679, the Dutch inventor of the microscope, Antoni van Leeuwenhoek (1632–1723), published the earliest quantitative estimate I have found of the maximum number of people the Earth can support. He estimated a maximum of 13.4 billion people. In 1765, a German regimental pastor, Johann Peter Süssmilch (1707–1767), compared his own estimate of 13.9 billion with three earlier estimates, by Leeuwenhoek (13.4 billion), the French military engineer Sebastien Le Prestre de Vauban (1633–1707) (5.5 billion) and the English writer and cartographer Thomas Templeman (who died in 1769) (11.5 billion). Dozens of additional estimates, making a variety of assumptions, have been published since then, most of them in ignorance of previous estimates (Appendix 3).

Part 4 reviews these estimates in two passes. In the first pass, I describe in detail eight estimates made since 1891. Looking closely at these examples brings out the issues and the unstated assumptions in the remaining examples. In the second pass, I go back to the (apparent) beginning with Leeuwenhoek and summarize more than 65 estimates of maximal global population and several estimates of local human carrying capacity for China, the United States, Australia and Brazilian Amazonia.

I then examine the concepts of carrying capacity in basic and applied ecology to see if they will serve for human populations. I conclude that the question "How many people can the Earth support?" cannot be answered using only ecological concepts. Human choices influence the Earth's human carrying capacity along with natural constraints. Water is a prime example of the natural constraints on human carrying capacity; like other natural constraints, limitations set by water interact strongly with human choices and with limitations of time.

To set the stage for an overview of human carrying capacity, I briefly retell the story of Easter Island, which has been proposed by others as a model for the rise and possible fall of the Earth's human carrying capacity.

I conclude that estimates of human carrying capacity may usefully serve as dynamic indicators of humans' ever-changing relations to the Earth. At any given time, a *current* but changing human carrying capacity is defined by the *current* states of technology; of the physical, chemical and biological environment; of social, political and economic institutions; of levels and styles of living; and of values, preferences and moral judgments.

As an aid to thinking about the dynamic interactions between population growth and human carrying capacity, I describe in Appendix 6 a playground for the mind. A simple mathematical model of the race between the growth in human carrying capacity and the growth in the human population highlights the diverse possible scenarios in a make-believe world system. The model shows that the recent historical record of superexponential population growth, accompanied by an immense improvement in average well-being, is logically consistent with very different possible futures, which depend on each additional person's effect on carrying capacity: continued expansion, or a rapid sigmoidal tapering off of the growth in both population size and carrying capacity, or oscillations (damped or periodic), or chaotic fluctuations, or overshoot and collapse. Logic alone will not choose among the alternatives. To believe that no ceiling to human population size or carrying capacity is in prospect you have to believe nothing will stop additional people from increasing the Earth's carrying capacity by more than, or at least as much as, they consume of the Earth's carrying capacity.

What to Do?

In Part 5, I review some suggestions for the future proposed by others and offer my own suggestions. Thoughtful suggestions are of three kinds: those intended to increase human productive capacities ("make a bigger pie"); those intended to reduce the number and expectations of people to be served ("put fewer forks on the table"); and those intended to change the terms of people's interactions ("teach better manners").

Approaches that put fewer forks on the table include ways to slow and stop population growth and ways to reduce material inputs and outputs per person. Without suggesting that other approaches matter less, I shall dwell on stopping global population growth.

The global population growth rate can fall from its present value of around 1.6 percent per year to zero or below only by some combination of fewer births and more deaths.[21] Hardly anybody favors more deaths.

International programs to slow population growth by lowering fertility began in the early 1950s, almost simultaneously with the greatest surge in population growth the world has ever known. The six main approaches have been: family-planning programs that promoted modern contraceptives and provided supporting services; economic development and modernization; reducing infant and childhood mortality so parents would feel secure with fewer children; empowering women through education, jobs, credit and other opportunities outside the home; educating men in general, and particularly about their responsibilities in sexuality, childrearing and homemaking; and combinations of the previous approaches. Whatever their impacts on fertility and population growth, all six of these approaches are worth pursuing simply because of the benefits they confer on mothers, fathers and children.

My four suggestions concern infrastructure for solving population problems. I suggest: developing institutions that balance the goals of efficiency and equality; improving accounting of social well-being, material flows and the consequences of actions; integrating knowledge of populations with knowledge of economies, environments and cultures; and creating a better understanding of mutual aid, including a quantitative documentation of the benefits that the well-off derive from helping the poor live better lives.

Numbers and the Law of Information

Numbers have played a large role in the study of populations since it began. In 1662, in a pioneering book on demography, John Graunt, "Citizen of London," begged his reader's indulgence for attention to numerical detail:

> I have taken the pains, and been at the charge, of setting out those *Tables,* whereby all men may both correct my *Positions,* and raise others of their own: For herein I have, like a silly Schole-boy, coming to say my Lesson to the World (that Peevish, and Tetchie Master) brought a bundle of Rods wherewith to be whipt, for every mistake I have committed.

Today scholars transmute sex and death (rugged Middle English words!) into the concepts of fertility and mortality (smooth Latinate words) and tame them with numerical measures and models. The numbers are inescapable and indispensable. Numbers alone, for example, reveal that a population that grows every year by 1.6 percent doubles its size in fewer than 44 years. Numbers alone reveal that a world population that continued to grow as it was growing, region by region, in 1990 would reach 11 billion by 2025. Numbers alone reveal that, in the long run, it is impossible for any population to have a long average lifetime, a high birth rate and a total size that is not growing; any two of the three are possible, yes, but not all three.

But numbers carry two dangers: they are partial descriptions, and they are not vivid enough as a means of communication. Numbers oversimplify the realities of the people whose births and deaths they describe.[22] To avoid being misled by the simplicity of numbers, it is important always to remember that behind demographic numbers are individual people. Births, migrations, marriages and deaths—the subjects of novels and demography—shape and are shaped by human psyches as they interact with economics, culture and biological and physical environments. Numbers also fail to stir emotionally and to motivate action on the part of many people who view them.[23] To avoid remaining unmoved by the stark abstraction of numbers, try to put yourself, in your imagination, in the place of the people described by demographic numbers. When you read that, in a poor country now (as in the United States or United Kingdom around 1915), one new-born in ten dies before the age of one year, imagine yourself that child's parent or sister. You can give the numbers human meaning.

How Many People Is a Billion People?

Numbers play a large role in this book, and they frequently count billions of people. The Earth has 5.7 billion. Its population is currently increasing by about a billion a decade. A billion people currently lack safe drinking water.[24] The world has nearly a billion Muslims, nearly a billion Roman Catholics and just over a billion Hindus and Buddhists combined.[25]

How many people is a billion people? I use billion in the American sense, not in the French or German sense. In the American sense, a billion is 1,000 million, or 1,000,000,000, or 10^9. The small superscript ^{9} means that 10 is to be multiplied by itself nine times, thus: $10 \times 10 \times 10 \times 10 \times 10 \times 10 \times 10 \times 10 \times 10 = 10^9$.[26]

Here are some ways to visualize a billion people. Imagine two American football fields side by side. That area is roughly 100 meters by 100 meters, or one hectare. If you stacked a city of 100,000 people (roughly the 1990 population of Albany, New York, or Sioux Falls, South Dakota[27]) on each square meter, you'd have a billion people on that hectare.

If a billion people spaced 38 centimeters (15 inches) apart (the distance from my elbow to the knuckles on my fist) formed a straight line, then, ignoring such minor physical constraints as gravity and the hazards of outer space, the line would go from the Earth to the moon (at the moon's average distance from the Earth).

In case you do not have a very good intuitive feeling for how far away the moon is, imagine a square field a bit less than 32 kilometers (nearly 20 miles) on each edge. If one person occupied one square meter of space, that field would hold a billion people.

Another way to get a feeling for a billion people is to think in terms of familiar nations or regions. In round numbers, a billion people equals four times the 1990 population of the United States (250 million); or five-sixths of the 1992 population of China (1.17 billion); or the sum of the 1992 populations of Latin America (453 million), all of Europe (511 million) and Oceania (28 million); or the combined 1992 populations of India (883 million) and Indonesia (185 million).[28]

The Limits of Statistics and the Law of Information: How Many People Has India?

Most people are aware that words vary widely in precision. "Living creatures" include plants, animals, fungi and bacteria, among others; animals

TABLE 1.1   Estimates of the population
of India in 1990 and 1991

date	population size	source
mid-1990	849.5 million	World Bank 1992, p. 218
mid-1990 "provisional"	827,057 thousands	United Nations 1992b, p. 146
mid-1990 "estimate"	853.4 million	Population Reference Bureau 1990
1990	853.09 million	World Resources Institute 1992, p. 247
1 March 1991 "provisional"	843,930,861	United Nations 1992b, p. 146
1 March 1991	844,324,222	Europa 1992, p. 1362 (attributed to Central Statistical Office, New Delhi)
July 1991	866,351,738	Central Intelligence Agency 1991, p. 141

include elephants; Jumbo was a famous circus elephant exhibited by P. T. Barnum in the United States; and Jumbo in his youth differed from Jumbo in his prime. Fewer people appreciate that numbers also vary widely in precision, and that the apparent precision of demographic numbers is frequently illusory.

Despite their superficial similarities, the numbers of mathematics and the numbers of statistics (including those of demography, economics and all the natural and human sciences) are different beasts. The numbers of mathematics come from logical calculations; the numbers either are exact or have known or estimable errors. The numbers of statistics come from empirical measurements; these numbers may have unknown errors, or estimates of error that are themselves vulnerable to error. For example, the 1990 census of the United States was estimated to undercount the population by 2.1 percent (an omission of more than five million people) until computer errors were discovered and statistical changes were made that lowered the estimated undercount to 1.6 percent (roughly four million).[29]

Uncertainty does not render statistical numbers worthless; even with uncertainty, statistical numbers are indispensable. They are often far more informative than verbal descriptions or intuitive hunches. But every statistical number should enter your consciousness with a penumbra of doubt. What is the precision of this number? How were this number and its uncertainty estimated?

Published figures for the population of India in 1990 and 1991 illustrate the point (Table 1.1). Since India's population is estimated to be growing at 2.1 percent per year (how accurate is that figure?), one would expect an annual increase of nearly 18 million on a base population estimated at 850 million. It is expected that estimates at different dates are substantially different. In addition, it would not be surprising if the Indian census had an uncertainty at least as large as that of the U.S. census of 1990, around 2 percent. On a base of 850 million, this could add an uncertainty of 17 million. The lowest and highest population figures in Table 1.1 differ, over one year, by 39,294,738, to be misleadingly precise.

Evidently the nine-digit precision of numbers like 844,324,222 and 866,351,738 for the Indian population is totally illusory. At most the first two digits have meaning. The second digit (counting tens of millions) could be off by three or more. The mid-1990 population of India was probably between 820 million and 850 million. India has one of the finest statistical bureaucracies and one of the most outstanding statistical traditions in the world. But the disease of spurious precision (apparent arithmetic precision that makes no scientific sense) is endemic in demographic and many other official statistics, and not only those of India.

Take an example from economic statistics. Is the 1990 gross national product per person of India U.S.\$300[30] or U.S.\$350[31] or something else altogether? How would a correction for the purchasing power of money in India affect the estimate? By definition, gross national product increases as capital depreciates, but fruit you can pluck from a tree counts for nothing. How good is the gross national product per person as a measure of what you want to know?

In this book, I avoid numerical estimates with three, four or even nine digits of precision when the estimates cannot be accurate to more than a few percent. I express all relative rates as a simple decimal fraction or as a percent, and avoid the plethora of demographic rates (often with illusory precision) given in units per thousand, per ten thousand, per hundred thousand and per million.

You are now warned. Every measurement of the real world carries a penumbra of uncertainty. In demography, the shadow of uncertainty is often longer than is conceded. Numerical measurements are an indispensable crutch, but every crutch has a bit of flex, and some numbers are a rubber crutch. The Law of Information states: 97.6 percent of all statistics are made up. Of course, the Law of Information applies to itself.

PART 2

———

PAST
HUMAN
POPULATION
GROWTH

2

Four Evolutions
in Population Growth

POPULATION GROWTH IS LESS LIKE IT USED TO BE
THAN IT EVER HAS BEEN BEFORE

THOUGH ISOLATED POPULATIONS have grown rapidly, never before World
War II did the entire human population grow as rapidly as it has grown
since then. Never has the human population of the Earth been nearly as big
as it is now. These are the main points of Part 2 of the book. Part 3 and
Part 4 together show that the current global rate of population growth cannot long continue—probably even for a century—with anything like present human behavior and institutions, technologies and expectations of well-
being (material, political and esthetic). It follows that the human species
either is passing through a transient peak of global demographic growth
(the more likely alternative) or, if rapid demographic growth continues, is
about to enter a period of revolutionary change in human behavior and
institutions, technologies and well-being that will make the changes of the
Industrial Revolution look staid. Barring the unlikely scenario of recurrent
large population booms and crashes put forward in 1963 by the British
astronomer Sir Fred Hoyle, the present peak of population growth is likely
to be unique in all of human history.

As I stated in the introduction, in 1995 the total number of people on the
Earth was approximately 5.7 billion and the annual increase in the total
number of people on the Earth was around 90 million. These two numbers
alone show that the present growth of the human population differs radically from its average growth over most of human history.

If the world's population had increased throughout its history by the same number of people as it increased over the last year, then the population would have started from zero 63 years ago,[1] and the original Adam and Eve of the 1930s would have had to have some 90 million offspring in their first year. This is not a plausible account of the world's demographic history.

The relative growth rate of the population during the previous year was 90 million, last year's increase, divided by the population size at the beginning of the previous year, or roughly 5.6 billion. This works out to about 1.6 percent.[2] (When you go to a ball game, you follow it with a score card. When you go to the opera, you follow it with a libretto, score or at least the plot summary—and binoculars, if you sit where I sit. You will have more fun with this book if you follow the calculations with your pocket calculator, and check me as we go.) If the world's population increased through its history at the same relative rate as over the last year, 1.6 percent per year, then the population would have started from Adam and Eve roughly 1,370 years ago, around A.D. 625.[3]

Even Archbishop James Ussher, Primate of All Ireland, who calculated that God created the universe in 4004 B.C., would agree that human history is much longer than 1,370 years, and therefore would have had to concede that the present relative growth rate could not have been sustained for most of human history. Ussher determined the moment of creation to be October 23 at noon.[4] The Oxford divine and Hebraist John Lightfoot revised Ussher's calculations and concluded that creation occurred on October 26 at 9 A.M., the date and time that are quoted in many texts.[5] I shall avoid taking sides in the controversy over whether the creation occurred on October 23 at noon or October 26 at 9 A.M.

As a further confirmation that the present relative growth rate of population could not have been sustained for most of human history, let's play just one more arithmetic game before turning to what actually happened in population history. The last ice age ended at various dates in different parts of the world, but let us take a typical figure of 12,000 years before the present. Archeological evidence is firm that there were by then substantial human populations on all the continents except Antarctica. If there had been only one person 12,000 years ago, and that population had grown (parthenogenetically, at first) at an average rate of 1.6 percent per year, the Earth's population now would be $(1+0.016)^{12,000}$ or approximately 5.3×10^{82} people.[6] Finding matter to construct this number of people would be a problem because the number of charged particles in the entire known universe is approximately 10^{80}, or 100 times smaller.[7]

If your calculator has not burned out yet, you should check how sensitive these conclusions are to errors in the two numbers on which the calculations are based. Would it make much difference to the conclusions drawn if the actual population of the Earth this year were 5.0 billion or 6.0 billion? Would it make much difference if the relative growth rate were 1.4 percent per year or 2.0 percent per year? (I know of no professional demographer who suggests that the current population size or growth rate lies outside of these ranges.) The answer, in every case, is the same. Even if the current

TABLE 2.1   Relation between relative change
per year and doubling time

relative change per year (*percent*)	estimated doubling time (*years*)[a]
0.1	693
0.5	138.6
1	69.3
1.5	46.2
2	34.7
2.5	27.7
3	23.1
4	17.3

[a]The estimated doubling time is equal to 69.3 divided by the relative change (percent per year), rounded to the nearest 0.1 year. The exact doubling time, which equals the natural logarithm of 2 divided by the natural logarithm of (1 + percentage change per year), is slightly larger in each case, but never more than half a year larger in the examples shown.

data are not exactly correct, the current absolute and relative change of population could not have been sustained over most of human history.

Firm conclusion: the current increase of the Earth's human population, in either absolute or relative terms, vastly exceeds the average increases that occurred over most of human history. Over most of its history, the human population experienced an average growth rate that must have been a tiny fraction of its current rate of growth, whether that growth is measured absolutely (in numbers per year) or relatively (in percent per year).[8]

Growth Rate and Doubling Time

For many people, an annual growth rate of 1.6 percent is much less vivid than saying that a population growing constantly at that relative rate would double in just over 43 years. There is a simple way to convert a constant annual relative growth rate into an approximate population doubling time, defined as the number of years of exponential growth required for a population to double. You divide the relative growth rate, expressed as a percent per year, into 69.3 (69 is close enough for most practical purposes, and 70 is easier to remember); the answer is the approximate number of years (Table 2.1). In this case, 69.3 / 1.6 = 43.3. If world population continues to grow at its present rate of 1.6 percent per year, it will double in 43 years. In general, if the annual relative change is small, then

doubling time (years) = 69.3 / annual relative change (percent per year).

To learn where the number 69.3 comes from, look in the notes for this chapter.[9]

More important than the formula is the meaning of the resulting numbers. So long as Ethiopia, with a 1990 population growth rate of 2 percent per year, grows at that rate, its population doubles in 35 years; while Mali and Niger, with 1990 annual growth rates estimated at 3 percent, double in 23 years if their population growth continues at that rate. These statements are not predictions that the populations of Ethiopia and Mali and Niger *will* continue to grow at these rates; in fact, continued growth at these rates is extremely *unlikely*. These statements, like a speedometer reading of kilometers per hour, describe how far their populations will have traveled *if* they continue in the same direction at their present rate of growth.

By contrast with present growth rates, the *average* global population growth rate for the 10,000 years prior to the birth of Christ was almost certainly less than 0.051 percent per year. (I give the details later.) At that growth rate, human societies and the Earth had 13 to 14 centuries to accommodate a doubling in human numbers.

So much for arithmetic. Now let's look at historical estimates of the human population.

AN OVERVIEW OF FOUR EVOLUTIONS
IN HUMAN POPULATION GROWTH

Historical knowledge of past human population sizes is a quilt of tiny pieces of fact (archeological remains, monuments, documents, observations of present human and nonhuman populations) patched together with large portions of conjectures and assumptions.[10] Estimates of past populations are often based on local, partial counts made for other purposes. The Babylonians probably counted population officially by 3800 B.C., the Chinese by 3000 B.C. and the Egyptians by 2500 B.C.[11] Governments organized these early counts to estimate taxes or to control military manpower. The counts were often limited to property holders or to men of military age. Such counts were probably at least as subject to efforts at evasion as some censuses are today. The fragmentary early census figures provide a flimsy basis for global population estimates. The Earth's population probably could not be known with an uncertainty of less than around 20 percent before the middle of the eighteenth century.[12]

The oldest surviving census of an entire state is found in a 1427 cadastre, or official land registry for taxes, of Tuscany. The first successive national censuses took place in New France (currently Quebec), starting in 1665. Because the Bible reported that God punished King David for the impudence of carrying out a military census, there was considerable trepidation when the United States instituted regular decennial censuses in 1790. After two U.S. censuses were completed without apparent divine retribution, Britain conducted its first census in 1801. Most Western countries counted their entire populations systematically and published detailed results only beginning in the second half of the nineteenth century. Civil authorities in most Western countries registered births and deaths systematically only in the nineteenth century.[13] Russia conducted its first census only in 1897, and few tropical African countries conducted censuses until after World War II.[14] Even today, there has not yet been one complete census of the world's population, and demographers still rely on estimates to help construct world totals.

Human demographic history differed from the hypothetical models of constant absolute growth or constant relative growth in at least two important ways. First, population growth differed from one place to another.[15] While Babylonian and Hittite cities were rising in what are now called Iraq and Anatolia (Asian Turkey), what is now Europe probably saw no comparable cultural or demographic growth, and parts of South America may have been still unpeopled.

Second, population growth varied as time passed: now faster, now slower, sometimes even negative. The population biologist and ecologist Edward S. Deevey, Jr., of Yale University suggested in 1960 that human population sizes experienced three periods of rapid rise (rapid by past standards, not rapid compared to twentieth-century population growth): first, before 100,000 B.C. when people discovered how to use and make tools; second, from 8000 B.C. to 4000 B.C. when people discovered or invented agriculture and cities; and third, in the eighteenth century when people discovered science and industry. Between these periods of rapid rise, Deevey suggested, were much longer periods of nearly stationary population size or very slow growth.[16]

Samples from today's human populations of the DNA in a cellular organelle called the mitochondrion suggest a different picture.[17] Modern humans may be the survivors of a dramatic reduction, from perhaps 100,000 to 10,000, in the numbers of an ancestral human. This drop in population probably occurred at the time of the last Pleistocene ice age, perhaps 80,000 to 100,000 years ago. The survivors slowly spread over the Old World and then began to expand rapidly at different times in different places—80,000 years ago in Africa, in a dozen other populations about 50,000 years ago and 40,000 years ago in Europe.

In sketching the history of global population sizes, I shall skip the incompletely known story before 10,000 B.C. and add two great changes that are absent from Deevey's summary: one, a great surge in population growth that started shortly after World War II, numerically the most important surge so far in human history; and two, the all-time peak in the global population growth rate in 1965–70 and then its initial decline. Neither Deevey nor anyone else foresaw this momentous crest and decline in the global population growth rate or even recognized it as it was happening.

I propose to summarize the surges and ebbs of human numbers over the last dozen millennia as four "evolutions": the local agricultural evolution (from the end of the last ice age until about 3000 B.C.), which took place at various times in Africa, the Middle East, Asia and Meso-America; the global agricultural evolution (from about A.D. 1650 to 1850), which pooled

TABLE 2.2   Four evolutions in human population growth

name of evolution	date in the middle	population (billions)	doubling time (years)	
			before	after
local agricultural	8000 B.C.	0.005	40,000–300,000	1,400–3,000
global agricultural	A.D. 1750	0.75	750–1,800	100–130
public health	1950	2.5	87	36
fertility	1970	3.7	34 (peak)	more than 40 (since 1990)

the cultivars developed on different continents and which coincided with the Industrial Revolution; the public health evolution (starting about 1945 and not yet complete); and, overlapping the two previous processes, the still-unfinished evolution in fertility (starting around 1785 in France and the United States and not yet begun in some places even today). The first three were increases in global population growth rates. The last is a halting decline in the global population growth rate as a result of reduced fertility. (A decline in the growth rate is not a decline in the number of people. A decline in the growth rate is only a decrease in the percent of increase per year.)

From the dates alone it is clear that these evolutions were hardly discrete events. Different evolutions lasted from millennia to decades. They overlapped in time because they occurred at different times in different places. Certainly the last two evolutions, and possibly the last three, are not independent: the current worldwide decline in fertility is at least partly driven by the consequences of the preceding population growth. Telling the story as four major steps is an expository convenience that should not disguise the coupling among the steps. Table 2.2 gives a glimpse of the story ahead in round numbers.

I prefer the word "evolution" to the more conventional term "revolution." The changes resemble more the biological pattern of cumulated, haphazard, small innovations leading to fundamental novelty than the political pattern of concentrated, intentional disruption leading, often, to new management of the same old store. The Italian economist Carlo M. Cipolla argued that the changes during what I named the local and global agricultural evolutions were revolutionary: "The Agricultural Revolution of the eighth millennium B.C. and the Industrial Revolution of the eighteenth century A.D. . . . created deep breaches in the continuity of the historical process. . . . The first 'Revolution' transformed hunters and food-gatherers into farmers and shepherds. The second one transformed farmers and shepherds into operators of 'mechanical slaves' fed with inanimate energy."[18] On the other hand, Donald L. Hardesty, an anthropologist at the University of Nevada, Reno, emphasized that England's population growth in the eighteenth century followed previous waves of population growth around

1300 and 1600 and previous spurts of economic development, including the mining and smelting of tin, lead and iron and the production of salt, pottery, wool for export and finished woolen goods. "A final population spurt in the eighteenth century brought about the 'industrial revolution' so well known to us all. It would better be called the industrial 'evolution,' since it merely continued trends started much earlier."[19] Evolution or revolution, choose the term you prefer; I won't argue.

3

People Control the Growth
of Nonhuman Populations

The Local Agricultural Evolution:
8000 b.c.–4000 b.c.

Before the several local inventions of agriculture, local human populations grew at long-term average rates just above zero. Where agriculture
was invented, local human populations grew ever so slightly faster.
Whether the invention of agriculture enabled the population to grow faster
or a faster-growing population was driven to devise agriculture, or both—
these remain questions for speculation.

A Latecomer to Domestication

The inventions of agriculture have ancient roots. The Earth formed some
4.6 billion years ago. Life has animated its surface for at least the past 3.5
billion years, and perhaps as long as 4.0 billion years.[1] By one billion years
ago, cells with nuclei wrapped in a membrane ("eukaryotic cells")
appeared. Early eukaryotic cells eventually led to plants and animals by a
sequence of steps that is still being investigated.[2] Among the animals,
within the last one-thousandth of the Earth's history appeared anatomically
modern *Homo sapiens*.

A remarkable feature of the earliest eukaryotic cells set the pattern for
much of later life. In addition to a nucleus (which is the defining characteristic of a eukaryotic cell), with its genetic material DNA, apparently all eukaryotic cells have organelles with their own genetic material. These organelles include chloroplasts in green plants (which contain the chlorophyll that

captures the energy of sunlight), various other plastids, and mitochondria (the powerhouses of cells). These genetically equipped organelles look like microbes that moved into the cell and stayed. Over the past half century, the theory has become generally accepted that these organelles originated in precisely this way.[3]

In time, both the host cell and each organelle came to depend on one another, to find one another indispensable and, ultimately, to reproduce together. This is an early example of a recurrent theme in the history of life. Initially separate organisms with different genomes (sets of genes) formed indissoluble partnerships in which the reproduction of each depended on the reproduction of the other. The combination developed vastly greater capabilities than either partner had separately.[4]

Many variations of this theme arose in all the kingdoms of life. Some of the most striking occur among the social insects.[5] For example, termites depend completely on their intestinal protozoans and bacteria to digest the cellulose in their diet of wood. The intestinal microorganisms depend on their termites to feed them wood and to propagate them to the next generation of termite hosts. Younger termites receive the protozoans that digest cellulose by feeding from the anus of older termites. This arrangement requires some social behavior and may have been a cause of social life in termites.[6]

Thousands of species of arthropods—from at least 17 orders, 120 families and hundreds of genera—live in mutually beneficial partnerships on or among social insects.[7] The ties that bind social insects to other social insect species, other arthropods and even vertebrate species are sometimes bizarre and beautiful. For example,[8] in England, when caterpillars of a certain lycaenid butterfly, the Chalk-hill Blue *(Agriades coridon),* are feeding on plants, ant workers (of the species *Lasius flavus*) stroke the backs of the caterpillars with their forelegs and antennae. In response, the larvae discharge beads of a certain crystal-clear fluid from a special gland on their seventh abdominal segment, which the ant workers then consume ("greedily," in the words of one observer). If the ants do not regularly remove the fluid exuded by this special gland, the caterpillars soon die. The ants protect the lycaenid caterpillars from predators and parasites, sometimes building "cattle-sheds" of earth around them like those they build for honeydew aphids.

In this comparative perspective, humans' discovery or invention of agriculture—the domestication of plants and nonhuman animals for food—after the last ice age is hardly a novelty. It is only a novelty for hominids, coming after more than 99 percent of their four-million-year history on the Earth so far.

The anthropologist Sidney W. Mintz of Johns Hopkins University observed:

Domestication really means controlling the reproduction of some other living thing, a process that human beings have been able to effectuate with animals and plants not just once, but at many different times and with different living things: rice, soybeans, and pigs in Asia; potatoes, llamas, and guinea pigs in the Andes; tomatoes, chocolate, chili, and turkeys in Meso-America; millet, okra, and one species of rice in Africa; olives and cabbage in Europe. Each was domesticated by nameless ordinary people and bequeathed to us by cultural inheritance. . . . Domestication is probably the single greatest technical achievement in the human record, more important than the internal combustion engine or nuclear energy. It was, from the beginning and long before these other triumphs, a remarkable way to capture and control energy.[9]

While humans naturally dwell on the benefits of domestication to themselves, from a more neutral point of view it is equally remarkable that all these domesticated species managed to engage the services of the adaptable and fecund *Homo sapiens* to further their own propagation, often at the expense of their ecological competitors. Men and women became the servants, as cultivators, of a dozen or so grasses, most importantly wheat, barley, oats, rye, maize, rice and the millets; and perhaps another dozen rhizomes or tubers, mainly manioc (cassava), sweet potatoes, potatoes, taro and yams. Most major societies in world history built their food supplies around sheep, goats, cattle, pigs and these dozen plants.[10]

Discovery of Agriculture, Invention of Cities

People began to practice agriculture roughly 10,000 to 12,000 years ago, after the glaciers withdrew from the hills north and east of Mesopotamia, in present Iraq. One theory is that the climatic change forced the withdrawal or extinction of the large ice-age mammals on which the hunters had depended. Another theory is that, with milder weather, the people survived better and hunted the large mammals to extinction.[11]

Either way, forest-dwelling hill people turned to plants in the woods for sustenance. They discovered that they did not have to wait for falling trees or other natural accidents to allow sunlight to reach the forest floor, where it would stimulate the growth of plants they could eat. Rather, with stone tools, they learned to cut away a belt of bark around trees. Girdling trees in this way killed the leaves and eventually the trees. The early farmers then seeded the litter of the forest floor with desirable plants. After a few years, when the standing dead trees had dried and the nutrients on the forest floor had been depleted, the farmers burned the trunks and enriched the litter with the ashes. After a few more years, when the yields again dwindled, the farmers moved to another patch in the forest. Such was "slash and burn" agriculture. Initially, the number of people was so small and the forest so big that each abandoned patch lay fallow for enough years to restore the patch's fertility.

These early farmers used three tools that had mattered little to hunters: axes to girdle and cut the trees, hoes to stir the leaf litter before seeding and sickles to harvest matured grain.[12] These technical advances over hunting and gathering whatever food nature happened to provide at the time had immense consequences. The ability to produce food allowed human numbers to increase greatly and made it possible, eventually, for civilizations to arise.[13]

Natural stands of wheat and barley were found on some hillsides. Though the details are surrounded by uncertainty, grasses began to be cultivated for their grains in the Middle East between perhaps 8500 and 7000 B.C. By this time, bands of hunters had probably not yet reached the southern tip of South America.[14] Grain cultivation may have spread from Mesopotamia westward into Europe and Africa; there is scholarly controversy about the possibility that it also spread eastward into Eastern and Southern Asia. Agriculture probably arose independently in the Americas (more than once), monsoon Asia and west Africa.[15] If the Middle East was the earliest hearth of domestication, it preceded the others by only a few thousand years.

People learned to domesticate indigenous animals as well as indigenous plants. Keeping dogs improved the effectiveness of hunting, making it easier for people to acquire meat and other useful animal products like bone (for tools and utensils), hides (for clothing and shelter) and sinews (for binding). By learning to milk domesticated sheep, goats and cows, people found substitutes for human milk. Because lactation delays the return of ovulation after pregnancy, the use of animal milk to supplement or replace human milk could have permitted women to begin menstrual cycling sooner than otherwise, increasing the number of potential births.[16]

With a more dependable food supply came a great surge in human numbers, compared to the population until then, along with substantial alterations of the natural environment and great changes in human behavior and social organization. An important change in social organization was the development of social hierarchies, in which some individuals commanded the labor of others. Settled villages in the Tigris and Euphrates river valleys became numerically important between 4000 B.C. and 3000 B.C. Around the same time or shortly after, urban communities or states also arose in the Nile and Indus river valleys. While hunter–gatherers followed the migrations of game animals and the seasonal availability of natural plants, farmers had to plant in the right season, to work the fields regularly and to save seed grain for the future.[17] Irrigation made it possible to cultivate more lands and to harvest rich crops from the same fields year after year. Building irrigation canals and dikes required cooperation among the field workers. Irrigated agriculture yielded surplus food that could support specialists in war, governance, healing, religion, art and eventually science.

Plows first appeared in the Sumerian plains of the Tigris and Euphrates river valleys, near the coast of the Persian Gulf, probably not long before 3000 B.C. When they coupled domesticated animals to tillage, Sumerian farmers benefited from the strength of their draft animals and thereby greatly increased their ability to produce an agricultural surplus from a variety of soils under varied climatic conditions. The plow thus contributed directly to further population growth. The plow had other equally important effects.[18] It created the farmer's field, a flat, smooth stretch of ground, because the plow could not easily turn or adjust to the ups and downs typical of a forest floor. Unlike a small, transient, burned patch in the forest, the field was a major investment of the farmer's labor and became a permanent alteration of the landscape. The plow tied the farmer to a place.

The plow also made cereal cultivation and animal husbandry mutually dependent and mutually beneficial, as animals could draw the plow and the crops could feed the animals, but may have intensified competition between those who wanted land for grazing and those who wanted it for cultivation.

On a longer time scale, the plow, by pulverizing the soil and weakening its cover of plants, made soil more vulnerable to erosion by wind and water. According to the soil expert Daniel Hillel, "In the history of civilization, contrary to the idealistic vision of the prophet Isaiah, the plowshare has been far more destructive than the sword."[19]

Like the plow, fruit trees also tied the farmer to a place. For example, date palms, which were very important in Mesopotamia, required several years of care before they bore fruit. The rest of the fascinating story of the rise, diffusion and interaction of civilizations is told elsewhere.[20]

In the local agricultural evolution, the global population growth rate increased. Since the growth rate of global population is its birth rate minus its death rate, it is natural to ask how the global population birth rate and death rate changed. Though no direct evidence is available to test speculations about Neolithic demography, a likely possibility is that both rates rose during the local agricultural evolution, with a slightly greater rise in birth rates.[21] Why would death rates have risen among the early farmers? Settled villages concentrated people in the vicinity of their own wastes, possibly contaminating water, food and soil. Dependence on crops could have increased vulnerability to crop failures due to crop diseases, pests and fluctuations of weather. In any event, if global death rates rose, then global birth rates rose slightly further.

Which Came First, Chicken or Egg?
A Digression on Explanation

Did the local agricultural evolution make possible a dramatic rise in the global population growth rate? Or, conversely, did a rise in the global population growth rate after the last ice age impel the local agricultural evolution? It is unfortunately impossible to prove a direction of causality in that remote period. The problem of inferring causes survives even today.[22]

Many have suggested that the invention or discovery of plant cultivation opened the way for population growth. But if people then had the option of hunting abundant animals and gathering abundant fruits and seeds, why would they have gone through the hard labor, and suffered the very long delays, of cultivating what must have been at first marginally satisfying grass seeds? Perhaps their own prior population growth exhausted the supply of game animals and drove people, in desperation, to cultivation; perhaps population growth stimulated the invention of agriculture, which in turn facilitated further population growth.[23] A third possibility is that an independent factor, such as climatic warming, eliminated the large game animals and simultaneously improved the survival of humans and of cultivable plants and animals. Archeological data do not support or exclude any of these possibilities; rather, archeologists interpret their data in terms of the theory that they find congenial.

The uncertainty about the directions of causation in the local agricultural evolution echoes through the interpretation of many later demographic changes. In fact, the theories of Malthus from 1798 on shaped archeologists' views of earlier events. Malthus was the first professional economist in Britain and the first Professor of Political Economy at Haileybury College of the East India Company.[24] He argued that unrestricted populations grow exponentially (that is, with a constant relative growth rate, like compound interest) while the production of food can grow at best linearly with increasing time (that is, by a constant absolute amount per year, like simple interest). Therefore, conditions permitting, populations grow to exhaust the available resources. If this were so, then a population could rise only after an increase in food production, through the opening of new lands or a change in the technology of food production. Malthus and his contemporary, the British economist David Ricardo (1772–1823), and others argued that, with a given supply of land and equipment, each additional worker could add to production, but the incremental product per worker decreased as the number of workers increased. As population grew, they argued, the addition to production would fall to the level that the additional worker considered just sufficient for survival, and population growth would then cease. By this process, the population would rise until it was in so-called equilibrium with its resources of land and equipment (or capital).

In opposition to this view, the French philosopher Marie-Jean-Antoine-Nicolas Caritat, Marquis de Condorcet (1743–1794), as well as twentieth-century economists such as Ester Boserup of Denmark and Julian Simon of the United States, and many others from the eighteenth century onward argued that necessity is the mother of invention, that population growth can stimulate technological innovation.[25] In a comment on Malthus in 1844, Friedrich Engels adopted this point of view even before he met Karl Marx:

> Has it been proved that the productivity of the land increases in an arithmetical progression? The extent of land is limited—that is perfectly true. But the labour power to be employed on this area increases along with the population; and even if we assume that the increase in yield due to this increase does not always rise in proportion to the labour, there remains a third element—which the economists, however, never consider important—namely science, the progress of which is just as unceasing and at least as rapid as that of populations. . . . Science increases at least as fast as population. The latter increases in proportion to the size of the previous generation. Science advances in proportion to the knowledge bequeathed to it by the previous generation and thus under the most ordinary

conditions grows in geometrical progression—and what is impossible for science?[26]

Part of Engels's point was espoused, perhaps unwittingly, by former president George Bush of the United States. When the Congress declared the week of 20 October 1991 as World Population Week, Bush issued a proclamation to recognize the legislature's resolution. His proclamation stated: "Population growth in itself is a neutral phenomenon . . . every human being represents hands to work, and not just another mouth to feed."[27]

Ronald D. Lee, a demographer at the University of California, Berkeley, called these viewpoints the "two grand themes in macro-demographic theory: the Malthusian one, that population equilibrates with resources at some level mediated by technology and a conventional standard of living; and the Boserupian one, that technological change is itself spurred by increases in population."[28]

Lee synthesized an ingenious theory in which the hypotheses of Malthus and Boserup both operate. Under additional important assumptions of his own, he investigated whether a combined Malthus-Boserup system would, in theory, expand forever. If diminishing returns will eventually set in as labor and technology increase while resources remain constant, and if maintaining any technological level requires maintaining the human and physical capital stocks that implement the technology, then "the system does not move onward and upward for ever, but rather, after first accelerating, then decelerating, it comes to rest at a high-technology–high-population stable equilibrium, beyond which neither increases in population nor technology can be sustained."[29] According to Lee's analysis, "progress to the highest technologies might occur by transition through a sequence of intermediate stable equilibria, at each of which the system might be indefinitely delayed. Premature population growth, or premature restraint, might render the passage from one stable equilibrium to a higher one much less likely."

By synthesizing two apparently conflicting causal explanations into a dynamic system governed by both, Lee showed that there are intelligible, analyzable alternatives to overly simple explanations of complex historical changes. We are not condemned to think linearly ("A causes B, B causes C, C causes D, . . .") about historical processes that don't work that way.

Population Patterns Depend on the Scale of Observation in Time and Space

Over long time periods, the global population grew on the average very slowly during prehistoric and early historic millennia. Over shorter periods, global population sometimes fell. For example, the fourteenth century saw what historian Barbara Tuchman called "the most lethal disaster of recorded history." Repeated waves of the Black Death, a form of bubonic plague, together with wars, heavy taxes, brigandage, insurrections and

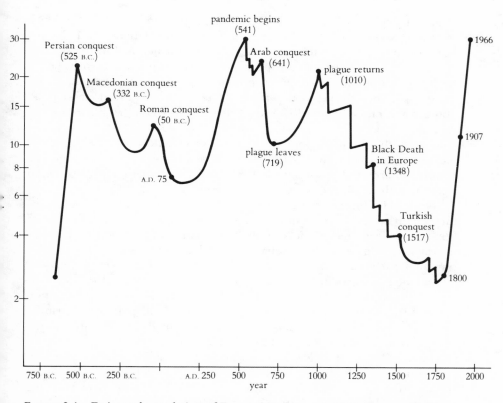

FIGURE 3.1   Estimated population of Egypt, 664 B.C.–A.D. 1966. SOURCE: Hollingsworth (1969, p. 311, Fig. 5)

poor and sometimes malicious governments "killed an estimated one third of the population living between India and Iceland."[30] The French demographer Jean-Noël Biraben estimated that global population fell at least three times in the last two millennia: between the second and fourth centuries, between the sixth and seventh centuries, and in the fourteenth century.[31] A widely cited British atlas of population history by historians Colin McEvedy and Richard Jones recognized only the fourteenth century as a time of global population decline.[32]

The general smoothness of global population changes concealed some dramatic local rises and falls. The examples of Egypt and England and Wales will make the point.

According to the reconstruction by a British historical demographer, T. H. Hollingsworth (summarized in Figure 3.1), the population of Egypt rose from less than 3 million in the seventh century B.C. to a peak in excess of 20 million at 525 B.C.[33] Following conquests by the Persians (525 B.C.), Macedonians (332 B.C.) and Romans (50 B.C.), the population fell to 7 million in the first century A.D. Population again rose for several centuries until, starting in A.D. 541, a sequence of plagues and Arab and Turkish conquests was accompanied by erratic falls in population. By 1750, the Egyptian population returned to the same level it had had in the seventh century B.C., around 3 million people. Population growth then began in earnest. Though the rises in population look very rapid in Figure 3.1, none exceeded 1.5 percent per year, a growth rate lower than the global population growth rate now and lower than that of every country in continental Africa in 1990.[34]

In 1966, the Egyptian population was approximately 30 million people, the same as its size just before the pandemic of A.D. 541. Since 1966, Egypt's population growth has continued. The estimated population in 1990 was 55 million, with an annual increase of 2.9 percent.

Some of Hollingsworth's population estimates prior to the twentieth century differ substantially from other estimates. An independent reconstruction by a team of geographers shows a population of 3 million in 500 B.C., instead of Hollingsworth's estimated 20 million at 525 B.C.; and a population falling from 3.4 million to 2.6 million between A.D. 400 and A.D. 600, instead of Hollingsworth's 30 million just before the pandemic of A.D. 541.[35] In spite of differences in the population sizes, this reconstruction shows a similar pattern of dramatic ups and downs: the population changes direction, from rising to falling or from falling to rising, 20 times in the interval from 4100 B.C. to A.D. 1800, with continuing growth since then.

The population of England and Wales grew steadily after the Norman conquest, long before the arrival of New World food plants or the Industrial Revolution, until the Black Death of 1348 killed a large fraction of the population. From its peak in the early 1300s to its trough in the early 1400s, the population of England and Wales dropped by roughly one-half, from 4 million to 2 million. By the middle of the fifteenth century, population was again on the rise, but leveled off for a full century from the mid–seventeenth to mid–eighteenth centuries.[36]

Another British historian of population, E. A. Wrigley, modestly conceded: "The causes of long-term fluctuations of this sort are obscure."[37] Among the possible causes of population decline that Wrigley considered were climatic cooling that shifted previously cultivable land to grazing or pasture only, and diseases such as bubonic plague, smallpox and virulent dysentery. Whatever the causes, the effects are clear: the population of England and Wales in 1400 was about the same as it was in 1200, in spite of having doubled between those dates.

These examples, and many others like them that could be offered, show that the apparent pattern of population growth (smooth steady growth versus wide fluctuation) depends heavily on the size of the region and the duration of time over which population growth is observed. For example, for nearly four centuries up to the pandemic of A.D. 541, and again for nearly 300 years from the departure of plague in A.D. 719 to the return of plague in 1010, Egypt's population experienced steady growth; viewed as part of a longer time interval, however, these periods of growth were each part of a cresting wave about to crash. The population of Meso-America fell by perhaps 80 percent or 90 percent during the sixteenth century, while the populations of Santo Domingo and Tasmania almost disappeared after early contacts with European explorers and settlers.[38] The smooth changes in global population size during the last dozen millennia averaged the wide fluctuations of many local populations. At least some of these local populations had an upward drift to their growth patterns, but many others declined or became extinct.

Two anthropologists at the University of California in Berkeley, Eugene A. Hammel and Nancy Howell, suggested that the search for global explanations of global population phenomena (growth or stasis) may be misguided, at least for the early stages of human history. From its earliest expansion on, the population of *Homo sapiens* was no longer a localized breeding population, but was rather a dispersed collection of such local populations.[39]

Evidence of fluctuating local populations does not conform to a neat ecological theory that has been proposed to interpret human population history. Some ecologists theorized that organisms fall along a continuum between two extreme types. At one extreme, according to this theory, organisms with small body size have prolific fertility but relatively poor survival of offspring. The parents produce large numbers of progeny but give them little care or protection. In this theory, populations of small organisms grow rapidly when the environment is favorable to the survival of offspring, but crash if the environment is unfavorable to their survival.

At the other extreme, still according to the theory, organisms with large body size have fewer offspring. The offspring tend to survive well because the parents protect them. Populations of large organisms grow slowly and steadily in propitious environments and are less prone to population crashes in unfavorable environments.

According to this theory, in fluctuating environments, organisms prodigal in their offspring are expected to experience wide fluctuations in population size as they are buffeted by the environment through periods of boom and periods of bust. Organisms with few, well-tended offspring are expected to experience slower but much steadier population growth.[40]

It has been suggested that humans practice the strategy typical of large-bodied organisms by controlling the demographic effects of a fluctuating environment and investing heavily in rearing the young.[41] But the examples of Egypt, England and Wales, Meso-America and others show that (at least until recently) local human populations have experienced wide swings and probably have not eliminated completely demographic responses to a fluctuating environment. Global human population growth appears relatively steady and smooth at least in part because the global population is the sum of many fluctuating local populations. The growth of a local human population may appear relatively steady if the interval of observation is as short as a century or two, but will appear much less steady over a longer period.

The underlying distinction in biological theory between the two "types" of nonhuman organisms may be partially an artifact, because larger organisms have longer generations than small ones.[42] If human beings observe populations of small and large organisms for equal time intervals, they will observe fewer generations of large organisms than of small. Hence human observers would be less likely to see population fluctuations in large organisms than in small.

THE GLOBAL AGRICULTURAL EVOLUTION:
1650–1850

Between 1650 and 1850, the human population more than doubled as its surging growth rate reached levels that were then unprecedented. The historian Alfred W. Crosby at the University of Texas considered the "population growth of the post-Columbian era . . . the most impressive single biological development of this millennium."[43] The increase in the growth rate resulted mainly from a fall in death rates, and especially from a decrease in the frequency and severity of episodes of catastrophic mortality; but in some places rising fertility also fueled the increasing growth rate.

Comprehensive quantitative evidence is still lacking that could measure precisely, region by region, the importance of nutrition, removal of human wastes, personal hygiene, the control of lethal infectious epidemics, increased trade and industrial production, increased migration and urbanization, more aggressive modification and exploitation of old and new lands for cultivation and other factors in the decline of mortality between 1650 and 1850.[44]

Life was perilous in Europe before the global agricultural evolution. In 1600, for example, Thomas Nashe published "A Litany in Time of Plague," which began:

> *Adieu, farewell, earth's bliss;*
> *This world uncertain is;*
> *Fond are life's lustful joys;*
> *Death proves them all but toys;*
> *None from his darts can fly;*
> *I am sick, I must die.*
> > *Lord, have mercy on us!*

As late as the early eighteenth century, the poet Thomas Gray (1716–1771), famous as the author of "Elegy Written in a Country Churchyard," was the sole adult survivor among his parents' twelve children.

The foods that European explorers brought back from the New World, as well as the foods European colonists introduced to the New World, helped to transform the Old and New Worlds demographically during the two centuries after 1650. Naturally, scholars debate whether the new foods

TABLE 3.1   Calories of Old World
and New World crops compared

American crops	million kilocalories per hectare	Old World crops	million kilocalories per hectare
maize	7.3	rice	7.3
potato	7.5	wheat	4.2
manioc	9.9	barley	5.1
		oat	5.5

SOURCE: Crosby (1972, p. 175), using Food and Agricultural Organization statistics for average soil and weather conditions.

were the principal cause of the concurrent rise in global population or were merely important contributing factors.

American food plants brought back to Europe, Africa and Asia included American corn (maize), potato, sweet potato, manioc or cassava or tapioca, many kinds of beans (including lima, sieva, butter, pole, curry, kidney, navy, haricot, snap, string, common and frijole beans, the obviously misnamed Rangoon, Madagascar, Burma and French beans, but not the soybean), tomato, peanuts, squashes, pumpkin, papaya, guava, avocado, pineapple, Chile pepper and cocoa. The detailed history of how maize reached Europe is complex and not fully known. Maize may have entered Europe before Columbus (in the Balkans, Italy and Granada), around the time of Columbus, and after Columbus (as milho into Portugal from Guinea).[45] In Crosby's view, "Collectively these plants made the most valuable single addition to the food-producing plants of the Old World since the beginnings of agriculture."[46]

Many New World plants grew well under conditions inhospitable for Old World cultivars. Maize grows on land too wet for wheat and too dry for rice, and gives roughly twice the yield of wheat, measuring yield by weight per unit of land. Potatoes yield several times more than wheat or any other grain. The sweet potato gives three to four times the yield of rice. Manioc generally produces a greater yield than any other tropical plant.[47] The American staples surpassed the Old World staples both in weight and in calories (Table 3.1).

Some of the New World cultivars spread rapidly. Maize soon reached southeastern Europe, Africa and southwestern China. In China the sweet potato flourished on hillsides and other lands where rice could not be grown. In Europe the cooler climate suited the Andean potato, though the summers were not warm enough to grow sweet potatoes.[48]

The increase of local food supplies was followed by a dramatic and widely dispersed rise in population in the eighteenth century. In western Europe, much of the rise coincided with the economic and social developments of the Industrial Revolution. Population rose at the same time in south China, where there was no parallel industrial revolution, and in Russia, where there was very little industrialization.[49] Population rose very rapidly in Russia even though Russians "then had virtually no access to the great new American or Eastern foods (potatoes, turkeys, maize, tomatoes, and rice). Access to sugar may have been another matter, however."[50] American crops such as maize may have made it possible for west African populations to produce the millions taken as slaves to the New World during the seventeenth and eighteenth centuries.[51] During the nineteenth century, the populations of north Africa, southwest and southeast Asia, the entire Indian subcontinent and central and south America all rose substantially, though those regions were far less industrialized and modernized than Europe.[52]

Thomas McKeown, a British scholar of social medicine, argued in 1976 that improved nutrition worldwide in the eighteenth century lowered the susceptibility of children to infectious and parasitic diseases and permitted many who formerly would have died in childhood to mature and reproduce. McKeown claimed that the simultaneous surge in population growth resulted principally from falling mortality, while fertility remained substantially unchanged.[53]

Episodes of catastrophic mortality decreased in frequency through the eighteenth and early nineteenth centuries, early in France, later in England and still later elsewhere in Europe. Such episodes became less frequent probably because some infectious disease became less virulent, public and private hygiene improved and transportation systems became better able to supply areas of incipient famine or other dire want. Possibly the period of lowered death rates in the eighteenth century did not differ from similar periods that had occurred before (as in the population history of Egypt); according to this hypothesis, the unusual aspect in the eighteenth century was that later epidemics, famines and other catastrophes failed to wipe out the population growth that accrued. The historian William H. McNeill of the University of Chicago suggested that improved transport and trade changed many infectious diseases from epidemic to endemic, as no population was long without exposure by contact from elsewhere.

> It seems plausible to connect the modern surge of population growth with this changed incidence of exposure to lethal infections. The fact that China and Europe led the way fits the hypothesis very nicely, for China and Europe had far more capacious and finely reticulated systems of internal transport in early modern times than other lands.[54]

McKeown's view that improved nutrition lowered death rates, which increased population growth rates, has been challenged by data on heights and fertility.[55] Average heights declined in England, the Hapsburg Empire and Sweden during the eighteenth century and the early decades of the nineteenth century, which would not be expected if average nutritional levels were improving, unless wars killed off all the tallest people.[56]

In many countries where both mortality and fertility have ultimately fallen, fertility rose before it eventually declined. The transient rise in fertility increased the population growth rate by amounts that varied from country to country.[57] In Europe between 1650 and 1850, birth rates rose more because a higher proportion of females were married than because fertility increased within marriage. In England in the second half of the eighteenth century, fertility rose at the same time that death rates fell.[58] At least part of the rise in fertility could have resulted from improved nutrition and a lowered age of menarche (first ovulation and menstruation); another contributing factor was probably the Industrial Revolution's increased demand for labor, which made it easier for people to marry earlier and to marry at all.

Among the factors not initially responsible for the rise in population up to the middle or end of the eighteenth century were scientific medicine and industrialization. Edward Jenner first published his experiments on vaccination by cowpox to protect against smallpox only in 1798. Through the end of the eighteenth century, scientific medicine had little or no influence in Europe, China and India, though higher growth rates were observed in these regions from the beginning of the seventeenth century.[59] In addition, many of the regions where population rose experienced no industrial revolution, though industrialization probably did contribute to European population growth during the nineteenth century.

4

People Control the Growth of Human Populations

THE DEMOGRAPHIC TRANSITION

DEMOGRAPHERS ORGANIZE MUCH of their thinking about population growth during the last two centuries and the coming decades in terms of, or in opposition to, a concept called "the demographic transition." The demographic transition refers to two different things: an idealized historical pattern of changes in birth, death and population growth rates; and a hypothesis about the mechanisms of these changes. When they use the term "demographic transition," demographers are often unclear about whether they refer to the pattern or to the hypothetical mechanism. Every time you see "demographic transition," you should ask which meaning is intended.

The idealized historical pattern of the demographic transition is simple. A population undergoes an idealized demographic transition in four stages. At stage one, the population has a high average birth rate, a high average death rate and the rates are nearly equal (so the initial average population growth rate is very low, or possibly zero); while the *average* birth and death rates are high, yearly rates of birth and death vary widely and population size may consequently fluctuate, though the long-term average size changes little. At stage two, the average death rate falls, while the average birth rate remains high or possibly rises a bit (so that the growth rate increases and the population grows much faster than before). Stage two is sometimes called the mortality transition. In stage three, while the death rate remains low and much less variable than at stage one, the average birth rate falls (so population growth slows). Stage three is sometimes called the fertility transition. At the fourth and final stage, the average birth rate is low, the average death rate is low and both are nearly equal (so the final growth rate is very low or possibly negative, but the population size is much larger than it was before the transition began). The process resembles the box step I learned in high school dancing class: you start with both feet together, then your right foot moves, then your left foot moves over to join your right foot, and you end up with your feet together again, but standing in a different place from where you started.

This idealized pattern describes a major historical fact: in the past two centuries, all the countries now considered "developed" at least doubled their average duration of life (from less than 35 years to more than 70 years) and reduced the average number of children born per woman by half or even more.[1] There is much room for variation within this pattern. Countries varied, for example, in the duration and extent of the declines in mortality and subsequently fertility, how long the delay was between them and how well synchronized the stages were within the country and with neighboring countries.

As a hypothesis, the theory of the demographic transition asserts that industrialization, urbanization, education and general modernization lead first to a fall in death rates (by various detailed mechanisms) and then to a fall in birth rates. Social and economic development causes the demographic transition, according to the hypothesis. Detailed historical research on the demographic transition in Europe and experience in the world's poor countries since World War II have not been kind to this hypothesis, even in the varied and vague forms it has sometimes assumed.

THE PUBLIC HEALTH EVOLUTION: 1945–NOW

The public health evolution since 1945 is epitomized by the experience of Algeria.[2] In 1946, the death rate of Algerian Muslims exceeded Sweden's in 1775. By 1954, in spite of the guerrilla war against France, the Muslim death rate in Algeria was lower than Sweden's in 1875.

Since the second quarter of the twentieth century, and especially since World War II, the poor countries of the world—often called "developing countries," more euphemistically and hopefully—have experienced phenomenal falls in death rates and equally phenomenal increases in numbers and share of world population. From 1930 to 1990, the population of the world's developing countries (that is, everywhere except Europe, North America, Australia, New Zealand and Japan) more than tripled from 1.3 billion to 4.1 billion, and grew from 64 percent of world population to 77 percent.[3]

By the second quarter of the twentieth century, improvements in administration and transport made it possible to prevent local epidemics and famines from causing massive deaths. The population history of India illustrates the effects of controlling major lethal episodes.[4] In 1891, the population of India was about 236 million, a bit less than the 1990 population of the

United States. Over the three decades from 1891 to 1921, the average annual population growth rate was about 0.17 percent. The population enumerated in the census of 1901 was slightly below that in 1891 because of severe famines during the decade. The population counted in 1921 was slightly below that in 1911 because of the influenza pandemic of 1918–19. After 1921, uncontrolled bursts of deaths from famine and disease stopped, while fertility remained high. From 1921 to 1951, the average annual population growth rate exceeded 1.2 percent. The rate of growth increased by a factor of more than six.

From 1929 onward, demographers observed the historical pattern and developed the theory of the demographic transition. Those who thought the depressed fertility of the Great Depression was permanent worried about the prospective decline of populations of European origin.[5] But the demographers who took seriously the historical pattern of the demographic transition, such as Frank W. Notestein, founder of Princeton University's Office of Population Research, foresaw a potential for demographic growth in the world's poor countries. They supposed that modernization in the less developed regions, which was necessary to alleviate poverty, would cause death rates to fall before birth rates. They forecasted rapid population growth in the large regions that had then hardly modernized, including most of Asia, Africa, Latin America, the Caribbean and the large island populations of southeast Asia. The less developed countries would benefit from population policies that could shorten the gap between the fall in the death rate and the fall in the birth rate.

The forecasts of some demographic transition theorists before and after World War II went in the right direction, but not nearly far enough. No one guessed how large the coming wave of population growth would be. Here are five examples, in the order in which they were published.[6] In 1936, Raymond Pearl and Sophia Gould projected 2.645 billion people by the end of the twenty-first century. (That population size was surpassed before 1955.) In 1949, an Australian economist, Colin Clark (of whom more will be heard in Chapter 10), projected a 1 percent annual increase to 3.48 billion people by 1990. (The actual population in 1990 was 5.3 billion.) Also in 1949, economist Joseph J. Spengler of Duke University, relying largely on demographic forecasts of others, estimated that world population would grow from 2.084 billion in 1940 to 3 billion in 1970 and to 3.345 billion by the year 2000.[7] (The world had 3.7 billion people in 1970 and is very likely to have more than 6 billion people by 2000.[8]) In 1950, Notestein estimated a total population of 3.3 billion by A.D. 2000.[9] The United Nations' projections published in 1951 estimated world population in mid-1950 around 2.4 billion people and projected a 1980 world population between 2.976 billion and 3.636 billion.[10] (The 1950 population was probably closer to 2.5 billion, and the 1980 population was 4.4 billion.)

As Ansley J. Coale of Princeton observed, "The error was in underestimating the pace of decline [in death rates], and over-stating the connection with over-all modernization."[11] After World War II, the rich countries of the world exported more health than wealth. Only late in the story did the export of wealth, in the form of the Green Revolution, become as prominent as the export of health. The contrast between the recent public health evolution and the earlier global agricultural evolution is dramatic. To simplify greatly, in and after the eighteenth century, new foods probably improved the resistance of large populations to infection, and the improved resistance to infection contributed to a gradual decline in death rates and a gradual rise in population growth.[12] By contrast, in the twentieth century, and especially after World War II, research laboratories and public health institutions in the modernized countries developed ways to attack infections directly. Western medicine introduced cheap death control: antibiotics, the biocide DDT to control insect vectors of infection and vaccines against smallpox, measles, whooping cough, neonatal tetanus, polio and diphtheria, as well as drugs that cured tuberculosis and malaria.[13] Public health measures included safer water supplies and ways of segregating and treating human wastes. Public health institutions and field techniques translated the new technologies into practices that affected the lives of hundreds of millions of people. These techniques, readily transferred from rich to poor countries without the necessity of great industrial or educational development, were absent or rare during the decline of mortality in eighteenth-century Europe.

By 1900, life expectancy at birth was 40 to 50 years in North America and most of northwestern Europe.[14] Now, life expectancy at birth in the more developed countries is about 78 years for women, 71 years for men.[15] By 1940, most people in the world still had the expectation of life at birth of western Europe in the Middle Ages, nowhere near that of North America and northwest Europe. Now, in the less developed countries, the expectation of life at birth for women is about 64 years, for men about 61 years. Africa lags with a current female expectation of life at birth of about 55 years and a male life expectancy at birth of about 52 years. Since World War II, the world's poor countries have lowered the death rates of their growing masses from medieval levels to below those of the most privileged people on the Earth at the start of the twentieth century.

An important technical digression is necessary here. How can demographers possibly know the life expectancy, or average duration of life, of infants born this year? They can't. What demographers mean by life expectancy at birth for infants born in, say, 1995 is the average number of years those children would live if they experienced the 1995 death rates of infants while they were infants, and then experienced the 1995 death rates of one-year-olds when they reached one year old, and then experienced the 1995 death rates of two-year-olds when they reached two years old, and at each subsequent age experienced the 1995 death rates for that age.[16] If death rates at each age decline in the future, then the infants born in 1995 will live longer on the average than the calculated life expectancy at birth for 1995; if death rates at each age rise, then the infants born in 1995 will live shorter lives on the average than the calculated 1995 life expectancy at birth.

The consequences of death control through public health technology and organizational improvement have been dramatic in the past half century.

Even countries with limited social and economic development increased their life expectancy by ten years in a single decade.[17] Such improvements require large decreases in death rates. In Sri Lanka, the chance of dying within a year fell from 2.2 percent in 1945 to 1.3 percent in 1950.[18] Spraying DDT against mosquitoes and a lower incidence of malaria probably played a major role in the decline.

In the poor countries as a group, during the first three decades after World War II, the expectation of life at birth rose from 32 years to 50 years, according to United Nations estimates, an increase of more than half. In the same period, the fertility rate fell only 4 percent.[19] Rapidly falling death rates and nearly steady birth rates made for rapidly rising population growth rates. In India, for example, from 1951 to 1991, the population grew from some 357 million to more than 850 million. The average annual rate of increase was about 2.2 percent, nearly double the average growth rate of the previous three decades, and nearly 13 times the growth rate of the three decades 1891–1921.

In retrospect, the demographic transition correctly described the change from high to low in the rates of death and birth in highly modernized societies. It correctly predicted that, in countries with high fertility and mortality at the end of World War II, death rates would drop before birth rates and population size would grow. It did not predict when the decline of fertility would begin or how fast the declines of mortality and fertility would proceed.[20] It wrongly assumed that falling death rates had to be preceded or accompanied by socioeconomic development.

Growth with Increasing Economic Inequality

Since World War II, the unprecedented growth of human numbers in the poor countries and of prosperity in the rich countries has been accompanied by an increasingly unequal distribution of real income between rich and poor people. Yet signs of plenty have increased: domestic animal stocks rose while animals consumed a smaller fraction of world grain production; prices of many commodities fell; the numbers and proportions of the chronically undernourished in developing regions decreased. Around 1990, the extremes of the world distribution of wealth were these: more than 800 million people enjoyed average annual incomes per person of $22,000; another 800 million people, day after day, failed to receive enough calories to grow normally and walk around.

For the world as a whole, from 1955 to 1980, world population increased from 2.8 billion to 4.4 billion, a rise of 57 percent, while world output of goods and services roughly tripled in real terms and income per person roughly doubled.[21] In the 1950s, the world's agricultural output rose 3.1 percent per year; in the 1960s, 2.6 percent per year; in the 1970s, 2.2 percent per year. From the early 1950s to 1980, world agricultural production, not counting China's, nearly doubled.

The average person in the poor countries saw less improvement in income and food supplies than these impressive gains in global output might suggest. A major reason is that, from 1955 to 1980, the population of the low-income developing countries grew at 2.1 percent per year and increased by roughly 68 percent over the period. In Africa, while the total food output grew by 2.7 percent per year in the 1960s, output per person increased only slightly; in the 1970s, production per person fell on average more than 1 percent per year, from levels that were already low. Food production per person in Africa in 1988–90 was only 96 percent of its level in 1979–81; total agricultural production per person in Africa was also down 5 percent over the same period.[22] Millions of people remained undernourished even in those countries that could import food.[23]

Between 1960 and 1989, the income (both total and per person) of the wealthy countries grew faster than the income of the poor countries, so that the wealthy countries' share of the world's income steadily increased. In 1992, the United Nations Development Program (UNDP) constructed statistics on the distribution of income from all sources by making a list of all the countries of the world, each with its population size and its gross national product (GNP). GNP traces transactions in markets and usually omits barter; it may bear little relation to well-being in societies not organized around markets. For each country, the GNP was divided by the population size to compute that country's GNP per person. The countries were sorted in decreasing order of GNP per person: the first country in the list had the highest GNP per person and the last had the lowest GNP per person. Then, starting at the top of the list, the population sizes were cumulated until enough countries were included to contain 20 percent of the world's population. In 1960, the combined GNPs of these rich countries came to 70.2 percent of the total GNP of all countries in the world. Similarly, starting from the country at the bottom of the list with the lowest GNP per person, the population sizes were cumulated until enough countries were included to contain 20 percent of the world's population. In 1960, the combined GNPs of these poor countries came to 2.3 percent of the global GNP. The share of global GNP of the countries with the poorest one-fifth of the world's population dropped from 2.3 percent in 1960 to 1.4 percent in 1989, while the share of the countries with the richest one-fifth of the world's population rose from about 70 percent in 1960 to almost 83 percent in 1989 (Figure 4.1).[24] The ratio of income (total and per person) between the richest and the poorest fifth of the population rose from about 30 to 1 in 1960, to 32 to 1 in 1970, to 45 to 1 in 1980, to 59 to 1 in 1989.

In 1989 U.S. dollars per person, the absolute gap between the top fifth and the bottom fifth of world population rose from $1,864 in 1960 to $15,149 in 1989.[25] These numbers show that economists are not immune to the disease of quoting more digits of precision than the underlying data could possibly justify. I would guess that these dollar values are accurate to at most one or two figures. If so, it would be more faithful to actual knowledge to say that the absolute gap in income, measured in 1989 dollars, increased by a factor of roughly eight between 1960 and 1989, starting from somewhere under $2,000 in 1960.

The Gini coefficient (named after the Italian statistician Corrado Gini,

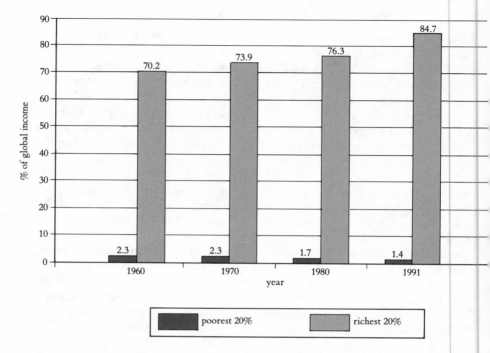

FIGURE 4.1 Fraction of global income received by the poorest 20 percent of people and the richest 20 percent of people from 1960 to 1991, according to the average gross national product per person of different countries. SOURCE: based on United Nations Development Program (1992, pp. 34, 36)

1884–1965) summarizes the inequality of an income distribution. When countries are the unit of measurement, this coefficient would be zero if the income per person of all countries were equal. It would be 1 if a single country had all the GNP and all other countries had nothing. The Gini coefficient rose steadily from 0.69 in 1960 to 0.71 in 1970, 0.79 in 1980, and 0.87 in 1989. The last value indicates an income distribution with nearly the maximum possible inequality among nations (which would be represented by a Gini coefficient of 1).

The figures I have just given compared the average incomes of countries rather than the incomes of individual people. A country with a moderate average income could, in principle, have a small number of fabulously rich people and a great majority of destitute people, or a uniform distribution of income with neither rich nor poor people. Because every country has some people who are richer than some others in the same country, the figures based on country averages understated the income gap between the world's richest 20 percent of people and the world's poorest 20 percent of people. Data on the distribution of income within countries, which could be politically embarrassing in cases of extreme disparity, were available for 41 countries in 1988. The industrial countries, where income disparities were

TABLE 4.1   Livestock populations of the world
(average, 1990–92)

livestock	billions	percentage change from 1980–82
cattle	1.3	4
sheep and goats	1.8	13
pigs	0.9	10
equines	0.1	7
buffaloes and camels	0.2	16
chickens	17.2	132

SOURCE: World Resources Institute (1994, p. 296)

generally smaller than elsewhere, were overrepresented among these 41. Using just these 41 countries, the UNDP compared the incomes of the richest fifth with the incomes of the poorest fifth, using both countries and individual people as the units of analysis. When the 41 countries were the units of analysis, the ratio was 65 to 1 in 1988.[26] When the income distribution within the 41 countries was considered, so that people were the units of analysis, the ratio was 140 to 1 ($22,808 to $163). Based on these figures, the UNDP estimated that the ratio of incomes between the richest fifth and the poorest fifth of the whole world's population around 1990 was at least twice that shown in Figure 4.1 "and may be well over 150 to 1."[27] Even if the dollar values are adjusted to reflect real purchasing power, it is estimated that the ratio in real income between the richest fifth of the population and the poorest fifth exceeded 50 to 1 around 1990.

In 1992,[28] the 830 million people in the world's richest countries enjoyed an average annual income of $22,000—a truly astounding achievement. But the almost 2.6 billion people in the middle-income countries received only $1,600. The more than 2 billion people in the poorest countries lived on an average annual income of $400, or a dollar a day. These figures are based on gross national products and national population sizes. Within the poorest countries some happy few lived far above the average. For each such person others barely survived on less than a dollar a day.

There were important signs of plenty, or at least of progressive global enrichment. In 1990 to 1992, the numbers of domestic cattle, sheep, goats, pigs, equines, buffaloes and camels totaled 4.3 billion, and all were rising (Table 4.1). The number of chickens, 17.2 billion, more than doubled over the prior decade. In 1992, domestic animals were fed 37 percent of all grain consumed, a reduction from 41 percent in 1972.[29]

In constant prices with the price in 1990 set equal to 100, the price of petroleum fell from 113 in 1975 to 76 in 1992, while the prices of metals and minerals fell over the same period from 135 to 83. The price of a basket of 33 nonfuel commodities fell from 159 in 1975 to 86 in 1992. Total food commodity prices fell from 196 in 1975 to 85 in 1992; cereal prices in particular fell from 259 in 1975 to 94 in 1992. Only timber prices increased, from 62 in 1975 to 112 in 1992.[30]

In developing regions, the absolute numbers and the fraction of the population that was chronically undernourished fell from 941 million and 36 percent in 1969–71 to 844 million and 26 percent in 1979–81 and still further to 786 million and 20 percent in 1988–90. This remarkable improvement still left one person in five hungry in the developing regions. In Africa, while the fraction of chronically undernourished declined by 2 percentage points from 1969–71 to 1988–90, the absolute number increased from 101 million to 168 million.[31]

How could world food prices drop by half while some 800 million people in developing regions do not receive enough calories? You have already seen the answer. The bottom billion are so poor that they cannot exercise effective demand in world commodity markets. They have too little money to buy food traded internationally, so they cannot drive up its price. They cannot compete for grain with the cattle and chickens of the world's wealthy people. The extremely poor are irrelevant to international markets; they are economically invisible. But they are people nonetheless.

The colossal modern rise of population, overwhelmingly in the world's poor countries, prompted Paul Ehrlich's alarum *The Population Bomb* in 1968. That book happened to appear just as the world's population growth rate peaked and began to decline—for the first time in centuries.

THE FERTILITY EVOLUTION: 1785–?

One of the most important and least heralded events in human history occurred between 1965 and 1970. The world's population growth rate reached an all-time peak and began to drop thereafter. The high-water mark of the global population growth rate in 1965–70 was 2.1 percent per year. If this rate had held constant, the population would have doubled in just over 33 years. After World War II, growth rates continued to fall in 37 early-transitional countries (those countries where fertility began to fall before 1950), and continued to rise in 67 pre-transitional countries (those where fertility had not begun to fall by 1990). The news was that, in 46 late-transitional countries (those where fertility began to fall between 1950 and 1990), growth rates dropped sharply from more than 2.5 percent in 1965–70 to below 1.9 percent in just one decade, and since have declined much more slowly to just above 1.8 percent in 1980–85.[32] The global population growth rate fell primarily because of the drop during and after 1965–70 in the fertility of such populous countries as China, India, Brazil, Egypt, Indonesia, Korea, Mexico and Thailand (Figure 4.2).

The United Nations estimated that the number of births per year declined from over 122 million in 1970–75 to a bit less than 121 million in 1975–80.[33] Given the limitations, or complete absence, of birth registration in

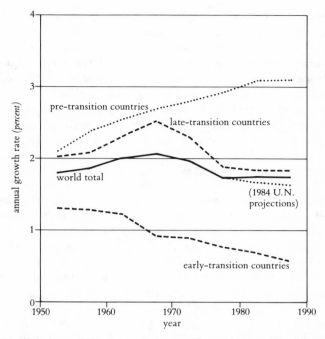

FIGURE 4.2   Global trends in the annual rate of population growth, 1950 to 1990, according to United Nations estimates. For the world total in 1990, the solid line shows the 1990 estimate and the dotted line just below it shows the growth rate projected in 1984; the anticipated decline in the population growth rate did not occur. SOURCE: Horiuchi (1992, p. 761, Fig. 1)

many parts of the world, I doubt that either estimate is accurate to better than 1 percent; but since both estimates are consistently derived, the downward trend in absolute numbers of births may be real.

The slight drop in the population growth rate after 1965–70 does not mean that the size of the population itself began to drop. On the contrary, the population of the world has risen steadily from an estimated 3.7 billion in 1970 past 5.3 billion in 1990. The slight drop in the growth rate also does not mean that the number of people added to the world's population each year began to fall. On the contrary, in 1970, world population increased by an estimated 72 million people per year. That number rose to around 92 million (realistically, 90 to 95 million) in the early 1990s. The peak in the world's population growth rate means only that the relative growth rate— the variable interest rate in the world's demographic bank account—reached a high point and began to fall.

The recent decrease in the global population growth rate is certainly the first since credible world population estimates became possible in the nineteenth century, and very probably the first since the Black Death grew rank in the fourteenth century. The global population growth rate fell after 1970 because birth rates fell faster than death rates. This momentous change in the direction of the human population growth rate during 1965–70 was the global expression and cumulation of gradual cultural, behavioral and technological changes that began as long as three centuries before.

The historical collection of patterns by which fertility fell from high levels typical of traditional societies to much lower levels typical of modern societies is called the fertility transition by demographers. I shall call it the fertility evolution. The fertility evolution began long before the public health evolution just sketched. It began even before the global agricultural evolution had finished. Yet because this colossal turning of the tide became visible on a global scale so recently, I view this prolonged and still incomplete evolution as the fourth and latest stage of the story of the human population.

The fertility evolution represents a new step in human consciousness, a step that places humans in the forefront of all species that have ever lived on the Earth. Changes in billions of beds and byways gave humans conscious control of their own fertility. Of course, not all humans have taken this forward step in consciousness. Some (such as the American Hutterites and other groups opposed to any form of birth limitation) view the control of fertility as contrary to their most fundamental values. But enough human beings have taken command of, and reduced, their fertility to bring the species past the peak of its global growth rate. The story is far from complete, as modern methods of contraception and cultural change are placing unprecedented control of fertility in the hands of women and men.

The First Wave: Fertility Falls in Europe and Japan

People have long found ways of limiting the numbers of mouths to feed. Some present hunter-gatherer groups, including Australian aborigines and !Kung bushmen in Africa, are reported to practice infanticide and probably have had the practice for a long time.[34] Abnormal ratios of male to female skeletal remains suggest that essentially modern people in the Upper Paleolithic period practiced female infanticide perhaps 20,000 years ago. Infanticide occurred in Hellenistic Greece and Rome; it continued in Christian Europe into the later Middle Ages in England, among other places.

Unambiguous written evidence to document the practice of family limitation by an entire social group first appeared in seventeenth-century France, in the family records of the upper classes of France, the dukes and peers of the realm.[35] How can today's demographers possibly know that the French nobility practiced family limitation?

If couples make no effort to influence the likelihood of another birth according to the number of children they have already borne, women tend to stop having babies when they are biologically unable to give birth, typically in their forties. This situation is called natural fertility.

But if couples stop having additional children once they have reached a particular number of children, then the age at which women have their last child falls below the biologically imposed upper limit. Such couples are said to practice family limitation when both partners survive beyond the birth of the last child. (If a couple's childbearing ends because one partner or the other dies, the couple can hardly be said to be limiting births.) The detection of family limitation through the mother's age of last childbearing requires no knowledge of how couples prevented births. It rests only on the unequivocal outcome of their behavior. Family limitation occurs when families with a particular number of children are more likely to have no more children than families who have fewer than that particular number.

From clerical, genealogical and royal records of the households of the dukes and peers of the French realm, demographers reconstructed the birth histories of individual women: the names and dates of birth of the children each woman bore, and the mother's age at each birth. By the end of the seventeenth century, according to the demographers Etienne van de Walle at the University of Pennsylvania and John Knodel at the University of Michigan, women were in their low thirties at the birth of their last child. In the same period, the French-speaking bourgeoisie of Geneva also underwent a notable decline in fertility, and the Italian nobility followed by the eighteenth century.[36]

By the last quarter of the eighteenth century, well before the French Revolution, family limitation spread from the nobility to the peasants in much of rural France. The French demographer Moheau (the entire pseudonym of Antoine J.-B. R. Auget, Baron de Montyon) wrote in 1776: "They cheat nature even in the villages!"[37] Recent quantitative historical studies of fertility in the French provinces confirm that Moheau was right.[38]

Family limitation differs from birth control, though it uses techniques of birth control, because it indicates couples' efforts to stop having any more children. Birth control techniques can also be used to influence the timing of births, to increase the interval between them or to prevent illegitimate births as a result of extramarital intercourse. The principal technique of birth control practiced in France starting in the seventeenth century is believed to have been withdrawal before ejaculation, or coitus interruptus.[39]

Couples' desire to control the number of their children, to the extent that it existed in the eighteenth and nineteenth centuries, had to counterbalance increases in women's physiological capacity to bear children. Better nutrition gradually decreased the age of menarche and gave more women the reserves of body fat required to bring a pregnancy to term.

By the beginning of the nineteenth century, evidence of family limitation appeared in rural Germany, Hungary, Sweden and New England. Family limitation spread to most European countries by the last quarter of the nineteenth century.[40]

When detailed data about the fertility evolution in Europe were scarce, it was possible to believe that fertility declined along a uniform path according to homogeneous mechanisms. The facts about the European fertility decline that have been assembled in the last three decades are not so simple. Starting in 1963, Ansley J. Coale at Princeton organized researchers

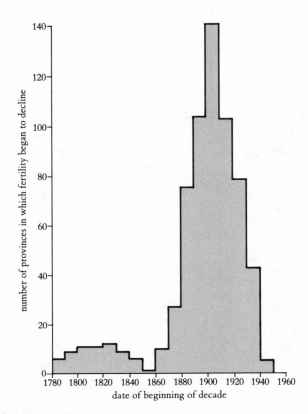

FIGURE 4.3 Number of provinces of Europe that experienced a 10 percent decline in marital fertility, by decade in which the decline first occurred. SOURCE: Coale and Watkins (1986, p. 38, Fig. 2.2)

to document and analyze changes in the rates of birth, death and migration in more than 700 provincial units of Europe (departments in France, counties in England and so on) in the nineteenth and twentieth centuries. The results should satisfy any historian's taste for richness and complexity. Here are some of the findings.

First, fertility declined at different times and rates in different places. A practical way to define when fertility began to decline in a particular province is to find the decade in which fertility within marriage in that province first fell by 10 percent or more.[41] The dates of decline of all the provinces of Europe may be summarized by a bar chart that shows how many provinces experienced a first fall in fertility decade by decade (Figure 4.3). The small hill on the left in Figure 4.3 represents primarily the provinces of France; the mountain on the right, mainly provinces in the rest of Europe. Fertility began to decline in more than half of the provinces of Europe between 1880 and 1910.[42] In some countries, fertility began to decline in different provinces over a long period, while in others fertility declined in almost all parts of the country nearly at once. In France, for example, family limitation first became demographically important in rural villages at the end of the eighteenth century, but some provinces showed very slight family limitation at the beginning of the twentieth century. By contrast, in England, in almost all 40 counties and London, fertility began to decline between 1890 and 1900. British couples who married in 1861–69 had 6.2 children, on average; those who married in 1890–99, 4.1; and those who married in 1920–24, 2.3—a drop in marital fertility of more than 60 percent in 60 years.[43]

Second, physical contiguity between countries was not needed for fertility to decline simultaneously. Countries that received many migrants whose home countries were in the midst of a decline in fertility quickly began to experience fertility decline as well. Birth rates followed remarkably similar paths in Australia, the United States, Britain, New Zealand and English-speaking Canada.[44]

Third, shared culture was more likely to produce a simultaneous decline in fertility than shared location. For example, in 1962, in doctoral research on the fertility evolution in Spain, William Leasure of Princeton mapped the level of marital fertility in 1910 in the 49 provinces of Spain. Provinces with similar marital fertility were adjacent, not scattered through the country, and often differed substantially in the level of literacy, the fraction of workers in agriculture and other economic characteristics. Without indicating that he had plotted levels of marital fertility, Leasure showed his map to a professor at Princeton who specialized in Spanish language, literature and culture. The professor immediately supposed that Leasure had mapped the linguistic regions of Spain. The Spanish statistical authorities divide Spain into regions that once constituted different kingdoms. These regions differ in language and traditions. Leasure's statistical analysis showed that more than 90 percent of the variation in marital fertility occurred between different standard statistical regions, and less than 10 percent within regions.[45] In Belgium and Germany also, being in the same neighborhood mattered less than speaking the same language or dialect and sharing the culture carried with that language. By contrast, in England, relative cultural homogeneity and extensive networks of communication made it possible for people throughout the country to accept family limitation almost simultaneously, though regions differed widely in urbanization and economic development.[46]

A fourth finding, just hinted at, is that it seems to be impossible to predict the onset of fertility decline from existing social or economic conditions.[47] For example, fertility began to fall when literacy was low in France, Bulgaria and Hungary, but when literacy was high in England and Wales. The English population was 28 percent rural, with only 15 percent of employed men in agriculture, while the populations of Bulgaria and Hungary were largely agricultural, as France had been when its fertility began to fall.

Going beyond such examples, van de Walle and Knodel concluded: "There is no evidence that other indicators of socioeconomic development, were they available for comparison, would explain the timing of the [fertility] decline. Clearly, large differences in the level of development existed among European populations at the start of their fertility transition and it seems safe to conclude that there was no easily definable threshold of social and economic progress required for it to begin."[48] An empirical relationship in one European country between the date at which marital fertility first declined and socioeconomic characteristics (like the proportion of the labor force in agriculture and the level of infant mortality) does not generally predict the date of decline in another country.[49]

This sweeping conclusion was disputed by Maria Sophia Lengyel Cook and Robert Repetto at Harvard University. They criticized the approach of the European fertility project for two reasons. First, by concentrating on aggregate statistics for whole provinces, the Princeton project neglected the difference between the average economic well-being of a province and the economic well-being of most households within a province. The average income could be moderate if a few households were very wealthy and the rest poor, or alternatively if most households had moderate income. Which of these alternatives actually held could have influenced the rate of change of fertility. Second, by considering the diffusion of fertility reduction only from one province to another, the Princeton project neglected the barriers to the spread of reduced fertility within a province. Cook and Repetto examined the fertility evolution in 48 Hungarian provinces from 1880 to 1910, when fertility began a sustained decline. They found that a province with a large gap between rich households and poor posed greater obstacles to the spread of lower fertility than a province with greater economic equality. Indicators of economic inequality explained the fertility transition in Hungary better than either cultural factors or extent of modernization. "If the fertility transition is a diffusion process, socio-economic stratification can evidently erect serious barriers to its rapid dispersion. There is, on the basis of these findings, no reason to interpret European experience of the nineteenth century to minimize the importance of development as a stimulus to demographic change."[50] This provocative finding is consistent with the twentieth-century experience of developing countries that have made serious efforts to promote economic equality.

A fifth conclusion of Princeton's European fertility project was that the timing of the declines in mortality and fertility was not very simple. Previously, the fertility transition was considered the dancing partner of the mortality transition, and the mortality transition was assumed to be definitely the leading partner in the dance: death rates were supposed to fall first and fertility rates were assumed to follow with a substantial lag. The gap between the falling death rates and the lagging birth rates generated population growth. While this pattern was observed sometimes (Figure 4.4), it was far from universal. In France, fertility fell simultaneously with, or soon after, mortality, and the resulting population growth was very moderate compared with that in some other European countries. In modern Germany, infant mortality rates hardly changed at all until after 1870, then fell

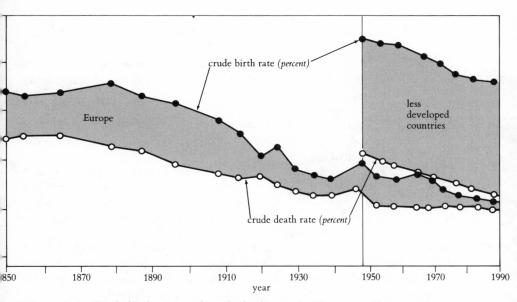

FIGURE 4.4   Crude birth rates and crude death rates in 13 western European countries and 106 less developed countries. The unweighted average understates the global impact of declines in large countries such as China and India. SOURCE: Kelley (1988, p. 1688, Fig. 1)

in parallel with marital fertility. The fall in fertility preceded the fall in infant mortality in about half the provinces of Germany, and followed in the other half.[51] Therefore the fall in mortality could not be the cause of the decline in fertility; some other common cause must be sought. Generally, ". . . in the last quarter of the 19th century, both marital fertility and infant mortality fell rapidly at the same time. It may be that the ability to determine a target family size through family limitation was a preliminary condition to any real progress in infant and child survival."[52]

Sixth, and finally, because demographers could not explain the fertility decline in Europe and in populations of European origin by geographic, social, economic or demographic characteristics, they resorted to cultural explanations. They supposed that shared language and standards of conduct contributed to the diffusion of the idea of family limitation through cultural groups. According to van de Walle and Knodel,

It is probably wrong to assume that the decline was triggered by the transfer of information on birth control techniques or actual contraceptive devices. Some diffusion of techniques clearly occurred among interested couples but this would have been too secretive and too subject to censure to have been responsible for the very fast drop of fertility in millions of individual families. The decisive factor was probably the spread of a new mentality—an openness to the idea of manipulating reproduction, a new willingness to explore methods of fertility control, or the new acceptability of already available methods which previously seemed scandalous, uncouth, or threatening to the sexual prerogatives of the male.[53]

The empirical support for the cultural hypothesis of fertility change is scant. No one seems to know precisely what social and cultural indicators reflected a receptivity to family limitation. The favored candidates are improvements in the status of women, more secular attitudes and an increasing preference for individual interests over traditions. Such factors may have been more important than economic growth in initiating the West's fertility transition.[54]

The detailed mechanisms by which cultural factors translate into reduced fertility have not been measured or analyzed with the same hard-headed precision as the demographic and economic facts. In the heyday of socio-economic explanations of the fertility transition (before the facts were in), it was fashionable to say that "development is the best contraceptive."[55] Since the conclusions of the Princeton European fertility project challenged that slogan, it became fashionable to suppose that improvements in the status of women and the spread of secular attitudes will bring about the fertility transition in countries with high fertility. This plausible belief has as little empirical support as did the equally plausible earlier slogan. Socioeconomic development, improvements in the status of women and secular attitudes may be neither necessary nor sufficient for a fertility transition, whatever other virtues or drawbacks they may have in the eyes of different observers.

A second problem with shared culture and communication as an explanation for the timing of fertility decline is that the early decline of fertility in France occurred almost simultaneously with a similar decline in Japan. Under the Tokugawa Shogunate, from 1603 to 1867, Japan excluded virtually all Europeans and was practically closed to foreign contacts. Japan and France can hardly be said to have fallen within the same cultural sphere. From a population of around 10 million at the start of the seventeenth century, the population of Japan grew rapidly to around 30 million (plus or minus 5 million) by 1720. During this period the average annual growth rate was around 0.9 percent. In the 150 years following 1720, growth slowed to 0.2 percent per year, and by 1870, just after the end of the Tokugawa dynasty, the Japanese population numbered about 35 million.[56]

Japanese women were clearly limiting their fertility. Women in the village of Yokouchi, for example, who were born before 1700 and married when 20 years old bore, on average, 5.5 children; those who married at the same age but were born between 1750 and 1800 averaged about 3.2 children. Massimo Livi-Bacci offered an interpretation: "Whatever the explanation, Japanese society seems to have found effective mechanisms for controlling population growth as the process of agricultural expansion encountered natural and insurmountable obstacles."[57] This interpretation harks back to the socioeconomic hypothesis of the demographic transition. Whether or not agricultural obstacles (insurmountable or otherwise) motivated or caused a Japanese decline in fertility, shared culture and communication are not the reason that Japan's fertility fell at the same time as France's.

In spite of all the complexities, the decline of European fertility was consistent with some important generalizations. After a decade of his project's studies, Coale offered three propositions that have been widely influential.

Three general prerequisites for a major fall in marital fertility can be listed:

(1) Fertility must be within the calculus of conscious choice. Potential parents must consider it an acceptable mode of thought and form of behavior to balance advantages and disadvantages before deciding to have another child. . . .

(2) Reduced fertility must be advantageous. Perceived social and economic circumstances must make reduced fertility seem an advantage to individual couples.

(3) Effective techniques of fertility reduction must be available. Procedures that will in fact prevent births must be known, and there must be sufficient communication between spouses and sufficient sustained will, in both, to employ them successfully.[58]

In short, as a student of Ansley Coale's once wrote, potential parents must be ready, willing and able to control their fertility.

The Second Wave: Global Fertility Begins Its Modern Fall

The fall of fertility in the early-transitional countries of Europe and North America was not sufficient to brake the rise in the global population growth rate. Only when birth rates began to fall in South America and east and southeast Asia (including China and India) did the global population growth rate peak and begin to fall. The reasons for the fall in birth rates are not clear.

The paths of falling fertility in developing countries after World War II were just as diverse as those in the provinces of nineteenth-century Europe. Around 1970, Thailand was judged to have entered the fertility transition because its marital fertility had fallen 10 percent below a peak level; the country was then still 85 percent rural. When Chile's fertility transition began in 1964, Chile was less than 30 percent rural. In 1964, the infant mortality rate in Chile was 10.3 percent, a high level, but when Taiwan started its fertility transition in 1963, Taiwan's infant mortality rate was 4.9 percent, less than half of Chile's.[59] Some people attributed Mexico's rapid fertility decline in the 1970s to "political will," by which they meant advocacy, policies and resources for family planning. But Brazil had a similar decline without strong government intervention; and India's strong government intervention in family planning was judged to be counterproductive.[60]

After passing its peak in 1965–70, the global annual population growth rate dropped sharply for about a decade (from 2.1 percent to about 1.8 percent), then remained flat for about a decade. China's falling fertility contributed importantly to the global fall. China's total fertility rate, or average number of children born per woman, dropped spectacularly from about 6.5 in 1968 to about 2.2 in 1980.[61] Chinese couples passed through a change in behavior in a dozen years that took 60 years (1865–1925) in Great Britain and still longer in France. At the same time, India's fertility fell, but by a smaller amount. Though the United States took 58 years to lower its total fertility rate from 6.3 to 3.5 children per woman, Colombia accomplished the same transition in 15 years, Thailand in 8 years and China in only 7 years.[62]

Since the early 1980s, the global population growth rate has hardly fallen. Seventy-eight million people live in countries with a total fertility rate above seven children per woman, and 708 million live in countries with six or more children per woman.[63] Three reasons why the decline in fertility stopped are visible.[64] First, the substantial fertility declines in China and India halted, at least for the time being, or were even slightly reversed. China relaxed its official prohibition of youthful marriage[65] and India backed off from family-planning programs viewed as too vigorous. Second, many women entered the childbearing years in the 1980s. These women were born in the 1950s and 1960s during the baby boom in the rich countries and during a rapid fall in infant and childhood mortality in the poor countries. The boom in the number of surviving children in the 1950s and 1960s had an echo in an increased number of women able and wanting to have children in the 1980s. Third, few additional countries began to have declining fertility in the 1980s. Of the 46 countries that initiated a fall in fertility after 1950 and before 1990, all but a handful had done so by 1975.

What does this analysis tell us of the future? The women who entered childbearing years during the 1980s will age beyond childbearing within little more than two decades, so one cause of the recent stagnation will be eliminated (though *their* children will probably still want to have children). But the first and third of the three reasons (that fertility stopped falling in China and India, and that few new countries entered the fertility transition) are really only descriptions at a finer level of detail of the global stagnation in fertility decline. The absence of credible explanations of the underlying individual fertility behavior over the last few decades cripples prediction of future fertility in countries where individual choice governs fertility. The absence of reliable predictors of governmental policies affecting fertility cripples prediction of future fertility in countries where official policies strongly affect fertility.[66] In 1992, Shiro Horiuchi, a demographer at Rockefeller University, on whose analysis I relied here, concluded cautiously: ". . . it is extremely difficult to predict when fertility declines will resume in China, accelerate in India, and begin in pre-transition countries."[67] Could anyone have guessed that, within a single year following the publication of Horiuchi's article, the Chinese total fertility rate would drop from 2.5 to 1.9 children per woman?[68]

Demographic data on national fertility rates do not describe or explain the individual motivations and choices that bring about falls in fertility, and therefore cannot provide more than a phenomenological understanding of the fertility transition. Anthropological studies of individual cultures claim to offer the possibility of understanding changes in fertility through changes that affect individuals and families. The American anthropologist W. Penn Handwerker assembled studies by others of culture and reproduction among U.S. college students, Alaskan Eskimos, Mexicans, Guatemalans and Mexican-Americans in the Western Hemisphere; peoples of Liberia, Tunisia, Botswana, Ghana, Gambia and Sierra Leone in Africa; and of Ireland and Java. To simplify, Handwerker's hypothesis is that fertility falls when children change from assets to liabilities for parents, and children become liabilities when they require formal education outside the home.[69]

This hypothesis must be only part of the story, however, for several reasons. It seems an unlikely account of the decline of fertility among French peasants in the eighteenth century. It does not encompass China's present direct social regulation of fertility by means of both positive and negative incentives. It would not explain the recent fall of fertility in Bangladesh unaccompanied by any changes in income or improvements in the status of women.[70] It ignores the differences between men and women in the incentives for having children, in the opportunities for work and education and in the determinants of personal material well-being.[71]

The Third Wave: Africa

Over the past quarter century, fertility in Africa remained high, and in some African countries continued to rise, while fertility fell in every other developing region. By 1990, however, sample surveys indicated that birth rates had fallen by 15 percent to 25 percent from their peaks in Botswana, Zimbabwe and Kenya, suggesting that a fertility evolution had begun. In Kenya in particular, the total fertility rate dropped from around 8 children per woman in 1977 to 7.7 in 1984, and then more sharply to 6.7 in 1989.[72] By 1991, fertility had declined more than 10 percent in southwest Nigeria (with over 36 million people).[73]

Why did fertility fall in Botswana, Zimbabwe and Kenya? Of the mainland African countries between the Sahara and South Africa, only Botswana, Zimbabwe and Kenya have infant mortality rates below 7 percent. They all have unusually high levels of education for girls, and uniquely high levels of contraceptive practice.[74]

In Kenya, at least one proximate cause of the decline in fertility is contraception. Whereas an estimated 7 percent of married women used a contraceptive method in 1975–77, 17 percent did in 1984 and 27 percent did in 1989.[75] By 1993, 33 percent of married women used a contraceptive method.[76] Abortion is officially illegal, but hospital admissions for complications arising from abortion have reportedly risen dramatically in the past decade.[77] Why did these married women turn to contraceptives? Perhaps because average ideal family sizes reported for both husbands and wives dropped from 6.2 children in 1977–78 to 5.8 in 1984 and 4.4 in 1989.

And why did the ideal family size drop? The reasons must be many and complex, and not all of them may be knowable. Among the plausible reasons are land distribution, education and propaganda through the mass media. First, the government of Kenya's land distribution policy created many rural agricultural landowners with fixed, small to moderate holdings. Replacing communal cultivation of lands held by a clan with privately owned lands shifted some costs of large families from the community to the private landowner, giving incentives to limit family size. Second, the government of Kenya capitalized on a widespread Kenyan hunger for education by investing massively in school construction, and by getting parents to help support the operating expenses of the schools through cost-sharing fees. Parents felt the financial cost of educating children directly. Feeling the pinch played a major role in changing parents' attitudes toward contraception and family size, in nearly all studies.[78] Third, a very successful soap opera, heard by 41 percent of the population, extolled the advantages of limiting family size. Exposure to such messages through the media was strongly associated with preferences for smaller families and with the use of contraception.[79]

Many demographic experts failed to foresee the decline of Kenyan fertility. They assumed an economic model of fertility that supposed that couples always know about ways to limit the number of their children and have access to the means to do so at a cost reasonable for them. They overemphasized the resistance to change of Kenyan culture, ignoring Kenya's modernization within the framework of its traditional values. They did not give the family-planning programs enough time to develop the necessary individual and institutional infrastructure to become effective.[80]

With fertility declining in only three or four countries, it is still very early to generalize about Africa's fertility evolution (if there is to be one). Nevertheless, the African demographic transition so far appears to differ from the European pattern.[81] In the African countries with a fertility decline, contraceptive use is apparently rising and fertility is falling among women of all ages (rather than only among married women trying to limit the number of their children, as in the European fertility evolution). Unmarried young women are seeking contraception to avoid becoming pregnant and being forced to marry as a result of pregnancy. Making contraception available through anonymous commercial channels to unmarried teenagers may result in a rising age of marriage. Married women are seeking contraception to space successive births, partly to compensate for the breakdown of traditional taboos on postpartum intercourse. Couples may eventually turn from contraception for child spacing to contraception for family limitation.

Organized Efforts to Lower Fertility in the Last Half Century

After World War II, demographers' expectations of a rapid increase in human numbers, particularly in the poorer countries of the world, generated concern and action. An early alarm bell rang in 1946. Radhakamal Mukerjee, an economist at the University of Lucknow, India, argued for massive planned emigration from India and China to the "vast open spaces in Southeast Asia, Africa, and the Pacific where the white man cannot undertake manual labor nor thrive on the land, but where the ban on immigration of the yellow and brown man resulting from a narrow racial, nationalistic, or industrial policy thwarts an expansion of the agricultural front that might materially reduce world food deficiency." While advocating massive emigration in the short term, Mukerjee conceded the importance of birth control: "No people, even if they jostle one another for lack of standing-room, have the moral right to go wherever there are open spaces on the earth. . . . Birth-control and not emigration should be regarded as the major cure of overpopulation."[82]

Mukerjee's slim, polemical book received a sympathetic preface by Harold L. Ickes, who served three terms (1933–46) as Secretary of the Interior of the United States. The book also received extended scholarly review[83] and notice in a 1953 report of the United Nations.[84] But Mukerjee's plea for massive emigration was not heeded. By 1981, for example, between 5 million and 5.5 million Indians were living outside of India, about 0.7 to 0.8 percent of the Indian population then.[85]

Political obstacles opposed action to support birth control. For example, in 1950, Prescott Bush, the father of later president George H. Bush, Jr., ran for election to the United States Senate in Connecticut. On the Sunday before election day, the newspaper columnist Drew Pearson published the information that Prescott Bush was involved with Planned Parenthood, an organization that evolved from a birth control clinic Margaret Sanger opened in Brooklyn in 1916. The elder Bush lost the election by a few hundred of the nearly million votes cast, and many observers said that his alleged contacts with Planned Parenthood cost him the election.[86]

As late as December 1959, President Dwight D. Eisenhower declared that "birth control . . . is not our business. I cannot imagine anything more emphatically a subject that is not a proper political or governmental activity or function or responsibility."[87] A man who joined the staff of Planned Parenthood in 1955 described his whole first decade of work as "trying to persuade people that the roof will not fall in on them if they mention or support birth control."[88] Mailing information about birth control devices, and mailing the devices themselves, through the United States mail was prohibited by law until 1970.[89]

In spite of such obstacles, in 1952 two institutions were founded that played leading roles in organized efforts to slow population growth.[90] The International Planned Parenthood Federation, with headquarters in London, took up the task of linking the family-planning programs in different countries. The Population Council, with headquarters in New York, undertook to expand the science behind efforts to limit population growth.

The possibility of food shortages in the mid-1960s and the continuing rise of global population growth rates into the late 1960s stimulated advocates of limiting population growth.[91] In 1967, the United Nations Fund

TABLE 4.2   Annual rates of birth, death and growth
of the human population since 1950

5-year period beginning in year	annual growth rate (percent)	annual birth rate (percent)	annual death rate (percent)
1950	1.79	3.7	2.0
1955	1.86	3.6	1.7
1960	1.99	3.5	1.5
1965	2.06	3.4	1.3
1970	1.96	3.2	1.2
1975	1.73	2.8	1.1
1980	1.74	2.8	1.0
1985	1.74	2.7	0.98

SOURCES: United Nations (for birth and death rates, 1991b, pp. 226–27; for growth rate, 1992c, p. 29)

for Population Activities was founded. It provided a politically neutral con-
duit, free of the taint of neo-colonialism, from countries that wanted to
support population-related activities to countries that wanted such support.
Population-related activities included censuses and statistical development
as well as family-planning services and education. Surveys of contraceptive
knowledge, attitudes and practices showed that many women between 15
and 45 years old who were not practicing contraception wanted to space
their children or to limit the total numbers of children they had.

In 1968, Paul Ehrlich wrote:

> Too many people—that is why we are on the verge of the "death rate solution."
> . . . The agencies most likely to result in a drastic rise in the death rate in the next
> few decades are exactly those most actively operating in pre-explosion human
> populations. They are three of the four apocalyptic horsemen—war, pestilence,
> and famine. . . . It now seems inevitable that death through starvation will be at
> least one factor in the coming increase in the death rate.[92]

In the quarter century since Ehrlich wrote, the global death rate fell steadily
from 1.3 percent per year in 1965–69 to 0.98 percent per year in 1985–
89 (Table 4.2). Nevertheless, Ehrlich's alarum raised concern about "the
population problem" in the minds of many people.

Six main approaches to slowing population growth by lowering fertility
have been taken since organized international programs began in the early
1950s. Why so many approaches? At least three reasons are obvious. First,
humankind's demographic situation in the second half of the twentieth century was utterly without historical precedent. So were large-scale organized
attempts to lower fertility. History could not pronounce one approach
superior to another. Second, different countries and regions with rapid population growth were differently situated in other respects (in population

density, level of education, economic development and natural resources, for examples), hence different responses could be argued to be appropriate. Third, different groups of people saw programs to reduce fertility as potential instruments to advance their own interests. Since these interests differed, different groups favored different approaches.

The six principal approaches may be summarized as six commandments: promote contraceptives; develop economies; save children; empower women; educate men; and do all of the above! Some of these approaches aim to make people ready to lower their fertility (empower women, educate men), some aim to make them willing (save children) and some aim to make them able (promote contraceptives). Some approaches have multiple effects (develop economies, do all of the above).

Organizations, both governmental and nongovernmental, promoted modern contraceptives through information and through free or low-cost delivery of products and services. Informational programs promoted the modern idea of controlling fertility,[93] advertised the benefits of small numbers of children, dramatized the problems of large families and conveyed factual information about how to control fertility. The messages were spread through mass media—radio, television, films, newspapers, comic books and posters—and by local means such as puppets shows, theater and presentations of dance and music. With an estimated 1.9 billion radios in the world (more than one radio for every three people), the mass media offered unprecedented ways to reach every family.[94] Family-planning services to enable women to space and to limit the number of their children were delivered sometimes through special programs, sometimes as part of maternal and child health programs. Depending on the time and place, participation in family-planning programs was sometimes strictly voluntary, sometimes encouraged by financial or other incentives and sometimes effectively or actually coerced.

The governments of some developing countries perceived that rich countries promoted family-planning programs in poor countries as a form of neo-colonialism, as a covert form of racism or to avoid transfers of wealth from richer to poorer countries. In reaction, the governments of some developing countries promoted a second approach: economic development and modernization. If fertility fell in Europe and North America and Japan as those regions industrialized and became wealthy, why should not the developing countries also enjoy wealth (achieved with substantial development assistance from the industrialized nations), letting fertility fall as a consequence? The catchword of this approach was the phrase quoted earlier, "development is the best contraceptive," which gained currency after the 1974 World Population Conference in Bucharest.

A third approach emphasized improving the survival of infants and children.[95] Proponents of this approach included the United Nations Children's Fund (UNICEF) and many demographers. They suggested that parents counted on children (or at least sons) to carry on the family name, to labor on behalf of the family and to support and care for the parents in their old age. Parents would insist on having extra children as insurance, the argument went, as long as parents expected a large fraction of their children to die young. Therefore parents in developing countries had to see that their children were likely to survive infancy and childhood before parents would reduce the number of children they wanted to bear. These and additional arguments for reducing childhood mortality as a means of lowering fertility came under various attacks. At least in the short run, improving child survival appeared to increase rather than diminish population growth. Historically, in some regions, a decline in infant mortality followed, rather than preceded, a fall in fertility. UNICEF responded by urging "measures of birth spacing and family planning as part of child survival and development, on the grounds that together they will do more to reduce child mortality and fertility than either alone."[96]

A fourth approach aimed to improve the status of women through education and employment. Among countries with varying levels of female education and fertility, proponents argued, "the more education women have, the more likely they are to have small families."[97] More opportunities for girls to remain in school may delay the age of marriage and postpone the onset of fertility. Higher levels of completed education may increase women's opportunities to work outside of the home and expose them to modern views of limited family size. Both effects of schooling may reduce the number of children women eventually have. In support of improving conditions for women, and in opposition to promoting contraceptives through family-planning programs, Lant H. Pritchett, a senior economist at the World Bank, argued

> that high fertility primarily reflects desired births and that couples are roughly able to achieve their fertility targets. . . . In this view men's and women's fertility choices, which are conditioned and constrained by the social, educational, cultural, and economic conditions they face, are the primary determinants of actual fertility. Furthermore, policies that improve objective conditions for women—raising their income, increasing their education, encouraging empowerment—are probably the most important voluntary and sustainable way to achieve the reductions in fertility necessary to slow population growth.
>
> . . . nearly all (roughly 90%) of the differences between countries in actual fertility are accounted for solely by differences in desired fertility. . . . although contraceptive use is an obvious proximate (or direct) determinant of fertility and hence an important correlate of fertility, contraceptive prevalence has no effect on excess fertility (or the fraction of births that are unwanted) and little independent effect on fertility, after controlling for fertility desires. Moreover, measures of a country's family planning effort also have only a small effect on fertility after controlling for fertility desires.[98]

Of course, if a country's family-planning effort changes people's fertility desires, then controlling for fertility desires eliminates the effect of the family-planning program on those desires.

While countries where women have better education and economic opportunities have lower fertility in general, the directions of causality are not clear. Perhaps cultures that are ready to invest in educating girls and women are also ready for fertility to fall.[99] In any event, in cultures where women are expected to marry early, raise many children and have no independent lives outside of their homes, improving the status of women through education and employment overthrows the traditional concept of the family. Reducing fertility by empowering women is the approach that most clearly aims to undermine the cultural values of societies with high fertility.

A fifth approach, educating men, has not yet achieved the visibility of the strategy of empowering women. In September 1993, at the meeting of the International Union for the Scientific Study of Population in Montreal, a male African demographer suggested that it might do little good to offer women contraceptives or educate women with the intention of reducing fertility if the decisions about fertility are taken by men. He advocated educating men about the benefits of small families and the means of achieving them. His recommendation is supported by a 1994 survey in Nigerian cities: 97 percent of men and 91 percent of women agreed that men want more children than women. Most agreed that a woman would be reluctant to practice family planning if she feared her husband would object. The author of the survey, Uche C. Isiugo-Abanihe, a demographer and sociologist at the University of Ibadan, concluded that programs to provide population information and awareness need to address the "prevailing high reproductive goals of Nigerian men."[100]

Finally, some advocates argued that different approaches would be more effective if combined with others.[101] Couples must be ready, willing and able to lower their fertility if fertility is to fall. Educated women are more likely to use contraceptives effectively, to avoid having more children than they want and to want fewer than uneducated women. Economic development is more likely to increase the demand for family-planning services when the institutions and people are already in place to deliver family-planning services and products.

The United Nations International Conference on Population and Development (ICPD), held in September 1994 in Cairo, advocated all conceivable voluntary approaches. By one count, the ICPD's final *Programme of Action,* a document of 115 single-spaced pages, offered more than 1,000 recommendations. Only a handful of the recommendations dealt with the desirability and means of reducing fertility and slowing population growth. The remaining recommendations urged governments to improve almost every aspect of human well-being, but specified no priorities.

There was something for almost everybody in the final report's mix of dream and sermon, of wish and prayer. Chapters dealt with general principles; the relationships among population, sustained economic growth and sustainable development; the empowerment of women; the family; population growth and structure; reproductive rights and reproductive health; health, morbidity and mortality; population distribution, urbanization and internal migration; international migration; education; technology, research and development; national action; international cooperation; the nongovernmental sector; and follow-up to the conference.

The ICPD's announced aim was to build a consensus among the world's nations on population and development over the next 20 years. One reason for the diversity (and frequent inconsistency) of the recommendations in the *Programme of Action* was that no single formula was appropriate for the 183 countries that sent delegations to the meeting. Another reason was that, as there was no consensus among scholars about the most effective means of lowering fertility before the meeting, one could hardly have expected the ICPD to take a single clear direction. And it did not.

Abortion, adolescent sexuality, homosexuality and extramarital sexual relations absorbed attention and generated rhetoric. Despite the controversies over these issues—which many saw as diversions from the principal problems the ICPD was intended to address—the ICPD can take credit for at least three major accomplishments.

First, contrary to the statement of former president Dwight D. Eisenhower, family planning and contraception were firmly established as proper subjects for discussion and action by almost all peoples and governments. The 2,000 journalists who covered the Cairo conference saw to it that family planning is no longer a taboo topic.

Second, the right of women to limit their own fertility was affirmed. Women took center stage in the conference's organization and proceedings, in its final document and among the 900 accredited nongovernmental organizations that attended. Women's health, jobs, credit, education, property rights and reproductive autonomy emerged as primary concerns.

Third, the United States resumed shared leadership along with other industrialized nations in promoting slower population growth to enhance human well-being. President Clinton requested $585 million for population activities in fiscal 1995. Both houses of Congress approved $10 million more than he asked for. The United States will become the largest single donor. Over the next seven years, Japan will spend $3 billion and Germany $2 billion for population activities.

An additional important accomplishment of the ICPD is that it was held at all, despite serious threats of disruption, and was held in Cairo. This venue recognizes that some Muslim countries are aware of their own population problems.

One such country, Indonesia, the fourth most populous country in the world in 1995, illustrates how different approaches interact.[102] From 1970 to 1980, the average number of children per woman fell from 5.6 to 4.1; in the next five years, it fell from 4.1 to 3.2. In 1980, 27 percent of women used contraception; in 1987, 47 percent. Women's mean age of marriage rose from 19.3 years in 1971 to 21.1 years in 1985. The fraction of children aged 7 to 12 years who were enrolled in school rose from under 50 percent in 1961 to 60 percent in 1971 and to 94 percent in 1985. Between 1980 and 1987, real wages for women rose by 65 percent and for men by 40 percent.

These were years of extraordinary social, behavioral and economic change.

What caused the fall in fertility? Econometric analysis indicated that 75 percent of the decline of fertility in Indonesia from 1982 to 1987 resulted from increased use of contraceptives, and that 87 percent of the increase in use resulted from improved education and wages. "Therefore the educational and economic impacts, working strictly through increases in contraceptive use, accounted for 65% of fertility decline. In contrast, changes in measures of family planning program inputs were responsible for only 4 to 8% of the decline."[103] However, the contraceptives were supplied on demand because Indonesia already had a highly responsive system that delivered both commodities and services.

Of the six principal approaches to lowering the fertility of a country, which achieves the greatest reduction per dollar spent? Given limited resources, will a government or a private organization do better to spread its resources on a combination of approaches, or to focus single-mindedly on one or another approach? No one seems to know for sure. Enthusiasts are disinclined to compare approaches that they don't favor in expensive field trials. Localities vary in so many important respects that it is extremely difficult to do a clean controlled experiment in the field.

In spite of such obstacles and difficulties, some things have been learned about what does work. As the percentage of married women aged 15 to 44 years who use contraception of any kind (the so-called contraceptive prevalence) goes up, the average number of children per woman at current rates (the total fertility rate) goes down (Figure 4.5). The contraceptive prevalence takes no notice of the age of marriage (it deals only with women already married), of the fertility of the unmarried or of the proportion of women voluntarily or involuntarily sterile within marriage; hence it could not be, and is not, a perfect predictor of fertility. On the average, however, for each 15 percentage points of increase in contraceptive prevalence, women give birth to one fewer child. Differences between countries in the contraceptive prevalence rate account statistically for about 90 percent of the differences between those countries in the total fertility rate. As Bryant Robey of Johns Hopkins University, Shea O. Rutstein of the Demographic and Health Surveys Program and Leo Morris of the U.S. Centers for Disease Control put it:

. . . although development and social change create conditions that encourage smaller family size, contraceptives are the best contraceptive. . . . changes in contraceptive use and in fertility depend as much on the strength of a country's family-planning effort as on its economic development.[104]

It is not too surprising that family-planning programs contributed to the fall in fertility, given that millions of women said at the outset that they were having more children than they wanted. What is surprising is the trigger that Robey, Rutstein and Morris identified as firing off the rapid drop in fertility in many developing countries in the last two decades. The trigger

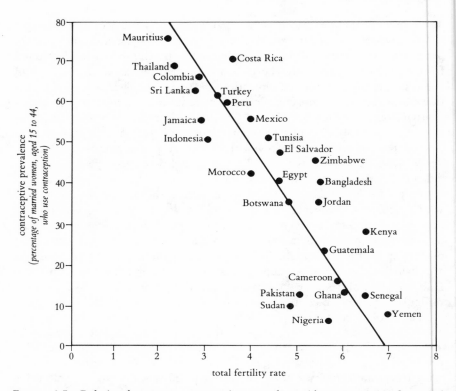

FIGURE 4.5   Relation between contraceptive prevalence (the percentage of married women, aged 15 to 44 years, who use any form of contraception) and the total fertility rate (the average number of children a woman bears in her lifetime, at current age-specific fertility rates) in some developing countries, 1984–92. SOURCE: Robey et al. (1993, p. 62)

they identified was none of the approaches described above, but was the same unwelcome cause that lowered fertility in the United States during the 1930s: hard times, or "the sharp economic contractions of the late 1970s and early 1980s. For the first time, many families found that their standard of living fell. In response, couples decided to limit their family size or to postpone the next birth. This trend is unlikely to reverse."[105] Would Malthus have been surprised?

UNINTENDED EFFECTS: THE LAW OF ACTION

The story thus far demonstrates the difficulty of doing just what is intended. Among the many examples that could be chosen, here are three. The plow increased food production in the short term but promoted soil erosion that undermined food production in the long term.

The insecticide DDT saved human lives from malaria after World War II and contributed materially to the rise in population in developing countries. Through widespread agricultural use, DDT probably also affected adversely many species other than the targeted pests.

The Green Revolution greatly increased grain production in developing countries, but favored owners of high-quality lands, for whom it was profitable to invest in irrigation, fertilizers and control of pests. In some countries, the net effect on the distribution of income was probably to increase the concentration of wealth in the hands of the wealthy.

In 1776, the Scottish philosopher and economist Adam Smith (1723–1790) devoted a chapter of *The Wealth of Nations* to illustrating the (benificent, in his case) unintended social consequences of individual actions, and contemporary economists have developed many more illustrations.[106] In 1963, the ecologist Garrett Hardin proposed a First Law of Ecology: "We can never do merely one thing." He intended to suggest that every action has "at least one unwanted consequence."[107] For me, "never" is a strong word, and not every unintended consequence is necessarily unwanted. But it is difficult to do one thing without entailing additional and often unexpected consequences. Even inaction achieves its desired consequences imperfectly, as the British statesman Neville Chamberlain (1869–1940) discovered on the eve of World War II. I propose a Law of Action: it is difficult to do just what you intended to do.

5

Human Population History in Numbers and Graphs

EVERETT MCKINLEY DIRKSEN (1896–1969), a conservative congressman and senator from Illinois, once commented on the ease with which the U.S. Congress dispensed the American taxpayers' money: "A billion dollars here, a billion dollars there, and pretty soon it adds up to real money." A similar remark applies to global population growth.

It took from the beginning of time until roughly 2,000 years ago for the Earth's human population to reach a quarter billion. It took until roughly A.D. 1600 to reach half a billion, and until sometime between 1800 and 1850 to pass one billion. After only one more century, around 1930, the population reached two billion. The next increase by a billion took only 30 years, from 1930 to 1960. The next billion took only 14 years, as the population passed four billion around 1974. The following billion took only 12 years: the population passed five billion around 1986. Demographers confidently expect more than six billion humans to be alive by the year 2000. A billion people here, a billion people there, and pretty soon it adds up to a real crowd.

I now tell the story of the human population from the beginning in somewhat greater detail, numerically and graphically. Why? Because the numbers are essential to prove historical generalizations, and the graphs could (but don't) reveal simple patterns in the history of population growth.

Did the Global Population Growth Rate Increase at Each Evolution?

In a verbal assertion that begs for quantitative proof, William H. McNeill began his magisterial *A World History* by claiming that the local agricultural evolution coincided with "an enormous multiplication of human numbers."[1] Was it really so? The numbers, though based on substantial guesswork, say yes: the average annual global population growth rate rose by a factor of ten to several hundred around the time of the local agricultural evolution.

Testing McNeill's claim requires population estimates at three points in time: at the origin of the human species, at 10,000 B.C., and at A.D. 1. When the human species originated, the minimum population size must have been two or more people. A more likely estimate is that the species began in a band of hominids grossly similar in social structure to today's chimpanzees or baboons. A plausible upper bound to the size of such a group is 200 individuals.[2]

How long ago did the individuals in an ancestral group become close enough to the present *Homo sapiens* to be called human? This imprecise question has no precise answer. Hominids, in the sense of the lines of descent leading to today's great apes and humans, originated perhaps 17 million years ago. The human lineage clearly existed 4 million years ago. Fossil tracks indicate that proto-humans were bipedal 3 million years ago. Flaked-stone tools manufactured by proto-humans date back 2.4 million years.[3] Humans with modern anatomy existed perhaps 120,000 years ago. Let us suppose that humans emerged between 1 million and 4 million years ago.

At 10,000 B.C., estimates of population size vary. McEvedy and Jones estimated 4 million people.[4] The demographic archeologist Fekri A. Hassan at Washington State University estimated approximately 8.5 million.[5] The French demographer Roland Pressat estimated between 5 and 10 million.[6] Cipolla estimated between 2 and 20 million.[7] The anthropologist Joseph B. Birdsell estimated 2.2 million people at 8000 B.C.[8] Since the estimates of Cipolla are consistent with all the other estimates and are the most modest about current knowledge of the remote past, I accept the range of 2 million to 20 million people at 10,000 B.C.

At A.D. 1, global population estimates also vary widely (Appendix 2). McEvedy and Jones estimated 170 million people.[9] Biraben estimated 252 million.[10] Hauser quotes a United Nations estimate of about 300 million.[11] The demographic historian John Durand estimated a range from 270 to 330 million.[12] I accept the range from 170 million to 330 million; as a single estimate, I would use a quarter billion because it suggests no more precision than the evidence justifies.

In absolute terms, an increase from 2–20 million people in 10,000 B.C. to 170–330 million people around A.D. 1 is enormous. McNeill's claim is correct for absolute numbers. A subtler question is whether the rate of population increase after 10,000 B.C. greatly exceeded that prior to 10,000 B.C. The estimates *least* favorable to an increased population growth rate would assume (first) the largest possible growth in the earlier period, from two individuals initially to 20 million at 10,000 B.C., over the shortest possible time, 990,000 years; and (second) the smallest possible growth in the later period, from 20 million at 10,000 B.C. to 170 million in A.D. 1. Under these assumptions, the average growth rate prior to 10,000 B.C. was roughly 0.0016 percent per year, that is, less than 1/500th of a percent per year, while from 10,000 B.C. to A.D. 1 the average growth rate was roughly 0.021 percent per year, that is, just over 1/50th of a percent per year. At a minimum, therefore, the average rate of population growth increased by a factor of 13 after the local agricultural evolution, compared to the earlier period.

The estimates most favorable to a rise in growth rates at the time of the local agricultural evolution would assume a rise from a high initial guess of 200 individuals (4 million years in the past) to a low of 2 million people (at 10,000 B.C.) to a high of 330 million (at A.D. 1). These estimates yield average annual growth rates of 0.00023 percent and 0.051 percent before and after 10,000 B.C., which is an increase in average rates by a factor of 221.

If instead of 200 people 4 million years in the past, I used Deevey's estimate of 125,000 people a million years in the past, the average annual growth rate for the period before 10,000 B.C. would range from 0.00028 percent to 0.00051 percent. These values fall nicely within the range of growth rates just estimated for the period before 10,000 B.C. and are both a small fraction of the estimated average annual growth rate after 10,000 B.C.

I conclude that the local agricultural evolution coincided with a rise in the average annual global population growth rate by a factor of at least ten to several hundred. The average annual growth rates before and after the local agricultural evolution were tiny compared to those that lay ahead. No matter how the population estimates and time spans are combined, the average annual growth rates up to A.D. 1 are a tiny fraction of a percent per year. Tiny average growth rates do not imply that births and deaths were exquisitely balanced in each year of these ten millennia, but just that the average is small.

On a millennial time scale and a global geographic scale, the demographic sailing was apparently smooth between the local and the global agricultural evolutions. From A.D. 1 to 1650, global population climbed from perhaps 170–330 million to perhaps 500–600 million. Supposing the population doubled in this period, the average population growth rate was about 0.042 percent per year, less than 1/24th of a percent per year. This estimate falls within the range from 0.021 percent to 0.051 percent of annual population growth rates already estimated for the period from 10,000 B.C. to A.D. 1. The agreement of the estimates before and after A.D. 1 suggests that there were no radical changes in the factors affecting global long-term average population growth from the local agricultural evolution to the global agricultural evolution.

The global agricultural evolution coincided with a further large increase in the average annual global population growth rate. The quantitative evidence can be pieced together from population estimates at three points in time: A.D. 1, 1750 (the midpoint of the period 1650–1850) and 1950. For A.D. 1, estimates already quoted ranged from 170 million to 330 million. For 1750, I accept Cipolla's range of 650 million to 850 million.[13] For 1950, I accept the United Nations estimate of 2,516 million[14] (a number with more precision than could possibly make sense), modified by the uncertainty of plus or minus 5 percent that Cipolla prudently attached to an earlier and different U.N. estimate for 1950.[15] I suppose that world population in 1950 numbered between 2,390 million and 2,642 million.

According to these guesses, the population trajectory (for A.D. 1 to 1750 to 1950) with the smallest increase in growth rate goes from 170 million to 850 million to 2,390 million. The average growth rates are 0.092 percent per year from A.D. 1 to 1750 and 0.52 percent per year from 1750 to 1950. Such a trajectory entails a nearly six-fold rise in the average annual population growth rate.

The population trajectory with the greatest increase in growth rate goes from 330 million to 650 million to 2,642 million. The average growth rates are 0.039 percent per year from A.D. 1 to 1750 and 0.70 percent per year from 1750 to 1950. This trajectory involves a nearly 18-fold rise in the average annual population growth rate.

From 1850 to 1900, world population increased from around 1.2 billion to around 1.65 billion, with an average population growth rate of around 0.6 percent per year (Appendix 2).[16] From 1900 to 1950, the average annual growth rate was nearly 0.8 percent. In the next quarter century, the average annual growth rate more than doubled, to 1.9 percent per year, as the population rose to 4.1 billion by 1975. Between 1975 and 1990, population rose to 5.3 billion, at an average growth rate of just under 1.8 percent per year (see Figure 4.2).

A PICTURE ALBUM
OF HUMAN POPULATION GROWTH

The pictures that follow display human numbers over the past million years. The numbers are assembled in Appendix 2. The making of these pictures should be viewed as part of the persistent human urge to seek simplicity and beauty in experience. If the pictures revealed simple patterns in past human population growth, then these patterns might serve as a guide to future population growth at the global level over millennia. Unfortunately, I have not yet discovered a form of graphing that reveals a beautiful simplicity in the history of the global human population. Whatever beauty you may find must arise from the complexity of the facts.

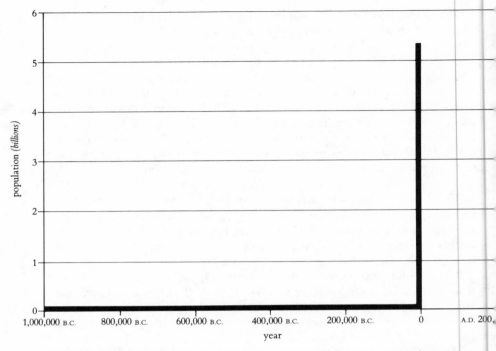

FIGURE 5.1   Estimated human population from a million years ago to the present.
SOURCE OF DATA: Appendix 2

The Conventional Portrait

The conventional formal portrait of the human population suggests an airport runway that terminates in a high stone wall (Figure 5.1). An immensely long period of time with very low numbers of people (the runway) is followed by a very short period of nearly vertical increase in numbers (the wall). Any airplane with a trajectory for takeoff like this would severely wrench its passengers and its mechanical parts.

To represent the uncertainty about population numbers, the precise-looking thin line should be replaced by a blurry-edged line of spray paint. The population size at 10,000 B.C. is probably accurate within a factor of ten or so; that at A.D. 1, within a factor of two or so; that at 1750, within a factor of 1.2 (20 percent) or so[17]; and that of today, within a factor of perhaps 1.05 (5 percent). Because of the dramatic rises in population in recent centuries, allowing for uncertainty would not seriously affect the shape of the curve.

Zooming in on the 12 millennia since the end of the last ice age expands the time axis 100-fold. The modern rise of population is only slightly less abrupt at this magnification (Figure 5.2). This figure hints that the global population growth rate was higher in the millennium before Christ than in the millennium after, but the calculations described above revealed no

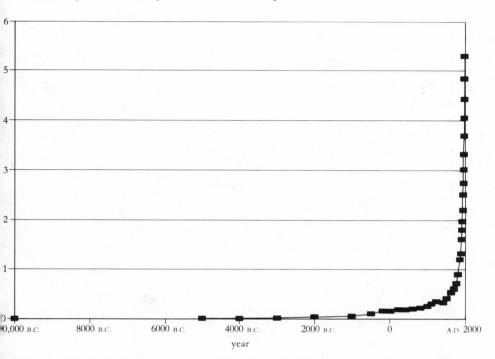

FIGURE 5.2   Estimated human population from the last ice age to the present. SOURCE OF DATA: Appendix 2

major change in the population growth rate around the time of Christ. The appearance of a slowdown could easily result from inadequate population data, especially from the millennium before Christ. Alternatively, a real slowdown might have been caused by greater mortality from infectious diseases in denser population aggregates.[18]

Zooming in closer on the last 2,000 years (another six-fold magnification of the time axis) shows an abrupt rise in numbers over the last four centuries. Figure 5.3 includes all the variant estimates of population size.

Photographers' Models: Exponential, Logistic, Doomsday and Sum of Exponentials

In reflecting on the history of the human population, it is useful not only to appreciate the complexities, as we have done, but also to seek the simplicities. Does the size of the human population follow any overall pattern that can be described in a simple way? Four idealized models of population growth will be described here, then compared with history. The models are known as the exponential, logistic, doomsday and sum-of-exponential models.

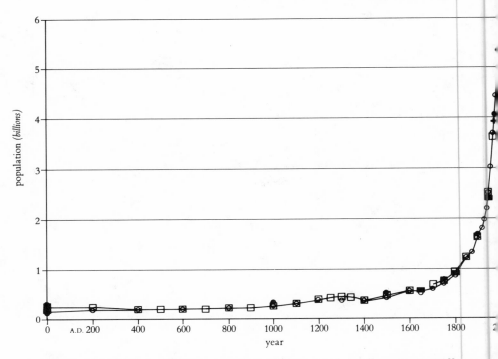

FIGURE 5.3   Estimated human population from A.D. 1 to the present. Different symbols represent estimates from different sources. SOURCE OF DATA: Appendix 2

The exponential curve. By definition, exponential growth means that the population size after *t* years from the start of observation equals the initial number of people multiplied times (1 plus the relative growth rate *r*)^t, where the exponent *t* is the number of years since the beginning of observation. On a graph, the location and curvature of an exponential curve depend on its initial population size and its growth rate *r*. Different values of time *t* are used to trace out the curve. In an exponentially growing population, the relative growth rate *r*, or percentage of increase per year, is constant as time passes.

In 1755, Benjamin Franklin, the American printer, polymath and patriot, estimated that the population of the American colonies was doubling approximately every 25 years and that "before long, the greatest number of *Englishmen* will be on this side of the water." In the 1830 edition of his work on population, Malthus took the population increase of the former English colonies in America as an example of "unfettered" growth. From U.S. censuses, he estimated that the population was doubling approximately every 25 years, after correcting for the contribution of immigration.[19] For several European countries, Malthus estimated doubling times of approximately 50 years.

Most countries that have been carefully observed have not had constant doubling times. For example, in the United States, the decadal increase

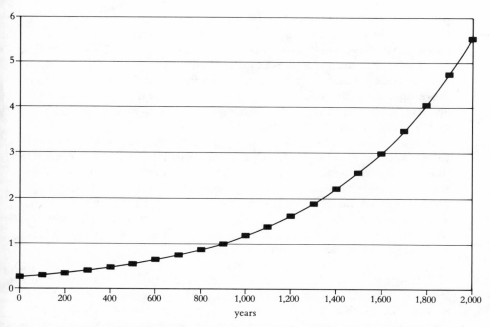

FIGURE 5.4 Hypothetical population growing exponentially from an initial value of 250 million people at 0.155 percent per year and reaching a population of 5.54 billion after 2,000 years. The population at year t is computed as $2.5 \times 10^8 \times (1.00155)^t$.

from one census to the next fluctuated between 32.7 percent and 36.4 percent from 1800 to 1860, then began to fall sharply: to 26 percent by 1880, to 21 percent by 1900 and to 15 percent by 1920. The U.S. population growth rate fell in spite of abundant food and space, and without Malthusian misery and vice.

In the nineteenth century, the Registrar General of the United Kingdom (a government agency analogous to the U.S. Bureau of the Census or the demographic statistical office of many other countries) published estimates of British population in the years after the most recent census based on strict exponential extrapolation of the penultimate and latest decennial censuses. In 1895, Edwin Cannan, a British economist, ridiculed these intercensal population projections because the exponential extrapolations were invariably far off the mark when the next census was made.[20] The growth rate of the decade just completed was then corrected to conform to the new census figure on the supposition that growth had been exponential, but at a rate that changed on the date of the previous census. The resulting "corrected" series of birth rates, marriage rates and death rates saw-toothed irregularly between one decade of supposed exponential growth and the next.

The exponential curve is no more successful for global population than for the American or the British. The starting and ending populations of the hypothetical curve in Figure 5.4 correspond roughly to the estimated real population sizes at the hypothetical starting and ending dates. Visual comparison of the exponential curve with the historical estimates shows that the exponential curve rises much more smoothly, unaffected by the Black Death of the fourteenth century. One could hardly expect a model as simple as a model of constant relative growth to reflect such fluctuations. A much more serious problem for the exponential model is that it lacks the gross acceleration of population growth observed in the twentieth century prior to 1970, and the deceleration since then.

Because of its great simplicity, the exponential model is remarkably useful for very short-term predictions: the growth rate of a large population during the next one to five years usually resembles the growth rate of that population over the past one to five years.[21] Because of its great simplicity, the exponential model is not very useful for long-term predictions, beyond a decade or two. Surprisingly, in spite of the abundant data to the contrary, many people believe that the human population grows exponentially. It probably never has and probably never will.

The logistic curve. The logistic equation asserts that the change in population size during the next time period equals the product (the result of multiplying) of three factors: a constant relative growth rate called the Malthusian parameter (which is assumed to be greater than zero, so that the population does not spontaneously go extinct); the current population size at the beginning of the period; and the difference between the carrying capacity and the current population. In one common notation, the Malthusian parameter is written r and the carrying capacity is written K. If P stands for the current size of the population, then the change in population size during the next time period equals $r \times P \times (K - P)$, according to the logistic equation.[22]

In the logistic equation, the Malthusian parameter and the carrying capacity are both assumed not to change in time. The population size P and the carrying capacity K are measured in the same units, usually the numbers of individuals or the aggregate weight (biomass) of the population, possibly per unit of area or per unit of volume of the environment.

The logistic equation assumes a population with neither immigration nor emigration. It assumes an environment with a steady supply per unit of time of the nutrients and resources required to support the species being considered. The spatial boundaries of the population are assumed to be fixed and known.

When a population increases according to the logistic curve, the relative growth rate is highest at the very beginning and ultimately drops to zero. Because the curve starts growing (nearly) exponentially at first, but decelerates as it approaches some fixed upper limit, it is sometimes described as S-shaped. The logistic curve has a constantly falling relative growth rate, unlike the constant relative growth rate of the exponential curve and still less like the increasing relative growth rate of the data up to 1970.

If the starting population P exceeds its carrying capacity K,[23] then the population declines, gradually settling toward its carrying capacity. As P approaches closer and closer to K, the population changes size more and more slowly.

When P just equals K, $K-P$ is zero and therefore the product $r \times P \times (K-P)$ is zero. Then the population size does not change during the next unit interval of time, or ever again, as long as the logistic equation governs its growth. The population is said to be stationary when it just equals its carrying capacity.[24]

The logistic equation was created by Pierre François Verhulst, a professor of mathematics at the École Militaire (Military College) in Brussels, Belgium. In 1838, 1845 and 1847 he published three memoirs in which he derived a new mathematical curve for human population, one that avoids predicting a population of infinite size. In 1845, he named it the logistic curve.[25] Verhulst fitted the logistic curve to three censuses of the American population. His predictions of future American population growth did not turn out well.[26]

In 1920, Raymond Pearl, an energetic professor of biometry and vital statistics at Johns Hopkins University, and his colleague Lowell J. Reed fitted the logistic curve to the U.S. census results from 1790 to 1910 (Figure 5.5).[27] Apparently they did not at first know that Verhulst had derived the same curve and fitted it to data more than 80 years earlier. Presumably they knew, but were not troubled by the knowledge, that the territory of the United States more than tripled between 1790 and 1910.[28] If the ceiling on population size assumed by the logistic theory were related to territory, it could not have been fixed over this period.[29] Their fitted curve predicted an upper limit to the U.S. population of 197.3 million people. The curve agreed quite well with the census results from 1920 to 1950. The baby boom arrived in the United States after World War II. By 1970, the U.S. population surpassed the upper limit of 197.3 million people. The 1990 U.S. population approximated 250 million.

In 1924, Pearl and Reed fitted the logistic curve to population histories of cities, countries and the world as if it were consistent to expect all of them to be logistic.[30] Unfortunately for them, a sum of logistic curves with different initial growth rates and different upper limits is not a logistic curve. Hence global population growth would not be expected to be logistic if national or regional growth were exactly logistic.

Listen to the sweet things Pearl and Reed said about the logistic curve: "We think that the evidence to be presented strongly suggests that [the logistic curve] may be regarded as an adequate description of the phenomena of population growth. It seems to us fairly to correspond, in a modest way, to Kepler's Law of the motion of the planets in elliptic orbits, but to lack the heuristic element which Newton added in showing that gravitation would account for elliptic orbits. . . ."[31]

The logistic curve can be trusted far into the past and far into the future, they claimed:

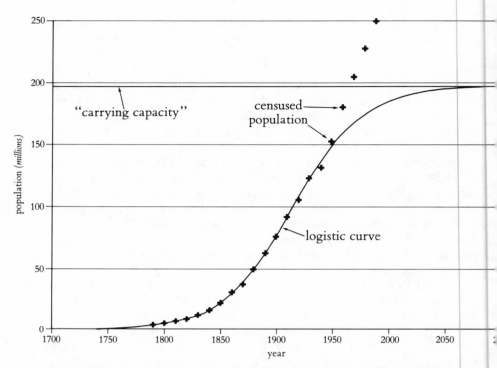

FIGURE 5.5   Censused population of the United States from 1790 to 1990 (+ symbols), and a logistic curve (solid sigmoid curve) fitted in 1920 to the censuses from 1790 to 1910. The horizontal solid line at 197.27 shows the upper asymptote or "carrying capacity" of the fitted logistic curve. SOURCES: Pearl and Reed (1924) for the logistic curve and the censuses through 1910; United States Bureau of the Census (1974) for the censused resident population 1920–40; United Nations (1993, p. 660) for the population estimates 1950–90

> Now if, as we believe to be the case, this curve states a first approximation to a descriptive law of nature, there is some justification for extrapolation in both directions from the period of known population history. That is to say, the curve enables and in some degree justifies the prediction of future populations, and the estimation of past populations before census counts were made. Accordingly we have in each case extended the curves to the upper and the lower asymptotic conditions realizing that in so doing we are inviting criticism.[32]

From a logistic curve fitted to estimates of world population size over two and a half centuries ending in 1914, Pearl and Reed in 1924 estimated an upper limit of two billion people.[33] Around 1930, world population surpassed this limit. As I mentioned in Chapter 4, Pearl and his associate, Sophia Gould, refitted the logistic curve in 1936, including the latest estimates of world population. They estimated an upper limit of just over 2.6 billion, which they predicted would be reached about A.D. 2100. Writing in the midst of the Great Depression, they emphasized that world population growth was slowing down. By 1955, world population numbered 2.8 billion and the annual population growth rate, far from falling from the 1 percent that Pearl and Gould estimated in 1936, had jumped to almost 1.9 percent.

Pearl was influential in the political world of science and promoted the logistic curve so effectively that some users attached his name to it, with or without Verhulst's. In 1945, Hornell Hart, a sociologist at Duke University, reviewed "logistic social trends" and enumerated 219 applications of the logistic curve, including the population growth of countries, the size of empires in Asia, the number of "independent countries in Europe and in North and South America which had adopted postage stamps" and the number of lynchings per million of the American population.[34]

In a 1977 study of world food prospects, a team at the Hudson Institute including the futurologist Herman Kahn wrote: "Our argument concerning population growth is that its rate is approximated by a flattened S-shaped (or logistical) curve, rather than by an exponential one. We do not envisage population growth continuing to a point where it encounters physical barriers, such as lack of living space or resources, and brings about widespread scarcities, famines, and intolerable pollution."[35]

Efforts to fit the logistic curve to the population sizes of England, Scotland, Australia and New Zealand appeared to be successful for a time, according to a 1992 report that promoted the use of the logistic for global population projection, "but a jump in the parameters occurred just after the Second World War. . . . Thus there are apparently logistic-type regimes which persist until some major event occurs."[36] That is, the logistic curve works until it doesn't.[37]

The principal assumption of the logistic curve, that the population growth rate declines in a straight line as the population increases, is flatly contradicted by the *increasing* population growth rate throughout most of the history of world population up to 1965. The three hypothetical logistic curves in Figure 5.6 all have the same initial population size, 250 million people. From the top curve to the bottom curve, the hypothetical ceilings K on population size are 10 billion, 20 billion and 30 billion and the relative population growth rates r are 0.19 percent, 0.17 percent and 0.165 percent. With these values, after 2,000 years, the hypothetical populations reach 5.33 billion, 5.49 billion and 5.55 billion. The higher the ultimate ceiling, the steeper the curve at the year 2000 and the more the curve resembles the exponential curve. Yet none resembles the course of global population size over the last two millennia.

The logistic curve describes well the growth of laboratory populations of fruit flies and bacteria[38] and has been applied to the population growth of yeast cells, honey bees and sheep. For human population projection, the logistic curve is not noticeably worse than other smooth curves for short-term prediction of human population sizes and no better for long-term prediction.[39] In spite of its poor performance in past long-term predictions of human population sizes, enthusiasm for the logistic curve survives in some quarters.

If a hypothetical population's growth rate responds with a lag to the cur-

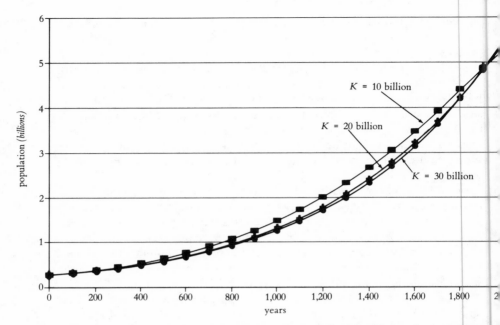

FIGURE 5.6   Three hypothetical populations growing logistically from an initial 250 million people with a ceiling of 10 billion people (solid rectangles), 20 billion people (+ symbols) or 30 billion people (• symbols). All three curves reach approximately 5.5 billion people after 2,000 years. For the curve with a ceiling at 10 billion people, the population at year t is computed as $10^{10}/\{1 + [10^{10}/(2.5 \times 10^8) - 1]1.0019^{-t}\}$; the other curves were computed with the ceilings and growth rates shown in the text.

rent population size according to what is called the discrete-time logistic equation,[40] and if r is sufficiently large, the population can behave very strangely. It may oscillate periodically or even fluctuate chaotically, that is, without any apparent determined pattern or repetition.[41] Widely regarded as a very tame beast for the first century and a half of its existence, since the 1970s the logistic equation has been discovered to be a mathematical wolf in sheep's clothing. For more chaos (of the mathematical variety), see Appendix 6.

The doomsday curve. A third model is called the doomsday equation.[42] In 1960, an electrical engineer at the University of Illinois, Heinz von Foerster, and his colleagues Patricia M. Mora and Lawrence W. Amiot suggested a model in which the relative growth rate of the world's population is neither constant, as the exponential model assumes, nor decreasing, as the logistic model assumes, but increases in direct proportion to the size of the population. That is, if a population doubles, its relative growth rate also doubles. A mathematical consequence of this assumption is that the human population will become infinite after a finite amount of time. At that point, presumably, all our problems would come to an end, though not a very

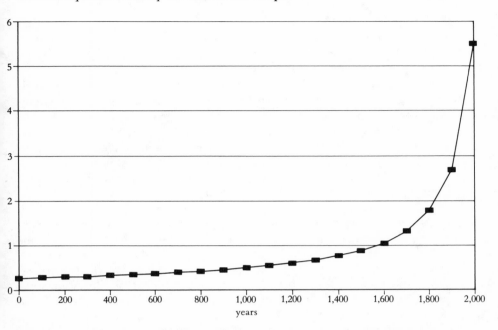

FIGURE 5.7 Hypothetical population growing according to the doomsday curve of von Foerster et al. (1960) from an initial 250 million people to 5.51 billion people after 2,000 years. The population at year t is computed as $2.5 \times 10^8 \times 2,095/(2,095 - t)$.

pleasant one. Don't worry; the conclusion is only as good as the assumption, and the assumption is no more plausible than the exponential curve's assumption of constant relative growth.

Von Foerster et al. originally fitted the doomsday equation to population data up to 1958. They estimated (deadpan, but good-humoredly) that population size would go infinite on 13 November 2026 (which just happens to be Friday the 13th). In 1994, two ecologists at the University of Georgia, H. Ronald Pulliam and Nick M. Haddad, reported, with precision that defies belief, that the global human population size fell below that projected by von Foerster et al. "for the first time on 5 May 1994."[43] The doomsday equation predicted the approximate observed population sizes for several decades after 1960 by predicting growth rates that were at first too low and then too high, compared to those observed.

To give the model the benefit of the doubt, it is necessary now to refit the model to more recent data. With an initial hypothetical population size (in year zero) of 250 million and a "doomsday" estimated at A.D. 2095, the model predicts a population of 5.51 billion after 2,000 years (Figure 5.7). Visual comparison of the data (Figure 5.3) with this theory (Figure 5.7) shows that, while the doomsday curve accelerates much more than the exponential or logistic curves, it does not accelerate quite as much as the data. Whereas the doomsday equation (when pegged to 5.5 billion at

$t = $ A.D. 2000) passes one billion people after 1,600 years, the real world population reached one billion only after A.D. 1800, and still accelerated to pass 5.5 billion before A.D. 2000.

In 1962, two years after von Foerster et al. published their doomsday equation, Dorn commented: ". . . this forecast probably will set a record, for the entire class of forecasts prepared by the use of mathematical functions, for the short length of time required to demonstrate its unreliability."[44] Dorn was right. Within the decade, the relative growth rate of the world's population began to drop while the population size continued to rise, contrary to the model's hypothesis that the relative growth rate would rise with rising population. Notwithstanding its theoretical and empirical failings, the doomsday equation still has at least one enthusiast.[45]

The sum-of-exponentials curve. A final model, the sum of exponentials, supposes that the population is divided into two subpopulations. One subpopulation starts out as a large majority, but grows slowly. The other subpopulation starts out as a tiny minority, but grows rapidly. The population size is the sum of the two subpopulation sizes. At first, the population grows slowly, because it is dominated by the slow subpopulation. After a while, the initial minority overtakes the slowly growing subpopulation and the growth rate of the whole population increases toward the growth rate

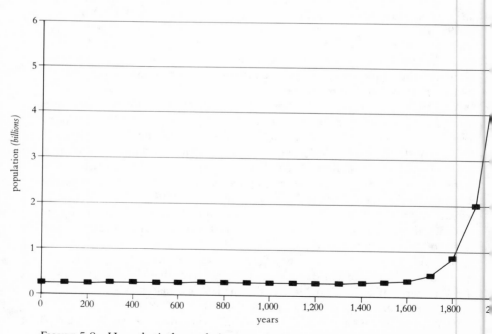

FIGURE 5.8   Hypothetical population growing as a sum of exponential subpopulations from an initial 250 million people to 5.52 billion people after 2,000 years. population at year t is computed as $2.5 \times 10^8 \times 1.0001^t + 1.01125^t$.

of the faster-growing subpopulation. A population growing as a sum of exponentials displays ever-increasing relative growth, like the doomsday model, but does not approach an infinite size in a finite time.[46]

A sum-of-exponentials curve requires estimates of the initial population size, the initial proportion in the slower-growing population and the growth rates of each subpopulation. In Figure 5.8, one person (obviously hermaphroditic) starts out with a growth rate of 1.125 percent per year while the other 250 million people increase in numbers at 0.01 percent per year. After 2,000 years, the population reaches 5.52 billion. The visual similarity to the data on population history (Figure 5.3) is not bad.

Change the Lens! A Semilog Portrait

I forced all the curves I have described to start with an initial population of 250 million and to rise to approximately 5.5 billion after 2,000 years. The differences among them reside in the pattern of growth during the intervening 2,000 years. But the method of graphing used so far conceals the relative growth rate of population size. A different way of graphing the data can distinguish which of these models most closely describes the historical facts.

To see what the problem is, please look at Figure 5.9 before you read the

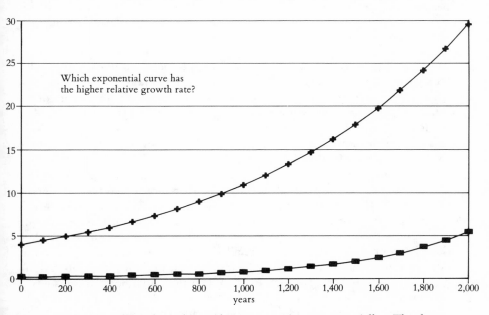

FIGURE 5.9 Two hypothetical populations growing exponentially. The lower curve is growing at 0.2 percent per year from an initial population of 100 million. The upper curve is growing at 0.1 percent per year from an initial population of four billion. The relative growth rate of the upper curve is half that of the lower curve, but its absolute growth rate is larger.

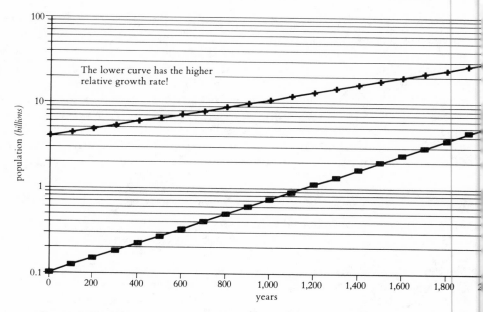

FIGURE 5.10   The same two hypothetical exponential populations as shown in Figure 5.9, plotted on a logarithmic scale for population. The lower curve rises 0.2 percent per year (solid rectangles). The upper curve rises 0.1 percent per year (+ symbols). The relative growth rate of the upper curve is clearly less than that of the lower curve.

caption, and put your finger on the curve that you think has a higher relative growth rate. No cheating! Think before you read on! Of the two hypothetical exponentially growing populations in Figure 5.9, the upper curve, which appears to be growing faster, is growing at half the relative rate of the lower curve. The upper curve appears to grow faster because the absolute increments in height, corresponding to population size, are much larger than the increments in the lower curve.[47]

The human eye is very poor at judging relative change or relative growth rates when population is graphed on a scale that allots equal physical increments to equal absolute changes in population size. Such a scale is called a linear scale or an arithmetic scale. On a linear scale, a population increase of one million people moves the graph upward by the same amount, whether the initial population is a million people or a billion people. When the initial population is a million people, the addition of a million represents a doubling, a substantial relative increment. When the initial population is a billion people, the addition of a million, one-tenth of 1 percent of the base population of one billion, is almost too small to notice.

Relative growth rates can be judged accurately by eye on a graphical scale that represents equal relative changes in population size by equal physical distances on the graph. The graph should rise by two millimeters, say, if the population increases by 10 percent, whether the initial population is one million or one billion. Such a scale is known as a logarithmic scale. When

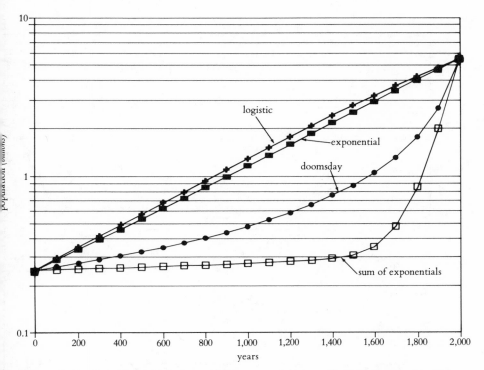

FIGURE 5.11 Four hypothetical populations growing according to the exponential (solid rectangles), logistic (+ symbols), doomsday (• symbols) and sum-of-exponential (open squares) models. Population size is plotted on a logarithmic scale.

population is represented on a logarithmic scale, equal relative increases in size appear as equal absolute increments in the physical height of the plot. On a logarithmic scale, a rise in population from 1 million to 10 million looks as big as a rise in population from 10 million to 100 million because both represent ten-fold increases, even though the absolute increment in the second case (90 million) is tremendously larger than that in the first (9 million). A logarithmic scale gives relatively more attention to the details of population growth when populations are small.

Since the relative increase of population size is constant as time passes if the population grows exponentially, exponential growth plotted with a logarithmic scale for population size and an arithmetic scale for time appears as a straight line. Such a graph is called a semilog plot, because one axis (for population) is logarithmic and the other axis (for time) is arithmetic. A semilog plot (Figure 5.10) of the two hypothetical curves previously plotted linearly (Figure 5.9) shows clearly that the lower curve is rising at a more rapid relative rate than the upper curve. This graph guides the eye to the correct conclusion.

A semilog plot of the hypothetical exponential, logistic, doomsday and sum-of-exponential equations shows a straight line for the exponential curve, as expected (Figure 5.11). The logistic curve appears slightly con-

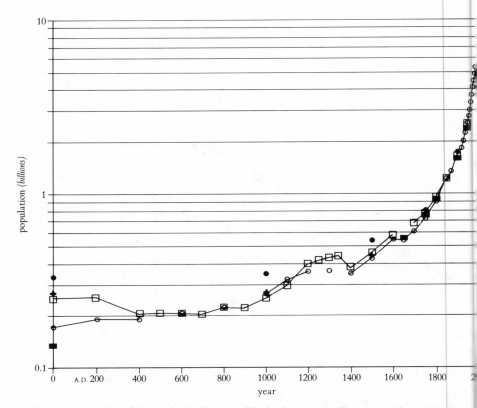

FIGURE 5.12   World population history for the last two millennia, with population plotted on a logarithmic scale. Different symbols represent estimates from different sources. SOURCE OF DATA: Appendix 2

cave, with gradually decreasing slope. The doomsday curve has a gradually increasing slope (like an exponential curve, but now on a logarithmic scale). The sum–of–exponentials curve appears more U-shaped than any of the others; it is approximately straight for the earliest years, and for the latest years, and strongly bowed in the middle. The eye can distinguish the doomsday and sum-of-exponential models from the other two models much more easily using a semilog plot than using an arithmetic plot.

What do the real data look like on a semilog plot? Since the data are least unreliable in the last two millennia, I confine the semilog plot in Figure 5.12 to those years. Except possibly for the first few centuries A.D., where the estimates are highly uncertain, the different estimates of population size make very little difference to the picture that emerges. The plot bears no resemblance to a straight line. Population growth was not exponential during these millennia, whatever Malthus and others may have thought. The observed history bears still less resemblance to a concave curve with a steadily declining slope, as the logistic model would predict. My eye cannot pick out the slight reduction in slope of the curve during the last 20 years, important though I believe that reduction to be. The data seem to fall somewhere between the doomsday and sum-of-exponential models, though neither predicts the recent deceleration of growth. A simple model that incorporates both global acceleration (for the history up to 1965–70) and global deceleration (for the history since then) is proposed, but not tested quantitatively, in Appendix 6.

A Wide-Angle Portrait: Deevey's Staircase

As I mentioned in Chapter 2, Deevey viewed population history through a wide-angle lens. He suggested that, on a graph with *both* axes, population and time, on logarithmic scales (called a log-log plot), the course of human population size would look like a series of rounded steps in a staircase (Figure 5.13). In fact, a log-log plot (Figure 5.14) of the estimated human population size for the last million years resembles Deevey's schema only slightly.[48] The initial rounded steplike rise in this plot is based solely on Deevey's largely conjectural estimates prior to the local agricultural evolution and is hardly a strong confirmation of his schema. This first step is followed by three nearly straight rising lines. The first straight line after the local agricultural evolution 10,000 years ago rises at a faster rate than Deevey's initial rounded step until about 2,000 years ago, when the population size first exceeds 100 million. The second nearly straight line rises less rapidly to a population in excess of four billion people a decade or two ago. The log-log plot, truly wide-angle, obliterates such minor deviations as the medieval Black Death and the global agricultural evolution. The third and last straight line, defined only by the last two points and greatly magnified

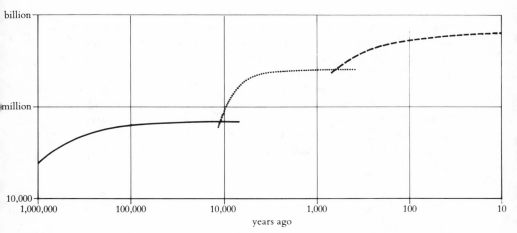

FIGURE 5.13 Deevey's schema of world population history for the last million years, with the number of years before the present and population size both plotted on logarithmic scales. SOURCE: Deevey (1960, p. 198)

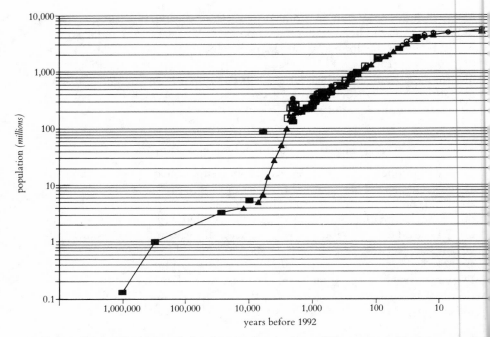

FIGURE 5.14   World population history for the last million years, with the number of years before 1992 and population size both plotted on logarithmic scales. Different symbols represent estimates from different sources. SOURCE OF DATA: Appendix 2

by its recency, shows the diminished population growth rate of the global fertility transition.

I know of no published mathematical model to explain Figure 5.14. The model that comes closest, by the Berkeley demographer Lee, predicts a straight line on a log–log plot. But in Figure 5.14 there is a noticeable bend in the curve, a decrease in the slope, 2,000 years ago. This bend may be an artifact of faulty estimates for the previous millennia.

In any event, the available simple models do not describe human population history. Some would say that the hope of finding a simple model that would describe past human numbers is naive, and that the search for such a model should be abandoned. Others who are attached to the power of simple quantitative models may take the absence of a working model as a challenge (Appendix 6).

6

The Uniqueness of the Present
Relative to the Past

GLOBALLY, PRESENT POPULATION growth vastly outpaces past population growth. This simple conclusion has been demonstrated theoretically and empirically. In recent centuries, the global average population growth rate accelerated so strikingly that roughly 90 percent of the increase in human numbers since the beginning of time has occurred since 1650, in fewer than 350 years.

Other major evolutions have accompanied the enormous growth of the human population. Here I describe four: the rise in the proportion of older people; the rise in each person's ability to affect the natural environment through the command of nonhuman sources of energy; the rise in the unevenness of the spatial distribution of people, largely through the development of cities; and the rise in the contact of cultures, through migration, travel and communication. Some other major evolutions may be equally important but are omitted here—for example, the spectacular rises in the command of information, in worldwide literacy and in the control of the properties of physical, chemical and biological materials.

AGING

The United States Census Bureau defines people who are 65 years old and older as "elderly." The number of elderly people in the developed regions (Europe, North America, Japan, Australia and New Zealand) grew at 2.4 percent per year from 1950 to 1980.[1] In countries where significant declines in fertility began before 1950 (which are the developed regions plus Argentina, Barbados, Cuba, Uruguay and Israel), the fraction of the population that was elderly climbed from 7.6 percent in 1950 to 12.1 percent in 1990, an increase by more than half.[2] As of 1992, the country with the highest proportion of elderly was Sweden: 18 percent, or close to one in five.[3]

In developing countries, the numbers of elderly are growing twice as fast as the number of people of all ages in the world. Demographers confidently expect the countries where fertility declined significantly after 1950, all of them in the developing regions except Albania, to see dramatically rising numbers and proportions of elderly in the first half of the twenty-first century, assuming that death rates do not rise in the interim.

Two causes drive the increases in the proportions of elderly: falls in fertility and improvements in survival. Declines in fertility lower the proportion of children who enter the population, automatically increasing the proportions in older age categories. Recent declines in death rates raise the fraction of children already born who survive to old ages.

Because female death rates are lower than male death rates almost everywhere, women outlive men. Consequently, within the elderly population, the ratio of women to men rises with age, sometimes dramatically. In the United States in 1985, in the age groups 65–69, 70–74, 75–79 and 80+ years old, the fractions of women were 55.4 percent, 57.9 percent, 61.3 percent and 68.1 percent.[4]

Barring unforeseen catastrophes, the numbers and proportions of the elderly will jump dramatically in the years after 2010.[5] Then the large cohorts born after World War II will begin to pass age 65. A 1987 report of the Census Bureau observed: "Rapidly expanding numbers of older people represent a social phenomenon without historical precedent, and one that is bound to alter previously held stereotypes of older persons."[6]

THE COMMAND OF ENERGY

The growing amount of energy available per person is one measure of the rise in the environmental impact of the average person.[7] Before agriculture was invented, the only sources of energy that an individual commanded were fire and his or her own muscle power. Human use of fire dates back 350,000 to 450,000 years in China and perhaps half as long in Europe, according to archeological finds; from early times, people used fire to alter natural vegetation, drive game animals and cook food. Even if an individual could compel the services of his fellows, the average muscle power of a pre-agricultural group of given size remained constant. For short periods, a man's muscles can work at a maximum of about 800 watts or a little more than one horsepower; for periods of a day or more, one-third horsepower is a more plausible maximum.[8]

A great leap in power came with the domestication of horses, oxen, pack mules, camels, elephants and other animals for draft and portage. The invention of the horseshoe around 400 B.C. permitted horses and oxen to

TABLE 6.1   Energy use in total and per person
from 1800 to 1987

year	world coal extraction per year (million tonnes)	energy from coal (million megawatt-hours per year)[a]	world population (millions)	coal energy per person (megawatt-hours per year per person)	inanimate energy from all sources (million megawatt-hours per year)	inanimate energy from all sources per person (megawatt-hours per year per person)
1800	15	120	900	0.13		
1860	132	1,056	1,200[b]	0.88	1,078	0.9
1900	701	5,608	1,625	3.5	6,089	3.7
1950	1,454	11,632	2,500	4.7	20,556	8.2
1980	2,728	21,824	4,448	4.9	68,354	15.4
1987	3,334	26,672	5,000	5.3	77,229	15.4

[a] 1 tonne of coal = 8 megawatt-hours.
[b] Estimate for 1850.
Source of coal and energy production estimates for 1800 to 1950: Cipolla (1974, pp. 56–59); for 1980 and 1987: Johnson (1991, p. 143). Source of population estimates: Appendix 2.

plow stony fields without injury.[9] The water mill, windmill and sailing boat gave people command of the energy of water and wind. While sailing vessels are known from Egyptian vases as far back as 3500 B.C., water mills and windmills were not extensively used until the Middle Ages.[10]

Around 1765, as England was running out of timber and found large stocks of coal, James Watt began experiments with the steam engine.[11] Beginning in 1785 the steam engine spread into commerce; coal became a strategic resource. Rapidly though the global population grew from 1800 to 1950, the annual energy available to the average person from coal extraction increased even faster during the same century and a half: 35-fold from 0.13 megawatt-hour per person in 1800 to 4.7 megawatt-hours per person in 1950 (Table 6.1). Each megawatt-hour per person of energy gives each person on the Earth one slave in energetic form, 24 hours a day, every day of the year.[12]

With the expansion of waterpower and the introduction of lignite, petroleum, natural gasoline and natural gas, inanimate energy per person climbed from 0.9 megawatt-hour per person in 1860 to 8.2 megawatt-hours per person in 1950. In 1990, global energy consumption per person was the equivalent of 1,567 kilograms of oil per year.[13] At 43 megajoules per kilogram,[14] this translates to an annual average energy consumption of almost 19 megawatt-hours per person—nearly 19 energetic full-time slaves per person.

Between 1900 and 1990, average energy consumption per person increased by a factor of five. Livi-Bacci commented: "The dependency of energy availability on land availability was again (and perhaps definitively) broken and the principal obstacle to the numerical growth of population removed."[15] In the U.S. economy of the mid-1980s, human muscle power supplied less than 0.2 percent of the work done, while oil, coal and natural gas supplied nearly 90 percent.[16]

Access to the colossal global flow of energy is not equal, but is less unequal now than in the recent past.[17] In low-income economies other than China and India, energy consumption per person in 1990 was less than 10 percent of the world average. In countries of the Organisation for Economic Co-operation and Development (OECD), energy consumption per person in 1990 was more than 3.3 times the world average, and it was higher still in the United States and Canada. The ratio of commercial energy consumption per person in OECD countries to that in low-income countries was nearly 34 in 1990, down from the ratio of 48 in 1965.

URBANIZATION

The increasingly uneven distribution of people in space, with immense concentrations of people in cities, is sometimes called urbanization.[18] The demographer Philip M. Hauser of the University of Chicago called it the "population implosion."[19] The implosion began with the local agricultural evolution some 10,000 years ago when perhaps the first built, long-lasting, communal settlements were established. The early rise of cities coincided with that early rise in population. By the period of the Akkadian empire, southern Mesopotamia had cities of more than 100,000 people. The city of Teotihuacan in the Valley of Mexico is estimated to have had 150,000 to 200,000 people by A.D. 600.[20] The fraction of the human population living in places with 20,000 or more people rose from about 2 percent in 1800 to perhaps 20 percent in 1950. In only one country in the world, Great Britain, did more than half of the population leave the farm for the city before World War I.[21]

Currently the United Nations uses each country's definition of "urban" population.[22] Because these definitions vary widely from country to country, the global statistics are blurry in meaning, but clear in trend: the percentage of the population that is urban rose from 29 percent in 1950 to 34 percent in 1960, 37 percent in 1970 and 40 percent in 1980.[23] (Evidently the United Nations' definition of "urban," which gave 29 percent in 1950, differed from Hauser's, which gave 20 percent in 1950. Remember the Law of Information.) Recent U.N. estimates found about 43 percent of the world's population urban in 1990 and 45 percent urban in 1995.[24]

In less than two centuries (1800 to 1990), the fraction of people who lived in cities surged from perhaps 1 in 50 to nearly 1 in 2. The absolute number of city dwellers rose from perhaps 18 million to 2.3 billion,[25] a 128-fold increase, while the total population size increased six-fold, from perhaps

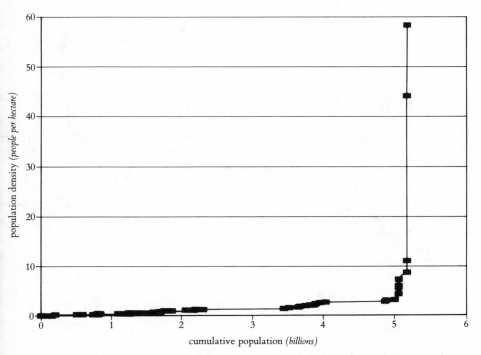

FIGURE 6.1   Population density of 148 countries as a function of cumulative population in 1989. Population densities are country averages. Countries are ranked from low density to high density. SOURCE: original figure, from data of the World Resources Institute (1992, data diskette)

0.9 billion around 1800 to 5.3 billion in 1990. Urbanization has greatly outpaced population growth. The present number of city dwellers is more than 100 times what it was two centuries ago, while the total number of people is more than 100 times what it was 3,000 years ago. Of current city dwellers, 1.4 billion live in less developed regions of the world.

Urbanization and aging interact because the migration of young people from the countryside to cities is a major contributor to urbanization.[26]

Using 1989 data[27] on the populations and areas of 148 countries, I computed the number of people per hectare in each country. The 148 countries had a total of 5.19 billion people and 13 billion hectares of land, so they included almost the whole Earth and its human population. For these countries combined, the average population density was about 0.4 people per hectare (or 40 per square kilometer or 104 per square mile).

For further description, I took Vietnam and Belgium as convenient points of reference. Vietnam had a density of two people per hectare (200 per square kilometer or 518 per square mile). Belgium had a density of three people per hectare (300 per square kilometer or 777 per square mile).

Using nations as the units of analysis greatly understates the concentration of people experienced by individuals because, for example, it averages

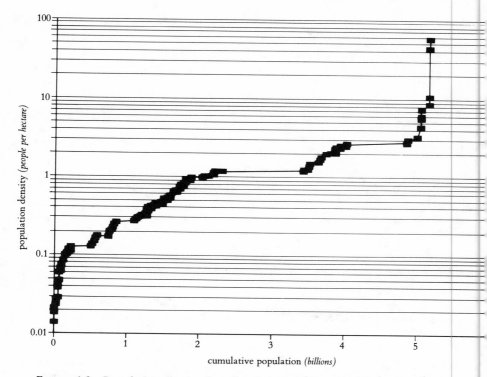

FIGURE 6.2 Population density (on a logarithmic scale) of 148 countries as a function of cumulative population in 1989. Population densities are country averages. Countries are ranked from low density to high density. SOURCE: original figure, from data of the World Resources Institute (1992, data diskette)

New York City with the deserts of Nevada, and Montreal with arctic tundra. About 3.8 billion people lived in countries with two or fewer people per hectare, so 1.4 billion lived in countries at least as densely settled as Vietnam. When the countries are ranked by population density from lowest to highest, a plot of population density (people per hectare) on an arithmetic scale as a function of cumulative population (Figure 6.1) shows the relatively small fraction of the total population living at very high density; replotting the same data with population density on a logarithmic scale (Figure 6.2) reveals more detail about the countries with low population density. About 4.9 billion lived in countries with three or fewer people per hectare, so about 0.3 billion lived in countries at least as densely settled as Belgium. Of these 0.3 billion, 0.29 billion lived in just four countries—Japan, Bangladesh, South Korea and the Netherlands, in order of decreasing population size.

In 1989, the least densely populated countries with a cumulative area equal to half the Earth's total land area had a combined population of about half a billion people, just under 10 percent of the total population; conse-

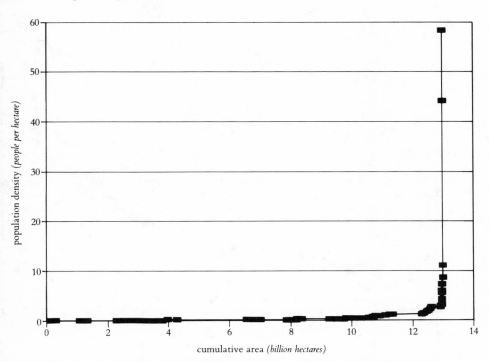

FIGURE 6.3   Population density of 148 countries as a function of cumulative area in 1989. Population densities are country averages. Countries are ranked from low density to high density. SOURCE: original figure, from data of the World Resources Institute (1992, data diskette)

quently 90 percent of the population lived in the more densely populated half of the Earth's land area. Of the 13 billion hectares of land in the 148 countries, 12.5 billion hectares were in countries with an average density of two people per hectare or lower, and 12.9 billion hectares were in countries with an average density of three people per hectare or lower (Figures 6.3 and 6.4). About a quarter of all people lived in countries with an average population density of two or more people per hectare (like Vietnam or denser), but the countries of such high density covered less than 4 percent of the Earth's land.

MIXING

Hauser used the term "population displosion" to refer to "the increasing heterogeneity of peoples who share not only the same geographic locale but, increasingly, the same life space, social, political and economic activities."[28] People come into increasingly direct contact who vary in culture, language, religion, values, ethnicity and race. Though such contacts could

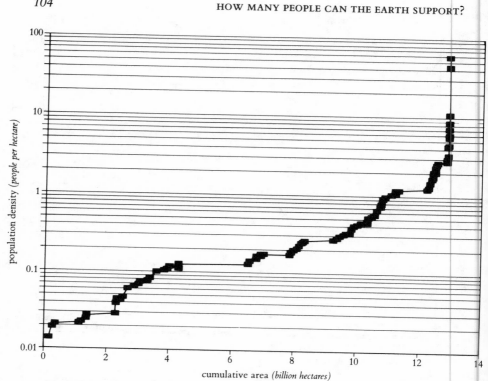

FIGURE 6.4 Population density (on a logarithmic scale) of 148 countries as a function of cumulative area in 1989. Population densities are country averages. Countries are ranked from low density to high density. SOURCE: original figure, from data of the World Resources Institute (1992, data diskette)

no doubt be documented in empires dating back beyond ancient Babylon, the current extent, multiple aspects and political symmetry of the contacts (unlike the asymmetry of conqueror and vanquished) are even more recent than urbanization. The resulting frictions are evident in all parts of the world.

The many cities or city-systems worldwide that cross national borders illustrate the simultaneous rise of urbanization and mixing.[29] The megacity of Los Angeles (U.S.)–San Diego (U.S.)–Tijuana (Mexico)–Ensenada (Mexico) spans California and Baja California. Other North American examples include El Paso (U.S.)–Ciudad Juárez (Mexico); Laredo (U.S.)–Nuevo Laredo (Mexico); and Detroit (U.S.)–Windsor (Canada). South America has Santa Ana do Livramento (Brazil)–Rivera (Uruguay); Posadas (Argentina)–Encarnación (Paraguay); San Cristóbal (Venezuela)–Cúcuta (Colombia); and the three-way Foz de Iguaçu (Brazil)–Puerto Iguazú (Argentina)–Ciudad del Este (Paraguay). In Europe, Trieste spans Italy and the former Yugoslavia, while Geneva (Switzerland) is linked with Annemasse (France); Liège (Belgium) with both Maastricht (Netherlands) and Aachen (Germany); and Trento (Italy) with Innsbruck and Salzburg (Austria) and Munich (Germany). International city-systems in Asia include Hong Kong and Guangzhou (China); Singapore and Johor Bahru (Southern Malaysia). Africa has Kinshasa (Zaire)–Brazzaville (Congo).

TEN THOUSAND YEARS:
A GLANCE BACKWARD AND FORWARD

To make the transition from the past to the future of the human population, consider a simple exercise in arithmetic. About 10,000 years ago, there were 5.7 million people. Today there are about 5.7 billion people. (Assume these plausible figures are correct.) So the human population increased by a factor of 1,000 in 10,000 years. An increase by a factor of 1,000 represents fewer than ten doublings in population size because $2^{10} = 1,024$. On the average, the human population doubled no more often than once per millennium. (That the population more than doubled twice in the last 200 years, and once in the last 40 years, emphasizes the unprecedented recent acceleration of population growth. The calculation I described concerns only millennial averages.)

Now look into the future. If the human population exists after another ten millennia, its average growth rate from now till then cannot exceed its average growth rate over the past ten millennia. Why not? If the population as much as doubled for each of the next ten millennia, it would increase by another 1,000-fold, from 5.7 billion now to 5.7 trillion (5.7×10^{12}) people. The total surface area of the Earth, including oceans, lakes, streams, ice-caps, swamps, volcanoes, forests, highways, reservoirs and football fields, is 510 million square kilometers. With a population of 5.7 trillion, each person would be allotted a square area less than 10 meters on a side. This area may be commodious as a jail cell, but is incapable, on average over the oceans and continents of the Earth, of supporting a person with the food, water, clothing, fuel and physical and psychological amenities that distinguish people from ants or bacteria. No optimist, if that is the right word, has suggested that the Earth could support 5.7 trillion people, and with good reason, as we shall see. It follows that, for the next ten millennia, the average future population growth rate cannot exceed a doubling every millennium, or an average growth rate of 0.069 percent per year.[30]

The same argument applies to the present population growth rate of perhaps 1.6 percent per year. If growth of 1.6 percent per year persists for 436 years, the population will have increased at least 1,000-fold.[31] If the Earth cannot support five trillion people in the distant future, it probably cannot support them 436 years from now either. If people and the planet will not tolerate a ten-fold, rather than a 1,000-fold, increase in population size, then the present global growth rate cannot continue even another 150 years.

The upper limits I have just mentioned (a ten-fold increase to 57 billion, or a 1,000-fold increase to 5.7 trillion) are probably far larger than the limits that most humans will accept, according to the recent declining trend of global fertility. The point of the calculation is that, even with extremely large limits on human population size, the amount of time remaining to bring the numerical (not spiritual, cultural or economic) growth of the human population to a halt is not extremely long. Within the next 150 years or so, and possibly much sooner than that, a drastic though not necessarily abrupt decline in the global population growth rate is inevitable. The longer a growth rate in excess of 0.069 percent per year is maintained from now on, the longer it will be necessary to experience periods of population growth below 0.069 percent per year—and possibly even negative population growth, depending on the scenario—if the average growth rate over the next ten millennia is not to exceed its absolute maximum of 0.069 percent per year.

While these calculations are uncontroversial, I believe, they are also uninformative about the possible trajectories of, and possible constraints on, human population sizes, globally and locally, in the coming century and a half. Understanding the possible trajectories and constraints comes next.

PART 3

———

FUTURE
HUMAN
POPULATION
GROWTH

7

Projection Methods:
The Hazy Crystal Ball

It is a good deal easier to utter warnings against
prophecy than to abstain from it. . . . The real
question is not whether we shall abstain altogether from estimating the future growth of population, but whether we shall be content with
estimates which have been formed without adequate consideration of all the data available, and
can be shown to be founded on a wrong principle.

—EDWIN CANNAN 1895[1]

THE FUTURE IS UNLIKE THE PAST
BECAUSE IT HAS NOT HAPPENED YET

POPULAR AND PROFESSIONAL accounts of population matters often fail to
make clear the real uncertainty about the demographic future. For example,
in 1990, the *Economist* magazine, a distinguished British source of generally
reliable information, published a graph of global population growth rates
for the period from 1950 to 2025.[2] The graph made no distinction between
the past and the future. It showed the world population growth rate flat for
the decade and a half prior to 1990, and then declining after 1990. The graph
gave the misleading impression that the future decline in the rate is just as
factual as the past estimates were. While a future decline is plausible, it is
anything but certain.[3] The *Economist* should have distinguished the future
from the past graphically—for example, by using a solid line to draw past
data and a dotted line to draw projections of the future. Still better would
have been a pair of diverging dotted lines from 1990 into the future to indicate a range of uncertainty about the future population growth rate.

In 1991, the United Nations published a similar figure for the period
1950–2025 in its official *World Population Prospects 1990,* with the identical
shortcoming.[4] Neither the caption nor the graphic content of that figure
gave any hint that the future of population growth is a matter of surmise,
not of fact. The true situation is better represented by the cartoonist Sidney
Harris (Figure 7.1).

Here is one of the best-kept secrets of demography: most professional
demographers no longer believe they can predict precisely the future

FIGURE 7.1 "How do you want it—the crystal mumbo-jumbo or statistical probability?" SOURCE: Harris (1992, p. 27)

growth rate, size, composition and spatial distribution of populations.[5] In 1979, in an official United Nations publication on the methodology of population forecasting, the eminent British demographer William Brass, a former president of the International Union for the Scientific Study of Population (the worldwide organization of population scientists), stated flatly: "The science of demography has not yet reached a stage of development where the future growth of population and its subgroups can be predicted."[6]

This uncertainty derives from the way demographers try to develop knowledge about the future of populations. The "how" and the "what" of demographic knowledge about the future are inseparable, for methods shape what people know as much as what people know shapes methods. Demographic knowledge of the future of a population focuses on its internal dynamics. Other views of the future of a population emphasize how ecological, economic, cultural and other factors may affect a population's internal dynamics. An example of a difference in perspectives appeared earlier at the end of Part 2. There I argued that the next 10,000 years will not see average human population growth as fast as 0.069 percent per year because such growth would cause a 1,000-fold increase, and such an increase is insupportable. That argument has two points of view: one demographic, one external to demography. The demographic part of the argument pertains to population dynamics without constraint from the environment, and asserts that, if the human population grows at 0.069 percent per year, the population will increase 1,000-fold over ten millennia. The ecological part of the argument pertains to the interaction of the population with its external environment, and asserts that people and the Earth cannot support a 1,000-fold increase in the human population.

All approaches to population prediction assume that some mechanism (whether deterministic or partially random) that has operated in the past will continue to operate in the future. (Even divination assumes that the oracle still functions effectively.) Approaches differ, sometimes radically, in the details of the supposed mechanism, including the number and kind of quantities that are assumed to matter. To keep life simple, I will concentrate on predicting total population size.

Attempts to predict total population size have followed three main paths. Mathematical extrapolation assumes that future population sizes are determined by present and past population sizes, and nothing more. A mathematical curve is fitted to the total sizes of a population at past times; then the curve is continued, by using the same mathematical formula, into the future. In most instances, the mathematical formula has no visible connection to the observable mechanisms of human population growth. A second approach, called the cohort-component method, assumes that the composition or distribution of the population according to age and sex plus past age-specific and sex-specific rates of birth, death and migration are enough to predict the future size of each subgroup of the population and hence the population's growth and size. Various methods are used to extrapolate from past age-specific and sex-specific rates of birth, death and migration to those of the future. Finally, system models, while typically ignoring the detailed age and sex composition of the population, posit quantitative interactions of population growth and size with nondemographic factors such as industrialization, agriculture, pollution and natural resources.

While it is desirable to embed population projections in models that represent the economic, political, environmental and cultural factors that interact with populations, the most ambitious efforts so far show that present knowledge is not up to the task. The following chapters of this book assume that population size and growth are not independent of the world's economies, environments, and cultures. But for quantitative projections of population, given present limited knowledge, we probably learn as much from the cohort-component method as from the largely untested assumptions of system models.

MATHEMATICAL EXTRAPOLATIONS

Mathematical extrapolations will not detain us long, enjoyable as they are to those in search of mental calisthenics. We have seen in Chapter 5 that the mathematical curves most commonly used for extrapolation—exponential, logistic and doomsday—as well as the sum-of-exponentials model all fail to describe adequately the last two millennia of human population growth. There is little reason to use them for long-term projections of the future. For short-term projections, they are all virtually equivalent.

All mathematical curves share a common weakness as a means of predicting future population growth in the short term: they ignore the age composition and sex composition of the population. Babies, young children and babushkas (old grandmothers) don't have babies. A population of one million people all over the age of 60 will have a much higher death rate and much lower (in fact, zero) birth rate than a population of one million people between the ages of 15 and 45. A pioneer population consisting mainly of men, such as gold-rush miners or settlers of newly opened land, will have a much lower birth rate and probably a higher death rate than a population of the same size and age composition with equal proportions of both sexes. In 1990, among 206 million East Africans, 47 percent were under the age of 15, while among 178 million Western Europeans, 18 percent were under the age of 15.[7] Even after allowing for the substantially higher death rates in East Africa (with life expectancies for men and women of 50 and 53 years, respectively) compared to Western Europe (with life expectancies of 73 and 79 years, respectively), it seems very likely that 18 years from now, a much higher fraction of the population will be in the prime reproductive years from 18 to 33 in East Africa than in Western Europe, and hence a much higher proportion of the whole population could be expected to give birth in East Africa than in Western Europe.

Extrapolation of mathematical curves fails because a human population has more dimensions than just its size. Most professional demographers no longer take curve fitting seriously as a means of predicting population sizes.[8]

THE COHORT-COMPONENT METHOD

In 1895, the British economist Cannan developed an arithmetic procedure to take account of age structure when projecting population. Apart from differences of detail, his procedure, called the cohort-component method, is now used by every major demographic institution, including the British Registrar General, as well as most individual demographers.

Here is how the modern cohort-component method works (Figure 7.2). Suppose you want to forecast the population of a country over the next 50 years. You start with the most recent census, say, from 1990. This census is an actual count or sampling estimate of people (whether or not adjusted by statistical means to correct census errors) according to sex (male or female) and according to age. Censuses commonly ask for age (completed years of life) at last birthday, but projections usually lump individual year classes into 5-year age groups: the numbers of men and numbers of women in the age ranges 0–4, 5–9, 10–14, 15–19 and so on up to the last age considered (for example, 95+). Cannan used 10-year intervals of age.

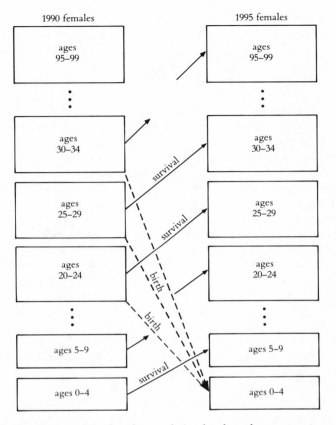

FIGURE 7.2   Projection of the female population by the cohort-component method.

You break the long-term forecast into a sequence of short-term forecasts, say, of five years each. Once you have a procedure to forecast a hypothetical census in 1995 from the actual 1990 census, you can apply the same procedure to the 1995 forecast to construct a hypothetical census for the year 2000. You can continue iteratively stepping five years into the future as long as you like.

To forecast the 1995 population from the 1990 census, first set aside migration into and out of the country and treat the population within the country as if it were closed. Since a population can increase only by births or by immigration, and can decrease only by deaths or by emigration, temporarily ignoring migration reduces the number of processes that have to be considered initially from four to two.

As a further temporary simplification, also set aside the male population and concentrate on the female population. It is often easier to tell which females are involved in reproduction than which males simply because women are physically linked to their babies at birth. Moreover, because giving birth is a nine-month commitment for a female but may require only a single insemination on the part of a male, the number of females is viewed as more likely than the number of males to limit the rate of births. The cohort-component method's initial concentration on females is really a pure convention, because there will obviously be fewer births if there are not enough males to go around. How many males are enough to go around depends on the conventions that govern male parenthood and how strictly those conventions are observed. For example, it will take more males to mate 1,000 females in a hypothetical culture where childbearing requires strict lifelong monogamy than in a hypothetical culture where childbearing is open to any fecund female regardless of any durable relation with a male. Beneath the mathematical formalism of the cohort-component method lie cultural assumptions that should be, but rarely are, checked when the method is applied to a real population.[9]

How many girls aged 5–9 will there be in 1995? Migration is excluded, so each such girl must have been 0–4 years old in 1990 (since time and age increase together and by equal amounts) and must have survived for five years. What fraction of girls aged 0–4 in 1990 will survive to 1995? Nobody knows for sure, but you can make a reasonable guess. From the death certificates filed with the national system of vital registration, or from special-purpose sample surveys, you can estimate the proportion of 0- to 4-year-old girls who survived for five years in some period in the past (perhaps from 1985 to 1990, or perhaps averaged over some longer or different interval). Now, with a long drum roll and a bugle fanfare, you *make some assumption* about the survival proportion from 1990 to 1995. You may *assume* that the survival proportion you estimated from the past will continue in the future; or you may assume, say, a 10 percent improvement in the survival proportion because you observed that death rates at 0–4 years have been falling in the past and you expect them to continue to fall; or you may expect the survival fraction to fall because of a spreading epidemic. Whatever the details, you have to *make some assumption* about the future survival proportion of 0- to 4-year-old girls from 1990 to 1995, and you multiply that assumed survival proportion by the censused or estimated number of 0- to 4-year-old girls in 1990 to project the number of girls aged 5–9 in 1995.

In exactly the same way, you project the number of females aged 10–14, 15–19 and so on in 1995 from the counted number of females aged 5–9, 10–14 and so on in 1990, each multiplied by the corresponding *assumed* future five-year survival probability.

You have yet to determine how many girls aged 0–4 there will be in 1995. Again, migration is excluded, so each baby girl must have been born between the last census in 1990 and the hypothetical census date in 1995. The girls aged 0–4 in 1995 will be contributed by mothers who were aged 15–19 in 1990 (assuming no girls aged 10–14 were mothers), plus the mothers who were aged 20–24 in 1990 and so on.

The number of baby girls who will be 0–4 in 1995, per woman aged 20–24, say, in 1990, is called the effective fertility rate of women aged 20–24 in

1990. A simple way to estimate the *past* effective fertility rate of women aged 20–24 from two successive censuses is simply to divide the number of baby girls aged 0–4 in 1990 whose mothers were aged 20–24 in 1985 by the number of women aged 20–24 in 1985. Then you could assume that the *future* effective fertility rate of women aged 20–24 from 1990 to 1995 is equal to (or some fraction smaller or larger than) the past effective fertility rate of women aged 20–24 from 1985 to 1990, or over some other past period.

Effective fertility rates can also be estimated without using two censuses, by pasting together age-specific birth rates and survival probabilities. First you must estimate the birth rates of mothers of each age. From historical records of birth certificates filed with the national system of vital registration, or from special sample surveys, you can estimate the number of baby girls born per year to mothers aged 15–19, to mothers aged 20–24, to mothers aged 25–29 and so on. From the 1990 census, you can count or estimate how many women were aged 15–19 years, 20–24 years and so on. The age-specific birth rate of women aged 15–19 is the ratio of the number of births born to women of that age divided by the number of women of that age. So from vital records and the census (or from special sample surveys), you can estimate all the age-specific birth rates. You already know the age-specific survival probabilities from the previous part of the projection.

An effective fertility rate can then be constructed from survival probabilities and birth rates. For a baby girl to be born in 1993 and alive in 1995, for example, her mother has to survive from 1990 to 1993 and has to give birth in 1993, and the baby girl has to survive from 1993 to 1995. So you multiply the survival probability from 1990 to 1993 for women aged 20–24 times the birth rate in 1993 for women of the age that the mother will then be, times the daughter's survival probability from 1993 to 1995. The product of these three numbers can then be summed with similar products for the baby girls born in 1991, 1992, 1994, and 1995, to obtain an effective fertility rate for women aged 20–24 from 1990 to 1995. This recipe for an effective fertility rate *assumes* that three events are all independent (maternal survival, giving birth and child survival) to justify multiplying the rates at which these events occur. Past effective fertility rates can be looked up in published tables.

Once you have constructed future effective fertility rates from the observed or estimated past effective fertility rates, you multiply the number of mothers aged 15–19 in 1990 by their future effective fertility rate to compute their contribution to the number of girls aged 0–4 in 1995. Similarly, you multiply the number of mothers aged 20–24 in 1990 by their future effective fertility rate, and so on for each of the other age groups of mothers, up to age 50–54, say. Then you add together the contributions of each age group of mothers in 1990 to arrive at the total number of girls aged 0–4 in 1995.

Now you have a complete projected census of the female population in

1995. What about the males? Practices among respectable demographers vary. In an influential set of projections, the Czech demographer Tomas Frejka simply doubled the female population.[10] The United Nations and many other demographers follow a slightly more refined procedure. As with the females, the males aged five years and over in 1995 must be the survivors of the males who were five years younger in 1990 (still excluding migration). Male survival coefficients for 1990–95 may be estimated from past male survival coefficients, as they were for the females. You estimate births of boys by multiplying the births of girls by the historically observed ratio of male births to female births, typically a number around 1.05 or 1.06. This number, called the sex ratio at birth, varies from culture to culture and sometimes reveals infanticide of one disfavored sex or the other. You now have projected the female and male populations to 1995, assuming no migration.

To allow for migration, in principle you again examine historical evidence of migration rates by age and sex. Such data, when they exist at all, are often of lower quality than data on births and deaths. Overall levels of migration may be nominally set by law but may include substantial illegal or undocumented migration. In the best of circumstances, when you know, for every country, the numbers of emigrants by age and sex, and the numbers of immigrants by age, sex and place of origin, you compute historical emigration and immigration rates by age, sex, origin and destination, and extrapolate these rates into the future according to some independent model. You can then apply the assumed future emigration rates to compute the number of emigrants, and subtract these; and apply the immigration rates for each sending country, and add these. Of course, all this depends on knowing how the populations of the sending countries will evolve, which makes it difficult to project countries or regions one at a time if migration is really important.[11] By hook or by crook, you make some guesses about the numbers of migrants, by age and by sex, and add them to or subtract them from the offspring and survivors of people counted in the 1990 census.

In the real world, practices in projecting migration vary among respectable demographers. Frejka assumed no international migration. Here is his justification:

> . . . it was felt that in the long run migration in most countries would probably not play a major role in the development of total numbers of respective populations (this does not mean that internal migration will be insignificant). Further, it certainly does not seem probable that the total world population could be influenced by either in- or out-migration during the foreseeable future. Finally, the inclusion of any migration assumptions would significantly increase the complexity of the project.[12]

In the long-run projections prepared in 1992,[13] the United Nations repeated the assumptions about international migration it used in its 1990 projections to the year 2025.[14] These assumptions were based on World Bank estimates of international migration prior to 1990. The United Nations did not try to project migration between countries after 2025: "Because of the irregularity and unpredictability of international migration over time and place, the long-range projections assume no net migration between major areas after 2025."[15] Projecting future migration is still an art.

In summary, the requirements for a projection according to the cohort-component method are an initial census or representative sample of the population by age and sex (and possibly by region or race or ethnicity, if these factors are believed to be important), and estimates of *future* rates of birth, death and migration according to age and sex (and region, race or ethnicity, as desired). If you are making a conditional prediction, you are free to choose the future rates of birth, death and migration as you please. In an unconditional prediction of future population, uncertainty about future rates of birth, death and migration renders projected future population sizes uncertain.

In the recent past, except during periods of famine, war or other catastrophe, survival probabilities generally have had a consistent trend with relatively small variation for short periods from a few years to a few decades. Demographic experts usually view the projection of gradually improving survivorship as easier than the projection of migration or fertility. Yet mortality has had its surprises in the past half century in both developed and developing countries. The planners of the Social Security system in the United States during the 1930s failed to anticipate the remarkable improvements in the survival of older Americans. The Utopias of the proletariat in Eastern Europe suffered an unexpected and embarrassing rise in adult mortality during and after the final years of Communism. In Russia, from 1990 to 1992, life expectancy for men fell from 63.9 years to 62.0 years, and for women from 74.4 years to 73.8 years.[16] Only a few comparatively recent students of future population, such as Bernard Gilland in Denmark, allowed for the possibility of an important future rise in global death rates.[17]

In the recent past, for large regions, demographers have had most difficulty predicting birth rates. Frejka put it simply: "As is generally recognized, it is practically impossible to predict future fertility trends."[18] Most demographers in major institutions appear to believe that the major source of uncertainty for the future lies in birth rates.

To predict how many children women will have, why not ask the women? In 1993, Charles F. Westoff of Princeton University suggested using the results of surveys that asked women, at various points in time, whether they want more births.[19] The future fraction of women who want no more births could be predicted from the present fraction of women who want no more births. The future prevalence of contraception is then predicted from the predicted future fraction of women who want no more births plus the present prevalence of contraception. Then the future total fertility rate is predicted from the predicted prevalence of contraception plus the present total fertility rate.

In April 1994, Westoff tested this ingenious approach using data on eight countries surveyed in rounds I and II of the Demographic and Health Surveys.[20] The predicted total fertility rate agreed with that observed five years later within one-tenth of a child for Egypt (forecast 3.9 children per woman, observed 3.9), Morocco, Kenya, Senegal, Dominican Republic, Peru and Indonesia. In the exceptional case, Colombia, where rounds I and II of the surveys were only three years apart, the forecast was 2.6 children per woman and the observed total fertility rate was 2.9. Thus far, the performance of this method is impressive. More extensive testing is required to build confidence.

The cohort-component method improves on simply guessing the future numbers of people in each grouping according to age and sex by moving the guesswork to a higher level. The required future rates of birth, death and migration are not divinely revealed, but must be posited (in a conditional prediction) or projected (in an unconditional prediction).

Two important features of the cohort-component method limit its ability to predict populations correctly. The method is ahistorical (or Markovian, in mathematical lingo), and it is linear. I will explain both of these properties.

The method is ahistorical because the present influences the future, but the past matters only through its effects on the present. For example, according to the cohort-component method, the hypothetical census in 1995 depends only on the 1990 census and the vital rates between 1990 and 1995, and not on anything in the history of the population prior to 1990. For a given 1990 census, it makes no difference to the calculation whether the 1990 population just emerged from a long war that depressed fertility and devastated the country, or just enjoyed a long period of peace and prosperity. Given the 1990 census, it makes no difference to the calculation whether the country is early, midway, or late in its demographic transition. The missing history may affect the rates of birth, death and migration to be expected during 1990–95, but the projection of those rates lies outside the cohort-component method. Whatever memory the cohort-component method may have is imposed from the outside by the user's choice of rates, rather than generated from within by the method.

In addition to being ahistorical, the cohort-component method is linear (setting aside the way immigration is sometimes computed). For example, according to the cohort-component method, if the number of females aged 0–4 in 1990 were somehow doubled, then the number of females aged 5–9 in 1995 would also be doubled, if nothing else changed. The number of females aged 5–9 in 1995 is called a "linear" function of the number of females aged 0–4 in 1990 because a plot of the calculated number of females aged 5–9 in 1995 on the vertical axis is a straight-line function of the observed number of females aged 0–4 in 1990 on the horizontal axis. Such a linear relationship holds for every age-sex group in the census. If the size of every group in the current 1990 census were multiplied by, say, 17, then the size of every group in the next hypothetical census in 1995, and every census thereafter computed with the same vital rates, would also be multiplied by 17. The population computed for 1995 would have the same fraction of people in each age class as before, but the total population size would be 17 times as large.

Because the cohort-component method is ahistorical and linear, it is easy to analyze mathematically.[21] For the same reasons, it is also, in the eyes of system modelers who emphasize ecological constraints, totally unrealistic.

STOCHASTIC POPULATION PROJECTION

Cannan did not anticipate one recent development of the cohort-component method. That is the combination of the cohort-component method with statistical models that forecast birth and death rates and their future uncertainty. The combination gives plausible stochastic population projections. ("Stochastic" means "with randomness" or "probabilistic.") The basic idea is very simple, though the technical details are not.[22]

First, you look at a long past history of age-specific birth and death rates (or the total fertility rate or life expectancy). Based on this history, you build statistical models (such as time-series models) to predict these vital rates and to derive estimates of their uncertainty in the future. Estimates of uncertainty are commonly expressed as confidence intervals. A confidence interval asserts, for example, that the total fertility rate in the year 2000 will lie between 1.9 and 3.2 children per woman with 90 percent probability. (I made up the numbers for illustration only.) In this part of the procedure, you learn from the variability of past vital rates how much variability you might encounter in the future. Past data tell you how uncertain to be about the future, assuming that the pattern and level of variability in the vital rates will remain constant as time passes. This is a much more sophisticated leap of faith than supposing that the vital rates themselves, or some deterministic pattern of change in them, will remain constant as time passes. In the second part of the process, you embed these statistical forecasts of rates into the cohort-component method. While conceptually simple, this step can present a serious computational problem.

A stochastic population projection produces confidence intervals for age-specific projections, not merely best guesses or a range of guesses. Estimates and confidence intervals can be derived for any characteristic of an age-structured population that you might want to know about, such as the size or fraction of the population above age 65 years or of school-going age.

Though it is an important advance, stochastic population projection shares some of the fundamental limitations of the cohort-component method. Like the cohort-component method, it is ahistorical in some respects. It sets aside unique events (such as the 1918 influenza epidemic or the return home of soldiers after World War II) and assumes that the underlying statistical patterns of vital rates in the past will continue into the future without change. But this is a more advanced way of being ahistorical. Also like the cohort-component method, stochastic population projection (as currently practiced) is linear: increase the initial population by a factor of 17, and you increase the predicted future populations by the same factor of 17. The realms outside of demography appear only as random perturbations of rates of birth, death and migration. Neglecting to measure and to model the world outside of demography can lead to major errors in both projected population sizes and their confidence intervals.[23]

SYSTEM MODELS

Why System Models?

The cohort-component method rests on the rates of birth, death and migration without explicit regard to any factors external to demography such as agriculture, ecology, economics, politics and culture, among others. On such grounds, Robert F. Chandler, the founding director of the International Rice Research Institute in Manila, the Philippines, criticized the World Bank's cohort-component projections for Asia:

> In my view it seems extremely unlikely that average Asian rice yields will ever exceed 6 [tonnes[24] per hectare], which is double the current level. Yet demographers estimate that world population will at least double before it becomes stabilized, and some predictions even place the ultimate population at twelve to fifteen billion. If such forecasts prove correct, global food production resources will be strained to the limit and . . . the environment will be severely damaged. . . . Bangladesh . . . now [ca. 1990] has an estimated population of 113 million, which is increasing at the rate of about 2.4 percent annually. The density is 2,028 people per square mile [783 per square kilometer], 80 percent of whom live in rural areas. The land area is about 55,000 square miles [142,000 square kilometers], roughly that of the state of Georgia [U.S.], which, by contrast, has a population of 6.2 million and a density of 106 per square mile [41 per square kilometer]. . . . More than half the rural population [of Bangladesh] is landless and is severely underemployed. Over 70 percent of the farms are less than one hectare in size. I cannot conceive of Bangladesh supporting the 342 million people predicted by the World Bank.[25]

Whether Chandler will prove to be right about the potential yields of Asian rice production, I do not know. While I defer to his technical expertise, I am aware that technical experts have been wrong before. That uncertainty is beside the point. What Chandler really objected to is that the World Bank's use of the cohort-component method neglected certain agricultural and social constraints that he assumed would apply in the future.

Chandler's criticism of the World Bank's projection as being too narrowly based is itself subject to the same criticism. An economist looking at Chandler's comment might object that Bangladesh need not necessarily grow enough to feed its people if it can produce something else of value and trade for food with areas that have an agricultural surplus. Places that do so include Hong Kong, Singapore and, increasingly, Israel. An anthropologist looking at the comments of Chandler and the imaginary economist might note that even if Bangladesh's current population density tripled to 6,000 per square mile, as the World Bank's projection implied, that density would be less than half of Hong Kong's population density of over 14,000 per square mile.[26] Whether Bangladeshis can make a stable transition to such densities may be constrained (or favored) by behavioral patterns, class differences or cultural norms long before agricultural or economic factors intervene.

Where Do System Models Come From?

Any attempt to model the influence on population of agriculture, the environment, economics, politics, culture and other factors quickly encounters two distinct problems, which are often treated as if they were a single problem. The first problem is understanding: how can one describe usefully, in quantitative form, the influence of present and past demographic and nondemographic factors on the future of a population? A second problem is computation: given equations that track all the factors that affect population growth, how can one solve all the equations numerically?

The computer is very good at numerically solving multiple equations but, so far, not very good at understanding complex human and natural systems without very close human supervision. If you hand the computer useful equations and an appropriate method of solving them, the computer is a whiz at solving the equations arithmetically. The results are as valuable as the understanding that went into the equations and the correctness of the method of solving them. Expertise in getting computers to solve complex systems of equations is not equivalent to expertise in translating reality into useful equations.

During and after World War II, military analysts developed methods, known by the general title of "systems analysis," to track and forecast very complex situations. As computers spread after World War II, concepts of systems analysis were applied to nonmilitary problems. At the Massachusetts Institute of Technology in the 1950s, Jay W. Forrester headed a group that used digital computers to solve the equations of system models. He then promoted the use of system models to simulate industrial and urban problems. In recent decades, numerous system models have tried to describe human populations interacting with energy, agriculture, pollution and other nondemographic phenomena.[27]

In 1972, protégés of Jay Forrester produced what was undoubtedly the best-advertised example at that time. With the financial support of the Club of Rome, a group of influential people from business and government, an M.I.T. study team led by Donella H. Meadows, Dennis L. Meadows, Jørgen Randers and William W. Behrens III published a small book, *The Limits to Growth*. The book predicted dire futures from a continuation of what it represented as current trends. According to the dust jacket of the twentieth-anniversary reprise, called *Beyond the Limits*,[28] the original *Limits* sold nine million copies in 29 languages. In *Limits*,[29] Meadows and her colleagues constructed a computer model for five variables: population, food, industrialization, nonrenewable resources and pollution. Their model, modestly called World3, was a refinement of earlier models, World1 and World2, proposed by Forrester.[30] Meadows et al. adjusted World3 to fit values of the five variables estimated from historical or putative data for the years 1900 to 1970. They then computed the consequences of various assumptions about the future. Alternatives included, among others, a simple continuation of previous trends, a doubling of resources with limitless energy and a doubling of agricultural yields with a four-fold reduction of pollution per unit of industrialization. These scenarios were presented as *conditional* predictions, as sketches of what would happen if the growth in human population and industrial output continued according to the authors' model of their past dynamics.

In all the scenarios considered, population and industrialization surged upward and then fell sharply. Meadows et al. concluded that this pattern, which they called "overshoot and collapse," is a fundamental property of World3.

> The basic behavior mode of the world system is exponential growth of population and capital, followed by collapse. . . . [T]his behavior mode occurs if we assume no change in the present system or if we assume any number of technological changes in the system.
>
> The unspoken assumption behind all of the model runs we have presented . . . is that population and capital growth should be allowed to continue until they reach some "natural" limit.[31]

Meadows et al. inferred that overshoot and collapse are fundamental properties both of their model and of the world itself.

The Limits to Growth excited a storm of public and scholarly argument.[32] Many articles, comments and letters were published in the leading British and American scientific journals, *Nature* and *Science,* between March and September 1972 and in *New Scientist* between April and July 1972. In one of the funniest denunciations, David Berlinski, a philosopher at the University of Puget Sound, wrote: "Friends . . . have sometimes asked why I spend so much time denouncing as worthless theories that *are* worthless. To this question I have no reasonable answer save the one that H. L. Mencken gave: for the same reason that men go to zoos. . . . It is the use of mathematical methods for largely ceremonial reasons that I deplore and denounce as pernicious."[33]

Even after two decades, there seems to be little consensus about the value of the conclusions of *The Limits to Growth*. In 1987, T. N. Srinivasan, an economist at Yale, dismissed the study as an example of "simple trend analyses and mechanical models devoid of economic content."[34] By contrast, Kingsley Davis, a demographer then at the University of Southern California and Stanford University, wrote in 1991 that "one cannot ignore developments in the last two decades that tend to support the study's findings."

After giving numerous examples, he concluded, "Thus the grizzly *[sic!]* truth may turn out to be that *Limits* was more prophetic than its detractors and even some of its defenders thought possible."[35]

In one critique, H. S. D. Cole, Christopher Freeman, Marie Jahoda and K. L. R. Pavitt at the Science Policy Research Unit of the University of Sussex, England, mounted the World2 model of Forrester[36] and the World3 model of Meadows et al.[37] on their own computer.[38] They showed that the models are by no means fated to overshoot and collapse. Meadows et al. considered the possibility of a one-time, large advance in technology, and found that population, industrial output and food still overshoot and collapse. Cole et al. found, on the contrary, that if a single, large technological advance is replaced by continuous, small incremental improvements in the technology of food production, resource recycling, fertility reduction and pollution control, then overshoot and collapse can be replaced by more or less steady growth in industrial output per person, population and food. The alternative assumptions may be more or may be less plausible than the originals, depending on your prejudices. Either way the exercise casts much doubt on the claim that overshoot and collapse are inevitable properties of the models and of the world.[39]

Limits argued that, if the *physical* relationships of production and consumption assumed in World3 (as an approximation to what happened in the real world from 1900 to 1970) persist unchanged, there will soon be a collision with the finiteness of the world, and therefore those physical relationships will be forced to change. In short, according to *Limits,* the absence of a change of technology implies a catastrophic change (or collapse) of technology. Is there useful news here? Most people are aware that the physical, economic, political and cultural relationships of production and consumption are constantly shifting in response to changing values, preferences, environmental conditions, technology and prices. Is it more plausible to posit a rigidly unchanging world system that collapses when it encounters constraints, or a world system that adapts incrementally (albeit sometimes inefficiently)?

The Limits to Growth publicized complex computerized modeling of the human population. Unfortunately, *The Limits to Growth* set a precedent that many subsequent system models followed: it did not give the detailed equations of the model along with the results. The equations of *Limits* were later revised and eventually published in a separate technical report. This practice implicitly suggested that the problem of understanding reality and formulating useful equations to describe it is less significant than the problem of solving the equations with a computer. It also greatly increased the difficulty of replicating the results and criticizing the equations. (Fortunately, the 1992 reprise, *Beyond the Limits,* made the computer model available.[40])

How Is Population Projected in System Models?

System modeling describes changes over time in numerical quantities known as state variables. Since the World3 model of *Limits* was an extension of the World2 model published in full detail in Forrester's 1971 *World Dynamics,* I will give the details of Forrester's treatment of population. World2 had five state variables: population, capital investment, natural resources, fraction of capital devoted to agriculture and pollution.[41] Population was not subdivided according to age, sex or geographical location. By contrast, the cohort-component method divides the population into many age groups but neglects nondemographic factors.

Forrester produced a prediction or projection into the distant future incrementally by stepping forward from the present, one time interval at a step. Each state variable changed as a result of flows in and flows out. For example, Forrester computed the world's population at the present time from the population at an earlier time by the unarguable equation: present population = past population plus (number of intervening years) times (the average number of births per year minus the average number of deaths per year during the intervening years).

To compute the numbers of births per year and deaths per year, Forrester relied on his intuitions about how these numbers depend on other state variables. He computed the number of births per year as a product of six quantities: the population size P, the "normal birth rate" which he assumed was 0.04, and four numbers that modified the "normal birth rate" up or down according to Forrester's view of how births respond to external conditions: the "birth-rate-from-food multiplier," the "birth-rate-from-material multiplier," the "birth-rate-from-crowding multiplier" and the "birth-rate-from-pollution multiplier." Under "normal" conditions, according to the model, every multiplier equals 1, so the "normal" birth rate was 4 percent of population size per year.

Forrester derived the birth-rate-from-food multiplier from the value of the food ratio, which is the ratio of food available per person at the current time to the food available per person in 1970. Forrester specified the connection by means of a table[42]:

food ratio	0	1	2	3	4
birth-rate-from-food multiplier	0	1	1.6	1.9	2

When there is as much food per person as there was in 1970 (the food ratio is 1) then the birth-rate-from-food multiplier is 1. When there is twice as much food per person as in 1970, the birth-rate-from-food multiplier is 1.6, and when there is four times as much, the birth-rate-from-food multiplier is 2. If there were 3.5 times as much food per person as in 1970, the BRFM would be 1.95 (halfway between the tabulated values of 1.9 and 2). The food ratio was computed from other variables in the model that described agriculture, economics and natural resources.

Forrester echoed Malthus: "It appears that the world has normally existed in that sensitive region where food regulates birth and death rates so that population maintains its precarious existence at the maximum number of people that the available food can sustain."[43] Decide for yourself how well this statement describes any region of the world of which you have *first-hand* knowledge.

The other multipliers of the normal birth rate were derived from similar, arbitrarily made-up tables. The same procedure gave the death rate with its own four multipliers and their made-up tables. As far as I can see, the only observed, not invented, data—of any kind—in *World Dynamics* are estimates of global population in 1900 and 1970 and global land area.

World2, the model Forrester used in *World Dynamics,* begat son-of-World2, called World3, the model Meadows et al. developed in 1972 for *The Limits to Growth.* The population subsystem of World3 was not described in detail in *The Limits to Growth.* More information became available in separately published technical reports and in a detailed criticism of the model.[44] As in World2, in World3 population was represented by a single aggregated state variable. According to the technical reports, decomposing the population into 4 or even into 15 age groups made only a marginal difference.[45]

In World3, the number of births was assumed to be determined by the total fertility, which in turn was affected by six factors: the population size, the fraction of fertile women in the population (set at a constant 22 percent), the reproductive lifetime (set at a constant 30 years), the maximum total fertility or biological fecundity (normally 12 children when life expectancy is 60 years, but changing with life expectancy), the average desired total fertility and birth control effectiveness. Birth control effectiveness was assumed to depend on service output per person, including health services. Desired total fertility depended on a "compensating multiplier from the perceived life expectancy" (assuming that, if parents perceive that their children will survive longer, they will bear fewer children to achieve the completed family size they want) and on the "desired completed family size" (normally set to four children). Desired completed family size was modified by a "family norm multiplier from income expectations," which in turn depended on income expectation, and by a "family norm multiplier from social structure." Both income expectation and the "family norm multiplier from social structure" depended on industrial output per person. A similarly complex set of relationships was posited to predict deaths per year.

In the 1992 reprise and refinement of World3, called World3/91, Meadows et al. maintained the structure of World3 but renamed the elements.[46] The 1992 model population had four age groups: 0–14 years old, 15–44, 45–64 and 65 and over. Meadows et al. found that the old World3 failed to predict the speed of decline in both global birth and death rates since 1972; they therefore adjusted World3/91 to bring it in line with historical experience.[47]

How Reliable Are System Models for Population Projection?

System models like World2 of Forrester and World3 of Meadows et al. can easily be nonlinear, and they can easily be historical. Making a system model nonlinear is no more difficult than writing a line of computer code with a nonlinear relation in it. Making a system model depend on past history is no more difficult than assigning arrays of computer memory to hold past values of the state variables and then including some dependence on past values in the computer code.

These advantages are gains in *potential* realism, but not necessarily in *actual* realism. The actual realism of a system model depends on whether the nonlinear relations embodied in the computer code correspond to historical realities, and on how long into the future the model's relations continue to be valid. In the failure to examine historical realities lies one great gap between the potential and the actual realism of system models such as World2 and World3.

For example, Forrester assumed that the number of births per year depends on five quantities: population size, food, the material standard of living, crowding and pollution. Forrester or his students and colleagues could have investigated how well these variables actually predicted the number of births, using historical series of observations. A whole academic industry is devoted to elucidating the so-called determinants of fertility by econometric and statistical means.[48] Historical demographers have encountered great difficulty in predicting population change from social and economic variables. You would never know it from *World Dynamics* or *The Limits to Growth*. The real question concerning system models, as Cannan put it in 1895, is "whether we shall be content with estimates which have been formed without adequate consideration of all the data available. . . ."

In a critique of *World Dynamics,* the Yale economist William Nordhaus wrote: "The treatment of empirical relations in *World Dynamics* can be summarised as *measurement without data.* The model contains 43 variables connected by 22 non-linear (and several linear) relationships. *Not a single relationship or variable is drawn from actual data or empirical studies.*"[49]

World Dynamics suffers from other omissions as well.[50] The model omits the possibility of devoting resources to reducing the production of pollutants or cleaning them up. The model omits technological progress, the discovery of resources and the invention of substitute materials. The model has no system of prices to reflect scarcities and induce substitutions and shifts in behavior.[51] The model treats all effects as instantaneous: there is no lag in the effects of crowding or pollution on the birth rate, no lag in the effect of any variable on any other.[52] The model ignores differences between poor and rich countries, differences among poor countries, differences among rich countries and differences within countries. All the system models omit shifts in goals, values and priorities, as well as the political processes that mediate the conflicts among goals, values and priorities.[53]

In strongly recommending World2 as a basis for policy and immediate action, Forrester paid no attention to the uncertainty of the estimates and relations embodied in the model and no attention to the costs that society would incur if his model turned out to be wrong. Forrester's *World Dynamics* reflected no more than his intuitive view of how the world works. It should be shelved with scientific Utopias and Dystopias like Aldous Huxley's *Brave New World,* Edward Bellamy's *Looking Backward* and J. B. S. Haldane's *Man with Two Memories,* even though Forrester used the literary device of the computer to work out the details of the plot.

Perhaps surprisingly, by 1992 Meadows et al. came to appreciate the limits of system models. One indication was the chapter in *Beyond the Limits* devoted to statistical data on factors that could limit the growth of population and industrial output. Another indication, relevant to the choice of a method of population projection, was the explicit disclaimer with which Meadows et al. introduced World3/91: "It is not possible to make accurate 'point [that is, numerically exact] predictions' about the future of the world's population, capital, and environment. No one knows enough to do that. And the future of that system is too dependent on human choice to be precisely predictable."[54]

What Conclusions Follow from System Models?

In 1972, the first of the three main conclusions of *The Limits to Growth* was:

1. If the present growth trends in world population, industrialization, pollution, food production, and resource depletion continue unchanged, the limits to growth on this planet will be reached sometime within the next 100 years. The most probable result will be a rather sudden and uncontrollable decline in both population and industrial capacity.[55]

The World3 model did not predict that the world's population growth rate would peak and begin to fall just after *Limits to Growth* was published. In 1992, in the first of the three main conclusions in *Beyond the Limits,* population no longer made the headlines, either as a cause of problems or as a probable victim of uncontrolled decline:

1. Human use of many essential resources and generation of many kinds of pollutants have already surpassed rates that are physically sustainable. Without significant reductions in material and energy flows, there will be in the coming decades an uncontrolled decline in per capita food output, energy use, and industrial production.[56]

Both the above quotations were not descriptions of the World3 model, but were inferences about the real world. The inferences assumed that World3 reflected useful understanding of the real world. "If I hit my thumb with a hammer, it will hurt!" This conditional prediction should get me to move my thumb out of harm's way rapidly. But what if I am using a foam-rubber hammer?

The conclusions of Forrester and Meadows et al. may or may not be correct. System modeling by computer has not made a compelling case that the conclusion of "uncontrollable decline" (in 1972) or "uncontrolled decline" (in 1992) is likely. Even some of the system modelers grant that system models cannot yet provide a reliable tool for projecting future population. Without placing faith in the conclusions from the modeling, I confess sympathy with many of the recommendations made in 1992 by Meadows et al. There are many things that could and should be done, things worth doing for their own sake (like improving efficiency in using energy and materials, avoiding inefficient use and pollution). It is not necessary to believe in system modeling with evangelical fervor to recognize that some of the actions recommended in 1992 by Meadows et al. make sense, though the level of priority they deserve remains to be analyzed.

Going beyond the models of Forrester, the Meadows and their groups, a review of a broader class of system models asked the question: "what use are large-scale economic-demographic simulation models to development planners?" The blunt answer was: "In policy evaluation, at any rate, we conclude that they are of little use."[57]

Can Local System Models Be Useful?

It may turn out (though it is not yet proved) that system models can be useful for detailed modeling on a small geographical scale. Without attempting a comprehensive survey, I offer a few examples. In one early application of system modeling (in the style of Forrester and Meadows) to a single country, Peter W. House of the University of California and Edward R. Williams of the U.S. Department of Commerce developed a model of the United States in 1975.[58] Their model involved assumptions and abstractions that limited its practical use, and it was too complex to provide theoretical illumination. In 1986, John Gever, Robert Kaufmann, David Skole and Charles Vörösmarty at the University of New Hampshire developed models of the energy supplies, agriculture and economy of the United States but did not document the model sufficiently to permit evaluation of it.[59] Both models included demographic projections.

A very large model of a small island was developed for Mauritius, an island republic 800 kilometers east of Madagascar in the Indian Ocean. Its population in 1990 was just over one million. With a land area of only 1,850 square kilometers, Mauritius is one of the most densely settled countries in the world. The most notable feature of its demographic history is that, following a dramatic increase in population during the 1950s and 1960s, the total fertility rate dropped from an average of around six children per woman to around three children per woman in just eight years, from 1963 to 1971. According to Wolfgang Lutz, leader of the population project at the International Institute for Applied Systems Analysis, Laxenburg, Austria, and Jawaharlall Baguant, head of the School of Engineering at the University of Mauritius, "This was probably the most rapid fertility transition in world history."[60]

Lutz, Baguant and their colleagues developed a detailed model with more than 1,000 state variables to aid policy-makers and planners in Mauritius.[61] The model runs on a personal computer, asks the user to specify certain assumptions and computes future scenarios in five-year intervals from 1990 to 2050 in accordance with the user's assumptions plus the built-in assumptions of the model. The four major components of the model are a population module, an economy module, a land-use module (keyed to a map of Mauritian urban land, sugar cane plantations, beaches and land used for any other purpose) and a water module (to track surface water in streams, groundwater and lagoons). The population module tracks the composition, by five-year age groups and by sex, of seven subpopulations: people in school or too young to attend school; people with a primary education who are in the labor force; people with a primary education who are no longer in school and not in the labor force; and four similar subpopulations for people with secondary or tertiary education who are currently in or out of the labor force.[62]

Each subpopulation is projected forward five years at a step by the cohort-component method. Where do the rates come from that are used in the cohort-component method? The user must supply them:

> Because the vast literature on socio-economic fertility determinants does not suggest any clear and simple functional relationship between fertility and a set of non-demographic parameters, we decided not to specify such a relationship when it could hardly be defended. Instead, the user can decide when and how in the course of running the model the fertility levels in the different population groups should be changed, based on either altering socio-economic or environmental conditions, or simply on assumptions about relevant cultural and behavioral change.[63]

This modest approach to specifying economic, environmental and cultural feedbacks to birth and death rates contrasts strongly with that of the global system models. It avoids pretending to knowledge that does not exist, but puts the burden of wisdom on the user.

The user also bears heavy burdens in the economy module: "International trade is exogenous and to be specified by the user. Government expenditure is a function of population size and age structure, and a user-provided profile of per person expenditure. . . . Foreign investments are user-defined."[64] Fixed prices are built into the model, though the changing price of imported petroleum fuels and the fixed or declining price of exported cane sugar have caused Mauritius economic grief.

In short, even for a small island of a million people, an elaborate and sensible system model is no panacea. Used intelligently, it may save planners from making some mistakes. If it does, the modeling is worthwhile. But it is still too early to tell.

How Successful Have Past Projections Been?

The United States Bureau of the Census published twelve sets of U.S. population projections between 1947 and 1975, usually with three or four alter-

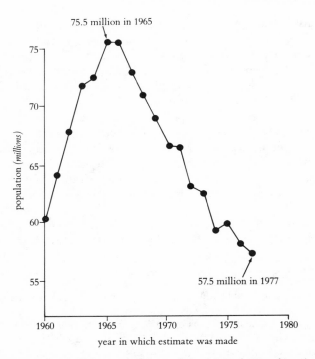

FIGURE 7.3 Projections of the population of the United Kingdom in A.D. 2001 made by the Registrar General of the United Kingdom from 1960 to 1977. SOURCE: Blaxter (1986, p. 27)

native sets of assumptions to cover a range of plausible uncertainty. The projections published in 1947 forecasted a U.S. population in 1950 of between 145 million and 148 million. The actual population in 1950 was 152 million, higher than the highest projection made three years earlier. The projections published in 1971 forecasted a U.S. population in 1975 of between 216 million and 218 million; the actual (estimated) population in 1975 was 213 million, lower than the lowest projection made four years earlier.[65]

These examples illustrate one way to measure the success of past predictions of population size in some future year: wait until that future year arrives, then compare the prediction with the current reality. The next example illustrates another way to evaluate predictions of population size.

Between 1960 and 1977, the Registrar General of the United Kingdom published 18 predictions of the population of the United Kingdom in A.D. 2001 (Figure 7.3). The predictions ranged from a high of 75.5 million, published in 1965, to a low of 57.5 million, published in 1977. Sir Kenneth Blaxter, the British nutritionist who assembled these projections, commented: "Obviously not all the estimates of the future population can be correct!"[66]

This example illustrates a second way to measure the success of past pop-

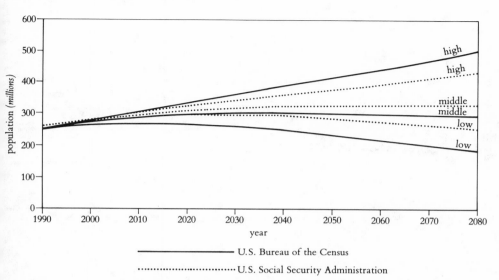

FIGURE 7.4 Total population of the United States projected by the U.S. Bureau of the Census and the Social Security Administration under high, middle and low scenarios. SOURCE: Grummer-Strawn and Espenshade (1991)

ulation projections: compare predictions for a fixed future target year, made at various times or by different sources or with different methods. If the forecasts vary widely, they cannot all be right. Of course, if various forecasts agree closely, nothing guarantees that any of the forecasts is nearly right. The concordance may well reflect little more than current conventional wisdom.

An extension of this approach shows how differently two agencies of the United States government assessed the demographic future.[67] The Bureau of the Census assumed a much wider range of uncertainty than the Social Security Administration did when predicting the future total population size of the United States (Figure 7.4). But the Social Security Administration assumed a much wider range of uncertainty when predicting the future old-age dependency ratio (the ratio of the population 65 years old and older to the population aged 20 to 64 years old) (Figure 7.5). The Census Bureau was more concerned than the Social Security Administration about mistaken estimates of total population size, while the Social Security Administration was more concerned about mistaken estimates of the retired or elderly population. Each was more cautious than the other in its own area of visible responsibility.

Sometimes the retrospective and comparative approaches can be combined. Between 1951 and 1980, the Population Division of the United Nations published high and low estimates of the population of the world for the target year 1980 (Figure 7.6). Until 1963, the high estimate fell below the actual 1980 population. Worse than being merely wrong, the low

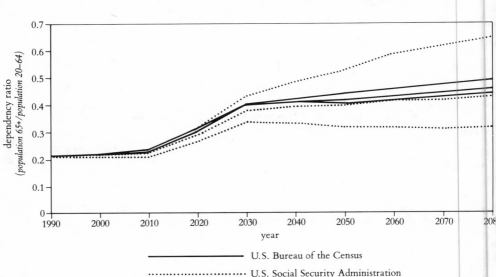

FIGURE 7.5   United States old-age dependency ratio (population aged 65 years and older divided by the population aged 20 to 64 years) projected by the U.S. Bureau of the Census and the Social Security Administration under high, middle and low scenarios. SOURCE: Grummer-Strawn and Espenshade (1991)

estimate of the 1957 projection was higher than the high estimate of the 1951 projection; and again the low estimate of the 1968 projection was higher than the high estimate of 1957 projection. Twice within 17 years, the estimated range from high to low shifted upward so far that it over-lapped not at all with a previously estimated range from high to low. Such extreme shifts in the range of uncertainty show that the earlier ranges of uncertainty were far too narrow.

The U.S. Census Bureau projections that went wrong within three or four years and the experience of the United Nations Population Division show that demographers who use the cohort-component method are not sure how uncertain they are about the future. Estimates of the range of uncertainty are frequently far too low; they often reflect far too much con-fidence in the projector's ability to foretell the demographic future.

All of the official projections just cited (by the U.S. Census Bureau, the U.S. Social Security Administration, the U.K. Registrar General and the United Nations Population Division) used the cohort-component method. The projections of Cannan, who invented the method, also have not fared very well (Table 7.1). The 1991 population of England and Wales was about one-third larger than the projected. Cannan underestimated the decline in death rates and assumed a constant number of births. Cannan could not foresee the baby boom after World War II.

Examples of the failures of past population forecasts abound. Reciting them seems to be one of demographers' favorite forms of self-flagellation,[68]

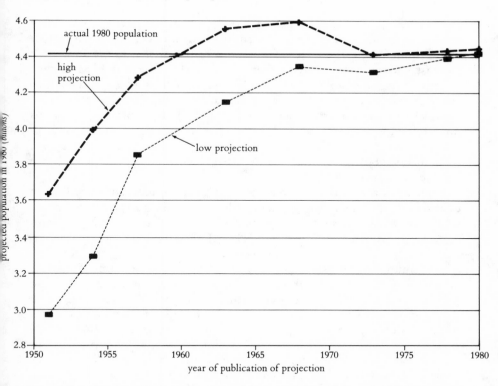

FIGURE 7.6   High and low projections of the population of the world in the target
year 1980 made by the Population Division of the United Nations from 1951 to
1980. SOURCE: original figure using data from Frejka (1981)

TABLE 7.1   Population of England and Wales:
Edwin Cannan's forecast in 1895 and later censuses

year	predicted population (millions)	censused population (millions)
1901	31.5	32.5
1911	33.5	36.1
1921	35.5	37.9
1931	36.5	40.0
1941	37.0	—
1951	37.3	43.8
1991	37.4	50.4

SOURCES: predictions from Cannan (1895, as I read them from his graph, p. 509, with an accuracy not
exceeding 0.5 million, and from p. 513); census figures: Mitchell (1978, p. 8) from 1901 to 1951; Office for
Population Censuses and Surveys (1993) for 1991 (adjusted for undercount from the unadjusted count of
48.9 million)

another being, of course, reading each other's academic publications. When enough examples are collected, patterns begin to emerge.[69] First, the farther in the future the target year of a population forecast lies, the lower the forecast's accuracy, measured either in absolute numbers or as percentage of error. Second, simple projection methods are at least as good as complicated ones for short-term forecasts. Third, forecasters are generally overconfident of the forecasts they produce and of the central assumptions underlying them.

Predictions based on system models are too recent to evaluate in terms of their success, but the 20 years of experience with the World3 model give grounds for serious doubt.

Population forecasts are prone to error. That is the bad news for the demographers who make population forecasts and for people who use them. The good news for demographers is that they are not the only forecasting professionals without a crystal ball. Political, economic, technological and cultural forecasts are also prone to error, not to mention forecasts of epidemics, volcanoes and the weather. Nathan Keyfitz, a mathematical demographer at Harvard, observed: "Demographers can no more be held responsible for inaccuracy in forecasting population twenty years ahead than geologists, meteorologists, or economists who fail to announce earthquakes, cold winters, or depressions twenty years ahead. What we are responsible for is warning one another and our public what the error of our estimates is likely to be."[70] Even that is difficult, because demographic projection techniques omit major factors that influence population change.[71]

CONFIDENCE: THE LAW OF PREDICTION

I offer a simple proposition about predictions by experts and others. Here is my Law of Prediction: The more confidence someone places in an unconditional prediction of what will happen in human affairs, the less confidence you should place in that prediction. If a prediction comes with an estimated range of error, then the narrower that range, the less you should believe it.

Many specific examples in demography and other fields support this law. General reasoning supports it also, by this argument. Events in the sphere of human affairs necessarily depend on the conjunction of a very large number of general preconditions and specific factors, any one of which is subject to change. Such events often involve the behavior of a large number of humans, whose individual and collective behavior is notoriously difficult to predict. Consequently, any prediction about human affairs necessarily rests on a very large number of assumptions. Someone, expert or not, who makes a prediction may make these assumptions explicit or may leave most of them implicit. If the predictor makes explicit the many assumptions behind a prediction, he or she can hardly have much confidence that they will all continue to hold in the future. If the predictor ignores, conceals or is simply unconscious of the many assumptions behind a prediction, he or she can display great confidence in foretelling the future. Thus a predictor's confidence in an unconditional prediction declines with increasing recognition of the many preconditions required for the prediction to come true.

You note that I am quite confident of the Law of Prediction. Does the Law of Prediction apply to my confidence? How much confidence should you place in the Law of Prediction?

8

Scenarios
of Future Population

Why, in heaven's name, should anyone suppose
that mere quantity of human organisms is a good
thing, irrespective either of their own inherent
quality or the quality of their life and their experiences?

—Julian Huxley 1950[1]

In 1992, the United Nations published seven projections of regional and
world population to the year 2150, together with historical estimates from
1950 to 1990. The United Nations modestly presented the projections as
conditional predictions: "Such projections, 160 years into the future, are in
no way a prevision of the future trend of population in the world. They do
illustrate, however, the evolution of population size and its characteristics
under possible—and very hypothetical—scenarios of future levels of fertility and mortality."[2]

The projections were presented for nine major areas of the world: Africa,
Latin America, Northern America, China, India, Other Asia (Asia excluding China and India), Europe, Oceania and the former USSR. These areas
were divided into two groups. Group I contained Northern America,
Europe, Oceania and the USSR, with 1.1 billion people in 1990. Group II
contained the other areas, with 4.2 billion people in 1990. Except for the
inclusion of Melanesia, Micronesia and Polynesia in group I and the inclusion of Japan in group II, group I was identical to what the United Nations
usually calls the "more developed regions," and group II to the "less developed regions."

All seven projections used the cohort–component method with five-year
intervals of age and time. All the projections assumed that death rates will
slowly decline, so that the life expectancy at birth of women will rise
smoothly and eventually plateau at 87.5 years, while that for men will rise
and level off at 82.5 years. Recall that the expectation of life, or life expectancy at birth, in some year, say 1990, is the average number of years a
newborn would live if he or she experienced the 1990 age pattern of sur-

vival. Group I areas were assumed to reach the ceiling on life expectancy sooner than group II areas. None of the projections explored a demographic future in which death rates rise and life expectancy falls. In this sense, the projections assumed that the demographic future will be free of surprises.

All the projections assumed the same international migration as was assumed in 1990 United Nations projections, which went only as far as the year 2025. From 2025 onward, net migration between major areas was assumed to be zero because no one knows what international migration then might be.

The seven projections differed only in their assumptions about fertility. Here the fun began. The assumptions about fertility were expressed in terms of the total fertility rate. Recall that the total fertility rate in some year, say 1990, is the average number of children a woman would have if she experienced 1990 age-specific birth rates for all her fertile years. To compute the 1990 total fertility rate of a woman in the United States, for example, you simply add up the U.S. 1990 birth rates of women at each age, for all ages. If women in the United States in 1990 started having children at age 15 and stopped at age 50, the 1990 total fertility rate of U.S. women gives the number of children that a girl born in 1990 will have, on the average, if she has the same likelihood of having a baby at age 15 as 15-year-old U.S. women had in 1990, plus the same likelihood of having a baby at age 16 as 16-year-old U.S. women had in 1990 and continues thus year by year until at age 50 (in the year 2040) she has the same likelihood of having a baby as 50-year-old women had in 1990.

Like the speed shown on your car's speedometer, the total fertility rate is not a prediction; it is only an indicator. American women are unlikely to have their lifetime fertility described by the 1990 total fertility rate of the United States. The total fertility rate measures the *current* rate or level of fertility.

The two most interesting projections assumed, first, that fertility would remain constant at its present levels and, second, that fertility would drop to the replacement level instantaneously. The United Nations labeled these two projections "illustrative,"[3] as if the other projections were not.

CONSTANT FERTILITY

The constant-fertility projection considered the seemingly innocent possibility that future total fertility rates in each area would remain as they were in 1990 (Table 8.1). The status quo: what would happen if women in each area went on having children at the rate they were having them in 1990?

The consequences of no change in the fertility rates of each area from 1990 onward, and a continued slow decline in death rates, were startling (Table 8.2). The average total fertility rate for the whole world increased over time as the areas with higher fertility grew to have a larger share of the world population. By 2025, when my 19-year-old daughter will have

TABLE 8.1   Total fertility rates in 1990, by region

region	1990 total fertility rate	region	1990 total fertility rate
world	3.3		
U.N. group I		U.N. group II	
Europe	1.8	Africa	6.5
Northern America	1.8	China	2.5
Oceania	3.2	India	4.4
USSR	2.4	Latin America	4.1
		Other Asia	5.0

SOURCE: United Nations (1992a, p. 10)

finished having whatever children she will have, the world would have 11 billion people, double its number today. The increasing portion of world population in the areas of faster-growing population would raise the world's total fertility rate to 4.3 by 2025, and another doubling would take only a bit more than an additional 25 years. A sum of exponentially grow-

TABLE 8.2   United Nations estimates and projections
of world population, 1950–2150, and
World Bank projections, 2000–2150 (billions of people)

	United Nations							World Bank base case
	low	medium/ low	medium	medium/ high	high	instant replacement	constant fertility	
eventual TFR[a]→	1.7	1.96	2.06	2.17	2.5	2.06	from 3.3 to 5.7	replacement level
year ↓								
1950	2.5	2.5	2.5	2.5	2.5	2.5	2.5	—
1975	4.1	4.1	4.1	4.1	4.1	4.1	4.1	—
1990	5.3	5.3	5.3	5.3	5.3	5.3	5.3	—
2000	6.1	6.1	6.3	6.4	6.4	5.8	6.5	6.2
2025	7.6	7.6	8.5	9.4	9.4	7.1	11.0	8.4
2050	7.8	7.8	10.0	12.5	12.5	7.7	21.2	10.0
2075	7.1	7.2	10.8	15.3	15.7	7.9	46.3	11.0
2100	6.0	6.4	11.2	17.6	19.2	8.1	109.4	11.3
2125	5.1	5.9	11.4	19.4	23.2	8.3	271.1	11.5
2150	4.3	5.6	11.5	20.8	28.0	8.4	694.2	11.5

[a]TFR = total fertility rate (average children born per woman in a reproductive lifetime at the current birth rates).

SOURCES: United Nations (1992a, p. 14, Table 1); for the World Bank projection, McNicoll (1992, p. 334)

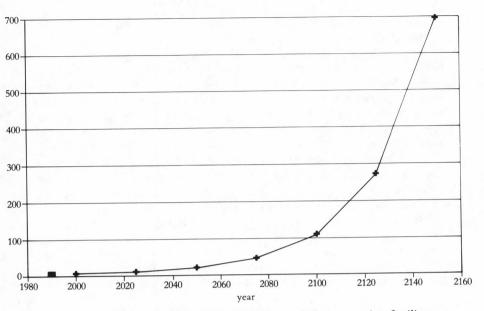

FIGURE 8.1 United Nations' projection of world population, assuming fertility remains constant at its 1990 levels in different regions. SOURCE: original figure drawn according to data of United Nations (1992a)

ing populations has a relative growth rate that increases toward the rate of the fastest-growing subpopulation. The same effect appears here.

At my daughter's centennial, in 2076, the population would have more than doubled again, passing 46 billion (Figure 8.1). The population would be still accelerating as it passed 109 billion by the year 2100. By 2150, the human population would number 694,213,000,000 individuals (here I use the amusing six digits of precision in the original United Nations publication). Population growth would be going stronger than ever with a total fertility rate of 5.7 children per woman. The proportion of the global population in the region with the highest fertility (which is Africa) keeps rising, and the global total fertility rate keeps increasing.

Of these 694 billion people, only 1.6 billion would live in the present "more developed areas" of group I. The other 99.8 percent would live in the present "less developed areas" of group II. By 2150, Europe and Northern America were projected to decline to 0.3 billion and 0.2 billion people, respectively. Africa would rise to 420 billion people (61 percent of the total) and Other Asia would rise to 181 billion (26 percent of the total).

The hypothetical population of 2150 would be very young, even younger than the population of 1990. Forty-six percent would be under age 15 (compared with nearly 33 percent in 1990). Only 3 percent would be aged 65–79, compared with 5 percent in 1990. The fraction aged 80 or over would be unchanged from 1990's 1 percent.

There, in 2150, the projections of the United Nations Population Division stopped. Perhaps they stopped because the numbers grew too long to print in their allotted column widths. Perhaps they stopped because the computers grew weary with the thought of so many births to celebrate, so many marriages to consummate, so many dead to bury. An unchanging urge to go forth and multiply left a hypothetical 4,700 people on every square kilometer of land (47 people per hectare; 12,100 people per square mile), at present sea levels; or 1,360 people in every square kilometer of the Earth's surface, oceans included (13.6 per hectare; 3,500 per square mile).

The United Nations commented drily: "To many, these data would show very clearly that it is impossible for world fertility levels to remain at current levels for a long time in the future, particularly under assumptions of continuing mortality improvement."[4]

Though there is tremendous uncertainty about the details of when, where and how, there is no uncertainty about the global alternatives for future population growth: either fertility will fall from present levels, or mortality will rise from present levels, or both, at most within the next century and a half. Our children, and their children, will likely see global rates of birth and death converge.

INSTANTANEOUS REPLACEMENT-LEVEL FERTILITY

The second projection called "illustrative" by the United Nations assumed that fertility would fall to the replacement level in 1990–95 in rapidly growing regions, and rise instantaneously to replacement fertility in Europe and Northern America. Replacement-level fertility means that the population will eventually neither grow nor decrease, given an assumed unchanging age pattern of death rates. The death rates assumed in the United Nations calculation of the replacement-level total fertility rate correspond to a life expectancy at birth of 87.5 years for women and 82.5 years for men, for all nine major geographical areas. The resulting replacement-level total fertility rate for the world is 2.06 children per woman, with negligible variations among major areas.[5] The different areas were not assumed to start out with these long life expectancies. Rather, mortality was assumed to fall slowly while fertility remained constant at what would become its replacement level.[6]

If all women henceforth had an average of 2.06 children while life expectancy gradually improved, world population size would rise from 5.3 billion in 1990 to 7.1 billion by 2025 and to 8.1 billion by 2100 (Figure 8.2). By 2150, the population would level off at 8.4 billion. From 1990's 5.3 billion, population would increase by 3.1 billion, more than half of the 1990 level (Table 8.2).

By 2150, Europe and Northern America would have 0.6 billion and 0.3 billion people, respectively. Africa would rise to 1.1 billion people (instead of the 420 billion projected with constant fertility) from 0.64 billion in 1990.

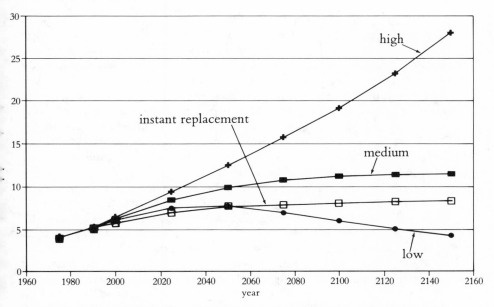

FIGURE 8.2 United Nations' projections of world population, according to high, medium, low and instant-replacement scenarios. SOURCE: original figure drawn according to data of United Nations (1992a)

Other Asia would rise to 1.9 billion (instead of the 181 billion projected with constant fertility) from 1.1 billion in 1990.

Why would world population increase by more than half even if fertility were at the replacement level from 1990 onward? The answer lies in the high fraction of young people in today's population. There are more young people now than there were when today's middle-aged and older people were young. So regardless of future births, the numbers of people in the middle and older ages will increase in the next several decades, as today's younger generations reach those ages (assuming no dramatic increase in death rates). In addition, the number of babies will also increase for a while, even if fertility remains at the replacement level. The number of babies will increase because there will be more mothers. For example, women now 25 years old were born 25 years ago, and there are more babies now than there were babies 25 years ago. So 25 years from now, the number of 25-year-old women will be bigger than it is now. Even if the birth rate for 25-year-old women remained unchanged from 1990 on, the number of babies born to 25-year-old women would increase in the coming years simply because there would be more 25-year-old mothers. The same argument applies to any other age at which women can have babies. Hence the number of births will continue to rise for some time even when fertility is at replacement level.

This explanation makes it clear why a big surge in population size, an increase of nearly two billion, would occur by 2025, in the first 35 years after 1990: the additional people are the children of the girls and young women of 1990. Demographers call the large increase of population size that occurs when a young, rapidly growing population switches abruptly to replacement-level fertility the "momentum" of population growth. The momentum of population growth makes many demographers think about achieving zero population growth as a process like bringing a very long train, a very big ocean liner or a very hot nuclear reactor to a safe halt. A population with many young people cannot stop growing quickly if each girl or young woman has, on the average, 2.06 children, or however many are required to replace her and her partner.

Nevertheless, there is nothing inevitable about population momentum. Population growth could end more rapidly if the total fertility rate fell below replacement. Even with fertility at the replacement level, the population growth rate can be reduced substantially by increasing the age at marriage and, to a lesser extent, by increasing the spacing between births.[7]

The hypothetical population of 2150 would differ dramatically from that of 1990 in size and in age. Less than 18 percent of the population would be under age 15 years compared with more than 32 percent in 1990. Fifteen percent would be aged 65–79 years compared with 5 percent in 1990. More than 9 percent would be aged 80 or over, compared with 1990's 1 percent. Altogether, nearly a quarter of the population would be 65 or older in 2150, roughly four times the share in 1990. An inescapable feature of zero population growth when people have a long life expectancy is a small fraction of young people and a large fraction of old people.

SENSITIVITY ANALYSES BY THE UNITED NATIONS

The United Nations made its medium projection the centerpiece of its seven long-range projections. In the medium projection, every area's fertility was assumed to move gradually to replacement level by 2100. The areas with high present fertility were assumed to experience a fall in fertility to a replacement level in the first half of the twenty-first century. Fertility in the areas with current below-replacement fertility was assumed to rise to replacement level at the end of the twenty-first century.[8]

In this scenario, world population would grow to 11.5 billion people by 2150 (Table 8.2), a 4.6-fold increase in the two centuries after 1950. Global population size would level off eventually at 11.6 billion people (Figure 8.2). The age structure of the population in 2150 would differ negligibly from that in the instant-replacement projection: the fraction of old people would be much higher and the fraction of young people would be much lower than at present. Both projections must reach the same eventual age structure because the eventual age structure of a population with replacement-level fertility is determined by the age pattern of death rates, which was assumed to be the same for both.

The United Nations carefully refrained from suggesting that its medium projection will actually happen. The detailed paths of fertility in the different areas were plausible but arbitrary. Why should fertility in today's wealthy areas rise to replacement level in the late twenty-first century after world population passes ten billion in 2050? Why should fertility anywhere move exactly to the replacement level?

The medium projection serves most usefully as a standard of reference for the United Nations' modest exercise in sensitivity analysis. In one comparison with its medium projection, the United Nations supposed that all areas might see fertility rise to a level 5 percent above the replacement level (the medium/high protection). In another comparison, the U.N. supposed that all areas might see fertility fall to a level 5 percent below the replacement level (the medium / low projection). The difference between the medium / high and the medium / low projections is about 10 percent of the replacement-level fertility, or two-tenths of a child on average, not a large difference, on the average, to an individual couple.

If the eventual total fertility rate were 1.96 children (one-tenth of a child less than the replacement level), the population size would rise from 5.3 billion in 1990 to 7.8 billion in 2050, then decline, dropping to 5.6 billion by 2150 and continuing steadily downward. If the eventual total fertility rate were 2.17 children (one-tenth of a child larger than replacement level), then the population would rise to 20.8 billion by 2150 and continue upward. The United Nations commented, and I agree: "Perhaps the major conclusion . . . is that there is a wide range of uncertainty regarding the future size of the world population. . . . At the level of the individual couple, if it is assumed reasonable that their behaviour will result in exactly 2.06 children on average (replacement level), it is probably just as reasonable to assume that the average might be 1.96 or 2.17 children."[9]

The United Nations' high and low projections formed a broader sensitivity analysis. The high projection assumed that, sometime between 2040 and 2100, each area's total fertility rate would become fixed at 2.5 children per woman. The low projection assumed that, between 2035 and 2100, each area's total fertility rate would become fixed at 1.7 children per woman (Figure 8.2). These were the first high and low long-range projections published by the United Nations to consider the possibility that the fertility might eventually become fixed at any level other than replacement. In the previous long-run projections, published in 1982, the high and low variants simply reached replacement level later and sooner than the medium variant. In this sense, the 1992 high and low projections were a radical departure for the United Nations.

According to the United Nations, "The high and low variants indicate the plausible range of future demographic trends."[10] I disagree. Around 1990 or 1991, the estimated total fertility rates of Italy and Spain were 1.3 and that of Germany was 1.4 children per woman.[11] At the high end, the estimated total fertility rates around 1990 or 1991 of Africa, Latin America and Asia excluding China were 6.1, 3.4 and 3.9 children per woman, respectively.[12] Compared to these current total fertility rates, the United Nations' hypothetical low total fertility rate of 1.7 and its hypothetical high of 2.5 children per woman hardly seem extreme.

At least one agricultural economist thinks the United Nations' low projection is more likely than any of the other U.N. projections.[13] As of 1993, the total fertility rate of the more developed countries as a whole had fallen to 1.8 children per woman, and as low as 1.7 or lower in Singapore, Hong Kong, Japan, South Korea, Macao, Taiwan, Antigua and Barbuda, Barbados, Denmark, Latvia, every country in western Europe except France (which had 1.8 children per woman), Bulgaria, Romania, most of former Yugoslavia and Russia.[14] China was not far behind with 1.9 children per woman. Just as the United Nations' high projections of the early 1950s were not nearly high enough, the projected fall in fertility of its present low projection may not be nearly low enough. After World War II, demographers failed dramatically to predict the rapid decline of mortality. It would be ironic if they made the same conservative error regarding the decline of fertility.

By 2050, when a child born in 1990 would be 60 years old, world population, according to the high and low projections, would differ by 4.7 billion people, a difference almost as large as the total present world population. By 2150, the high population (28.0 billion) would be more than six and a half times the low population (4.3 billion). The differences in age structure in 2150 would be nearly as dramatic as the differences in total size. The high population would have 23 percent under age 15, the low 14 percent. The high population would have 18 percent aged 65 and over, the low 31 percent.

These sensitivity analyses show unmistakably that there is a wide range of uncertainty concerning both population size and age structure. That much seems clear. However, the United Nations' approach to assessing just *how* uncertain they are could appear as unreliable to future demographers as the nineteenth-century Registrar General's exponential extrapolations of population size (based on the previous two decadal censuses) appeared to Edwin Cannan in 1895. Though the United Nations' approach of constructing high, medium and low projections based on fixed assumed paths of fertility, mortality and migration is conventional among most institutional demographers, it has logical problems.[15]

For example, if I do not know whether the total fertility rate over the next five years will be about 2.1 (the replacement level) or 2.5 or 1.7 children per woman, then after five years have passed, why should I assume that the total fertility rate over the *next* 150 years will be exactly what it was during the five years that just passed? If I am uncertain about the immediate future now, then presumably I would also be uncertain about the immediate future five years hence. (My uncertainty five years hence may not be exactly the same as my uncertainty now, because then I will have five more years of experience, but still I will have some uncertainty then if I have some uncertainty now.) The conventional approach's trio of high, medium and low projections starting from the present should be replaced, conceptually at least, by a branching bush of projections with an additional trio of possibilities sprouting every five years from every projection that exists so far. If there are three projections for the next five years, there should be nine projections for ten years from now, and 27 for 15 years from now and so on. It is probably not feasible to compute every possibility in this branching bush of projections, but it may well be possible to estimate the shape of the bush (for example, the range and quartiles of projected population sizes) using selective computations in combination with probability theory.

A second problem is that different demographic processes interact in a way that is more complicated than the conventional approach recognizes. For example, how many children will be born during 2025–29? The conventional "high" projection multiplies the high value of each age-specific birth rate by the high value of each age group of women. But in 2025, which is 35 years after 1990, the women who are then 15 to 35 years old will all have been born since the projection was launched in 1990. Unless the total fertility rate is constant in time (in which case a single projection suffices anyway), some of those women will have been born in years of high fertility and some will have been born in years of low or medium fertility. To compute the number of births during 2025–29 for the projections in which the total fertility rate is high, I should multiply the high age-specific birth rates by the number of mothers born in some years with high birth rates, the number born in some years with medium birth rates and the number born in some years with low birth rates. Consequently, the number of births should be lower than the results of multiplying all birth rates by the number of mothers born supposing all years had high birth rates. Moreover, the variability (the range or standard deviation or any other quantitative measure of statistical fluctuation) of the number of births, the birth rates and the total population size should all be different.

By similar reasoning, the number of deaths in 2025–29 is the product of the assumed age-specific death rates during that interval times the size of the corresponding age groups. Since the age groups less than 35 years old were born after 1990, some of them should be assumed to be high, some medium and some low. In general, the conventional approach via high, medium and low projections fails to allow for the demographic interactions between uncertainty at a given target date in the future and the cumulative effects of uncertainty between the time the projection was launched and the time of the target date. Recently developed methods give more sensible estimates of uncertainty, but they are not in widespread use.[16]

A year after publishing its 1992 long-range projections,[17] the United Nations published new projections.[18] For the year 2025, in the low, medium and high variants, the United Nations' new projected global populations were 7.9 billion, 8.5 billion and 9.1 billion. The 1993 high-variant projection of 9.1 billion is lower than the high-variant projection of 9.4 billion produced a year earlier, and the low-variant projection of 7.9 billion is higher than the low-variant projection of 7.6 billion produced a year ear-lier.[19] The range from low to high fell by 0.6 billion in one year, more than one-tenth of the present human population size, as if the United Nations' confidence in its knowledge about the future were improving. Did the U.N. really know that much more in 1993 than it knew in 1992? Doubtless this new estimate of uncertainty will be adjusted further in the future.

OTHER LONG-TERM PROJECTIONS

Like the United Nations, the World Bank uses the cohort-component method to prepare detailed projections to the year 2150 for its annual *World Development Report*. The World Bank's base-case projection is remarkably similar to the United Nations' medium projection (Table 8.2). The similar-ity results from applying similar assumptions to the same national censuses up to 1990. Both the United Nations and the World Bank assume gradually lengthening life expectancy and fertility that gradually moves to replace-ment level.[20]

Until recently, the Bank prepared a single scenario. The projections in the 1992 report considered "slow" and "rapid" falls in fertility in addition to the standard "base-case" projection. Rapid declines in fertility were mod-eled on Costa Rica, Hong Kong, Jamaica, Mexico and Thailand. Slow fer-tility declines were modeled on Paraguay, Sri Lanka, Suriname and Turkey. In the scenario where fertility fell quickly, the population leveled off at 10.1 billion. When fertility fell slowly, the population increased more than four-fold to about 23 billion, and leveled off late in the twenty-second century.[21]

Frejka published five projections from 1970 to 2150.[22] He assumed that, starting in 1970, fertility would fall in a straight line until it reached replace-ment level by one of five dates: 1970 (instant replacement), 1980, 2000, 2020 or 2040. If fertility had dropped instantaneously to the replacement level in 1970, world population would have leveled off at around 5.7 billion by 2100 (Figure 8.3). It now seems highly likely (demographers would say "virtually certain," but there is more to life than demography) that popula-tion size will exceed 5.7 billion by the middle of the 1990s. If fertility declined linearly to reach replacement level by 2040, the global population in 1990 would have been almost 5.5 billion (in fact the population was about 5.3 billion) and would level off near 15.1 billion around 2100. From 1970 to 1990, the actual global total fertility rate fell but not on a straight line: it declined rapidly in the 1970s but less rapidly in the 1980s. Frejka's highest projection lies between the medium and medium / high projections of the United Nations,[23] closer to the latter.

The projections of the United Nations, the World Bank and Frejka all assumed business as usual: continuous social and economic development, no large-scale epidemics, famines or wars, no agricultural or environmental crises, no surprising developments in technology or social organization that would greatly reduce the desire for children and no radical changes in gov-

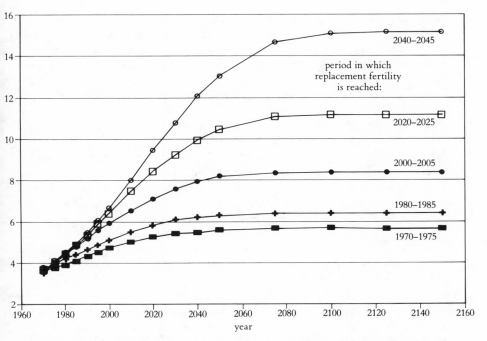

FIGURE 8.3 Frejka's projections of world population, assuming that fertility falls to replacement level at various dates from 1970–75 to 2040–45. SOURCE: original figure drawn according to data of Frejka (1973, p. 220, Table A)

ernments' population policies. Such projections provided an image of gradual change that is comforting to the public and to politicians, more comforting than the facts can guarantee.

As an alternative scenario, Gilland proposed the concept of a "demographic interlude."[24] In this scenario, the death rate falls due to health improvements, then rises to match or exceed the birth rate due to starvation, malnutrition and disease, while the birth rate remains constant or possibly even rises. Gilland refrained from carrying out numerical projections based on the scenario of the demographic interlude.

WILL TODAY'S POOR COUNTRIES EXPERIENCE A FERTILITY TRANSITION?

As we saw in Chapter 4, by 1990 about 77 percent of the world's population lived in countries, largely poor ones, where no fertility transition had yet begun and population growth rates were still rising (17 percent of the world total) or in countries with population growth rates that were still very high by historical standards, though somewhat lower than their peak (60 percent of the total). These facts contrast with the assumption of most conventional population projections that, while mortality gradually improves, fertility in every country will eventually fall just to replacement level and remain there. The big question is: should today's poor countries be expected to experience a fertility transition? Arguments have been offered on both sides.

Why should the poor countries *not* be expected to have a fertility transition? Since no one really understands the fertility transition in places where it has already occurred, there is no way to identify the precise conditions that lead to it, and therefore there are no grounds for asserting that today's poor countries will obey these conditions. When I say that no one "really understands" the fertility transition, I mean that no one so far has been able to predict the fertility transition's date of onset and the rate of passage, whether in Europe or in countries that have recently experienced it. Retrospective interpretations abound; but interpretations after the fact are words papering over the cracks in the intellectual plaster.

A second argument against the likelihood of a fertility transition for today's poor countries is that the European fertility transition took place in a setting of rich resources and opportunities for expansion and colonization. From 1500 to 1900, people of European origin and descent increased in numbers from perhaps 100 million to nearly 550 million, and as a fraction of world population from roughly one-sixth to about one-third.[25] Occupying about 7 percent of the Earth's land area in 1500, they occupied or controlled five-sixths of the area in 1900, including North and South America, Australia and its adjacent islands and Africa; and dominated southern Asia and its nearby islands. During this period, usable land and capital (precious metals, raw materials and finished goods) increased more rapidly than population.

The 400-year boom in population and resources that peoples of western European origin enjoyed is unlikely to be repeated for the peoples of Africa, Asia and Latin America. According to the American demographer Harold F. Dorn, writing in 1962,

> Although there are many thinly populated areas in the world, their existence is testimony to the fact that, until now, these have been regarded as undesirable living places. The expansion of population to the remaining open areas would require large expenditures of capital for irrigation, drainage, transportation facilities, control of insects and parasites, and other purposes—capital that the rapidly increasing populations which need these areas do not possess. In addition, this land is not freely available for settlement. The entire land surface of the world is crisscrossed by national boundaries.[26]

The European experience and that of today's poor countries differ in other respects as well: in awareness of the possibilities of wealth, and in rates of population growth.

The Europeans of the eighteenth, nineteenth and early twentieth centuries had no images from television, radio and newspapers to confront them with the vastly better life enjoyed by richer peoples.[27] By contrast, today many of the poor of Asia, Africa and Latin America are aware of the level of living of the rich countries. The awareness may bring about reductions in fertility, in the most favorable case. In a less favorable alternative, the awareness could lead to political changes that stymie a fertility transition in poor countries and adversely affect the rich. According to Dorn, "There is small likelihood that the two-thirds [by 1990, three-fourths] of the world's population which has not yet passed through the demographic revolution from high fertility and mortality rates to low fertility and mortality rates can repeat the history of western European peoples prior to the development of serious political and economic problems."[28] Of course, serious political and economic problems are hardly novel in the Old World and New. The economic development experienced by many previously poor countries over the last 30 years suggests that, with important exceptions, Dorn's view may have been too pessimistic.

European countries, especially those in western Europe, never had to contend with population growth rates as high as those of some poor countries recently.[29] There are two reasons for this difference. First, while the fertility of married couples in the West was as high as, or higher than, fertility within marriage in today's developing countries, overall birth rates in the West were substantially lower because couples in the West typically married at much later ages, a large fraction never married and those who never married had low fertility. Second, death rates in the West fell more slowly than they have in the developing countries since World War II. For a given decline in fertility, western death rates were higher, and hence population growth rates were lower, than in today's less developed countries.

Contrast Sweden and Taiwan, for example. In 1855, about 40 years before fertility began its long-term decline in Sweden, the Swedish birth rate was 3.3 percent and the death rate was 2.2 percent. The annual population growth rate was 1.1 percent, for a doubling time of 63 years. Taiwan's fertility evolution began in 1963. In 1953, ten years earlier, the birth rate was 4.5 percent and the death rate was 0.9 percent. Taiwan's 1953 annual population growth rate was 3.6 percent, equivalent to a doubling time of 19 years.[30]

Maurice King, professor of public health at the University of Leeds in Britain, argued that poor countries may be prevented from completing a demographic transition by what he called "demographic entrapment." His argument combined elements of several of the preceding arguments with an emphasis on ecological resources.[31] The idea of entrapment is that if a country's mortality falls much more rapidly than its fertility, the population will grow so rapidly that the ecological supports of the country (topsoil, trees, biological diversity) will be consumed before a rise in wealth triggers a fertility decline. If its people cannot emigrate to more favorable conditions, the country may then be "trapped" with high fertility, a rapidly growing population and few ecological resources.[32] King had in mind the "78 million people in countries whose total fertility is over 7, and 708 million where it is over 6."[33] He suggested that it might not be a very good idea to lower infant and childhood mortality in such a situation, because it would only accelerate population growth and deepen the trap. Robert H. Cassen, a development economist at the University of Oxford, found this argument "egregious" and pointed out that there was no evidence for the existence of any such "trap."[34]

Why *should* today's poor countries be expected to pass through a demographic transition? Scholarly ignorance about the factors responsible for past fertility transitions is no reason to believe that the same factors have ceased to be at work in today's poor countries. On the contrary, to some eyes, recent changes have only made the fertility transition more likely. According to Dudley Kirk, a Stanford University professor of population studies, "The prospect for reductions in the birth rate in the less industrialized countries has never been more hopeful. . . ."[35] In 1967, Kirk gave six reasons to be hopeful.

First, family planning is no longer unmentionable. Government policies and propaganda now legitimate family planning in many developing countries, and organized family-planning programs provide information, services and products. Modern methods of communication facilitate the spread of new attitudes, information and behaviors. By contrast, family limitation in Europe initially occurred in spite of institutional hostility toward birth control, restrictive legislation, religious opposition (Protestant and Catholic) and public denunciation of birth control.

Second, according to Kirk, religious doctrine in developing countries does not oppose family planning, except in Latin America where fertility has fallen anyway. Apart from the official positions of the Roman Catholic and the Orthodox Churches, most religions do not clearly ban the use of contraceptives and often permit abortion, at least prior to quickening.[36] I shall say more about religion as a possible obstacle to fertility decline in Chapter 13.

Third, new contraceptive methods developed by biomedical research offer women, men and couples wider choices, improved reliability and greater convenience. Recent developments of long-term implantable but reversible contraceptives such as Norplant and morning-after antigestational agents have widened choices further since Kirk wrote.

Fourth, the surprising speed with which mortality has fallen since World War II in many poor countries makes the improvement in survival more obvious. Death rates dropped within a single generation or even a decade or two. Visibly improved infant survival favors more rapid acceptance of family planning. By contrast, the declines in mortality of most European countries were much more gradual and would have been less apparent to individuals and couples.

Fifth, the notion of numeracy in fertility has spread more widely.[37] As Kirk put it, "Today it is increasingly appreciated among all cultures and strata of people that, within nature's limits, man can control his destiny over births as well as deaths."[38]

Sixth and finally, according to Kirk, more governments are recognizing that rapid population growth renders economic progress more difficult.[39]

For example, the final communiqué of the August 1992 Summit Meeting of the Non-Aligned Movement in Jakarta, as well as the final *Programme of Action* of the International Conference on Population and Development held in Cairo in September 1994, emphasized that population growth makes it more difficult to solve the problems of social and economic development.[40]

Van de Walle and Knodel found reasons to hope for a fertility transition in poor countries, not in the differences between them and the European countries, but in their common features.[41] These features include the diversity of social, economic and demographic conditions that preceded and accompanied the fertility transition in Europe; the absence or minimal effect of intentional birth control within marriage before the fertility transition in spite of the evidence that a considerable fraction of births were not wanted; the coincidence of the decline in fertility with an abrupt adoption of birth control practices; the concentration in time of the dates at which the declines started, and the rapidity with which they spread, once started; the irreversibility of the resulting drastic changes in reproductive behavior, once they were observable in aggregated statistics; and the major role of cultural influences on the start and spread of the fall in fertility. "These same features can be identified in many less developed countries today," van de Walle and Knodel observed hopefully in 1980. Further, cultural boundaries influence the initial date and rate of fertility decline in today's poor countries as they did in the countries of European descent.

In 1987, the United Nations published a lengthy final report on the World Fertility Survey (WFS), a decade-long series of studies of fertility and development in 38 developing countries. The study established that, among both families and countries, fertility was lower where various indicators of social and economic development were higher. The first sentence of the final paragraph of the report asserted: "In the final analysis, the WFS data confirm the inevitability of a demographic transition [meaning 'fertility transition'] by documenting common patterns and changes occurring across certain socio-economic groups in a variety of settings."[42] The asserted "inevitability" rests on at least two major assumptions: that the cross-sectional correlations established by the World Fertility Survey arise because increasing socioeconomic development causes fertility to fall, and that universal socioeconomic development is inevitable. At the same time, the report recognized that governmental policies, such as support for or opposition to family-planning programs, can accelerate or retard declines in fertility.

Fertility has fallen far in many of the poor countries Dorn described rather pessimistically in 1962 and hardly at all in others. In the last two decades alone, in developing countries, the fraction of couples who use family-planning methods rose from about one in eight to about one in two while the number of births per woman fell from about 6 to 3.8, a drop of more than 37 percent.[43]

There may be a simple reason why it can be argued, with some factual and logical support, both that poor countries should and that they should not pass through a fertility transition. Perhaps a fertility transition is neither inevitable nor impossible in any given country. Perhaps policies and programs can either accelerate or retard, promote or obstruct, a fertility transition. Perhaps people can *choose* to have for themselves, and to help others have, a fertility transition; or they can choose otherwise. If this view is even partially right, then population projections that assume a universal smooth transition to replacement-level or lower fertility are conditional predictions that leave unstated a key assumption: that people will choose lower fertility (Chapter 13).

The demographic future has none of the inevitability that population projections convey to some viewers. One of the many reasons population projections are uncertain is that no one knows what people will choose to want.

9

What Do We Know for Sure about the Future of Global Population?

> Just as Thomas Malthus, at the end of the 18th century, could not foresee the effect upon the peoples of western Europe of the exploration of the last great frontier of this earth, so we today cannot clearly foresee the final effect of an unprecedented rapid increase of population within closed frontiers. What seems to be least uncertain in a future full of uncertainty is that the demographic history of the next 400 years will not be like that of the past 400 years.
>
> —Harold F. Dorn 1962[1]

THE LAW OF PREDICTION asserts: the more confidence someone places in an unconditional prediction of what will happen in human affairs, the less confidence you should place in that prediction. Considering the Law of Prediction, it may seem impudent or self-defeating to suggest that anything can be known for sure about the future of global population. Nevertheless, a few modest but important certainties emerged from our critical look into the future. I summarize them under four headings: uncertainty, zero population growth, momentum and Methuselah's choice.

UNCERTAINTY

The future of human population growth is uncertain; that much is sure! What we do not know for sure is exactly how uncertain. There is no reliable way (so far) to construct a 90 percent confidence interval for the population or population growth rate of the United States, Thailand or the world in the year 2025. However, we do know, from the United Nations' sensitivity analyses, that the total population size and the age structure are highly sensitive to whether parents have more or fewer children than required for replacement.

As the horizon of prediction recedes into the future, some characteristics of global population become more uncertain while other characteristics become less uncertain.

The farther into the future we try to predict the size or structure of a population, the more uncertain prediction becomes. If global population is around 5.7 billion in 1995, it is a biological certainty that it will not be 10 billion in 1996 (there are just not enough women of reproductive age), but it is highly uncertain whether it will be 10 billion in 2025. Similarly, since about 6 percent of the world is elderly (65 years old or older) in 1995, the world could have 8 percent elderly in 1996 only if massive deaths removed many people aged less than 65 years in the intervening year; but the possibility that 8 percent of the population would be elderly in 2025 falls well within the range of variation of the United Nations' projections.[2]

Unlike population size, the average global population growth rate over the next ten years is less certain than the average global population growth rate over the next 10,000 years. If global population over the next 10,000 years is to remain between 5.7 million people (the 1995 population divided by 1,000) and 5.7 trillion people (the 1995 population times 1,000), then the average annual global population growth rate must remain between -0.0007 and $+0.0007$, that is, close to zero. The absolute uncertainty from high to low in the average population growth rate over the next ten millennia is less than one-seventh of 1 percent $[+0.0007 - (-0.0007)]$. During the next ten years, however, the global population growth rate could probably change as much as it changed within any decade in the last half century. In the decade from 1965–70 to 1975–80, the global population growth rate dropped by 0.4 percent, following a comparable rise in the previous decade. The range of uncertainty about the global population growth rate over the next decade (say, 0.4 percent) is more than twice the range of uncertainty about the global population growth rate over the next ten millennia (say, 0.14 percent).

ZERO POPULATION GROWTH

Statements about zero population growth take at least three forms: long run, short run, and weak. The long-run formulation of zero population growth goes like this: "Every demographer knows that we cannot continue a positive rate of increase indefinitely. The inexorable arithmetic of compound interest leads us to absurd conditions within a calculable period of time. Logically we must, and in fact we will, have a rate of growth very close to zero in the long run."[3] I know of no scholar of populations who disagrees, regardless of propaganda for space colonization. The Earth's human population must ultimately approach a long-term average growth rate of zero. This is a simple mathematical fact, not subject to the whims of wars or elections or wish or chance. It is the one irrefutable proposition of demographic theory.

The catch here is that the statement applies equally to a growth rate of one-millionth of a percent per year and to a growth rate of 2 percent per year. The long-run formulation of zero population growth is uncontroversial because, in pure form, it implies no present concern or action. While the long-run formulation of zero population growth seems irrefutable to me, often it is quoted to suggest some short-run version of zero population growth.

The short-run formulation of zero population growth varies. A modest form, based on the United Nations' constant-fertility projection,[4] is that the regional levels of fertility observed in 1990 cannot persist to 2150 together with slowly improving mortality, because if they did the human population would then exceed 694 billion. Therefore, sometime before 2150, the global population growth rate must fall to zero (though it need not necessarily stay there). This statement seems extremely probable.

Less modest short-run formulations claim that current population growth cannot continue for one, two or three more decades without catastrophe. Meadows et al. quoted U Thant, Secretary-General of the United Nations, as saying in 1969:

> I do not wish to seem overdramatic, but I can only conclude from the information that is available to me as Secretary-General, that the Members of the United Nations have perhaps ten years left in which to subordinate their ancient quarrels and launch a global partnership to curb the arms race, to improve the human environment, to defuse the population explosion, and to supply the required momentum to development efforts. If such a global partnership is not forged within the next decade, then I very much fear that the problems I have mentioned will have reached such staggering proportions that they will be beyond our capacity to control.[5]

In 1986, a report on the future of energy and agriculture in the United States, carried out at the Complex Systems Research Center at the University of New Hampshire, asserted:

> Most of us wouldn't care if our use of resources were unsustainable for the next five hundred years; this time scale is too large to affect today's decisions. The problem is that current patterns of resource use, including the ways in which we respond to perceived scarcities, are not sustainable even for the next forty or fifty years.[6]

In 1993, representatives of 58 of the world's scientific academies met in New Delhi and signed a brief report that concluded:

> In our judgement, humanity's ability to deal successfully with its social, economic, and environmental problems will require the achievement of zero population growth within the lifetime of our children.[7]

Between the claims that zero population growth must occur within one or two decades and that it must occur within at most a century and a half is a continuum of claims with increasing credibility.

The weak form of zero population growth asserts that a long-term average global population growth rate of zero is very unlikely to apply uniformly to every province, country, region or continent and all future time. Zero population growth, though inevitable, does not have to be boring. A long-term average of zero is consistent with many different combinations of population growth and decline, as in the history of Egypt. Future people might find attractive a global schedule of nine centuries of slow or moderate population growth, followed by a fertility holiday of relatively rapid population decline; or perhaps a rotating schedule in which different continents take turns growing and declining in population size, for a century at a time, while global population remains constant. Future populations might decide that certain regions are best as net producers and exporters of people and that others are best as net importers of young adults raised elsewhere. According to the weak form of zero population growth, the least likely alternative is that people will choose to give up all their demographic alternatives.

MOMENTUM

The remaining things we know for sure about the future of population are conditional predictions. From the United Nations' instant-replacement projection, we know for certain that population would rise substantially even if fertility changed to replacement levels today and mortality gradually improved. Similarly, we can be sure that the longer fertility takes to fall to the replacement level, the greater will be the population at that time and subsequently, provided that mortality does not worsen notably in the ages before the end of reproduction.

METHUSELAH'S CHOICE

The long-run version of zero population growth guarantees that the human population must ultimately approach a long-term average growth rate of zero. This means that the long-term average number of births must equal the long-term average number of deaths. This in turn means that, on average, the global birth rate (that is, the number of births divided by the total population size) must equal the global death rate (that is, the number of deaths divided by the total population size).

In a population with a constant size and with constant fractions in each age group (called a stationary population), the life expectancy at birth equals 1 divided by the death rate. For example, if the death rate is 2 percent per year (as it was in 1992 in Niger and Ethiopia,[8] though these were not stationary populations), and if the population is stationary, then the life expectancy must be $1 / 0.02 = 50$ years. It is easy to see why: if 1 / 50th (that is, 2 percent) of the people die every year, then the average person gets to live

50 years. If the death rate is 1.5 percent per year in a stationary population, then the life expectancy must be 1 / 0.015 = 66.7 years.[9]

We just saw that in a stationary population, the birth rate equals the death rate. Since life expectancy equals 1 divided by the death rate, life expectancy also equals 1 divided by the birth rate.[10] I glorify this elementary fact about any stationary population by calling it the equation of Methuselah's choice:

average length of life in a stationary population = 1 / birth rate.

People who live in a stationary population must choose: they can have a long average length of life together with a low birth rate, or they can have a high birth rate together with a short life expectancy. A short life expectancy for a population, being an average of everyone's length of life, usually means nowadays that many children die young, not that everybody lives happily to middle age and then disappears. In today's world, a population with a short life expectancy is a population living in misery. People cannot have both a high birth rate and a long life expectancy, and still have a stationary population. By creative use of the weak form of zero population growth, the constraints imposed by Methuselah's choice can be temporarily or locally weakened, but they cannot be altogether evaded. High fertility and high mortality will still be coupled, though in complex ways.

Methuselah's choice has a corollary. If people in a stationary population prefer long life and choose low fertility, like today's rich countries, there will be many more old people and many fewer young ones than if they choose high fertility and short lives. For example, if worldwide mortality improves and fertility falls as assumed in the United Nations' 1992 medium projection, the global median age will rise from 24 years in 1990 to 42 years in 2150, and the fraction of people aged 65 and over will rise from 6 percent to 24 percent.[11]

PART 4

———

THE HUMAN CARRYING CAPACITY OF THE EARTH

10

Eight Estimates of Human Carrying Capacity

> I believe it is worth while to prepare estimates of the maximum population that can be supported and to revise these as new information becomes available, . . . since this constitutes a rational effort to comprehend the implications of the increase in population.
>
> —HAROLD F. DORN 1962[1]

HOW MANY PEOPLE can the Earth support? The question is obviously incomplete. Support with what kind of life? With what technology? For how long? Leaving what kind of Earth for the future? I will return to these and many additional questions in Chapter 13. First I skip to the finish line and review eight case studies of how many people the Earth can support. I summarize the logic and principal numerical claims of these studies as neutrally as I can. After each summary, I offer my own comments in a separate subsection. Warm up your calculator again, and check me as I go.

"LANDS OF THE GLOBE STILL AVAILABLE FOR EUROPEAN SETTLEMENT" (1891)

The nineteenth century witnessed what the historian William McNeill called "the Western explosion." Powered by "firm belief in the value of their own inherited institutions, together with burgeoning numbers, the world's most powerful weapons, and most efficient network of transport and communication,"[2] European settlers or their descendants occupied the entire temperate regions of Central, North and South America and much of Australia, New Zealand and South Africa, while Russian settlement extended farther into Siberia and central Asia. Most of Africa, southeast Asia and Oceania fell under European political control by 1914.[3]

By 1890, Alexandrina Victoria was in the forty-seventh year of her reign as queen of Great Britain. Parliament had titled her Empress of India in 1876. On 8 September 1890, as one fleck of spume on the British Empire's advancing wave, E. G. Ravenstein read a paper entitled "Lands of the Globe Still Available for European Settlement" at the joint meeting of the Geographical and Economic Sections of the British Association for the Advancement of Science in Leeds. The paper, published in 1891, aimed "to determine:—(1) The present population of the world, and its probable increase. (2) The area capable of being cultivated for the yield of food and other necessaries of life; (3) The total number of people whom these lands would be able to maintain."[4]

Leaving aside the polar regions, where perhaps 300,000 people lived by hunting, fishing and gathering, Ravenstein estimated the portions of each continent that were "fertile," "steppes" and "desert" (Table 10.1). Ravenstein defined a region as "fertile only in as far as within it lies most of the land which is capable of remunerative cultivation. It cannot be assumed for an instant, that the whole or even the greater part of it could ever be converted into fields yielding the fruits of the earth. There are within it mountains, which will never tempt the agriculturist, sandy tracts, capable of supporting only forest, and even steppes or poor savannahs, not fit for anything except the raising of cattle."[5] The steppes are "poorer grass lands, and as within the 'fertile' region we met with comparatively sterile tracts, so within these 'steppes' there exist large areas which can be rendered highly productive, especially where means for irrigating the land are available. The third region includes the deserts, within which fertile oases are few and far between."[6]

Ravenstein then cautiously approached "the difficult task of estimating the number of people whom this earth of ours would be capable of supplying with food and the other necessaries of life, once it had been fairly brought under cultivation."[7] He set aside the possibility that humankind would become vegetarian along with the hope, expressed by some, "that the day would come when food, as toothsome as meat and equally nutritious, might be grown in our fields, thus obviating the necessity of keeping up large herds of cattle and sheep."[8] He also remarked that

> it has been asserted that our present methods of cultivation are capable of vast improvement; that the earth might be made to yield much larger harvest than it yields now; and that population might thus be permitted to increase without correspondingly increasing the cultivated areas. This no doubt is true as respects many countries, but it is hardly true of the world at large. In the United States, for instance, and generally speaking in all newly-settled countries, where large tracts of unoccupied land are still available, agriculture is carried on in a wasteful style, the cultivator looking only to immediate returns and having no thought of the prosperity of his descendants. . . . These things, however, will be mended in course of time; the exhausted soil of the eastern states will recover; and the forests, where wantonly destroyed, will be replanted. In proportion as the population increases, so will the resources of the country be more carefully husbanded.[9]

In estimating the supportable population density, Ravenstein "assumed that the available areas would be rationally cultivated, and . . . even admit-

TABLE 10.1 Ravenstein's (1891) estimates of population size and growth and of type of land

region	population in 1890 (millions)	population per square kilometer[a]	fertile region (square kilometers)	steppe (square kilometers)	desert (square kilometers)	total (square kilometers)	increase in a decade (percent)	estimated population in 1900 (millions)[b]
Europe	380.2	39	7,479,927	1,727,532	0	9,207,459	8.7	413.3
Asia	850	22	24,035,224	10,955,711	3,108,003	38,098,938	6	901.0
Africa	127	4.2	14,918,415	9,137,529	5,765,346	29,821,290	10	139.7
Australasia	4.73	0.6	3,022,533	3,903,134	1,590,262	8,515,929	30	6.1
North America	89.25	5.4	12,810,153	3,638,954	246,050	16,695,157	20	107.1
South America	36.42	1.9	10,950,531	6,640,767	116,550	17,707,848	15	41.9
total[c]	1,467.6[d]	12.4	73,216,783	36,003,626	10,826,211	120,046,620	8	1,609.1
supportable people per square kilometer	NA[e]	NA	80	3.9	0.4	NA	NA	NA
total supportable population (millions)	NA	NA	5,851	139	4	5,994	NA	NA
polar regions	0.3	0.02	NA	NA	NA	12,662,005	NA	NA

[a] I converted Ravenstein's figures in units of square miles (given to the nearest thousand) to equivalents in units of square kilometers (1 square kilometer = 0.3861 square mile). Ravenstein's calculations neglect the population of the polar regions.

[b] My calculation from Ravenstein's estimates of population in 1890 and percentage increase in a decade.

[c] Excluding polar regions.

[d] This total, shown by Ravenstein, is incorrect; the correct total is 1,487.6 million.

[e] NA = not applicable.

SOURCE: Ravenstein (1891, pp. 27, 28, 32)

ted a slight improvement in the yield of each acre." For the fertile regions, considering continental Europe from the North Sea and the Atlantic to the Black Sea along with India, China and Japan, "I find that their mean population is 207 to the square mile"[10] or 80 people per square kilometer. He supposed that the entire fertile region could support that density of population. "The 'steppes,' with their large tracts of land capable of cultivation, I believe to be capable of supporting ten inhabitants to the square mile [roughly four per square kilometer], whilst the 'deserts' would be fully peopled if they had even one inhabitant to a square mile. The total possible population would consequently amount to 5,994,000,000."[11]

Ravenstein worried that the tropical regions lack a climate suitable for permanent European colonization. His interpretation of temperature and humidity in the tropics carried the stamp of Victorian Britain: ". . . broadly speaking, the tropical regions are not adapted for colonisation by Europeans. For the present, at all events, the white man must be content to settle there temporarily, to teach the natives the dignity of labour, and to lead him on to a higher plane of civilisation."[12] These pleasantries are unremarkable for their time and are not why the paper is remembered.

To show that the limit of 5,994 million people does not lie in the remote future, Ravenstein estimated a current global population growth rate of 8 percent per decade (0.77 percent per year).

> By the close of this [nineteenth] century, the 1468 millions who now dwell upon the earth will have increased to 1587 millions; in the year 1950 there will be 2332 millions; in the year 2000, 3426 millions; and in the year 2072, or 182 years hence, there will be 5977 millions. These estimates are not presented as a prophecy. I have already hinted at voluntary checks to the growth of population, which will come into play in proportion as civilisation advances, and the demands for the comforts of this life shall become more general. At all events, as far as we personally are concerned, one hundred and eighty-two years is a long period to look forward to; but if we look back . . . we are bound to admit that it is but a short period in the lifetime of a nation.[13]

In calculating the future world population, Ravenstein evidently assumed a constant global population growth rate instead of projecting each continent according to its own growth rate. He would have obtained more rapid population growth had he projected each continent separately.

A printed discussion followed Ravenstein's paper. The first commentator was Alfred Marshall, the distinguished economist who was then the president of the Economic Science and Statistical Section of the British Association. He thanked Ravenstein for "his admirable paper, . . . but before sitting down would venture to remark that Mr. Ravenstein had not explicitly called attention to the question of fuel. There were many who thought that a check to population in the future in temperate regions would come from the scarcity not of food but of fuel,"[14] while others thought a copper wire a few yards thick from the Sahara to England could supply England all the heat and force England could want. Marshall concluded by raising, but not answering, a question that troubled him: "Supposing they were careful not to over-populate, how were they to be sure that the world would not be over-populated by people who were less careful, and whom for that very reason, perhaps, the world would less care to have?"

Comments

How good are Ravenstein's estimates of current and future populations in today's perspective? In 1979, Biraben estimated regional populations in 1900.[15] When I combined Biraben's estimates into the regions used by Ravenstein, I found that Biraben's estimate of total population size was less than 2 percent larger than Ravenstein's estimate for 1900, and the regional totals were also close.[16] In retrospect, Ravenstein's estimates of the then-current population look remarkably good. His extrapolations into what was then the future look much less good, apart from questions about his arithmetic. Doubtless he would be surprised to see that his estimate of the world's maximum possible population, six billion, will very probably be surpassed before the year 2000.

Ravenstein assumed that the potential population of fertile lands, steppes and deserts could be estimated from present areas of high population density within each type of land, that the future maximal population density of each type of land would not change materially and that the area of each type of land would not change materially. Though Ravenstein seemed to consider the production of food as the principal factor limiting human population, he did not explicitly say so. By using current population densities as his guide, Ravenstein implicitly allowed for all the requirements necessary to support populations with the technologies then available.[17]

"THE CHIEF PROBLEM OF PHYSICAL ANTHROPOGEOGRAPHY" (1925)

In 1924, the Weimar Republic was in its sixth year of a feverish childhood that was soon to be cut short. The first Nazi *Putsch* in 1923 had been suppressed. In November 1924, while under house arrest for his role in the attempted coup, Adolf Hitler finished writing *Mein Kampf*.

In September 1924, at the Prussian Academy of Sciences, Albrecht Penck lectured on "the chief problem of physical anthropogeography," namely, "the relation between the Earth's surface and man, whose nutritional needs will be produced from it."[18] Penck's lecture was printed in the 1924 proceedings of the Prussian Academy. It was quickly reprinted, with a minor correction of formulas, in the 1925 *Zeitschrift für Geopolitik* (*Journal of Geopolitics*). Penck's contemporaries, like Ravenstein's, viewed his calculations in a geopolitical perspective.

Penck proposed some simple equations that relate food production and population density. I will replace most of his symbols by the words they represent, but will use P to represent the number of people on the Earth. According to Penck,

food production $= P \times$ average nutritional requirement of a single person.

The food production also equals the product of the productive area times the average production per unit of area. Therefore

productive area $\times$ production per unit of area
$= P \times$ average nutritional requirement of a single person.

Dividing both sides of this equation by the average nutritional requirement per individual gives

$$P = \frac{\text{productive area} \times \text{production per unit of area}}{\text{average nutritional requirement of a single person}}.$$

In Penck's words, "the number of people on the Earth equals the productive area times its average production per unit of area, divided by the average nutritional requirement per individual. All of the quantities just mentioned are finite, and since the nutritional requirements of people cannot become equal to zero, the number of people on the Earth is limited."[19]

If there are neither imports nor exports, the same equation applies to each region, Penck said. Differences among regions in the production per unit of area result from differences in the climate, in the soil and in the intensity of cultivation or management. Though the nutritional requirements per person vary from place to place, they vary within a very limited range. The production per unit of area is the product of the highest possible productivity per unit of area, which is conditioned by climate and soil, times the variable intensity of agricultural cultivation. While the highest possible productivity per unit of area has the dimensions of output per area, the intensity of cultivation is a pure number, a fraction. In an economically closed region without imports or exports,

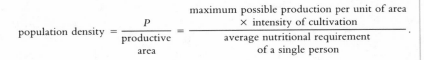

Penck emphasized: "The intensity of cultivation . . . is essentially dependent on the level of culture, and thus it is clear in what large measure the population density of a region is determined by its level of culture. . . . We must always take into consideration both the advantage of natural conditions and the level of culture when we want to explain the population density of a region."[20]

Trade in foodstuffs requires that the previous formula be corrected for imports and exports, so that

$$\text{population density} = \frac{\begin{array}{c}\text{maximum possible production per unit of area} \times \text{intensity of cultivation} \\ + \text{ imports per area } - \text{ exports per area}\end{array}}{\text{average nutritional requirement of a single person}}.$$

According to Penck, "while world trade raises or lowers the natural population density of individual lands, it brings about no general increase in the number of people on the Earth; this is and remains finally dependent on the size and productivity of the Earth and on the intensity of cultivation, as well as on the nutritional requirements of the individual."[21]

Taking the Earth's area and maximal productivity as fixed, and the nutritional requirements of the individual as only slightly variable, the maximum population can rise no higher than the maximal intensity of cultivation permits. Penck called this maximum population the potential population consistent with the capacity of the land. Because soil and other physical conditions vary within any large climatic region, Penck did not adopt the highest observed population density within a region as the density that the entire region could support; "the plant cover of the land gives a good basis for estimating the gradations of the productivity of soil and climate. This permitted us to draw up plausible values of the average potential population density of a climatic region and, using the areas determined by [Hermann] Wagner, to deduce the probable largest possible number of inhabitants."[22]

Penck then estimated the average, and the highest conceivable, potential population density of each of 11 climatic zones. To give an idea of his methods, it suffices to quote his analysis of the climatic zone with the largest potential population density and largest absolute population, the moist warm primary forest climate.

> In the moist warm primary forest climate, the highly cultivated island of Java, with its population density of 266 inhabitants per square kilometer, is outstanding; this density increases to 350 in the western parts of the island. At the same time, the island is only partly under cultivation, and Woeikof [writing in *Annales de géographie* 1901] considers possible an average population density of 800. Accordingly he believes that the entire tropical zone between 15°N and 15°S could feed on average 400 inhabitants per square kilometer and 10 billion in total. We remain far below this estimate, in that we put the highest potential population density in the moist warm climatic zone at 400; for the conditions on Java are extraordinarily favorable.[23]

Penck then discussed the volcanic origin of the soil in Java and the estimates of other authorities for the potential population density of the tropics, and concluded: "We probably do not overestimate the average population density if we express it as 200" people per square kilometer. The ten other climates received briefer treatment.

Penck quoted Wagner's estimates of the areas of the 11 climatic regions (column I of Table 10.2) and gave his own examples of thickly settled lands and his assumed maximum populations (column II of Table 10.2). "As our

TABLE 10.2   Penck's (1925) estimates of the potential population of the Earth (both highest conceivable and probable), by climatic zone

climate	(I) area (million square kilometers)	most thickly settled lands (people per square kilometer)	(II) assumed maximum population density (people per square kilometer)	(III) highest conceivable number of inhabitants (millions)	(IV) probable average population density (people per square kilometer)	(V) probable largest possible number of inhabitants (millions)	(A) product of columns I and II (millions)
1. moist warm primary forest climate	14.0	West Java (400)	350	**5,600**[a]	200	2,800	4,900
2. periodically dry savanna climate	15.7	Madras	115	1,806	90	1,413	1,806
3. steppe climate	21.2	Region of the Don (10)	21	**212**	5	106	445
4. desert climate	17.9	Egypt (3)	14	**54**	1	18	251
5. warm climate with dry winter	11.3	Bengal	228	2,576	110	1,243	2,576
6. warm climate with dry summer	2.5	Italy	125	**312**	90	225	313
7. wet temperate climate	9.3	Southern Japan	220	2,046	100	930	2,046
8. cold climate with moist winter	24.5	Poland	106	2,597	30	735	2,597
9. cold climate with dry winter	7.3	Chile	96	701	30	219	701
10. tundra climate	10.3	Greenland	0.02	0	0.01	0	0
11. climate of eternal frost	15.0	Antarctica	0	0	0	0	0
total	149.0		107	15,904[b]	51[c]	7,689	15,634

[a]The four entries in this column set in boldface type indicate the four arithmetic discrepancies in Penck's multiplication of columns I and II (compare with column A). See note 24 to Chapter 10.

[b]See correct figure in column A.

[c]Penck's figure is mistaken; should be 52.

Source: Penck (1925, p. 340), except for last column

TABLE 10.3   The distribution of global population by continent: the actual distribution in 1920 compared with the potential population according to Penck (1925) and the estimated 1993 population

region	1920 population (millions)	1920 (percent)	potential population (millions)	potential population (percent)	1993 population (millions)	1993 (percent)
Eurasia	1,440	80	2,080	26	4,055	74
Africa	126	7	2,320	29	677	12
Australia	9	0.5	480	6	28[a]	0.005
North America	162	9	1,120	14	287	5
South America	63	3.5	2,000	25	460	8
Earth total	1,800	100	8,000	100	5,507	100

[a] All of Oceania (Australia, New Zealand, Papua New Guinea and Pacific islands).

SOURCES: Penck (1925, p. 343) for percentages and totals of 1920 and potential populations; Population Reference Bureau (1993) for 1993 estimated populations

table makes clear, the highest conceivable number of inhabitants of the Earth is 15.9 billion, which presupposes an average population density of 107 [per square kilometer]. These numbers seem to us to be the most extreme limits, which could be reached only with difficulty. The probable largest number of inhabitants of the Earth is given as only half as large, 7.689 billion, and thus not essentially different from the corrected estimate of von Fircks."[24]

As minor variations in the assumed maximal densities of a few regions lead to an increase of nearly 400 million in the estimated maximal total population, Penck inferred that "our final result has an uncertainty well in the hundreds of millions, and we may without hesitation round it off to 8 billion. But even this number appears in no way assured." Penck concluded that "the potential population of the Earth may be set between 8 and 9 billions. This compares with a present population of around 1.8 billion. Thus the living space [*Lebensraum*] of mankind is only one-fifth full."

Penck remarked that of the estimated 1920 population of 1.8 billion, roughly 80 percent lived in Eurasia, while of the potential population of 8 billion, Eurasia's share would shrink to 26 percent, largely as a result of major increases in Africa and South America (Table 10.3).

Based again on estimates done by Hermann Wagner, Penck calculated that world population had grown by 0.57 percent per year over the previous half century. Were this rate of growth to continue, the temperate zones would be "filled" in roughly a century and a half, and the world as a whole in less than three centuries. "Whether the space will be filled in the long run so quickly as in the last 50 years can easily be doubted,"[25] Penck suggested, because rapidly expanding world trade had opened up large areas of easily cultivated lands; in the future, additional lands could be won only with great difficulty.

Comments

Penck's procedure for estimating maximum population density represented an advance in theory, but not in method, over Ravenstein's. Penck made no attempt to measure the quantities in his equations, such as individual nutritional requirements, maximal possible productivity of food per unit of area or intensity of cultivation. Rather, his estimates of population density were, like Ravenstein's, lower than the highest existing population densities and higher than the lowest. Penck assumed, but did not show, that population densities were constrained by supplies of food. The observed population densities on which Penck based his estimates of maximal population densities could have been limited by water, soil, cultural preferences for space or factors in addition to or other than food. Like Ravenstein's, Penck's estimates were intuitive judgments.

Penck's formula for the maximum supportable population,

$$P = \frac{\text{productive area} \times \text{production per unit of area}}{\text{average nutritional requirement of a single person}},$$

was used by later investigators.[26] However, it is seriously incomplete as a theory of maximum supportable population.

The major assumption underlying Penck's equations is that human numbers are limited by food alone. Subject to that major assumption, a further assumption is that individual food requirements are constant in every place and time. Most estimates of the average energy per person required for subsistence, averaged over national populations, fall within the range from 2,000 to 2,700 kilocalories per person per day (Appendix 5). However, the amount of plant food that must be grown (or grazed) to supply, say, 2,500 kilocalories depends heavily on the composition of the diet. To take hypothetical extreme cases, if the diet were purely vegetarian, then only 2,500 kilocalories of humanly edible plant food would have to reach the consumer. At the other extreme, suppose that 30 percent of the average daily diet came from animal sources. If the animal sources required ten kilocalories of feed for every kilocalorie of energy eaten by the consumer,[27] then the amount of edible food energy that would have to be grown to supply 2,500 kilocalories per person would be $0.7 \times 2,500$ (for the vegetable portion of the diet) $+ 0.3 \times 2,500 \times 10$ (for the animal portion) $= 9,250$ kilocalories. In this case, 3.7 times as many edible calories would have to be grown or grazed as are eaten. However, some of the calories animals eat may be in forms inedible to humans, so the multiplier of humanly edible calories might be less than 3.7. In some developing countries, diets are shifting toward more consumption of animal products, including eggs and meat; in some rich countries, diets are shifting toward less consumption of animal products. The assumption of invariant caloric requirements is justified only under the implicit, implausible assumption that every person eats a uniform vegetarian diet at a bare subsistence level.

Penck's first equation,

food production $= P \times$ average nutritional requirement of a single person,

assumed that the food produced equals the food consumed by people. A more accurate accounting would recognize that, of the food produced each year, some may be consumed by people, some put into storage, some consumed by warm-blooded animals, insects or microbial pests before or after retail sale, some spoiled in transport, handling and cooking and some simply wasted. Moreover, not all food consumed by people may be formally cultivated; some may be hunted, fished or gathered. All these factors may be combined into a more detailed accounting equation for the annual food flows of a closed region, such as the globe:

food consumed = food grown + food gathered and hunted − food stored + food taken from storage − food consumed by pests before harvest − food never gathered or spoiled in harvest − food wasted after harvest before final sale − food lost between final purchase and consumption.

As much as 40 percent of food may be lost between production and consumption, including a loss of 10–15 percent after food leaves retail establishments.[28] While such estimates of losses are subject to error and to change, the food consumed may be substantially less than the food grown.

Penck asserted wrongly that world trade could have no effect on the agricultural productivity of the Earth and hence on the number of people who could be fed at any given level of nutrition.[29] Contrary to this assertion, developing countries have supplied potash to fertilize the soils of rich countries; rich countries have supplied to poor countries the technology to develop better strains of rice and corn, chemical fertilizers and pesticides and tools and machinery to cultivate, harvest and process crops. The exchanges increased the "potential population" of both rich and poor regions. Penck's assertion that trade does not affect global potential population cannot stand today. As a result it is difficult to assess the potential population, however it may be defined, of individual regions in isolation.

Penck's estimate of the global population growth rate over the half century prior to 1925 lies within the range of today's estimates for that period, but Penck did not foresee that the world population growth rate would more than triple within less than half a century from the time he wrote. He might be surprised to see that the estimated 1993 population of Eurasia was twice his estimate of its potential population (Table 10.3).

Penck's views met with approval by the powers that were soon to be in Germany. By 1941, Penck was invited to write the leading chapter (following a formal introduction) in a two-volume collective treatise on *The Ques-*

tion of Living Space for European Peoples (Lebensraumfragen europäischer Völker). By then Penck held two honorary doctorates in addition to his earned doctorate and was professor-at-large of geography at the University of Berlin and honorary president of the German Geographical Meetings. His chapter's title was "The Carrying Capacity of the Earth." His first reference was to the paper he presented in September 1924 at the Prussian Academy of Sciences, which I have just described. Most of the chapter reviewed his earlier work and related work by others before and since. Penck should be remembered for his scholarship and not for the final paragraph of his chapter. After a reference to Germany's losses at Versailles, the chapter ends:

> Today the whole German people struggles under its leader [*Führer*] for the final victory, not only for the recovery of a possession taken from it, but also for its acceptance by the world, which is indispensable for its collaboration in the large tasks of humanity.[30]

"The Potential Productivity of Earth and the Population It Could Support" (1967)

The years around 1965 will probably stand for a long time, and possibly forever, as the high-water mark of global human population growth. As we have seen, the population growth rate then, estimated at greater than 2.1 percent per year, resulted from the baby boom in some rich countries and an unprecedentedly rapid fall in mortality in many poor countries. In 1966, American prosperity and power were higher than ever before. The American military presence in Vietnam was only building up, and victory appeared to be just around the corner.

In October 1966, the International Minerals and Chemical Corporation sponsored a symposium to commemorate the opening of a new laboratory in Libertyville, Illinois. The title was "Harvesting the Sun: Photosynthesis in Plant Life." One of the five distinguished contributors from outside the United States was C. T. De Wit of the Institute for Biological and Chemical Research on Field Crops and Herbage in Wageningen, the Netherlands.

De Wit posed a modest, conditional question: "How many people can live on earth if photosynthesis is the limiting process? To answer this question, the potential photosynthetic capability of green crop surfaces has to be estimated and related to the energy requirements of man. In calculating the potential rate of photosynthesis, we must assume that neither water nor minerals are limiting."[31]

The potential rate of photosynthesis depends on multiple factors: how much photosynthate is produced as a function of the incident light intensity and temperature; the scattering coefficient, which describes how the leaves and seeds of a crop scatter the light coming from the sky; the leaf area index (the area of leaf surface exposed to light per unit of area of ground surface[32]); how the plant displays its leaves; the light intensity; and the direction of the arriving light. The direction of the arriving light depends on whether the sky is cloudy or clear and the height of the sun. The height of the sun depends on the season and the latitude. A computer model of the photosynthesis of leaf canopies combined all these factors to predict the kilograms of carbohydrate produced per hectare per year. (Yield measured in kilograms per hectare is close to yield measured in pounds per acre; see Appendix 1.) De Wit did not mention a particular crop, so presumably he chose a crop or crops with characteristics optimal for maximizing yield. De Wit calculated the gross tonnes per hectare per year of carbohydrate that could potentially be grown in each 10-degree belt of latitude, assuming no constraints of water or minerals (column 4 of Table 10.4).

The theoretical figure for the gross carbohydrate produced allowed nothing for the losses due to plant respiration, nor did it allow for the possibility that "the crop surface is not always closed [that is, some sunlight reaches the ground, rather than crop leaves]. To correct for these factors, we can assume half this value. Now there is one other factor which affects . . . the number of individuals which can be fed per hectare. Not all of the . . . [kilograms of] carbohydrate are usable for human consumption. This figure must again be halved."[33] One-quarter of the potential gross carbohydrate shown in column 4 of Table 10.4 is the net carbohydrate available for human consumption, according to De Wit. But each gram of net carbohydrate eaten yields about four kilocalories of energy, so the potential weight of gross carbohydrate produced per hectare per year (in grams) just equals the kilocalories of humanly consumable food energy; that is, the division by four to allow for respiration and incomplete crop cover just cancels the multiplication by four to convert grams of net carbohydrate to kilocalories. For example, at 70 degrees north, if one hectare can potentially produce 12 tonnes or 12 million grams of gross carbohydrate per year, then it can produce 12 million kilocalories of humanly edible net carbohydrates per year.

De Wit continued, "What does this mean in terms of population? . . . Each human requires about 1 million kilocalories per year [about 2,740 kilocalories per day] as food."[34] In the example just given, if one hectare can potentially produce 12 tonnes of gross carbohydrate and 12 million kilocalories of humanly edible net carbohydrates per year, then it can feed 12 people for a year, assuming for all a largely vegetarian diet of carbohydrates. De Wit used Penck's formula, possibly without being aware of its source:

$$P = \frac{\text{productive area} \times \text{production per unit of area}}{\text{average nutritional requirement of a single person}}.$$

Per hectare, at 70 degrees north, the numerator on the right was 12 million kilocalories and the denominator was one million kilocalories, so $P = 12$ people. In general, the number of tonnes of gross carbohydrate per hectare (shown in column 4 of Table 10.4) equals the number of people who could be fed per hectare.

Table 10.4 De Wit's (1967) estimates of the Earth's potential carbohydrate production (assuming photosynthesis were the sole limit on growth) and the human population that could be fed from the calories grown

north latitude[a] (degrees)	land surface (100 million hectares)	number of months above 10°C	carbohydrate per hectare per year (1000 kilograms)[b]	square meters per person to support life				percentage of agricultural land
				no allowance for urban and recreational needs		750 square meters per person for urban and recreational needs		
				square meters per person	number of people (billions)	square meters per person	number of people (billions)	
Column 1	2	3	4	5	6	7	8	9
70	8	1	12	806	10	1,556	5	52
60	14	2	21	469	30	1,219	11	38
50	16	6	59	169	95	919	17	18
40	15	9	91	110	136	860	18	13
30	17	11	113	89	151	839	20	11
20	13	12	124	81	105	831	16	10
10	10	12	124	81	77	831	11	10
0	14	12	116	86	121	836	17	10
−10	7	12	117	85	87	835	9	10
−20	9	12	123	81	112	831	11	10
−30	7	12	121	83	88	833	9	10
−40	1	8	89	113	9	863	1	14
−50	1	1	12	833	1	1,583	1	53
total	131				1,022		146	

[a] De Wit (1967, p. 318) says that each row corresponds to a 10-degree interval of latitude but does not specify the interval corresponding to each number. My guess is that the number shown is the midpoint, so that 70 degrees north means the interval from 65 to 75 degrees north, while zero degrees means the interval from 5 degrees north to 5 degrees south.
[b] Also equal to the number of people who can be supported per hectare.

Source: De Wit (1967, p. 317)

Since there are 10,000 square meters in one hectare, the required area (in square meters) of cropland per person (column 5) is 10,000 divided by the potential gross carbohydrate (tonnes) per hectare (column 4), allowing for the fact that column 4 is rounded to the nearest whole number. For example, at 70 degrees north, if $P = 12$ exactly, each person consumes the yield of $10,000 / 12 = 833$ square meters of land. In fact, P must lie between 11.5 and 12.5, so the square meters per person must lie between 800 and 870. All the figures of square meters per person shown in column 5 are consistent with those in column 4, within the error of rounding.

To obtain the number of people that could be fed with the net carbohydrate grown in each belt of latitude, De Wit multiplied the land surface (column 2) by 10,000 to convert it from hectares to square meters, then divided by the square meters per person (column 5). For example, at 70 degrees north, the land surface covers 800 million (8×10^8) hectares or eight trillion (8×10^{12}) square meters; because each person consumes the product of 806 square meters, the number of people P who could be fed carbohydrates by this land is 8×10^{12} square meters divided by 806 square meters per person, which equals 9.9×10^9; after rounding, this appears in column 6 as 10 billion people.

De Wit wrote:

> The staggering conclusion to be drawn from this table is that 1,000 billion people could live from the earth if photosynthesis is the limiting factor!
> This is how many could live *from* the earth; not *on* the earth. A dense population can only be maintained in an affluent society and an affluent society has been estimated [by L. H. J. Angenot in 1966] to require at least 350 square meters (0.087 acres) per person for urban use. Additional recreation areas may add another 350 square meters per person to the total. This figure is probably underestimated since the region from Boston to Washington covers an area of 138,000 square kilometers and includes metropolitan areas of 27,500 square kilometers occupied by 37 million people. This amounts to about 750 square meters (0.19 acre) per person for urban needs only.[35]

Try to visualize 750 square meters. An American football field is a rectangle roughly 50 meters wide by 100 meters long. Your 750 square meters of space "for urban and recreational needs," including your share of housing, highways, parks and gardens, is a strip across the field with dimensions 50 meters by 15 meters (roughly 55 yards by 16 yards). If your strip is at 70 degrees north latitude or 50 degrees south latitude, it will have a temperature below 10 degrees centigrade (50 degrees Fahrenheit) 11 months of the year. Your strip may lie on a rocky mountain slope, but no matter. Of course, parts of "urban and recreational" space are shared, so 750 square meters may be a bit less constraining than it seems; but it's hardly much space.

De Wit estimated the total land required per person (column 7 in Table 10.4) as 750 square meters plus the area for growing food in column 5. "Division of the amount of land available by the total land needed for each individual gives a figure of 146 billion people. This figure, 146 billion, may be somewhat too high since some land is not suitable for urban use, agriculture, or even recreation. On the other hand, the value may be increased by shifting a part of the population from highly productive areas in the tropics to more northern latitudes."[36] If population were shifted from the more productive regions to the extreme latitudes, then more than six billion people (a number greater than the Earth's present population) would live closer to the poles than 70 degrees north or 50 degrees south.

Future increases in yield per unit of area would not change the picture greatly because most land is used for living space, not for growing food, in De Wit's scenario. According to De Wit,

> A yield increase of 30% leads only to an increase of the maximum number of people by 3%. Even if all the production could be obtained from the sea, the maximum number would increase only 20%, from 146 billion to 175 billion.[37] The sea can be neglected as a source of food because the amount of minerals that must be added to keep so much water in a reasonable nutritional status is prohibitive. The organic matter produced by plankton at the present nutritional status is only 5% of the potential photosynthesis of a comparable land area. Of this organic matter, only 1% can be harvested in the form of fish, so food production of the sea is only 1/500 of food production on land. With a population of 146 billion, 2,500 square meters of sea surface is available per man. This is the equivalent of 2500 / 500 = 5 square meters of land.[38]

Adding 200 grams (0.4 pound) of meat to the daily diet would reduce the potential population from 146 billion to 126 billion, because "About 5,000 kcal in the form of vegetable fodder products is necessary to grow this amount of meat which contains, on an energy basis, 500 kcal. In that case, each man will need about two times more land for agricultural purposes."

What really limits the maximum population is the use of land for non-agricultural purposes, under De Wit's assumption of unlimited water and soil nutrients. Raising the non-agricultural requirement to 1,500 square meters rather than 750 square meters per person lowers the 146 billion maximum population to 79 billion. Always assuming no limitations of water or minerals, De Wit estimated that "the agricultural land required for 79 billion people would equal about 7% of the earth—an area which is readily available. The number of persons on earth is, therefore, ultimately limited by the amount of space a man needs to work and live in reasonable comfort and not by the production of food. In the long run a situation of over-population without starvation must be visualized."[39]

De Wit's last words: ". . . today many, many persons go hungry in a world where the technical ways and means to prevent this are available."[40]

Comments

Unlike the calculations of Ravenstein and Penck, De Wit's calculation was conditional. *If* photosynthesis *and nothing else* limited human numbers, the sunlight reaching the Earth could drive enough photosynthesis, according to De Wit's computer model, to satisfy the caloric requirements of 1,022 billion people, more than one trillion people. *If* people wanted a million kilocalories a year plus 1,500 square meters per person to live, work and play (roughly three people per American football field, over every desert and ice field, forest and meadow, mountain and valley), and *if there were no other limits,* then 79 billion people could be accommodated. If people want meat, fewer can be fed. *If* people wanted only 750 square meters per person for living and recreation, *then* 146 billion could be supported. De Wit concluded that population size is likely to be constrained by other factors, including non–agricultural uses of land, long before it is constrained by photosynthesis.

De Wit did not attempt to consider the physical problems of supplying soils everywhere with the water and minerals his calculations assumed; or the biological problems of preventing all forms of damage and spoilage before final consumption; or the economic problems of providing infrastructure, of preparing soils for maximal productivity, of delivering credits, seeds, fuels and equipment to the farmer, of getting crops from the farm to the consumer; or the cultural problems of assuring that the diets grown at a maximal level of photosynthesis are acceptable, region by region, to those who have to eat them, that the required farming practices are compatible with the values of the people who have to implement them, that the farmers have the education required to carry out those practices and the motivation to do so. This list of what De Wit omitted does not pretend to be exhaustive.

An example illustrates the details that did not trouble De Wit. Most cereal grains require a growing season of at least three to four months. Tropical rice grows to maturity in not less than 90 days. Temperate spring wheat grows for four months; winter wheat grows for nine months from planting to harvest. When the growing season (determined by temperature and light) is shorter than three months, the land cannot be used to grow such crops. While plants could photosynthesize at extreme northern and southern latitudes as De Wit calculated, cereal crops could not reach maturity in the time available to them there. De Wit's estimates for high latitudes presupposed fast-maturing crops, or transplantation to other latitudes in mid-season or enclosure in greenhouses; in the latter case, his concern about outdoor temperatures was irrelevant. Higgins et al., whose work is described later in this chapter, treated the length of the growing period more realistically.[41]

Roger Revelle, an oceanographer who directed the Center for Population Studies at Harvard University, defined "arable land" as "land areas covered with soil in which crops can be grown."[42] According to Revelle, "The panel on the world food supply of the [United States] President's Science Advisory Committee concluded after an intensive study in 1967 that only about 3.2 billion hectares of the total 13 billion hectares of the earth's ice-free land surface can be cultivated."[43]

De Wit's highly abstract exercise offered no realistic estimate of how many people the Earth can actually support. If De Wit's estimates of the Earth's photosynthetic capacity are correct, his calculations are useful precisely because they direct attention *away* from photosynthesis as a potential limiting factor and toward other potential limits on human numbers.

It is impossible to judge the details of De Wit's computer model of photosynthetic capacity from his published paper because the model was described in a technical report published separately. Hence it is useful to have some independent check on the plausibility of De Wit's estimate that annual gross production of carbohydrate could be about a trillion (10^{12}) tonnes. Plant production is sometimes measured by the weight of carbon fixed, rather than by the weight of carbohydrate, and by *net* primary production (NPP) rather than by gross primary production (GPP). NPP is GPP minus what the plant burns up or respires to drive its own metabolism. Carbohydrate is 40 percent carbon by weight, and NPP is half of GPP,[44] averaged over the Earth. So De Wit's GPP measured in weight of carbohydrate may be converted to NPP measured in weight of carbon by dividing by 5. De Wit estimated that, unconstrained by water and minerals, terrestrial NPP could fix 200 billion (2×10^{11}) tonnes of carbon.

For comparison, the oceans have an NPP of 20–44 billion tonnes of carbon annually and the continents an NPP of 48 billion tonnes of carbon annually.[45] Taking the high estimate for oceanic NPP gives a total of 92 billion or roughly 10^{11} tonnes of carbon annually. De Wit's prediction that net production on land could total 2×10^{11} tonnes of carbon represents at least a doubling of present global net production and more than a four-fold increase over the present net production of the continents. In hydroponic experiments with controlled temperature, it is possible to quadruple biomass yields of wheat, compared to record yields of wheat grown in the field, by supplying additional carbon dioxide, water, nutrients and four times the photosynthetic radiation of summer sunlight.[46] You may decide for yourself whether such productivity could be reached globally under natural conditions.

In the field, the record wheat yield is 14.5 tonnes per hectare, measured in Washington State in a one-hectare field of the winter wheat cultivar Gaines.[47] Winter wheat is in the field for nine months, so only a single crop per year is possible. Assuming that dry edible grain is half the total dry mass of plant tissue, as De Wit does, and assuming that net production is half of gross production of carbohydrate, the record yield results from gross production of about 60 tonnes per hectare. To attain gross production of 10^{12} tonnes annually would require about 16.7 billion hectares.[48] De Wit's estimate of the Earth's total land is 13.1 billion hectares. In practical terms, De Wit's estimate of total potential food production is equivalent to assuming that 127 percent of the Earth's total land surface produces the all-time record yield of wheat, or that some other crops yield an equal total number of calories.

"Optimum World Population" (1970)

In 1970, world population approached 3.7 billion people. In that year, H. R. Hulett, then in the Department of Genetics of the Stanford University Medical School, estimated that the *optimal* population of the world must be less than one billion people. No surprising advances in data or theory occurred between 1967 and 1970. The difference of more than 1,000-fold between the numbers obtained by De Wit and Hulett results from radically different approaches and assumptions.

According to Hulett, "the average U.S. citizen would certainly assume that the amount and variety of food and other raw materials available to him are not greater than optimum. The ratio of current world production of these materials to current average American consumption [per person] then can be used as a rough indication of the upper limit of optimum world population at present production rates."[49]

Hulett estimated the ratio for food, forest products and selected nonrenewable resources. First, food. In 1966, Americans purchased about 3,200 kilocalories per day of food and consumed about 2,600 kilocalories per day.[50] About 1,100 of the 3,200 kilocalories per day came from animal products such as meat, milk and eggs. The remaining 2,100 kilocalories per day came from plants. Hulett estimated that the animal products required animal feeds of 6.3 million kilocalories per person per year, which is 15.7 times the energy in the purchased animal products. This amount of animal feeds, and the nearly 770,000 kilocalories of plant energy per person consumed directly, brought the total annual American food energy consumption per person to just over seven million kilocalories, "about six times what it would have been on a strictly vegetarian diet."[51]

Based on estimates of Walter R. Schmitt[52] at the University of California, San Diego, Hulett estimated the total energy value of all the world's plant crops at 4.2×10^{15} kilocalories per year.

> If this is doubled to include grazing by domestic animals, the total production would be less than 10^{16} kcal per year, enough to provide for only about 1.2 billion people at American food standards.[53] . . . These figures show the impossibility of lifting the rest of the world to our [American] dietary standards without a several fold increase in world food production or a massive reduction in population.[54]

Hulett dismissed food from the ocean as the present source of only 1 percent of food calories and 4 percent of total protein.

Hulett then considered wood. World wood production in 1965 for all uses, such as lumber and paper, was estimated at 2.0 billion cubic meters; of this total, 0.33 billion cubic meters were consumed in the United States. "If the present cut could be maintained, it would supply a world population of a little over one billion people at the U.S. level of consumption." How is that? The U.S. population was approximately 200 million people when Hulett wrote. The wood consumption per person in the United States was 0.33 billion cubic meters divided by 200 million, and the global wood production divided by the U.S. consumption per person was $[2 \times 10^9/(0.33 \times 10^9)] \times 2 \times 10^8 = 1.2 \times 10^9$ or 1.2 billion.

According to Hulett,

> The picture is even bleaker in terms of present production and use of many nonrenewable resources. . . . World production of energy in 1967 was equivalent to about 5.8 billion tons of coal, that of the United States was equivalent to almost two billion tons. Thus, fewer than 600 million people could have used energy at the rate we did. [Check the arithmetic!] . . . If all the material currently photosynthesized on land were burned, it would provide energy at the U.S. rates of consumption for about one to four billion people (and, of course, there would be nothing left for food).[55]

By similar calculations, Hulett estimated that steel sets a limit of 700 million people, fertilizer a limit of 900 million and aluminum a limit of 500 million, and similarly for other mineral resources. "The world's present industrial complex is sufficient to provide fewer than a billion people with the U.S. standard of affluence. Production of all these substances can be increased, but the increases will be slow because of the heavy capital investment required." Increases would also deplete mineral reserves faster and increase pollution, Hulett wrote. He concluded:

> In all the areas treated, it appears that of the order of a billion people is the maximum population supportable by the present agricultural and industrial system (and the present work force) of the world at U.S. levels of affluence.
> It would obviously be very difficult to produce food and raw materials at the present rate with the smaller work force consistent with a world population of about a billion people; therefore, this number is, if anything, too large to be self-supporting at U.S. affluence levels. As our technology, knowledge, and industrial and agricultural systems expand so can the optimum population. . . .[56]

Comments

Hulett's ratio of 15.7 between the caloric value of animal feeds and the caloric value of the consumed animal products is higher than the ratio of 10 that De Wit used,[57] and much higher than Revelle's estimate of 4.5,[58] but almost the same as the ratio of 16 estimated by Gever et al.[59] If Revelle's estimate were more nearly correct, and if there were no problems with other aspects of Hulett's method, the estimate of "optimal population" determined by food supplies would be nearly double Hulett's estimate.

Hulett asserted, "This optimum population can increase no more rapidly than the production of these essential raw materials can increase."[60] This ignores shifts in technology. For example, consumption of steel per person in the United States has fallen recently. The "optimum population" calculated by Hulett's method could increase even if global steel production remained constant or fell while American consumption per person fell more rapidly. If Hulett applied his method to comparable statistics for 10,000 B.C. (had such statistics existed), he would have had to conclude that "the maximum population supportable by the present agricultural and industrial system (and the present work force) of the world at [Mesopotamian, or the then equivalent of U.S.] levels of affluence" is on the order of a few million people.

Hulett computed the ratio of world production to U.S. consumption per person for one material at a time. This procedure assumed that a limitation imposed by one material is independent of a limitation imposed by any other: that ceramics could not be substituted for steel, fiberglass for wood, more intensive cultivation for more land.

A much more serious problem is Hulett's failure to make explicit a major assumption underlying his approach. Hulett assumed that a world populated with a smaller number of people who enjoy U.S. levels of resources would produce and consume exactly the same amount of everything as the world now produces and consumes. Unfortunately, Hulett never stated the assumption, and therefore never examined it. How plausible is it?

For concreteness, take the example of food. To keep the numbers simple, assume a U.S. population of 200 million and a world population of 3.5 billion for the period in the late 1960s. The key equation is $P = 8.4 \times 10^{15}/(7 \times 10^6) = 1.2 \times 10^9$ or 1.2 billion people. The numerator 8.4×10^{15} is Hulett's estimate of total annual kilocalories of food supply. The denominator 7×10^6 is Hulett's estimate of American annual kilocalorie consumption per person. The equation is Penck's. Hulett interpreted this to mean that, in addition to the 0.2 billion people in the United States, at most an additional 1 billion people could be fed at U.S. levels of consumption. He assumed that the resulting 1.2 billion people, all fed at the U.S. level (and, in his later arguments, supplied with other resources at the U.S. level of consumption), would consume and produce exactly the same supply of food calories (and other products) as the actual population of 3.5 billion.

If 200 million Americans consumed seven million kilocalories each per year on average, their aggregate annual consumption would be 1.4×10^{15}. This would leave 7.0×10^{15} kilocalories $= 8.4 \times 10^{15} - 1.4 \times 10^{15}$ for the 3.3 billion non-Americans. The average consumption of non-Americans would be 424,000 kilocalories per year or less than 1,200 kilocalories per day. That is less than the minimum required to sustain even the basal metabolism, let alone the normal activity, of any human population, even one with many children and with adults substantially smaller than American adults. A male weighing 58 kilograms or 128 pounds who spent 24 hours resting in bed would consume 1,560 kilocalories.[61] Daily intakes on the order of 1,200 kilocalories per day are not pure fantasy. In a 1955 survey[62] of 2,800 individuals in the town of Vellore, Madras State, in southern India, the average daily intake of energy ranged from 1,260 kilocalories to 1,725 kilocalories. Protein intake ranged from 32 grams to 45 grams. In every income group in Vellore, the diets provided from 65 percent to 90 percent of the physiological requirements for calories and protein. Unskilled laborers, the poorest class, with an energy intake of only 1,260 kilocalories per day, were incapable of prolonged heavy labor. I spent February 1966 in Vellore; the level of energy of the average person seen on the street was obviously low, even to casual observation. Miller estimated that for adult men, energy intakes below 1,500 kilocalories per day have adverse health effects and that "it is a useful rule of thumb to say that the average energy requirement per head of any population is about 2000 kcal per day or 8.4 [megajoules] per day for every man, woman and child."[63]

As I mentioned in Chapter 4, in the period 1969–71, an estimated 941 million people in developing regions (36 percent of their population) were chronically undernourished.[64] One reason there was not worldwide famine then is that the United States and some other countries exported food, net of food imports. For example, in 1965, on the average, one U.S. farm worker supplied 31 people at home and six people abroad; in 1970, one U.S. farm worker supplied 40 people at home and seven people abroad.[65] Roughly, one-sixth of farm production appears to have been exported. Is it implausible to suppose that an additional billion non-American people, supplied with resources at the U.S. level, could also produce more food than they consume, and therefore feed even more people?

Of course this argument could be correct only up to the point where the finiteness of the Earth imposes diminishing returns; otherwise the supportable population would be infinite. But Hulett offered no evidence about where diminishing returns set in. He failed to argue that a global population which enjoys a U.S. level of consumption of all resources would be constrained by diminishing returns to under a billion people.

Hulett argued in the opposite direction: "It would obviously be very difficult to produce food and raw materials at the present rate with the smaller work force consistent with a world population of about a billion people; therefore, this number is, if anything, too large to be self-supporting at U.S. affluence levels." This argument suggests that a billion people with American levels of consumption cannot produce what they consume. If a billion cannot, why should three-quarters or half a billion be able to do so? The logical extension of this argument is that a human population consuming resources at the U.S. level should collapse altogether. There is no sign of such a collapse. The argument must fail to be correct at some point. Hulett gave no evidence to suggest at what point the argument would fail.

From Hulett's evidence, there is no telling what the poor masses of Asia, Africa and Latin America could produce given an equal distribution of resources at the American level. Hulett's calculations are the simplest example of an approach used in 1945 by Frank A. Pearson and Floyd A. Harper; in 1981 by Arthur H. Westing, an ecologist at Hampshire College, Massachusetts; and in the late 1980s by *The Hunger Reports* of Brown University, which are described later in this chapter. Pearson and Harper assumed that population size is constrained solely by grain production.[66] They divided the 1945 total grain production by the 1945 Asiatic, European and North American average grain consumption per person to estimate that 1945 grain supplies could support 2.8 billion people at Asiatic standards, 2.1 billion at European standards and 0.9 billion at North American standards. Westing extended Hulett's assumptions and approach from the United States to two groups of countries—the 27 richest nations and 43 nations of average wealth according to 1975 data on gross national products—and to five resources: total land, cultivated land, forest land, cereal grain consumption and wood consumption. He estimated that 2.0 billion people could live at an "affluent" level and 3.9 billion could live at an "austere" level.[67]

Hulett, Pearson and Harper, Westing and the Hunger Reports all assumed that the global supply of a limiting resource remains fixed when the number of producers changes and the distribution of consumption among them becomes equal. This assumption seems doubtful.

"The Resources Available for Agriculture" (1976)

In 1967, under U.S. president Lyndon Johnson, the President's Science Advisory Committee (PSAC) published extensive studies on "The World Food Problem."[68] Based on the PSAC studies, one leading participant, Roger Revelle, published two widely read estimates of how many people the Earth could feed: 38–48 billion people[69] and 40 billion people.[70] Here I describe the major steps by which he arrived at his second estimate. He used Penck's formula, assuming that food limits population size.

The PSAC panel classified the Earth's soils into 13 geographic types and estimated the arable area of each. "The 3.2 billion arable hectares cover 24 percent of the land area of the earth, about 2.3 times the currently cultivated area and more than three times the area actually harvested in any given year. Of this total .3 billion hectares require irrigation for even one crop."[71] However, water was available to irrigate less than a third (82 million hectares) of the land that was potentially arable with irrigation, so the total potentially arable land, with irrigation, was reduced to around three billion hectares.

> . . . the potential increase of the gross cropped area (that is, the sum of potentially arable areas multiplied by the number of four-month-growing-season crops that could be raised in each area) through irrigation development is limited to 1.1 billion hectares. Without irrigation three crops could be grown on .5 billion hectares in the humid Tropics and two crops on .8 billion hectares in subhumid regions. One crop could be grown without irrigation on 1.5 billion hectares. Hence the potential gross cropped area without irrigation is 4.6 billion hectares and with irrigation is 5.7 billion. Of this total, however, 1.5 billion hectares lies in the humid Tropics—where, except for the island of Java and a few other areas

. . . , no technology is currently available for high-yielding agriculture on a large scale. The potential gross cropped area accessible to relatively high-yielding cultivation with present technology is therefore somewhat more than 4.2 billion hectares.[72]

This estimate appears as the total of column 7 in Table 10.5.

Detailed calculations were carried out for each of seven large regions (Table 10.5). The gross cropped area in column 5 of Table 10.5 is not the sum of the arable areas in columns 2 and 3 because some lands were taken to yield multiple crops per year. The sum of columns 5 and 6 is column 7. Except for some 200 million hectares of arable land for which no water is available, the ratio of potentially arable land to total land in the world is about one hectare in five.[73]

How much food could be grown on this land? Revelle estimated that 10 percent of the gross cropped area would be used for nonfood crops such as fibers and beverages. The remaining 3.8 billion gross cropped hectares outside the humid tropics could produce human food. Assuming that the lower quality of the soils and the uneven topography would limit the average yields to three tons per hectare instead of the U.S. Midwest yield of six tons per hectare,[74] this potential gross cropped area could yield 11.4 billion tons of food grains or equivalent food energy, "enough for a minimum diet of 2,500 kilocalories per day for nearly 40 billion people (if pest losses and nonfood uses could be kept to 10 percent of the harvest)."[75]

Revelle described the resources required to achieve this level of production: nitrogen fertilizer (nitrogen production from fossil fuels cost "less than 10 percent of the value of the resulting crop yield"[76]), phosphorus ("Some abundant resources can be substituted for scarce ones, but there is no substitute for phosphorus in plant and animal metabolism"[77]), mechanical energy (which, he wrote, could be produced by fermenting less than half of the humanly inedible crop residues), biological resources (the gene pool of crop plants and domestic animals, microorganisms for fermentation, earthworms) and capital investments to modernize agriculture.

In 1976 dollars, the capital investments Revelle envisioned to increase crop yields in favorable regions would cost more than $700 billion, Revelle estimated. Dams, barrages, canals and watercourses would store and distribute river waters for irrigation. Wells with motorized pumps would tap aquifers. (An aquifer is a permeable region of earth or rock that stores and transmits groundwater.) Farmlands would be drained by grading land and building drainage channels or underground drains. Better roads would enable villages to acquire fertilizer and other farm inputs from markets and to deliver harvests to markets. Better structures to store crops would protect harvests against vermin and moisture. Better marketplaces would improve the efficiency of trading in farm commodities. Specialized farms would multiply the seeds of high-yielding crop varieties. People could build most of these facilities in poor countries with little modern machinery, finding productive employment in the task. But costly machinery and

TABLE 10.5 Revelle's (1976) estimates of total potential gross cropped area

column 1	2	3	4	5	6	7
	net arable area in humid tropics (*millions of hectares*)	arable without irrigation outside humid tropics (*millions of hectares*)	irrigation required for even one crop (*millions of hectares*)	gross[a] cropped area without irrigation (*millions of hectares*)	gross[a] cropped area added by irrigation (*millions of hectares*)	total potential gross cropped area (*millions of hectares*)
Africa	105	490	10	705	290	995
Asia	80	450	15	625	475	1,100
Australia, New Zealand	0	115	2	123	2	125
Europe	0	170	0	205	40	245
North America	10	440	8	535	160	695
South America	300	350	24	635	80	715
USSR	0	325	23	325	30	355
total	495	2,340	82	3,155[b]	1,077	4,230

[a]Potential gross cropped area is defined as the potentially arable land area multiplied by the number of crops that could be grown in a four-month growing season, where climatic conditions allow.

[b]Slight discrepancy presumably due to rounding.

SOURCE: Revelle (1976, p. 168)

TABLE 10.6 Revelle's (1976) estimates of cultivated area, population and cropped area per person in 1970 and 2000 (projected), compared with estimates for 1990

column 1	2[a]	3	4	5	6	7	8	9	10	11
date →	1970				2000		1987–89	1990	1987–90	1990–92
region ↓	cultivated area (millions of hectares)	population (millions)	cultivated area per person (hectares)	potential gross cropped area (millions of hectares)	projected population (millions)	potential gross cropped area per person (hectares)	cropland (millions of hectares)	population (millions)	cropland per person (hectares)	cereal yields (tonnes per hectare)
Africa	165	345	0.48	995	750	1.33	186	642	0.29	1.2
Asia	475	2,055	0.23	1,100	4,090	0.27	454	3,113	0.15	2.9
Australia, New Zealand	20	20	1.00	125	35	3.57	49	26	1.88	1.7
Europe	150	460	0.33	245	580	0.42	140	498	0.28	4.3
North America	240	320	0.75	695	530	1.31	274	427	0.64	4.0
South America	80	190	0.43	715	440	1.63	142	297	0.48	2.2
USSR	230	245	0.94	355	340	1.04	232	289	0.80	1.8
total	1,360	3,635	0.37 (average)	4,230	6,765	0.62 (average)	1,477	5,292	0.28 (average)	2.8 (average)

[a]Columns 2, 5 and 8 compare total observed or projected cultivated areas; columns 3, 6 and 9 compare observed or projected populations; columns 4, 7 and 10 compare observed or projected cultivated area per person. Revelle projected an average cereal yield of 3 tons per hectare. Cropland per person in 1987–90 (0.28 hectare per person) was less than half that projected for 2000 (0.62 hectare per person).

SOURCES: Revelle (1976, p. 170) for 1970 and 2000; World Resources Institute (1992, pp. 262–63, 246–47) for 1987–89 cropland and 1990 population; my calculations for 1987–90 cropland per person (column 8 divided by column 9); World Resources Institute (1994, pp. 292–93) for 1990–92 cereal yields. In columns 8–11, North American statistics include Central America; Australia and New Zealand statistics include Oceania.

materials would be required to manufacture farm machinery, chemical fertilizers and pesticides.[78]

Revelle estimated world agricultural land and population in 1970, and projected the potential gross cropped land and population in 2000 (Table 10.6).

Of the 1,360 million hectares under actual cultivation in 1970, only a tiny fraction yielded more than one crop a year. The potential gross cropped area of 4,230 million hectares projected for A.D. 2000 represents a figure that could be achieved by growing more than one crop a year on roughly a third of some 2,900 million net arable hectares. Asia will be hard pressed to obtain the projected ratio of gross cropped area per person. Africa and South America currently offer the largest opportunities for expansion of agricultural production.[79]

Comments

To what extent have the possible improvements and extensions of agriculture that Revelle projected in 1970 been realized? The answer is that the glass is half full, or half empty, depending on how you look at it.

Cereal production expanded more than 50 percent from 1.2 billion tonnes in 1970 to an average 1.9 billion tonnes in 1990 to 1992.[80] Production of fruit, vegetables, meat, milk and fish also increased, while production of root crops remained steady. According to the World Resources Institute in 1992, "Every region of the developing world has substantially increased its food production since 1970. . . . Most of these production increases came from increases in yield rather than increases in cropland."[81] Total cropland hardly changed from 1,448 million hectares in 1980[82] to 1,442 million hectares in 1991.[83]

Unfortunately, the rise in food production did not keep up with population growth in Africa, and barely kept up in Latin America and the Near East. Only the Asian centrally planned economies (largely China) managed to increase food production faster than their populations grew.[84]

Revelle posited both an increase in cereal yields (tonnes of cereal per cultivated hectare) and a great extension of cultivated lands, amplified by irrigation and multiple cropping where possible. From 1990 to 1992, cereal yields (nearly 2.8 tonnes per hectare[85]) almost reached the level Revelle postulated as possible (3 tonnes per hectare). But the areas under cultivation (1.4 billion hectares in 1991,[86] down from 1.5 billion hectares in 1987–89) were nowhere near the gross cropped areas (4.2 billion hectares) Revelle suggested were possible by 2000 (Figure 10.1), even if some of the projected gross cropped areas for 2000 are substantially deflated to remove the assumed multiple cropping.

Cropped areas may have failed to increase as Revelle suggested they could because the investments he anticipated in irrigation never materialized. Between the mid-1960s and the early 1990s, the rate of growth of irrigated land dropped about 60 percent globally and by 72 percent in Asia.

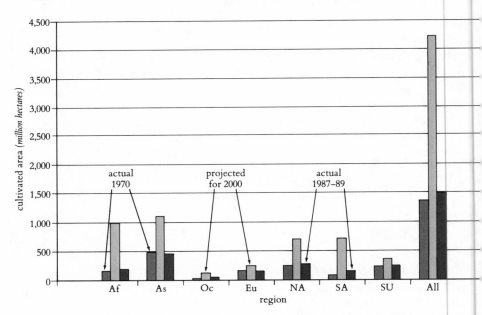

FIGURE 10.1   Cultivated area in 1970, potential gross cropped area in 2000 and cropland in 1987–89, by regions of the world: Africa (Af), Asia (As), Australia and New
Zealand or Oceania (Oc), Europe (Eu), North America (and Central America)
(NA), South America (SA), the former USSR (SU) and total (All). SOURCE: Table
10.6

The four main financial donors—the World Bank, the Asian Development
Bank, the U.S. Agency for International Development, and the Japanese
Overseas Economic Cooperation Fund—cut support for irrigation by half
between 1977–79 and 1986–87. Though India increased its domestic spend-
ing for irrigation, most countries—including Indonesia, the Philippines and
Thailand—spent less for irrigation.[87]

Unlike the slow growth or declines in the cultivated area, since 1970 population sizes have grown far toward the levels Revelle projected for 2000
(Figure 10.2). The cultivated area per person has fallen in Africa, Asia,
Europe, North America, the former Soviet Union and for the world overall. The dramatic rise in Oceania, mainly Australia, and the small rise in
South America are overshadowed by the falls everywhere else (Figure
10.3).

Paul Ehrlich, Anne Ehrlich and Gretchen Daily, ecologists at Stanford
University, reported that Revelle's estimate of a supportable population of
40 billion was adopted by some authorities in the Catholic Church.[88] But
Ehrlich, Ehrlich and Daily found Revelle's estimate problematic.

Revelle assumed, among other things, that the amount of cultivated land could
be increased more than twofold (when actually most of the world's suitable land

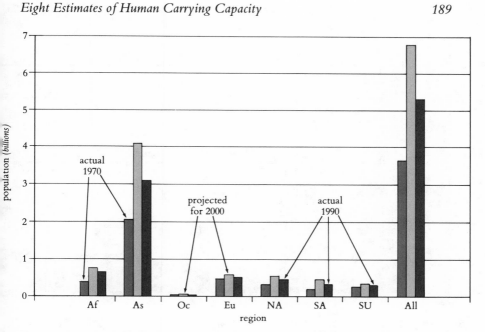

FIGURE 10.2   Population in 1970, projected population in 2000 and estimated population in 1990, by regions of the world: Africa (Af), Asia (As), Australia and New Zealand or Oceania (Oc), Europe (Eu), North America (and Central America) (NA), South America (SA), the former USSR (SU) and total (All). SOURCE: Table 10.6

is already under cultivation and much prime farmland is now being degraded or lost); that losses to pests would be minimized to 10 percent (perhaps a third of their present level); that postharvest wastage of food would be negligible (when it may be as high as 40 percent); that the present impact of agriculture on environmental systems could be greatly increased without penalty (although today's impact is not sustainable) and that food would be perfectly equitably distributed among people with no grain diverted to livestock. In addition, Revelle's calculations did not include the possibility that global change could reduce productivity.[89]

In retrospect, Revelle's assessment in 1976 that cultivated areas could be increased to feed 40 billion people on a vegetarian diet was not followed by the global investments and social arrangements that would translate that possibility, if indeed it was a possibility, into reality.

One interpretation is that the areas under cultivation did not expand as predicted because the market invested elsewhere; if you assume that whatever happens in the marketplace is economically rational, then there could have been no economic reason for cultivated areas to expand because they evidently did not expand. Another interpretation is that the areas under cultivation did not expand as Revelle projected they could because the peo-

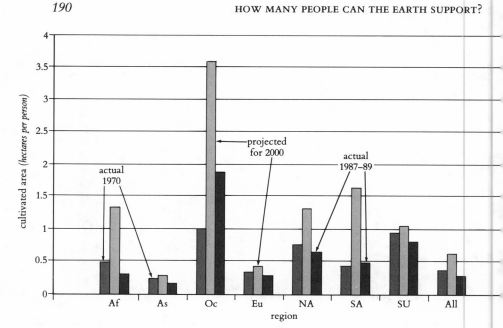

FIGURE 10.3   Cultivated area per person in 1970, potential gross cropped area per person in 2000 and cropland per person in 1987–89, by regions of the world: Africa (Af), Asia (As), Australia and New Zealand or Oceania (Oc), Europe (Eu), North America (and Central America) (NA), South America (SA), the former USSR (SU) and total (All). SOURCE: Table 10.6

ple most in want of more food lacked the capital, or the control of capital, to invest in expanding cultivated areas.

"POPULATION GROWTH AND LAND USE" (1977)

The Australian statistician and economist Colin Clark published two estimates of how many people the Earth could feed. His first estimate of 28 billion, published in a short paper in the scientific journal *Nature* in 1958, is much less widely known than his second estimate of 157 billion, published in an influential book in 1967. It is worth looking at both to see how a single author's estimates grew by a factor of 5.6 in less than a decade.

Clark derived his earlier estimate in one paragraph.

The world's total land area (excluding ice and tundra) is 123 million sq. km., from which we exclude most of the 42½ million sq. km. of steppe or arid lands, discount anything up to half the area of certain cold or sub-humid lands, but could double 10 million sq. km. of tropical land capable of bearing two crops per year. We conclude that the world possesses the equivalent of 77 million sq. km. of good temperate agricultural land. . . . [T]he most productive farmers in Europe, the Dutch, . . . feed 385 people (at Dutch standards of diet, which give

TABLE 10.7   Clark's (1977) "Potential agricultural area of the world expressed in terms of equivalents of standard farm land (million hectares)"

column 1	2	3	4
		of which	
	total	standard-farmland equivalents of two–crop tropical areas are	standard-farmland equivalents of cold–climate areas are
U.S. and Canada	1,006	4	367
Central and South America	1,835	736	29
Europe (excluding USSR)	403	0	47
USSR	1,109	0	539
Africa	1,555	732	0
China	409	0	88
India and Pakistan	305	43	13
rest of Asia	791	464	7
Oceania	268	60	0
world	7,680	2,039	1,090

SOURCE: Clark (1977, p. 149)

them one of the best health records in the world) per sq. km. of farm land, or 365 if we allow for the land required to produce their timber. . . . [This density is equivalent to 3.65 people per hectare of *farm*land, or 2,740 square meters of *farm*-land per person.] Applying these standards throughout the world, as they could be with adequate skill and use of fertilizers, we find the world capable of support-ing 28 billion [≈ 77 million × 365] people, or ten times its present population. This leaves us a very ample margin for land which we wish to set aside for recre-ation or other purposes.[90]

Should the sea and land prove incapable "in the very distant future" of feed-ing a growing population, Clark added, people could then build and occupy artificial satellites.

In 1967, Clark explained the estimate of 77 million square kilometers or 7.7 billion hectares in more detail (Table 10.7). His classification was "based entirely on climate," making no deductions for poor soils, mountains or steeply sloping land or swamps. He defined "standard land" as "the sort of farm land to which we are accustomed in the humid temperate countries [for example, England], capable of producing one crop a year, or substan-tial quantities of grazing throughout the summer." Where inadequate rain-fall limits production, lands are expressed as fractions of "standard land." "The limiting factor is taken as moisture rather than temperature, which is in fact the case over most of the world." However, each unit of tropical

TABLE 10.8   Clark's (1977) "Land required per person
to produce U.S. type diet"

column 1	2	3	4
dietary items	square meters per person	kilocalories per kilogram	annual kilocalories
cereals, sugar, etc. (180–195 kilograms[a])	500	3,300	600,000
pig and poultry meat (42 kilograms)	500	4,000	168,000
beef and mutton (42 kilograms)	400	2,800	117,600
milk (250 kilograms)	400	650	162,500
eggs (18 kilograms)	200	1,450	26,100
total	2,000	NA[b]	1,074,200

[a] My calculated kilogram range for this entry (see text).
[b] NA = not applicable.
SOURCES: Clark (1977, p. 153) for columns 1 and 2; Watt and Merrill (1963) for column 3 (kilocalories per kilogram = 2.2 × kilocalories per pound); my calculations for column 4 (kilograms in column 1 × kilocalories per kilogram in column 3)

land with high temperature and high rainfall counts as two units of standard land, assuming that two crops could be grown each year. Based on experience in Australia, where semi-arid land is used for grazing only, semi-arid land counts as one-thirtieth of standard land.

Taking the tropical lands as equivalent to only 2 units of standard land, the world possesses the equivalent of 7.7 billion hectares of standard land. If we apply the maximum co-efficient of five to the tropical lands, this figure becomes 10.7 billion hectares.[91]

Clark estimated the land per person required for two styles of life, which he called American and Japanese. Clark considered only the land required to raise food and wood and ignored any other uses of land. To produce what he called a "U.S. type diet," he estimated that 2,000 square meters of land were required per person (Table 10.8). In detail:

Each kilogram of pigmeat corresponds to 1.3 kilograms of live pig, requiring, in the hands of a good pig man, 5.3 kilograms of cereals to produce it; a kilogram of poultry meat (1.5 kilograms of live bird) only 3.7 kilograms feed, equivalent however to about 4 kilograms of cereals, if we take into account the agricultural value of protein and other supplements included in poultry feed. The pork and poultry half of such a meat ration could be produced from the cereals grown on 540 sq. m.

If the 42-kilogram ration of pork and poultry consisted of 21 kilograms of pork and 21 kilograms of poultry, then Clark here assumed that

$21 \times (5.3 + 4) = 195.3$ kilograms of cereals are required. To grow this amount of grain on 540 square meters, the yield per hectare must be 3.6 tonnes. To grow this amount of grain on 500 square meters, which is the area shown in Table 10.8, the yield per hectare must be 3.9 tonnes.

The remainder of the meat ration, that is, 42 kilograms of beef and mutton, would be produced, Clark assumed, by fertilizing grasslands to grow 15 tonnes of dry weight of grass per hectare per year, sufficient to raise 2 tonnes of live weight of beef per hectare, or 1 tonne of consumed beef or mutton. Then producing 42 kilograms of meat to be consumed would require 420 square meters of land, hence Clark's figure in Table 10.8 of 400 square meters. This assumed level of productivity is five times better than that achieved currently by "good English farmers," according to Clark.

As for milk production and consumption, Clark estimated that the average North American or British cow produced 3 tonnes of milk per year and required 7.5 tonnes dry weight of grass, hay and silage (after allowing for the cost of breeding replacement stock and the value of meat from old cattle). Again assuming that 15 tonnes dry weight of grass could be raised per hectare, he calculated that the 3 tonnes of milk required half a hectare of land. These 3 tonnes of milk could feed 12 Americans 250 kilograms of milk each per year (Americans then consumed 285 kilograms per person per year of raw milk equivalent of all dairy products). Hence, for dairy products at a level close to that of the American diet, each person would require one-twelfth of one-half a hectare, or a little over 400 square meters.

Finally, to produce 18 kilograms of eggs per person per year, the U.S. level of consumption then, would require 72 kilograms of cereal, which would in turn require 200 square meters of land (at an implied yield of 3.6 tonnes per hectare).[92]

Clark did not specify how much grain and sugar he assumed an American eats per year, but given cereal yields of 3.6–3.9 tonnes per hectare, the land requirement of 500 square meters for cereals and sugar (Table 10.8) implies a consumption of 180 to 195 kilograms per person per year, a bit more than a pound a day.

In total, Clark calculated that 2,000 square meters are required to feed one person American style. One hectare could feed five people an American diet, according to Clark's assumptions, and one square kilometer could feed 500. However, additional land is required for wood.

To estimate the land required to produce wood, Clark listed estimates of the average sustained yield in various forests. He converted each ton of dry weight of roundwood to two cubic meters. The estimates he quoted ranged from 1.1 cubic meters per hectare per year for the USSR (although it is not clear whether Clark included forest land only or all land) to 58 cubic meters per hectare per year in planted coniferous forests in Queensland. The only figure he quoted that referred specifically to a hardwood was 47 cubic meters per hectare per year for beech forest in Denmark. He settled on the production of Burma bamboo at 20 cubic meters per hectare per year as a global average figure.[93]

"Consumption of wood (other than fuel wood, which will probably soon become obsolete) ranges from 2 cu. m. [per] person / year round wood in the United States and Canada to about 0.5 cu. m. in certain Western European countries which have to import nearly all their wood, and where prices are correspondingly high."[94] Clark considered U.S. wood consumption "wasteful" and assumed that Americans require only 0.5 cubic meter of wood per person per year, like Europeans. With an assumed yield of 20 cubic meters per hectare per year, one-fortieth of a hectare, or 250 square meters, would provide 0.5 cubic meter of wood per person per year.

Clark summarized: "Each person's land requirements for American type food consumption are some 2000 sq. m., or one-fifth of a hectare (half an acre), or 2250 sq. m. including requirement of forest land. If we take world resources of agricultural land at 10.7 billion hectares of standard land equivalent, this could feed, at maximum standards, 47 billion people."[95] Allowing for food and wood, each square kilometer could support 444 people.

Clark also estimated how many people could be supported on a subsistence diet with minimal wood consumption. He determined calorie requirements from data on adults in central Africa, India, southeast Asia and China who ranged in weight from 45 kilograms to 57.5 kilograms.[96] (A typical adult male in rich countries weighs 70 kilograms.) Clark estimated that if men work four hours a day, the population average calorie requirement may be as low as 1,625 kilocalories per day (based on Indian body weights), but if men work eight hours a day, requirements could be as high as 2,012 kilocalories per day (based on central Africa). He then translated these caloric requirements into grain. "Cereals yield about 3.2 calories / gram; the minimum and maximum requirements of 1625 and 2012 [kilo]calories / day . . . can therefore be met by the consumption of 185–230 kilograms / person / year of cereals." Clark measured agricultural production in "grain equivalents" by replacing other agricultural products with "their exchange value against grain in the local markets. Allowing for a small quantity of animal products, of green vegetables, and of textile fibres, the minimum agricultural requirements of a population can be put at somewhat below 250 kilograms / person / year of grain equivalent. . . ."[97]

Implicitly assuming a yield of 3.9 tonnes of grain per hectare "under the most productive conditions, as in Japan," Clark calculated that the production of subsistence requirements equivalent to 250 kilograms of cereals requires 640 square meters of land. The minimum land required to produce half a cubic meter per person per year of roundwood (the minimum Western European standard) was 250 square meters. "If however we are considering real minimum standards, wood consumption per head in Asian countries, mainly bamboo, is only about one-third of this. For people living at Japanese standards of food consumption and Asian standards of timber requirements only 680 sq. m. / person is required, and the world's potential agricultural and forest land could supply the needs of 157 billion people."[98]

Clark's estimate of the supportable population grew dramatically between 1958 and 1967 because he changed his assumptions. In 1958, he assumed that an average of 365 people could be fed per square kilometer, based on Dutch *farm*land; in 1967, 500 people, "for American type food consumption."[99] In 1958, he assumed 77 million square kilometers or 7.7 billion hectares of "standard land" equivalent to humid temperate croplands; in 1967, 107 million square kilometers or 10.7 billion hectares, based on five-fold cropping of grass or fodder from tropical lands. In 1958, he concluded that 28 billion people could be fed at Dutch standards; in 1967, that 47.6 billion people[100] could be supported "at maximum standards" and around 157 billion at a subsistence level.

Comments

Clark's 1958 estimate that the world has the equivalent of 77 million square kilometers of "good temperate agricultural land"[101] is remarkably close to Ravenstein's 1891 estimate (in Table 10.1) that the world has 73 million square kilometers of "fertile lands," but Clark's 1967 estimate of 107 million square kilometers of "standard land" equivalent is substantially higher than Ravenstein's. Clark's estimate that 47 billion people could be supported "at maximum standards" is more than seven times Ravenstein's estimate of 6 billion for two principal reasons: first, because Clark's estimate that requirements for food and wood of 444 people could be raised on one square kilometer of "standard land" was 5.6 times higher than Ravenstein's estimate of 80 people per square kilometer of "fertile land"; and second, because Clark's estimate of 107 million square kilometers of "standard land" equivalent was 1.4 times higher than Ravenstein's estimate of 73 million square kilometers of "fertile land" equivalent.

Clark appeared to pay little or no attention to the possible loss of food between its growth in the field and its final consumption by people.

Clark's estimates are sensitive to the details of his assumptions. For example, his estimate of the wood requirement is only a quarter of reported American consumption. Two cubic meters of roundwood per person per year would require 1,000 square meters of land, still assuming a yield of 20 cubic meters per hectare per year.[102] If tropical lands could only be doubly cropped instead of quintuply cropped, then the number of people who could be supported "at maximum standards" would be 7.68×10^{13} square meters divided by 3,000 square meters per person, or 25.6 billion. The number would fall further if average yields of cereals, grasses and wood were lower than those Clark assumed.

Clark suggested in 1967 that the use of wood for fuel will soon become obsolete. Since then, the use of wood for fuel has not become obsolete. Of the 3.43 billion cubic meters of roundwood produced annually in the period 1987–89, 1.76 billion cubic meters, a bit over half, were used for fuel and charcoal. In Africa during this period, 89 percent of roundwood production was burned for fuel and charcoal, in Asia 74 percent, but in Europe only 15 percent.[103] More than three-fourths of fuelwood used in developing countries is collected free,[104] much of it by the labor of women and children who receive no cash for their labor. When wood becomes scarce around cities, a market usually develops in which the costs of collection are included; even so, wood is cheap compared to kerosene or bottled gas.[105]

As of 1980, in developing countries, noncommercial fuel often supplied 90 percent of all energy used. In many countries, deforestation and desertification both resulted from and intensified the lack of fuelwood. According to D. O. Hall, a biologist at the University of London King's College, "The implications for nutrition and wellbeing are serious . . . ; about half the world's population relies mainly on wood fuel for their cooking . . . and heating. It often costs more to heat the pot than to fill it."[106]

China is an important case. According to Jing-Neng Li, director of the Institute of Population and Development Research, Nankai University, Tianjin, China, "The most frequently cited cause of deforestation in China, especially in rural areas, is the need for cooking and heating fuel."[107] In southwest and northeast China, fuelwood and hay provide about 80 percent of the total energy used. In Jingdong and Shipin counties of Yunnan Province, the average person uses one cubic meter of fuelwood per year. In Xishuang-Bana, the average household uses 3.4 cubic meters per year.

The scarcity of fuelwood has grave consequences. Of 170 million rural households in China, more than 70 million (350 million people) have serious fuel shortages. Up to six months in each year, crop residues are used up and no wood is available in deforested areas. Likewise, in west Africa, where two cooked meals each day were traditional, many families now eat cooked meals only once daily or once every other day because wood is scarce. According to one peasant in Senegal, "one can starve with a full granary if one has no fuel with which to cook the meal." In Upper Volta and in Haiti, where nutritious soybeans have been introduced, they have grown well but have not been widely used because they take too long to cook. A scarcity of fuel to boil water and heat foods contributes to the spread of some diseases and diverts a family's labor or income from improving other aspects of the household's level of living.[108]

Shortages of fuelwood reduce food production, because agricultural wastes are traditionally used to fertilize crop fields. Where fuelwood is scarce, people may burn crop wastes or animal dung instead. Each metric ton of cattle dung burned as fuel rather than used as fertilizer reduces potential grain output around 50 kilograms. Around 1985, an estimated 400 million tonnes of dung were burned annually in Africa, Asia and the Near East. Hence potential food output was reduced by 20 million tonnes in aggregate, more than 10 kilograms of grain per person in these areas.[109]

"POTENTIAL POPULATION SUPPORTING CAPACITIES OF LANDS IN THE DEVELOPING WORLD" (1983)

From 1971 to 1981, the Food and Agricultural Organization (FAO) of the United Nations published the first complete soil map of the world. The

FAO undertook the project because different countries had incomparable systems of naming, classifying and surveying soils. While mapping the world's soils, FAO also developed ways to estimate how much of various kinds of crops could be grown on various soils, given assumptions about the inputs used in farming. The FAO estimated potential crops by matching the soil and climatic requirements of crops with soil and climatic surveys.[110] In 1978, the FAO evaluated the crop potential of Africa, in the first of four volumes (completed by 1981) that cover the world.

The report on Africa prompted the United Nations Fund for Population Activities (UNFPA) to ask the FAO whether the "crop potential estimates [could] be converted into estimates of potential population supporting capacities; if so, can these population potential estimates be compared with data on present and projected populations to identify critical areas where land resources are insufficient to meet food needs."[111] The FAO answered yes to both questions. Hence in 1978 the UNFPA commissioned the FAO and the International Institute for Applied Systems Analysis (IIASA), a nongovernmental research institute in Austria, to evaluate potential "population supporting capacities." The final technical report by five authors described the methods, results and interpretation of the results in 150 pages.[112] I will summarize.

The research team estimated the physical potential "population supporting capacities" of lands in five regions of the developing world: Africa, Southwest Asia, South America, Central America and Southeast Asia. They excluded developed countries and East Asia (including China and Korea). "Factors limiting attainment of this physical potential, i.e. social, economic and institutional factors, are not included nor are land requirements for non-food crops and demands for diets above the minimum requirement level."[113]

The team considered two years, 1975 and 2000. For 1975, the areas of rain-fed and irrigated agriculture as well as population sizes were observed or estimated. For the year 2000, the study relied on national plans for irrigation and on the most recent United Nations medium projection of population sizes.

The study started from an overlay of FAO maps of climate on FAO maps of soil at the 1:5,000,000 scale (2 millimeters on the map represented 10 kilometers or 6 miles on the ground). The soil map was based on 26 major kinds of soil, 106 refinements of these and 12 soil phases that affect production. The climatic inventory distinguished 14 major climates (for example, warm tropics, defined quantitatively in terms of monthly and daily temperatures during the growing period) and zones according to the length of the growing period at 30-day intervals (for example, 120 to 149 days). The land potentially available for rain-fed cultivation was the total land reduced by the irrigated land (estimated from national data and satellite observations) and by the non-agricultural land requirements (estimated at 0.05 hectare per person, less than De Wit's 0.075 hectare per person for urban and recreational use). Land potentially available for rain-fed cultivation was estimated for each country, and within each country separately for each combination of soil conditions and climate. Africa alone required more than 35,000 "agro-ecological cells" to represent the details of country, soil conditions and climate.

For each agro-ecological cell, the team selected crops that could grow in the cell's climate and temperature. They estimated the potential productivity of each crop on each cell of land by combining multiple factors: the length of the growing period, the soil type, the soil phase (for example, stony, lithic, fragipan or saline), the slope (level, rolling to hilly or steep), the soil texture (coarse, medium or fine), the requirements for a fallow period, the risks of soil degradation, the possibilities of multiple cropping and deductions for waste and for future seeds. They converted the amount of each crop that could be produced to calories.

The researchers assumed three levels of inputs to agriculture: low, intermediate and high (Table 10.9). Low inputs entailed hand labor for subsistence, using only the cultivars currently grown. Intermediate inputs entailed allocating half the land to present cultivars, and half the land to a selection from the 16 major cultivars (which are listed at the top of Table 10.9) that produced the maximal calories, provided that the optimal selection also yielded a minimal required level of protein. High inputs entailed allocating all land to maximal calorie production (provided that protein requirements were met) as well as full mechanization and making optimal use of fertilizers and chemical controls for pests, diseases and weeds. To calculate the selection of cultivars that maximized calories and satisfied protein requirements, the team used linear programming, a mathematical technique for finding the best solutions to complex problems with constraints (such as airplane scheduling).

The team observed that the optimal crop ignored local crop preferences: "An instant change in crop pattern (i.e. new crops instead of currently grown crops), to obtain maximum calorie-protein production, is not considered a realistic short-term possibility."[114] The net result thus far was the maximum number of calories that the rain-fed portion of each cell could produce (depending on the level of inputs). "In quantifying irrigated production . . . , produce from non-food crops was converted to grain equivalents by crop substitution," using FAO tables of the calorie and protein composition of crops.[115] The researchers added the maximal rain-fed production plus the irrigated production to estimate the maximal total production for the chosen level of inputs.

The FAO estimated calorie and protein requirements per person based on each country's population by sex composition and age structure, as estimated in 1975 and as projected for 2000. Illustrative energy requirements (in kilocalories per person per day) using 1973 FAO standards with zero wastage allowance were, at the low end, 2,006 for India and 2,020 for Thailand and, at the high end, 2,220 for Chile and 2,293 for Turkey.[116] Dividing a cell's maximum potential calories (that met protein requirements) by the calorie requirements per person gave that cell's "potential population supporting capacity."

TABLE 10.9   Definitions of levels of inputs and crops considered in the Food and Agricultural Organization–IIASA–United Nations Fund for Population Activities study

crops of the assessment:	pearl millet, sorghum, maize, rice, wheat, sweet potato, white potato, cassava, *Phaseolus* bean, soybean, barley, oil palm, groundnut, banana/plantain, sugarcane, grassland		
	level of inputs		
	low	intermediate	high
production system	rain-fed cultivation of currently grown mixture of crops	rain-fed cultivation with part change to optimum mixture of crops	rain-fed cultivation of optimum mixture of crops
technology employed	local cultivars; no fertilizer or chemical pest, disease and weed control; rest (fallow) periods; no long-term soil conservation measures	improved cultivars as available; limited fertilizer application; simple extension packages including some chemical pest, disease and weed control; some rest (fallow) periods; some long-term conservation measures	high-yielding cultivars; optimum fertilizer application; chemical pest, disease and weed control; minimum rest (fallow) periods; complete conservation measures
power sources	manual labor with hand tools	manual labor with hand tools and/or animal traction with improved implements	complete mechanization including harvesting
labor intensity	high, including uncosted family labor	high, including part costed family labor	low, family labor costed if used
capital intensity	low	intermediate with credit on accessible terms	high
market orientation	subsistence production	subsistence production plus commercial sale of surplus	commercial production
infrastructure requirements	market accessibility not necessary; inadequate advisory services	some market accessibility necessary with access to demonstration plots and services	market accessibility essential; high level of advisory services and application of research findings
landholdings	fragmented	sometimes consolidated	consolidated

SOURCE: Higgins et al. (1983, p. 10)

The report of the study aggregated the results for individual cells in four ways: for the region (for example, Africa), for the country (for example, Guinea), for the regional growing-period zone and major climate aggregation (for example, all African cells in the moderately cool tropics where the growing period was from 240 to 269 days long) and for an individual-country growing-period zone (for example, cells in Guinea where the growing period was from 240 to 269 days long).

The researchers defined a "critical" area (a region, country or zone) as one that could not produce enough calories to feed the people it had, given the assumed inputs. For the year 2000, a "critical" area could not feed the people it was projected to have after allowing for planned additional irrigation. But ". . . it has not been possible to take into account existing or projected trade of food between countries."[117]

So much for the methods. In summarizing the results, I shall emphasize the year 1975 (Table 10.10). I shall skip most results for the year 2000 because the estimates of future irrigation and future population size are unreliable. The growth rate of irrigated area in the world has declined remarkably in recent decades, substantially below some earlier projections.[118] Likewise, predicted population size is changeable. The 1979 United Nations medium projections[119] of the regional population sizes for 2000 differ considerably from the 1992 United Nations medium projections[120] (Table 10.10). The African population in the year 2000 was projected at 780 million in 1979, but at 856 million in 1992, a 10 percent increase. The combined populations of South and Central America (including Mexico) were projected at 608 million in 1979, but at 523 million in 1992, a 14 percent reduction. The projected population in 2000 of Southwest Asia rose by 10 million from 1979 to 1992 while that of Southeast Asia fell by 43 million. The projected population sizes of many individual countries were far less stable than these regional totals. Because neither irrigation nor population size could be forecasted reliably, it did not seem worthwhile to review the results for the year 2000 in detail.

Even the 1975 regional population sizes reported by Higgins et al. differed from the regional population sizes in 1975 as they were assessed ten years later.[121] For example, the presumed population of Africa in 1975 rose by 35 million from 1983 to 1993. This comparison should increase your skepticism about the solidity of the numbers given for 1975. The population of other regions changed by trivial amounts (Table 10.10).

Now to the results. Regions differed enormously in their 1975 endowment of moisture, temperature and soil for food production. The fraction of land suitable for rain-fed crop production ranged from 18 percent in Southwest Asia to around 85 percent in South America and Southeast Asia. The fraction of land where the soil had no inherent limitations of fertility ranged from 8 percent in Southwest Asia to 44 percent in Central America, averaging 21 percent in the regions studied. Suitable soil was not overabundant in any region.

The available land was reduced by soil degradation in the absence of

TABLE 10.10   Regional characteristics of land, production and population according to Higgins et al. (1983)

characteristic	region					
	Africa	Southwest Asia	South America	Central America	Southeast Asia	total
land area[a] (million hectares)	2,878.1	677.4	1,770.2	271.6	897.6	6,494.9
land climatically suitable for rain-fed crop production (percentage of region's land area)	53.3	17.9	85.5	63.7	84.2	63.1
land with no inherent fertility limitations[b] (percentage of region's land area)	18.6	7.6	20.3	43.8	36.2	21.4
non-agricultural land requirements in 1975[c] (percentage of region's land area)	0.7	1.0	0.6	2.0	6.2	1.5
effects of unchecked soil erosion on productivity, assuming low inputs:						
decrease in area of rain-fed cropland (percent)	16.5	20.0	9.7	29.7	35.6	17.7
decrease in rain-fed crop productivity (percent)	29.4	35.1	22.6	44.5	38.6	28.9
decrease in total land productivity (percent)	24.9	4.9	20.6	24.6	12.4	18.5
1975 population (millions)	380.2	136.3	215.8	106.6	1,117.7	1,956.6
1975 population assessed by United Nations (1993) (millions)	415.1	132.6	214.6	105.5	1,123.1	1,990.9
1975 population density (persons per hectare)	0.13	0.20	0.12	0.39	1.25	0.30

TABLE 10.10   *continued*

characteristic	region					total
	Africa	Southwest Asia	South America	Central America	Southeast Asia	
1975 potential population supporting capacity (persons per hectare), with:						
low inputs	0.39	0.16	0.72	0.64	1.39	0.61
intermediate inputs	1.53	0.25	2.92	1.65	3.76	2.11
high inputs	4.47	0.40	6.97	4.51	6.34	5.05
potential population (millions), with:						
low inputs	1,122.5	108.4	1,274.5	173.8	1,247.7	3,961.9
intermediate inputs	4,403.5	169.4	5,169.0	448.1	3,375.0	13,704.2
high inputs	12,865.1	271.0	12,338.3	1,224.9	5,690.8	32,799.2
fraction of total potential population supporting capacities contributed by irrigated production, with:						
low inputs	9	80	6	38	39	
intermediate inputs	<5	49	<5	14	14	
high inputs	<5	32	<5	5	8	
ratio of 1975 potential population to 1975 actual population, with:						
low inputs	3.0	0.8	5.9	1.6	1.1	2.0
intermediate inputs	11.6	1.3	23.9	4.2	3.0	6.9
high inputs	33.9	2.0	57.2	11.5	5.1	16.6
total number of countries	51	16	13	21	16	117
number of critical countries, with:						
low inputs	22	15	0	11	6	54
intermediate inputs	7	12	0	4	1	24
high inputs	2	9	0	1	1	13

characteristic	region					
	Africa	Southwest Asia	South America	Central America	Southeast Asia	total
population of critical countries (millions of people above, percentage of regional total below), with:						
low inputs	188.4	96.2	0	17.1	770.5	1,072.2
	49.6%	70.6%		16.1%	68.9%	54.8%
intermediate inputs	25.5	45.1	0	3.6	2.3	76.5
	6.7%	33.1%		3.4%	0.2%	3.9%
high inputs	0.4	18.9	0	0.2	2.3	21.8
	0.1%	13.9%		0.2%	0.2%	1.1%
population in excess of potential supporting capacity (millions of people above, percentage of regional total below), with:						
low inputs	66.9	34.0	0	8.6	168.2	277.7
	17.6%	24.9%		8.1%	15.0%	14.2%
intermediate inputs	5.1	18.7	0	0.4	2.3	26.5
	1.3%	13.7%		0.4%	0.2%	1.4%
high inputs	0.4	8.2	0	0.2	2.3	11.1
	0.1%	6.0%		0.2%	0.2%	0.6%
year 2000 population projected in 1979, according to United Nations medium variant (millions)	780.1	264.8	392.6	215.2	1,937.1	3,589.7
year 2000 population according to United Nations (1993) medium variant (millions)	856.2	274.6	344.5	178.5	1,894.2	3,548.0

[a] Excluding areas mapped as water bodies on FAO/Unesco Soil Map.

[b] Land with no inherent fertility limitations is land where the growing period may be short (75–179 days) or long (180–365 days) or humid year-round; with no severe temperature constraints; and with fertile soils (andosols, chernozems, cambisols, fluvisols, regosols, luvisols, phaeozems, nitosols, podzoluvisols, kastanozems).

[c] 0.05 hectare per person.

Sources: Higgins et al. (1983, pp. 14, 16, 19, 24, 27, 34, 47, 106); United Nations (1993, pp. 154–57) using lists of countries in each region from Higgins et al. (1983)

countermeasures and by non-agricultural uses of land. The quantitative estimates of the extent of soil degradation and non-agricultural uses of land in Table 10.10 were admittedly based on inadequate data and rough calculations. Remember the Law of Information!

Soil degradation includes erosion by water or wind, salinization and alkalization, waterlogging, depletion of nutrients and organic matter, the deterioration of soil structure and pollution. (In salinization, irrigation water dissolves naturally occurring salts from the soil as it runs over and through the topsoil. When the water evaporates or is transpired, it leaves the salts in the soil.) Soil degradation reduced the productivity of productive land and rendered it unsuitable for crops in extreme cases.

Requirements for non-agricultural land were crudely estimated at 0.05 hectare per person. This estimate was invented in the absence of more detailed data for much of the developing world. On this rough basis, regional requirements for non-agricultural land were less than 2 percent of the total land except, as might be expected, in Southeast Asia where high population densities required more than 6 percent of total land for non-agricultural uses. In extreme cases, the fraction of land devoted to non-agricultural uses varied among countries from almost none to 33 percent.[122]

The importance of irrigation differed greatly from region to region, but in every region diminished as the hypothetical level of other inputs increased. In Africa and South America, the fraction of total potential population supporting capacities contributed by irrigated production did not exceed 9 percent, whatever the level of inputs. In Southwest Asia, with low inputs, 80 percent of the potential population supporting capacities depended on irrigation; with high inputs, as much as 32 percent depended on irrigation. In Central America and Southeast Asia, the contribution of irrigation dropped from just under 40 percent to 8 percent or less as inputs rose from low to high. Irrigation mattered much more in some places than in others, and the effect of additional inputs on the importance of irrigation varied from region to region.

With low inputs, the 1975 "potential population supporting capacity" expressed as persons per hectare exceeded the 1975 population density in all regions but Southwest Asia. There the population density of 0.20 person per hectare exceeded the potential of 0.16 person per hectare. In Southeast Asia, the 1975 potential capacity of 1.39 persons exceeded the actual density of 1.25 persons, but not by a wide margin. Even with low inputs, Africa had the physical potential in 1975 to support three times its estimated 1975 population, and South America almost six times its estimated 1975 population. With intermediate inputs, the 1975 regional "potential population supporting capacity" exceeded the regional population density by factors ranging from 1.3 for Southwest Asia to 23.9 for South America. With high inputs, the 1975 regional "potential population supporting capacity" exceeded the regional population density by factors ranging from 2.0 for Southwest Asia to 57.2 for South America.

These comparisons assumed the possibility of "massive and unrestricted movement of surplus potential food production and labour within . . . all five regions," because the aggregate crop potential of all countries within each region was compared with the aggregate food requirements within each region. Surpluses or deficiencies of different countries within a region were assumed to cancel out.

The estimates of the 1975 "potential population supporting capacity" for the five regions of the developing world combined presuppose still more: the possibility of "massive and unrestricted movement of surplus potential food production and labour within and between all five regions." For all five regions of the developing world treated as a single unit, without barriers to food or labor, the ratio of 1975 potential population to 1975 actual population is 2 with low inputs, nearly 7 with intermediate inputs and almost 17 with high inputs.

If the 1975 regional "potential population supporting capacity" expressed as persons per hectare is multiplied by the regional land area,[123] the result is the regional aggregate 1975 "potential population" (Table 10.10). The total of the five regions is 4.0 billion people with low inputs, 13.7 billion with intermediate inputs and 32.8 billion with high inputs. These estimates of regional and total potential population make the same assumption of complete mobility of food or people or both across national borders within regions and, for the total, among regions.

The researchers reported, "A more realistic assumption is that of movement of surplus potential food production *within countries*. On this basis, 54 countries (out of the total of 117 studied) have insufficient land resources to meet the food needs of their 1975 populations with low level of inputs."[124] Among these 54 "critical" countries are 22 in Africa (of 51 African countries), 15 (of 16) countries in Southwest Asia and 11 (of 21) countries in Central America. There are no "critical" countries in South America and 6 (of 16) in Southeast Asia. With intermediate or high inputs and 1975 populations, 24 or 13 countries remain "critical."

Higgins et al. calculated the population of "critical" countries and the population in excess of their potential population of "critical" countries, and summed them within regions and over all five regions (Table 10.10). The aggregate population of "critical" countries in 1975 with low inputs exceeded 1.07 billion; India alone accounted for more than 60 percent of this total. With intermediate and high inputs, the aggregate population of "critical" countries dropped to 77 million and 22 million, respectively. The 1975 population in excess of the potential population dropped from 278 million (14 percent of the total population) with low inputs to 27 million with intermediate inputs (1.4 percent of the total population) and 11 million with high inputs (0.6 percent of the total population).

International food trade between "critical" countries and neighboring countries with potential food surpluses could apparently eliminate national food deficits. For example, with low inputs, the 22 "critical" countries of Africa fell into ten geographical groups. Each group combined countries that had potential food deficits with one neighboring country that had a potential food surplus. The 22 "critical" countries lacked food for 66.9 million people; the 10 countries with common borders had a surplus potential population supporting capacity of 256.4 million people. Thus "the 22 deficit countries require[d] 26.1 percent of the surplus production potential of 10 countries. In comparison, at the Africa regional level, the total food surplus in the region is equivalent to a population excess supporting capacity for 741.7 million person[s]."[125]

With high inputs, two "critical" countries, Western Sahara and Cape Verde, which lacked food for 0.4 million people, would require about 0.2 percent of the surplus potential food production of Guinea, which had surplus food potential sufficient for 170.2 million people.[126]

The results for the year 2000 suggested that, even if the 1975 plans for irrigation by 2000 were realized, more countries would be "critical" at each level of inputs, more people would live in "critical" countries and the population in excess of the maximum potential supporting capacity within each country would be larger.

This entire analysis assumed that all potentially cultivable land would be used to grow food crops, not cash crops for export, contrary to the reality in many developing countries. According to the report, "Should present cash crop land requirements be considered, additional countries may have difficulty in meeting their future food needs. On the assumption that at least one-third of the potentially cultivable land is required for cash crops and/or food crops to take account of inequities in food distribution," the number of "critical" countries would increase further, whatever the level of inputs.[127]

Comments

The term "critical" used by Higgins et al. requires critical interpretation. The "critical" countries in 1975 with high inputs were Cape Verde, Western Sahara, Bahrain, Qatar, Oman, Kuwait, United Arab Emirates, Jordan, Saudi Arabia, Lebanon, Israel, Netherlands Antilles and Singapore. Some of these countries (notably Cape Verde and Western Sahara in Africa) are poor; some have immense oil wealth but largely lack a modern economy; and some have diversified industrial economies. The countries that have the means to trade for food do so. The assumption of no food trade between countries, which stands behind the classification of a country as "critical," seems just as extreme as, not "more realistic" than, the assumption of complete mobility of food or population across national or regional boundaries.

De Wit and Higgins et al. both gave *conditional* limits on population size, assuming only physical limitations on food production. Both applied Penck's formula, estimating maximal total food production and dividing by average individual requirements.

Higgins et al. applied Penck's formula at a very fine level of geographic resolution. They based their estimates on much more information about soil, climate, crops and dietary requirements than any other application of

Penck's formula, before or since. They showed that soil, water and climate severely limit the ability of available sunlight to drive photosynthesis. Assuming that each person required only 500 square meters (0.05 hectare) of land for non-agricultural uses and taking as given the 1975 distribution of population in developing countries, Higgins et al. calculated that, with 1975 irrigation and high inputs, the lands of the developing world (except East Asia, which was not included in the study) could feed 33 billion people a subsistence diet. This total includes 7.1 billion people in Brazil alone, an estimate regarded by Philip M. Fearnside, a human ecologist in Brazil, as "incredible."[128] With 1975 (low) inputs and the 1975 choice of crops, the developing regions (except East Asia) could feed four billion. By their estimates, changing from low to high inputs could multiply the maximum supportable population by a factor of more than eight.

Of the authors reviewed so far, Higgins et al. are the first to recognize that, when a country grows just enough food to feed everyone a subsistence diet, if somebody gets more than a subsistence diet then somebody else gets less. If a country wishes to assure that everyone in it could eat a subsistence diet, and if some people eat better than that, then the country must increase its production above, or reduce its population below, the levels calculated here.

Though the non–agricultural land requirement assumed by Higgins et al. was one-third of the largest requirement considered by De Wit, their maximum population with high inputs (33 billion) was less than half of his (79 billion). Part of the difference has an obvious explanation: Higgins et al. excluded East Asia and the developed world while De Wit included the entire land surface. More important, Higgins et al. recognized that soil, water and climate can limit photosynthesis before sunlight does.

However, it may not be possible to convert Amazonia to high-input mechanized agriculture, as Higgins et al. supposed. For example, as Amazonia has hardly any phosphate deposits, phosphate would have to be imported and distributed at great cost; heavy use in an area as extensive as Amazonia could exhaust global supplies of phosphate.[129]

Higgins et al. also assumed that land in areas not now cultivated is as productive as land currently cultivated. In their high estimates of potential productivity in tropical regions, they overlooked that warm nights in the tropics cause plants to respire more of the photosynthate they produce during the day. Warm temperatures year-round accelerate the degradation of soil and do not discourage weeds and pests, as cold seasons do in temperate zones.[130]

Higgins et al. intentionally set aside nonphysical factors. Such factors have real effects and may further constrain the "physical potential population supporting capacities." In drawing attention to these nonphysical factors, I do not criticize Higgins et al. for what they did, but urge caution in interpreting their results. I will illustrate the omissions of demography, economics and culture.

Demography appeared only in the FAO calculations of nutritional requirements, which depended on the composition of the population by age and by sex. No migration was considered, and no demographic constraints on the supply of labor were mentioned. For example, Higgins et al. estimated that, with high inputs, Guinea in 1975 could have exported enough food to feed 170.2 million people, far more than enough to feed the 0.4 million people in Western Sahara and Cape Verde who could not be fed from the produce of their own countries. The estimated population of Guinea in 1975 was 4.4 million. Could the farmers within this population of 4.4 million produce enough food to feed 174.6 million domestic and foreign consumers? To do so, every man, woman and child of Guinea would have to produce food for 40 people. Such productivity is not impossible in principle; would high inputs have made it possible in Guinea in 1975?

The research team did not consider the role of economics in determining which crops are grown, and with what level of technology. When intermediate or high inputs were assumed, Higgins et al. used a sophisticated linear programming model to select cultivars that yielded maximal calories. If national planners in developing countries were to use linear programming for optimal planning, they might seek to maximize calorie production as Higgins et al. did, but it seems at least as likely that they would use the technique to maximize export earnings or tax revenues. Owners of large plots of agricultural land might use linear programming to maximize calorie production, but it seems at least as likely that they would use the technique to maximize cash profits.

Africa increased its production of export crops throughout its periods of drought and famine. Large international firms in Ethiopia produced alfalfa to feed cattle in Japan, while Ethiopian peasants starved to death. Millions of Indian citizens remain malnourished while India exports food. William Murdoch, an ecologist at the University of California, Santa Barbara, observed that "poor countries, even in the worst of famines, have always produced enough food to feed their people, if the food were evenly distributed. The simple idea—too many people, too little food—is simply not tenable."[131] Producing the maximum possible calories would require overcoming physical, institutional and economic obstacles. To say that people who lack money cannot buy food is a tautology; but multiplied to a national and international scale, the tautology implies that very poor people are not able to exercise economic demand in economic markets—they are just sidelined, unable to give incentives to farmers to produce more food for domestic consumption.

The Yale economist T. N. Srinivasan objected that the projections of Higgins et al. included no economic analysis. If millions of peasant farmers pursue their private economic interests, they will not necessarily produce the kinds and amounts of crops that are agroclimatically and technologically possible. Unless there are adequate economic returns, no one will make "the investments in land, capital equipment, livestock, technical skills and knowledge needed to attain the potential output. . . ."[132]

Srinivasan also observed that the projections for 2000 treated population growth as totally independent of economic developments, unresponsive to either improvement or deterioration in the food supply and other economic conditions. The analysis also ignored any effects of population growth on the environment (specifically, on desertification, soil erosion, droughts and floods) and on the fragmentation of farms if land is divided among children within families.[133]

Finally, culture matters. Higgins et al. recognized that farmers might not easily switch from crops they know how to grow and like to eat (or export) to crops that satisfy protein requirements and maximize calories. Other cultural factors were not mentioned, and no cultural factors affected the calculations. For example, high inputs were defined to include capital-intensive farming, including full mechanization; a full complement of chemical pesticides, herbicides and fertilizers; the consolidation of land into large holdings; orientation of producers toward the market rather than toward subsistence; low use of labor; and high use of advisory services and other sources of advanced technological information. The image is closer to Iowa than to Bangladesh. Where high inputs are plausible, how plausible is the assumption, maintained throughout, that everybody, including the farmers, would remain on a subsistence diet? Not very. How plausible is the assumption that people would continue to require 0.05 hectare for nonagricultural uses? Not very. If high inputs were available, how plausible are the substantial levels of fertility assumed in the United Nations medium projections? Not very. And finally, how plausible is the assumption that different cultures in the developing world would be equally receptive to the massive changes in attitudes, education and behavior that would have to accompany changes from low to intermediate or high inputs? Not very.

"THE POPULATION POTENTIALLY SUPPORTED BY THE PRIMARY FOOD SUPPLY" (1991)

At Brown University, Providence, Rhode Island, Robert Kates and his colleagues in the World Hunger Program issued *The Hunger Report* annually for several years starting in 1988.[134] Each report or update included an estimated "population potentially supported by the primary food supply." For example, the 1991 update estimated that the 1989 primary food supply could potentially support 5.9 billion people (113 percent of world population then) on a "basic diet (principally vegetarian)"; 3.9 billion people (75 percent of world population then) on "an improved diet (about 15 percent of calories from animal products)"; and 2.9 billion people (56 percent of world population) on a "full-but-healthy diet (about 25 percent of calories from animal products)."[135] Each of these three figures is 0.1 billion people lower than the corresponding figure estimated on the basis of the 1986 primary food supply.

The population estimates equaled the ratio of the primary food supply to the average per-person food requirement (Penck's formula again). Kates et al. estimated the primary food supply from data in the *1986 FAO Production Yearbook* on cereals, roots and tubers, vegetables, fruit, oil seeds and other crops. They converted the total tonnes of roots, tubers, vegetables and fruit to an equivalent weight of grain by multiplying by 0.15.[136] They then increased the results by 5 percent to allow for animal and fish products derived from forage or waste.

To estimate the demand for food, Kates et al. relied on population estimates provided by the United States Department of Agriculture and the Population Reference Bureau. They considered three types of diet: "basic," "improved" and "full but healthy." For the basic diet, they derived an average requirement of 2,350 kilocalories per person per day from FAO caloric standards and U.N. data on the age distribution of the world's population. They converted the dietary requirements into grain by assuming that each gram of grain yields 3.5 kilocalories and that 40 percent of grain is lost between production and consumption, including a loss of 10–15 percent after food is sold at retail.

The "improved" diet allowed a 10 percent increase, and the "full-but-healthy" diet a 20 percent increase, in the share of food calories from animal products. Supposing that 600 kilocalories of primary foods yield 100 kilocalories of animal products such as meat, milk and eggs, they estimated that the "improved" diet increases the demand for primary food by 50 percent and the "full-but-healthy" diet increases the demand for primary food by 100 percent.[137]

Losses of calories after food is sold at retail were counted twice, because the FAO's national caloric requirements already allowed for a 10 percent loss after retail sale. According to Millman et al., "The implication is that our estimates . . . should be viewed as quite conservative indications of how many people could receive a given diet based on total food supply."[138]

Millman et al. recognized that food production responds to economic incentives as well as to physical and technical constraints: "Of course, more food probably could and would have been produced if more people had had the means to purchase it."[139]

Comments

*The Hunger Report*s estimated a supportable population by the same method as Hulett,[140] though the estimates in *The Hunger Report*s of the primary food supply were factually better based and the average individual caloric requirements referred to different populations. Hulett took the average American as the average individual, while *The Hunger Report*s took a world average. The "basic" diet of 2,350 kilocalories per person per day was higher than the range Clark considered for less developed countries (1,625 to 2,012) but lower than that assumed by Revelle (2,500).

Hulett estimated the total energy value of all the world's plant crops in the middle 1960s at 4.2×10^{15} kilocalories per year.[141] For comparison,

Millman et al. estimated the primary food supply in 1989 at 7.9×10^{15} kilocalories per year.[142]

As I mentioned earlier, *The Hunger Reports* and Hulett shared a major unstated assumption. They assumed that, if food were uniformly distributed to all people (which it is not), and if the number of producers differed from the actual number of producers, then the total food supply would remain equal to the actual food supply. Given the social and economic changes that a uniform distribution of food either presupposes or would rapidly create, it seems likely that incentives to farmers to produce food would be different, and therefore unlikely that the total supply would remain unchanged.

Now it is time to step back from these eight close examinations to a survey of estimates of how many people the Earth can support.

11

Estimates of
Human Carrying Capacity:
A Survey of Four Centuries

THE EARLIEST KNOWN estimates of how many people the Earth could support formed part of the intellectual explosion of the seventeenth century. William Harvey proved the existence of the circulation of blood in *De Motu Cordis* (1628), John Graunt began demography and modern statistics in *Natural and political observations made upon the bills of mortality* (1662), Gottfried Leibniz published *Ars combinatoria* (1666) and discovered the fundamental theorem of the infinitesimal calculus (1672–76), Antoni van Leeuwenhoek published the first of his letters on microscopy to the Royal Society in the *Philosophical Transactions* (1673), Isaac Newton explained why heavenly bodies move in their orbits in the *Principia* (1687) and John Locke published his *Essay on Human Understanding* (1690).

On 25 April 1679, in Delft, Leeuwenhoek wrote down what may be the first estimate of the maximum number of people the Earth can support. Around 1695, Gregory King in London estimated the population that the Earth's "Land If fully Peopled would sustain," in a manuscript notebook first published in 1973. At first a trickling and then a steady stream of estimates of how many people the Earth could support followed these early calculations. More than 65 estimates are summarized briefly in chronological order in Appendix 3. You are encouraged to read Appendix 3 whenever you feel the urge to learn more details about these estimates.

ESTIMATES OF GLOBAL
HUMAN CARRYING CAPACITY: LEVELS

The estimates of how many people the Earth can support vary from less than one billion to more than 1,000 billion. The low estimates indicate that more people are already on the Earth than can be supported (for some time period, usually not stated, in some mode of life considered plausible or desirable by the estimator). Low estimates imply that a decline in human numbers below the present 5.7 billion is inevitable. The intermediate estimates indicate that human numbers are on the verge of exceeding what the Earth can support (again, for some time period, usually not stated, in some mode of life considered plausible or desirable by the estimator). Since the Earth's population would exceed 8.4 billion by 2150 if fertility had fallen to the replacement level in 1990 (Chapter 8), the intermediate estimates of the Earth's maximum supportable human population could range from 5.7 billion to—any choice is bound to be arbitrary—perhaps 10 billion or 15 billion. The high estimates indicate that the Earth could sustain substantially more than 10 billion or 15 billion people, even as many as 10 or 100 times more (once again, for some unstated time period in some mode of life considered plausible or desirable by the estimator).

Out of curiosity, I plotted the estimates as a function of time, on a logarithmic scale of population size (Figure 11.1). Where an author gave a range of estimates or indicated only an upper bound, I plotted in Figure 11.1 only the highest number stated. I omitted one estimate of 10^{16}–10^{18} people, by

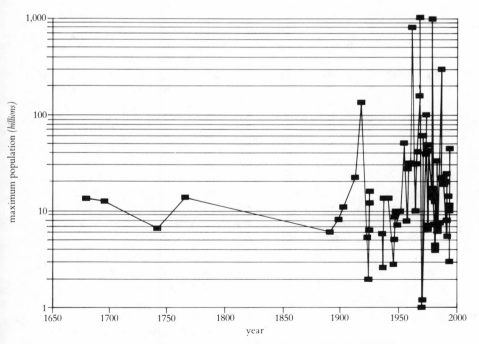

FIGURE 11.1   Estimates of how many people the Earth can support, by the date at which the estimate was made. When an author gave a range of estimates or indicated only an upper bound, the highest number stated is plotted here. The 1964 estimate by J. H. Fremlin would be off the scale and is omitted. SOURCE: Appendix 3

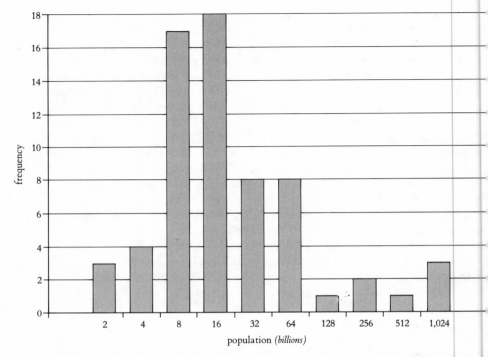

FIGURE 11.2 Frequency distribution of estimates of how many people the Earth can support, based on the highest estimate given by an author. The height of the bar for 4 billion shows the number of estimates greater than the next lower population size shown, that is, 2 billion, and not exceeding 4 billion. Each bar (after the first two) covers a range of population sizes twice as wide as the preceding bar. The 1964 estimate by J. H. Fremlin would be off the scale and is omitted. SOURCE: Appendix 3

the University of Birmingham physicist J. H. Fremlin, not because it deserves to be taken any less seriously than many of the other estimates, but simply because it is so large: including it in the graph would require such a severe compression of the graph's scale that the variations among all the remaining estimates would be obscured.

One striking feature of Figure 11.1 is that there is no clear increasing or decreasing trend in the estimated upper bounds. Leeuwenhoek's 1679 estimate of 13.4 billion and King's 1695 estimate of 6.3 billion to 12.5 billion hardly differ from the estimates of 7.7 billion by Meadows et al. in 1992 and 12 billion to 14 billion by Gerhard K. Heilig in 1993.

A second striking feature of the graph is that the scatter among the estimates seems to increase with the passage of time, as more and more extreme (both high and low) estimates are proposed, challenged and defended. Had I included Fremlin's estimate, the appearance of an increasing scatter in Figure 11.1 would be even stronger. The increasing scatter,

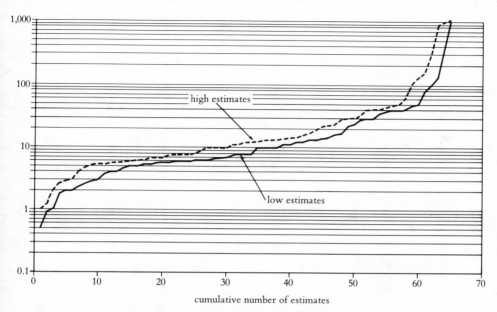

cumulative number of estimates

FIGURE 11.3   Cumulative distribution of high (upper dashed line) and low (lower solid curve) estimates of how many people the Earth can support. For example, according to the high estimates, 30 sources listed in Appendix 3 stated that the Earth can support 10 billion people or fewer; according to the low estimates, 30 sources listed in Appendix 3 stated that the Earth can support 7 billion people or fewer. The 1964 estimate by J. H. Fremlin would be off the scale and is omitted. SOURCE: Appendix 3

or at least absence of convergence, is the opposite of the progressive refinement and convergence that would ideally occur as time passes when a constant of nature like the speed of light or Avogadro's number is measured. The variation of these estimates of human carrying capacity hints that the Earth's human carrying capacity is not a constant of nature.

Considering only the highest number given when an author stated a range, the most frequent categories for estimates are 4–8 billion and 8–16 billion; these two categories include more than half of the estimates (Figure 11.2). However, just because most estimators thought the largest supportable population falls in these intervals is no proof that they are right. When the high estimates are ranked from smallest to largest, one-quarter of the estimates fall below 6.1 billion, half the estimates fall below 12 billion and three-quarters fall below 30 billion (Figure 11.3).

If the lowest number given is used when an author stated a range of estimates, the most frequent categories are again 4–8 billion and 8–16 billion; the interval 4–8 billion contains nearly a third of all the estimates (Figure 11.4). When the low estimates are ranked from smallest to largest, one-quarter of the estimates fall below 5 billion, half the estimates fall below 7.7 billion and three-quarters fall below 22 billion (Figure 11.3). Thus the

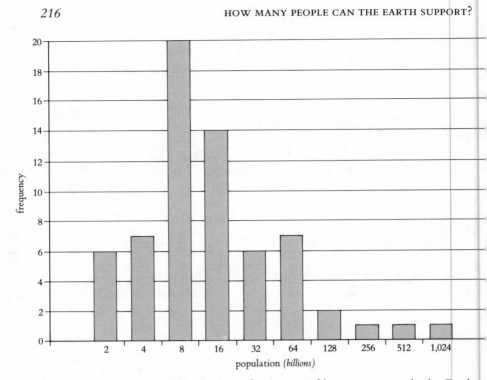

FIGURE 11.4   Frequency distribution of estimates of how many people the Earth can support, based on the lowest estimate given by an author. The height of the bar for 4 billion shows the number of estimates greater than the next lower population size shown, that is, 2 billion, and not exceeding 4 billion. Each bar (after the first two) covers a range of population sizes twice as wide as the preceding bar. The 1964 estimate by J. H. Fremlin would be off the scale and is omitted. SOURCE: Appendix 3

median of the low estimates is 7.7 billion and the median of the high estimates is 12 billion. Both medians fall in the range of intermediate estimates I suggested above.

The diversity of the estimates suggests that the people who made them were trying to measure different concepts, or had different data at their disposal or made different assumptions when data were lacking. By themselves, the numerical results do not explain the sources of variation; it is necessary to look at the methods used to reach them.

ESTIMATES OF
HUMAN CARRYING CAPACITY: METHODS

Though the numerical details of each estimate are unique, the methods fall into a few broad groups: categorical assertion, curve fitting, generalizations from observed population density, constraint by a single resource, constraint by multiple resources converted to a single resource, constraint by multiple independent resources, and system models.

Categorical Assertion

It's so because I say it's so. This venerable method is the choice of several authors in Appendix 3 who make quantitative assertions without any derivation from quantitative data. You can identify these authors yourself. There are no upper or lower limits (other than zero) on the estimates of the Earth's maximum population that can be achieved by this powerful technique. I am reminded of a remark of M. Roy Schwarz, M.D., of the American Medical Association. Question: What's the difference between genius and stupidity? Answer: Even genius has its limits.

Curve Fitting

Some mathematicians and computer scientists fitted mathematical curves to population sizes and extrapolated them into the future. For example, as I mentioned earlier, from a fitted logistic curve (which they likened to Kepler's elliptic orbits), Pearl and Reed in 1924 confidently estimated a maximum world population of two billion.[1] They may perhaps be excused for failing to test alternatives to the logistic curve because the labor of doing the arithmetic was prohibitive then. More recent proponents of other favored curves have no such excuse. For example, in 1971, Arthur L. Austin and John W. Brewer at the University of California, Davis, invented a modified logistic curve that predicted a maximum population between 40 billion and 60 billion. They considered no alternative models.

Curve fitting is no ignoble activity when it leads to a reliable general theory. Kepler's enthusiasm for fitting ellipses to planetary orbits followed naturally from his earlier mystical enthusiasm for explaining the radii of the orbits of the then-known planets by their putative relation to the five Platonic solids (read Arthur Koestler's *The Watershed*). In remembering, as Pearl did, only the brilliant success (in Newton's hands) of Kepler's elliptical curve fitting, it is easy to forget Kepler's previous numerological mysticism. Much of the fitting of curves to population sizes will share the fate of Kepler's mystical orbital radii rather than that of his ellipses.

Generalizations from Observed Population Density

King in 1695, Ravenstein in 1891, Fircks in 1898, Penck in 1925 and others divided the Earth's land into regions, assumed a maximum supportable population density of each region, multiplied each assumed maximal population density by the area of the corresponding region and summed over all regions to get a maximum supportable population of the Earth. The assumed maximum regional population density did not exceed the maximum observed regional population density, but there seemed to be no clear procedure by which the assumed maximum regional population density was selected. For example, Penck's two estimates, one the probable maximum and the other the highest conceivable maximum, seem arbitrarily selected. Estimates obtained by this method have superficial plausibility because they fall within the range of present experience, but there is no guarantee that present experience represents either the maximum desirable or the maximum possible population density, or one that can be sustained for any desired period of time in a desirable mode of life.

Constraint by a Single Resource

Many studies focused on a single assumed constraint on population size, without checking whether some other factors might intervene before the assumed constraining factor comes into play. Probably the single factor most often selected is food.[2] De Wit treated photosynthesis as the limiting factor, before he allowed for non-agricultural uses of land. Fremlin considered only the constraint of heat removal. Many other potential natural constraints on human carrying capacity have been proposed.

This apparently objective method can lead to extremely different estimates of maximum supportable population, as the examples just mentioned illustrate. Still more extreme results are possible, as I will now show by creating low and high estimates of the maximum population. These invented estimates are intended only to demonstrate the frailty of the method.

First, I construct a low estimate of the world's supportable population. Hulett estimated that Americans in the middle 1960s consumed seven million kilocalories of total plant calories per person per year[3] (about 19,200 kilocalories per day, an extremely high figure even if most of the calories are used as animal feed). Now assume that no population will be content until it can consume seven million kilocalories of plant calories per person per year. Assume also that the primary food supply could be no higher than that Millman et al. estimated for 1989, 7.9×10^{15} kilocalories per year.[4] Under these two assumptions, by Penck's formula, the maximum supportable population is 1.1 billion people.[5] This is Hulett's method of calculation.

Daily and Ehrlich of Stanford argued that the assumption that a primary food supply of 7.9×10^{15} kilocalories per year could be sustained indefinitely is far too generous, because the present population is consuming its natural capital, such as topsoil, nonrenewable groundwater, biodiversity and the quality of the atmosphere.[6] If Daily and Ehrlich are right, then the maximum population that can be supported indefinitely at this level of caloric luxury is lower than 1.1 billion.

Now I construct a high estimate of the world's supportable population using the same formula. Assume Colin Clark's 1977 estimate of 1,625 kilocalories per day or nearly 594,000 kilocalories per year as the minimum caloric requirement. This amount is less than one-tenth of the previous; if wheat gives 3.5 kilocalories per gram, 594,000 kilocalories per year would require fewer than 170 kilograms of grain per person per year, an extremely low figure. Assume, again with Clark, that 10.7 billion hectares (counting multiple cropping) could be cultivated each year, that these hectares could produce the caloric equivalent of 14.5 tonnes of winter wheat (the record from Washington State) and that each gram of wheat yields 3.5 kilocalories. Neglect any wastage of food between production and consumption. These generous assumptions give a potential primary calorie supply of 5.4×10^{17} kilocalories per year (nearly 100 times larger than the 1989 estimate of Millman et al.). Then the supportable population is 915 billion people, nearly 1,000 times larger than the previous result.

If this estimate makes you skeptical, double the caloric requirement per person to an ample 3,250 kilocalories per day and halve the assumed yield to 7.25 tonnes per hectare. In 1988–90, Belgium, Luxembourg, France, Ireland, the Netherlands and Switzerland all averaged yields of more than 6 tonnes per hectare of cereals nationally,[7] so an assumption of 7.25 tonnes per hectare may not appear outlandish (so to speak). These assumptions give a supportable population of 229 billion. Still uncomfortable? Divide the gross cropped area by 8, to get 1.34 billion hectares, *less* than the 1989 cropland of 1.48 billion hectares.[8] The maximum population drops to 28.6 billion. Halve the average yield again and you halve the supportable population again, to a mere 14.3 billion.

This activity is more than just playing games with numbers in Penck's formula. The results can be interpreted as useful *conditional* assertions about maximal population size. If you assume no constraints will restrict population size before food does, and if you want the average person to have a daily food supply of 3,250 kilocalories before losses due to seed, pests, handling, spoilage and waste are deducted, and if you assume that food will be based on crops grown in conventional agricultural fields on land, and if you grow cereals that yield on the average 3.5 kilocalories per gram, *then* to support a population of 28.6 billion you have to have at least 1.34 billion hectares under cultivation year after year with average yields of 7.25 tonnes per hectare, or some other combination of cultivable fields and yields that nets you the equivalent in calories of about 9.7 billion tonnes of cereals a year. Nothing less will suffice. Change any of the assumptions, and you may change the supportable population.

Constraint by Multiple Resources
Converted to a Single Resource

Several studies recognized that man and woman do not live by bread alone. People also require wood, fiber, fuel and amenities. Several authors reduced all requirements to the amount of land required to produce them. For example, Colin Clark expressed both food and wood requirements in terms of land, then divided the cultivable land by the summed land requirements for food and wood. De Wit combined agricultural and non-agricultural uses of land. Revelle allowed 10 percent of gross cropped area "to grow fibers, beverages and other nonfood crops." S. R. Eyre, a geographer at the University of Leeds, estimated in 1978 the land required for food, paper, timber and other forest products. Other factors that cannot be reduced to an area of land, such as water or energy, are sometimes recognized indirectly as constraints on the extent of cultivable land or on its possible level of productivity. Some authors favored energy rather than land area as a single limiting resource into which other constraints could be converted. The authors who combined different constraints into a single resource assumed without question that their chosen resource intervened as a constraint before any other factor.

Constraint by Multiple Independent Resources

Hulett recognized that population size can be constrained by food, wood products and multiple nonrenewable resources. Marchetti sketched a world designed to satisfy 1,000 billion people's requirements for housing, other structures, energy (for manufacturing, transportation, communication, lighting and air conditioning), food, water, transport and communication. Whatever you may think of the plausibility of his sketch, you cannot accuse it of technological narrowness. He paid no attention to the institutional hurdles that face the transition from today's world to the world he envisioned. Westing estimated the independent constraints of total land area, cultivated land area, forest land area, cereals and wood.

From a formal point of view, constraints from multiple independent resources are easily combined. For example, if

$$\text{population that can be fed} = \frac{\text{food supply}}{\text{individual food requirement}}$$

and

$$\text{population that can be watered} = \frac{\text{water supply}}{\text{individual water requirement}},$$

and if both constraints must be satisfied *independently,* then

$$\begin{matrix}\text{population that can be fed} \\ \text{and watered}\end{matrix} = \text{minimum of} \left(\frac{\text{food supply}}{\begin{matrix}\text{individual food} \\ \text{requirement}\end{matrix}}, \frac{\text{water supply}}{\begin{matrix}\text{individual water} \\ \text{requirement}\end{matrix}} \right).$$

The same approach extends to three or any number of independent constraints. This approach neglects the possibility of interactions among the constraints. For example, in reality but not in this formula, changes in the water supply, through irrigation, do affect the food supply.

System Models

Interactions among resources argue for the use of system models. If the interactions among potential constraints were well enough understood to be modeled reliably, system models would be attractive for conditional estimates of how many people the Earth can support in various modes of life.

Unfortunately, system models of the Earth are not yet so attractive. For example, in the World3/91 model of population, capital, food, nonrenewable resources and pollution, Meadows et al. reported in 1992 that a population of 7.7 billion people could be supported until the year 2100 if people bought only U.S.$350 of consumer goods per year. However, when Brian Hayes, a former editor of *American Scientist,* computed the same scenario for an additional three centuries beyond 2100, using the software provided by Meadows et al., he found that life expectancy, industrial output and population size all fell dramatically before 2300.[9] Meadows et al. neglected to mention that, according to their model, the population of 7.7 billion was not supportable for more than a century or two at most. Of course, because World3/91 embodied relationships and assumptions that were neither mechanistically derived nor quantitatively tested, neither the sustainability of 7.7 billion nor the collapse can be interpreted seriously as claims about the real world.

LOCAL ESTIMATES OF HUMAN CARRYING CAPACITY

The demand for estimates of the human carrying capacity of national and local regions is growing. For example, delegates to the United Nations Conference on Environment and Development in Rio de Janeiro adopted Agenda 21 in June 1992 as their statement of plans for the next century. In paragraph 5.23 of that lengthy document, the delegates recommended "assessment . . . of national population carrying capacity in the context of satisfaction of human needs and sustainable development, and special attention should be given to critical resources, such as water and land, and environmental factors, such as ecosystem health and biodiversity."[10]

To give an idea of what this recommendation involves and of the small likelihood that it can be satisfied in a useful way, I now sketch estimates of the national carrying capacity of the United States, China and Australia, and anthropological estimates of carrying capacity for shifting cultivators and Amazonian colonists.

The one important conceptual innovation among these estimates is due to Philip M. Fearnside, a research professor in the Department of Ecology at the National Institute for Research in the Amazon, Manaus, Amazonas, Brazil, and also a research associate of the Chicago Academy of Sciences. He was the first to recognize that the carrying capacity for colonists in the Brazilian rainforest depends on an individual's (or a family's) *probability* of survival or failure. Deterministic models of average resource availability say little about this probability.

The United States

In the mid-nineteenth century, President Abraham Lincoln compared the United States to Europe and inferred that the United States had a "capacity to contain 217,186,000" people.[11]

In 1909, Albert P. Brigham began an article on the "Capacity of the United States for population" with a skeptical review of the prophecies of others.

> . . . is a great population [in the United States] probable? Our list of prophets is distinguished. Mr. O. P. Austin thinks there is no good reason for our failing of three hundred million people in the year 2000. Mr. James J. Hill expects an increase to two hundred million in less than fifty years, and Mr. Andrew Carnegie a few years ago thought five hundred million a proper figure. Mr. Justin Winsor allows two hundred million for the Mississippi Valley. Mr. F. A. Ogg raises the figure by fifty million, and Professor A. B. Hart does not hesitate to go up to three hundred and fifty million. We are by no means disposed to dispute all of these figures, but there are considerations which point in the other direction, as for example that the percentage of increase went down in the decades between 1860 and 1900.[12]

Brigham recognized that it was important to specify a standard of living and to identify the factors that could impede meeting that standard. "[I]t is not of interest to know how many Chinese could exist on American soil, but how many occidental citizens could live here in comfort and progress. The largest single element in our problem must always be food." However:

> Population capacity would afford a less baffling inquiry if food alone were needed. . . . we must at once include clothing, of vegetable fibers, animal fibers, furs and skins, nearly all requiring land for their production. Man must have shelter and a long catalogue of objects of domestic utility, for the household and for the tillage of the soil. These things may become chiefly derivable from subterranean sources with the single exception of a minimum demand on the forest. . . . it seems certain that we could not for many generations supply iron for as many millions as we can feed. It may be doubtful whether our ultimate expansion will receive its first effective check above or below the surface of the earth.
>
> We must include also a wide range of objects of public utility, such as roads and all appliances of transportation and manufacture, and public structures for education, worship, government, health and charity, adding instruments of knowledge and pleasure such as books, music, ornaments and all works of art.
>
> Almost as fundamental as food is the requirement of power. Here, however, the supply seems ample and perma[n]ent. Long before the stores of buried fuel are exhausted, other natural forces, particularly that of moving water, will meet the needs of any population which we can feed. The maximum of population therefore for the whole world hinges upon the supply of material substances derived from the atmosphere, the water, the soil and the rocks.
>
> For a given country the problem is complicated by exchange. The exchange values, however, must be won on the home ground. England has, for example, a far greater population than she can feed, but her coal and iron have enabled her to manufacture and to carry for other nations.[13]

At the end of a long analysis, largely based on the population densities of comparable regions, Brigham ventured to guess that the United States could support 305 million people, but attached little confidence to his guess.

Estimates continued to be made before and after World War II. In an influential 1923 book (which looks racist in retrospect), *Mankind at the Crossroads,* Edward M. East, a botanist at Harvard University, estimated an upper limit of 331 million people.

In 1954, while a member of the staff of the Institute for Nuclear Studies at the University of Chicago, Harrison Brown observed that the high intake of calories and animal protein per person in North America resulted more from low population density than from high crop yields, while the then "low levels of nutrition in Asia result far more from high population densities than from low crop yields. If North Americans obtained the caloric yield per acre characteristic of Eastern Asia, a population of 350 million persons could be supported at our present nutritional standards, or 670 million persons could be fed at standards now characteristic of Western Europe [where the consumption of food still suffered from postwar shortages]. If we lowered our per capita caloric intake to that characteristic of Asia, the North American continent, with maximum calorie yields per acre, might well support a population of 1,300,000,000 persons without increasing the acreage of our crop lands."[14]

While most earlier estimates emphasized that the United States had the capacity to support much further population growth, several recent estimates argued that, because of its reliance on fossil fuels, the United States has already surpassed the level of population that it can sustain for an unspecified period at present levels of affluence. For example, in 1991, the Cornell ecologists David and Marcia Pimentel estimated that the current population of the United States far exceeded the numbers that could be supported by solar energy, directly or indirectly, at present levels of consumption:

> With a self-sustaining solar energy system replacing our current dependence on fossil energy, the energy availability would be one-fifth to one-half the current level. Then if the U.S. population remained at its present level of 246 million, a significant reduction in our current standard of living would follow, . . . even if all the energy conservation measures known today were adopted. If, however, the U.S. population wishes to continue its current high level of energy use and standard of living and prosperity, then its ideal population should be targeted at 40–100 million people [which was the U.S. population between the Civil War and World War I]. . . . On the positive side, however, we do have sufficient fossil energy, especially coal, to help us make the needed transition in energy resources and population numbers over the next century, if we can manage the environmental impacts.[15]

In 1994, the Pimentels and colleagues Rebecca Harman, Matthew Pacenza and Jason Pecarsky at Cornell University estimated that a future United States energy supply could be based on available technologies for capturing solar energy on about 900,000 square kilometers of land, without reducing agricultural and forest production. This is the area of a square roughly 950 kilometers or 600 miles on a side. Their idealized calculations assumed that some 200 million Americans (rather than the present 250 million or so) would use half as much energy as they do now and only 5,000 liters of oil equivalents per year, would conserve soil and water, reduce air pollution and recycle resources efficiently.[16]

According to journalist Monique Miller in 1992, Dr. Robert Constanza of the University of Maryland estimated that the United States' ideal population, living at half of current levels of consumption and based on renewable resources, would be 170 million people. She concluded, "Whether such estimates are accurate or not, it is obvious that U.S. population growth is not sustainable."[17] This conclusion is not universally shared.

China

Jian Song and Jingyuan Yu, two politically influential professors in Beijing, reviewed studies of Chinese carrying capacity conducted since the 1950s. They concluded that "the long term strategic goal of China's population policy should be the control of the population at a figure below one billion, or ideally, below 700 million."[18] The political history of these estimates would make a fascinating case study in the relations between scholarship and power, but that is another story.[19]

Australia

Australian political leaders have traditionally seen Australia's "population problem" as insufficient numbers of people to occupy, exploit and defend the country.[20] For some years in the 1880s, Australia's population growth rate from immigration and the excess of domestic births over deaths exceeded 3 percent per year—a rate of growth comparable to that of some of the fastest-growing sub-Saharan African nations today. Australian politicians viewed with alarm the collapse of immigration in 1891 and the fall in domestic fertility, which coincided roughly with the fertility decline that spread through England between 1880 and World War I. The Australian states adopted various measures to encourage local fertility, such as limitations on abortions and restrictions on the advertising, sale and distribution of contraceptives. These measures had no apparent effect on demographic indicators of fertility, which continued to fall through the Great Depression of the 1930s. Following World War II, politicians reemphasized Australia's vulnerability to invasion. The government's population policy aimed for a population growth rate of 2 percent per year, 1 percent from natural increase and 1 percent from immigration.

By the 1970s, public and political opinion voiced reservations about continued rapid population growth in Australia. Some argued that immigration brought workers without wanted skills, exacerbated problems of unemployment, created ethnic pockets of poor social and educational conditions and worsened the life of cities. The Zero Population Growth movement in other countries had its Australian partisans, who argued that

TABLE 11.1   Estimates of how many people Australia can support (in chronological order)

millions of people, author and year	methods and limiting factors considered
50 R. G. Thomas 1921	Food limitation.
20–65 Griffith Taylor 1922, 1937	Based on temperature, rainfall, elevation and coal reserves, he estimated an index of habitability for Australia and other regions of the world. When Taylor estimated the maximum population of Australia from the living standards of western Europe, he obtained an upper limit of 65 million people. When he later used the living standards of the United States, he obtained an upper limit of 20 million.
less than 40 Edward M. East 1924	Food limitation
480 Albrecht Penck 1924, 1925	Penck assumed that the vegetation in a region prior to human settlement indicated its natural fertility. He estimated Australia's maximum population from the maximum density of other regions with comparable primary vegetation, assuming people would live at a subsistence level.
20–40 C. H. Wickens 1925[a]	(p. 10) "With our present rate of growth Australia's population would reach 10 millions by the end of 1951 [it was actually 8.2 million in 1950], 20 millions by the end of 1986 [it was actually 16.9 million in 1990], 40 millions by the end of 2021, and 80 millions by the end of 2056, or 131 years from the present time; that is, it would double itself every 35 years. . . . I think it unlikely that this rate will be extended indefinitely into the future, and while it is probable that the 10 million mark will be reached at about the middle of the century, and the 20 million mark some time in the last quarter of the century, the attainment of the other positions is much more doubtful."
15–20 Ellsworth Huntington 1925	Previously Taylor had distinguished six regions of Australia according to the abundance of rainfall. Huntington estimated the maximum population each of these six regions could support from the population densities of the regions of the United States that received comparable rainfalls.
10–15 F. C. Benham 1928	Estimated optimum population using economic theory.
30 Henry Barkley 1928	Barkley followed Huntington's method with improved data on Australian rainfall. His standard of reference was the area west of the Mississippi River according to the 1920 census of the United States.
12.6 M. H. Belz 1929	Belz fitted a logistic curve with an asymptote of 12.6 million. The population was supposed to pass 12 million in A.D. 2000.
40–50 H. A. Mullett and S. Wadham 1933	Food limitation.
20–25 H. C. Trumble 1937, 1946	Food limitation, based on climate and soil. Trumble carried out experiments in South Australia to measure potential production.

TABLE 11.1   *continued*

millions of people, author and year	methods and limiting factors considered
70 Commonwealth Scientific and Industrial Research Organization 1973	Food limitation, but water limits agriculture. "More than 60 per cent of current rural production is exported. Were it consumed entirely within Australia, it would probably support a population of 30–35 million people. Assuming therefore that the area under crops could be doubled, Australia could potentially support 70 million people in terms of food production based on current technology. However, constraints from water supplies are likely to impose limits well below this, and it seems probable that a substantial proportion of our rural production must continue to be exported. . . . food supplies are unlikely to be a prime determinant of the ultimate Australian population or the rate of population growth" (pp. 10–11).
37 Aston et al. 1973	Water limitation. As of 1973, Australia supported 13 million people on approximately one acre-foot of water per person per year. The known reserves of about 24 million acre-feet per year could sustain another 24 million people, for a total of 37 million.
280 J. W. Holmes 1973	Water limitation. Water used for industrial, urban and rural domestic purposes averaged about 0.7 percent of the total run-off from the Australian continent. From a map of water and population potential, *and with no other limiting factor,* Holmes estimated that Australia could support 280 million people. This estimate makes no allowance for changes in the proportion of groundwater used, water recycling and reuse, desalination or other technological change.

^aI checked the original source.
SOURCE: Australian Government (1975, pp. 180–91, 715–21), where citations to original sources are given

Australians should practice what they preached for others. Some added that Australia's survival depended on the cessation of population growth among its Asian neighbors.

In 1975, a major government inquiry into Australia's population history and future policies reviewed scholarly estimates of Australia's human carrying capacity (Table 11.1). The methods used reflect those used elsewhere to estimate the Earth's human carrying capacity, with some additional sophistication. For example, as we have seen, in 1925 Penck asserted that trade could not increase the world's carrying capacity (ignoring what Ricardo had demonstrated a century earlier). In the same year, the Australian Commonwealth Statistician C. H. Wickens wrote:

> Apart from inquiries as to the possible maximum for the world, that for Australia is of great interest but is probably a more difficult subject for prophecy than the world's total. The possible population of the world depends on the supplies of the necessaries of life furnished by the whole globe; but that of a portion of the

earth's surface is clearly not limited to the supply of necessaries provided by that portion, as is indicated by the case of our great cities.[21]

Like estimates of the Earth's human carrying capacity, those for Australia ranged widely, from 10 million to 480 million. Prior to World War II, the economists, geographers and agricultural scientists who estimated Australia's human carrying capacity emphasized soil fertility, rainfall and river systems, even though most people already lived in cities and worked in industry, manufacturing and the services.[22]

Political and academic debate over Australia's human carrying capacity continued in 1994. An inquiry into Australia's human carrying capacity led by former science minister Barry Jones received conflicting submissions from senior academics about the necessity and urgency of setting limits on Australia's population size and growth.[23] According to a newspaper report, two academics told the committee that Australia should have between 12 million and 18 million people, the exact level to be determined by a political debate. "The present population of nearly 18 million is already large enough to support almost all social goals and too large to support others," they argued. A submission by two other academics opposed setting population targets because, they asserted, the government has no policy tools that could be effective in achieving those targets; they recommended instead that the government create contingency plans to cope with various possible scenarios of population size and distribution.

The Maximum Supportable Population under Shifting Cultivation

Anthropologists have estimated local carrying capacities by various formulas at least since 1949, when W. Allan studied the land use of shifting cultivators in Northern Rhodesia (now Zambia).[24] An estimated 200 million people still practice slash–and–burn agriculture.[25] Rather than review examples of population estimates, I will present a formula proposed by Robert L. Carneiro, an anthropologist at the American Museum of Natural History, in 1956 and published in 1960.[26] Most of the formulas used are minor variations of this one.

Shifting cultivation and slash–and–burn agriculture leave land fallow for extended intervals between periods of active cultivation. Hence not all of the available arable land can be used at any one time to provide food. For example, if a garden plot can be farmed for three years and must be allowed to lie fallow for 15 years to regenerate its initial fertility, then a community must have six times as much arable land as it cultivates at any one time, because $6 = (3 + 15)/3$. The ratio 6 in this example is called "the cultivation factor"; it expresses the multiple of actively cultivated land that is required as available arable land (including the cultivated land) to permit a sustainable cycle of cultivation and fallowing. The cultivation factor C is calculated by the formula

$$C = \frac{\text{cultivation period + fallow period}}{\text{cultivation period}}.$$

If A represents the area of actively cultivated land that grows the amount of cultivated food that an average individual consumes, then the population P that "can be supported permanently in one locale" is

$$P = \frac{\text{total area of arable land within walking distance of the village}}{A \times C}.$$

This is Penck's formula applied to cultivated land, with the cultivation factor C inserted to adjust for fallowing.

Practical use of this formula raises several problems. The amount of food that can be raised from a given area depends on the farmer's ability to work. That ability depends in turn on the adequacy of the available diet (not only what is raised but also what is hunted and gathered and fished), the difficulty of the terrain, climatic conditions (extremes of heat, cold or rain, for example) and disease. These factors may cause the requirement of cultivated land A to change even though they are not explicitly expressed in the formula.

The formula also assumes no change in farming technology; no change in the crops grown; and no changes in weeds, pests and crop diseases. The cultivation factor is usually estimated from current practice without checking whether current practice allows enough fallow time for land to recover its fertility. If the land is already under pressure and fallow time has been shortened, then the cultivation factor will be too low and the estimated maximum sustainable population will be too high.

The Maximum Population
with an Acceptable Probability of Colonist Failure

In analyzing concepts of carrying capacity, Fearnside observed that some estimates are instantaneous, while others refer to an indefinite period, or long-term sustainability.

> The definitions can be further broken down according to whether they are static or dynamic; deterministic or stochastic; based on a single limiting factor, several possible limiting factors, or a combined measure representing the contributions of several factors. In static systems the values of all variables are constant through time, while dynamic estimates allow for changes with time. Deterministic estimates are based on fixed values for all parameters, while stochastic estimates include random variation in at least some of the parameters (with the result that the probability of an outcome is less than one). Since the real world is characterized by both changes with time and variability, dynamic stochastic estimates should lead to the most realistic estimates of carrying capacity.[27]

In Brazil's Amazonian rainforest, some colonists fail, abandon their deforested plots and depart. Other colonists succeed in establishing home-

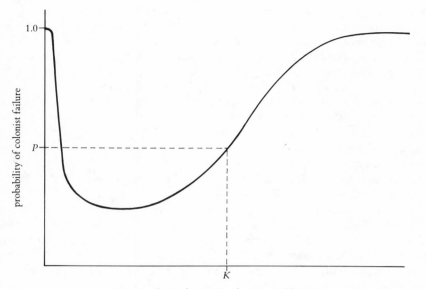

population density *(people per square kilometer)*

FIGURE 11.5   A hypothetical graph of the probability of colonist failure as a function of human population density. Philip M. Fearnside defined carrying capacity as the maximum population density (marked by K on the horizontal axis) for which the failure probability lies below a socially defined maximum acceptable level (marked by P on the vertical axis). SOURCE: Fearnside (1986, p. 80)

steads and farms. To develop a dynamic stochastic estimate of the rainforest's carrying capacity for colonists, Fearnside supposed that for each possible human population density (number of people per square kilometer), it is possible to measure or to estimate a probability of failure per year.

> Failure rates are those sustainable over some long time period at the corresponding human population densities. The criteria for failure can be defined in a variety of ways and can include multiple limiting factors or combinations of factors. They can include measures of environmental degradation as well as individual consumption. Focusing on individual consumption levels contrasts with the area-wide average consumption criteria implied by most definitions.[28]

Fearnside further supposed that a graph of the failure probability as a function of the possible population density would be U-shaped but asymmetrical (Figure 11.5). When colonists first settled a territory, the probability of failure would decline rapidly with increasing long-term population density, as increased capacity for mutual aid and specialization improved survival probabilities. At increased population densities, Fearnside assumed, the failure probability would fall to a minimum and then begin to rise as the average plot sizes available to each colonist diminished.

Fearnside assumed that low probabilities of failure would be socially acceptable but that there was some socially defined ceiling on acceptable failure probabilities. He defined the carrying capacity as the maximum population density (marked by K on the horizontal axis of Figure 11.5) for which the failure probability lies below a socially defined maximum acceptable level (marked by P on the vertical axis). If high levels of risk caused the curve of failure probabilities to lie above the maximum acceptable level P at every population density, Fearnside defined the carrying capacity as the maximum population density at which the failure probability was minimal.

To make practical use of Fearnside's concept of carrying capacity, it is necessary to estimate the curve of failure probability as a function of population density. The curve could be estimated empirically by observing many colonists who lived at different population densities, recording annual failure probabilities and smoothing the data to estimate failure probabilities at all population densities.

Fearnside estimated the failure curve by means of an elaborate computer simulation of the agricultural ecosystem of a population of colonists settled along a stretch of the Transamazon Highway. His labyrinthine computer program[29] should not be accepted any less critically than the system models of Forrester and Meadows et al. But there are notable differences between Fearnside's model and theirs. Fearnside based his model in part on his own field study of the area simulated, and he documented extensively the empirical support for the components of his model.

The model allowed for 20 possible combinations of crops (including upland rice, maize, *Phaseolus* beans, *Vigna* cowpeas, bitter manioc, sweet manioc, cacao, black pepper) and four noncropped uses of the land. The failure probability was the fraction of colonist-years in which minimal standards of consumption were not met.[30] The model computed the probability of failure separately on the basis of five potentially limiting factors—calories, total protein, animal protein, cash per family and the proportion of land cleared—and on the basis of a combination of these factors.

In computing failure probabilities, the model allowed for two forms of technological change: improved crop yields, and changing use of the land, "for example, a switch from annual crops to ranching or perennial crop strategies based on turnover in the colonist population."[31] The model could simulate a population with a fixed average family size or a population that changed according to demographic processes. When run with a fixed family size, different lot sizes could be taken to generate different population densities, and the failure probability could be computed under each assumed set of conditions.

The results were both illuminating and unexpected. What was illuminating? A sample simulation of 25 years' duration fixed the population density at 24 people per square kilometer (four 25-hectare lots per square kilometer with one family of six persons on each lot). In this simulation, the average (over all colonists) of the food energy grown changed from year to year around a middle value of roughly 3,500 kilocalories per person per day and never fell below 2,900 kilocalories per person per day. Yet, in the same simulation, the fraction of lots that provided less than the minimum standard of 2,550 kilocalories per person per day (in other words, the fraction of colonist failures per year as determined by food energy) ranged as high as 70 percent in two years and as low as 20 percent in seven years, and never fell below 20 percent. The illuminating observation was that, though average food-energy supplies were comfortably above the minimum standard, a variable but always substantial fraction of colonists fell below the standard. This observation is consistent with completely independent observations[32] on Hungarian development from 1880 to 1910: the average of some index of well-being may reflect poorly the experience of most, or a large fraction, of the population.

The shape of the simulated curve of failure probability as a function of colonist population density was, unexpectedly, not an asymmetrical U-shape (as was expected from Figure 11.5). For the five population densities simulated (24, 38, 50, 60 and 120 colonists per square kilometer), failure probabilities (based on calories, total protein, animal protein and cash per person, each considered separately) rose and fell irregularly, rather than rising smoothly with increasing density.[33] Contrary to expectation, these simulated curves suggest that the major source of variation in the probability of colonist failure is something other than population density, over the range of densities simulated. Whether the discrepancy between the simulated and the expected curves of failure probability is due to a mistaken expectation about the form of the curve or unrealistic features of the simulation model is impossible to say now.

Fearnside found that his simulated probabilities of failure exceeded the probabilities of failure envisioned in official standards for classifying land, and concluded that tropical regions like his study area could yield enough annual crops to support very few agriculturalists.[34]

Variability

Variability affects more than the Amazon. It affects local, national and global human carrying capacities, however they may be defined.

On the local level, environmental variability buffets tropical agriculture, through weather, malarial epidemics, accidents, crop diseases and pests and other hazards. A large buffer of land must be planted each year in case yields are lower than desired. This reserve lowers the carrying capacity of a given area of land.[35] Similarly, for the aborigines around the early Spanish missions in Baja California, who made little effort to store food, the carrying capacity was determined by the poorest season of several years, not by the average food supply. When food was scarce, survival could depend on a food that was available only in small quantity and usually ignored.[36]

The carrying capacity of a local population is also vulnerable to distant economic fluctuations if the population depends on trade for part of its sustenance. When farmers in northeastern Brazil switched to growing sisal for cash, they could no longer buy the same quality of diet that subsistence agriculture had formerly provided. Variations in the market price of a cash crop can cause colonist failure.[37]

Variability affects the carrying capacity of modern national populations.

The dry continent of Australia, for example, has one of the most erratic rainfalls in the world. Because of variable rains in the Murray-Darling Basin, which holds Australia's largest river system and which covers one-sixth of the mainland, flows in the Murray River vary widely. Most Australian irrigation by surface water depends on the Murray.[38] An official 1975 report on Australia's population asked: ". . . is . . . water . . . the Achilles heel of Australia?"[39]

Variability may affect the whole Earth's human population. A single volcanic eruption, such as that of Mt. Pinatubo in the Philippines, can inject enough material into the atmosphere to cool weather over a wide region for a time. The El Niño Southern Oscillation in the Pacific Ocean can affect coastal fish catches, rainfall and crop yields on multiple and distant continents. Genetic variability can give rise to mutant forms of influenza and other viruses that lead to unpredictable diseases. Variability in international financial and political arrangements can affect the carrying capacity of major regions or the globe. The risk-free, deterministic, static notions that underlie the estimates of carrying capacity (apart from Fearnside's) seem out of touch with reality.

VERBAL DEFINITIONS OF HUMAN CARRYING CAPACITY

A verbal definition of a scientific concept may be viewed as a target at which the operational definitions of the concept, such as methods of measurement and calculation, should aim. Appendix 4 gives 26 verbal definitions of human carrying capacity published since 1975. The definitions vary very widely and occasionally contradict one another. Human carrying capacity is a collection of concepts with no single generally accepted meaning.

Almost all of the definitions recognized that ecological concepts of carrying capacity must be extended to allow for the role of technology in enhancing nature's productivity. Most recognized that culturally and individually variable standards of living, including standards of environmental quality, set limits on population size well before the physical requirements for sheer subsistence.

Definitions varied widely in addressing the issue of the time horizon. If a definition refers to a number of people that can be sustained into the indefinite future,[40] it signals that this definition is not being used in practice, because the indefinite future cannot be measured now; it is simply unknowable. One definition recognized that any technology that uses nonrenewable resources necessarily has a finite lifetime, but viewed the difficulty of estimating that lifetime as insurmountable.[41] Many definitions were vague or silent about the assumed time horizon.

Another recurrent issue is whether human carrying capacity is necessarily a global concept or could be useful locally or regionally. One definition gave conditions under which an isolated locality or country has a carrying capacity[42]; another emphasized that trade and requirements of inputs from outside any region render carrying capacity inapplicable on any scale less than the globe.[43]

Some definitions rejected altogether the notion that the Earth has a finite human carrying capacity.[44] Human ingenuity can push back natural constraints without limit, they claimed. More moderate definitions recognized the major role of human choices, now and in the future, in defining human carrying capacity.[45]

Additional factors mentioned as factors to consider in human carrying capacity include congestion of infrastructure; institutions to extend new technology to farmers; productivity growth; possibilities of emigration for unemployed workers; seasonal and random changes in the environment; egalitarianism; social discipline; energy supplies; the speed of adaptation to shortages; cultural amenities; political institutions; educational resources; systems of land tenure; systems of contracts and incentives; physical and financial capital; management skills and traditions; ecosystem services; public policies; individual freedom; and the ability to mobilize to deal with major threats such as local crop failures, natural disasters and epidemics.

CONCLUSIONS

The "human carrying capacity of the world" is not a unitary concept on which there is universal agreement. Factors quite different from the obvious physical ones of land, photosynthesis and energy influence human carrying capacity. Notwithstanding their cloak of quantification, many of the published estimates of human carrying capacity are probably less dispassionate analyses than they are political instruments, intended to influence actions one way or another.

The nutritionist Sir Kenneth Blaxter concluded that, while

the carrying capacity of the world cannot be expressed with any certainty . . . , what is certain is that there are limits. Limits are set by the land area which determines the earth's interception of photosynthetically active radiation, by the efficiency of photosynthesis and by the support energy required to ensure that the biological systems on which we depend work at high efficiency. . . . There must be a limit to the human population when numbers reach the carrying capacity of the land. This general statement is in complete accord with Malthus' view.[46]

The equally distinguished nutritionist and former president of Tufts University, Jean Mayer, argued in 1964 that food and population might be "the wrong problem":

. . . how dangerous it may turn out to be for the population problem to have been linked so closely to food as a number of writers have done. . . . they have turned to the threat of a worldwide shortage of food as an easily understood, imperative reason for large scale limitation of births. Had they consulted nutritionists, agriculturists, and chemists, they might have chosen a more appropriate battle ground. For if we can feed an ever-increasing number of people—even if we feed them as badly as many of our contemporaries are fed—their argument fails. And yet there is a need for the establishment as soon as possible of a sound population policy for the world at large.

Our [American] population is increasing faster than it ever has; our major nutrition problem is overweight, our major agricultural problem is our ever-mounting excess production. Does anyone seriously believe this means that we have no population problem? Our housing problems, our traffic problem, the insufficiency of the number of our hospitals, of community recreation facilities, our pollution problems are all facets of our population problem.[47]

Having examined how different authors estimate and define what Blaxter calls "the carrying capacity of the world" brings to light some important assumptions behind Blaxter's comment. First, while Blaxter refers to "the carrying capacity of the world" as if it were a unitary concept, the diversity of approaches to measuring and defining it shows that not everybody is talking about the same thing when speaking of "the carrying capacity of the world."

Second, while I agree with Blaxter's categorical assertion that "what is certain is that there are limits," it is not so obvious that the operative limits are set by the factors Blaxter mentions. Long before land, photosynthetic efficiency and the energy required to support agriculture intervene to limit population, limits may be set by couples' desires for prosperity and freedom for themselves and their children, by infectious diseases, by the instability of social institutions or by a host of other factors including deliberate human choices.[48] What Blaxter called "the carrying capacity of the land" may or may not set the human carrying capacity of the Earth.

Third, if Blaxter meant to say that human population size cannot go *beyond* the biophysical limitations set by land and light, I would add that even those limits are very flexible and are not independent of human culture. For concreteness, consider why Harrison Brown estimated a supportable population of 50 billion in 1954,[49] and only three years later the same Brown, together with James Bonner and John Weir, estimated a supportable population of 7.7 billion.[50]

In 1954, Brown estimated that 100 million acres (40.5 million hectares, a bit more than the size of Paraguay and a bit less than the size of Sweden) of algae farms could produce twice as much as the entire existing food production; and a billion acres (405 million hectares, less than a third of the land area being cultivated in 1989) of algae farms could produce 25 times as much food as was then being produced.[51] Brown remarked: ". . . if food habits were to change sufficiently so that the people of the world were content to derive their main nourishment from the products of algae farms and yeast factories, a world population of 50 billion persons could eventually be supported comfortably from the point of view of nutritional requirements."[52]

Three years later, algae farming disappeared entirely from a chapter on world food production by Harrison Brown, James Bonner and John Weir. The estimates of the Earth's supportable population were derived entirely from conventional agriculture. The following chapter, on "New knowledge and new food," devoted two paragraphs to algae farming. The first described the technologies, and the second described the obstacles: preparing land for algal culture costs 10 to 100 times more than preparing it for conventional agriculture.

> And when the algae have been finally grown and harvested, we have merely a nasty little green vegetable, the consumption of which presents the same sorts of technological and psychological problems as are associated with the utilization of, for example, alfalfa as food for man. It seems logical to conclude that expansion of our food supplies by the more familiar agricultural techniques will precede expansion of our food supplies by the cultivation of algae.[53]

I suspect that Brown et al., confronting "merely a nasty little green vegetable," felt like the last hunters at the dawn of the local agricultural evolution; unable to find game, the hunters glumly faced the prospect of surviving on pulverized grass seeds, today's staff of life.

I once read or heard, but cannot now trace, this story, alleged to be true. When African slaves first arrived in Haiti, they were adequately nourished because they brought with them the African practice of consuming rodents, a plentiful source of animal protein. As the rats ate food the slaves would not, the practice of eating rats amplified the available food supply in addition to diversifying it. Once the slaves learned from the French colonists to disdain the eating of rats and mice in favor of French white bread, the nutritional state of the slaves fell rapidly.

The French anthropologist Claude Lévi-Strauss once commented that foods must be "good to think" before they can be "good to eat." Starting from this remark, anthropologist Sidney W. Mintz of Johns Hopkins captured the key role of culture in defining what constitutes a resource:

> The emphasis on the social and symbolic nature of human acts, including food-consuming behavior, the idea that socially learned behavior (culture) always determines the relationship between bodily needs and their satisfaction, is probably the single most important assertion anthropology has to offer on this subject. Biology may eventually tell us everything that we need to know about what we need to eat. However, it tells us little about why we eat what we eat, and next to nothing about how to change food habits.[54]

The Silence of Demography

Not one of the 95 symposia at the 1992 annual meeting of the Population Association of America dealt with estimates of regional or global human carrying capacity. At the 1993 annual meeting of the Association, three of roughly 120 sessions dealt with population and environment, but again none dealt directly with the estimation or meaning of human carrying capacity for any region of the Earth. It is strange. Demographers fear to tread where ecologists rush in. Many estimates of global and local human carrying capacity have been published in recent decades by scholars or academic politicians trained in ecology, economics, sociology, geography, soil science and agronomy, among other subjects.

Why have recent demographers eschewed questions of human carrying capacity? One can only speculate. A distinguished demographer suggested to me that demographers shy away because the interactions involved are very complex. The criteria employed so far are very subjective and past efforts look very silly (to that demographer). Another suggested that questions of human carrying capacity have been unanswerable but could eventually become answerable with improvements in the natural and social sciences.

I speculate that the present theoretical framework of demography focuses attention on the composition and growth of populations and diverts attention from their absolute size, much as the theoretical framework of economics focuses attention on problems of allocation and distribution and away from problems of the scale of an economy. If this speculation is even partially correct, then an enlightening theory of demographic and economic scale could be helpful.

12

Carrying Capacity in Ecology and Applied Ecology

> The results of human reproduction are no longer solely the concern of the two individuals involved, or of the larger family, or even of the nation of which they are citizens. A stage has been reached in the demographic development of the world when the rate of human reproduction in any part of the globe may directly or indirectly affect the health and welfare of the rest of the human race. It is in this sense that there is a world population problem.
>
> —HAROLD F. DORN 1962[1]

PEOPLE HAVE DEFINED and measured the Earth's maximum human population in many different ways, as we have seen. Many of the definitions refer to the ecological notion of the carrying capacity of a nonhuman population as if the latter were a simple concept. Before trying to make sense of human carrying capacity, it is essential to understand that ecology as a *basic* science uses at least four different concepts of carrying capacity. The specialties of *applied* ecology (such as range management, wildlife management, fisheries management, forest management and agriculture) require at least five additional concepts of carrying capacity. On examination, none of the existing concepts of carrying capacity in basic or applied ecology turns out to be adequate for the human population.

CONCEPTS OF CARRYING CAPACITY IN BASIC ECOLOGY

The key distinction between the basic ecology and the applied ecology of nonhuman populations is that basic ecology aims at description, understanding and ultimately prediction without immediate reference to satisfying human wants.

The Parameter K in the Logistic Equation

Introductory courses in ecology often introduce the concept of carrying capacity as the parameter K of the logistic equation.[2] Here is a definition of K from a widely used textbook of ecology: "Number of individuals in a population that the resources of a habitat can support; the asymptote, or plateau, of the logistic and other sigmoid equations for population growth."[3] Other versions of this concept of carrying capacity have slight differences in wording (Table 12.1). This definition carries with it all the assumptions and limitations of the logistic equation, which I described in Chapter 5.

The Population Size at Which the Birth Rate Equals the Death Rate

In some biological populations, the birth rate and the death rate are "density dependent." Density dependence means that, as the population size (or population density per unit of area or per unit of volume) increases, the birth rate changes or the death rate changes or both.[4] If a population is growing when it is first observed, and if it has neither immigration nor emigration, then the birth rate must exceed the death rate—otherwise, the population would not be growing. As the population grows, density dependence often appears as a decreasing birth rate or as an increasing death rate or as both. In such a case, there may come a population size at which the declining birth rate just equals the increasing death rate. If that population size is reached, some ecologists[5] define it as the carrying capacity (Table 12.1). This concept is more general than defining the carrying capacity as K in the logistic curve because this one does not assume that a logistic equation describes the curve of population growth.

The Average Population Size When the Population Neither Grows Nor Declines

The size of a population of breeding birds may be remarkably steady from year to year, perhaps because the number of nesting sites or the supply of appropriate food is steady from year to year. In other cases, a population size may fluctuate substantially from year to year (for example, because of epidemics or fluctuations in predator populations) but the running average of the last three or five years may display neither an increasing nor a decreasing trend. In both situations, some ecologists[6] define the average size of a population that is neither increasing nor decreasing as the carrying capacity for that population (Table 12.1).

This concept is more general than defining carrying capacity as the population size where birth and death rates are equal because this one does not assume a closed population. The average population size could be steady

TABLE 12.1   Definitions of carrying capacity in ecology

source	definition
Odum (1971, p. 183)	"Populations have characteristic patterns of increase which are called population growth forms. . . . In the sigmoid form, . . . represented by the simple logistic model . . . [t]he upper level, beyond which no major increase can occur, as represented by the constant K, is the *upper asymptote* of the sigmoid curve and has been aptly called the *carrying capacity*."
Wilson and Bossert (1971, p. 18)	In the logistic equation: "The carrying capacity K is therefore not only the upper bound of the growing population size, it is an equilibrium population size that will be approached in time from any initial population size."
Moen (1973, p. 333)	". . . to determine the number of animals that can be supported on a given area of land[, b]oth the supply of resources on the range and the requirements of the animals must be known. . . . The numerical determination of carrying capacity is very complex since biological organisms, including both the animals and plants on the range, are . . . changing continually."
Gever et al. (1986, p. 4)	"Populations of some plant and animal species seem to oscillate about a certain level that ecologists term the *carrying capacity*. Carrying capacity is defined as the number of individuals of a given species that a given area can support indefinitely. This sustainable population size is set by the amount of resources available and the rate at which individuals use them. . . . Since individual needs change very slowly, the carrying capacity for a plant or animal population can be estimated straightforwardly from the total supply of resources and per capita needs."

Begon et al. (1990, pp. 203–5, 847)	". . . as density increases, the per capita birth rate eventually falls and the per capita death rate eventually rises. There must, therefore, be a density at which these curves cross. . . . At the cross-over density itself, the two rates are equal and there is no net change in population size. . . . This density is known as the *carrying capacity* of the population and is usually denoted by K. . . . It is called a carrying capacity because it represents the population size which the resources of the environment can just maintain ('carry') without a tendency to either increase or decrease.
	    "However, while hypothetical populations . . . can be characterized by a simple carrying capacity, this is not true of any natural population. There are unpredictable environmental fluctuations; individuals are affected by a whole wealth of factors of which intraspecific competition is only one; and resources not only affect density but respond to density as well. . . .
	    "Indeed, the concept of a stable density settling at the carrying capacity, even in caricatured populations, is relevant only to situations in which density-dependence is not strongly overcompensating. Where there is over-compensation, cycles or even chaotic changes in population size may be the result."
	    "*Carrying capacity*. The maximum population size that can be supported indefinitely by a given environment, at which intraspecific competition has reduced [the] *per capita* net rate of increase to zero. An idealized concept not to be taken literally in practice."

Ricklefs (1990, p. 803)	"Carrying capacity *(K)*. Number of individuals in a population that the resources of a habitat can support; the asymptote, or plateau, of the logistic and other sigmoid equations for population growth."

TABLE 12.1   *continued*

source	definition
Daily and Ehrlich *(1992, p. 762)*	"Ecologists define carrying capacity as the maximal population size of a given species that an area can support without reducing its ability to support the same species in the future. Specifically, it . . . is specified as K in the biological literature. "*Carrying capacity* is a function of characteristics of both the area and the organism. A larger or richer area will, *ceteris paribus,* have a higher carrying capacity. Similarly, a given area will be able to support a larger population of a species with relatively low energetic requirements (e.g., lizards) than one at the same trophic level with high energetic requirements (e.g., birds of the same individual body mass as the lizards). The carrying capacity of an area with constant size and richness would be expected to change only as fast as organisms evolve different resource requirements. Though the concept is clear, carrying capacity is usually difficult to estimate."
Pulliam and Haddad *(1994, pp. 143–44)*	"Social behaviors such as dominance hierarchies and territorial defense . . . appear to be significant in the regulation of many animal populations, particularly vertebrates. . . . Since populations may reach an equilibrium well below the carrying capacity set by resources, it is not appropriate to equate the parameter K of the logistic equation with carrying capacity. . . . In our opinion, carrying capacity is a useful concept only when used in the original sense of a limit set to population size by the availability of resources. . . . the carrying capacity set by available resources may be above or below the predation stable point and/or a threshold for disease transmission. Given all of these factors, carrying capacity may or may not be reached by a population, but it is still a useful concept and can be measured independent of actual population size."

even if the average birth rate exceeds the average death rate provided that emigration removes the average excess of births over deaths. Similarly, the population size could be steady even if the death rate exceeds the birth rate provided immigration makes up the difference. This concept of carrying capacity makes no assumptions about density dependence. A population size could be steady, on the average, because environmental fluctuations (such as storms, waves or changes in climate) remove individuals above a certain level, even if birth and death rates did not depend on population density.

The Population Size Set by Liebig's Law of the Minimum

To explain why the carrying capacity of a nonhuman species varies from one place or period to another, some ecologists define carrying capacity in terms of Justus Freiherr von Liebig's law of the minimum.[7] Liebig (1803–1873) was a prominent organic chemist who did much in the middle of the nineteenth century to establish the scientific foundations of agriculture. The law of the minimum asserts that, under steady-state conditions, the population size of a species is constrained by whatever resource is in shortest supply.

Liebig stated this law for agricultural chemistry. He had in mind fields of a single crop, that is, monocultures. At the outset, Liebig simplified the measurement of yield to a single number, the weight of grain harvested. This simplification ignored many other aspects of the human value of a crop, such as its robustness in harvesting, durability in storage and palatability and nutritional value on consumption. The qualitative aspects of yield were replaced by a single numerical index. When Liebig's law is applied to human carrying capacity, the use of population size as a single numerical index is likewise a great simplification.

Liebig's law was often illustrated by analogy to a tub made of wooden staves of various lengths.[8] The staves represent the resources necessary to support a population, and the level of water in the tub represents the size of the population that the resources can support. Water poured into the tub rises to the level of the shortest staff, then ceases to accumulate as it overflows. If the shortest staff is lengthened, the water can rise higher until it overflows at whichever other staff becomes the lowest. Lengthening any of the longer staves does not permit the water level to rise.

Agricultural experiments showed that the yield of a field planted to a crop might be limited by a paucity of nitrogen in the soil. When nitrogen was added, the yield jumped until it was again limited by the shortage of another essential nutrient, such as phosphorus. When phosphorus was added to the nitrogen supplement, the yield again jumped until the crop became water limited. Thus crop yields were limited by the most constraining factor in a series of limiting factors such as nitrogen, phosphorus, water and light.

In the Wuxi area of Jiangsu Province, China, for example, applications of nitrogen fertilizer in the 1960s substantially increased rice yields. In the 1980s, an additional unit of nitrogen produced no increase in yields at all. While nitrogen was a limiting factor in the 1960s, by the 1980s nitrogen applications rose so much that then phosphorus and potassium became the constraints on bettering the yield.[9]

However, Liebig's law of the minimum often fails.[10] In many experiments with fertilizers, for example, one element at a very low concentration should be the limiting factor, and yield should increase only as more of that element is supplied. In reality, the yield responds to other elements, water and changes in other conditions. Liebig introduced the "Law of Compensating Factors" to describe the fact that other factors may partially compensate (an economist would say "substitute") for the element held at a low concentration. Unfortunately, the mechanism and extent of compensation remained unknown, and the law of the minimum was in effect canceled.

In the century following Liebig's 1855 treatise, published simultaneously in English and German for maximum effect, biologists eagerly took up the law of the minimum. Physiologists applied the law to the rates of any physiological process: *"When a process is conditioned as to its rapidity by a num-*

ber of separate factors, the rate of the process is limited by the pace of the 'slowest' factor. "[11] The distinction between the rate and the yield of a physiological process is like the difference between the rate of growth and the size of a firm.

Ecologists used the law of the minimum to understand both yields and rates in nature: the chemical conditions that determine the presence (yield) or absence of species in natural communities, as well as the rates of growth and turnover of the populations of individual species. Ecologists found that, in many natural systems, nonhuman populations are limited by nutrients, especially nitrogen and phosphorus.[12]

But natural communities are far more complex than the monocultural experiments on which the law of the minimum is based. Different species have different requirements for a given element, as Liebig knew. Consequently, when one element is limited in a community of species, population growth typically does not grind to a halt; rather, a species that is less constrained by that limiting element replaces another that is more constrained, in a process called succession.[13] For example, in experimental lakes in Canada, phosphorus was a limiting factor. When ecologists added phosphorus, nitrogen became limiting; consequently, cyanobacteria, the only photoplankton that can fix atmospheric nitrogen, took over and drew nitrogen into the lakes.[14] If Liebig's law applies anywhere at all, it probably applies to single-species populations, not to communities of species.[15]

This observation is extremely important when Liebig's law of the minimum is used to think about human carrying capacity. For humans, different technologies, like different species in nature, are ways of extracting life from the physical, chemical and biological environment. In ecological succession, as time passes some species become less abundant and other species become more abundant, in a more or less repeatable pattern. Analogously, in human ecology, some technologies decline and are replaced by others. The changes in technologies imply changes in how people live and how they make a living, but do not necessarily imply constraints on human numbers. More will be said later about the use of Liebig's law of the minimum as a concept of human carrying capacity.

Whether or not Liebig's law of the minimum is true in a particular instance, the so-called law can be used to calculate carrying capacity quantitatively. The arithmetic is easy, but the result is meaningless unless the population is constrained in size by limiting factors that act *independently*.

In oceanography, for example, the law of the minimum works well because the assumptions it makes do hold. In 1934, Alfred C. Redfield, a physiologist at Harvard University and the Woods Hole Oceanographic Institution, discovered that bottled water samples from open oceans around the world contained nearly fixed proportions of carbon, nitrogen and phosphorus, though the concentrations varied widely from place to place.[16] These proportions, now known in oceanography as Redfield ratios, reflect closely the chemical composition of plankton. In modern form, the Redfield ratios assert that, for each phosphorus atom in plankton, there are 106 carbon atoms, 263 hydrogen atoms, 110 oxygen atoms, 16 nitrogen atoms and 0.7 sulfur atom. To oxidize this quantity of organic matter with oxygen as dead plankton settle and decompose, 276 atoms of oxygen (or 138 molecules of O_2) are required.[17]

Now suppose that, at the mouth of a river or in an estuary, the nutrients in seawater are not in the Redfield ratios but are, say, 1,000 carbon atoms, 900 hydrogen atoms, 800 oxygen atoms, 700 nitrogen atoms, 600 phosphorus atoms and 500 sulfur atoms per microliter of seawater. (These numbers I have made up are not remotely realistic.) Which element will limit the size of the plankton population? What will be the resulting carrying capacity?

Let's call the quantity of plankton that contains one phosphorus atom a single plankton unit (1 PU). The PU is chosen for convenient calculation; it would take many PUs to make a single plankton cell. The 1,000 carbon atoms could produce $1,000/106 = 9.43$ PU, if all other elements were available in abundance. The 900 hydrogen atoms could produce $900/263 = 3.42$ PU, if all other elements were available in abundance. The 800 oxygen atoms could produce $800/110 = 7.27$ PU, the 700 nitrogen atoms could produce $700/16 = 43.75$ PU, the 600 phosphorus atoms $600/1 = 600$ PU and the 500 sulfur atoms $500/0.7 = 714.29$ PU, assuming in each case that all the other elements were available in abundance. The least, or minimum, number of PU that could be produced with this hypothetical nutrient soup is the 3.42 PU permitted by the 900 hydrogen atoms. In this (unrealistic) example, hydrogen is the limiting factor, and the carrying capacity of this soup is 3.42 PU per microliter of seawater.

To summarize this calculation in a single formula, suppose the population size or biomass were limited by three factors—say, factor 1, factor 2 and factor 3. (There were six limiting factors in the previous example.) Call the quantity of factor 1 that is required to sustain one individual the factor 1 ratio; similarly for factor 2 and factor 3. According to Liebig's law of the minimum, the carrying capacity can be calculated from the available quantities of the three factors (as in the example just given) according to a simple formula:

$$\text{carrying capacity} = \text{minimum of} \left(\frac{\text{available quantity of factor 1}}{\text{factor 1 ratio}}, \frac{\text{available quantity of factor 2}}{\text{factor 2 ratio}}, \frac{\text{available quantity of factor 3}}{\text{factor 3 ratio}} \right).$$

Once again, this formula simplifies all qualitative aspects of carrying capacity to a single numerical index. A special case of this formula appeared in Chapter 11 when human carrying capacity was calculated from the availability of food and water as if they were independent constraints: there factor 1 was food and factor 2 was water. Penck's formula for a population constrained by food is the special case of Liebig's law of the minimum in which only a single factor, food, limits population size. Liebig's formula is easy to use even when the assumptions it is based on are false. As the continuation of the oceanographic example will now show, the formula does not guarantee that the results are meaningful.

Ocean surface waters in three separate regions (off Antarctica, in the eastern tropical Pacific and in the subarctic Pacific) have high concentrations of major phytoplankton nutrients (nitrate, phosphate and silicate) not incorporated in phytoplankton.[18] Why don't the phytoplankton consume these nutrients? In 1988, oceanographers John Martin and S. E. Fitzwater collected water samples from the subarctic Pacific by special techniques.[19] The techniques were designed to prevent iron from the ship's hull from contaminating the samples. The more iron Martin and Fitzwater added to the bottled samples, the more phytoplankton there was in the bottles on shipboard four or five days later. In 1990, Martin proposed that the plankton populations off Antarctica, in the eastern tropical Pacific and in the subarctic Pacific were limited by the scarcity of iron, a micronutrient that was not included in the original Redfield ratios. In October 1993, in an experiment designed by Martin and carried out by his colleagues shortly after his death, the *Columbus Iselin* dumped half a ton of iron into a patch of ocean about 500 kilometers south of the Galápagos Islands. By the next day, the chlorophyll concentration in the patch was twice that in the surrounding ocean.[20] As a result of these studies, for every 1 phosphorus atom, 16 nitrogen atoms and 106 carbon atoms, the revised "Redfield ratios" now include 0.005 iron atom. Even after scientists had studied for decades the factors that limit the size of plankton populations, with all the advantages of laboratory experiments and a biochemical composition of plankton that was not changing in time, they were still surprised to discover a trace limiting factor (iron, in this case) that no one had attended to before. Similar surprises may be expected in estimates of human carrying capacity.

It can be difficult to determine limiting factors even when experimentation can be carried out in a laboratory. For example, suppose one wanted to determine the limiting factors for the rate of assimilation, the process by which a plant converts nutrients into protoplasm. Among the possible limiting factors are obviously the amount of carbon dioxide, the amount of water and the intensity of light. A controlled experiment would consist in placing two similar leaves side by side under conditions that were comparable in all respects except the concentration of the one factor being investigated. Suppose no difference in assimilation were found. One might conclude that the factor that was varied had no relation to assimilation, whereas in fact assimilation in both leaves may have been constrained by the low concentration of available carbon dioxide, or the moderate light, or the low temperature, that affected both leaves. If the unrecognized constraints were removed, the factor that was varied might well show an effect.[21] Thus the experimental determination of limiting factors is not simple.

At least four empirical limitations of Liebig's law of the minimum should be kept in mind when anyone uses it to think about the carrying capacity of nonhuman populations.

One limitation is that if different components of a population have heterogeneous requirements, aggregated estimates of carrying capacity based on a single Liebig's formula will not be accurate. For example, the proportions of elements are much more variable among terrestrial plants than among oceanic plankton. Calcium accumulates in the permanent tissues of plants while phosphorus and potassium concentrate in the transient foliage, so different species with different amounts and kinds of woody supporting structures have different ratios of these elements.[22] Therefore it is not possible to use a single Liebig's formula for "terrestrial plant biomass." The heterogeneity in the requirements of different species must be recognized when it exists. Heterogeneity in the requirements of different portions of the human population would have to be recognized if Liebig's law were to be applied to it.

A second limitation is that Liebig's law of the minimum does not apply in a fluctuating environment. When the supplies of nutrients change and they are not all proportional as time passes, different nutrients may be limiting factors at different times. The carrying capacity then can fluctuate randomly because it depends on randomly fluctuating quantities. In human applications, the notions of a single limiting factor and a fixed carrying capacity do not apply when inputs fluctuate in unforeseen ways (for example, due to short-term fluctuations of weather or long-term fluctuations of climate).

A third limitation is that Liebig's law of the minimum assumes the carrying capacity is strictly proportional to whatever factor is limiting (within the range where that factor is limiting). For example, if rice yields are limited strictly by nitrogen, Liebig's formula predicts that each additional kilogram of nitrogen applied per hectare should yield the same increment in rice yield per hectare until, at some point, nitrogen ceases to be limiting and some other factor takes over. In most places, the reality is not so simple as the example mentioned above from the Wuxi area of Jiangsu Province, China. For example, in the 1980s, nitrogen applied in Zhejiang and Shandong Provinces increased rice yields by amounts that were only 50 percent to 60 percent as large as the increments from an additional unit of nitrogen applied in the 1960s.[23] In these provinces, additional nitrogen produced gradually decreasing returns, rather than all or nothing as the model of the tub and staves would predict.

A fourth limitation of Liebig's law of the minimum is that it assumes no interactions among the inputs. If nitrogen is the limiting factor, then a simultaneous increase in supplies of nitrogen and potassium should increase rice yields no more than an increase in nitrogen alone. Such independence among inputs is not generally observed. For example, a plant that is grown in an atmosphere with increased carbon dioxide may keep its stomata closed longer, thereby reducing the water it transpires as well as the nitrogen that it takes up with the water from the soil. Hence increasing atmospheric carbon dioxide and soil nitrogen could enhance the plant's growth more than if each were increased separately.[24] In another example, the biocide DDT is not soluble in seawater, but is soluble in oil, so an oil spill where there is DDT affects a vulnerable population much more than either DDT or an oil spill separately.[25]

Liebig's law is useful when the population has homogeneous resource requirements, and when the environment does not fluctuate enough to invoke different limiting factors at different times, and when nonlinear responses can be usefully approximated as linear, and when interactions between limiting factors are small enough to neglect, and when the time interval over which the carrying capacity is to be estimated is short enough that adaptive responses, within the life span of individuals or during biological evolution, will not alter the estimated carrying capacity. The last condition is a special case of the more general assumption that the system will not change under one's feet, an assumption made by any measure of carrying capacity that is a fixed number. I discuss this more general assumption further below.

When Liebig's law of the minimum is applied to rates of turnover (not yields) in natural populations, recycling of nutrients must be considered. In the well-lighted top 100 meters of the open ocean, for example, when externally supplied nutrients are scarce, up to 94 percent of plant plankton growth may use nutrients recycled from the death and decay of other plankton.[26] The recycling of nutrients by microbes in the upper open ocean is so intense that marine biologists call the process "the microbial loop."[27] In forests, 60 percent to 80 percent of the total nutrients used consist of recycled atoms.[28] The growth rates of plankton in the ocean and plants in the forest are increased by recycling, while their steady-state densities are constrained by the steady-state level of available nutrients.

The formula for Liebig's law of the minimum was used as the so-called production function in the World3 system model[29]:

$$\text{output } Q = \text{minimum of} \left(\frac{\text{available capital}}{\text{capital/output ratio}}, \frac{\text{available labor}}{\text{labor/output ratio}} \right).$$

This production function gives the output Q of industrial production obtained from the inputs of capital and labor. Here the available capital is factor 1, the available labor is factor 2 and output Q corresponds to the carrying capacity. The capital/output ratio is the factor 1 ratio, and the labor/output ratio is the factor 2 ratio. The formula was dignified in the technical report on the World3 model as a production function "of the Walras-Leontief-Harrod-Domar type." This was just Liebig's law of the minimum in new clothes.[30] Meadows et al. apparently used the same production function in their revised model World3/91 in *Beyond the Limits*.[31] The limitations of the law of the minimum as a concept of carrying capacity apply equally to the production function of Meadows et al.[32] The inability of the law of the minimum to represent substitution among inputs may be one reason why many economists prefer other formulas for the production function.

Features of Ecological Concepts of Carrying Capacity

The carrying capacity of any nonhuman species is conditional on the population size and welfare of the other living species with which it interacts, though the other species are not mentioned in any of the definitions. Other species may compete for resources required by the population of interest. Other species may provide essential resources for the species of interest. Other species may prey on or infect the species of interest. Any natural or human perturbation of the other species may affect the given species' carrying capacity.

The carrying capacity of any nonhuman species also depends on the physical and chemical environment in which it lives, though these conditions are also not mentioned in the definitions. Changes in these conditions may change the carrying capacity.

Further, any concept of carrying capacity as a fixed number fails to take account of the adaptability of organisms within a single life cycle and in the course of evolutionary time. For example, certain African fish live in lakes that dry up from time to time. When the water gets turbid and shallow, the fish burrow into the lake floor. There they persist in the dried, caked mud for long periods in a state of suspended animation until the water returns and dissolves the mud. If one of these fish is suddenly picked out of the lake when it is swimming in water, it will die. Water is an essential limiting factor for the fish under normal conditions, but the fish can adapt to changed conditions if the change is not too quick. In another example, certain plants in western America are killed by fire, but their seeds, stored in the soil, require fire to germinate. The absence of fire is an essential condition for these plants under normal conditions but abnormal conditions (fires) provoke renewal of the population. These are examples of adaptability within a single life cycle.

Evolutionary adaptability is also common.[33] For example, any sufficiently large sample of bacteria from nature has so much genetic variation that some individuals will be able to synthesize practically any biochemical requirement from a limited set of nutrients in a laboratory culture dish, and some individuals will be able to detoxify practically any antibiotic. While the limited nutrients or the antibiotics may kill off most of the initial sample of bacteria (that is, the carrying capacity is low at first), the few survivors will reproduce. Succeeding generations of bacteria will have higher proportions of successful individuals. A new higher carrying capacity will become established. This is evolutionary change in a laboratory. It is a change in the biochemical technology of the bacteria that increases the carrying capacity of the environment for the new bacteria. In other famous examples, the evolution of plants to capture the energy of sunlight with chlorophyll dramatically increased the Earth's carrying capacity for plants; the adaptation of animals to life on land did likewise for animals.

Though most nonhuman species are unable to invent technology as humans do, they do evolve through natural selection to prosper under conditions previously hostile to them. Consequently the carrying capacity of nonhuman populations may be constant on the time scale of a few generations but not on the time scale of many generations. In ecology, the four definitions of carrying capacity listed at the beginning of this chapter are useful only to the extent that the behavior and ecological relationships of nonhuman species change slowly on the human time scale.

CONCEPTS OF CARRYING CAPACITY
IN APPLIED ECOLOGY

Basic ecology married to human purpose begets applied ecology. Applied ecology aims first and foremost at satisfying human wants. What people want and how they organize themselves in relation to nature affect the concept of carrying capacity in every branch of applied ecology. Consequently, applied ecology includes almost as many concepts of carrying capacity as there are human purposes.[34]

To illustrate the next three definitions of carrying capacity, imagine a simplified, hypothetical ecological system that consists of two populations, one a resource, the other a consumer, in a rudimentary food chain. You may think of the resource as the grasses of a rangeland and the consumer as the steers put out to graze on it; or think of the resource as the vegetation of an East African nature reserve and the consumer as the elephants that eat the vegetation; similarly for browse and deer in New York State; and for krill and whales in the Antarctic Ocean. To make description easy and concrete, I will refer to the resource as the plants and to the consumer as the animals (though krill are shrimps, not plants).

The Population Size at Which
the Standing Stock of Animals Is Maximal

Suppose the manager of the game reserve wants to have as many animals (elephants) as possible standing around for the tourists to photograph. His or her goal is to maximize the population size, standing stock or steady-state biomass of the animal population. He will cull (remove or shoot) the animals only when the plants begin to look overgrazed. Preventing overgrazing reduces the risk of a later decline in animal numbers. This was the sense of carrying capacity when the term was apparently first used. A 1922 publication by the United States Department of Agriculture on the management of reindeer populations introduced into Alaska defined carrying capacity as the number of stock which a range can support without injury to the range.[35] If the animal population grows according to a logistic curve, the manager will let the population get as close as possible to the asymptote K.

The Population Size at Which
the Steady Yield of Animals Is Maximal

Suppose the manager of the grazing land wants to harvest as many animals as possible from the population, subject to the condition that next year's yield should not be less than this year's yield. Applied year after year, this harvesting strategy amounts to aiming for a maximal steady yield or maximal sustainable yield.[36] If birth rates decrease with increasing population density or if death rates increase with increasing population density, then the manager should let the population grow until the difference between the number of animals born per year and the number of animals dying per year is maximal, and then harvest the excess of births over deaths. If the animal population grows according to a logistic curve, the population size for the maximal steady yield is just half of the asymptotic level called K.

The Animal Population Size for Maximal Plants

Suppose the manager wants to maximize the standing crop of the plants because he caters to tourists who delight in rare orchids, which are eaten by the hypothetical animals; or because the plants are fixing nitrogen during a fallow period, and more plants fix more nitrogen.[37] SInce the animals eat the plants, the manager may eliminate the animals altogether and let the plant population increase until it is constrained by competition between plants for light or water. More realistically, since an excessive density of plants might be followed by a catastrophic plant virus, fungus or other pathogen, the manager might maintain just enough animals to curtail unwanted variability in the plant population. When the manager maximizes the plant standing stock, the carrying capacity for the animals is at or near zero. Similarly, if the manager wants to maximize the steady yield of the plants (perhaps he is growing hay for feed or for sale), he will reduce the animals to a minimum because the animals compete with him in consuming the plants.

The Size of a Harvested Population
That Belongs to a Sole Owner

Suppose a single person, corporation, government or consortium with a single board of management owns a nonhuman population. The owner wants to maximize the present financial value of the population. The present financial value of a population is the net income (that is, gross income minus costs) from harvesting the population this year plus the discounted net income of all future years. I will explain the meaning of discounting in the next paragraph. First I want to state the main point. Under optimal management, the carrying capacity of the population depends heavily on the relation between the discount rate and the population's growth rate and mode of growth (exponential, logistic or otherwise).

The discount rate measures the rate at which people are willing to trade money for time. Roughly speaking, if a person is willing and able to save or invest one dollar this year in return for $1.07 one year from now, but not willing to save in return for less than $1.07 and unable to invest for more than $1.07, then her discount rate is 7 percent. This crude definition sets aside questions of risk and uncertainty. If the net income three years in the future is, say, $4, the discounted present value of that income (using a 7 percent discount rate) is $4/(1.07 \times 1.07 \times 1.07) = $3.27. The farther in the future income (or expense) occurs, and the higher the discount rate, the smaller the present value of that income (or expense). The discount rate is influenced by both technology and human values, among other factors. Technology affects the productivity of people, of capital made by people and of natural resources. Therefore technology affects the rate of growth that can be expected of future income. Human values determine the relative weights people give to income now versus income in the future: would I rather have the income from a stand of trees that I own or would I rather let them grow for possible harvesting by my (or your) children?

When the discount rate exceeds the relative growth rate of an exponentially growing population, the *economically* rational policy for the owner is to harvest the entire population as quickly as possible and invest the proceeds in another activity that produces net income at the discount rate. On the other hand, if the discount rate is less than the exponential rate of growth of the population, the owner's economically rational policy is to harvest nothing until the end of the planning period, and then harvest everything at once.[38]

Why is immediate, complete harvesting economically rational if the discount rate is higher than the population's growth rate? Colin W. Clark, an applied mathematician at the University of British Columbia, Canada, explained:

> The sole owner considers a resource asset to be a form of capital. If the asset fails to provide a suitable return on its capital value (in comparison with alternative forms of investment), it is profitable to liquidate the asset. . . . Most temperate-zone forests . . . cannot sustain a growth rate of much more than 5% per annum. When discount rates greater than 5% are employed, forest management may become unprofitable; virgin forests may simply be chopped down and the land abandoned.[39]

Clark did not applaud this presumptuous form of economic rationality, which may entail the extinction of species that live in the forest, and neither do I. However, timber companies may have behaved exploitatively for reasons that have nothing to do with the rational management of a renewable resource. Just as a miner views a vein of gold as a resource to be extracted and abandoned when depleted, timber companies may, until recently at least, have viewed their forest lands as nonrenewable resources to mine.

Mathematical analyses of hypothetical populations that grow according to the exponential, logistic and other curves give conditions when complete harvesting is economically optimal and when it is not.[40] These conditions assume that the population growth curve, the cost curve (cost per unit of harvesting as a function of the population size), the price of a harvested unit and the discount rate are all constant into the indefinite future. These assumptions of fixity are clearly unrealistic and can be removed at the cost of increasingly complex mathematics. Nevertheless, these simple mathematical models show why, when humans manage ecosystems for their own purposes, the carrying capacity of the nonhuman population depends, at least in part, on the relation between the discount rate and the population's growth rate.

Basia Zaba of the London School of Hygiene and Tropical Medicine and Ian Scoones of the International Institute for Environment and Development in London commented:

> In the same area, with the same animal and plant species a manager may choose three (or any number of) different carrying capacities. Carrying capacity in this context has . . . less to do with biology, but more to do with particular economic (or aesthetic, cultural, conservation) management decisions. These are not the ecological carrying capacity levels of theoretical biology, but economic carrying capacities.
>
> Three questions are asked by the manager in each case. First, what is the economic (or other) objective of management of this resource? Second, what is the way of ensuring this objective by adjusting animal numbers? And finally, what is the permissible level of environmental change? All of these questions are value judgements. Measuring carrying capacity, under these settings, is not a mechanical, scientific (in the positivist sense) procedure; it is a socially, economically, politically constructed decision. . . . [In applied ecology,] any specific definition of carrying capacity must be precisely defined in relation to a particular objective. . . .[41]

The Population Size of an Open-Access Resource

The previous four concepts of carrying capacity in applied ecology all refer to a single manager or owner of a nonhuman population. The carrying capacity of an open-access resource is quite another concept. "By definition, an *open-access resource* is one in which exploitation is completely uncontrolled: Anyone can harvest the resource."[42] The standard example is a fishing ground with unrestricted fishing rights.

Economists sometimes distinguish an open-access resource, which is owned by nobody, from a common-property resource, which is owned by everybody.[43] However, if a community that owns a resource in common has no effective institutions or traditions to govern its own members' access to the resource, then the members of the community see the resource as open access, even though outsiders may be excluded from access. Typical examples would be public grazing land, or commons,[44] where any citizen can put his or her cattle to feed; and a communal forest, where anyone from the village that owns the forest can gather fuelwood.

For concreteness, I will describe the carrying capacity of an open-access fishery.[45] The carrying capacity is determined by two ingredients: a revenue curve and a cost curve. Both may be visualized by plotting dollars on a vertical axis and the fishing effort, or the daily average number of fishing boats in the water, on a horizontal axis (Figure 12.1).

Suppose that for each amount of fishing effort, there is some level of steady yield, that is, some number (possibly zero) of tonnes of fish that can be caught per day, day after day. The standard models suppose that the

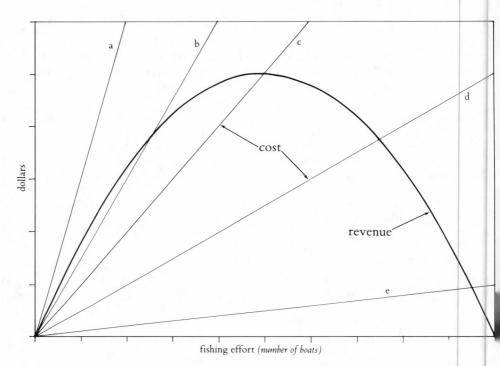

FIGURE 12.1   Economics of an open-access fishery. The inverted-U curve shows the total revenue (on the vertical axis) as a function of the fishing effort (on the horizontal axis). Each straight line shows the total cost (on the vertical axis) as a function of the fishing effort (on the horizontal axis); the lower the line, the lower the cost per boat-day of fishing effort. When the total cost is too high (line a), it does not pay to fish at all. Cost line c cuts the revenue curve at the maximum revenue; the corresponding fishing effort gives the maximum steady yield. When the cost of fishing is very low (line e), there is biological overfishing: the number of boats is so large that the fish population is greatly reduced. SOURCE: after Clark 1990

curve of yield as a function of fishing effort is shaped like an inverted U: the yield is zero if there are no boats, increases to a maximum for an intermediate number of fishing boats and declines again toward or to zero as the fishing fleet depresses the steady-state population of fish below the level that would produce the maximum steady yield.

   If a tonne of fish sells for a fixed price, then the total revenue of the fishery is just the product of the price times the yield. As the yield curve is shaped like an inverted U, the curve of revenue as a function of fishing effort is also shaped like an inverted U: it is zero if no boats are fishing, rises to a maximum at the same intermediate level of fishing effort where total yield is maximal and falls again to zero when there are so many boats in the water that they can catch no fish (see the solid curve in Figure 12.1).

   How do total costs depend on the fishing effort? To keep life simple, suppose that one day's fishing for a standardized fishing boat costs a fixed amount, including the cost of capital, independent of the number of such boats. Then the total cost of the fishing fleet is just the daily cost per boat times the number of boats. The total cost increases in direct proportion to the fishing effort. In Figure 12.1, the straight lines a, b, c, d, e show total costs as a function of fishing effort, for five different costs per boat-day, decreasing from a to e. Each cost line passes through the origin at the intersection of the axes in the lower left corner of the figure, where no boats cost nothing.

If the cost line is steeper than the beginning of the revenue curve (like line a), so that the two intersect only at zero fishing effort, then it does not pay to launch even one fishing boat to catch this particular kind of fish. Otherwise (assuming the revenue curve is a nice concave inverted U as shown in Figure 12.1, like half a grapefruit facedown), the cost line will intersect the revenue curve exactly once. The major result of the theory developed by H. S. Gordon in 1954 is that, in an open-access fishery, fishing effort will move to that number of boats at which the total revenue equals the total cost.[46] The corresponding level of fishing effort, where the cost line intersects the revenue curve, is called the bionomic equilibrium.[47]

Intuitively, it is easy to see why the number of fishing boats should approach the bionomic equilibrium. If there were more boats than the bionomic equilibrium, the cost line would be higher than the revenue curve. The fishery as a whole, and therefore at least some fisherfolk, would be losing money and eventually some of them would have to leave the fishery, reducing the number of boats. If there were fewer boats than the bionomic equilibrium, the revenue curve would be higher than the cost line, and fisherfolk would be making a profit. Under the assumption of open access, this profit would attract additional fisherfolk and fishing boats. Fishing effort would rise until it reached the bionomic equilibrium.

The cost per boat per day of fishing, the price per tonne of fish and the ecologically determined shape of the yield curve jointly fix the location of the bionomic equilibrium. If the cost is very high, but not too high to prevent fishing altogether (as in line b), then the fishing effort will be very small and the fish population will be only slightly below its maximum value. If the cost is a little lower, the bionomic equilibrium will lie a little higher, but still below the level that produces the maximum steady yield. If the cost line (line c) cuts the revenue curve just at its peak, the bionomic equilibrium will produce the maximum steady yield. If the cost is still lower (line d), the bionomic equilibrium engages more fishing boats and the yield falls below the maximum steady yield. This situation is called biological overfishing. If the cost is very low (line e), the bionomic equilibrium lies very near the maximum number of boats that can catch any fish at all, and the population is fished nearly to extinction.

The bionomic equilibrium in an open-access fishery is economically inefficient. For any number of fishing boats *smaller* than the bionomic equilibrium, the fishery as a whole could be making a profit, potentially benefiting the fisherfolk or the whole society or both. But that potential benefit is eliminated at the bionomic equilibrium. Clark called this situation economic overfishing.[48]

To see the difference between biological overfishing and economic overfishing most sharply, suppose that costs and prices just happened to place the bionomic equilibrium exactly at the peak of the revenue curve. In Figure 12.1 then, suppose that line c represents total costs, and ignore all the other cost lines. The fishing boats collectively harvest exactly the maximum steady yield. There is no biological overfishing. But if there were fewer fishing boats than the bionomic equilibrium, total revenue would exceed total cost and the fishing fleet as a whole would make a profit. By definition, the level of effort that would produce the maximal profit is economically efficient. That level of effort would harvest substantially less than the maximum steady yield.

Perhaps surprisingly, when the level of fishing effort is at the bionomic equilibrium or anywhere above the economically efficient level, it would be economically rational for some of the fisherfolk to pay others to leave the fishery; those who stayed in the fishery could share part of their profits (what economists call the "rent" of the fishery) with those who left, and all would be better off. If the fisherfolk could not negotiate such an agreement among themselves, an enlightened government could help, in principle.

It takes a little thought to see why an open-access fishery is economically inefficient, but the underlying principle is so important to human carrying capacity that the mental effort is worthwhile. The average revenue per boat (or per unit of fishing effort) is just the height (the vertical coordinate) of any point on the revenue curve (the total revenue) divided by the horizontal coordinate of that point (the number of fishing boats). So the average revenue per boat at any point on the revenue curve is the slope of a straight line from the origin (the lower left corner of Figure 12.1) to that point on the revenue curve. Take a pencil and fix one end of it at the origin; starting from alignment with the dollar axis (vertical), rotate the pencil slowly to the right (clockwise). This gradual rotation represents a gradual increase in the number of fishing boats corresponding to the point where the pencil intersects the revenue curve. As the fishing effort increases, the pencil becomes more nearly horizontal and the average revenue per boat declines. *Each additional boat lowers the average revenue of all boats.* The owner of the latest boat to join the fleet may be earning more by fishing than by not fishing, but by joining the fleet he (or she) lowers the average revenue of all boats previously in the fishing fleet. Each additional boat generates a "social cost" or "externality," the aggregate of the resulting reductions in average revenue suffered by each boat, but does not have to pay for that social cost because the fishery is open access. Because individuals do not bear the social costs they impose in drawing on open-access resources, humans generally overexploit such resources relative to the level of exploitation that is economically efficient. This is what the ecologist Garrett Hardin called the tragedy of the commons.[49]

Comparing the fish population size of an open-access fishery at bionomic equilibrium with the fish population size of a fishery that belongs to a sole owner (which would stay at the point of maximum profit) shows that, given the same biology, the human institution of ownership (or non-ownership) can make a dramatic difference to what is economically defined as the carrying capacity of a nonhuman population. This conclusion, demonstrated here under simplifying assumptions like fixed costs, fixed prices and no environmental fluctuations, remains true under much more realistic assumptions.

Practical ways to deal with shared ownership of a common-property resource are known. In oil production, oil reservoirs that underlie the lands of several owners are sometimes managed communally through "unitization." By contractual agreement or governmental regulation, the owners extract oil at rates that maximize its total value and each receives a fraction of the proceeds. The same approach has been proposed for extracting water from large aquifers like the Ogallala aquifer in the United States.[50]

Along with armed conflicts within or between countries, poorly conceived governmental policies for modernization and other human-induced hazards, human population growth in developing countries may undermine communal institutions for managing open-access resources. Demand from increasing numbers of people may overwhelm traditional systems of managing open-access resources. But community management can sometimes be strengthened. For example, when freely gathered fuelwood becomes scarce, some communities find ways to substitute other fuels for wood or develop profitable markets in fuelwood, which induce farmers to devote some land to growing trees. While population growth may aggravate the problems of open-access resources, it is far from being their sole cause.[51]

Private ownership may reduce some problems in managing a resource that would suffer if treated as open access, but private ownership is not necessarily a panacea. Under present social conventions, a private owner often does not bear the full costs that his management imposes on other resources and other people. For examples, wastes from privately owned mines, runoff from clear-cut forests and nutrient-laden waters from agricultural fields may adversely affect freshwater fisheries and downstream communities, imposing costs on people and other species that are typically not borne by the upstream resource owners. Economic markets to trade the interests of the owners of resources against the interests of those affected by the resource management are not yet widespread; and efforts to balance these competing interests through political institutions seem generally slow, cumbrous and inefficient.

CAN ECOLOGICAL CONCEPTS OF CARRYING CAPACITY SERVE FOR HUMANS?

The four concepts of carrying capacity in basic ecology that are defined at the beginning of this chapter would make sense whether or not people lived on the Earth. The five concepts just defined for applied ecology would not make sense if no people lived on the Earth, for there would be no range managers, no owners, no prices and no costs; there would be no applied ecology. These five concepts apply to an interaction between nonhuman biological populations and human social and economic systems, not to either separately. The concepts characterize upper limits on the size of biological populations, given the human objectives, values and institutions. If you accept humans as an integral part of the world that interacts with nonhuman species, then I think there is no choice but to accept these diverse concepts as carrying capacities of nonhuman species.

Can any concept of nonhuman carrying capacity from basic and applied ecology serve as a concept of human carrying capacity? Consider first the concepts of carrying capacity in basic ecology, then those of applied ecology.

The parameter K in the logistic curve cannot serve because the logistic curve has not accurately predicted long-term global human population in the past, and there is neither evidence nor likelihood that it can do so in the future. The population size at which the birth rate equals the death rate is useful under the assumption that increasing human population density will imply a rising death rate and a falling birth rate, and that these rates will become equal at some determinable population size. At some extremely high human population densities, beyond any so far experienced, such relations between population density and the rates of birth and death may be observed, but historically nothing like that has been observed. For example, in the United States, as its population increased after World War II, the birth rates first surged in the baby boom and then fell. Meanwhile, with rising population, death rates continued their steady fall. Apart from some worrying local exceptions, global birth and death rates appear to be falling and no one knows if and when they will become equal.

The average population size when the population neither grows nor declines is, like the previous concept, unknowable at present. It does not apply to the recent and current human population because human population size has been growing dramatically since around 1650. Defining the carrying capacity as the average population size when the population neither neither grows nor declines makes sense if applied to the human population in the millennia before the local agricultural evolution, when the change in population size was negligibly slow. It makes some, though less, sense if applied to the millennia before the global agricultural evolution; at least human numbers were tied to the productivity of the land and population size suffered reverses as well as advances. But the definition simply does not apply to the growing human population of the last few centuries. Apart from demographic projections by the cohort-component method in which a plateau of population size is assumed at the outset, it is not readily calculated from available facts or simple assumptions.

The population size set by Liebig's law of the minimum does not readily apply to human populations for reasons already described: because the human population is not homogeneous in its resource requirements, and because the environment varies enough in time and place to invoke different limiting factors at different times and places, and because nonlinear human responses cannot be usefully approximated as linear, and because interactions among limiting factors (sometimes appearing as economic substitutions) are not small enough to neglect, and because the time interval over which the carrying capacity is to be estimated is not short enough to justify the neglect of adaptive economic, technological and cultural responses.

Several concepts of carrying capacity from applied ecology also achieve limited success. The population size at which the standing stock of human animals is maximal may approximate the concept of human carrying capacity in a poor agricultural region or country if the region or country has little or no trade; few technological options available to improve agriculture; no institutions for agricultural extension or credit to spread appropriate technological improvements; no escape valve for surplus population; no additional arable land that is as productive as the land already cultivated; and a population growth rate that exceeds the growth rate of productivity.[52] But when people who can afford it set aside wilderness areas all over the world and establish zoning requirements for spacious minimum lot sizes in the United States, they are clearly not trying to maximize the standing stock of humans. That concept has little relevance to humans.

The population size at which the constant yield of humans is maximal is inappropriate since no one seems interested in cropping people. The human population size required to maximize the standing stock of plants might be favored by ardent botanists but is empirically a poor description of the global destruction of forests and other flora and fauna in recent centuries.[53] Defining carrying capacity as the size of a harvested population that belongs to a sole proprietor assumes the existence of a single profit-maximizing owner of the human species and a single discount rate, neither one of which exists.

The only remaining concept of carrying capacity from applied ecology is the population size of an open-access resource.

Open-Access Reproduction and the Second Tragedy of the Commons

The model of an open-access resource has some relevance to human carrying capacity. However, the size of the fishing fleet, rather than the size of the fished population, is the analogue of the human population. As I explained above, in an open-access fishery, additional vessels enter the fleet until the total revenues of the fishery coincide with the total costs. This level of fishing effort is called the bionomic equilibrium. The bionomic equilibrium is economically inefficient because the potential profit that could be extracted from the fishery is lost. Each fishing boat imposes a cost on all the other boats by lowering the other boats' opportunity to make a profit from the fishery, but each boat does not have to bear that cost. Each boat has to absorb only its own fishing costs, and receives the full benefit of its catch, without any deduction for the amounts by which it reduces the catch of others.

The entry of additional fishing vessels into the fishery is analogous to the entry of additional people into the human population. Children don't support themselves: the new individual reaps the benefits of living, and the family and community may eventually reap benefits from the additional individual, but the parents and the child do not bear the full costs that his or her presence imposes on others already in the population.[54] The Berkeley demographer Ronald D. Lee called the right of free access to common resources through reproduction "the second tragedy of the commons."

> In the real world . . . externalities to childbearing are pervasive. Among the most important are environmental externalities, since many enjoyable and productive aspects of the environment are not privately owned: air shed, water shed, ozone layer, parks, climate, freedom from noise, and so on. . . .
> The optimal level of use per person [of an open-access resource] depends on the number of people. Under optimal management, when the population is larger each person will be entitled to use the resource less—to visit Yosemite less often, to turn up the volume on his stereo less high, to burn less firewood, to discharge less waste. Furthermore, with a larger population, the optimal level of total use will generally be slightly higher (although less than proportionately so) and so each person will have to live with slightly more congestion, pollution, and degradation. Because each additional person is born with a birthright to public resource use, each birth inflicts costs on all others by reducing the value of their environmental birthright. Free access through reproduction is the second tragedy of the commons.[55]

Open access to reproduction affects employment. While each household makes hardly any difference to the supply of workers in a developing country, when all households hope to increase their income by having many children, the rapid increase in the number of available workers tends to depress pay, lower the quality and availability of education and health care and dilute the existing capital stock among a larger number of workers. Poorly educated, unhealthy and undercapitalized workers have lower productivity, and it becomes more difficult to modernize the country's economy.[56]

In fact, human reproduction has always been socially regulated to some extent, and potential parents have probably never been able to reproduce freely. Even among nonhuman primates, the reproductive success of males and females is linked to social status. In the Babylonian epic of Atrahasis, quoted at the very beginning of this book, certain classes of women were given responsibilities in temples and prohibited from reproducing, so that the gods would not be disturbed by the noise of an excessively large human population on the Earth.[57] Ecclesiastical constraints on reproduction in Western cultures underlie the notion of a "legitimate birth." Chinese social control of reproduction is new in degree but not in kind.[58] Because fertility is and has long been socially regulated, the analogy between the reproduction of the human population and an ideal free-access resource is less than perfect from the point of view of parents, but is widely applicable from the point of view of the child. Except where infanticide is still practiced, the birthright of the child, once born, is generally unchallenged.

The economist Julian L. Simon and others have argued that the so-called externalities of each additional birth are positive on balance.[59] From this point of view, a child confers benefits on his or her family, community, country and the world that outweigh whatever costs he or she may impose. To illustrate this point of view, I offer the remark of a scientific visitor from Tokyo, who went first to a scientific meeting in sparsely populated northern Florida, then came to my laboratory in crowded Manhattan, New York. I asked him how he liked Florida. He said, "It was lonely. There weren't enough people on the sidewalk. Here in New York, I feel at home, as in Tokyo." Even after allowing for his politeness (he was, after all, in New York), I cannot discount the empirical observation that, for various reasons, many people are attracted to the high population densities of cities.

Many people are also repelled by those same high densities. Opposing Simon, the World Bank economist Herman Daly and the theologian J. B. Cobb asserted that "the scale of human activity relative to the biosphere has grown too large. . . . Further growth beyond the present scale is overwhelmingly likely to increase costs more rapidly than it increases benefits, thus ushering in a new era of 'uneconomic growth' that impoverishes rather than enriches."[60]

It is possible for economists, demographers and others to take passionately held and opposite positions about the net external benefits or net external costs of each additional birth because, to my knowledge, these externalities have never been quantified precisely. There are many difficulties in doing so.

Our present reproduction and our use of the Earth affect past and future generations as well as the present generation. The present generation affects the welfare of past generations by giving their projects meaning and bringing them to fruition, or alternatively by nullifying and frustrating them, according to the British philosopher John O'Neill at the University of Sussex.[61] For successive generations, O'Neill suggested, the Earth may be viewed as a temporal "commons" even if all resources are privately owned at any one time. If any generation exploits the Earth's resources to the limit within the lifetime of that generation, without regard to the future, that generation receives the benefit and all successive generations share the loss. By this logic, each self-interested generation would be expected to deplete the resources it bequeaths to the following generations. To avoid one generation's depleting the resources of the Earth, O'Neill argued, each generation must view its own identity as part of a chain of generations, and must express its identity through projects that require to be continued and given meaning by future generations. The never-completed enterprise of science is an example of such a project. Land viewed as the shared property of a family that endures across generations will be conserved better than land viewed as a parcel to be bought and sold like a sack of potatoes. "The mobilization of labour by the market, like the mobilization of land, has undermined a sense of community across generations. Both lie at the basis of the temporal myopia of modern society."[62]

This generation inherited the Earth and will surely leave it to future generations. The view that your generation and mine take of the role and importance of future generations will influence how we treat the Earth today.

13

Human Choices

. . . there is no country in the world in which
people are satisfied with having barely enough to
eat.

—Kingsley Davis 1991[1]

A LITTLE BOY WANTED to know the sum of one plus one. First he asked a physicist, who said, "If one is matter, and the other is antimatter, then the answer is zero. But if one is a critical mass of uranium and the other is a critical mass of uranium, then that's an explosive question." Unenlightened, the little boy asked a biologist. She said, "Are we talking bacteria, mice or whales? And for how long?" In desperation, the boy hired an accountant. The accountant peered closely at the little boy and said, "Hmmm. One plus one? Tell me, little boy, how much do you want one plus one to be?"

There were more dimensions to the question than the little boy had considered. In addition to the pure mathematics, there were physical and biological constraints (the laws of matter and antimatter, critical masses, bacteria, mice and whales). And there were choices (for how long? and what do you want from one plus one?).

Estimating how many people the Earth can support requires more than demographic arithmetic. Like calculating one plus one, it involves both natural constraints that humans cannot change and do not fully understand, and human choices that are yet to be made by this and by future generations. Therefore the question "How many people can the Earth support?" has no single numerical answer, now or ever. Because the Earth's human carrying capacity is constrained by facts of nature, human choices about the Earth's human carrying capacity are not entirely free, and may have consequences that are not entirely predictable. Because of the important roles of human choices, natural constraints and uncertainty, estimates of human carrying capacity cannot aspire to be more than *conditional* and *proba-*

ble estimates: *if* future choices are thus-and-so, *then* the human carrying capacity is *likely to be* so-and-so.

No sharp line separates human choices and natural constraints. For example, technology obeys the laws of physics, chemistry and biology, but humans choose how, and how much, to invest in creating and applying technology. Hence the technology that people use depends jointly on human choices and natural constraints. In another example, how the human body responds to chemicals is a natural constraint on health, but individual choices (about food, smoking, alcohol and other drugs) and social and economic decisions (about the use of lead in gasoline and paints, about the production and disposal of radioactive wastes) determine the extent to which human bodies are exposed to chemicals.

The fuzzy zone between choices and constraints shifts as time passes. Changes in knowledge can reveal constraints that had not been recognized previously, and can also make possible new choices.

Further, a choice open to rich people may be a constraint for poor people. People from rich countries who become infected with malaria, tuberculosis or trachoma generally choose to get the infection specifically diagnosed, treated and cured. People in poor countries may be unable to make the same choice because they cannot afford to pay for prevention, diagnosis or treatment. A rich landowner may choose to leave forest uncut and cropland idle; a subsistence farmer with small holdings may not enjoy the luxury of choosing.

This chapter presents some questions of human choice that make the question "How many people can the Earth support?" more precise:

1. How many at what average level of material well-being?
2. How many with what distribution of material well-being?
3. How many with what technology?
4. How many with what domestic and international political institutions?
5. How many with what domestic and international economic arrangements?
6. How many with what domestic and international demographic arrangements?
7. How many in what physical, chemical and biological environments?
8. How many with what variability or stability?
9. How many with what risk or robustness?
10. How many for how long?
11. How many with what values, tastes and fashions?

Each of these questions could be the topic of a book. I aim here to amplify each question enough to indicate why it bears on how many people the Earth can support. The remaining sections of this chapter are all variants on the accountant's question to the little boy: "How much do you want one plus one to be?"

TYPICAL LEVEL OF MATERIAL WELL-BEING

The human carrying capacity of the Earth will obviously depend on the typical material level at which people choose to live. Material well-being includes food (people choose variety and palatability, beyond the constraints imposed by physiological requirements); fiber (people choose cotton, wool or synthetic fibers for clothing; wood pulp or rag for paper); water (tap water or Perrier or the nearest river or mudhole for drinking, washing, cooking and watering your lawn if you have one); housing (Auschwitz barracks with two men to a plank, or Thomas Jefferson' Monticello); manufactured goods; waste removal (for human, agricultural and industrial wastes); natural hazard protection (against floods, storms, volcanoes and earthquakes); health (prevention, cure and care); and the entire range of amenities such as education, travel, social groups, solitude, the arts, religion and communion with nature.

Standard economic measures do not capture all important features of material well-being. A rural village far from a source of fresh water is worse off than one close to a source, even if every economic indicator of income or wealth is identical in the two villages and even if neither pays a cash price for fresh water. A town with a river contaminated upstream by industrial or agricultural wastes is worse off than an economically identical town with a clean river in which it is safe to swim and boat. My son, robbed on the street in Manhattan at age 12 and again at age 14 by children only a little older than he, is materially (as well as psychologically) worse off than a child of identical economic income who can walk home from school without the risk of robbery and without fear of attack. An economist might respond that the less attractive village or town would have lower property values and that people would require higher pay to live in Manhattan if the fear of crime mattered to them; nonmonetary amenities would have cash consequences. Whether these cash consequences would fully capture all features of material well-being is for you to decide.

The typical level of material well-being could be measured by the mean or average (for dimensions of well-being that can meaningfully be added and divided), by the median (for dimensions that can be ranked), by the mode (the commonest category, for dimensions that can only be categorized) or by other reasonable indicators of central tendency.

Most but not all of the methods of estimating human carrying capacity recognize explicitly the importance of the typical level of material well-being. Two methods that do not are categorical assertion and curve fitting.

DISTRIBUTION OF MATERIAL WELL-BEING

The average or median material level at which people choose to live obviously affects the Earth's human carrying capacity. Less obviously, the scatter or distribution of material well-being around the mean or other central value also affects the Earth's human carrying capacity. Even if global average material well-being is satisfactory, people who live in extreme poverty may be unable to take a longer-term view because of the press of present wants.[2]

An example will illustrate the point that, for a fixed average level of material well-being, the scatter or distribution of well-being affects the human carrying capacity. Recent research in plant biotechnology makes it possible to isolate genes from many organisms and to introduce those genes into living plants so that they form a stable part of the genes of these plants. If the foreign genes are restructured appropriately they usually function predictably after being introduced into plant cells.[3] Aside from the importance for basic science of such gene transfers, the introduced genes can protect the new host plant against fungal diseases and insect pests (thereby reducing the demand for environmentally damaging chemicals), increase its tolerance to environmental stress, facilitate the production of hybrid seeds, enhance the nutritional quality of food crops and make it possible for plants to produce important commodities and valuable pharmaceuticals.

Any country or region with a few Ph.D.s in molecular plant biology and a modestly equipped laboratory can apply genetic technology to its own crops. The introduction of isolated genes into crops is sometimes difficult, but relatively low-tech methods suffice and do not require very heavy investment. If the available scientific and technical resources are distributed over the world so that no region is too poor to improve its own crop plants, the Earth can support more people than if the same total is distributed so that some regions are too poor to help themselves.

An apocryphal story is told about an ecologist, an economist and a statistician who went on a deer hunt with bow and arrow. As they were creeping through the forest, they saw a deer. The ecologist shot first, and his arrow landed five meters to the left of the deer. The economist shot next, and her arrow landed five meters to the right of the deer. The statistician looked at both arrows, looked at the deer and jumped up and down shouting: "We got it, we got it!" Use of the average well-being, without attention to the distribution of well-being, is no better for assessing global human carrying capacity than the average arrow is for hunting deer. Yet hardly any of the methods used to estimate human carrying capacity explicitly recognizes the importance of the distribution of material well-being.[4] This distribution is largely a matter of human choices, individual and collective.

TECHNOLOGY

Will people collectively choose to develop technologies for mass transportation or for individual cars? Will people develop new electrical generators based on sunlight, oil, coal, uranium, plant wastes, refuse from cities, agriculture, industry, wind, tidal motion, wave motion, falling water or heat deep in the Earth's crust? The human carrying capacity will depend on the choices made by voters, businesses, research organizations, civic groups and governments. Those choices will depend in turn on the economics, environmental effects, cultural acceptability, institutional governability and other features of the technologies.

In the early days of electricity in the United States, businessmen who wanted to generate electricity centrally and sell it over a network opposed those who wanted to sell household generators (analogous to home hot-water heaters) for independent local use. Investors in technology for solar power now face a similar choice between centralized and local generation. Different choices have different implications, though they are far from fully understood, for the quality of the environment as well as for material well-being.[5]

Some writers appear to believe that without human population growth there would be no need for technological change. On the contrary, as long as humans extract nonrenewable raw materials (for example, ores that bear metals or nonmetallic minerals) from the Earth's crust, technological change would be required to maintain average human well-being even if there were no population growth, because extraction and use modify a non-renewable natural resource. Typically the highest-grade ores, the richest concentrations, the most easily accessible deposits are used first. In the case of American use of petroleum, first the oil seeps of Pennsylvania were exploited; then the convenient domestic oil fields of Texas and Oklahoma; then the convenient but remote oil fields of the Middle East; then the inconvenient oil fields of Alaska and elsewhere. The next generation inherits only the resources that have not been extracted before, plus the durable products, good and bad, of the previous generation's activities.

Nonrenewable resources are not limited to minerals and fossil fuels, such as coal, oil and natural gas. Therefore the need for technological change is not limited to mining. For biological and freshwater resources, management and rates of exploitation determine what constitutes a nonrenewable resource. A mountain forest that is clear-cut and abandoned so that its soil washes away is a nonrenewable resource in both the short term and the long term; if it is clear-cut and replanted in time to conserve the soil, it may be renewable in the long term though it is nonrenewable until the trees mature; if it is selectively cut at a rate below its maximum steady yield, it is a renewable resource. The rising price of stumpage[6] and the increasing use of composite boards in place of whole-plank lumber signal a declining availability of mature forests. The animal species living in a forest are locally nonrenewable if the forest is clear-cut, whether or not the trees are replanted; local populations may be reestablished if they are reintroduced or if corridors for natural dispersal survive the clear-cutting.[7] A groundwater supply that is recharged at a rate of centimeters per year is renewable if exploited at less than the recharge rate, but is nonrenewable for periods of less than a century or so if pumped out at a rate of meters per year. The supply may be nonrenewable for more than a century if changes in the surface soil prevent water from filtering into the earth.

While technological change will be required as long as people exploit any nonrenewable resource, even when population size is constant, a growing population greatly increases the demand for technological change.

The Princeton demographer Ansley J. Coale observed that, in 1890 (when the U.S. population was 63 million), most reasonable people would have considered it impossible for the United States to support 250 million people, its approximate population in 1990; how would 250 million people find pasture for all their horses and dispose of all their manure? The essence of the argument over technological choices and natural constraints goes like this.

Ecologist: When a natural resource is being consumed faster than it is being replenished or recycled, an asset is being depleted, to the potential harm of future generations.

Technologist: If new knowledge and technology can produce an equivalent or superior alternative, then future generations may turn out to be better off.

Taxpayer: Which natural resources can be replaced by technology yet to be invented, and which cannot? Will there be enough time to develop new technology and put it to work on the required scale? Could we avoid future problems, pain and suffering by making other choices now about technology or ways of living? (No answer from ecologist or technologist.)

This imaginary dialogue is not far from recent actual discussions about human carrying capacity. In 1992, ecologists Gretchen Daily and Paul Ehrlich began with a polite but brief bow in the direction of the technologist:

> . . . human beings possess considerable ability to adapt to new conditions (such as resource scarcity) through rapid social and technological changes.
> Given present technologies, levels of consumption, and socioeconomic organization, has that adaptability made today's human population sustainable? The answer to this question is clearly no, by a very simple standard. The present population of 5.5 billion is being maintained only through the exhaustion and dispersion of a one-time inheritance of natural capital. . . . Essential elements of this diminishing capital include high grade agricultural soils, groundwater that accumulated during the end of the last ice age, and biodiversity; each is being depleted globally at rates orders of magnitude in excess of regeneration and has no known substitute that could be feasibly supplied at levels close to those required. . . . it is evident that the human enterprise has not only exceeded its current carrying capacity, but is actually reducing future carrying capacity. . . . Our descendants will have fewer of the essential requisites of life-support than we have today.[8]

In 1984, the economist Julian Simon and the technologist Herman Kahn began with an equally perfunctory nod in the direction of ecology:

> Global problems due to physical conditions (as distinguished from those caused by institutional and political conditions) are always possible, but are likely to be less pressing in the future than in the past. Environmental, resource, and popula-

tion stresses are diminishing, and with the passage of time will have less influence than now upon the quality of human life on our planet. These stresses have in the past always caused many people to suffer from lack of food, shelter, health, and jobs, but the trend is toward less rather than more of such suffering. Especially important and noteworthy is the dramatic trend toward longer and healthier life throughout all the world. Because of increases in knowledge, the earth's "carrying capacity" has been increasing throughout the decades and centuries and millennia to such an extent that the term "carrying capacity" has by now no useful meaning. These trends strongly suggest a progressive improvement and enrichment of the earth's natural resource base, and of mankind's lot on earth.[9]

Our hazy knowledge does not justify the assurance with which either of these views of the future is expressed. In different regions of the globe, both views were true at times in the past and may continue to hold true locally. Richard E. Benedick, an officer of the United States Department of State who has also served in the World Wildlife Fund, worried:

> While it is true that technology has generally been able to come up with solutions to human dilemmas, there is no guarantee that ingenuity will always rise to the task. Policymakers must contend with a nagging thought: what if it does not, or what if it is too late? . . . Markets may be imperfect, information may be lacking or not factored in. It seems reasonably clear, for example, that contemporary fossil fuel and water prices do not adequately reflect long-term ecological costs; they cannot, therefore, be expected to stimulate either more efficient use of resources or the development of alternative technologies. The economists' tautological long-term equilibrium between supply and demand may eventually be reached via laissez-faire, but policymakers must ask themselves whether the costs en route for generations struggling with the adjustment process may be unacceptably high.[10]

The time required for adaptation can be a serious constraint on human carrying capacity.

Domestic and International Political Institutions

Political organization and effectiveness affect human carrying capacity. For example, the United Nations Development Program estimated that developing countries could mobilize for development up to $50 billion a year (an amount comparable to all official development assistance) if they reduced military expenditures, privatized public enterprises, eliminated corruption, made development priorities economically more rational and improved national governance.[11]

Conversely, population size, distribution and composition affect political organization and effectiveness. Richard N. Gardner, professor of law and international organization at Columbia University, put it simply: "Where in the range of 7.8 to 28 billion population does finally stabilize will fundamentally determine the prospects of the human race not only for a habitable planet but for human rights, political stability, and world peace."[12]

Politics and Population in Ancient Iraq

In ancient Iraq, the human carrying capacity of the region depended on an effective political organization. The Lower Diyala Basin in what is now Iraq was first settled in the fifth century B.C. By the Sassanian period (A.D. 226–637), most arable land in the Diyala Basin had been brought under cultivation.[13] Archeologists infer that only a strong, well-organized central government could enforce the maintenance of the irrigation networks, and population sizes rose and fell with the strength of the central government. When the Sassanian state collapsed, dikes collapsed also, canals silted, captured foreigners departed with evacuating armies and entire valleys were depopulated. (I do not know if the data are good enough to show that the collapse of government caused the collapse of the irrigation system, and not vice versa.) In all, at the end of the Sassanian period, nearly half of the settled area in the Diyala Basin was abandoned. Population fell dramatically as the irrigation network and the subsistence base collapsed.

Citizen Effectiveness and System Capacity

How will political institutions and civic participation evolve with increasing numbers of people? As numbers increase, what will happen to two key dimensions of quality in democracies and other forms of government, namely, citizen effectiveness and system capacity? The Yale political scientist Robert Dahl and the Yale statistician Edward Tufte defined citizen effectiveness as the extent to which "citizens acting responsibly and competently fully control the decisions of the polity," and system capacity as the extent to which "the polity has the capacity to respond fully to the collective preferences of its citizens," that is, the polity's ability to solve problems for its citizens and assure their welfare.[14]

In theory, individuals in a group are more likely to act voluntarily to support some common purpose shared with all other individuals when the group is small than when the group is large.[15] If the group, such as a labor union, produces a benefit that will be shared by all members, then a large group tempts each member to go along for a free ride and to avoid personal effort on behalf of the group's goals. By contrast, in a small group, each individual sees that obtaining the group's goals depends on his or her personal effort. It is not rational to expect that groups of individuals with a common interest will voluntarily act to further that common interest unless the group is small. Theory predicts that increasing population size affects adversely the likelihood of voluntary civic participation.

Empirically, Dahl and Tufte related various concrete measures of citizen effectiveness to population size in different countries and political subdivisions within countries. Small polities (measured by population size) permitted citizens to participate politically and communicate better with political leaders, but large polities made it easier for citizens to find "an ally in dissent and an opportunity to participate in an organization with policies deviating from majority views."[16]

Dahl and Tufte also related several measures of system capacity to population size. They found "that on the whole, representative democracy in a large country is neither more nor less prone to destruction from internal conflict than in a small country."[17] Countries with smaller populations consistently had a higher ratio of foreign trade to gross national product. The increasing importance of trade for a democracy of smaller population size makes it "dependent—officially or not—on the actions of people outside the country."[18] They concluded "that a country's chances of survival do not depend significantly on its size" but that, in general, "[t]he *larger* a country's population, the more per capita it spends for defense."[19] Losses from war do not appear to be higher in smaller democracies than in larger.[20]

Dahl and Tufte argued strongly that there is no single optimum size for a political system. "Different problems require political units of different sizes [within and between nations]. Practically every modern state recognizes this fact in practice. . . . The central theoretical problem is no longer to find suitable rules, like the majority principle, to apply within a sovereign unit, but to find suitable rules to apply among a variety of units, none of which is sovereign."[21]

Liberty, Political Change, Public Goods and the Resolution of Conflicts

Several more specific questions link politics with human carrying capacity.

What standards of personal liberty will people choose?[22] When I drive my car in New York State, I am legally required to carry my state driver's license, to have written evidence of collision insurance in the car, to wear a seat belt, to drive on the right side of the road, to obey all traffic signs, signals and police and if it is raining to have my headlights lighted. I accept these and other legal constraints in return for the willingness of most other drivers to accept them. Thanks to traffic laws, all drivers share a limited road system with some safety and occasional efficiency. Without the laws and their acceptance by most drivers, the road system could not accommodate a fraction of the drivers that it does accommodate. My only alternative to accepting all these constraints on my liberty is to use public transportation or stay home. If there were far fewer people, vehicles could drive cross-country at will, as I have done in unsettled parts of Kenya and the Sinai Peninsula.

How will people bring about political change within existing nations? At least in the short term, armed revolution, insurrection and civil war impose constraints on human carrying capacity that differ from those imposed by peaceful elections or referendums; compare the violent and destructive breakup of the former Yugoslavia with the peaceful breakup of the former Czechoslovakia in the first half of the 1990s. As people choose how to bring about political change, they will set different limits on human carrying capacity.[23]

How effectively and efficiently will governments supply or promote the supply of "public goods" to their constituents? The definition of a public good is that its use by one person does not impair its use by others. Information, scientific knowledge, lighthouses and national defense are common examples of public goods. Highways and parks, though sometimes cited as public goods, become congested if used by enough people and no longer can be treated as public goods. According to Daly and Cobb,

> Whenever use by one person is at no cost to others, [economic theory claims that] the price should be zero. But the cost of production . . . is greater than zero. There is no market incentive for any firm to supply costly goods for a zero price, and so they would never be supplied by the market alone. And yet such goods are clearly beneficial and wanted by individuals. They are also the physical [and sometimes intellectual] infrastructure of community. . . . Markets need the help of governments to provide public goods efficiently.[24]

How will people choose to settle differences between nations, for example, over disputed borders, shared water resources or common fisheries? Preparation for and the conduct of war consume human and physical resources. Negotiation consumes patience and often requires compromise. When adopted repeatedly in response to disagreements, war and negotiation impose different constraints on human carrying capacity.[25]

National Security

How will people choose to define "national security"?[26] The American political essayist Walter Lippmann gave a traditional definition in 1943: "A nation has security when it does not have to sacrifice its legitimate interests to avoid war, and is able, if challenged, to maintain them by war."[27] Richard Ullmann, a political scientist at Princeton University, gave a broader definition forty years later: "A threat to national security is an action or sequence of events that (1) threatens drastically and over a relatively brief span of time to degrade the quality of life for the inhabitants of a state, or (2) threatens significantly to narrow the range of policy choices available to the government of a state or to private nongovernmental entities (persons, groups, corporations) within the state."[28] This definition may be too broad for some people: signing a treaty to ban the use of nuclear weapons in war or to abolish certain tariffs narrows the options available to a government, but might be viewed less as a threat to national security than as wise restraint.

Whether national security is defined by Lippmann or by Ullmann makes an immense difference to the problems that governmental leaders attend to and how they approach them. The threat to the ozone layer from chemicals used for refrigerators and spray cans was probably not a matter on which the United States could successfully maintain its interests by war; hence it fell outside Lippmann's concept of national security. It clearly fell within the scope of Ullmann's definition and could be dealt with only by achieving national and international consensus. Using Ullmann's broad definition, Joseph J. Romm, a researcher at the Rocky Mountain Institute, reviewed in 1993 the nonmilitary aspects of national security, including drug policy, environmental security, energy security and economic security. He viewed problems connected with population as one of the major threats to environmental security.[29] The definition of national security matters because the way people and their leaders choose to view national security will affect the attention and other resources they devote to problems connected with population, the environment and the economy, all of which will in turn affect the Earth's human carrying capacity.

The importance of the definition of national security illustrates a more general fact, which may be unsettling to natural scientists of empirical bent: the concepts and theories (political, economic, social, genetic and psychological) that people hold about the world will affect people's attention, actions and interpretation of the consequences of their actions. Concepts and theories are a factor (though not the only factor) in shaping what happens in reality.

Domestic and International Economic Arrangements

What levels of physical and human capital are assumed? Productive machinery and equipment, such as tractors for the farmer and lathes and computers for the metal worker, and higher levels of education and health make workers in rich countries far more productive than those in poor. Define the North / South productivity ratio as the ratio of value added per employee in the North to value added per employee in the South, where "North" is a sample of developed countries and "South" is a sample of developing countries.[30] In 1980, the North / South productivity ratio varied from a low of 1.9 in the manufacturing of footwear (that is, roughly 2 to 1, considering the Law of Information) to a high of 8.1 in the manufacturing of tobacco (let's say 8 to 1), and was at least 3 to 1 for manufacturers of food products, textiles, wood and cork, furniture and fixtures, printing and publishing, non-industrial chemicals, pottery and china, mineral products other than glass and metals and professional and scientific equipment. Wealthier workers make more wealth and can support more people.

What regional and international trade in finished goods and mobility in productive assets are permitted or encouraged? When an additional worker, or an increment in any other factor of production, creates more value in one place than another, then economists infer that a world in which people, capital or other factors of production are mobile could produce more than a world in which they are immobile.

In a hypothetical example,[31] countries A and B each have 1,000 hectares of land. Country A has 1,000 workers and 100 mules. Country B has 100 workers and 1,000 mules. Suppose one worker together with one mule can cultivate one hectare per year, but neither a worker alone nor a mule alone can cultivate anything. (The production function is assumed to take the form of Liebig's law of the minimum: the number of hectares of land cultivated equals the lesser of the number of workers and the number of mules.) If neither workers nor mules can move between countries A and B, then in country A only 100 hectares can be cultivated; likewise in country B. If country B could ship 900 mules to country A, then the combined cultivated land of the two countries would rise from 200 to 1,100 hectares. Instead of shipping mules, the migration of 900 workers from country A to country B would increase the total cultivated land equally. If cultivated land were the limit on human carrying capacity, then countries A and B could raise their combined human carrying capacity more than five-fold by permitting mobility of labor or capital (mules) or some combination.

This simple example illustrates a general point: integrating separate economies can achieve gains in output. Integration can be achieved by the movement of labor or by the movement of other factors of production, as long as the other factors are not specific to their original location. When the costs of transporting labor and capital are about the same (an assumption *not* satisfied in many real cases), mobility of one can be substituted for mobility of the other to achieve efficient production.[32] International trade can also permit small populations to achieve economies of scale in markets, eliminating one incentive for domestic demographic growth.[33]

World economic integration occurs when economic activity is reorganized to increase production without increasing inputs.[34] Economic integration brings risks as well as benefits.[35] Without presuming to summarize all the arguments, I offer some examples of the risks. When nations specialize in producing the goods that they are able to produce most efficiently, they give up the choice whether to trade for other goods. Specialization entails some loss of independence. The gains from long-distance international trade may be inflated by subsidies that artificially reduce the costs of the energy required to move goods around the world, and by the omission of the environmental costs of burning fossil fuels to power transport. More than half of international trade involves swapping essentially identical goods, as when Americans buy Danish butter cookies and Danes buy American butter cookies; such trade seems less efficient than home production. When trade occurs between countries with very different environmental regulations, the country with the more stringent regulations may be disadvantaged. If the prices in one country internalize the true costs of production over the entire cycle from acquisition of raw inputs to disposal of final products and by-products, while the prices in a trading partner take no account of the costs that production imposes on others, the first country will be unfairly handicapped in free competition with the other. The World Bank economist Herman Daly argued that "free international trade encourages industries to shift their production activities to the countries that have the lowest standards of cost internalization—hardly a move toward global efficiency."[36] If capital moves out of one country to profit from lower-cost labor in another, the country that sends the capital forgoes jobs for its own citizens, at least in the short run; and if population growth in the capital-receiving country is high enough to keep the people there poor in spite of the influx of capital, the capital-receiving country may never become a market for the products of the capital-sending country. Trade sometimes separates the place where the costs of environmental damage are incurred from the place where the benefits are enjoyed, as when tropical hardwoods are enjoyed in temperate industrialized countries. This spatial separation makes it more difficult to compare the costs and the benefits, and increases the risk of excessive exploitation.

Politicians, economists and environmentalists debate fiercely where the balance lies.[37] The choices that are made about world trade will substantially affect the Earth's human carrying capacity.

Many additional questions of human choice remain to be answered. How much does the individual worker benefit from the product of his labor? The incentives for a worker in a factory who receives hourly wages differ from those for a worker who owns a share in the factory or its profits. How much do governments regulate economic activity, and with what intelligence, effectiveness and goals? What roles do social and political customs play in the economy? For example, in a traditional farming culture, is the parental plot of land inherited by a single child, or is it divided among several children?

How will work be organized in the future? The invention of the factory organized production to minimize idleness in the use of labor, tools and machines. It was an economic rather than a technical invention. Factory production is economical only when a market demands a large total output. The creation of large markets through transportation, urbanization and international trade made factories efficient.[38] What new ways of organizing work should be assumed to estimate the future human carrying capacity?

How equitable will the distribution of income be? In 23 developed countries of the Organisation for Economic Co-operation and Development (OECD), life expectancy had a weak positive correlation to GNP per person in 1986–87. Between 1970 and 1987, the increases per year in life expectancy had hardly any connection with the increases per year in GNP per person. But the national distribution of income strongly affected national life expectancy. In nine OECD countries, data were available for 1979 to 1981 on the share of total income received by each tenth of the population: the tenth with the least income, the tenth with the next lowest level of income and so on up to the tenth of the population with the largest income. In these countries, life expectancy clearly increased with the percentage of family net cash income received by the poorest 70 percent of the population.[39] The more even the distribution of income in a country, the higher its life expectancy, even after controlling statistically for differences among countries in the average level of GNP per person.

Recycling

Recycling is not a human invention. The Bible observed that humans come from the dust of the Earth and return to the dust. In the oceans as well, carbon and other major nutrients are efficiently recycled. As organisms, living and dead, and feces settle through the oceans, they are constantly consumed and decomposed by bacteria and other organisms. Only a small fraction of the biological particles in the upper sunlit waters of the ocean escape directly into the deep.[40]

Recycling by humans deserves special attention among the economic choices that will determine human carrying capacity. Recycling can greatly increase the value derived from nonrenewable resources, such as high-grade nonmetallic and metallic ores, as well as renewable resources like water, and can reduce problems of waste disposal. Recycling is not costless, however. Additional energy and changes in human behavior may be required. The extent of recycling will depend on economic incentives (including alternative investments), governmental regulation and a culture's ability to promote behavioral change. Hence it is appropriate to discuss recycling here among other human choices.

As a concrete example, consider the recycling of metals. Without recycling, metal refined from ore gives a single use. However, if you can recycle 90 percent of refined metal after each use, then 1 kilogram of newly refined metal yields 0.9 kilogram of metal for a second use, giving a total of 1.9 kilograms of primary or secondary use. After secondary use, 0.9 kilogram of metal yields $0.9 \times 0.9 = 0.9^2 = 0.81$ kilogram for tertiary use, for a total of 2.71 kilograms of usable metal, and the tertiary 0.81 kilogram yields 0.9^3 kilogram for fourth use, and so on. The total amount of use from 1 kilogram of newly refined metal is equivalent to $1 + 0.9 + 0.9^2 + 0.9^3 + \ldots = 1/(1 - 0.9) = 1/0.1 = 10$ kilograms of metal.

In general, if a fraction f of a resource (mineral, water or other material) can be recycled ($f = 0.9$ in the example just given), and if the recovery rate f does not change with the number of prior uses, then the total amount of use that results from one primary unit is $1/(1 - f)$. The closer f is to 1, the more dramatic the increased use per primary unit of the resource. For example, if $f = 1/2$ (half the primary material is lost in each use or reuse), then one unit of primary material does double duty: $1/(1 - 0.5) = 2$. But if $f = 0.99$, then one unit of primary material does the work of 100: $1/(1 - 0.99) = 100$. Moreover, if it is possible to double the recovery rate, then a doubling of the recovery rate more than doubles the gain in use per primary unit.[41]

So much for theory. How fares recycling in reality? The Netherlands recovered 55.2 percent of its glass in the mid to late 1980s; this was the highest recovery rate at that time among OECD countries.[42] Each primary unit of glass was used more than 2.2 times. The United States recovered 8 percent of its glass, gaining a bit less than 1.09 uses from each primary unit of glass. If the United States doubled its recovery rate to 16 percent, it would gain a bit more than 1.19 uses from each primary unit. In 1975, U.S. industry as a whole used water brought into a plant 2.2 times before discarding it.[43]

Recycling can change from being profitable to being unprofitable when the regulatory environment changes. For example, when the United States had just one telephone company, the Bell System owned almost all the telephones in the country and recycled their components completely when they were replaced or upgraded. After the divestiture of the Bell System under the antitrust laws, it was no longer profitable for many of the smaller competing suppliers of telephone equipment to recover and recycle telephones.[44]

The platinum-group metals are used for catalytic converters (about 34 percent of consumption) and for fabrication, manufacturing and jewelry (about 60 percent of consumption). Virtually all of the platinum-group metals used for fabrication, manufacturing and jewelry are recovered, while only about 12 percent of these metals used in catalytic converters are recovered. No single economic entity can profit from recycling the platinum-group metals used in catalytic converters.[45]

DOMESTIC AND INTERNATIONAL DEMOGRAPHIC ARRANGEMENTS

Almost every aspect of demography (birth, death, age structure, migration, marriage and family structure) is subject to human choices that will influence the Earth's human carrying capacity. These demographic choices are not independent. They involve trade-offs of competing goods (or competing bads).

I have already described some demographic choices that a future stationary global population will face. One is the choice between a long average length of life and a high birth rate. Another is the choice of a single average birth rate for all regions, on the one hand, and a demographic specialization of labor on the other (in which some areas have fertility above their replacement level while other areas have fertility below their replacement level).

The level of migration is another choice that could materially alter the Earth's human carrying capacity. By the early 1990s, some 100 million people lived in countries of which they were not citizens, fewer than 2 percent of world population.[46] Most people who moved across international borders migrated from one developing country to another. In the late 1980s, about 8 percent of all migrants were refugees in Pakistan and Iran from war in Afghanistan and 44 percent were in sub-Saharan Africa. Relatively few were migrants from the developing to industrial countries. The stability in the ratios of immigrants to population through the middle of the 1980s showed that the mobility of workers could not explain the increased global economic integration of national economies since the 1950s. Most governments tended to discourage foreigners from entering; some restricted emigration by their own citizens. In all, though internal migration was substantial in Germany, for example, and in some other countries and regions, global labor mobility across national boundaries was not massive and had not increased over recent decades. Whether the migration of people will remain at its present low level is a choice to be made in the future.

The example above of mules and farmers showed that massive migration is not necessary for economic integration, provided that other factors of production are mobile. For example, if a British entrepreneur hires an Italian company to design a new line of clothing, produces those designs in a clothing factory in southern China and employs a shipping company in Hong Kong to transport the finished clothes to the United States to be sold by American retailers, no worker has to cross a national border for workers in five countries to exchange services.[47]

In 1986, as part of the Immigration Reform and Control Act, the Congress of the United States created a Commission for the Study of International Migration and Cooperative Economic Development. The two fundamental conclusions of the Commission's 1990 report were that "the search for economic opportunity is the primary motivation for most unauthorized migration to the United States; and . . . [d]evelopment and the availability of new and better jobs at home . . . is the only way to diminish migratory pressures over time."[48] How effectively developing and developed countries in concert are able to create more and better jobs could materially influence future migration.

Choices that govern migration have significant political and moral consequences.[49] How should the world's 17 million refugees be treated? For a country that receives refugees, moral questions arise about how many to admit, by what criteria and under what terms. How should those who are admitted (legally or not, recently or not) be treated? What are the standards for repatriation of unwanted entrants? How should a receiving country deal with another country that produces migrants and refugees that the first country does not want?

Patterns of marriage and household formation will also influence human carrying capacity. For example, the public resources that have to be devoted to the care of the young and the aged depend on the roles played by families. In China, national law requires families to care for and support their elderly members[50]; in the United States, each elderly person and the state are largely responsible for supporting that elderly person.

PHYSICAL, CHEMICAL AND BIOLOGICAL ENVIRONMENTS

What physical, chemical and biological environments will people choose for themselves and for their children? Demographer Paul Demeny assembled a splendid list of current environmental problems. It reads like a drum-roll at a beheading: "Loss of topsoil, desertification, deforestation, toxic poisoning of drinking water, oceanic pollution, shrinking wetlands, over-grazing, species loss, shortage of firewood, exhaustion of oil reserves and of various mineral resources, siltation in rivers and estuaries, encroachment of human habitat on arable land, dropping water tables, erosion of the ozone layer, loss of wilderness areas, global warming, rising sea levels, nuclear wastes, acid rain."[51]

Choices about the environment may be made indirectly, as a consequence of technological or economic choices (for example, when the burning of fossil fuels increases atmospheric carbon dioxide, or when the creation of water reservoirs for hydropower drowns habitats), or directly (for example, when reserves and parks are set aside as wilderness areas, or when people refrain from throwing trash out the car window).

Much of the heat in the public argument over the environment arises because the consequences of present and projected choices and changes are uncertain. Some people fear the consequences will be very bad and would like to stop the changes; other people view the costs and unpredictable effects of stopping the changes as worse than the likely consequences. Will global warming cause great problems, or would a global limitation on fossil fuel consumption cause greater problems? Will toxic or nuclear wastes or ordinary sewage sludge dumped in the deep ocean come back to haunt future generations when deep currents well up in biologically productive offshore zones, or would the long-term effects of disposing of those same wastes on land be worse? The choice of particular alternatives could materially affect human carrying capacity.

It seems prudent to avoid irreversible physical, chemical and biological changes to the environment because their effects may be uncontrollable. In many cases, present knowledge cannot distinguish changes that are reversible from those that are irreversible. Species extinction is irreversible, and will remain so unless there are truly remarkable advances in genetic and cellular technology. From a purely selfish human point of view, important moral issues aside, extinguishing species is like yanking loose threads out of a new suit: you may remove just the thread, but you run the risk of having a sleeve drop off. The economic benefits of extinguishing a species—in lumber extracted or woodland converted to pasture, for example—usually accrue to people who are not in any market or position to trade with those who will bear the economic costs, and therefore it is impossible to defend species extinction on the grounds that it may be economically rational. As understanding grows of the ecological, pharmaceutical and agronomic roles of species both prominent and obscure, regret over human-induced extinctions and caution about preventing further extinctions seem likely to grow also.[52]

Environmental goals interact with economic choices.[53] For example, in the belief that "widespread poverty is no longer inevitable,"[54] the 1987 report, *Our Common Future,* of the World Commission on Environment and Development assumed that economic and environmental goals could be achieved, given reasonable choices of technology and social organization. The report is generally known as the Brundtland report after the Commission's chairwoman Gro Harlem Brundtland, former prime minister of Norway.

Faye Duchin and Glenn-Marie Lange at New York University's Institute for Economic Analysis tested the assumption that the Brundtland report's economic and environmental goals were compatible by using a detailed input-output model of the world economy with 16 geographic regions and about 50 interacting economic sectors.[55] They explored the environmental consequences of achieving the Brundtland report's economic goals through a variety of projections of technology that could be used in developed and developing economies. They assumed that future population would follow the United Nations' medium projections and made additional assumptions about future energy prices, regional shares of world exports of goods and services and quantities of foreign aid.[56] While the scenario of the Brundtland report reduced emissions of the three pollutants that were tracked in the model (carbon dioxide, sulfur oxides and nitrogen oxides) compared to a reference scenario (business as usual), the emissions of these pollutants still increased substantially from 1990 to 2020, and carbon emissions nearly doubled. Most pollution shifted from today's rich to today's poor countries, where most population growth is predicted to occur.[57] Duchin and Lange concluded "that the economic and environmental objectives of the Brundtland Report cannot simultaneously be achieved. To the extent that our results about the physical reality are convincing, no amount of social organization and political will can make the *Our Common Future* Scenario work."[58]

Though skepticism about the United Nations' medium projections is surely justified, and though exploring alternative demographic and political scenarios might make the conclusion more compelling, the main point of Duchin and Lange stands firm: economic goals are achieved through physical technology that has environmental consequences. People cannot freely assume that economic goals and environmental goals are compatible.

Environmental goals also interact with political choices. For example, one way to increase power production while avoiding the unwanted by-products generated by burning fossil or radioactive fuels is through hydroelectric power. But hydroelectric projects pose other environmental problems. Major hydroelectric projects in China and India may place multilateral and bilateral aid agencies in politically awkward situations.[59] On one side, nongovernmental environmental groups may try to block such projects with the announced goal of preserving environmental values such as endangered habitats and species. On the other side, national governments may object to aid agencies placing limits on national sovereign rights to develop economically as local government sees fit.

The entire 1992 *World Development Report* of the World Bank was devoted to the interactions of development and the environment. The optimistic conclusion was: "The Report demonstrates that much [environmental] damage takes place with little or no benefit in the form of increased income and that a careful assessment of benefits and costs will result in much less environmental damage."[60] In 1990, the World Bank established a Global Environmental Facility of $1.3 billion, to be operated as a pilot program for three years by the Bank, the United Nations Environmental Program and the United Nations Development Program. The GEF aimed to pay the additional costs that developing countries incurred to achieve global benefits in four areas: climatic change, conservation of biodiversity, international waters in oceans and international river systems and protecting the ozone layer.[61] At the United Nations Conference on Environment and Development in Rio in 1992, developing countries moved to extend the GEF to cover desertification and deforestation and to modify its governance. The GEF is an experiment in governance, economics and the environment all rolled into one. It is an experiment worth watching and strengthening.

VARIABILITY OR STABILITY

How many people the Earth can support depends on how steadily you want the Earth to support that population. If you were willing to let the human population rise and fall, depending on annual crops, decadal weather patterns and long-term shifts in climate, then the average population would be higher than if you insisted on a steady level that could be guaranteed through good times and bad. The average population with ups and downs would include the peaks of population size, whereas the guaranteed level would have to be adjusted to the level of the lowest valley. Similar reasoning applies to variability or stability in the level of well-being, the quality of the physical, chemical and biological environments and many other dimensions of choice.

RISK OR ROBUSTNESS

How many people the Earth can support depends on how controllable you want the well-being of the population to be. One possible strategy, for example, would be to maximize numbers at some given level of well-being, ignoring the risk of natural or human disaster. Another possibility would be to accept a lower population size in return for increased control over random events. For example, when someone settles in a previously uninhabited hazardous zone (like the flood plain of the Mississippi River or the hurricane-prone coast of the southeastern United States), he demands a higher carrying capacity of the hazardous zone but must accept a higher risk of catastrophe. When farmers do not give fields a fallow period, they extract a higher carrying capacity along with a higher risk that the soil will lose its fertility (as agronomists at the International Rice Research Institute in the Philippines discovered to their surprise).

The distinction between risk (in this section) and variability (in the previous section) is that risk may lead to an unwanted fluctuation in human carrying capacity whereas variability may be desired. An analogous distinction arises in the design of a superhighway. Early designers, particularly in the western states of the United States, planned immensely long straight stretches; later designers preferred occasional gradual curves to enhance the alertness of drivers, even when the terrain did not require curves. The choice of straight or curved paths is analogous to the choice of a level of stability or variability. The choice of a width of lane corresponds to the choice of a level of risk: the wider the lane, the lower the risk that a vehicle's unforeseen wobble or swerve will lead to an accident.

TIME HORIZON

Human carrying capacity depends strongly on the time horizon people choose for planning. The population that the Earth can support at a given level of well-being for 20 years may differ substantially from the population that can be supported for 100 or 1,000 years.

The use of topsoil dramatizes the difference between temporary and long-term support. Suppose a newly opened crop field has 60 inches (roughly 1.5 meters) of topsoil on top of bedrock. Suppose the crop requires 18 inches of topsoil to keep its roots happy, and farming practice consumes an inch of topsoil for each annual crop. For the first $42 = 60 - 18$ years, the crop yield gives no indication that the loss of topsoil has any adverse effect. In the forty-third year, the roots confront bedrock. Yields rapidly worsen year by year. Practices that are acceptable in the near term may not be in the longer term.

If the farmer could see that the crop's roots were approaching the bedrock floor, he might have time to modify his erosive farming or breed a miraculous crop with roots insensitive to rock. If he cannot foresee the problem coming, he may not have time, when it arrives, to take corrective action. If more eroded land begins to sell for a lower price than less eroded land, the entire community may get a signal that it is time to correct erosion.

The time horizon is crucial in energy analysis. How fast oil stocks are being consumed matters little if one cares only about the next five years. In the long term, technology can change the definition of resources, converting what was useless rock to a valuable resource; hence no one can say whether industrial society is sustainable for 500 years. When it makes any sense at all, human carrying capacity makes most sense when it refers to a well-defined and limited time horizon.[62]

Some definitions of human carrying capacity refer to the size of a population that can be supported *indefinitely*. Such definitions are operationally meaningless. There is no way to know what human population size can be supported indefinitely (other than zero population, since our sun is expected to burn out in a few billion years and the human species as we know it is likely to be extinct long before then). Experts can predict tomorrow's stock prices and weather with limited precision at best. The precision of prediction declines very rapidly as the horizon of prediction recedes into the future. Think back 20 years: how many foresaw the collapse of the Soviet Union and Yugoslavia, the unification of West and East Germany, the rise of the fax and the personal computer, the spread of AIDS, the thinning of the ozone layer and the possibilities of reconciliation in Israel and South Africa? The concept of indefinite sustainability is a phantasm, a diversion from the difficult problems of today and the coming century.

The Static Reserve Index

Some people seem to believe that, at least for nonrenewable resources, there is a natural time scale, called the "static reserve index." The static reserve index is defined as "the number of years present known reserves of that resource . . . will last at the *current* rate of usage."[63] The static reserve index (in years) is calculated as the reserves (measured in tonnes, for example) divided by current consumption (measured in tonnes per year, for example). To illustrate, around 1970, copper reserves were 308 million tons and the annual global consumption of copper was 8.6 million tons, so the static reserve index was about 36 years (308 divided by 8.6).[64]

Some people view the static reserve index as an overstatement of the actual time scale, because it neglects any growth in consumption.[65] For example, the American physicist Albert A. Bartlett wrote in 1978: "The consumption of resources is generally growing exponentially, and we would like to have an idea of how long resources will last. . . . Imagine that the rate of consumption of a resource grows at a constant rate until the last of the resource is consumed whereupon the rate of consumption falls abruptly to zero."[66] The years required to exhaust a fixed reserve under this model (called the exponential index[67] or the exponential expiration time[68]) may be calculated by this formula (assuming a *positive* annual growth rate of consumption):

$$\text{exponential index} = \frac{\text{natural logarithm of } (1 + \text{annual growth rate of consumption} \times \text{static reserve index})}{\text{annual growth rate of consumption}}.$$

For example, if consumption of copper was growing annually by 4.6 percent on average around 1970, the exponential index of copper was 21 years (to the nearest year).[69] Naturally, when consumption grows at any positive rate, the life of the resource according to the exponential index is shorter than its life according to the static reserve index.

If the assumptions underlying the calculation of the exponential index were true, copper should have been completely exhausted by 1991 (which is 21 years after 1970). According to Meadows et al. in 1972, the exponential index predicted that by 1993 there would be no more copper, gold, lead, mercury, silver, tin, zinc and petroleum; by 1994 natural gas would be gone.[70] In fact, none of these resources was exhausted. The assumption of a reserve that could only be depleted, not replenished by exploration, discovery and improved efficiency of extraction, as well as the assumption of exponential growth in demand both failed.

Some other people view the static reserve index as a gross understatement of the time scale, because it neglects the reduced consumption, enhanced recycling, intensified exploration, development of reserves and substitution of alternative resources that would follow from rising prices, under appropriate conditions.[71] However, these ideal responses of the market are far from automatic in the real world. For example, if the resource is an open-access resource, there may be no incentive for any private interest to develop it as it is being depleted. One thoughtful economist, Robert N. Stavins, wrote: "It is obviously not enough to say that markets will automatically respond appropriately to scarcity. Imperfections in markets and imperfections in public policies clearly reduce the effectiveness of these responses. Common property resources, externalities, the tax treatment of resources, and price controls are more than just rare exceptions."[72]

Faced with the static reserve index, the exponential index and the economic arguments that both indices are gross underestimates of the likely lifetime of nonrenewable resources, what's a body to do? All three viewpoints rest on highly idealized models of future behavior. The static reserve index assumes constant reserves and consumption; the exponential index assumes constant reserves and exponentially growing consumption; the market model assumes prices that accurately reflect complete information, smooth substitutions and rational economic actors, among other assumptions. None of the three ideal models corresponds closely to reality in most cases. Like demographic projections, all three are no more than conditional predictions. Nevertheless, conditional predictions can suggest that caution may be in order. If your speedometer says you are traveling at 40 kilometers per hour, you do not expect to be exactly 40 kilometers straight ahead of where you are now after an hour's travel, but you know you can stop or turn more easily than if your speedometer says you are traveling at 100 kilometers per hour.

FASHIONS, TASTES, AND MORAL VALUES

In 1966, I was privileged to visit Vellore, a small town in southern India, to interview businessmen (no businesswomen were involved) about the consequences of a course they had taken to develop entrepreneurial attitudes. As I mentioned in Chapter 10, nutritional surveys taken then showed severe shortages of calories in the diets of most people in Vellore. One afternoon, a graduate of the course and I were standing next to his small grain warehouse. A rat inside the warehouse poked its head out through a coin-sized hole in the metal siding, squeezed its well-fed body through the hole and waddled out of sight. I asked the businessman why he didn't plug up the hole. He said, "The rat has as much right to live as I do." This answer surprised me so much that I was speechless. I would still, today, be inclined to plug the hole. The decision depends on human values, not only on facts or constraints of nature.

The American anthropologist Donald L. Hardesty observed in 1977: "A plot of land may have a low carrying capacity, not because of low soil fertility but because it is sacred or inhabited by ghosts."[73] The citizens of Manhattan, the central island of New York City, devote substantial amounts of land that could be prime commercial real estate or housing to their churches, synagogues, mosques and other places of worship.

In 1976, Roger Revelle asserted that the Earth could support 40 billion people on a vegetarian diet of 2,500 kilocalories per day.[74] If he were right (which I do not claim), the same hypothetical calories could supply 10 billion people a diet rich in animal products based on 10,000 kilocalories of plant products per day. While the arithmetic is indifferent between these two uses of the sun's energy, the people involved might not be indifferent between diets with animal products for 10 billion and universal subsistence for 40 billion. People certainly differ on how desirable they consider animal products in the diet.

How many people the Earth can support depends on what people want from life. Moral and ethical values, tastes and fashions affect all of the choices discussed in this chapter. For the remainder of this chapter, I focus on choices that have two characteristics: the choices could materially affect human carrying capacity, and the choices do not seem to be determined by the facts of a situation, that is, different reasonable people make different selections, given free choice and the same apparent facts. An immense variety of choices have both characteristics. I will give examples.

How Do You Measure the Well-Being of a Population?

Human values determine the answer to a major question often left unexamined: how do you measure the well-being of a population, given a measure of the well-being of every individual in the population? To keep life simple, suppose you can measure every person's well-being by a single number, such as his daily intake of calories or her annual income or his headache-free days per year. Obviously any single number is a ridiculously simple measure of well-being for a creature as complex as a human being. I start with the simplifying assumption of a single number to emphasize the freedom of choice one has in evaluating the well-being of a population. For concreteness, I will use calories as a measure. Ignoring the problems of overweight people, I will assume that more calories are better than fewer calories. Economists prefer to measure well-being in utiles, which are units of utility (whatever that may mean)[75]; physicists prefer energy. I like to eat and I like physically measurable quantities, so I will use calories.

TABLE 13.1   Hypothetical populations and daily calorie supplies,
to illustrate three measures of population well-being:
total, average and minimum

| individual | population | | | | |
	A	B	C	D	E
1	2,000	3,000	2,200	2,450	2,100
2	2,000	3,000	2,200	2,450	2,100
3	2,000	3,000	2,200	2,450	2,100
4	2,000	3,000	2,200	2,450	2,100
5	2,000	3,000	2,200	2,450	2,100
6	2,000	3,000	2,200	2,450	2,100
7	2,000	3,000	2,200	2,450	2,100
8	2,000	3,000	2,200	2,450	2,100
9	3,000	3,000	2,200	1,900	2,100
10	3,000	3,000	2,200		2,100
11		3,000	1,900		
total	22,000	30,000	23,900	21,500	21,000
average	2,200	3,000	2,173	2,389	2,100
minimum	2,000	3,000	1,900	1,900	2,100

Three of the infinite number of ways of combining individual calories to measure a population's well-being are the total (the sum of the calories consumed by the individuals in the population); the average (the total calories consumed divided by the number of people); and the minimum. Each of these three measures has staunch defenders among philosophers, economists and demographers.[76] The name of Jeremy Bentham is often associated with the total; most economists use average income, and attribute it to John Stuart Mill; and Franklin Delano Roosevelt defended the minimum when he wrote: "The test of our progress is not whether we add more to the abundance of those who have much; it is whether we provide enough for those who have too little."[77] A despot would insist on measuring a population's well-being by the individual maximum in the population, namely, his own, but that approach is out of fashion in most countries and I will not pursue it here. My goal is not to defend any measure but to make clear that a choice among measures reflects human values, not natural or logical constraints.

To show that the total, the average and the minimum have different consequences for estimating human carrying capacity, I have invented some fictional populations (Table 13.1). Suppose population A, our reference population, consists of ten people, eight of whom eat 2,000 kilocalories per day and two of whom eat 3,000 kilocalories per day. The total is 22,000 kilocalories, the average is 2,200 kilocalories and the minimum is 2,000 kilocalories. Population B, our first comparison population, consists of ten people, all of whom eat 3,000 kilocalories per day. By all three measures (total, average, minimum), population B is better off than population A. (If populations of ten people seem too unrealistic to interest you, replace each person by a billion people.)

That was an easy comparison. Now consider three more hypothetical populations. In population C, the total will be higher but the average and minimum both lower than in population A. In population D, the average will be higher but the total and minimum both lower than in population A. In population E, the minimum will be higher but the total and average both lower than in population A. Try to invent such populations yourself first!

Let population C have eleven people: ten who eat 2,200 kilocalories per day and one who eats 1,900 kilocalories per day; the total (23,900) is bigger but the average (2,173) and the minimum (1,900) are smaller. Let population D have nine people: one who eats 1,900 per day and eight who eat 2,450; the total (21,500) and the minimum (1,900) are lower than in population A, but the average (2,389) is higher. Let population E have ten people: all eat 2,100 kilocalories per day; the total (21,000) and the average (2,100) are lower than in population A, but the minimum (2,100) is higher. Would you prefer population A or population C? A or D? A or E? Ask someone else and see if you get the same answers.

To conclude the example, suppose that natural constraints prevent everyone from getting 3,000 kilocalories per day (population B) and that social constraints limit the options to populations C, D or E. Depending on whether you choose to maximize the total, the average or the minimum among these three alternatives, you will evaluate the Earth's human carrying capacity as eleven, nine or ten people. Economics cannot tell you whether it is better to have eleven people eating on the average 2,173 kilocalories per day (as in population C) or nine people eating on the average 2,389 kilocalories per day (as in population D)[78] or ten people in which everyone is assured a minimum of 2,100 kilocalories per day.[79]

From Fashion to Questions of Life and Death

If people choose to be clothed in cotton clothes, then there must be enough land and water to grow the required cotton plants. Growing one kilogram of cotton in Oklahoma uses about 29,000 kilograms of water, or 29 tonnes.[80] If people prefer wool, then water and land are wanted to grow the fodder or provide the grazing that feeds the sheep that provide the wool. Nylon is a polyamide derived from adipic acid, which in turn comes from oat hulls or corncobs[81]; nylon clothing could require no additional land and water beyond that already used for food or fodder. Rayon is cellulose ordinarily obtained from wood pulp,[82] so rayon clothing requires forest land. Recently a major paper company developed transgenic bacteria with the cellulose gene from plants so that cellulose could be produced industrially in bacterial fermenters. The land and water required per person for clothing depend materially (so to speak) on fashions, as well as on new technology. It makes no sense to think in terms of fixed ratios of land and water per person when human choices of fabrics strongly affect these requirements and ultimately human carrying capacity.

Though few people attach moral significance to tastes in fabrics, some do to the use of leather and furs for clothing. Dogs and swine are traditional Chinese foods; Europeans gladly consume swine but are horrified at the thought of eating dogs; Muslims and Jews define the consumption of dogs and swine as divinely prohibited.[83] Many people attach moral significance to the choice of animal or vegetable foods.[84] The choice of animal or vege-tarian diet, whether based on gastronomy or on morality, can have a major effect on human carrying capacity.

Some cultures routinely accept infanticide; others accept geriatricide; still others accept neither. Hardly any culture is indifferent to the control of demographic events, and most cultures attach emotional and moral mean-ing to birth, marriage, migration and death.[85]

Choices that appear to be economic also depend on individual and cul-tural values.[86] For examples, should industrial societies use the available supplies of fossil fuels in households for heating and for personal transporta-tion, or outside of households to produce other goods and services? Do people prefer a high average wage and low employment or a low average wage and high employment (if a high average wage and high employment are not simultaneously attainable)? If the use of energy for agriculture is to be lowered, is it better to cut surplus production using existing technology or to seek more energy-efficient technology? Should industrial economies seek now to develop renewable energy sources that maximize the deposits of fossil fuels that remain for future generations, or should industrial econo-mies continue to consume the available resources and leave the transition to other energy sources to future generations?

Should women work outside of their homes? It depends on the culture.[87] In the traditional Muslim societies of North Africa and Western Asia, women are discouraged from leaving home to work for others. Official statistics in Egypt report that fewer than 10 percent of women are in the labor force. As many as one-third of women participate in the labor force in sub-Saharan Africa and in some Asian countries, where women work in agriculture and marketing. In Latin America, about one-fifth of women of working age were in the labor force around 1990. In socialist countries, such as China and Vietnam, a large fraction of women work in the labor force. How women allocate their labor between their homes and the paid labor market, and what they do at home and in paid jobs, can alter the Earth's human carrying capacity in ways that are difficult to predict.

Even in apparently objective labor statistics, values play a role. People see what they want to see. Women's paid employment is underreported in labor surveys and censuses where culture frowns upon women working outside the home. For example, in Egypt, a careful survey estimated that

42 percent of agricultural workers in 1960 were women, not the 4 percent reported in the census.[88]

Most economic analysis that compares the present and the future discounts future income and costs. The British nutritionist Sir Kenneth Blaxter disowned this practice: "To me, and to many economists, the device of an intergenerational discount rate is repugnant and immoral. . . . we in our generation are in a monopolistic situation with respect to future generations. The more gloomy we are, the higher the intergenerational discount rate we will select and the greater will be our concern for the present rather than for our grandchildren."[89] Economists who disagree with Blaxter point to the observable preference many people have for a dollar of income now rather than ten years from now. People's willingness to defer income in return for greater compensation later is measured by the discount rate. I don't wish to take sides, only to underline two realities: values stand behind impeccable mathematics, and different people have different values.

Is it ever moral for people, by collective agreement, to extinguish a living species? Before you answer too quickly, hear the World Health Organization Commission on Health and Environment:

> Biodiversity is acknowledged as a condition for the long-term sustainability of the environment and its current destruction must be halted. . . . However, the protection of biodiversity cannot be unconditional; there may be conflict between the need to improve health or provide necessities and the need to preserve a species. In such instances the health cost of ensuring the survival of species that are pathogenic to humans or are pests of food crops will need to be carefully taken into account. There seems for example to be little ground for preserving the human immunodeficiency, smallpox, or poliomyelitis viruses, malaria parasites, or guinea worm.[90]

The elimination of these infectious agents could substantially increase human carrying capacity. Would it be worth risking the gain in health by failing to extinguish the agents altogether? What would the grain merchant I interviewed in Vellore say?

Are Organized Religions an Obstacle to Fertility Decline?

In the last few years, I spoke about topics presented in this book at colleges, universities and public meetings. Two questions were raised every time. One question was whether Roman Catholicism is a serious obstacle to the decline of fertility. Islam is sometimes also mentioned. The second question is whether AIDS (the acquired immunodeficiency syndrome) will "solve the population problem." I will respond to the second question in Chapter 15. Here I offer some observations on the role of religions in fertility decline.

In summary, the Catholic religion as practiced by many of its adherents is quite consistent with lowered fertility, but official Church doctrine has inserted substantial friction into the process of lowering fertility. Catholics use modern methods of contraception throughout the developed and most of the developing world. In Islam, by contrast with Roman Catholicism, there do not appear to be specific doctrinal prohibitions against modern methods of contraception, but the traditional roles that are permitted to women dramatically slow the spread of modern methods and the decline of fertility.

While factors other than religion seem to be decisive in the average levels of fertility for both Roman Catholics and Muslims, religious beliefs can influence when people have children. For example, the Years of the Dragon, including 1976 and 1988, are years of the Chinese zodiac considered particularly favorable for having children.[91] As the fertility of the Chinese in peninsular Malaysia declined from 1960 to 1990, the level of fertility spiked in 1976 and 1988, while the fertility of the Malay population continued its slower decline in those years (Figure 13.1). Such observations are close to a laboratory demonstration of the power of religion to influence the timing of fertility, because there is nothing special, economically or politically, about Years of the Dragon, and nothing that should affect the Chinese population differently from the Malay.

Granting that religion can affect when people have a child, can it affect how many they will have over a lifetime? To find out whether organized religion is a serious obstacle to fertility decline, it is impossible to do a controlled experiment, running history twice, once with and once without a major religion. Analyzing observational data on religion and fertility is full of pitfalls.[92] For example, some studies have compared differences in fertility between different religious groups without allowing for the economic differences between those groups. Differences that are attributed to religion could have been due to differences in income and wealth. Even the simple question of who is a Catholic is not so simple. Studies that select wives who consider themselves Catholic include converts who were not raised as Catholics as well as born Catholics with a wide range of religious practices; such samples exclude ex-Catholics and usually make no allowance for the religion of the husband. Within most major religions, including Roman Catholicism and Islam, orthodoxy varies from place to place; monolithic conclusions are probably unjustified. Because of limitations of data and methods, what follows is factually based and plausible but not definitive.

Roman Catholicism is not the only religion with an official position opposed to fertility control by modern methods. The Hutterites, the Amish and some Orthodox Jewish groups are similarly opposed.[93] Public attention focuses on the Catholic Church because it has a billion adherents[94] and political influence, and not because it alone is opposed to modern methods of contraception.

France was the first country to experience a fertility transition. France was and is a largely Catholic country. In 1992, the three geopolitical entities with the lowest total fertility rates in the world were Hong Kong (1.2 children per woman), Spain and Italy (both 1.3 children per woman).[95] The last two are Catholic, and Italy is host to the Vatican. In largely Catholic

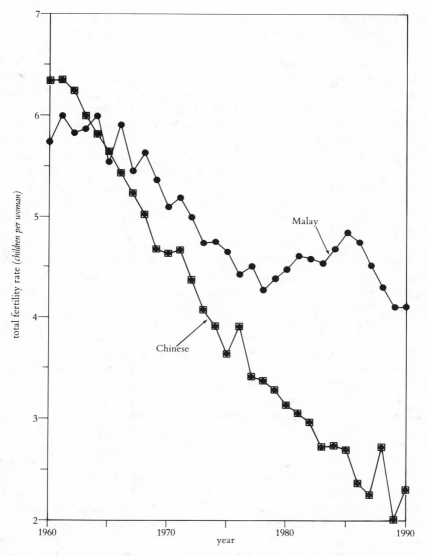

FIGURE 13.1   Total fertility rates (children ever born per woman, at current levels of fertility) of the Chinese and Malays in peninsular Malaysia from 1960 to 1990. The peaks in Chinese fertility in 1976 and 1988 coincided with the Year of the Dragon in the Chinese zodiac. SOURCE: Goodkind 1992

Latin America, fertility has been falling rapidly. While France's fertility transition predated the invention of modern methods of contraception, modern methods played a major role in recent fertility declines in Catholic countries and continue to play a major role in maintaining their present low levels of fertility.

In the United States, the fertility of Catholics has gradually converged to that of Protestants except in some cities with large concentrations of Catholics.[96] Using current religious status to determine whether a person was a Catholic inflated the positive effect of Catholicism on fertility. The inflation arose because Catholics who preferred smaller families were inclined to leave the Church, while respondents who wanted many children were inclined to join it. Catholic norms significantly increased fertility among respondents born before 1920, but a Catholic upbringing bore little relation to variations in fertility for respondents born after 1920.[97]

A Gallup poll in late 1992 reported that 83 percent of U.S. Catholics believe that the Catholic Church should approve of condoms to prevent the spread of AIDS. Some 87 percent said that couples should follow their consciences in deciding whether to use modern contraception. A poll conducted for *Time* magazine and CNN television reported that 79 percent of Catholics surveyed believed "people should make up their own minds about family planning and abortion."[98]

According to Daly and Cobb, "Catholicism encourages other-regarding behavior as a natural virtue."[99] So do many other religions. The Catholic Church's official doctrine does not yet appear to have caught up with the many modern Catholic couples in developed countries who are exercising the traditional Catholic sense of responsibility for family and community; in 1988, Pope John Paul II reaffirmed the Church's rejection of modern contraception. In some developing and developed countries, official Church positions have interfered with the frank recognition of couples' wants for modern contraception and have posed obstacles to governmental and nongovernmental family-planning programs.

For example, in March and April 1992, at the fourth preparatory committee session for the United Nations Conference on Environment and Development (UNCED) (which was held in June 1992 in Rio de Janeiro), the Holy See, Argentina, Ireland and Colombia managed to eliminate references to family planning and contraceptives from the chapter on population in Agenda 21, a comprehensive planning document for future governmental policies.[100] Such actions excited the ire of Prime Minister Brundtland of Norway: "I have been stunned to see how the Rio conference seems to fail to make workable decisions on how to curb population growth. States that do not have any population problem—in one particular case, even no births at all [the Vatican]—are doing their best, their utmost, to prevent the world from making sensible decisions regarding family planning. Family planning services must clearly be made universally available."[101]

On the positive side, through its promotion of literacy for adults, education for children and the survival of infants in developing countries, the Church has helped bring about some of the social preconditions for fertility decline.[102]

Catholicism, like most orthodoxies, shelters a diversity of views. On 15 June 1994, the Italian bishops' conference issued a report by a lay panel of the Pontifical Academy of Sciences that stated: "There is a need to contain births in order to avoid creating the insoluble problems that could arise if we were to renounce our responsibilities to future generations." Falling mortality and improved medical care "have made it unthinkable to sustain indefinitely a birth rate that notably exceeds the level of two children per couple—in other words the requirement to guarantee the future of human-ity."[103] The report does not say how couples should achieve that low level of fertility but recognizes an "unavoidable need to contain births globally." Pope John Paul II was reported to be infuriated by the report.

The world's Muslims, perhaps 935 million strong, are largely concentrated in northern and central Africa, the Middle East through Pakistan and India, and southeast Asia, Indonesia and the Philippines.[104] The average completed family size of Muslims is about six children, larger than that of any other major religious group.[105] Arab fertility rates are twice the world average and infant death rates are far higher than those in Western countries. Even in wealthy Saudi Arabia 8.3 percent of babies die before age one, whereas in northern Europe only 0.9 percent die.[106]

Muslim doctrine is not opposed to birth control. Companions of the Prophet Muhammad practiced coitus interruptus, and neither the Prophet nor the Qur'an prohibited it.[107] In 1988, the same year that Pope John Paul II confirmed the Catholic Church's rejection of modern contraception, the grand mufti of Al-Azhar in Egypt proclaimed an official religious decree or *fatwa* declaring that Islam accepts birth control.[108] While Muslim doctrine forbids abortion after quickening of the fetus except when pregnancy threatens the mother's life, some Muslim legal schools do not oppose abortion before quickening.[109]

In spite of doctrines favorable to modern contraception, birth rates and death rates in many Islamic countries have been slow to fall. According to the Italian demographer Massimo Livi-Bacci,

> Improved education, and especially female education (because of the woman's decisive role in childrearing, domestic hygiene, and food preparation), appears to be a necessary prerequisite to improved sanitary conditions. The fact that certain Islamic countries still have high levels of mortality in spite of considerable economic development has been explained by the subordinate status of women and the limited instruction they receive.[110]

The engineer Walter J. Karplus viewed "religious fundamentalism" as one of the two major obstacles to fertility decline (the other being "strident nationalism").[111] The ecologist William Murdoch argued, on the contrary, that "Religious beliefs have only small, although sometimes significant, effects on family size. Even these effects tend to disappear with rising levels of well-being and education."[112] Though Karplus's view is a common view, the evidence seems to me to favor Murdoch's.

What Happens When Moral Values Conflict?

Tastes and moral values that affect the Earth's human carrying capacity commonly conflict. Here is a striking example from the Harvard demographer Nathan Keyfitz: "Every couple has a right to as few or as many children as it wishes. That sounds fair enough, until one meets up with the parallel assertion that every child has the right to adequate nutrition. Suppose the world is made in such a way that these two rights cannot both exist once density goes above a certain point? Such incompatibilities of moral principles are not usually acknowledged in official documents."[113]

I will cite some additional examples, mention some proposed responses (not necessarily responses I accept) and suggest one way of organizing conflicts of values.

Kristin Shrader-Frechette, a philosopher at the University of Florida, Gainesville, analyzed three ethical issues[114]: First, should the wealth and environmental well-being of the world be distributed primarily according to egalitarian, utilitarian or libertarian values? Egalitarian principles would aspire to give future generations and today's poor equal opportunities to compete with today's rich and powerful for a share of the world's pie. The underlying axiom of egalitarianism is "that all human beings, within and among different generations and countries, share a social contract according to which all are to be treated as morally equal."[115] Of course, the notion and practice of equality are far subtler than these simple words suggest.[116] Utilitarian principles would aspire to maximize the well-being of all people, even if equal opportunity and equal treatment had to be sacrificed in the short term because they would delay eventual social improvement. Libertarian principles would aspire to fairness (no enslavement, theft, fraud or force) in the procedures by which the world pie is divided, whatever the equity or social utility of the resulting distribution of goods.

Shrader-Frechette argued in favor of egalitarian values. Virginia Abernethy, a professor of psychiatry at the Vanderbilt University School of Medicine, argued against them: "One-world ideology, which implies a commitment to sustaining the needy wherever they may be, creates ambiguity over the ownership of resources. As with most 'commons,' it fosters a preference for short-term consumption over long-term saving. The redistribution ethic not only undercuts incentives to conserve, but in a vastly overpopulated world may be impracticable. Uneven distribution seems a requisite of conservation under conditions where many are absolutely destitute and cannot afford to forgo consumption of their capital stock."[117]

Similarly, another author, who supposed that world supplies of phosphate rock would limit the global growth of population in the long run, thought it would be unethical to transfer food grown elsewhere to rapidly growing populations that cannot feed themselves.[118]

Zaba objected that Abernethy's view neglects "the problems caused by high per capita consumption. . . . Abernethy seems to believe that only the growing aspirations of growing populations are dangerous. . . ."[119] Abernethy, Hardin[120] and others, Zaba wrote, "concentrate on the threat that population growth in less-developed countries poses to the standard of living in the United States, whereas the threats to the local environments and social fabric of countries actually experiencing these growth rates are of a far higher order of magnitude."

The conflict between egalitarian and utilitarian values takes a very practical form in Kenya, Thailand, Brazil and Italy. In each country, one region (the arid northeast of Kenya, northeast Thailand, northeast Brazil, southern Italy) lags far behind the rest of the country in agriculture, natural resources, human skills, roads, communication facilities and industry. The people who live in the backward regions are poor, and often more fertile than the rest of the country; their skills and natural and economic resources do not make it easy for them to get richer. No easy technological fixes, like applying nitrogen or water to otherwise suitable soil, could make the backward regions as profitable for investments of capital as the more advanced regions. Where should national authorities and international lenders like the World Bank invest their funds? Public investments in a backward region may yield low returns for both the region and the country. Pushing more rapid growth in a more advanced region might make all areas better off.

For example, several donors combined to finance substantial investments in very low-yielding irrigation projects in northeast Thailand. These projects satisfied the government's desire to show that it did not discriminate against this region and the donors' desire to aid the poorest people. But these investments had a high opportunity cost: the money would have been more productively spent elsewhere.[121] The choice between egalitarian and utilitarian values can directly affect the human carrying capacity of such countries.

The second ethical problem Shrader-Frechette analyzed was: do the rights of individuals have priority over the rights of governments and groups, or vice versa?[122] For example, does a government have the right to sanction industrial emissions of dangerous pollutants on the grounds that further reductions are not cost effective, or do individuals have the right not to be exposed to the risks of cancer caused by those pollutants? Does a state or do potential parents have the ultimate right to control the number and spacing of children? Present-day Hutterites and Amish consider the control of marital fertility by conscious choice to be immoral.[123] What if they are surrounded by a majority who, like John Stuart Mill, regard "the producing of large families . . . with the same feelings as drunkenness or any other physical excess"?[124]

More generally, what if the childbearing decisions by independent couples or women lead to a level of fertility that the society decides it does not want (however the society arrives at and expresses its wants)? In Nepal, because of high fertility, people in the hill areas were gathering more fuelwood than forest growth was replacing, and were clearing forests to grow food. People were then migrating to lowland resettlement areas called *terai*. Children, as additional helping hands, became economically more valuable in the hill areas when traditional environmental monitoring and communal support broke down there. Children, again as laborers, also became economically more valuable in the *terai* because the mixed communities of immigrants there lacked traditional communal support and environmental monitoring. Density itself brought about social changes that made families find large size more attractive; large family size aggravated the problems of density.[125] Similarly, families in Bangladesh confronted with recurrent famines and floods sustained high fertility to counterbalance the economic and mortal risks. By trying to reduce their own vulnerability to disaster, families collectively worsened the risk and magnitude of disaster. Again, if farmers try to produce more food to feed more people by shortening fallow periods, soil fertility may decline and food production may fall. Does the farmer have the right to do as he or she sees fit, or does a government have the right to compel agricultural practices that it sees as more beneficial?[126]

In 1992, then-senator Al Gore proposed a solution to the conflict between individuals and groups that some might accept: "The emphasis on the rights of the individual must be accompanied by a deeper understanding of the responsibilities to the community that every individual must accept if the community is to have an organizing principle at all."[127] Will this hortatory principle solve some of the practical conflicts just described?

The third ethical conflict Shrader-Frechette raised was: should policies regarding population and the environment center on the values of people, all sentient beings (including animals, who are evidently capable of suffering), all living beings (including trees and viruses and fungi), everything on the Earth (do rocks have rights?) or whole ecosystems? Shrader-Frechette argued that anthropocentric values are theoretically preferable and practically more workable than ecocentric values. By contrast, a high government official, N. H. Biegman, writing in 1992 as Director General for International Cooperation of the Netherlands Ministry of Foreign Affairs, preferred ecocentric values:

> I, personally, find it hard to accept the tendency passed down to us by the Jewish, Christian and Islamic religions to see man as the centre and the measure of all things on earth. I think that even without man the earth would be a very worthwhile place and that as a latecomer on the scene man should show the necessary modesty. If one takes this view, the protection of nature and the environment requires no further argument. Nature can manage very nicely without man, but man cannot manage without nature.[128]

Edwin Dobb, a magazine editor writing on humankind's place in nature, argued that seeing an opposition between humans and nature is itself the problem, and the dichotomy is a false one: ". . . any definition of nature that excludes people and their works has always been indefensible, as has any definition of humanity that excludes nature. Wherever we stand, in the Gila Wilderness or in Times Square, we stand at the intersection of nature and culture."[129]

A simple framework for organizing conflicts of moral values is useful (Table 13.2). Conflicts of values can be classified as within persons or between persons, and within time periods or between time periods. A conflict of values within persons occurs when a single person, group or government holds two values that are incompatible with each other to some extent. Such conflicts require what have been called "tragic choices,"

TABLE 13.2   Classification of moral conflicts, with examples[a]

	conflict between two goods at the present time	conflict between a present good and a future good
conflict of two values held by the same person, group or government	Governments want to protect both health and the environment: "Priority given to human health raises an ethical dilemma if 'health for all' conflicts with protecting the environment." (WHO Commission on Health and Environment 1992, p. 4)	Rich countries' compassion for poor people in rapidly growing populations vs. rich countries' desire to conserve natural resources for the future: "Uneven distribution seems a requisite of conservation under conditions where many are absolutely destitute and cannot afford to forgo consumption of their capital stock." (Abernethy 1991, pp. 323–24)
conflict of two values held by different persons, groups or governments	Shall I have clean air or shall you? "Tall chimneys for coal-fired or oil-fired power stations can greatly reduce air pollution within their immediate environment, but they contribute to acid deposition at a considerable distance." (WHO Commission on Health and Environment 1992, p. 14)	Parents' present right to have children vs. children's future right to eat well: "Every couple has a right to as few or as many children as it wishes. . . . every child has the right to adequate nutrition. Suppose the world is made in such a way that these two rights cannot both exist once density goes above a certain point?" (Keyfitz 1991, p. 16)

[a] I do not necessarily accept the oppositions stated in these quotations; I cite them to illustrate what some people see as conflicts of values.

because a closely held value is doomed to be denied.[130] (The government and people of the United States value equal opportunity for all, but also protect procedurally fair exchanges that result in unequal distributions of wealth and well-being and, subsequently, unequal opportunities. In one view of population control in China, the government and people of China both accept the necessity of limiting Chinese population growth, but also value an abundance of sons to continue the family line and care for parents in their old age.[131]) A conflict of values between persons holds when one person, group or government holds values that are incompatible to some extent with the values of another person, group or government that exists at the same time and can defend its values. (A landowner has the right to clear-cut the trees on her property, but a local government has the right on behalf of all its citizens to prevent flooding and siltation in its watershed, which includes that private property. The conflict in China between the desire to limit population growth and the desire to have children, especially sons, has also been framed as a head-to-head conflict between the regime and the peasants.[132])

Both kinds of conflicts may oppose one present good against another (as in some of the parenthetical examples above) or a present good against a future good (a timber company wants to cut an old forest now to meet the market demand for wood products, but conservationists want to preserve the rare or endangered species that live there for the benefit of future generations).

A poor population with a high child death rate faces a conflict of values. On the one hand, a lowered child death rate is good for children now and may eventually contribute to the lowering of future birth rates. On the other hand, a lower child death rate now accelerates present population growth; more rapid immediate population growth may overwhelm the population's ecological supports, impoverish the population further and render a future fall in fertility more difficult.[133]

The WHO Commission on Health and Environment gave an important example of a conflict between values held by itself:

> Priority given to human health raises an ethical dilemma if "health for all" conflicts with protecting the environment. Two extreme positions may be envisaged. The first stresses individual rights, societal good being seen as the aggregate of everyone's personal preferences and any controls over the individual's use of resources as an infringement of the individual's freedom. The other extreme—a response to increasing environmental degradation—gives priority to the environment and to the maintenance of the ecosystem. All species are seen as having rights as people do, environmental welfare thus coming before human welfare. A middle ground between these extremes can be found by distinguishing between first-order and second-order ethical principles. Priority to ensuring human survival is taken as a first-order principle. Respect for nature and control of environmental degradation is a second-order principle, which must be observed unless it conflicts with the first-order principle of meeting survival needs.[134]

And who decides which principles are first order, which are second order?

The WHO Commission on Health and Environment also identified short-term local conflicts between improving health by the cheapest means and maintaining a clean environment. Power stations that burn coal or oil can reduce local air pollution by venting combustion products through tall chimneys; doing so increases acid deposition elsewhere. A country rich enough to import minerals and timber transfers the environmental costs of mining and logging to the exporting country.[135]

Humans seem to resolve conflicts of values by personal and social processes that are poorly understood and virtually unpredictable at present. How such conflicts are resolved can materially affect human carrying capacity, and so there is a large element of choice and uncertainty in human carrying capacity.

I emphasized in this chapter that the Earth's human carrying capacity depends on human choices, including human values. Not all of those choices are free choices. Natural constraints restrict the possible options, as the next chapter will show by example.

14

Water: A Case Study
of Natural Constraints

> I know of nine-year-old farm lads in jail for mur-
> der over water disputes.
>
> —SYED AYUB QUTUB 1993[1]

THE EARTH IS the sole planet in the solar system where water is abundant in liquid form. Though ice, steam and the liquid form of water are all abundant on the Earth, only the liquid supports active life.

Brian J. Skinner, a geologist at Yale University, claimed that "More than any other factor, availability of water determines the ultimate population capacity of a geographic province."[2] To prove that claim would require varying the availability of water and every other factor in a system model that has never been constructed. By selecting water for a case study, as I do in this chapter, I do not assert water's primacy. I do assert that water is important, among other important natural constraints.[3] Water illustrates the questions that must be answered to determine how any natural resource constrains the human population, as well as the difficulty of answering these questions.

1. How much water is available?
2. What is the minimum requirement for subsistence?
3. How many people can the available water support, now and in the future?
4. How does water interact with other resources that potentially constrain human population?
5. How does water limit human population size?
6. How could radical developments affect water supplies?

The best short answers to these questions show that much remains to be learned about natural constraints, and that natural constraints cannot be viewed other than through the lens of human purposes.

1. The amounts of each kind of water vary from place to place and from time to time, and are not known with much precision. The availability of water depends heavily on human choices.
2. The minimum requirement for subsistence depends on how you define subsistence.
3. I answer one question with two questions: How much water do people want to use, and how much are they willing to pay for it?
4. Water interacts strongly with other resources, human and natural.
5. Water can limit a human population in extreme circumstances. When time and means permit people to adapt to water constraints, other factors can constrain population size before water does.
6. Cheap energy, nonconventional agriculture and interventions in the hydrologic cycle could make a huge difference; incremental improvements seem more likely.

In dry regions, water is a major constraint on the distribution of nonhuman and aboriginal human primates. For example, in the semi-arid savanna of East Africa, baboons congregate where groundwater comes to the surface; there water permits plants to flourish and animals to drink.[4] In Australia, among aborigines that depended strictly on local rainfall to provide water for drinking and plant growth (thus excluding tribes dependent on coastal marine resources or rivers), the area occupied by a tribe increased roughly 16 percent for each 10 percent decrease in the mean annual rainfall.[5] As tribes had a geometric mean population size of some 500 people, regardless of area, the population density increased about 16 percent for each 10 percent increase in the mean annual rainfall. Granting that water may constrain the population density of people living by means of Old Stone Age technology, what role does water play for today's global population?

Even a summary list of some of the ways people currently use water shows the scope for choice, efficiency, recycling and waste. People use water to drink and cook; wash themselves; wash clothes, homes and other possessions; air-condition; remove excreta; purify sewage; play (swim, canoe, boat, skate, sled, ski, garden); grow food, fibers, domesticated aquatic and land animals, forests and other cash crops; sustain wildlife and natural ecosystems; transport people and goods; generate electrical power; and in industry to cool, heat, clean and flush.

How many people water can support depends on how people use or misuse it. Reducing leakage in the delivery of water to homes, farms and industries, reducing the use of water to dilute contaminants, more recycling of water after use and more sensible pricing of water are more likely to alleviate existing and prospective water shortages than spectacular technical advances.[6]

How Much Water Is Available?

The Earth's stocks of water are immense. Geologists define free water as water that is not locked in the minerals of the crust. The estimated 1.4 billion cubic kilometers of free water would cover the entire Earth to a depth of 2.75 kilometers (1.7 miles).[7] For comparison, if all the present humans were reduced to soup and spread evenly over the Earth's surface, including oceans and continents, the film would be about half a micrometer—half a millionth of a meter—thick. Now *there's* a fun calculation for you.

Only a few percent of the Earth's water is fresh. The Russian hydrologist Igor A. Shiklomanov estimated 2.5 percent is fresh. The Harvard engineer Peter P. Rogers estimated 5.8 percent is fresh,[8] mainly because he estimated six times more fresh groundwater than other water experts (Table 14.1). Remembering the Law of Information, you should take the estimates of fresh water with a grain of salt.

Of global fresh water, 69 percent is locked in glaciers, permanent snow cover and aquifers more than a kilometer deep. Such aquifers are generally considered inaccessible. Roughly 30 percent of fresh water is accessible groundwater. The estimates of Rogers roughly reverse these proportions.[9] Less than 0.3 percent of all fresh water, 93,000 cubic kilometers (about seven parts in 100,000 of all fresh and salt water), is found in freshwater lakes and rivers (Table 14.1).

The stock of renewable fresh water is constantly depleted and regenerated by the hydrologic cycle—the perpetual circulation of water down from the sky as precipitation and back up again through evaporation (primarily) and transpiration (secondarily). Transpiration is the removal of water from the ground into plants and its evaporation from plants back to the atmosphere. It is difficult to measure evaporation independently of transpiration. Evapotranspiration includes both processes. The hydrologic cycle of precipitation and evapotranspiration has been understood scientifically only in the last two centuries.[10]

How much rain, snow and other precipitation fall annually on the Earth's islands and continents? Estimates vary.[11] At the high end, Shiklomanov estimated 119,000 cubic kilometers per year, an average of roughly one meter of precipitation per year over the entire land surface of the Earth.[12] At the low end, the geophysicist Frank Press of the Massachusetts Institute of Technology and the geologist Raymond Siever of Harvard University estimated precipitation over land at 90,000 cubic kilometers per year.[13] Between these extremes, the World Resources Institute estimated it at 110,000 cubic kilometers per year; the Russian hydrologist M. I. L'vovich estimated it at 113,500 cubic kilometers per year.[14] This range of variation shows that there is much more uncertainty than the significant digits of any single estimate would suggest (another grain of salt, please). Of the—shall we say?—113,000 cubic kilometers of annual precipitation,[15] about 72,000

Table 14.1   Global water stocks

type of water	Shiklomanov			Press and Siever			Rogers		
	volume (thousand cubic kilometers)	percentage of total water	percentage of fresh water	volume (thousand cubic kilometers)	percentage of total water	percentage of fresh water	volume (thousand cubic kilometers)	percentage of total water	percentage of fresh water
all	1,385,984	100		1,387,601	100		1,454,000	100	
salt water (world ocean, saline lakes and inland seas)	1,350,955	97.5		1,350,000	97.3		1,369,000	94.2	
fresh water	35,029	2.5	100	37,600.6	2.7	100	84,400	5.8	100
glaciers, icecaps, permanent snow	24,064	1.7	68.7	29,000	2.1	77.1	24,000	1.7	28.4
fresh groundwater	10,530	0.76	30.1	8,400	0.6	22.3	60,000	4.1	71.1
freshwater lakes and rivers	93	0.007	0.27	200	0.01	0.53	281.2	0.02	0.33
other[a]	341	0.025	0.97				85	0.006	0.10
biosphere	1		0.003	0.6	4×10^{-5}	0.002			

[a] "Other" includes soil moisture, ground ice, permafrost, swamp water. Atmospheric water, which is approximately 0.001 percent of total water (Skinner 1969, p. 130; Shiklomanov 1993, p. 13), is included under "other" in the estimates of Shiklomanov and apparently excluded from the estimates of Press and Siever and of Rogers.

Sources: Shiklomanov (1993, p. 13); Press and Siever (1986, p. 167); Rogers (1985, p. 262)

cubic kilometers evaporate or are transpired back to the atmosphere, leaving about 41,000 cubic kilometers to replenish aquifers or return to the ocean as runoff. These estimates also vary.[16]

The PETRI equation is a convenient way to account for the water flowing through the hydrologic cycle.[17] For a given land area, Precipitation = Evaporation from soil and plants + Transpiration + Runoff of surface water + Infiltration into the soil, or $P = E + T + R + I$. Of the water that infiltrates into the soil, some remains available to plants in the shallow root zone and some recharges groundwater. In arid areas, where precipitation is much less than potential evapotranspiration, runoff and infiltration are relatively small and $P = E + T$. By contrast, in humid areas, where precipitation is much larger than evapotranspiration, runoff and infiltration are important. In the subhumid and semi-arid areas where precipitation roughly balances potential evapotranspiration, all the water goes into evapotranspiration in dry years, but wet years bring runoff (possibly flooding if the soil surface has become impermeable) and infiltration (if the soil surface remains permeable).

The annual 41,000 cubic kilometers of freshwater runoff and infiltration correspond to $R + I$ in the equation $R + I = P - E - T$. The global volume or stock of river water at any instant is about 2,000 cubic kilometers; this water empties into the oceans and is renewed every 16 to 18 days or so, making the total annual river flow $R + I$ about 20 times larger than the stock of river water at any moment.[18] The flood runoff R is about 28,000 cubic kilometers and the renewable infiltration I of stable underground flow into rivers is about 13,000 cubic kilometers[19] or 14,000 cubic kilometers.[20] This renewable groundwater I explains why big rivers keep flowing even after it has not rained for a while; the rivers are fed from beneath. Renewable groundwater and meteoric water (rain, snow, hail and sleet) are natural water supplies that people can count on without human intervention.

People can capture for use only a fraction of the freshwater runoff and infiltration of 41,000 cubic kilometers per year. Of the 28,000 cubic kilometers per year of flood runoff, the usable portion depends on the capacity of human-made dams and lakes and on how often the water in such reservoirs is turned over. Of the total of 13,000 to 14,000 cubic kilometers per year of water that infiltrates the soil, about 5,000 cubic kilometers per year falls on uninhabited areas; how much of this 5,000 cubic kilometers per year can be used depends on technology for capturing and transporting water. This leaves about 9,000 cubic kilometers of infiltrated water or stable underground flow in regions where people live. The world's *available* renewable fresh water lies somewhere between the 9,000 cubic kilometers per year of stable underground flow in inhabited regions[21] and the 14,000 cubic kilometers per year if the stable underground flow in uninhabited regions is included, plus the usable capacity of human-made reservoirs.[22]

Local supplies of renewable fresh water vary greatly from place to place, from year to year and from season to season within any year. The natural unit for describing the spatial variation of renewable fresh water is the river

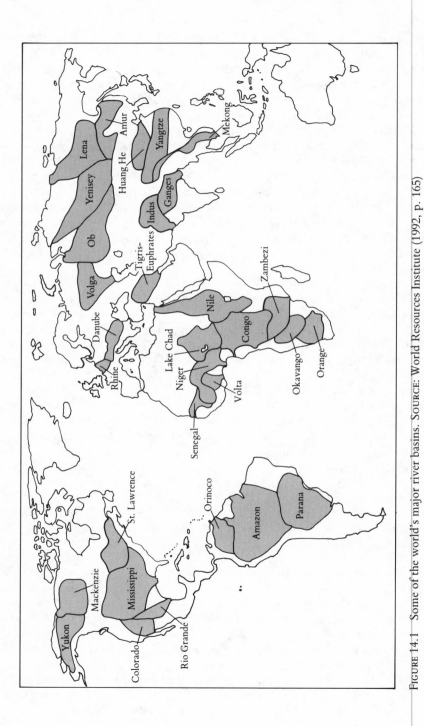

FIGURE 14.1   Some of the world's major river basins. SOURCE: World Resources Institute (1992, p. 165)

basin, simply because streams and rivers do not carry water across the boundary of a river basin. If one neglects groundwater flows across the boundary of a river basin, the input of water to a basin can be easily measured by measuring precipitation, and the water is counted only once on its way from the sky to the ocean. Though the number of streams and rivers is enormous, half the runoff of the world's land is carried by about 70 major river systems[23]; about half of these systems are shown in Figure 14.1.

Regional renewable water supplies vary widely. The Amazon basin and parts of south and southeast Asia generally receive heavy rainfall; the Middle East, north Africa, north-central Asia, parts of south Asia and central Australia receive little rain.[24] Over short periods, the difference between places may be very wide: in the Chilean desert at Iquique, no rain fell for one stretch of 14 years, while Cherrapunji, India, had 22 meters of rain in one year. In the United States, the average annual rainfall in parts of Hawaii exceeds ten meters per year but in some deserts is near zero.[25] The Pacific Northwest receives 382 cubic kilometers of renewable water per year (and consumes 4.5 percent of it), while the Rio Grande river basin receives 7.5 cubic kilometers (and consumes 59 percent of it); people in the Lower Colorado river basin consume more than 100 percent of their renewable water supply by mining groundwater.[26]

Estimating renewable fresh water for countries is trickier than for river basins because countries do not generally correspond to watersheds. An estimated 214 river basins and lake basins (areas drained by a lake) are shared by two or more countries; these basins are home to 40 percent of the Earth's human population and cover more than half of its land area.[27] Many aquifers cross international borders. Who has the right to use the water in such rivers, lakes and aquifers, for either withdrawals or discharges? If a river flows through several countries, the same water may be counted multiple times and its usefulness to downstream countries may be altered by how upstream countries use it. The Danube River touches more than a dozen countries; the Nile supplies eight countries before it reaches Egypt.[28] Both rivers are constantly in contention. In such situations, national supplies of renewable fresh water may be unclear.

In spite of the difficulties of definition and measurement, Peter H. Gleick, a water expert at the Pacific Institute for Studies in Development, Environment, and Security, estimated renewable water resources (stream flows corrected for evaporation plus international inflow from rivers) for 149 countries. Robert Engelman and Pamela LeRoy, of the program on population and the environment at Population Action International, Washington, collated these estimates with 1990 population estimates and ranked the countries from least to greatest according to the annual available fresh water per person.[29] The average person in Djibouti, the most water-scarce country in the world, has available some 23 cubic meters of fresh water per year; the average person in Iceland has available about 29,000 times as much. These are the extremes. Israel, with 461 cubic meters per person, has half the available fresh water of Somalia, with 980 cubic meters per person, though Israel's 1989 gross national product per person was roughly 57 times Somalia's.[30] The United States has about 9,900 cubic meters of renewable fresh water per person per year.

Overall, in 1990, when the world's population was about 5.3 billion and the renewable supply of fresh water totaled 41,000 cubic kilometers per year, the average renewable fresh water per person per year totaled about 7,700 cubic meters. In 1987 people withdrew 3,240 cubic kilometers (about 660 cubic meters per person) of fresh water.[31] For historical comparison, in 1680, people numbering perhaps 600 million withdrew less than 100 cubic kilometers (less than 200 cubic meters per person) of fresh water.[32]

Intermittent freshwater supply could be related to poverty at the national level.[33] Malin Falkenmark, a hydrologist at the Natural Science Research Council in Stockholm, compared three world maps: one of countries with annual income per person below U.S.$500, one of regions with a low "human capability index" (a composite measure of purchasing power, life expectancy and literacy) and one of regions where at least part of the year is dry. She observed that in most currently poor countries, part of the year is dry or recurrent drought years are part of the climate or both. She suggested that there could be a causal connection between the intermittent freshwater supply and poverty.

Freshwater supplies vary in both space and time. The average over time of freshwater supplies is often a misleading guide to how much water is available in most years because the average may combine a few years of flooding with many years of little precipitation. Some countries suffer flooding in a rainy season and near-drought the rest of the year; others receive steadier precipitation. In general, the lower the average annual level of rainfall, the wider the swings from year to year, from season to season and from place to place.[34] In the Indus basin, the average amount of water available annually is 169 cubic kilometers (or 137 million acre-feet), but one year in five flows are less than 152 cubic kilometers (or 123 million acre-feet).[35] Roughly 40 percent of the world's population, living in 80 dry or partially dry countries, face serious periodic droughts.[36] In such countries, the amount of water that can be counted on, say, 95 years in 100, is commonly less than half of the annual average.[37]

How much people can use the water that nature provides depends heavily on human investments in cisterns, dams, wells, pipelines and facilities for the treatment and recycling of water. Visitors to the Negev desert in Israel today can see immense cisterns built beneath every house and every public building in Nabatean cities that are at least two millennia old. These cisterns permitted Nabatean outposts to prosper along trade routes in the desert. Before the Nabateans, the Second Book of Chronicles recorded that King Uzziah, who succeeded Solomon as a king of Judah, "built towers in the wilderness and hewed out many cisterns."[38] In the Petén jungle of northern Guatemala, in spite of four virtually rainless months a year, Mayans built an empire around a city, Tikal, that once supported as many as 90,000 people. They used paved areas of the central city to catch fresh water during the eight rainy months. An elaborate system of reservoirs watered homes and surrounding farms year-round.[39]

Today human–made reservoirs have a useful capacity globally of 3,000 to 5,000 cubic kilometers, roughly twice the stock of water in all the world's rivers.[40] Around the world, more than 36,000 dams more than 15 meters high prevent flooding and smooth the supply of useful water.[41] In the United States, San Francisco gets water from the Sierra Nevada hundreds of kilometers away while Los Angeles depends on waters from as far away as the Colorado River.[42] New Yorkers drink and bathe in water delivered by a far-flung network of reservoirs and aqueducts. Wells can draw from renewable groundwaters, if the technological capacity to drill and maintain them and the energy to pump them are available.

The question "How much water is available?" makes sense by itself if water is viewed only in physical terms, but is incomplete if viewed in human terms. I would complete it by asking, "Available to whom? When and where? At what cost?" For example, in 1980 about 43 percent of the population of developing countries reportedly had "reasonable access" to safe supplies of drinking water.[43] The chief limitation in these countries was not physical supply. How quickly water supplies could be improved depended, rather, on each country's costs, financial resources, trained personnel and community organization. To mobilize these resources requires finding means appropriate for each country's natural and social environment.

How Much Water Is Required?

In describing how people use water, hydrologists distinguish consumption from withdrawal. Withdrawal means the removal of water from a natural source, such as a river, lake or aquifer. This definition is unambiguous and is the measure most hydrologists use because it is difficult to measure water consumption. Water is consumed when it evaporates, is transpired or is used in a way that leaves it unfit for any further use.[44] While evaporation and transpiration are clearly defined, "unfit for any further use" depends on the further uses you may have in mind and the available processes for treating and using water. The definition of water consumption is less clear cut than that of withdrawal.

For example, you might think that the water that people drink is consumed. In fact, a small fraction evaporates (and is therefore consumed by definition) but most is excreted. What happens to the excreted water is a matter of choice: it can be a source of pollution or a resource. Thirty years ago, 757 cubic meters of human urine and 400 tonnes of human feces from St. Louis daily fertilized the Mississippi River.[45] Now, human and other wastes from the Calcutta sewage system feed the largest single waste-fed aquaculture system in the world.[46] Sewage and water are fed into two lakes that cover approximately 25 square kilometers (the area of a square three miles on a side). Following an initial algal bloom and a delay to let the water re-aerate, the lakes are stocked with carp, tilapia and other fishes. Additional sewage is applied monthly. This system yields 7,000 tonnes of fish a year, or 2.8 tonnes per hectare. Simple measures prevent the fish from transmitting human pathogens. In the Calcutta aquaculture system, human drinking water is a withdrawal with a large rate of return, rather than consumption.

The portion of the withdrawn water that is not consumed may later be returned—discharged—to the same or a different natural source. Different human activities consume widely varying fractions of water withdrawals. About 25 percent of agricultural water withdrawn returns to streams as wastewater, about 86 percent of industrial water flows back to rivers and coastal waters and about 60 percent of water withdrawn for domestic purposes returns to rivers.[47] Worldwide in 1987, 69 percent of water withdrawals were for agriculture, 23 percent were for industry and only 8 percent were for domestic use.[48]

The regional balance of agricultural, industrial and domestic withdrawals varied widely. The fraction of water withdrawals used for agriculture ranged from 88 percent in Africa and 86 percent in Asia to 33 percent in Europe and 34 percent in Oceania. The fraction of water withdrawals for industry ranged from 54 percent in Europe and 42 percent in North America to 5 percent in Africa and 2 percent in Oceania. The fraction of water withdrawals for domestic use varied from 64 percent in Oceania to 6 percent in Asia and the former USSR and 7 percent in Africa.

A crude estimate of the global fraction of withdrawn water that is discharged can be obtained by multiplying the global fraction of water withdrawn for each sector by the global fraction that sector discharges. Thus 0.69×0.25 (for agriculture) $+ 0.23 \times 0.86$ (for industry and mining) $+ 0.08 \times 0.60 = 0.4183$ or 42 percent of water withdrawn was discharged in 1987. (Check me with your calculator please!) If this water could be used again and again for its primary purposes, then the effective freshwater supply could be increased by 70 percent.[49] This estimate of the global fraction of discharged water is crude because the fraction discharged by each sector might be correlated with the size of that sector (for example, if those who use more agricultural water were less efficient). The 42 percent discharge rate, while only a first approximation, does suggest a substantial potential worldwide for expanding the usable fresh water if users could avoid polluting the water they discharged. In 1985, Rogers estimated that, as of 1970, the world's people withdrew about 3,500 cubic kilometers of fresh water per year and contaminated about 5,800 cubic kilometers, roughly two-thirds more than they withdrew.[50] Opportunities to use water more efficiently were, and are, ample.[51]

Water Quality Matters

There is more to water than just quantity. The fraction of discharged water that can be put to secondary use depends on the nature and quantity of the physical, chemical and biological agents in the water, as well as the possibilities for human management of discharged water. Nutrients from sewage and eroded soil support algal and other microbial blooms. These blooms exhaust the dissolved oxygen in water that fish require, and may produce toxins dangerous to the health of humans and wildlife. Evaporation of water from agricultural soils may concentrate in the soil the mineral salts that occur there naturally; subsequent rainfall or irrigated water may carry these salts into groundwater or runoff and render well water unfit for human consumption. Bacterial and viral pathogens from human excreta and other sewage may spread disease; in developing countries, more than 95 percent of urban sewage goes into surface waters without treatment.[52] Heavy metals, pesticides and other synthetic organic compounds from mining, agriculture and industry may be concentrated in microscopic aquatic plants, further concentrated in the small animals that eat those plants and concentrated still further in the fish that eat small water animals and the water birds that prey on both. The process by which toxins are concentrated along a food chain is called bioaccumulation. Because of bioaccumulation, the New York State Department of Health advises people not to eat any freshwater fishes caught in New York State more often than once a week, and some bottom-feeding or fatty fishes not at all.

The quality of water is crucial to human health. Nearly half the people in the world—practically all of them in developing countries, and most of them poor—suffer from diseases related to insufficient or contaminated water.[53] Two billion people are at risk of waterborne and foodborne diarrheal diseases. These diseases are the main biological reason nearly four million children die each year. Schistosomiasis infects some 200 million people through contact with infested fresh water. Dracunculiasis infects 10 million through drinking water that contains the disease vector, a nematode called the guinea worm. In addition, insect vectors that breed in water transmit malaria (which infects 267 million people—specious precision!), filariasis (which infects 90 million), onchocerciasis (which infects 18 million) and dengue fever (which infects 30 million to 60 million people each year). In addition to biological agents, trace chemicals in water can significantly affect human health.[54]

In addition to affecting human health, water pollution interferes with the ecosystem services provided by lakes, streams and groundwaters. Water pollution raises the cost of water as an input to industry and diverts resources from economic development to water treatment and management. For all these reasons, water quality matters.

Individual Water Requirements

To estimate human water requirements per person quantitatively, consider drinking, domestic uses (washing and cooking and sanitation), food and other uses of water.

How much drinking water does one person require? In temperate climates, people drink about two liters (roughly two quarts) of water per day.

Two liters of water weigh two kilograms, so a year's supply weighs $2 \times 365 = 730$ kilograms and occupies 0.73 cubic meter. One cubic meter of water weighs one tonne or 1,000 kilograms. In arid climates, up to three times as much drinking water may be required to avoid dehydration. Even allowing for water-drinking sprees, as a global average one to two cubic meters of water per year per person suffice for drinking.

In a developing country, for all household purposes, including drinking and cooking, a typical urban resident uses 7 to 15 cubic meters per year and a rural person two to four cubic meters per year. Falkenmark proposed that water-deficient countries should strive to assure 100 liters per person per day for health and minimal personal well-being.[55] This amounts to 36.5 cubic meters per year per person and is about half of typical domestic water consumption in North American towns.[56]

Except for the physiologically required drinking water, people use less water if they have to pay more for it. In 1978, for example, the citizens of Boston, Massachusetts, paid $0.26 per cubic meter for fresh water and used 323 cubic meters per year per person (much of which leaked away), while the citizens of Frankfurt, Germany, paid $0.75 per cubic meter, nearly three times as much, and used only 55 cubic meters per year per person, about one-sixth as much.[57] When water meters were introduced in Boulder, Colorado, domestic water use for all purposes dropped 35 percent; watering of lawns alone dropped by 49 percent. In Israeli households with no lawns to water, households with water meters used 25 percent less water than carefully matched households without meters. Economists estimate that when the price of water rises by 10 percent, say, the ordinary person (distinguished from the farmer or the industrialist) generally uses between 1.5 and 7 percent less water.[58] For many discretionary uses (and that includes most uses beyond drinking), people respond to the price of water.

In addition to drinking, people like to eat, and that requires much more water than might at first appear. The one or two cubic meters a year required for drinking—even the lofty goal of 37 cubic meters per year for all domestic uses—are a mere drop in the bucket compared to the water required to grow food, because the plants that people eat are very thirsty. Wheat, rice, corn, other cereals and tubers dominate the plant crops. The thirst of each crop is described by its transpiration ratio. The transpiration ratio is the number of kilograms (or liters) of water a plant transpires to produce one kilogram (dry weight) at maturity. The transpiration ratio of wheat is 500; that of sorghum, 250; of corn, 350; of potato, 636; of cucumber, 713; of alfalfa, 800 to 900.[59] If half the weight of the wheat plant is wheat to be milled, and if most of the weight of bread is wheat, then one kilogram of bread requires two kilograms of wheat plant. Ignoring ingredients other than wheat, one kilogram of bread requires the final consumption, through transpiration alone, of 1,000 kilograms, or one cubic meter, of water.[60] Similarly, the transpiration ratio of rice under field conditions is 200 to 400. About half the dry weight of the mature rice plant is in the edible grain. So 400 to 800 kilograms of water are transpired for each kilogram of edible rice grain.[61] There is no way for people to recapture the water transpired by wheat plants or rice plants grown in an open field, short of waiting for it to condense and fall again as rain or snow. The natural dynamics of the hydrologic cycle set the rate of recycling of transpired water.

A transpiration ratio is typically measured in a laboratory or greenhouse using a plant in a pot with a cover over the soil to prevent water from evaporating. Growing that same plant in a farmer's field provides many ways to lose water in addition to transpiration. In the Indus basin of Pakistan, only 30 percent of diverted water at canal heads reaches crop roots[62]; the rest evaporates or seeps away on the way to the field or as it is applied in the field. To harvest a kilogram of wheat in Oklahoma, American farmers use not the theoretical minimum of one tonne, but four tonnes of irrigation water[63]; even if one of those four tonnes runs off and could theoretically be recycled, the remaining three tonnes are three times the theoretical minimum. To harvest one kilogram of corn in Colorado, U.S. farmers use 600 kilograms of irrigation water (though the transpiration ratio is 350); for one kilogram of rice in a tropical climate, farmers use five tonnes (5,000 times its weight) of irrigation water.[64] The global average water consumed (not withdrawn) per kilogram of grain was estimated at 3.3 tonnes in 1979.[65]

Systems of irrigation that deliver water directly to the roots of the plant can use water much more efficiently. In some cases, sensors inform a computer of the light intensity and temperature; the computer calculates how much water the plant transpires and controls a pump to deliver the right number of drops. While efficient in water use, such systems are vastly more demanding of capital equipment and human skills for design, installation, operation and maintenance.

Farmers, even more than city folks, generally reduce their use of water when the price rises. In the United States, a 10 percent increase in the price of water for irrigation induces farmers to buy between 3 percent and 20 percent less of it. Farmers respond to a change in water prices with roughly twice the change in water consumption of households. Prices make a huge difference to water use. But so does biology: conventional wheat plants cannot be persuaded to produce a kilogram of edible grain for much less than a tonne of water, though wheat plants do not care whether the water falls naturally or arrives as irrigation. To avoid trying to guess the future price of irrigation water and farmers' responses to that price, I will use only the theoretical minimum of a tonne of water (from precipitation or irrigation) for a kilogram of wheat grain to make my subsequent calculations. I will use wheat for illustration, though perhaps two-thirds of the world relies on rice as the staple grain.

How much water per year is required to give one person 1,000 kilocalories of daily energy from wheat for a year? Wheat flours vary in energy content, but a useful figure is that one gram of wheat flour supplies 3.5 kilocalories, or one kilogram supplies 3,500 kilocalories.[66] Bread purchased in U.S. stores supplies considerably fewer calories per kilogram; for example, enriched white bread made with 5 to 6 percent nonfat dry milk yields only 2,740 kilocalories per kilogram.[67] A thousand kilocalories daily amounts to 365,250 kilocalories yearly, which could be supplied by 365,250 / 3,500 = 104.4 kilograms of wheat flour. The growth of this much wheat flour would transpire 104.4 cubic meters of water. The underlying data justify no more precise statement than the rule of thumb that 1,000 daily kilocalories of energy from wheat require about 100 yearly tonnes of water from precipitation or irrigation, minimum.

How many calories people eat daily depends on their biological requirements, on their cultural traditions and on their economic ability to buy or produce food. Estimates of biological requirements and economic demand—you guessed it—vary widely (Appendix 5). Variation in requirements for subsistence is not surprising. From a historical study of food supplies, heights and weights, the historian Robert W. Fogel at the University of Chicago concluded:

> Subsistence is not located at the edge of a nutritional cliff, beyond which lies demographic disaster. . . . [R]ather than one level of subsistence, there are numerous levels at which a population and a food supply can be . . . indefinitely sustained. However, some levels will have smaller people and higher "normal" (noncrisis) mortality than others.[68]

According to the manual of the Food and Agricultural Organization,[69] the average caloric requirements of a national population depend on the age and sex composition of the population, average body weights for each group by age and sex, basal metabolic rates based on body weight and sex and physical activity levels by age and sex. They depend only slightly on the average annual temperature because people modify their behavior through clothing and housing to adjust for climate. The average requirements per person range from 1,884 kilocalories per day in Ethiopia to 2,390 kilocalories per day in the United States. In very round numbers, people consume about 2,000 kilocalories per day. To produce a wheat diet of 2,000 kilocalories per day requires 200 tonnes per year of water, as an absolute minimum set by transpiration alone.

These calculations take no account of losses as the wheat grows and is harvested, processed, distributed and consumed. If 40 percent of wheat were lost between production and consumption,[70] the water requirement would rise to 330 to 350 cubic meters per year per person. Assuming that people eat 2.5 pounds of bread a day and neglecting any losses, Charles C. Bradley estimated that a vegetarian diet would require 415 cubic meters of water a year (or 300 gallons a day).[71]

Eating meat demands more water than eating wheat. Estimates of how many calories of plant food must be grown to obtain a calorie of animal food range from 4.5 to 16.[72] I shall use a ratio of ten as a middle figure. You can repeat the calculation with higher and lower values of the ratio.

If 20 percent of calories come from animal products, each 1,000 kilocalories has 800 kilocalories from wheat and 200 kilocalories from, let us say, beef. If growing the plants to feed the beef requires ten times as much water as the wheat for each calorie on the consumer's plate, then the annual water requirement for each 1,000 kilocalories of this diet is 0.8×100 (for the wheat) $+ 0.2 \times 100 \times 10$ (for the meat) $= 280$ cubic meters per 1,000 kilocalories. A diet of 2,000 kilocalories per day would require 560 cubic meters per year per person. This amount of water could be supplied by precipitation or irrigation.

The factor of ten used to estimate the water required to raise beef may be checked against the report that one kilogram of beef steak produced by a typical California cattle operation uses 20.5 cubic meters of water.[73] One kilogram of raw choice T-bone steak yields approximately 4,000 kilocalories.[74] Thus raising 1,000 kilocalories of steak consumes about 5.1 cubic meters of water. To produce 1,000 kilocalories of steak every day for a year therefore consumes about 1,872 tonnes of water, which is roughly 19 times the 100 tonnes of water required to grow 1,000 kilocalories of wheat every day for a year. Thus the factor of ten may underestimate the real water requirements for feeding and watering beef cattle; other forms of meat may require less water.

These calculations take no account of food losses during production and distribution. A 40 percent loss between production and consumption would increase the water requirement per person for a diet of wheat and meat to 933 cubic meters per year. This estimate exceeds by nearly half the actual renewable water withdrawals per person for all purposes in 1987, which came to 660 cubic meters per year. The water requirements for a diet of wheat and meat could exceed the actual renewable water withdrawals for several reasons. Most people are not eating a diet of 2,000 kilocalories per day with 400 kilocalories from meat. In 1989 to 1991, about 83 percent of the world's cropland was not irrigated but rain-fed; thus rain-fed cropland far exceeded irrigated farmland.[75] Food losses may have been smaller than 40 percent in some cases. And the Law of Information (most statistics are made up) should not be forgotten: the statistics of global water withdrawals are surely approximate.

For comparison, Revelle estimated that Americans consume nearly 10,000 kilocalories of humanly edible plant products per person per day, either directly as food or indirectly as feed for domestic animals.[76] If the animals are fed grains with a transpiration ratio close to that of wheat, the water requirement for a diet of 10,000 kilocalories per day would be 1,000 cubic meters per year per person.

National and Global Freshwater Requirements

Whereas a single country can prosper using less water than required to grow the food and fiber it consumes, the world as a whole cannot. One region may buy food from another, but everyone's food has to grow somewhere.

I calculated a bit earlier that a diet of 2,000 kilocalories per day, with 20 percent of calories from animal products, would require 560 cubic meters of water per year per person. If a single country uses less water than 560 cubic meters per year per person, its people are not necessarily underfed. In Israel, for example, where most people are remarkably well fed, the 1986 withdrawals were 447 cubic meters per person, 88 percent of the renewable fresh water available per person.[77] Most Israelis ate and drank well, and some went to the swimming pool from time to time, by producing goods and services that they exchanged for food grown in other countries. What food they grew at home, they grew with a maximum of water efficiency, using drip irrigation and recycled water. Foreign aid, particularly from the United States, contributed to the infrastructure that made this efficiency possible.

In 1987 annual water withdrawals ranged from a low of 244 cubic meters per person in Africa and 476 cubic meters per person in South America to a high of 1,330 cubic meters in the former USSR (in 1980) and 1,692 cubic meters in North and Central America. In the United States, 1985 water withdrawals approximated 2,162 cubic meters per person.[78]

Falkenmark proposed that a population with more than 1,670 cubic meters per year per person of available fresh water is unlikely to experience water shortages.[79] In her definition, "available fresh water" includes rivers and groundwater aquifers (runoff and infiltration in the PETRI equation), but not water that evaporates or is transpired before it reaches rivers or aquifers (not evaporation or transpiration in the PETRI equation). She classified a population with less than 1,670 cubic meters per year per person but more than 1,000 cubic meters per year per person as water stressed, and one with 1,000 cubic meters per year per person or less as water scarce.

Countries differ in the fraction of available fresh water that can be captured for human use. It is difficult to store much water in a flat country and to prevent evaporation in a hot one. In hot, flat countries (including many in Africa) it may be difficult to capture for use more than 20 percent or 30 percent of the available water.[80] In Europe, serious problems of water management began to arise when the demand for water rose above 20 percent of the available supply; and the United States, withdrawing 19 percent of its internal renewable water resources in 1985,[81] had regional water shortages in California, Arizona, New Mexico, Florida and New York City, to name a few. If people can capture only 20 percent of available water in rivers or aquifers, countries that are water scarce by Falkenmark's definition can use at most 200 cubic meters per year per person, and water-stressed countries not more than about 330 cubic meters per year per person.

I estimated above that a vegetarian diet of 2,000 kilocalories per day, with a 40 percent loss between production and consumption, would require 330 to 350 cubic meters of water per person per year. Comparing the requirements with the supplies suggests that water-stressed countries that use 20 percent of the available fresh water can just barely grow their own food with irrigated water, if they use water from rivers and aquifers for practically nothing else, and water-scarce countries simply cannot grow all their own food by irrigation alone.

Using Falkenmark's scarcity threshold of 1,000 cubic meters per year per person, Engelman and LeRoy compared Peter H. Gleick's estimates of water supplies with the United Nations' estimates of population in 1990 and found that 20 of 149 countries were water scarce in 1990.[82] These countries, concentrated in north and east Africa and the Middle East, were home to 131 million people. Engelman and LeRoy also compared the same estimates of water supplies with U.N. population projections for the year 2025. By 2025, if the low-variant projections come true, they calculated that 817 million people will live in water-scarce countries; if the high-variant projections come true, 1,079 million will. The number of people living in water-stressed countries will rise from an estimated 335 million in 1990 to between 2.8 billion and 3.3 billion by 2025, depending on which of the U.N. projections comes closer to the actual trajectory of population; the numbers would increase largely because population growth would push large countries (including India but not China) into the category of water stressed. In addition to the demographic assumptions, these estimates of future scarcity or stress assume that renewable supplies will neither rise nor fall as a result of changes in climate, flood control, water recovery or environmental factors that affect water supply, such as plant cover and soil quality.

If the water scarcity spreads as populations rise, then abundant, cheap water will not be able to lubricate economic development, as it did in many now-developed countries. Rather, increasing capital and labor will have to be devoted to supplying water by means of dams and pipelines. Tensions over water within and between countries will rise. As Falkenmark observed, *"population growth can therefore be seen as equivalent to futures foregone in terms of water-dependent societal activities, such as industry and irrigated agriculture."*[83]

In addition to supporting human activities, renewable fresh water supports the forests, grasslands and wetlands that are of value in their own right and that supply essential services to humans. Forests serve indigenous peoples and wildlife as homes; smooth the flow of runoff; promote infiltration of water into the ground; diminish soil erosion; provide wood, charcoal, fruits, medicinals and industrial gums and exudates; and stabilize climate.[84] Deforestation in the Cherrapunji region of northeast India, just on the border with Bangladesh, aggravated floods during one-third of the year and drought during the rest.[85] Wetlands buffer floodwaters, nurse the young of many forms of aquatic life, settle silt and filter out some water pollutants. Grasslands provide forage for domestic animals, wild relatives of cultivated cereals with desirable genetic properties and habitat for wildlife. Humans depend on many of these ecosystem services,[86] though the water requirements of natural ecosystems are not routinely quantified along with human water withdrawals.

Water shortages make it more difficult to maintain the quality of both water supplied and wastewater removed. To restrict water consumption, developing countries commonly provide water only intermittently during the day or year. I remember my surprise, while staying at an academic guest house in Xi'an, China, at discovering that water was available in my room at best two to three hours each day. One drawback of this approach to conserving water is that when the water supply is stopped, the pressure in the pipes drops. Instead of leaking from the pipes into the surrounding earth, water leaks in the opposite direction, bringing with it bacteria and whatever else is in the vadose water. Water of high quality, free of contaminants, may go into a city's distribution system, but heavily contaminated and possibly dangerous water may be delivered to the faucet.[87] A second drawback is that rich customers may build storage tanks on their housetops to tide them over the intervals when supply is interrupted. Filling these tanks increases the demand for water when it is available. The tanks, unless scrupulously cleaned and maintained, may further contaminate the water consumed.

If water to remove wastes is limited, sewage, industrial effluents and runoff from farms and cities overload the capacity of bodies of water to decompose biodegradable wastes and to dilute other wastes.[88]

How Many People
Can the Earth's Water Support?

How many people the Earth's renewable water supply can support at a given level of well-being cannot be calculated without knowing how much water is required to maintain viable ecosystems; how much water future industry will be prepared to buy under future arrangements for the delivery and sale of water; how much flood runoff can be captured; how much fresh water can be recycled; how efficient water piping systems will be; and a host of other factors equally difficult to predict. I can estimate a number, however, such that more people *cannot* possibly be supplied with enough water for domestic use and for food grown by conventional irrigated—I emphasize *irrigated*—agriculture. In dividing the Earth's terrestrial renewable water supply—rivers and aquifers only—into a maximal number of equal portions, I am assuming that the people who, by accidents of geography, have more such water will share it evenly (at some price) with those who have less; that there are no obstacles of technology, economics or politics to transporting the water to the people and farms where and when it is wanted, or equivalently no obstacles to transporting the food produced where water and soil are abundant to the people who want it; that variations from year to year in this water supply can be smoothed so that the average and not the minimum or the 95–years–in–100 water supply constrains population size; and that fertile soil is available in excess to grow as much as this water supply will support.

I am not making these assumptions because I believe them—I do not believe them. For example, the last assumption is false in most of central and western Africa, where sandy, relatively infertile soils derived from granite erode severely when cleared of forest. Large areas of Africa cannot be economically irrigated because of topography and geology.[89] Why make assumptions known to be false? I make these assumptions so that I can do some arithmetic and learn something from the result. An estimate of maximum supportable population made on these assumptions is an *extreme upper bound* on the additional population that could be supported by irrigated agriculture alone.[90]

I calculated freshwater requirements under two extreme assumptions about the fraction of available water ($R + I$, river runoff plus infiltration to aquifers) that can be captured for use (20 percent and 100 percent), two extreme assumptions about the average dietary calories of plant food consumers might demand (2,350 kilocalories per day and 10,000 kilocalories per day) and two extreme assumptions about losses during plant growth, processing and distribution (10 percent and 40 percent). With all possible combinations of extreme assumptions, I considered $2 \times 2 \times 2 = 8$ scenarios. Each one is summarized in one row of Table 14.2.

The world's annual supply of renewable fresh water (runoff plus infiltration) in 1990 was approximately 41,000 cubic kilometers.[91] As mentioned, experts estimated the annual available renewable fresh water at 9,000 to 14,000 cubic kilometers. In my calculations, I assumed for illustration three levels of available fresh water: 41,000, 14,000 or 9,000 cubic kilometers per year (as shown in the last three columns of Table 14.2).

When 100 percent of available water is assumed to be used for domestic purposes and agriculture, no water is set aside for industry or ecosystem services. In the scenarios with 100 percent use of 41,000 cubic kilometers of water, I assume that no drop of groundwater or runoff reaches the sea or evaporates without passing through human households or agriculture. With no water whatsoever for nature or for manufacturing, it might be difficult to store water and transport it to its place of use. I regard such scenarios as illustrative, not as remotely realistic.

The choices among these scenarios are likely to be determined by relative prices and by cultural factors that are even more difficult to predict than prices. I am unable to construct a plausible model to forecast all the relevant prices in response to changes in the fraction of available water that is used, the global demand for calories from animal products, the fraction of food lost before people eat it, capital investments in water infrastructure, energy prices and other factors that affect the amount of available renewable fresh water. Consequently, Table 14.2 describes alternative scenarios of water availability and use without mention of prices.

The estimated agricultural water requirements in Table 14.2 range from 261 cubic meters per year per person (with 100 percent use of the available water, low dietary requirements and low food losses) to 8,333 cubic meters per year (with the opposite assumptions). If (unrealistically!) all 41,000 cubic kilometers of renewable water are available, the upper bounds on the size of the population that could be fed from irrigated agriculture range

TABLE 14.2   Renewable freshwater requirements per person for irrigated agriculture, and the maximum population that can be provided with domestic water and food produced entirely from irrigated agriculture, under various assumptions[a]

If the fraction of available renewable fresh water in rivers and aquifers that can be used is (percent)	and the average diet requires the growth of wheat that yields (kilocalories per day)	and the fraction of calories lost is (percent)	then the amount of renewable fresh water that must be available for irrigated food crops alone is (cubic meters per year per person)	If 41,000 cubic kilometers per year of water are available, then maximum population is (billions)	If 14,000 cubic kilometers per year of water are available, then maximum population is (billions)	If 9,000 cubic kilometers per year of water are available, then maximum population is (billions)
20	2,350	10	1,306	30.5	10.4	6.7
20	2,350	40	1,958	20.5	7.0	4.5
20	10,000	10	5,556	7.3	2.5	1.6
20	10,000	40	8,333	4.9	1.7	1.1
100	2,350	10	261	137.5	47.0	30.2
100	2,350	40	392	95.6	32.7	21.0
100	10,000	10	1,111	35.7	12.2	7.8
100	10,000	40	1,667	24.1	8.2	5.3

[a]Calculations assume that 1,000 kilocalories per day of humanly edible wheat require 100 cubic meters per year of usable fresh irrigation water. (Actual use of water in the United States is about four times this minimal amount.) The amount of renewable fresh water that must be available (in cubic meters per year per person) = (kilocalories per day)/[10 × fraction of water used × (1 − fraction of calories lost)]. Example: 2,350/(10×0.2×0.9)=1,306. The maximum population supportable with 37 cubic meters of water for domestic uses plus food from irrigated agriculture (in billions) = 41,000/(37 + cubic meters per year per person for food). Example: 41,000/(37 + 1,306) = 30.5.

from 137.5 billion with the lowest water requirements down to 4.9 billion with the highest water requirements. If 80 percent of renewable fresh water from runoff and infiltration is reserved for other than domestic and agricultural use, and if people want a diet that requires the equivalent of 10,000 kilocalories per day of wheat, and if losses of food are reduced to only 10 percent, then the maximum population supportable by irrigated agriculture is 7.3 billion (under all the above idyllic assumptions about sharing and distribution of water and availability of fertile land). The upper bounds range from 30.2 billion people down to 1.1 billion people if only 9,000 cubic kilometers of renewable fresh water are available.

The assumptions required to obtain these figures are numerous and doubtful. Nevertheless, it is instructive to compare the estimates of Table 14.2 with prior estimates of the maximum supportable population (Appendix 3). The hydrological cycle does not supply enough river water and groundwater to irrigate food grown by conventional agriculture for the populations at the upper extremes estimated by Clark[92] (157 billion) and De Wit[93] (1,022 billion). Unless there is an unanticipated revolution in the productivity of rain-fed agriculture, the Earth's production of human food is likely to be limited by renewable fresh water for irrigation before it is limited by photosynthesis, as in De Wit's calculation.

For the year 2150, the United Nations' low, medium and high projected populations are 4.3 billion, 11.5 billion and 28.0 billion; the instant-replacement projection gives 8.4 billion and the constant-fertility projection gives 694.2 billion [94] (see Table 8.2). The limited renewable freshwater supply of the Earth is too small for the constant-fertility projection to come true. If every drop of the 110,000 cubic kilometers of water that fall on land were used domestically and for *rain-fed or irrigated* agriculture, and if people ate only 2,350 kilocalories per day and lost only 10 percent of food before consumption, the maximum possible population would be 369 billion; if people captured only 20 percent of the total precipitation over land for domestic use and agriculture (rain-fed or irrigated), the maximum population would be 82 billion people. (Check me, using the formula in the note of Table 14.2.)

As the desired average daily energy supplies increase, the population that can be supported by conventional irrigated agriculture decreases (Figure 14.2). The special assumptions underlying the two curves shown in Figure 14.2 (namely, 20 percent use of all available water for homes and irrigated agriculture, and 10 percent loss of food between growth and consumption) are no more plausible than various other assumptions that could equally well have been chosen for illustration. The larger the desired daily food energy, the smaller the difference between the curves for annual water supplies of 14,000 cubic kilometers and 9,000 cubic kilometers. As daily calories rise from very low levels, the supportable population drops rapidly at first, then more slowly.

It would be desirable to carry out such calculations for individual countries, because these global calculations have little relevance to humid, tem-

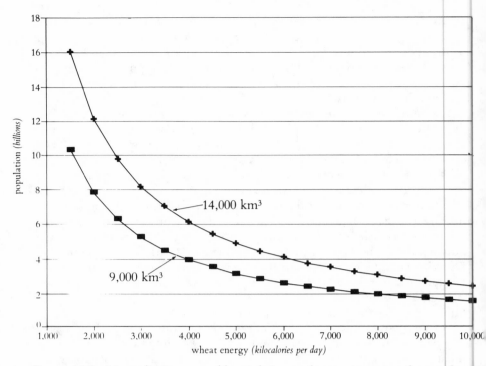

FIGURE 14.2   Upper limits on world population set by requirements of water for domestic use and irrigated agriculture of wheat, assuming 20 percent use of available water and 10 percent loss of food between growth and consumption. The upper curve assumes available renewable annual water supplies in rivers and aquifers of 14,000 cubic kilometers per year; the lower curve assumes 9,000 cubic kilometers per year. Important additional assumptions are set out in the text. SOURCE: original calculations

perate regions like Sweden or the eastern United States.[95] In those regions, the growth of plants is limited more by light and temperature than by water. On the other hand, food production in drought-prone regions in Africa and southern Asia, for example, is limited by the water available for irrigation, along with other factors. In these regions, additional food production will have to be irrigated to maintain yields in spite of droughts. These regions have the most rapid population growth. It would be instructive to see whether the conventionally projected populations and the available renewable fresh water are consistent with self-sufficiency in food of drought-prone countries. Countries that cannot grow their own food will then have to depend on food from elsewhere. Some countries with insufficient water have mineral wealth to trade for food; some do not. Will the physical capital (ships, trucks, roads and railroads), the political, institutional and administrative infrastructure and the energy required to transport the food be available?

HOW DOES WATER CONNECT WITH OTHER CONSTRAINTS?

Supplies of fresh water are very closely linked to other potential constraints on how many people the Earth can support.[96] The links are so interdependent that there is no easy way to measure the importance of each link separately. I shall describe the links under four headings: economics (including agriculture); the environment; culture and politics; and population. Many links fall under more than one of these headings.

Economics

Economic development and economic systems. Water use and abuse depend on the stage of economic development and on the economic system. Developing countries with less efficient agricultural and industrial technology may use more water per person or per unit of output than more developed countries. In the United States, for example, total water withdrawals and offstream consumption increased to a peak around 1980 and then declined,[97] while the real gross national product rose substantially.[98] Since 1985 U.S. water use has again begun to increase, but far more slowly than it rose from 1960 to 1980. By 1990 the United States still used less water than in 1975.[99] In the 1970s and 1980s, in industrial countries with competitive market economies, the throughputs of major resources and the discharges of pollutants into the air, water and soil began to fall. During the same two decades, in the Soviet Union and European socialist countries, throughputs of resources and environmental pollution increased even during economic stagnation.[100]

Open-access resource. Problems of water supply and quality are closely connected with the economic institutions, or lack of them, that govern people's access to fresh water. Because freshwater supplies in many places are treated as an open-access resource, they are overexploited relative to their economically efficient level of exploitation. Where water withdrawals are unregulated, two neighboring farmers who withdraw water from the same aquifer may lower the water table for each other, but neither may have to pay for the costs (such as increased energy costs for pumping) that he or she imposes on the other.[101] In the lower Rhine river that flows through the Netherlands, boaters, swimmers and drinkers want to enjoy clean water without having to pay for the privilege; upstream, Belgians, Germans and French do not want to be charged when they dump untreated wastes into the upper Rhine. Markets that do not exist could permit upstream and downstream users of the Rhine to trade wants. The absence of prices and the very low level of prices in imperfect markets poorly reflect social values.[102]

The same problem of externalities (costs freely imposed on others by an individual's actions) arises in the use of agricultural water.[103] A farmer who uses water for irrigation may transmit salts, agricultural chemicals and sedimentation to downstream users of the discharged water. This imposition of costs on other farmers is likely to intensify as the demand to produce more food from the same land increases the use of agricultural chemicals in developing countries. And farmers are very reluctant to change practices that cost themselves nothing in order to reduce their effects on others.

Energy for pumping. Conventional freshwater supply depends heavily on energy for pumping, which often grows more costly as time passes.[104] For example, four-fifths of Mexico's surface water is found in the low-lying coastal regions, but three-fourths of the population lives in the dry central highlands.[105] Groundwater under Mexico City (elevation 2,380 meters or about 7,800 feet) is being pumped out 40 percent faster than it is being recharged[106]; the water table has dropped, streets and buildings are subsiding and the energy cost of pumping is rising. In addition to mining its groundwater, Mexico City pumps water from remote sources that are progressively farther away and lower in altitude. The mined water is dispersed over the globe through the hydrologic cycle and only a tiny fraction returns to Mexico. Similarly, in the Ludhiana district of India's Punjab, groundwater is being extracted one-third faster than it is being recharged and water tables are dropping almost one meter per year.[107] The costs of pumping are also rising in the Middle East and in 50 Chinese cities including Beijing, where water tables are falling on average one to two meters per year.

In the United States, by the 1980s, nearly one-quarter of the groundwater withdrawn was not being replenished, and the water table was falling an average of two meters per year under some six million hectares of land irrigated by groundwater.[108] Falling groundwater levels and higher energy costs substantially increased the costs of groundwater irrigation from the Rio Grande to Nebraska and in Arizona and California. Withdrawals from many rivers and streams of the United States' main irrigated areas exceeded available supplies. Kenneth R. Farrell and his colleagues at Resources for the Future, Washington, concluded: "The availability and price of water and energy, rather than land, may be the critical natural resource variables for agriculture in the West in the years ahead."

Electric power generation. The quality of much water depends on the technology used to generate electricity.[109] In 1990, 48 percent of all off-stream water use was to cool electric power utilities.[110] The temperature of the water withdrawn is usually raised several degrees and the water is then discharged. The increased temperature eliminates cold-water fishes and shellfish; stimulates the growth of aquatic plants; and increases the vulnerability of some fishes to toxic wastes, parasites and other diseases. Other technologies that could recapture or avoid generating this waste heat could avoid thermal pollution.

The cooling technology that an electric power utility uses depends on the price of water.[111] In the United States, an electricity-generating plant powered by fossil fuels would use "once-through" cooling as its most economical technology if water costs less than $0.013 per cubic meter ($0.05 per 1,000 gallons); this technology withdraws up to 189 kilograms (50 gallons) of water per kilowatt-hour of generated electricity. Above $0.013 per cubic meter, the utility's economically optimal strategy is to use a cooling tower, which withdraws about 3 kilograms (0.8 gallon) per kilowatt-hour. Above $2.11 per cubic meter ($8.00 per 1,000 gallons), the firm's least-cost strategy would be to invest in a dry cooling tower, which uses no water. Like city folks and farmers, industries use less water when it costs more. The pricing of water strongly influences how well water is used to serve social and economic goals.

What we have just seen is a two-way street. In one direction, the price of water affects the technology and the cost of producing electrical power. In the other direction, the price of electrical power affects the cost of pumping water. Water connects with the rest of the world via feedback loops, not via unidirectional cause and effect.

Dams and pipes. Supplies of fresh water depend on dams to retain and control river flow, and on capital investments for water transport within and between river basins. China alone has more than half of the world's dams over 15 meters high (in 1991, 18,820 of a world total of 36,562 dams).[112] Only very rich countries (like the United States) or very desperate ones (like China) can undertake extensive piping of water from one river basin to another.[113] The engineering and the maintenance of piping systems make a large difference to water deliveries: more than half the water supplied to Cairo, Jakarta, Lima, Manila and Mexico City leaks away or is not accounted for (the North American standard is about one-sixth).[114]

Agriculture. Water shortages hamper efforts to improve agricultural yields in developing countries. When a plant is short of water, its leaves do not expand fully and the flux of photons that it can absorb is reduced.[115] To increase yields of grain from one tonne per hectare to four tonnes per hectare, as hoped in some development plans and some optimistic calculations of human carrying capacity, may require an increase in transpiration from 1,000 cubic meters per hectare to 4,000 cubic meters per hectare. If the required water is not available, the increased yields are simply unattainable with existing plants.[116]

Agricultural chemicals. Agricultural water pollution depends on the intensity of use of fertilizers and pesticides. The use of these chemicals depends on the development of the local chemical industry, subsidies or tariffs for chemical imports, the available alternatives for biological control or integrated pest management, consumer preferences for organically grown versus chemically treated produce and farmer education. Concentrations of nitrates in groundwater exceeded allowable limits in many localities in England, where nitrogenous fertilizers are heavily used.[117] In the early 1970s, nitrate concentrations in Dutch groundwater used for drinking started to rise sharply. By the early 1980s, they just exceeded the standard set by the European Community,[118] which was two and a half times higher than the U.S. standard.

Livestock. Water quality depends on how much meat people eat and how domestic animals are managed. In 1990–92, the world's domestic animals outweighed and outnumbered the human population several-fold (see Table 4.1). Their solid, liquid and gaseous (notably methane) wastes presented formidable threats to the quality of the land, water and air, as well as opportunities, depending on management. A typical large farm in the former Soviet Union with 108,000 pigs produced effluents to water bodies and to the atmosphere about equal to those of an industrial city of 300,000 people.[119] More efficient livestock management and production, especially in developing and formerly socialist countries, and consequent reductions in the livestock herd, could compensate for some impacts of world population growth, temporarily at least.

Soil. How long irrigated agriculture can be maintained depends sensitively on how the soil is managed to minimize salinization, the accumulation of naturally occurring salts in the soil.[120] To prevent the salts from building up ordinarily requires flushing the soils with a higher volume of water over a shorter period of time than is applied in irrigation. Salvaging salinized fields is delicate and expensive. Farmers must balance the costs of water to flush salts from their soils against the costs of losing the use of the soil.

After the Aswan Dam was built in Egypt, the farmers downstream came to appreciate the service formerly provided by the rise and fall of the river's water. With nothing to flush the salt away, many once-fertile fields were ruined by salt.[121]

The Environment

Alterations in the flow of rivers and the drainage or drowning of wetlands affect aquatic ecosystems, with consequences for environmental quality and human well-being that are diverse and not fully understood.[122] Three specific aspects worth special attention are the management of forests, the disposal of toxic chemicals and climatic change.

Forests. Forest management can reduce the demand for dams to prevent flooding. In the heavily wooded Adirondack Mountains of New York State, for example, beaver dams impound streams and regulate flooding.[123] By contrast with the Adirondacks, deforestation in tropical forests adversely affects watershed functions in at least 1.4 million square kilometers of catchments and humid tropical valleys where some two billion people live.[124]

In the middle hills of Nepal, geological forces generated flooding, landslides and shifts in river channels well before humans were a major presence. Even before the twentieth century, people cut forests to make room for shifting cultivation and to provide charcoal for the local smelting of metals. In the twentieth century, tree lopping continued to provide animal fodder and fuelwood.[125] In recent decades, deforestation in Nepal and India has probably contributed materially to major floods downstream in Bangladesh, which impede increased agricultural productivity.

Water control is largely a public good; it is possible only in the presence of institutions to organize collective action.[126] The inequalities between the rich and the poor in Bangladesh and the struggles over wealth interfere with the creation of the necessary new institutions there. Visualize the chain: in the north, a poor Nepalese family, in search of fuelwood or an additional plot of land, cuts some trees; the rain, instead of sinking into the forest floor, runs off in the south; for want of dams and waterworks, which are blocked by the society and institutions of Bangladesh, a Bangladeshi farmer is flooded; the poor of Bangladesh get poorer; and meanwhile in Nepal the soil that the Nepalese farmer hoped to plant has eroded.[127] Examples such as these show the intimate links among social organization, land use and water use.

Chemicals and ocean dumping. To protect groundwater against contamination by toxic chemical wastes, some marine engineers have considered depositing these chemicals in the ocean. They have argued that excluding the possibility of disposing of some wastes in the oceans may damage groundwaters through leakage from dump sites; under some conditions, they argued, oceanic disposal may be preferable to disposal on land.[128] People must choose among putting groundwaters at risk, putting oceans at risk or modifying industrial processes of production. Local populations have a stake in preserving groundwater supplies; several or many nations may have a stake in preserving the local and regional productivity of the oceans; and local or multinational companies have a stake in shifting the costs of toxic waste disposal to others. There is no free market and there are few forums of any kind in which local health officials, foreign governments and industries can come together to trade or balance their interests.

Global warming. Global warming could shift patterns of rainfall and the spatial distribution of freshwater supplies.[129] Warming could also melt Antarctic and Greenland ice, raise sea levels, flood low coastal areas and cause seawater to intrude farther into coastal freshwater aquifers. Rising concentrations of atmospheric carbon dioxide are believed to increase the risk of global warming. The burning of fossil fuels to generate power contributes to increased atmospheric carbon dioxide. As already mentioned, many power plants use fresh water for cooling; power plants also provide electricity to pump fresh water. The production of carbon dioxide (when fossil fuel is burned for power generators) and the possibility of an increased risk of global warming link freshwater supplies and the technology used to generate energy.

Culture and Politics

Politics. Countries or provinces are responsible for distributing renewable water supplies. Unfortunately for the solution of water problems, political units and river basins rarely coincide. Fifty rivers or freshwater lakes border more than four countries; two or more countries share almost 150 rivers and lakes.[130] Perceived inequities in water use have caused and aggravated regional and international tensions. Nations have cut off, or have threatened to cut off, the water supplies of other nations for political and military reasons.[131] Economic development and population growth could aggravate conflicts over water if national belligerence is seen as a productive policy, or could drive neighbors into win–win collaborations if foresight and wisdom suffice. For example, Sandra Postel suggested that Israel could provide technical assistance to Jordanian farmers to reduce their water use by one-third, as Israeli farmers have done, in return for a share of the water saved.[132] Peace between Israel and Jordan may make it possible to realize some of these potential gains.

The political stability of nations and international economic arrangements often determines how effectively scientific knowledge and technical knowledge are applied to environmental management and how wisely new knowledge and technology are developed. The efficient development of water resources depends on a congenial political setting.[133]

Women. The infrastructure available to distribute water affects the status and welfare of women. Women and children are the primary carriers of fuel and water in countries too poor to have mechanical distribution systems[134]; women account for about one-third of the world labor force but about two-thirds of the work-hours. Better infrastructures for water would increase women's opportunities for other work as well as for education.

Population

Cities. The cost of freshwater distribution depends on the concentration of the population. Networks for water supply and wastewater removal are more efficient per person in cities than in the countryside, but the benefits of a concentrated population can be realized only if governments or private water companies can supply the required infrastructure and supporting services. Most urban squatter settlements in developing countries have at best rudimentary systems of water supply and no sewers or drains.[135]

Population growth and economic development. Water and other natural resources interact with rates of population growth in affecting economic development. Population growth is most likely to hinder growth in output per person where water and arable land are scarce or costly and the ownership of water, land and other natural resources is poorly defined.[136] Conversely, abundant water and other natural resources are most conducive to a favorable effect of population growth on output per person.

Summary: Water Flows in Every Person's Veins

Renewable fresh water is connected, often both as a cause and as an effect, with many factors that affect the number of people and the quality of life the Earth can support: energy, capital investments, forest management, wildlife preservation, social and economic institutions, social and economic equity, soil conservation, urbanization, sewage treatment, the status and welfare of women, economic development, the type of economy (market oriented versus command oriented), agricultural intensification, chemical industries and tariffs, integrated pest management, dietary preferences (wheat versus rice, grain versus meat), animal husbandry, power generation technology, international politics, ocean dumping and global warming.

IS WATER A LIMITING FACTOR FOR HUMAN POPULATION?

The complex connections between fresh water and a host of other aspects of human life show the complexity of the question "Is water a limiting factor for human population?" If water is a limiting factor for human population, it must act through birth, death or migration.[137] Water affects birth, death and migration in many ways along a spectrum from very directly to very indirectly. Water's most important roles as a limiting factor for human population are probably highly indirect.

Water shortages cause death directly only in the extreme cases in which the people affected lack help from regions with water and cannot migrate to such regions. Water shortages and the contamination of water with biological and chemical pollutants contribute massively to diarrheal diseases of infants and waterborne diseases at all ages, as already mentioned. Wastage of agricultural water yields less food, and economically inefficient uses of water generate less well-being, than optimal water uses. Water waste and inefficiency in use slow the decline of death rates in developing countries.

Water shortages have long been an important factor in migration. As a result of drying in the north Mesopotamian plain around 2200 B.C., the population within 15 kilometers of Tell Leilan probably dropped by between 14,000 and 28,000 people and the Hurrian, Gutian and Amorite populations moved into southern Mesopotamia.[138] The Book of Genesis recorded the flight from drought of Jacob and his family. Water shortages may be expected to continue to add to other pressures for large-scale emigration, particularly from northern and western Africa and western Asia.[139]

Migration is not the only possible response to water shortages. For example, migrants of European origin who settled the arid western regions of the United States promoted the building of dams, reservoirs and other waterworks to exploit the little water available. This option is foreclosed in flat countries because dams do not create reservoirs where there are no valleys.

The connection of water to birth rates is, except in extreme drought, entirely indirect and as diverse as the ways economics, the spatial distribution of population, politics and culture affect fertility.

How Could Radical Developments Affect Water Supplies?

The upper limits on population in Table 14.2 assume a conventional world much like the present one. Radical developments could have an immense effect on supplies of fresh water. I call such radical developments "wild cards," because in card games a person who holds a wild card can set its denomination for his own convenience. Three major wild cards are new sources of energy, major changes in food production and new technologies for intervening in the hydrologic cycle.

Sufficiently cheap energy could make widespread desalinization of seawater feasible and economically competitive. Desalinization is accomplished mainly by distillation or reverse osmosis, both very costly in energy. Currently desalinization costs U.S.$0.40 to $0.60 per cubic meter of brackish water and U.S.$1.05 to $1.60 per cubic meter of seawater.[140] At these prices, desalinizing a cubic kilometer of water costs between $0.5 billion and $1.5 billion. Conventional sources of fresh water cost up to one-third as much. Farmers in the western United States pay an estimated $0.01 to $0.05 per cubic meter for water while urban users pay about $0.30 per cubic meter.[141]

As a handy example of a new source of large amounts of energy, I take controlled fusion, without prejudice against any other sources. Promising tests of controlled fusion were carried out in England at the Joint European Torus in 1991 and in the United States at the Princeton Plasma Physics Laboratory in 1993.[142] Under the most favorable prognosis with present and likely future levels of funding, the first commercial generators based on fusion energy could not begin operating before 2030 or 2040, according to the physicists involved. For the long run, developments of alternative energy sources could be immensely important. There is little sign, however, that a miracle in energy production or funding devoted to energy research is just around the corner.[143]

Another major wild card is nonconventional agriculture. Some of the possibilities include the development of cereal crops that transpire less water or tolerate brackish or saline water. Plants transpire when they open their stomata to absorb carbon dioxide from the atmosphere. Cultivation in greenhouses could be carried out with elevated carbon dioxide, which would reduce the plants' opening their stomata, and hence reduce the water transpired[144]; transpired water could be condensed and recycled. Industrially fermented microbial food sources including algae, bacteria and filamentous fungi have a higher protein content than conventional foods, require less land and water than conventional agriculture, are independent of climate and generate far less waste than conventional agriculture.[145] Some technological optimists have estimated that the single-celled protein grown on fewer than four square kilometers of land could meet the requirements of a billion people.[146] Even if that estimate is too small by a factor of 1,000, the land requirement would be small compared to that of conventional agriculture. Costs of production per unit of product drop dramatically as the scale of production increases, but the capital for the initial investment and a marketable product must be in hand. As long as conventional agriculture is subsidized (for example, by underpricing water), nonconventional agriculture is economically handicapped. Globally significant changes away from conventional agriculture for human food will probably require decades or human generations at least.

A third class of wild cards, major interventions in the hydrologic cycle, still lies largely in the realm of science fiction, except for desalinization. Two possibilities that have been just over the horizon for decades are cloud seeding and towing icebergs to inhabited zones. I would suggest another possibility that does not seem to have been explored: capturing rain that falls on the oceans. The oceans receive a share of precipitation (78 or 79 percent) that is greater than their share (about 71 percent) of the Earth's surface.[147] Vast floating plastic sheets or other collectors could capture some of the fresh water that falls on the oceans, at a minimal cost in energy and a potentially enormous cost in capital. Floating oceanic collectors of fresh water could be tethered offshore or could float freely in the open sea. They could be visited and drained periodically by fleets of tankers based at nearby oceanic islands. The effects of such collectors on planetary albedo and the oceans' biological productivity would have to be investigated.

FRESHWATER OVERVIEW

The Earth's vast stock of salt water feeds fresh water to the hydrologic cycle through evaporation; in return, it receives the world's rivers and a disproportionate share of the world's precipitation. The much smaller stock of fresh water lives in two different worlds. A portion lives in underground aquifers largely filled before the evolution of agriculture; fossil water withdrawn from these aquifers can be recharged at best very slowly and is nonrenewable on the time scale of human generations. A renewable portion of the Earth's fresh water participates in the hydrologic cycle: it precipitates, then evaporates, is transpired, runs off to the sea or infiltrates the soil (think $P = E + T + R + I$).

Humans can use the runoff if they can capture it in surface dams and reservoirs and belowground aquifers. Humans can tap the infiltrate through wells or by diverting the stable flow that emerges into rivers. The runoff and infiltrate are renewable resources. Their total annual volume is fixed by the hydrologic cycle. People can greatly increase or decrease the use they derive from the renewable flow of fresh water by recycling or polluting discharged water.

Currently, the variation, and not the aggregate, of freshwater supplies poses the chief obstacle to meeting people's desires for water. The vast excesses of fresh water currently available in some regions could readily meet present requirements elsewhere. Today's problems are to get the right amounts of water in the right places at the right times, and to get the most use from the available fresh water. If population growth continues in the future, present water shortages could become more severe in many regions, and people could encounter limits set by aggregate renewable freshwater supplies. As long as freshwater supplies are limited, further growth of the human population will reduce the range of choices about how to use the available fresh water. Obvious improvements in recycling, pricing and the efficiency of delivering and using water could postpone water shortages.

15

Natural Constraints
and Time

Had we but world enough, and time, . . .

—ANDREW MARVEL,
"To His Coy Mistress," 1681

FOOD, WATER, ENERGY, land, soil, space, diseases, waste disposal, nonfuel minerals, forests, biological diversity, biologically accessible nitrogen, phosphorus, climatic change—all have been proposed as potential natural constraints that do or could limit the Earth's human population. These factors are closely interconnected, as the case study of water illustrated.

For most goods and services (like food, energy, aluminum, nitrogen or natural removal of wastes), one could ask the same six questions just considered for water: How much is available? (This question divides naturally into two parts: What are the physical, chemical or biological supplies? What are the economic, social and cultural limitations on using the supplies?) How much is required? (This question also divides: How much for subsistence? How much for a wealthy style of life?) How many people can the available supply support (at different levels of well-being)? How does each good or service connect with others? Does a good or service limit human population through its effects on birth, death and migration? How could radical developments affect the good or service? The same questions that are asked of goods could be asked of bads, like disease, earthquakes and the unwanted effluents of industrial or agricultural production.

Each potential natural constraint has its scholarly and popular enthusiasts. Each has inspired a vast number of technical reports and popular books. For each potential constraint that someone claims is crucial, someone else denies that it matters much at all.[1]

HOW CAN NATURAL CONSTRAINTS BE ORGANIZED?

A major problem in thinking about natural constraints is how to organize them. Many taxonomies of natural constraints have been proposed. Here is a sample of taxonomies. None is perfectly satisfactory.

N. H. Biegman, a Dutch government official in charge of international cooperation, proposed in 1992 a three-part classification of natural functions: the supply of inputs; environmental regulation, including the removal of wastes; and genetic memory. Each function implies a natural constraint over some time period that has to be determined. According to Biegman, people cannot draw more inputs than nature can provide "sustainably"; people cannot dump more wastes or otherwise disrupt the environment more than the environment can tolerate "sustainably"; and people cannot deplete the genetic memory of nature faster than biological diversity is renewed "sustainably." By the word "sustainably," Biegman meant that "Consecutive generations must protect the environment so that nature can continue to fulfill its functions for us."[2] Biegman's taxonomy fails to distinguish dangerously rapid from negligibly slow depletion or degradation of natural functions; he does not specify over what time scale the natural functions operate as global constraints.

Also in 1992, Daily and Ehrlich classified natural resources according to three dichotomous dimensions[3]: nonrenewable (at current rates of use) versus renewable; not necessarily degraded or dispersed in use versus necessarily degraded or dispersed in use; and essential (nitrogen in diets and fertilizers[4]) versus substitutable (horses used for transportation can be replaced by motor vehicles). Making one choice for each dichotomy (for example, fossil petroleum is nonrenewable, dispersed in use and substitutable) gives eight[5] categories of resources. Depending on the source and the quantity of use, fresh water can be both a renewable and a nonrenewable resource. Catalysts and materials for chemical processing may be dispersed or not dispersed in use depending on the design of the processing system. These dichotomies of natural constraints depend on human modes of use.

Again in 1992, Thomas F. Homer-Dixon, a political scientist at the University of Toronto, identified several dichotomies, in addition to those of Daily and Ehrlich, that could be useful for classifying natural constraints.[6] Some resources are stocks (petroleum in the ground); some are flows (sunlight reaching the Earth, precipitation). Some are intermediate goods (water used to cool power plants); some are final goods (drinking water). Some are material goods (timber for construction); some are material services (the retention of soil and water by the roots of trees); some are amenities (beautiful wilderness). Some are currently open-access resources (whale populations); some are priced resources (property). Some priced resources are public (timber in national forests; minerals under lands owned by a government); some are private.

Dorn in 1962 emphasized the difference between localized problems of resources and global problems.[7] Tropospheric carbon dioxide and strato-spheric ozone are global concerns, but tropospheric ozone (in the smog in Los Angeles) and the availability of fresh water are largely local problems.

None of these classifications does justice to the complexity of the interactions among constraints, though the interactions strongly influence human carrying capacity. The variety of possible taxonomies of natural constraints shows that there is no uniquely correct scheme of classification. Instead of pretending to give encyclopedic coverage of the important natural constraints, either one by one or according to some taxonomy, this chapter will follow a single thread that links most constraints: time.

A TALE OF TIME

A large truck sets out from a town called Here to a big, beautiful city called There. The city of There lies on the other side of a range of mountains. The route from Here to There is subject to rockfalls, freezing bridges and persistent fog. It can be traveled safely provided the truck goes slowly enough for the load it carries. The heavier the load, the slower the truck's maximum safe speed at the hairpin turns.

The truck is the Earth, its cargo the human population. The likelihood of serious mishap depends on how much cargo the truck carries, how fast it travels, how securely fastened the cargo is and the hazards of the road.

The image is imperfect, of course, because the cargo, the Earth's human population, has billions of hands on the steering wheel, billions of feet on the accelerator and billions of feet on the brake. People influence the changes they undergo. But every change interacts with physical, chemical and biological laws still shrouded in fog, as well as economic, social, political and cultural responses that are even less well understood. The time required for transitions constrains every aspect of human carrying capacity.

Rapid population growth and a rising environmental impact per person in many regions give present societies less time to adjust socially, economically and technologically than in the past. In one long lifetime, most of North America's easily accessible oil was and is being consumed. In West Africa, one-tenth of the forest reportedly disappeared between 1980 and 1990.[8] Within a decade after large-scale fishing began, whole populations of bottom-dwelling fish species around Antarctica were depleted.

The remainder of this chapter looks at some constraints of time in greater detail.

TIME CONSTRAINTS IN ENERGY

The time required for a transition from one major source of energy to another could constrain the Earth's human carrying capacity. Consider two prognostications, one about oil and gas, the other about fusion energy. (I select controlled fusion for convenience here without ranking it as more promising than solar or other energy sources.) Gever et al. predict that known reserves and future discoveries of United States oil and gas stores "will be effectively empty by 2020. World oil and gas supplies will last perhaps three decades longer, or more if Third World economies fail to develop, as is beginning to appear likely."[9]

In December 1993, physicists at the Princeton Plasma Physics Laboratory carried out a successful experiment to demonstrate the feasibility of fusion energy. Just before the test, the *New York Times* reported: "If all goes well during the planned tests, and if Congress subsequently makes a long-term commitment to support a continuing fusion research program, scientists believe a commercial fusion power plant could begin operating by the year 2040."[10] Just after the first successful test, the same reporter reported in the same newspaper: "Physicists believe that if the current series of high-power experiments is successful—and two more advanced fusion reactors now planned are actually built—the first commercial fusion power reactors could begin operating around the year 2030."[11]

If Gever et al. and the newspaper reports were both right (I make no estimate of the probability that they were right), there could be a gap in U.S. energy supplies in the decade or decades starting in 2020. Various responses are possible: discounting the prognostications, conserving oil and gas (which means slowing the rate of consumption), accelerating the development of fusion energy, developing other renewable or nonrenewable sources of energy (such as oil from shale or the conversion of coal to the equivalent of petroleum products) or taking diplomatic, economic or military action to assure U.S. access to foreign sources of oil and gas until fusion energy is feasible and economically competitive with alternative sources of energy. Time is a constraint: no problem would arise if fusion energy could be made economically competitive with other energy sources within one decade, at a price for research and development that people were willing to pay.

Fortunately or unfortunately, predictions about the future of energy supplies are frequently unreliable. To illustrate, in 1981, the National Geographic Society published a special report on energy. The first page of the first article headlined "conservative estimates" of $80 a barrel for oil in 1985, four years into what was then the future.[12] A decade after 1985, oil prices are closer to $20 a barrel. Though the details of any energy projection are highly uncertain, the constraint of time remains.

TIME CONSTRAINTS IN AGRICULTURE

World grain production rose by a factor of 2.7 from 1950 to 1991, while the area harvested for grain grew only 17 percent.[13] In the past three decades alone, world grain production doubled.[14] If world population doubles in the next few decades, as some people confidently expect (given their confidence, I am agnostic), world grain production will have to double again just to keep the average grain supplies per person at their present level. Better agricultural extension—bringing to farmers better varieties, equipment and knowledge already in hand—might increase present harvests worldwide by as much as 50 percent.[15] To keep average grain supplies per person from falling, additional new technologies, including new crop varieties, will be required.

Developing new varieties takes time. From the time research began on the genetics of plant breeding, 50 years passed before applications of the results increased agricultural production significantly.[16] In one example, the Max Planck Institute for Plant Breeding in Cologne began breeding a variety of barley which was eventually called Vogelsanger Gold, after the district of Vogelsang where the institute is located. Breeding began in 1938. The aim was to improve a variety of barley that was desirable agriculturally but was very sensitive to a fungal disease. A wild barley that could be crossed with the domestic variety was resistant to unwanted fungus. When both genomes were mixed to combine their genetic properties, the first hybrid was useless because it had many agriculturally undesirable traits of the wild parent. From 1938 to 1962, the hybrid was repeatedly backcrossed to the agriculturally desirable variety. The breeders selected the offspring that combined the best yields with resistance to the fungus. Creating improved crops by even the most advanced techniques of breeding still labors under what Jozef St. Schell, a German molecular plant biologist, called "the constraint of time."[17]

As the poet wrote, "Had we but world enough, and time . . ."

TIME CONSTRAINTS IN MINERAL RESOURCES

Views of the limitations imposed by mineral resources diverge widely. Gever et al. argued that during the nineteenth century, the state of human knowledge and social organization limited economic growth more than the availability of high-quality natural resources, at least in the United States.[18] Today, Gever et al. suggested, the chief limit on economic growth in the United States has become "the supply of resources needed to implement our still-growing knowledge. . . . [O]ur present [American] economy and our understanding of its operation were both formed during the period of relative resource abundance and knowledge scarcity. It will take some time, at least a few decades, to adjust to the new order."[19]

Whether or not this view of the history of American economic growth is correct, it seems doubtful as a description of world natural resources so far. World reserves of copper, iron, aluminum and lead were larger in 1980 and 1990 than in 1950, in spite of substantial world production of these metals between 1950 and 1980 (Table 15.1). This apparent paradox is possible because "reserves" refer only to the working inventory of the mining industry. Since reserves cost money to develop or "prove" and are taxed in many

TABLE 15.1   World reserves and production of selected minerals (millions of tonnes of metal content), 1950–80 and 1990

mineral	1950 reserve	production from 1950 to 1980	1980 reserve	1990 reserve
copper	100	156	494	321
iron	19,000	11,040	93,466	64,648
aluminum	1,400	1,346	5,200	3,576[a]
lead	40	85	127	70

[a]Calculated as 200 (world reserve life index of aluminum) × 17,877,900 tonnes (1990 metal consumption) from World Resources Institute (1992, p. 320).

SOURCES: Vogely (1985, p. 458) for 1950–80; World Resources Institute (1992, pp. 320–23) for 1990. The figures for reserves in 1990 may not be strictly comparable with the earlier figures for reserves.

jurisdictions, mining companies have little incentive to explore for, report and develop more reserves than they want for the immediate future. As an economist views mining, "reserves are created from the underlying resource base by investing in exploration, technology, and mine develop-ment, just as capacity is generated in the nonmineral goods sector. Minerals are scarce because they have production costs [which increase as lower grades are mined, plus exploration costs, which increase as discovery diminishes]. The issue of future supply is whether they will become more scarce—that is, more expensive."[20] I would prefer the words "located in" or "made accessible from" to the words "created from" because people do not create the resource base that underlies reserves. People recognize the elements of reserves in nature and transform them for economic use; these activities may be viewed as creative or exploitive.

In strong contrast with the conclusion reached by Gever et al.,[21] William A. Vogely, a mineral economist at Pennsylvania State University, con-cluded: "Minerals and materials (such as metals and ceramics) have not lim-ited society's welfare in the past. Nor do they have the potential for limiting the welfare of mankind in the future, so long as certain institutional condi-tions are maintained."[22] Mines, and their customers, should pay for envi-ronmental damages they cause; raw materials should be freely traded worldwide; all of the Earth's crust should be open for exploration; and both sellers and buyers should be prevented from controlling markets by collu-sion or cartels. "If these rules of the game are followed, mineral markets will provide supplies and ration use so that minerals and materials will be available to meet society's needs without significantly increasing costs for a very long time, probably forever."

This view ignores the possible limits imposed by the abundance of mate-rials in the Earth's crust, and should be balanced against the recognition that doublings of resources in the past do not guarantee future abundance.[23] At present, not enough is known about world mineral resources to justify any claim that an absolute shortage worldwide of any strategic mineral is imminent. The problem is rather that exploration, discovery and commercial development of mineral resources take a long time.

According to Hatten S. Yoder, Jr., a former director of the Geophysical Laboratory, Carnegie Institution of Washington, most of the currently operating mines of mercury, silver, tin, tungsten, lead, copper, barium and zinc have a life expectancy of approximately 15 to 20 years. By early in the twenty-first century, they will have to be replaced. How much of each resource is available within the United States remains unknown, because a geochemical census of the United States has never been adequately supported. "Optimistic reports based on 'near term' (3–5 years) and the 'foreseeable future' (25 years) clearly disregard the needs of future generations. *The lead time and geochemical limits are major factors underlying the present lack of understanding of the nonfuel minerals problem.*"[24] Beyond constraints of time lie physical limits.

The mining industry has no incentive to undertake basic research devoted to understanding how ores form, as an aid to discovering new ore not now exposed at the Earth's surface, because the fundamental knowledge gained would not benefit any particular company immediately or exclusively. Published scientific knowledge is an open-access resource, though much specific knowledge is governed by intellectual property rights in some societies. In their reluctance to support publishable basic research, the mining companies behave exactly like the peasants in developing countries who refuse to plant trees on government-owned land because someone else may reap the benefit later.

In 1982, a decade before the war in the Persian Gulf, Yoder wrote of the great danger to world peace in the scramble for the Earth's limited mineral resources. He predicted that nations would ultimately learn to share the mineral wealth of the world. "In the meantime, this nation should look to its own survival by developing secure alternative sources of mineral resources, preferably within its own borders."[25]

Reserves are typically concentrated under the control of a few scattered nations.[26] The concentration of reserves leads to institutional and political problems that are no less difficult than those of research and exploration. Policy-makers should encourage a cooperative, long-term view of creating and sharing knowledge of the Earth's resources. Both mineral exploration and learning to cooperate to keep strategic minerals flowing take time.

"Had we but world enough, and time . . ."

TIME CONSTRAINTS IN BIOLOGICAL DIVERSITY

Harvard's impassioned naturalist Edward O. Wilson wrote: "The one process now going on that will take millions of years to correct is the loss of genetic and species diversity by the destruction of natural habitats. This is the folly our descendants are least likely to forgive us."[27] I want to describe some evidence and arguments that stand behind this statement.

Biological diversity—or biodiversity, for short—names the observation that different living organisms differ genetically.[28] Biologists organize the genetic variations among individuals into a hierarchy. Individuals vary genetically within a local population of a single species (such as the mice in my house in the woods), between species (the mice differ from the voles), between higher taxonomic categories (rodents differ from insects), between ecological communities (the terrestrial collection in my house differs from the aquatic collection in a nearby stream) and between ecosystems (the woods in New York State differ biologically from a coral reef in the Red Sea or a rainforest in Costa Rica).

Zooming back down to my mice, selecting one and turning up the magnification reveals that an individual can be a genetic mosaic. Different cells of one individual often vary genetically because genes sometimes mutate as the cells of the body divide. Eukaryotic cells (cells with distinct nuclei bounded by a membrane) probably originated as symbioses of different organisms.[29] Hence even single eukaryotic cells have genetic diversity: one genome for the nucleus, another for the mitochondria, another for the chloroplasts and possibly others for other organelles. Within a chromosome in the nucleus, two complementary strands of the genetic material DNA (deoxyribonucleic acid) may specify slightly different versions of the same gene. Diversity runs rampant at every level of biological organization.

Most public attention focuses on the diversity of species. A species is defined variously, because definitions good for species that reproduce by means of sex usually don't apply to asexually reproducing species (of which there are many). A sexually reproducing species is often defined as a set of individuals with enough in common genetically to be capable of interbreeding and producing offspring as fertile as the parents.[30] About 1.8 million species have been named, but as many as 20 to 40 percent of different names may refer to the same species. The number of distinct named species may be closer to 1.4 million or 1.5 million.[31] Estimates of the number of species on the Earth have ranged from fewer than 1 million to more than 100 million, but both extremes seem implausible. Missouri botanist Peter H. Raven[32] guessed 8 million to 10 million. Harvard entomologist Edward O. Wilson[33] guessed 10 million in rainforests alone. Oxford ecologist Robert M. May considered estimates from 3 million to 30 million.[34]

If God created species, he or she also disposed of them fairly often.[35] Among marine animal species found in the fossil record, the average life span is about four million years; for other groups of organisms, estimated species' life spans range from one million to ten million years. If, on the average, about one fossil species in five million went extinct each year for reasons unrelated to human intervention, and if there were 30 million living species today, six species would be expected to go extinct on average each year.

The fossil record naturally describes only species with enough hard parts, abundance or luck to leave a fossil record. Rare and local species could have gone extinct without leaving a trace. So the estimated life expectancy of four million years for a species could be several times too large. Consequently, the derived estimate of six or so extinctions a year could be several times too small. On the other hand, a guess of 30 million species alive today may be several times too large. Both the University of Chicago geologist David M. Raup and Harvard's Wilson arrived at a "background rate" of extinction of ten or a few tens of species per year, averaged over long periods of time.

Based on very incomplete information, estimates of how many species were going extinct in the early 1990s varied widely: 18,000 to 55,000 species per year according to the ecologist and writer Norman Myers,[36] 27,000 per year according to Wilson.[37] These estimates rest largely on inferences from the areas of habitat being destroyed to the numbers of species, largely unsampled and unstudied, in those areas. Even if the background rate of extinction were as high as 100 species a year (far higher than the highest estimates), and even if the present rate were 1,800 species per year (one-tenth of the lower estimate of Myers), still far more species would be going extinct yearly than the background rate would predict.[38]

No one has suggested that the rate of creation of new biological species greatly exceeds the background rate of extinction. Consequently, these very rough numerical estimates imply a current reduction in the diversity of living species on the Earth. If there were 55,000 species extinctions a year (Myers's high estimate) and no more than the 1.4 million named species, the rate of extinction of species would be nearly 4 percent per year. At the other extreme, if there were 18,000 species extinctions a year (Myers's low estimate) and 40 million species extant, the rate of extinction would be nearly 0.05 percent per year.

Two obvious questions are: Why are species disappearing so much faster than they disappeared for most of the history of life? And so what? I give the briefest responses.[39] First, why? People are converting the habitats in which many species live to human uses, driving out the native species. If the uprooted species are endemic, they disappear forever; if the uprooted species have a refuge elsewhere, they can be reintroduced eventually. Natural habitat is converted to human settlements, ranches, cultivation and timber plantations. Water reservoirs for power, water supply and recreation drown habitats. Direct and indirect outputs of industry, mining, agriculture and individual consumption acidify or eutrophicate lakes, warm or contaminate streams and pollute coasts. Habitats are also destroyed by accidental pollution from transport (grounded oil tankers, truck spills), runoff from winter salt and some recreational uses. The second major cause of extinction after habitat loss is hunting for meat, fur, hides and live trade. A third major cause of extinction is the introduction of predatory or competitive species from other habitats. Of the animal extinctions since 1600, the destruction of habitat caused 36 percent, hunting caused 23 percent, and the introduction of alien species was responsible for 39 percent; other causes accounted for 2 percent.

Human population growth intensifies many of these threats to the survival of nonhuman species. For example, population density is statistically associated with rates of deforestation, though the strength of the association is sensitive to how deforestation is measured (for example, as a fraction of remaining forest or as an absolute area or as an amount of logging).[40] In 60 tropical countries in 1980 (excluding eight arid African countries), the larger the number of people per square kilometer, the smaller the percentage of land covered by forest. The higher the deforestation in these countries, the higher food production also; forests were cleared to open the land for agriculture. In some poor countries, logging is driven primarily by domestic uses of timber, not by demand for luxuries in the rich countries.

Between 1973 and 1988, developing countries transformed around 400,000 square kilometers of forest to farms and around 856,000 square kilometers of forest to houses, roads and factories; deforestation in this period totaled about 1,450,000 square kilometers.[41] This deforestation resulted from both population growth and a rising demand for individual well-being.

To estimate the extent of deforestation per additional person between 1973 and 1988, divide the total deforestation of 145 million hectares[42] by the estimated rise of 1.2 billion in world population during the same interval.[43] The area of deforestation is 0.12 hectare per additional person. This area, some 1,200 square meters, may be visualized as a rectangle 50 meters by 24 meters, roughly one-quarter of an American football field. Paul Harrison, the author of The Third Revolution, estimated that each additional person needs about one-quarter hectare of land.[44] If each additional person requires 0.12 to 0.25 hectare of additional land, each additional billion people require 1.2 million to 2.5 million square kilometers of additional land, land that may have been habitat for wildlife.

So what if a lot of species are going extinct? The economist Julian L. Simon and the political scientist Aaron Wildavsky argued that species extinction might not be a bad idea because it could make room for the evolution of new species that are even better for human beings than the ones now on the Earth.[45] True, new species could be more wonderful than the ones now alive; then again, they might be no better, or worse, or far worse. New species are most likely to be what gardeners regard as weeds, that is, species adapted to exploiting environments disturbed by human action. Wonderful new species are unlikely to appear at a rate anywhere near the rate at which present species are being extinguished unless people create them. The net effect of continued species losses at present rates (whatever they may be) would surely be progressive impoverishment in diversity.

The potential consequences of the loss of species can be illustrated by resuming the tale of time that I started to tell early in this chapter. In the back of the truck are some people who are breaking up bits of the wooden flooring and burning them to warm their hands through the long, cold trip; others are tearing off scraps of metal from the walls to fashion spoons and pots for dinner; others are throwing truck parts of unknown function out of the back of the truck so they will have a little more room to stretch out and relax. In one corner a few passengers are feverishly trying to decipher and understand the truck's instruction manual, even as others tear out odd pages to light their evening fires. It is a race between the rate of consumption of the truck and the rate of understanding why the truck's parts are there, which parts are essential, which are beautiful and which—like the male teat—are neither ornamental nor useful.

Anecdotes of serendipitous discoveries from humble species abound.[46] An entire industry is based on the polymerase chain reaction (PCR), a method of amplifying tiny bits of DNA to useful quantities. Applications include diagnostic tests for strep throat, DNA testing of crime specimens and evolutionary studies of the DNA of fossil animals (which inspired the novel and movie *Jurassic Park*). The PCR depends on an enzyme discovered in the humble bacterium *Thermus aquaticus* that lives in a hot spring in Yellowstone National Park. Taxol, a chemical useful in the treatment of breast cancer, originated from the bark of the Pacific yew—a northwestern United States evergreen considered a trash tree until recently. Penicillin was accidently discovered as a product of a soil mold. An estimated half to three-quarters of all pharmaceuticals originate biologically, mostly from plants. Wild relatives of domestic crops continue to contribute genes resistant to disease and pests. Bacterial toxins and specialized fungi offer alternatives to dangerous chemicals for the control of plant pests. Novel microorganisms decompose spills of oil and other chemicals.

The conservation of species brings three kinds of benefits: benefits to human values; direct economic benefits; and indirect benefits through ecosystem services.[47] The human fascination with other forms of life, the esthetic enjoyment they offer, the compassion they deserve and their right to exist as fellow travelers on the only known planet with life are arguments for conservation based on human values. Direct economic benefits include medicinal applications, sources of novel foods and improvements of existing food crops, agents of biological control and other products. The least visible and most pervasive benefits are the ecosystem services. Living species regulate the atmosphere, climate, fresh water, soils, waste disposal, cycling of essential nutrients, pest control, disease control and pollination. They provide wild foods and store genetic history. They continuously tune genetic diversity to the demands of shifting environments at a rate limited by the mechanisms of natural selection. Each of these topics deserves, and has, many treatises.

In addition to all these values, living species provide the subject matter of the basic sciences of individual organisms (such as molecular biology and biochemistry) and the basic sciences of populations in relation to their environment (such as ecology and behavior). These sciences may offer unexpected insights in the future, as they have in the past.

Each esthetic, ethical, economic, ecosystemic and scientific value has to be negotiated against other, conflicting values; none is absolute. For example, I would favor the extinction of smallpox, though I strongly favor species conservation in general. I concede that my judgment on smallpox may prove shortsighted in the future. A balance of values likewise applies to each wonder chemical discovered in an obscure species. Economically minded observers will ask whether the chemical is available elsewhere, or could be synthesized, at a cost that is comparable to or lower than the cost of conserving the species in which it was discovered. Fair enough.

But human ignorance is so extensive that people know only a few of the right questions to ask when trying to balance the costs and benefits of preserving biological diversity. What services does living nature provide for us that we do not yet recognize? Given the present primitive state of understanding of how the biological world works, the suggestion that market mechanisms could be relied on at present to govern species conservation seems preposterous. Moreover, many of the benefits that result from conserving species are open-access resources, but the costs of conservation may be privately borne. Hence the conservation of species is drastically undervalued by current market mechanisms of assigning value. The race is on between understanding what the parts of our vehicle the Earth are doing, and tossing them out the back of the truck.

TIME CONSTRAINTS IN INFECTIOUS DISEASE: "WILL AIDS SOLVE THE POPULATION PROBLEM?"

One of the questions I am most frequently asked during talks on human carrying capacity is "Will AIDS solve the population problem?" Only people who have neither experienced nor observed AIDS could see it as a solution to a problem. Deaths from AIDS—about two million by 1993[48]—are painful and wasteful, wherever they occur. The losses are concentrated among people in their most productive years. In the poor countries, deaths from AIDS aggravate the difficulty of agricultural and economic development, worsen the plight of the surviving young and old who depend on the middle-aged for care, dilute already thin resources for health care and weaken incentives for the voluntary reduction of fertility.

I assume that what is intended is a question like "Could AIDS substantially lower the population growth rates in countries with high population growth rates?" As you might by now expect, expert opinions differ. Different models predict that, if 30 percent of adults are infected with the human immunodeficiency virus (HIV), the population growth rate could be lowered as little as 1 percentage point or as much as 3 percentage points (Figure 15.1). The range of effects on the population growth rate increases with an increasing prevalence of HIV infection. A report of the United Nations complained:

> . . . the number and diversity of models of the AIDS epidemic and its demographic impact are staggering, and each model purports to have some decisive advantage. The diversity of models has inevitably led to diversity in outcomes:

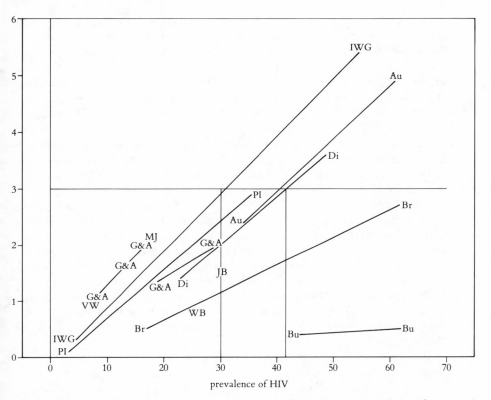

FIGURE 15.1 Estimates of the decrease in the rate of population growth as a function of the adult prevalence of HIV infection. Each set of initials summarizes a result of one study, which is identified by the initials of its authors. When a study considered a range of estimates, the extreme values of HIV prevalence and of reduction in the growth rate are shown as the endpoints of a line segment. For example, the line segment labeled "Bu" in the lower right corner identifies the estimates of a model by Rodolfo A. Bulatao. Different authors defined adult prevalence in different ways; some included one sex only and some included both. SOURCE: Zaba 1994

answers to a single query are multiple while the range of projections is broad and usually unaccompanied by a measure of their uncertainty. Currently, no criterion exists to facilitate a choice among the models. This situation is discouraging to policy-makers, who are interested in unambiguous answers to what appear to be simple questions.[49]

Nevertheless, the United Nations Population Division has come up with its official estimates of the demographic impact of AIDS. Before describing these estimates, I will place AIDS in a larger picture of human infectious diseases.[50]

Human infection by a biological agent requires three ingredients: people who are susceptible to infection, an infectious agent capable of infecting people and an environment that brings people and the infectious agent together enough for the infection to occur. Infection is necessary but not sufficient for infectious disease. Millions of people harbor malarial protozoa and the bacteria of tuberculosis without suffering apparent disease. Often an infection turns into a disease when the body is weakened by poor nutrition, stress or other infections. In some cases, signs of infectious pathology are not defined culturally as a disease. For example, in parts of Africa, serious damage to the urinary bladder by a bilharzial parasite (*Schistosoma haematobium*) causes boys to lose blood through their urine. Where infection is so common that local people assume boys menstruate as well as girls, the infection is not viewed as a disease. Infectious disease is not purely a matter of biology.

Infectious diseases may be epidemic, surging from a low frequency to high and then eventually subsiding again, or endemic, maintained at a steady frequency. They may be virulent, injuring or killing the infected person, like bubonic plague, or avirulent, causing no major impairment, like herpes. They may cause permanent immunity, rendering a second infection unlikely, like measles, or they may leave the person open to reinfection, like malaria. Whether an infectious disease is epidemic or endemic, virulent or avirulent, depends in large part on the size of the human population in which it occurs and on how long the population has experienced that infection.

Before the local agricultural evolution, human groups were probably too small and isolated to maintain endemic infections that were immunizing or highly virulent. Virulent infections might wipe out an entire group of human hosts, leaving the infectious agent nowhere to go. Natural selection acting on the biological agent would disfavor virulence when the human hosts were organized in small, isolated groups. Infections that confer permanent immunity might sweep through a human group, leaving the group immune, and the infectious agent nowhere to go, until the infected generation died and was replaced by susceptible youngsters.

Nonhuman animals may have transmitted virulent and immunizing infections to human groups from time to time, as swine in Asia today are believed to transmit influenza viruses to people. Infections of animal origin are called zoonoses. Small, scattered human groups probably could not sustain virulent or immunizing zoonoses on their own. Small bands, innocent of these infections, crossed into the Western Hemisphere, Australia and Tasmania, setting the stage for infectious catastrophes millennia later. Until the local agricultural evolution, shortages of food and the hazards of acquiring it, rather than infectious diseases, may have been the principal controls on population growth.

Settled agriculture and the rise of cities opened a golden age for infectious diseases. Human exposure to human and domestic animal excrement increased in towns and fields, creating a newly favorable environment for infectious agents, from viruses to worms, to cycle through the human population. Ancient domestic commensals like mice and rats, while not intentionally domesticated, brought their own parasites, like fleas, and their parasites' infections, like the bubonic plague. Larger urban populations provided larger annual supplies of susceptible babies and children to sustain immunizing infections. By various means, the major civilizations of the Old World acquired a broad repertoire of infectious diseases. In time, their populations acquired some genetic and immunological resistance to those infections. At the same time, small groups of people moving from southeast China and Taiwan across Polynesia probably lost many infections of the major civilizations for the same reasons that small groups of hunters and gatherers could not sustain those infections.

In spite of their adaptations to infection, most people in major civilizations probably died of infectious diseases. Ill nourished by modern standards, they often died as children.[51] Adaptations to familiar infections gave limited protection against novel infections. For example, as I mentioned earlier, in repeated epidemics in the fourteenth century bubonic plague, a new entrant probably from east Asia, reduced the human population from India to Iceland by as much as one-third.

Starting about five centuries ago, emissaries of the immunologically experienced Old World encountered populations of the New World, Australia and South Pacific that lacked prior exposure to Old World infectious diseases. In the first century following contact between Western Europeans and aborigines in the New World, the aboriginal populations fell dramatically, mainly as a result of the disasters wrought by smallpox, tuberculosis, measles and other newly introduced infections.[52]

Some simple lessons emerge from this brief history. When people come into new, closer contact with other human or nonhuman animals, they stand an improved chance of contracting their infections. When people establish new, denser forms of settlement, they create opportunities for novel infections that could not be sustained or transmitted in less dense settlements. A new infection can be widely lethal.

This background makes AIDS more intelligible, though it in no way determines either the origin of the human immunodeficiency virus or the most likely future course and demographic effect of AIDS. One theory of the origin of HIV is that it is, or derives from, a monkey virus. The so-called simian immunodeficiency virus could have infected people who entered new forest habitats or ate poorly cooked monkey flesh. Another theory, compatible with the first, is that HIV had long been a human infection in small, isolated African villages, where it was not virulent and possibly not even recognized as a disease. A dead village provides a virus no hosts for the future, so there may have been natural selection for avirulence, a low probability of transmission or a very slow progression from infection to disease and death. Selective pressure for viral moderation may have been relaxed when the virus spread to a larger, denser population that offered more opportunities for transmission.

As of 1990, about eight million people had HIV infections.[53] Of these, about five million lived in sub-Saharan Africa, and of these 4.5 million lived in just 15 countries. Twelve of these 15 countries were located in a continuous belt across middle and eastern Africa; three were in west Africa. For comparison, as of 1990, 200 million people had schistosomiasis (also called bilharzia) and 200,000 died of it every year[54]; of the roughly 267 million with malaria, 107 million people were clinical cases and an estimated 1 million to 2 million of them died of it every year (three-quarters of them children under five years old)[55]; and 1.7 billion—one in three humans—were infected with the tubercle bacillus (including half the population of Africa), 10 million to 20 million people had active tuberculosis and 3 million of them died of it every year.[56]

To shed light on the future demographic impact of HIV infection and AIDS, the United Nations Population Division and the World Health Organization's Global Program on AIDS convened a meeting at U.N. headquarters in December 1989. The aim of the meeting was to find out why various models of the demographic impact of HIV infection produced such different results. To eliminate differences due to variations in the assumed initial population, the organizers distributed detailed assumptions[57] about a hypothetical population and the transmission of HIV infection to the eight groups of invited modelers and asked them to project the hypothetical population 25 years into the future.

According to the standard input distributed by the organizers, the hypothetical population had 100,000 males and 100,000 females. Life expectancies at birth were assumed to be 53 years for females and 50 years for males. The population was assumed to be growing exponentially at 3.5 percent per year, a very high rate of increase by world standards but typical of sub-Saharan African countries where AIDS was most serious. Females were assumed to marry at a median age of 17 years to men who were five years older, and 95 percent of women were assumed to marry eventually. The average age of childbearing was assumed to be 29 years. (This does not mean that the average woman waited from age 17 to age 29 to have her first child. It means that the average of all the ages at which all women had all of their children was assumed to be 29. For example, a hypothetical woman who had five children at ages 18, 23, 29, 35 and 40 would have an average age of childbearing of 29 years.) One-quarter of the population was assumed to be urban.

Most cases of AIDS were assumed to occur among heterosexuals. An infected mother was assumed to transmit HIV infection to a newborn infant 40 percent of the time. This pattern of AIDS occurs in more than a dozen countries of sub-Saharan Africa and some countries of South America, Central America and the Caribbean. The assumed initial prevalence of HIV infection mimicked the results of surveys in Kenya, Malawi, Uganda and Tanzania.[58] Half of newly infected adults were assumed to have frank AIDS within ten years and 90 percent within 18 years. Half of individuals newly diagnosed with AIDS were assumed to be dead within one year, 100 percent within five years.

The empirical gaps in formulating the standard input were staggering.

No published or unpublished data could be found on the sexual activity of people after they were diagnosed with AIDS. Physicians reported that some AIDS patients acquired other sexually transmitted diseases after the patients were diagnosed with AIDS. Based on these anecdotal reports and the presumption that a far higher proportion of HIV infections and cases of clinical AIDS go undiagnosed in African countries, the working group decided to assume that patients with AIDS remain sexually active.[59]

A more important gap in knowledge concerned the transmission of HIV infection. If a man infected with HIV has a single unprotected intercourse with a woman not infected with HIV, what is the probability that the woman will become infected with HIV as a result? Similarly, if an infected woman has a single unprotected intercourse with an uninfected man, what is his probability of acquiring HIV infection from her? Controlled experiments to answer these questions are ethically impossible. The organizers had to consider three scenarios—called best, intermediate and worst—to allow for the uncertainty in this and a few other important quantities. "These three scenarios were defined according to variation in three factors: (a) rate of infectivity, that is, the probability of infection from sexual contact with an infected partner; (b) number of sexual contacts of males with prostitutes; and (c) proportion of sexual acts with condom use."[60]

The best scenario assumed a probability of infection (or rate of infectivity) from male to female of 3 per 1,000 and from female to male of 1 per 1,000; 12 sexual contacts per year with prostitutes by men who frequented prostitutes; four sexual contacts per year with non-prostitutes by men who did not frequent prostitutes; and the use of condoms in 20 percent of sexual acts. In all scenarios, condoms were assumed to be 80 percent effective in preventing infection in a single act of intercourse. The worst scenario assumed a probability of infection from male to female of 1 in 10 and from female to male of 1 in 10; 36 sexual contacts per year with prostitutes by men who frequented prostitutes; 12 sexual contacts per year with non-prostitutes by men who did not frequent prostitutes; and the use of condoms in 2 percent of sexual acts. The intermediate case assumed the arithmetic average of the assigned minimum and maximum values, except for the probabilities of infection, which were set at 3 per 100 from males to females and 1 per 100 from females to males.

(Remember these numbers, ladies and gentlemen, girls and boys! If you are not infected with HIV and you have unprotected intercourse with an infected partner, the best guess is that your chance of acquiring HIV is 3 percent if you're female and 1 percent if you're male. But your chance of infection could be as large as 10 percent. One in ten. Is it worth it?)

The modelers were sent to their corners and asked to prepare a standard demographic and epidemiological summary of the hypothetical population for the next 25 years (Table 15.2). Even the standard set of starting assumptions posed problems. Some of the input values were not used at all by some of the models, while other models required data that were not included in the set of inputs. Each modeler had to specify some values that

TABLE 15.2 Selected demographic and epidemiological outcomes projected by six models, 25 years in the future, for three scenarios of the AIDS epidemic in a hypothetical population

model

outcome:	Auvert			Brouard			Bulatao[a]		
	best	intermediate	worst	best	intermediate	worst	best	intermediate	worst
HIV[b] prevalence (percent)	0	31.0	55.0	0.2	15.0	55.0	0.3	39.5	57.5
AIDS[b] prevalence (percent)	0	3.0	5.80	0.0	1.9	7.0	0.0	4.5	4.4
cumulative AIDS cases (percent)	0	21	23	0.7	5	13.8	0.2	3.4	50
cumulative AIDS deaths (percent)	0	20	22	—[c]	—[c]	—[c]	—[c]	—[c]	—[c]
life expectancy at birth (years)	60	26	16	—[c]	—[c]	—[c]	61	47	45
rate of natural increase (percent)	3.0	0.5	-2.0	3.3	2.4	0.16	3.0	2.5	2.4
population (thousands)	464	236	146	467	426	344	449	409	382

model

outcome:	Dietz			Interagency Working Group			Palloni		
	best	intermediate	worst	best	intermediate	worst	best	intermediate	worst
HIV prevalence (percent)	0	21.2	43.9	0	3.5	42.4	0.1	2.8	30.3
AIDS prevalence (percent)	0	1.8	4.7	0	0.8	12.0	0.0	0.4	5.2
cumulative AIDS cases (percent)	0	6.9	17.2	0.7	21.2	21.3	0	2.8	16.6
cumulative AIDS deaths (percent)	0	6.3	17.4	0.7	19.9	21.4	0	2.6	15.4
life expectancy at birth (years)	61	36	24	65	58	28	60	42	22
rate of natural increase (percent)	3.2	1.5	-0.7	2.9	2.6	-2.5	3.1	2.8	-0.0
population (thousands)	470	355	120	392	378	245	446	427	260

[a] Values correspond to the interval 20–25 years after the beginning of the projection.
[b] AIDS = acquired immunodeficiency syndrome; HIV = human immunodeficiency virus.
[c] Not available as output.

Source: United Nations (1991, pp. 52–53, Table 10).

were not specified by the organizers. Some of the models started with an assumed distribution of HIV infection by age, sex and region, as specified by the organizers; other models started with the introduction into the population of a few HIV-infected persons.

In the best scenario, the probabilities of infection were too low to sustain the epidemic, and all the models agreed that HIV infection would gradually disappear from the population. In the worst scenario, all but one of the models agreed that after 25 years the population growth rate would be near zero or negative. From 30 percent to 58 percent of the population would be infected with HIV and from 4 percent to 12 percent of the population would have AIDS.

Life (or death) became much more complicated in the intermediate case, in which the assumed rates of infectivity were thought to be closest to those actually operating. In this case, the models predicted that the epidemic would continue, but the differences among the models led to enormous differences in predicted outcomes. The projected prevalence of HIV infection after 25 years ranged from 3 to 40 percent. The projected cumulative number of AIDS cases ranged from 34,000 to 275,000. The projected rate of population growth ranged from 0.5 to 2.8 percent per year, and the projected life expectancy at birth ranged from 26 to 58 years.[61]

The models differed widely in the intermediate case because they made very different assumptions about how couples formed and how people behaved sexually. To specify couple formation, the standard input included an age pattern at which men and women first married and a fixed difference in the ages of partners; a distribution of people according to their sexual behavior; a range of values for the frequency of sex with partners; and three values for infectivity per sexual contact. Implicit in these apparently neutral standard values were several strong assumptions about sexual unions. Practically all women were assumed to enter a union according to the given age pattern as long as men could be found in the proper age categories. Once a union was formed, it was assumed to dissolve only on the death of one partner. If partners were available in the appropriate age categories, the surviving spouse was assumed to reenter a union according to the same age pattern of probabilities that governed first unions.

The standard input assumed that monogamous females sought partners only among monogamous males and that non-monogamous females entered into unions only with non-monogamous males. No assumptions were specified for relations between non-monogamous females and monogamous males, or vice versa. Among the non-monogamous persons there was an implicit distinction between regular unions and casual unions. The standard input assumed that the probability of infection for a member of a couple was a function of the rate of infectivity and the frequency of sexual contact and nothing else.

These assumptions could have been changed without changing the standard input given to each modeler. For example, it could have been assumed that males and females, whether monogamous or non-monogamous, engaged in premarital sex before they entered unions. It could have been assumed that unions might end through the death of a partner or divorce and that individuals entered no further unions once their first union ended. Instead of assuming that sexual contacts could occur only among persons with like sexual preferences, random mating or other mating patterns could have been assumed. The probability of transferring infection from one member of a steady or a casual union could have been made to depend on the duration or the type of the union.[62]

In short, ignorance about biology (probabilities of transmission) and behavior (frequencies of extramarital intercourse and condom use) made it necessary to specify three scenarios. Additional ignorance about behavior left open many ways to interpret each scenario. This remarkable study showed unmistakably that no one knows whether the AIDS epidemic will or will not stop or reverse rapid population growth in countries with a high prevalence of HIV infection.

Yet the lesson was not learned. The urge to fabricate "unambiguous answers to what appear to be simple questions"[63] seems to be irresistible. Just two years after this study was published, the United Nations Population Division published the 1992 revision of its regular biennial *World Population Prospects*.[64] For the first time, the *Prospects* offered a detailed country-specific discussion of the projected demographic impact of AIDS in 15 sub-Saharan countries. These were the countries where more than 1 percent of the population age 15 years and older had HIV antibodies in 1990. The prevalence of antibodies to HIV in blood sera ranged from 1 percent to 15 percent and averaged 4.5 percent. The projections relied on a single epidemiological model developed by the Global Program on AIDS of the World Health Organization, plus the United Nations Population Division's standard demographic model. The United Nations Population Division's own study[65] on the uncertainty of such forecasts was neither mentioned nor cited, not in the descriptive chapter and not in the technical chapter on methods. Instead, the new account of *World Population Prospects* gave a single projection from 1980 to 2005 of what the population would have been in the absence of AIDS and another single projection of what it was expected to be in the presence of AIDS. The difference was presented as the impact of AIDS. The uncertainty of such an estimate was nowhere mentioned. In 1994, the United Nations published an expanded version of the AIDS estimates in its *AIDS and the Demography of Africa*. Once again, the U.N.'s own comparative study of the uncertainty of modeling was neither mentioned nor cited.[66]

The projections indicated that with AIDS, the 138 million people of these 15 countries will increase to 298 million by the year 2005, whereas without AIDS they would have increased to 310 million. AIDS decreased the aggregate population in 2005 by 4 percent. The difference of 12 million people resulted from 9 million additional deaths and 3 million fewer births, because fewer women survived into and through the ages of childbearing.[67] In Zambia, where AIDS caused the largest proportional decrease (10.1 percent), the population would rise from 5.7 million in 1980 to 12.1 million in 2005 with AIDS, but to 13.5 million without AIDS.[68] Either way the population would more than double in 25 years.

At the end of the projection period, in 2000–2005, the aggregate population growth rate for the 15 countries would be 2.88 percent per year with AIDS, but 3.13 percent per year without AIDS.[69] The projected time for the 15 countries to double from their 1980 size would be 22.3 years with AIDS, but 21.3 years without AIDS.[70] If these calculations described the real world, it would be difficult to argue with the conclusion: "Very high fertility in those countries will influence their future population growth far more than the effect of the AIDS epidemic or any other demographic parameter."[71]

While these official projections[72] forecasted a moderate demographic impact of AIDS, the British epidemiologists Geoff P. Garnett and Roy M. Anderson argued on the contrary that AIDS could stop or reverse population growth in some African countries. Garnett and Anderson cited reports that in some urban centers of sub-Saharan Africa, 20 percent to 30 percent or more of pregnant women aged 15 to 40 years were infected with HIV. In their mathematical model "a level of HIV infection of 30 percent in pregnant women could be sufficient to reduce a 3 percent per annum population growth before the epidemic to below zero once an endemic situation has been attained."[73]

Analysts at the United States Bureau of the Census reported a single projection of the demographic impact of AIDS in 13 sub-Saharan countries (omitting only Benin and Mozambique from the 15 countries in the United Nations' AIDS projections), as well as in Brazil, Haiti and Thailand. They projected that, for the year 2010, AIDS would increase the aggregate crude death rate of the 13 sub-Saharan countries by 150 percent. Unlike Garnett and Anderson, they found that, because the projected fertility remained so high, the aggregate difference between crude birth and death rates never dropped below about 2 percent. The U.S. Census Bureau analysis indicated that at least half the adults nationally would have to test positive for HIV in sub-Saharan Africa to drive the population growth rates below zero.[74] Four sub-Saharan countries were expected to have population growth rates at or below 1 percent in 2010, compared to rates without AIDS in excess of 2 percent; Thailand's growth rate in 2010 was projected to fall from 0.9 percent increase per year to 0.8 percent decrease per year.[75]

The calculations of the United Nations, Garnett and Anderson and the United States Census Bureau fell within the range of possibility.[76] But the earlier comparative study of models showed that there is little reason to accept any of these calculations with much confidence. The real lesson of the United Nations' modeling workshop was that too much remains to be known to say with confidence what will happen.

In the good old days before the AIDS epidemic, demographers knew they could not predict the future of population because they knew little about the future of fertility. The AIDS epidemic has increased the uncertainty about the future of fertility, and added uncertainty about the future of mortality. The uncertainty about the future population of countries with substantial AIDS epidemics (a growing number of countries) has thus increased considerably. That's progress.

The present realities and even the most favorable projections are horrifying enough. One estimate is that between 6 percent and 11 percent of the children under age 15 years in ten sub-Saharan countries will be orphaned by AIDS during the 1990s.[77] The virus of AIDS may interact disastrously with the bacillus of tuberculosis, harbored by an estimated half of the African population, especially if the bacillus can resist the major tuberculosis drugs.[78] As a result of AIDS, infant mortality rates are projected to nearly double in Zambia and Zimbabwe and to more than double in Thailand.[79]

The appearance of AIDS is retrospectively intelligible as an instance of what can happen when people press into new habitats; come into closer contact with nonhuman animals; and establish new, denser patterns of settlement and interpersonal contact. Yet AIDS surprised scientists as much as it surprised the public. The final chapter of an excellent book on infectious diseases published in 1972 by the Australian Nobel laureate in medicine and physiology, Sir Macfarlane Burnet, together with Professor David White, had this paragraph:

> On the basis of what has happened in the last thirty years, can we forecast any likely developments for the '70s? If for the present we retain a basic optimism and assume no major catastrophes occur and that any wars are kept at the "brush fire" level, the most likely forecast about the future of infectious disease is that it will be very dull. There may be some wholly unexpected emergence of a new and dangerous infectious disease, but nothing of the sort has marked the past fifty years. There have been isolated outbreaks of fatal infections derived from exotic animals. . . . Similar episodes will doubtless occur in the future but they will presumably be safely contained.[80]

Contrary to the complacent vision of Burnet and White, it now seems prudent to expect unpleasant microbial surprises to continue to occur. As human populations continue to expand, people will enter new habitats and have closer contacts with nonhuman animals and their infections. As gigantic cities with primitive or no sanitation continue to grow in developing countries, while jets transport passengers between continents, people will mingle ever more closely. Bulk international shipments of foods, fuels and finished products will increasingly carry insects, rodents and their infections across the seas, just as the first Polynesians to reach Easter Island introduced the Polynesian rat (Chapter 16).

People who are dying of AIDS today waiting for a vaccine that they hope will come tomorrow or the next day feel acutely the constraint that time imposes on human carrying capacity. The processes that drive microbial surprises are happening faster than in the past, leaving less time than ever for humans to adapt. Global mixing has raised the stakes. In the fifteenth and sixteenth centuries, the Europeans had at least a few millennia of settlement to adapt to smallpox and measles; Africans and Mediterranean peoples had far longer to develop genetic adaptations to malaria. When they brought their microbes to the New World they put the American aborigines at risk, but not the whole human species.

While human vulnerability to new infections is great, so is the potential to slow some of the processes that increase vulnerability and to gain advance warning of others. Slowing population growth could slow migration into novel habitats and reduce contacts with novel infectious agents. (But slowing population growth is not the only, and not necessarily the most efficient, way to keep people from migrating into new habitats.) Improved urban sanitation and health education for mothers everywhere could slow the spread of human infections and diminish contact with infections of domestic animals. (Improved sanitation and health education would also improve the survival of children, which could lead to lower fertility eventually.) Better surveillance of diseases worldwide, including systematic searching for new viruses, could contain and control novel outbreaks when other forms of prevention fail.[81] The foundations of viral, bacterial and protozoal research could be strengthened internationally, so that progress made anywhere is shared everywhere, and so that local competent people can deal with outbreaks wherever they occur. Occur they will.

TIME CONSTRAINTS IN POPULATION GROWTH

The immense momentum of human population growth resembles the very long stopping time of a fully loaded truck. As we have already seen from U.N. projections, if the world's women had maintained replacement-level fertility from 1990 onward while life expectancy gradually improved, total world population would increase from 5.3 billion in 1990 to 8.1 billion by 2100 and level off at 8.4 billion by 2150—a rise of 3.1 billion in 160 years. The lag between the time when individuals or couples achieve replacement-level fertility and the time when the population stops growing means that even an instant success in reducing fertility today will not eliminate increasing numbers tomorrow.

Many factors that interact with population have similarly long lags.[82] Chlorofluorocarbons accumulate in the stratosphere before the ozone layer erodes, and are there even longer before human skin cancers rise. Atmospheric carbon dioxide from the burning of fossil fuels accumulates in the atmosphere long before a temperature change can be detected; in some computational models (pass the salt, please!), temperature rises are expected to continue two decades after carbon dioxide concentrations level off.

Preparing the infrastructure for future human populations entails long lags.[83] How many schools, universities, housing projects, health clinics, hospitals, water reservoirs, aqueducts, sewers, power lines, steam pipes, power plants and irrigation canals should be built, and where? How many highways, bridges, rail lines, ports and airports should be built, and where?

How many and what kind of parks and nature reserves should be planned, and where? How many teachers, doctors and nurses should be trained? How should military technology, strategies and tactics respond to projections of the future pool of available personnel?

The answers to all these questions depend in part on demographic projections. When differing projections are available, the user must recognize and plan for an uncertain future. Opportunities are wasted by creating excess capacity; shortages result from too little.

For most poor countries with large numbers of underemployed, poorly educated workers, inadequate physical and economic infrastructure and limited institutional development, fast population growth interferes with economic development and social well-being, even though estimates of the effects of rapid population growth appear to fluctuate with the ideological winds. In 1971, a committee of the National Academy of Sciences of the United States emphasized that rapid population growth is a serious obstacle to economic development.[84] In 1986, another committee under the same sponsorship offered a more qualified view: rapid population growth affects development negatively in many developing countries, but the connections between population growth and development are complex and difficult to measure quantitatively; through adaptation and substitution, markets may reduce adverse effects.[85]

In 1992, the United Nations Fund for Population Activities convened a meeting of economists (some 30 attended) on the relationship between population growth and economic development. The report of that meeting concluded that fertility rates can fall rapidly in the absence of dramatic economic improvements; full economic development is not a prerequisite for lowered population growth rates. In a cautious and blandly worded statement of consensus, the report emphasized that rapid population growth makes it more difficult for developing countries to provide and improve education and productive employment. Consequently, "the potential gains that might have accrued from having a rapidly growing stock of younger workers are offset by lower productivity of workers and reduced competitiveness in a global economy where gains from trade depend primarily on productivity. When low productivity is coupled with low earnings, efforts to alleviate poverty are undercut."[86]

One economist at the meeting, George J. Stolnitz, a retired professor of economics at Indiana University, attached to the report a passionate dissent. He gave a long list of adverse effects of population growth faster than 2 percent per year and concluded that today's newly developing countries, "both individually and in aggregate, are demonstrably incapable of feeding, sheltering, educating, employing or servicing the great majority of their populations even today, despite claiming a doubling of income. Why, then, should further rapid population growth be expected to have equal developmental and welfare implications than would considerably lower rates of such growth?"[87]

The balance of present scholarly judgment is that slower population growth would benefit most developing countries, and that rapid population growth exacerbates many other problems of which it is not the sole or principal cause.[88] The adverse effects of rapid population growth are felt macroeconomically and at the level of individuals and households.

At the macroeconomic level, raising a baby and providing it with the physical and educational resources to become a modern productive worker require major investments. A rapidly growing population has a higher proportion of babies and, compared to a slowly growing or stationary population, requires adults to sacrifice more consumption (including leisure) in favor of investing in the next generation. Adults have generally proved unwilling to forgo their own consumption to the extent required by very high rates of population growth.

In the United States, for example, where the population currently grows at a rate near 1 percent per year, raising each additional baby requires an investment of $20,000 for housing, 20 years or so of feeding that cost at least another $20,000, an education averaging $100,000, plant and equipment at the work site that run to $80,000 and transportation worth an additional $20,000. Developing a new infant into a worker in the American economy requires investing about $240,000. New technology will probably require still more investment in plant, equipment and education, raising further the initial investment required to make each new worker productive. According to the M.I.T. economist Lester Thurow, a population growth rate of 4 percent per year would require the United States to invest half of its gross national product in its new members.

Thurow asserted that adult Americans probably would not agree to lower their standard of living to the extent required, "just as the wealthy people in those countries with rapid population growth rates haven't been willing to make the personal sacrifices that would make rapid population growth and economic development consistent. The result: continued poverty in those nations with high rates of population growth."[89]

One recent, extensive, balanced review of empirical studies concluded that economic output in many developing countries would have grown more rapidly with slower population growth, even though population growth probably had negligible, or rarely positive, impact in some countries.

> Population's adverse impact has most likely occurred where arable land and water are particularly scarce or costly to acquire, where property rights to land and natural resources are poorly defined and where government policies are biased against the most abundant factor of production—labor. Population's positive impact most likely occurred where natural resources are abundant, where the possibilities for scale economies are substantial, and where markets and other institutions (especially government) allocate resources in a reasonably efficient way over time and space.[90]

Individuals and households also feel negative consequences of rapid population growth, and the effects may be long term.[91] Mothers with many pregnancies have elevated risks of dying in pregnancy or from unsafe abortions. Children with many siblings, especially older siblings, generally receive less parental attention, all else being equal, and, in poor societies, may receive less food, less education and less health care. In many poor families, girls are less likely than boys to receive formal education. Lack of education for girls promotes another generation of poverty: it prevents girls from getting jobs outside the home, increases their difficulty in controlling their own fertility and makes them more dependent on their own subsequent children for support.

In contrast to the developing countries, some developed countries face the prospect of population decline. In 1992, three countries—Germany, Bulgaria and Hungary—reported slight dips in population.[92] A slow decline is easier to accommodate than a fast one. The more rapid the decline, the greater the fraction of the population over age 65 and the smaller the fraction of people below working age. With an aging population, the increased total costs of assuring the well-being of the older population are partly compensated by the reduced total costs of rearing and educating young people. More gradual change in population size risks fewer surprises than more rapid change.

NATURAL CONSTRAINTS, TIME, INGENUITY, AND ORGANIZATIONAL COMPLEXITY

Time is required to solve problems of energy, agriculture, minerals, biological diversity, disease and infrastructure. While time is necessary, it is not sufficient to solve such problems. The will to solve them plus the ingenuity and the organizational means to implement solutions are also required.

In 1963, the British astronomer Sir Fred Hoyle forecasted that the limit to population growth in technological societies would come not from food, as Malthus predicted, but from organizational breakdown: "It is the organization that ultimately becomes overloaded and collapses. For instance, it would be impossible to maintain the organization necessary to support hundreds of thousands of millions of people if the ration of standing room really were reduced to one square yard per person."[93]

Under the load of a large population, Hoyle argued, the organizational structure of a technological society would be less likely to degrade smoothly, like melting butter, than to collapse abruptly, like a snapped violin string. "With the effectively discontinuous collapse of society there will be an effectively discontinuous rise in [the death rate], simply because the very organization that permitted vast numbers to be fed and kept alive will have disappeared."[94] The curve of population as a function of time would be saw-toothed, Hoyle predicted. After each collapse of population, an expansion phase would follow that would favor individuals with exceptional qualities of cooperation and intelligence. In 5,000 years, plus or minus a millennium, a new, cooperative breed of humans—a new species, in Hoyle's view—would emerge and the oscillations in population size might be damped away.

Hoyle offered no details about why and how a rising population would lead to an organizational overload and collapse. For developing countries, the Canadian political scientist Thomas Homer-Dixon provided a fuller picture of how environmental scarcity, aggravated through rapid population growth, could lead to an "ingenuity gap."

With rising populations and consumption, economic and political decision-makers will face multiple, simultaneous, interacting and urgent problems of conservation, resource substitution and technological innovation. "Rapidly unfolding environmental scarcities will require decision makers to make fast and accurate decisions about, for example, strategies for investment in research and development, institutional and organizational procedures for channeling expertise, and programs for convincing people to change their resource consumption behavior."[95] Because of unanticipated thresholds and nonlinear responses, decisions and responses may have highly unpredictable and far-reaching consequences.

Ingenuity, defined as "intelligence that is applied to solve practical social and technical problems," will be in short supply for four reasons: social friction, capital shortages, market failure and cognitive limits. According to Homer-Dixon,

> The most damaging impacts of population growth and resource scarcity . . . occur in the political and social sphere, because scarcity weakens the society's capacity for institutional innovation, that is, its capacity to supply social ingenuity. This is Malthus in the real world, a world evermore fraught with the pushing and pulling of powerful groups that struggle to protect their narrow interests. . . . [T]he greater the severity of environmental scarcity, the greater the social turmoil caused by this scarcity, and the lower the probability that a poor society can supply the ingenuity required to adapt.[96]

Time will tell.

16

Human Carrying Capacity: An Overview

> The question of how many people the world can support is unanswerable in a finite sense. What do we want?
> Are there global limits, absolute limits beyond which we cannot go without catastrophe or overwhelming costs? There are, most certainly.
>
> —GEORGE WOODWELL 1985[1]

CASE STUDY: EASTER ISLAND

THE CONSTRAINTS ON the Earth's human carrying capacity are just as real as the wide range of choices within those boundaries. The history of Easter Island provides a case study of human choices and natural constraints in a small world.[2] While exotic in location and culture, Easter Island is of general interest as one example of the many civilizations that undercut their own ecological foundations.[3]

The island is one of the most isolated bits of land on the Earth. The inhabited land nearest to Easter Island is Pitcairn Island, 2,250 kilometers northwest; the nearest continental place, Concepción, Chile, is 3,747 kilometers southeast. The island is roughly triangular in plan, with sides of 16, 18 and 22 kilometers and an area of 166.2 square kilometers (a bit larger than Staten Island, a borough of the city of New York). About 2.5 million years old, the volcanic island rose from the sea floor 2,000 meters below sea level. A plateau occupies the middle of the island and a peak rises nearly 1,000 meters above sea level.[4]

Radiocarbon dating suggests that people, almost certainly Polynesians, occupied the island by A.D. 690 at the latest; scattered earlier radiocarbon dates from the fourth and fifth centuries are uncertain.[5] The first arrivals found an island covered by a rainforest of huge palms. The islanders were probably isolated from outside human contact until the island was spotted by Dutch sailors in 1722.[6]

During this millennium or millennium and a half of isolation, a fantastic civilization arose. Its most striking material remains are 800 to 1,000 giant statues, or *moai,* two to ten meters high, carved in volcanic tuff and scattered over the island.[7] Many are probably still buried by rubble and soil. The largest currently known is 20 meters (65 feet) long and weighs about 270 tonnes. It was left unfinished.

According to pollen cores recently taken from volcanic craters on the island, a tree used for rope was originally dominant on the island.[8] At different times, depending on the site, between the eighth and the tenth centuries, forest pollen began to decline. Forest pollen reached its lowest level around A.D. 1400, suggesting that the last forests were destroyed by then. The deforestation coincided with soil erosion, visible in soil profiles.[9] The Polynesian rat introduced for food by the original settlers consumed the seeds of forest trees, preventing regeneration. Freshwater supplies on the island diminished. In the 1400s or 1500s, large, stemmed obsidian flakes used as daggers and spearheads appeared for the first time; previously obsidian had been used only for tools.[10]

While early visitors in 1722 and 1770 do not mention fallen *moai,* Captain Cook in 1774 reported that many statues had fallen next to their platforms and that the statues were not being maintained.[11] Something drastic, probably some variant of intergroup warfare, probably happened between 1722, when the Dutch thought the statue cult was still alive, and 1774, when Cook thought it finished.[12] A visitor in 1786 observed that the island no longer had a chief.[13]

The population history of the island is full of uncertainties.[14] The prehistory is based on the dating of sites of agricultural and human occupation. The best current estimate is that the population began with a boatload of settlers in the first half millennium after Christ, perhaps around A.D. 400.[15] The population remained low until about A.D. 1100. Growth then accelerated and the population doubled every century until around 1400. Slower growth continued until at most 6,000 to 8,000 people occupied the island around 1600. The maximum population may have reached 10,000 people in A.D. 1680.[16] A decline then set in. Jean François de Galaup, Comte de La Pérouse, who visited the island in 1786, estimated a population of 2,000, and this estimate is now accepted as roughly correct. Smallpox swept the island in the 1860s, introduced by returning survivors among the islanders who had been enslaved and taken to Peru. The population numbered 111 by 1877. In 1888, the island was attached to Chile. Since then, Chileans have added to the population. The present population of 2,100 includes 800 children.

The plausibility of these numbers can be checked from the annual rates of population growth or decline that they imply. An increase from 50 people in A.D. 400 to 10,000 people in A.D. 1680 requires an annual increase of 0.41 percent. If the number of original settlers were 100 instead of 50, the implied population growth rate would be 0.36 percent; if 25 instead of 50, 0.47 percent. The long-term growth rate of around 0.4 percent per year is within the historical experience of developing countries before the post–World War II public health evolution. If the population declined from

10,000 in 1680 to 111 in 1877 (including removals by Peruvian slave trad-
ers), the annual rate of decline was 2.3 percent. If the population maximum
in 1680 was only 6,000 instead of 10,000, then the annual rate of decline
was 2.0 percent. A population decline from 10,000 in 1680 to the 2,000
reported by La Pérouse in 1786 requires an annual decline of 1.5 percent. In
round numbers, Easter Island's human population seems to have increased
by about 0.4 percent per year for about 13 centuries, then to have declined
by about 2 percent per year for about two centuries before resuming a rise
in the twentieth century.

Paul Bahn, a British archeologist and writer, and John Flenley, an ecologist and geographer in New Zealand, synthesized the archeological and historical data in an interpretive model.

> Forest clearance for the growing of crops would have led to population increase,
> but also to soil erosion and decline of soil fertility. Progressively more land would
> have had to be cleared. Trees and shrubs would also be cut down for canoe build-
> ing, firewood, house construction, and for the timbers and ropes needed in the
> movement and erection of statues. Palm fruits would be eaten, thus reducing
> regeneration of the palm. Rats, introduced for food, could have fed on the palm
> fruits, multiplied rapidly and completely prevented palm regeneration. The over-
> exploitation of prolific sea bird resources would have eliminated these from all
> but the offshore islets. Rats could have helped in this process by eating eggs. The
> abundant food provided by fishing, sea birds and rats would have encouraged
> rapid initial human population growth. Unrestrained human population increase
> would later put pressure on availability of land, leading to disputes and eventually
> warfare. Non-availability of timber and rope would make it pointless to carve
> further statues. A disillusionment with the efficacy of the statue religion in pro-
> viding the wants of the people could lead to the abandonment of this cult. Inade-
> quate canoes would restrict fishing to inshore waters, leading to further decline
> in protein supplies. The result could have been general famine, warfare and the
> collapse of the whole economy, leading to a marked population decline.
>
> Of course, most of this is hypothesis. Nevertheless, there is evidence, as we
> have seen, that many features of this model did in fact occur. There certainly was
> deforestation, famine, warfare, collapse of civilization and population decline.[17]

Supposing you accept this summary of the island's history, would you
accept the following conclusion of Bahn and Flenley? "We consider that
Easter Island was a microcosm which provides a model for the whole
planet."[18] Easter Island shares important features with the whole planet and
differs in others. Draw your own conclusion.

Living in the Land of Lost Illusions: Human Carrying Capacity as an Indicator

A number or range of numbers, presented as a constraint independent of
human choices, is an inadequate answer to the question "How many people

can the Earth support?" While trying to answer this question, I learned to question the question.

If an absolute numerical upper limit to human numbers on the Earth exists, it lies beyond the bounds that human beings would willingly tolerate. Human physical requirements for bare minimal subsistence are very modest, closer to the level of Auschwitz than to the modest comforts of the Arctic Inuit or the Kalahari bushmen. For most people of the world, expectations of well-being have risen so far beyond subsistence that human choices will prevent human numbers from coming anywhere near absolute upper limits. If human choices somehow failed to prevent population size from approaching absolute upper limits, then gradually worsening conditions for human and other life on the Earth would first prompt and eventually enforce human choices to stop such an approach. As different people have different expectations of well-being, some people would be moved to change their behavior sooner than others. Social scientists focus on the choices and minimize the constraints; natural scientists do the reverse. In reality, neither choices nor constraints can be neglected.

An ideal tool for estimating how many people the Earth can support would be a model, simple enough to be intelligible, complicated enough to be potentially realistic and empirically tested enough to be credible.[19] The model would require users to specify choices concerning technology, domestic and international political institutions, domestic and international economic arrangements (including recycling), domestic and international demographic arrangements, physical, chemical and biological environments, fashions, tastes, moral values, a desired typical level of material well-being and a distribution of well-being among individuals and areas. Users would specify how much they wanted each characteristic to vary as time passes and what risk they would tolerate that each characteristic might go out of the desired range of variability. Users would state how long they wanted their choices to remain in effect. They would specify the state of the world they wished to leave at the end of the specified period. The model would first check all these choices for internal consistency, detect any contradictions and ask users to resolve them or to specify a balance among contradictory choices. The model would then attempt to reconcile the choices with the constraints imposed by food, water, energy, land, soil, space, diseases, waste disposal, nonfuel minerals, forests, biological diversity, biologically accessible nitrogen, phosphorus, climatic change and other natural constraints. The model would generate a complete set of possibilities, including human population sizes, consistent with the choices and the constraints.

If Meadows et al. aspired to create such a model, they did not achieve it, nor could they have been expected to. In the present primitive state of human intellectual capacity and knowledge, one cannot blame anyone for failing to achieve such a model. In trying to answer a superficially much less ambitious question (how has rapid population growth affected economic development in Third World countries during recent decades?), the Duke

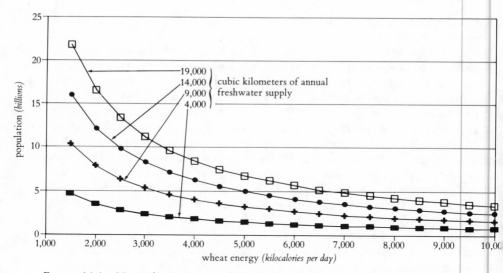

FIGURE 16.1   Upper limits on population set by requirements of water for domestic use and daily energy requirements from irrigated agriculture, assuming 20 percent use of available water and 10 percent loss of food between growth and consumption. The four curves assume available renewable annual water supplies of (from top to bottom) 19,000 cubic kilometers, 14,000 cubic kilometers, 9,000 cubic kilometers and 4,000 cubic kilometers. Important additional assumptions are described in Chapter 14. SOURCE: original calculations

University economist Allen C. Kelley indicated that a good model would be the best way to answer the question. He added: "Unfortunately, the problems of constructing such a model are formidable."[20] To that, I say amen.

Between the inadequacy of a single number for human carrying capacity and the impossibility of an ideal model for human carrying capacity are some imperfect, feasible and useful alternatives for thinking about human carrying capacity. For example, it was easy to calculate the maximum population that could be supplied with water for domestic use and irrigation, given any volume of freshwater supply. The two curves in Figure 14.2 are among the four curves in Figure 16.1, which represent the trade-off between maximum population and daily calories from irrigated agriculture, for available renewable annual water supplies of 4,000 cubic kilometers, 9,000 cubic kilometers, 14,000 cubic kilometers and 19,000 cubic kilometers. I ask you now to imagine a third axis in Figure 16.1 perpendicular to the plane of the page, extending from the origin (lower left corner of the figure) behind the paper, to represent the amount of the available renewable annual water supplies. The four curves in Figure 16.1 would then be lines on a surface that shows maximum population as a function of both daily calories and available renewable annual water supplies. Figure 16.2 gives a perspective view of this surface. In this view, human carrying capacity is

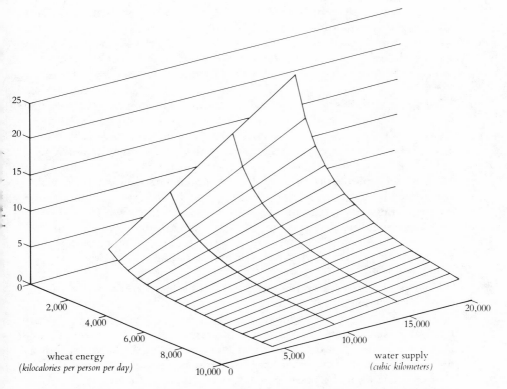

FIGURE 16.2 Upper limits on population (vertical axis) set by requirements of water for domestic use and daily energy requirements from irrigated agriculture (left axis) and renewable annual water supplies (right axis). This surface plots the same information as Figure 16.1. SOURCE: original calculations

not a single number for population size but is a "population surface" above a plane of choices and possibilities.

The curves in Figure 16.1 and the surface in Figure 16.2 all assume 20 percent use of available water and 10 percent loss of food between growth and consumption. A collection of population surfaces for different fractions of use of available water and different fractions of loss of food between growth and consumption would show maximal population as a function of four variables: water supplies, daily calories, percentage of use and percentage of loss. Permitting the other fixed assumptions behind Figure 16.1 to vary would incorporate the effects of additional variables on the maximal population; for example, instead of considering only wheat, other crops with different transpiration ratios and caloric values could be considered.

Population surfaces of this sort could be constructed for different countries or regions (while recognizing that the surfaces are not independent) and for different times (to reflect changes in technologies and everything else).

The representation of human carrying capacity by population surfaces leaves open the question of optimal human population size: "What is the *best* number of people for the Earth to have?"[21] But it sheds light on that question. Look again at the curve for 9,000 cubic kilometers of fresh water in Figure 16.1. If you want people to consume at least 3,500 kilocalories per day of wheat energy (as food, feed or seed) from irrigated agriculture, then you have to believe that the optimal population to be supported by irrigated agriculture is below five billion people. You can look at the same curves another way. If you want to support at least ten billion people with at least 2,000 kilocalories per day of wheat energy from irrigated agriculture, then according to the assumptions embodied in Figure 16.1, you must assure 14,000 cubic kilometers or 19,000 cubic kilometers of annual renewable water supplies (by recycling or damming nearly every river or establishing human settlements in currently empty regions or somehow). The only way irrigated agriculture could support more than ten billion people with just 9,000 cubic kilometers of annual fresh water (under the other assumptions of Figure 16.1) is to feed people on average 1,500 kilocalories per day, which is the edge of starvation.

The speed registered on the speedometer of a car, the current total fertility rate of a population and the gross national or domestic product of an economy are, every one, indirect and incomplete summaries of more complicated realities: they are summary indicators, approximate but useful. Likewise, estimates of the human carrying capacity of the Earth are indicators. They indicate the population that can be supported under various assumptions about the present or future. Estimates of the Earth's human carrying capacity are conditional on current choices and on natural constraints, all of which may change as time passes. This view of estimates of human carrying capacity as conditional and changing differs sharply from a common view that there is one right number (perhaps imperfectly known) for all time.

Human carrying capacity is more difficult to estimate than some of the standard demographic indicators, like expectation of life or the total fertility rate, because human carrying capacity depends on populations and activities around the world. The expectation of life of a country can be determined entirely from the mortality experienced by the people within the country. But that same country's human carrying capacity depends not only on its soils and natural resources and population and culture and economy, but also on the prices of its products in world markets and on the resources and products other countries can and are willing to trade. When the world consisted of largely autonomous localities, it may have made sense to think of the Earth's human carrying capacity as the sum of local human carrying capacities; but no longer.

BEYOND EQUILIBRIUM

Think of a man engaged in four activities: lying on his back on the floor with his arms and legs relaxed; standing erect but at ease; walking at a comfortable pace; and running. When lying on his back, the man is at a passive equilibrium. If you push him gently on one side, he may rock a bit but will roll back to his original position. If you push him hard enough, he may switch from a passive supine equilibrium to a passive prone equilibrium. Whether he is supine or prone, he can remain in his present equilibrium without effort.

Standing is a much more complicated matter. Opposing muscles are constantly adjusting their tension to maintain upright posture, under the guidance of the body's sensory and nervous systems for maintaining balance. The man may not appear to be working, but his oxygen consumption increases and he will fall to the floor if he relaxes completely. If pushed hard, he may not be able to stay standing. His apparent equilibrium is dynamically maintained by constant control.

Walking is controlled falling. The man's center of gravity moves forward from his area of support and he puts one foot forward with just the right timing and placement to catch himself. He then pivots over the forward foot and continues to fall forward with just-in-time support from alternating legs. Anyone who has watched a child learn to walk, or an adult learn to walk with crutches, appreciates the complex sequential coordination, muscular strength and balance required to walk. The equilibrium of walking is not a stationary state at all, but a sustained motion.

Finally, running is more than an acceleration of walking because the runner may have both legs off the ground at once. The effort required, the speed of the motion and the vulnerability to collapse increase compared to walking. On a rocky mountain ridge or a crowded city street, running is impossible; simplification and control of the environment are required to sustain the equilibrium of steady running.

The purpose of this foray into kinesiology is to find some old and new analogies for the situation of humans on the Earth. If the population size of the human species was ever in a passive equilibrium regulated by the environment, it must surely have been before people gained control of fire. By using fire, early peoples massively reshaped their environment to their own advantage,[22] with the effect of increasing their own population size. For example, they periodically burned grasslands to encourage plants desirable to themselves and to the game they hunted. After the mastery of fire, people moved from a supine equilibrium to a controlled balance analogous to standing. With the invention of shifting cultivation some ten or so millennia ago, and then settled cultivation, the human species initiated a form of controlled forward falling analogous to walking. Humans invented cities and farms and learned to coordinate them. Where agriculture failed, civilizations collapsed. In the last four centuries, surpluses of food released huge numbers of people from being tied to the land and enabled them to make machines and technologies that further loosened their ties to the land. Machines for handling energy, materials and information released people from old work, imposed new work and transformed much of the natural world. More than ever before, the land that still supported people became a partly human creation. For humans now, the notion of a static, passive equilibrium is inappropriate, useless. So is the notion of a static "human carrying capacity" imposed by the natural world on a passive human species.[23] There is no choice but to try to control the direction, speed, risks, duration and purposes of our falling forward.[24]

PART 5

CONCLUSION:
HUMAN
CARING
CAPACITY

17

Entering the Zone

> No species has ever been able to multiply without
> limit. There are two biological checks upon a
> rapid increase in number—a high mortality and a
> low fertility. Unlike other biological organisms,
> man can choose which of these checks shall be
> applied, but one of them must be.
>
> —Harold F. Dorn 1962[1]

Recapitulation

THE HUMAN POPULATION of the Earth now travels in the zone where a substantial fraction of scholars have estimated upper limits on human population size. These estimates are no better than present understanding of
humankind's cultural, economic and environmental choices and constraints. Nevertheless, the possibility must be considered seriously that the
number of people on the Earth has reached, or will reach within half a
century, the maximum number the Earth can support in modes of life that
we and our children and their children will choose to want.

This conclusion emerges clearly from the three main elements of the
book up to this point: human population history, scenarios of future population and estimates of the maximum number of people the Earth can support (Figure 17.1).

The history: since 1600, the human population increased from about half
a billion to nearly six billion. The *increase* in the last decade of the twentieth
century exceeds the *total* population in 1600. Compared to all human history prior to World War II, the world's population growth rate since 1950
has been and still is unprecedented. Within the lifetime of some people now
alive, world population has tripled; within the lifetime of everyone over 40
years old, it has doubled—yet never before the last half of the twentieth
century had world population doubled within the life span of any human.

The future: human populations, like economies, environments and cultures, are highly unpredictable, and only conditional predictions are credible. In the United Nations' high projection published in 1992, if worldwide

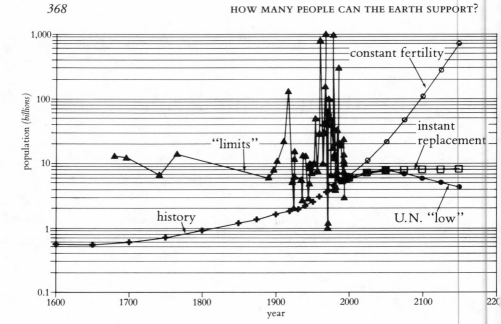

FIGURE 17.1   Human population size 1600–1990, three United Nations scenarios of future population growth 1990–2150 and estimates of the Earth's maximum human population ("limits") by year of publication 1679–1994. The constant-fertility projection assumes that fertility in each region of the world remains at its level in 1990; in this scenario, the global average total fertility rate rises from 3.3 children per woman in 1990 to 5.7 children per woman in 2150 as the faster-growing regions become a larger share of world population. The instant-replacement projection assumes that the total fertility rate dropped to 2.06 children per woman in 1990 and remains at that level. The low-fertility projection assumes that the total fertility rate gradually moves to 1.7 children per woman everywhere. By the year 2050, according to these three projections, the world's population would number 21.2 billion, 7.7 billion and 7.8 billion. The plotted estimates of the Earth's maximum human population are the highest given when an author stated a range. SOURCE: for history, Appendix 2; for future scenarios, Table 8.2; for "limits," Appendix 3

average fertility falls to 2.5 children per woman in the twenty-first century, then population will grow to 12.5 billion by 2050. In the United Nations' 1992 low projection, if worldwide average fertility falls to 1.7 children per woman, population will peak at 7.8 billion in 2050 before beginning to decline. The projected range for 2050 is 12.5 billion to 7.8 billion.

The Earth's human carrying capacity: estimates range from fewer than 1 billion to more than 1,000 billion. This enormous spread follows from widely varying concepts, methods and assumptions. Estimates fall most frequently in the range from 4 billion to 16 billion. Counting the highest estimate when an author gave a range of estimates, and including all estimates given as a single number, the middle value, or median, of the estimates was 12 billion; counting the lowest estimate when an author gave a range, and the single number otherwise, the middle value, or median, of the estimates was 7.7 billion. These static and deterministic estimates are inadequate to picture human-planetary interactions that are intrinsically dynamic and full of surprises.

Tying together the three chief elements—population history, population projections and estimates of potential limits—are two threads that are woven into the book: the insufficiency of our present understanding, and the finiteness of time.

Three laws of intellectual modesty describe the insufficiency of our present understanding. The Law of Information asserts that 97.6 percent of all statistics are made up. Knowledge of the present and past is highly imperfect. The Law of Action asserts that it is difficult to do just what you intended to do. Action and inaction achieve desired consequences imperfectly. The Law of Prediction asserts that the more confidence an expert attaches to a prediction about future human affairs, the less confidence you should attach to it. Knowledge of the future is highly imperfect.

The finiteness of time, the second thread in the book, limits the abilities of individuals and of societies to solve problems. For each human being, time is finite. I want to eat and drink today. As a privileged inhabitant of a wealthy country, I can postpone buying a new car for several years, but the requirements of poor people for subsistence are not so elastic in time. Those who want firewood to cook a meal today will break branches from the last tree standing if they believe that otherwise their children may not survive to lament the absence of trees 20 years hence. In the American legal system, the finiteness of time to satisfy basic human wants is recognized in a phrase: justice delayed is justice denied.[2]

Efforts to satisfy human wants require time, and the time required may be longer than the finite time available to individuals. There is a race between the complexity of the problems that are generated by increasing human numbers and the ability of humans to comprehend and solve those problems. Educating people to solve problems takes time. Developing traditions of stable, productive cooperation takes time. Building institutions with the resources to make educated people into productive problem-solvers takes time. Even with educated, cooperative people and appropriate institutions at hand, understanding and solving problems take still more time.

DEALING WITH POPULATION PROBLEMS: BIGGER PIE; FEWER FORKS; BETTER MANNERS

A population problem arises whenever human welfare—any value held by the people concerned—suffers because of more or fewer people, or a different age distribution of people, or a faster or slower population growth rate, or a changed spatial distribution of population.[3] Thus a population problem can arise when any aspect of human welfare is affected by population size, composition, change or distribution. A population problem can sometimes be ameliorated by changing other factors that affect human welfare, as well as by changing the demographic situation.

Proposals for dealing with population problems confront an intellectual and ideological minefield. While plausible, well-intentioned suggestions for mitigating population problems abound, no one knows exactly what will work across the whole range of population problems, or will work most efficiently in a given situation. Since generally accepted conclusions about what works in which circumstances are scarce, almost all proposed actions are motivated by some explicit or implicit ideology.

Suggestions for ameliorating population problems fall into three main groups: those intended to amplify human productive capacities, given the number and expectations of people to be served (the "bigger pie" school); those intended to reduce the number and expectations of people to be served, given human abilities to find well-being (the "fewer forks" school); and those intended to change the terms under which people interact, whatever the technology or population (the "better manners" school). The enthusiasts of one school often neglect and suspect suggestions from the others.

The "bigger pie" school calls for new industrial, agricultural and civil technology of all types for both developed and developing countries. One enthusiast of technology, Jesse H. Ausubel, of the Program for the Human Environment at Rockefeller University, wrote: "The only way to meet the challenge of the multiplication of needs is to substantially enhance the contributions of science and technology to development and to enhance the cooperation between the science-rich and the science-poor."[4]

The "fewer forks" school calls for family-planning programs, for more effective and more acceptable contraceptives and sometimes for vegetarian diets (to reduce demand for animal feeds). Some proponents of the "fewer forks" school view technology as responsible for many adverse human impacts on the environment. Some argue, at the opposite extreme from Ausubel, that "the only way" to save the natural systems that support human life is to decrease human population growth rates, human numbers or human levels of consumption.

The "better manners" school calls for freer markets[5] or socialism (depending on taste), the breakup of large countries or the institution of world government or new forms of shared governance for sovereign states (depending on taste), democratic institutions, improved public policies, less corruption and the full life-cycle costing of business products. If poverty is the problem, the "better manners" school would propose to help poor people obtain increased access to credit, land, public infrastructure, education and health. In this approach, "a family planning program that emphasizes health services to the poor may be more easily justified on the grounds that it directly redistributes health resources to the poor than on the grounds that lower fertility may decrease poverty."[6]

How to Slow Human Population Growth

I focus here on large-scale efforts to slow or reverse human population growth because such efforts are less mature, more recent and less rewarded by existing economic institutions and incentives than are technological innovations. In my review of population history, I summarized six principal approaches to slowing population growth. In slogans, these approaches are promoting contraceptives; developing economies; saving children; empowering women; educating men; and doing everything at once. The Oxford economist Robert Cassen rightly emphasized that "virtually everything that needs doing from a population point of view needs doing anyway."[7]

Here I give a few examples of the people and institutions who have adopted one or more of these approaches. My sketches are drawn from political figures; private research institutions like the Population Council in New York; scientists; international organizations like the United Nations Fund for Population Activities; and nongovernmental advocacy groups.

A Politician

Shortly before his election to the vice-presidency of the United States, Albert Gore offered five "strategic goals [to] direct and inform our efforts to save the global environment."[8] His five goals were, first, to stabilize world population "with policies designed to create in every nation of the world the conditions necessary for the so-called demographic transition"; second, to create and develop "environmentally appropriate technologies— especially in the fields of energy, transportation, agriculture, building construction, and manufacturing—capable of accommodating sustainable economic progress without the concurrent degradation of the environment"; third, to change economic ways of measuring human effects on the environment to "a system of economic accounting that assigns appropriate values to the ecological consequences of both routine choices in the marketplace by individuals and companies and larger, macroeconomic choices by nations"; fourth, to negotiate and approve new international agreements required to carry out the overall plan; and fifth, to establish "a cooperative plan for educating the world's citizens about our global environment."

To accelerate or induce a global demographic transition, Gore proposed three major approaches.[9] First, programs should be funded to assure "functional literacy [in] every society where the demographic transition has yet to occur. Although the emphasis should be on women, the programs should be directed to men as well. Coupled with this program should be a plan for basic education, emphasizing simple techniques in sustainable agriculture, specific lessons on preventing soil erosion, planting trees, and safeguarding clean water supplies." Second, programs should be developed "to reduce infant mortality and ensure the survival and excellent health of children." Third, programs should "[e]nsure that birth control devices and techniques are made ubiquitously available along with culturally appropriate instruction. At the same time, scientists must be charged with stepping up research into improved and more easily accepted contracepti[ve] techniques. Depending upon the culture, delayed marriages and birth spacing should also be emphasized, along with traditional practices such as breast feeding (which simultaneously improves the health of children and suppresses fertility)." Contraception, Gore emphasized, is a preferable alternative to abortion; and the Roman Catholic Church, as an advocate of education and lowered infant mortality, should be enlisted as an ally in efforts to achieve a demographic transition.

A Private Research Institute

The Population Council in New York is one of the world's leading private, nonprofit population institutes, and one of the few to carry out research in both the biomedical and the social sciences related to population. It created the long-acting implantable contraceptive called Norplant and carried out long-term evaluations of the effectiveness of family-planning programs.[10] It shapes and reflects the view of many demographers and national and international officials responsible for population-related policies.

John Bongaarts, a vice-president in charge of research at the Population Council and a leading demographic researcher, analyzed quantitatively three factors responsible for the anticipated rise in the population of the developing countries.[11] His analysis started from a World Bank projection that the developing countries would grow from 4.5 billion people in 1995 to 10.2 billion in 2100, an increase of 5.7 billion. Bongaarts attributed to population momentum an increase of 2.8 billion; to unwanted fertility an increase of 1.9 billion; and to high desired family size an increase of 1 billion. He proposed programs to counteract each of these factors.

The biggest source of population growth, population momentum, responsible for nearly half the anticipated increase, results from the very high fraction of young people in developing countries, including young people of an age to bear children and those still too young to bear children. Today's high fraction of young people in developing countries is a legacy of the failures of both developed and developing countries over the past few decades to create the conditions for a rapid fall in fertility. One way to counteract population momentum is to induce women to have far fewer than an average of two children each, as in the one-child policy of China. Bongaarts considered this possibility briefly and discarded it. Instead, he recommended trying to raise the average age of women at childbearing in developing countries. His simulations suggested that if all women, now and henceforth, delayed having children by five years compared to the present ages at which they bear children, the rise due to population momentum could be reduced from 2.8 billion to 1.6 billion, assuming that fertility were just at replacement level.

Policy options to raise the age of childbearing include raising the legal age of marriage and prolonging the education of girls, especially in secondary schools. In a sample of women who had ever been married and who were aged 30 to 34 years at the time of the study in 23 developing countries, the median age of the mother when she had her first birth was 22.8 years among women with secondary education, while that of women with no education was 19.3 years. These data suggest that achieving a five-year delay in childbearing (as assumed in Bongaarts's simulations above) could require a greater social change than assuring all women a secondary education.

Bongaarts also recommended making contraceptive information and services available to adolescents. Adolescents often use contraception sporadically or not at all when they become sexually active, and consequently begin to bear children much earlier than they would if they had better information and services. Bongaarts understated the difficulty of implementing this suggestion when he remarked: "Governments have been reluctant to address these problems of adolescents for social and political reasons."[12]

The second largest source of increased population (an additional 1.9 billion) in developing countries over the next century was unwanted fertility, in Bongaarts's analysis. Bongaarts estimated that, in the developing countries outside China, about 100 million women—one married woman in six—has an unmet demand for contraception and about one birth in four is unwanted; further, a large fraction of the approximately 25 million abortions annually are conducted illegally or unsafely, or both. "Many of these undesirable pregnancies can be prevented if women are given greater control over their sexual and reproductive lives."[13] Family-planning programs would provide women and men with the information and means to decrease the number of mistimed and unwanted pregnancies. Such programs would also be likely to improve the health of women and children, in part by putting them in regular contact with providers of medical services.

The source of an additional billion people in developing countries by 2100 was the desire for large families, according to Bongaarts. Surveys in the late 1980s in 27 countries in Africa, Asia and Latin America found that desired family sizes everywhere exceeded two children; in sub-Saharan Africa, people wanted nearly six children. Bongaarts proposed to lessen the desire for large families by "investments in human development"[14] so that parents would value smaller families and invest more in the children they have. Governments could aim for improvements in levels of education, the status of women and the survival of children.

Educational opportunities for children diminish the immediate value of children as workers and make them more expensive because the children require books, uniforms and school fees. According to Bongaarts,

> Of all the social and economic factors that have been studied for their potential effect on reproductive behavior, the level of education stands out as the most

consistent. This relation is attributable to shifts in the costs and benefits of children but also, and perhaps more importantly, to an acceleration in cultural change and the adoption of new, mostly western values that are facilitated by the introduction of mass schooling.[15]

Improving the legal, social and economic status of women also raises the cost of children by giving women potential roles other than motherhood and encouraging women to act independently and innovatively in contraception. "Empowering women is also likely to lead to reductions in the dominance of husbands (or other household members) over women, the societal preference for male offspring, and the value of . . . children as insurance against adversity (for example, in old age) and as securers of women's positions in families."[16]

Public health programs to reduce death rates among infants and children would reduce the fatalism of parents, encourage investments in the health and education of children and increase the likelihood that the desired number of children will survive to adulthood. Bongaarts asserted that "no population in the developing world has experienced a sustained fertility reduction without first having gone through a major decline in infant and child mortality."[17]

Other tactics to encourage parents to have fewer children include monetary incentives for contraception and disincentives for large families, and messages in mass media about styles of life incompatible with large families.

In preparation for the 1994 International Conference on Population and Development in Cairo, the Population Council set out an agenda of action and research for the coming decades. In a pamphlet entitled *Population Growth and Our Caring Capacity,* the Population Council took a broad view of the effects of rapid population growth on global resources, on the capacity of national and local institutions to supply the services and protections of civil society and on the welfare of families and individuals.

> Reducing the numbers of human beings should not be a goal in itself, but rather a means toward achieving improved human welfare through a more sustainable balance of population and resources, a reduction of disparities in life opportunities, and a realignment of the risks and benefits of reproduction. The fundamental question behind concerns about population growth must be not only "Will there be sufficient resources?," but also "How will they be distributed?"
>
> If rapid population growth is understood to be of interest because of the ways it diminishes the present and future quality of human life and environmental integrity, then we must seek a broader spectrum of solutions than the international and national communities typically have promoted.[18] . . .
>
> It is time to advocate—without ambiguity or timidity—positive social investments that are good in themselves and have a demonstrable fertility-reduction impact. . . . In short, one can promote a smaller world by promoting a just world.[19]

The Population Council's pamphlet proposed loosening governments' widespread identification between demographic goals and family-planning programs in two respects. First, governments should try to achieve their demographic goals through all the social and economic programs available to them, not just through family-planning programs. Second, family-planning programs should be viewed not merely as instruments for achieving demographic goals, but as "key social investments" to help people reproduce voluntarily and healthily, when and to the extent that they choose.

Academies of Science

In October 1993, representatives of 58 scientific academies signed a brief report called *Population Summit of the World's Scientific Academies.*[20] The report reviewed the United Nations' long-term population projections; essayed to identify the key determinants of population growth; sketched relations among human population size, economic development and the natural environment; and made recommendations for action. The report urged that "all reproductive health services must be implemented as a part of broader strategies to raise the quality of human life." These strategies include reducing and eliminating inequalities between men and women in sexual, social and economic life; convenient reproductive health services (including family planning), regardless of ability to pay; "elimination of unsafe and coercive practices" in family planning (a two-edged reference, presumably, to reportedly forced abortions in China and backroom abortions in countries where abortion is illegal); and more attention to clean water, sanitation, primary health care, education and power for the poor and for women.

The report reserved its most specific, detailed and ambitious suggestions for scientists, engineers and health professionals. It urged them to study and offer advice on an enormous range of topics, including "cultural, social, economic, religious, educational, and political factors that affect reproductive behavior, family size, and successful family planning; . . . economic inefficiencies; social inequalities; and ethnic, class or gender biases; global and local environmental change . . . , its causes (including the roles of poverty, population growth, economic growth, technology, national and international politics), and policies to mitigate its effects"; education, especially of women; improved family-planning programs, maternal and child health care and primary health care generally; transitions to economies that consume less energy and materials; increasing the capacity of developing countries in the natural sciences, engineering, medicine, the social sciences and management; "technologies and strategies for sustainable development (agriculture, energy, resource use, pollution control, materials recycling, environmental management and protection); networks, treaties, and conventions that protect the global commons; strengthened world-wide exchanges of scientists in education, training, and research."

Among the signers of this report were representatives of six African national academies, including those of Ghana, Kenya, Nigeria and Uganda from sub-Saharan Africa. However, the African Academy of Sciences, one of the 15 academies that convened the summit meeting, did not sign the

main report but issued its own statement instead.[21] Acknowledging that
rapid population growth rates may be a problem for some countries, the
dissent argued that "for Africa, population remains an important resource
for development, without which the continent's natural resources will
remain latent and unexplored. Human resource development must therefore form part of the population / resource issue." Because population
problems vary widely among countries and regions, not all countries can
share the same population goals. ". . . for certain parts of Africa, infertility
is a major problem. . . . In Africa, many of the so-called impediments to
family planning have a rationality which require[s] careful assessment." As
for natural limits on population, the African dissent stated: "Whether or not
the earth is finite will depend on the extent to which science and technology
[are] able to transform the resources available for humanity. There is only
one earth—yes; but the potential for transforming it is not necessarily
finite."

An Agency of the United Nations

The United Nations Fund for Population Activities (UNFPA) is foremost, though not alone, among the U.N. agencies that attempt to affect
population growth. Other agencies with related responsibilities include the
World Health Organization (with responsibilities for reproductive health
and sexually transmitted diseases), the Food and Agricultural Organization,
the U.N. Development Program, the U.N. Environmental Program, the
U.N. Children's Fund (UNICEF) and the U.N. Educational, Scientific and
Cultural Organization (which has sponsored studies of the Earth's human
carrying capacity).

The UNFPA's 1993 *Population Issues: Briefing Kit* highlighted the
agency's major concerns in ten chapters of two pages each.[22] These concerns were rapid population growth; the special burdens of developing
countries ("Continued rapid growth in developing countries has brought
human numbers into collision with the resources to sustain them"); more
adequate financing for population programs; family planning as a human
right; comprehensive national population policies embracing family planning, demographic research, data collection, the wants of children and the
elderly, urbanization, migration, education and communication; "gender
equality: a country's best investment," to be achieved through equal educational opportunities for girls and boys, men and women; the degradation of
air, land, water and biota "from ever-increasing numbers of people, ever-
increasing demands for resources and ever-increasing pollution"; urbanization and migration; information, education and communication adapted to
local cultures; and population data.

The UNFPA estimated that the world spent about $4.5 billion per year
on population programs in the early 1990s, a bit less than one United States
dollar per person per year. Developing countries spent about $3.5 billion of
their own resources and received about $958 million as population assis-

tance. In 1991, only 1.3 percent of total official development assistance went for population programs, and more than one-third of that ($352 million) came from the United States. Funding for the UNFPA was constant in real terms for the few years before the 1993 report. Not surprisingly, the UNFPA called for doubled funding for population programs by the year 2000.

A Private Foundation

In addition to governments, several private foundations support population programs. Though most private foundations cannot supply as much money as some governments, they are freer to do experiments that demonstrate what works or does not work. In 1992 the population program of the John D. and Catherine T. MacArthur Foundation in Chicago, Illinois, spent $12.1 million on population programs: $6.1 million for women's reproductive health, $0.6 million for population and natural resources, $2.3 million for communications and popular education, $1.1 million to develop individual leaders in population programs in developing countries and $2.0 million for other initiatives. The program emphasized activities in Mexico, Brazil, Nigeria and India.

Overview

This small sample shows that diverse approaches are being advocated, and in some cases funded, to slow population growth. "The issue now is where to put the marginal population-control dollar,"[23] wrote journalist Peter Passell during the wrangling at the United Nations in April 1994 in preparation for the International Conference on Population and Development. A major issue is whether to focus on increasing the supply and lowering the cost of contraception, or to focus on increasing the demand for reduced fertility, for example through economic development, improvements in the status of women and mass communications.[24]

Unfortunately, there appears to be no believable information to show that a dollar spent to put girls through primary school will lower the total fertility rate more, now or a decade from now, than a dollar spent on radio programs about small families or a dollar spent on health clinics for mothers and children or a dollar spent to distribute contraceptives.[25] The experiences (described earlier) of Indonesia, which had a very rapid fall in fertility from 1970 to 1985, and Kenya, where fertility began to fall in the last half of the 1980s, suggested that well-developed family-planning programs interacted with educational, cultural and economic changes to lower fertility by more than the sum of their separate effects.

Asking whether family-planning programs or desires for children are the primary determinants of fertility resembles asking whether airline passengers fly because airplanes exist or because passengers want to go somewhere. Aristotle, who distinguished efficient causes from final causes (or means from goals) more than two millennia ago, would have been amused. People can travel without airplanes, but the great convenience of airplanes promotes travel. People can reduce their fertility without family-planning programs, but the great convenience (relative to the alternatives) of modern contraception facilitates lowered fertility.

QUESTIONS

An end to long-term average population growth is inevitable, very probably within the twenty-first century. Questions under debate are: just how soon and by what means and at whose expense? Here are eight issues that remain to be resolved.

1. How will the bill for family planning and other population activities be distributed between the developing countries (who now pay perhaps 80 percent) and the rich countries?
2. Who will spend the money, and how? How will the available monies be allocated between governments and nongovernmental organizations? How much will go for family planning and how much for allied programs like reproductive health?
3. How will environmental goals be balanced against economic goals? For example, if reducing poverty requires increased industrial and agricultural production in developing countries, can the increases in production be achieved at acceptable environmental costs?
4. How will cultural change be balanced against cultural continuity? In some cultural settings, the goal of empowering women directly contradicts the goal of maintaining "full respect for the various religious and ethical values and cultural backgrounds." Both goals were often repeated in the final document of the 1994 International Conference on Population and Development. Women achieved the vote in the United States only in 1920 and only after considerable struggle. Asking for equality for women now asks some cultures to make far greater change in far less time. I fully support such demands, but they should be made with a clear and sympathetic understanding that they require profound cultural change.
5. How will the often-asserted right of couples and individuals to control their fertility be reconciled with national demographic goals if the way couples and individuals exercise that right happens not to bring about the demographic goals?
6. How will national sovereignty be reconciled with world or regional environmental and demographic goals? This question arises in the control of migration, reproduction and all economic activities that involve the global commons of atmosphere, oceans and international water bodies, and the management of the plant and animal populations that inhabit them.

7. How will the desire and moral obligation to alleviate poverty and suffering as rapidly as possible be reconciled with the use of local scarcities as an efficient market signal?

8. In efforts to protect the physical, chemical and biological environments provided by this finite sphere, how will rapid population growth and economic development in poor countries be balanced against high consumption per person in the rich countries?

18

Looking Beyond
the Next Hill:
Some Suggestions

I NOW SUGGEST WAYS of improving some population problems. These suggestions concern the infrastructure for solving population problems; they are not solutions in themselves. The approaches I propose do not depend on complete knowledge of the past, present or future. I offer them in addition to, and not instead of, the suggestions offered by others. I aim in this book not to sell any particular approaches, but to promote a view of the Earth's human carrying capacity that is more modest, more in touch with a complex reality and more likely to enable you to think through your own choices of action than many of the simpler alternative views.

The four suggestions I will offer here are: to develop institutions that balance the goals of efficiency and equality; to improve the accounting of social well-being, materials and the consequences of actions; to integrate thinking about populations with thinking about economies, environments and cultures; and to create a better understanding of mutual aid, emphasizing the benefits that the well-off derive from helping the poor live better lives.

INSTITUTIONS TO RECONCILE EFFICIENCY
AND EQUALITY

In developing countries, as elsewhere, investments that help the poor directly (egalitarian investments) may differ from investments that yield the largest growth in aggregate economic output (efficient or utilitarian investments). The choice between enhancing the well-being of the poor directly and maximizing aggregate output illustrates the practical conflict between egalitarianism and utilitarianism. Social and political institutions could mediate this conflict by assuring the poor a share of the increase in output that would result from more efficient (utilitarian) investments. For such arrangements to succeed domestically or internationally, the wealthier regions must understand and concede that they have a stake in the well-being of the poorer regions and must justify the trust that the poorer regions would be required to place in them.

I recall an example described earlier. The Thai government and the World Bank faced a choice in placing investments in Thailand. Northeast Thailand is poor in natural resources, poor economically and backward in human development compared to the rest of the country. Irrigation projects in northeast Thailand, partially financed by international donors, were expected to yield very low returns, by purely economic yardsticks, for both the region and the country. They were nevertheless attractive because the government wanted to demonstrate that it did not discriminate against the northeast and because donors wanted to direct assistance to poor people. However, a consultant for the World Bank estimated that pressing more rapid growth in better-endowed regions could make all areas better off.[1] Choice: should the government and the Bank invest limited capital in the poor northeast or in other, more developed regions?

All regions *might* be better off if the World Bank invested in better-endowed regions, but all regions *would* be better off only if the regions that benefited from the World Bank investment actually shared a portion of their increased income from the investments with the people in the poorer region. If the people in the poorer region knew beforehand that they would benefit more by having investments made in the richer region than by having the same investments made in their own region, they would have every reason to support investments in the richer region, and the investing agencies would be free to choose according to economic efficiency.

Social and political institutions can reconcile efficiency with equality[2] (at least partially). An example of such an institution exists in Germany (and existed since the founding of the Federal Republic of Germany in 1949).[3] Germany has a national government, states and localities. Periodically there is a debate in the second chamber (Federal Council, or *Bundesrat*) of the national parliament among the heads of the states in a process called *Länderfinanzausgleich*. *Länder* means states; *finanz* means finances or spending; *ausgleich* means equalization, settlement, adjustment, arrangement, agreement or compensation. The process aims to balance living conditions in the wealthy industrial states with those in the poor agrarian states. Equalization is based on statistical indicators. The debate concerns which statistical indicators to use and how to interpret them. A special kind of *Länderfinanzausgleich* is used to integrate the relatively poor former East Germany with the economically more advanced former West Germany. Similar mechanisms could balance oil-rich Lagos with the destitute rural districts of Nigeria; the richer parts of Kenya with the poor, arid northeast; the rich and poor regions of other developing countries; and neighboring rich and poor countries.

Social and political institutions that can reconcile efficiency with equality are particular examples of "features of social organization, such as networks, norms, and trust, that facilitate coordination and cooperation for mutual benefit."[4] In an extended field study of regional governments in Italy, the Harvard political scientist Robert D. Putnam found that communities with traditions of civic engagement, including soccer clubs and choral societies, developed economically, while atomistic communities did not. Putnam concluded that social integration amplifies the benefits of investments in human and physical capital.

ACCOUNTING

Demographers joke that a demographer is somebody with a flair for numbers who doesn't have the personality to become an accountant. The implication is that demography is even duller than accounting. I reject the implication that accounting is dull. Accounting matters. What gets counted in accounting often guides action.

Accounting should recognize and correctly assign positive or negative values to more of the effects of current economic and non-economic activities, especially the effects on the stocks and flows of physical, chemical, biological and human resources.[5] If economic actors bore the full costs of economic activities, including costs that are now evaded as externalities, environmental damage might be greatly reduced. Much more knowledge is available to define the full effects of present activities than is used, but still more knowledge is required.

To illustrate, I shall describe problems in accounting for national income, hazardous wastes (a problem for the wealthy as well as for the poor), fresh water, soil, human behavior and childrearing. Warning label: the critical remarks on accounting that follow are likely to be controversial, as the existing methods have reasonable defenders.

Inappropriate accounting for national income distorts the goals and misrepresents the achievements of economic development. Many national governments and international lenders like the World Bank and the International Monetary Fund define economic development as increasing the gross national product (GNP) per person, after adjusting for inflation or deflation.[6] The definition of GNP in the national income accounts is fairly complicated; it includes all monetary market activity along with a few non-market activities that are assigned monetary values intended to reflect individual welfare, such as the rental value of housing occupied by its owner. All else being equal, the greater the depreciation of the capital assets of business in a year, the larger the GNP in that year; in this case, GNP goes up as national wealth goes down. If a developing country obtains 5 percent of its GNP by exporting timber, of which 1 percent is steady yield and

4 percent is achieved by deforestation, the GNP takes no account of the deforestation. This is a double omission. The deforestation reduces the country's future maximum steady yield of timber, and also eliminates the unpriced natural services provided by the forest. If a country spends millions to clean up pollutants from consumers (for example, smog generated by cars) or from factories, and residues from mining, these defensive expenditures are counted positively in national income, rather than deducted from the economic production available for a people's use. The more people spend on health care institutions and personnel for the care of patients with AIDS or any other incurable disease, the higher the GNP; the lost production of the patients is deducted from GNP, but the illness they experience counts for nothing. The GNP omits positive indicators of human development and well-being such as a rising life expectancy and an increasing rate of literacy as well as negative indicators such as rates of homicide, suicide and addiction to drugs. The Human Development Index created by the United Nations Development Program combines the expectation of life at birth, adult literacy, years of schooling and the real gross domestic product per person; this index is a step in the right direction.[7]

Better accounting could improve the management of hazardous wastes.[8] Toxic chemicals could be tracked from production to disposition with the same care that a dollar in sales is tracked from receipt to expenditure. For example, chemicals are sometimes legally dumped on land bought or rented for that purpose. Better understanding of the fate of such chemicals in the soil and subsurface aquifers would clarify the long-term impact of such dumping both on the natural environment and on humans who may settle on the land later or who may use the groundwater. If there are adverse effects, as were reported in Love Canal, near Niagara Falls, New York, and in Times Beach, Missouri, the costs of such effects should be counted as part of the costs of making, using and disposing of hazardous chemicals. A careful accounting of where toxic chemicals come from could stimulate companies to reduce the production of those chemicals in the first place, rather than try to dispose of them after they are created.

Better accounting could make the use of natural resources such as water and soil more rational. The Ogallala aquifer, which lies under more than 40 million hectares in seven states[9] in the center of the United States, supplies water to vast fields of wheat and other important crops. That water is being extracted from underground reserves faster than it is being replenished by percolating groundwater. The aquifer is reported to be more than half depleted beneath almost a million hectares in Kansas, Texas and New Mexico.[10] When the wheat grown with mined water and the beef fed on grain grown with mined water are sold at home or abroad, the price takes no account of the likely replacement cost of the water. Thus when the wheat and beef are sold, water is given away. At the same time, to prevent surplus crops from depressing prices, the U.S. government pays farmers not to cultivate rain-fed cropland. The cost of replenishing the Ogallala aquifer or finding alternative sources of fresh water or going without the services the

Ogallala aquifer might have provided will be borne by future Americans, who may not benefit from the current profits or consumption of wheat and beef. Future generations are subsidizing some people in the present generation.

Better accounting, based on better understanding, could make the conservation of soil more rational. The difficulty is to compare the future income earned when soil is conserved today with the future income forgone when soil is eroded today.[11] Farmers who pay the cost of regenerating the soil concurrently as their cultivation erodes it may be a short-term disadvantage in competing with other farmers who mine the soil. But farmers who conserve soil contribute to the long-term productivity of the land. Their contribution may be imperfectly reflected in the market price of well-conserved land. Better accounting could reflect more of the value of conserving soil.

Much better accounting is needed for human behavior and its consequences. Some behavior that is economically profitable has bad consequences that are not charged to the actors. Such behavior is currently rewarded more than is economically or socially rational.

For example, successful producers and advertisers of tobacco are not charged for the effects of tobacco on health. "Why should they be?" you might ask. "After all, nobody charges makers of ice cream and candy for tooth decay." True, but ice cream and candy are not addictive in the same way as tobacco, and the consumer has a fairly full picture of the consequences of use. At the opposite extreme, many societies do penalize makers, purveyors and sometimes users of addictive drugs. If there were an economic justification for penalizing them, it would probably be that drug dealers should bear more of the externalities of addictive drugs, which impose large costs on both users and non-users. Pushing tobacco falls on a spectrum between pushing hard drugs and pushing ice cream. Better accounting could make clearer where on that spectrum the tobacco industry lies and what its real costs are.

Behavior that is economically unprofitable but has good consequences is insufficiently rewarded. For example, homemakers and childrearers, who are overwhelmingly women, do work that has great value to families and societies. They bring home, prepare and serve food; maintain, clean and decorate the home and dispose of wastes; procure, repair and clean clothing and other personal effects for people in the home; and—most undervalued of all—love, raise and teach children language, etiquette and basic concepts of morality and culture. The time, effort and skill spent on all these activities are largely omitted from accountings of productive work. The foundations of what economists tenderly call human capital are laid in the home. There is virtually no economic accounting for the contributions of homemakers, mostly women, to increased investment in human capital.[12]

In the United States, the most visible public incentive for childrearers is the exemption from federal income tax for minor children living at home. An adult parent or guardian is permitted to exclude from taxation a certain amount of income for each child who meets certain criteria. The more children a couple has, the greater the amount of income exempted. Surely such a crude estimate of the contribution of childrearers could be refined or supplemented. For example, guardians could receive an additional exemption for each child (not disabled by disease or injury) who completes the sixth grade and meets certain minimal standards of nonviolent behavior, physical fitness and literacy; and a similar exemption could apply for each child who completes high school and satisfies agreed standards of competence. Such a proposal is sure to be controversial, and rightly so; a political process is required to sort out the proper criteria. The example is intended only to suggest that much better accounting for productive behavior on the part of both parents and children is possible and may be desirable, depending on the values of the polity.

When businesses close factories and governments change neighborhoods through urban renewal and public housing projects, better accounting could measure the effects on old and new social networks. These effects go beyond the effects on individuals. Putnam remarked, "The fact that these collective costs are not well measured by our current accounting schemes does not mean that they are not real. Shred enough of the social fabric and we all pay."[13]

Some people may object to better, or to any, accounting in spheres such as childrearing, efforts to save human lives and the conservation of species. They would hold that no possible accounting can adequately measure the value of human life or a species. For example, though soil scientist Daniel Hillel called for improved environmental accounting, he also claimed: "The environment has an intrinsic value beyond all present-day economic measure. Just as we no longer trade with human lives or ask what slaves are worth, just as we have learned to accept the ethical principle that human life has inalienable rights and is not merely an economic object, so it must be with the environment which is, after all, the source and sustenance of life."[14] True, human life is no longer traded directly. But the unromantic fact is that an economic value is imputed to human life with every decision to spend more or less money on safety for road vehicles, airplanes, the space shuttle or trains, and with many decisions to spend more or less money on preventive and curative medicine. An economic value is imputed to childrearing with every decision to support, or not to support, day-care centers, after-school programs, vaccination programs, textbooks for schools and educational television. An economic value is imputed to the environment every time a decision is made about how much money to spend lining a landfill to limit leakage from it, or reducing unwanted effluents from automobiles, homes and factories. Any accounting for what is precious must be recognized as partial and incomplete; but the alternative of no accounting is a sure road to neglect and exploitation.

As facts and understanding change, what is accepted as satisfactory accounting must also change. The laissez-faire hope that the market would automatically price goods in a way that maximized everyone's well-being had to be abandoned when it was realized that markets underprice public goods or open-access resources and that market prices can be distorted by open or hidden subsidies. The Marxist faith that every good could be valued by the human labor required to produce it would have assigned no value to species of plants and animals, clean air and clean water.[15] In earlier times, when a few farmers on the American Great Plains withdrew less water from the Ogallala aquifer than was being replenished, it was reasonable to treat the water as free. When the scale of withdrawals increased enough to begin depleting the aquifer, the accounting still could not be modified because the implications of the depletion were not understood. But now the water table is dropping rapidly. Drops in water level of three meters or more were reported during the 1980s under 19 percent of the aquifer's area.[16] The immediate consequences are visible (higher costs for pumping; subsiding land), and some future consequences are predictable. It has become time to take account of the expenditures for research, for capital and for labor that will be required in the future to supply the same stream of benefits currently derived from the mined water.

If the human condition is like a continuing forward fall, ever-evolving systems of accounting can help maintain an upright dynamic equilibrium, and can even improve our posture as we move forward. Better accounting is required by the difficulty of doing just what was intended.

RESEARCH ON POPULATION, CULTURE, ECONOMICS AND ENVIRONMENT

To understand present population problems, to examine the possible paths by which the human population growth rate will drop to or below zero and to make more credible concepts and estimates of the Earth's human carrying capacity, scientists must learn more of the four-way interactions of population, the environment, economy and culture. It is useless to imagine that population interacts with the environment while economics and culture have no effect and are unaffected; and equally useless to pretend that population growth interacts with economic development independently of the environment and culture. Populations, the environment, economics and culture all interact *jointly*. Think of a string quartet: the combined effect exceeds that of any single player or pair or trio of players.

Population, environment, economy and culture should be interpreted broadly. Population includes size, growth rate and age structure (how many young people want schooling? how many old people want pensions?), health (are people free of parasites? are they well fed? are they in good mental health?), spatial distribution (are people in cities or rural areas? near or far from fresh water?) and migration (are people moving from poor countries to other poor countries or to rich countries?). The environment includes soil, fresh water, salt water, air, all nonhuman living creatures and the Earth's stage of soils, rocks, mountains, rivers, plains, oceans, volcanoes, earthquakes, meteorites and solar flares. The economy includes all the human and material arrangements for the production and exchange of goods and services to satisfy people's wants. Culture includes values (what do people want? what do people think is right?), technology (what knowledge and artifacts, including machines, do people inherit and create?) and social and political institutions (how do people interact in satisfying their wants?). The boundaries are fuzzy: for example, law and technology belong both to culture and to the economy.

Any proposed description or solution of a population problem that does not include all four of population, environment, economy and culture is incomplete. In any partial description or solution, the omitted aspects are explicitly or implicitly assumed to remain constant. A partial description or solution is vulnerable to failure when one, or more, of the omitted aspects changes.

Let me give an analogy. The hydraulic engineers of the Roman Empire knew that the bigger the diameter of a pipe, the bigger the flow (volume of water per second) that could come out of the pipe. They did not know that the flow also depends on the head of pressure on the water supplied to the pipe. Consequently, when they wanted a copious flow, they built large-bore pipes. Sometimes the large-bore pipes delivered only a trickle. The Roman hydraulic engineers stubbed their toes on what today's scientists call the problem of dimensionality. Their description of flow in terms of the pipe's diameter omitted the dimension of pressure.

Too often, descriptions and proposed solutions of population problems lack sufficient dimensionality. For example, trying to predict life expectancy (an aspect of population) from GNP per person alone (an aspect of economics, and far from a perfect measure of real income, as we have seen) is like trying to predict water flow from the pipe diameter alone. When different developing countries are compared, those with a higher GNP per person tend to have a higher life expectancy. However, the connection between survival and income is affected by culture and social structure. Among developing countries with a given GNP per person, some have notably longer life expectancies than the average for such countries, while others have notably shorter life expectancies than the average.[17] For example, in 1988, both Haiti and Sri Lanka had GNP per person of about $400. During the interval 1985–90, Haiti's life expectancy was 55 years while Sri Lanka's was 70 years. The Ivory Coast and the Dominican Republic had GNP per person of about $750 and life expectancies of 52 and 66 years, respectively. With GNP per person of $1,700, Syria had a life expectancy of 65 years, Costa Rica one of 75 years.

The education of women is one key missing dimension required to explain these large differences in life expectancy, according to the Italian demographer Massimo Livi-Bacci. "Improved education, and especially female education (because of the woman's decisive role in childrearing, domestic hygiene, and food preparation), appears to be a necessary prerequisite to improved sanitary conditions. . . . The examples of China, Sri

Lanka, Cuba, and Costa Rica—politically diverse countries which have made considerable efforts in this area [of education]—show that low mortality is within reach of even the poorest populations."[18]

In rich countries as well, life expectancy depends on more than the average income per person. As I mentioned when discussing economic choices in Chapter 13, among the richer developed countries, differences in life expectancy are apparently more related to the degree of inequality in the income distribution than to differences in each country's average income.[19] Variations in the environment may be responsible for some of the remaining variation in life expectancy.

The four-way interaction of population, environment, economy and culture also affects agricultural development. The use of high technology in agriculture requires a favorable confluence of soil, water, climate, economic development, social development and population density and distribution. The society must be able to produce the material inputs required to modernize agriculture. Farmers must be able to purchase those inputs, and must be able to absorb and apply new knowledge and skills. Hence agricultural modernization requires industrialization and effective public and private institutions to provide education and credit. At the same time, industry requires investments that are possible only if agriculture is producing a surplus. These simultaneous requirements lead to what may be called Revelle's paradox, after Roger Revelle who stated it thus:

> Social and economic development that brings an increase in per capita income and a more equitable income distribution is probably also a necessary condition for a continuing reduction of rates of population growth, and ultimately for a stationary world population. Here we are faced with a paradox: attainment of the earth's maximum carrying capacity for human beings would require a high level of agricultural technology which in turn calls for a high level of social and economic development. Such development, however, would be likely to lead to a cessation of population growth long before the maximum carrying capacity is reached.[20]

Sometimes population, the economy, the environment and culture are all recognized implicitly. For example, in its 1992 report on *Development and the Environment,* the World Bank displayed an equation[21] to relate economic activity and the environment. According to the World Bank's equation, the quality of the environment equals the scale of the economy (income per person × population) × output structure (what people demand as final products, such as private cars or public transport, beef or rice and beans) × input–output efficiency (the amount of various resources consumed to produce each final product) × environmental damage per unit of input.[22] Here population, the environment and the economy all appear explicitly. Culture appears implicitly in the output structure and input–output efficiency (what do people want the economy to produce? how important are formal education and economically productive work in the culture? how well do workers apply knowledge to their economic activities?).

In another example, the United Nations studied the effect of female education on reproduction in 38 developing countries. The study showed that "although education generally exerts a negative influence on fertility levels, the shape and strength of the association is contingent on [the] level of development, social structure and cultural milieu. The study also concluded that the pattern of the relationship is not static over the course of the fertility transition."[23] Here the economy, population and culture appear explicitly. The environment appears implicitly in the level of development and possibly in the changing pattern of the relationship as fertility falls.

To visualize the interactions of population, environment, economy and culture, picture a tetrahedron, a pyramid with a triangular base and three triangular sides. At the top vertex is "population." At the three corners of the base are "environment," "economy" and "culture."[24] The pyramidal arrangement of these major dimensions of population problems emphasizes graphically that each interacts with all three of the others. The symmetry of the pyramid means that culture or ecology or the economy could be placed on top without changing the message.

The pyramid of population, economy, environment and culture is my mental prophylaxis against omitting important dimensions when I listen to discussions of population problems. Of course, the pyramid of population, economy, environment and culture may omit additional important dimensions. But it is handy for practical purposes because it is easy to remember.

Each corner of the pyramid has its own academic devotees. Some scholars, usually senior enough to risk scandalizing their brethren, have studied the links between one corner of the pyramid and another. Ansley J. Coale's and Edgar M. Hoover's 1958 analysis of connections between population growth and economic development in poor countries gained wide attention, and many economic-demographic models followed.[25] At a meeting on population and the environment, the American demographer Kingsley Davis complained that "no one specializes in the study of population and resources as an integrated discipline. One is either a demographer or a natural scientist, but not both at once."[26] The anthropologist Eugene Hammel of the University of California, Berkeley, propounded a theory of culture for demographers; after all, what the neighbors will say affects whether I am happy to have no children or ten.[27] Herman E. Daly, an economist at the World Bank, Colin W. Clark, a mathematician at the University of British Columbia, Charles Perrings, an economist at the University of Auckland, Faye Duchin, an economist at New York University, and others developed theories to link economies with their environments.[28] Nathan Keyfitz, who taught demography at Harvard, attempted in 1991 to relate three of the pyramid's four corners: population, economics and the environment. He also recognized the crucial role of culture in population questions.[29]

The image of a pyramid of population, economy, environment and culture does not yet embody enough knowledge to guide action or support prediction. Research should be systematically planned and carried out to put some factual muscle on the bones of this conceptual skeleton. Two possible approaches are case studies of particular populations and trying to measure the consequences of an average single birth.

A potential subject for a case study is the huge Brazilian city of São Paulo, where population, the economy, the environment and culture interact visibly.[30] Increasing numbers of poor people immigrate to São Paulo (population). The fleet of more than two million private motor vehicles in the metropolitan area grows by 5 percent per year (economy). In 1989, motor vehicles produced more than 800,000 tons of carbon monoxide. Less than a quarter of the metropolitan area's sewage is fully processed. Carbon monoxide, ozone and particulates degrade air quality as diseases of the heart and lungs increase. People living in squatter settlements on hills around the city remove forests and make landslides more frequent. Sediment in the rivers increases, inducing flooding (environment). The gap between rich and poor persists, and critics claim that governmental policies aid wealthy landowners at the expense of the landless rural poor, who migrate to cities (culture). Planners in São Paulo have termed the situation "environmental chaos."

Another approach would measure comprehensively the consequences of one additional birth (on the average) in some particular population at a particular time. Parts of what I have in mind have already been developed by demographers, economists and educators. Demographers have already calculated age-specific and sex-specific schedules of survival and fertility for various populations and times. These schedules show, respectively, at each age for each sex, the probability of surviving to the next year and the average number of children borne in the next year. The schedule of survival is the core of the life insurance industry as well as the basis of annuities and pension planning. The schedule of fertility is the key to current and projected future rates of population growth. Economists have lifetime schedules of employment (the fraction of people who are employed, at each age, for each sex) and earnings (the average income, at each age, for each sex). Educators have lifetime schedules of school enrollment (the fraction who are enrolled in school in each group by age and sex). My suggestion is to develop age-specific schedules for direct and indirect consumption or use of water, food, electric power, petroleum products, timber products, metals, nonmetallic minerals, vegetable and artificial fibers, pharmaceuticals, wildlife areas, other recreational areas, services by major activities (health, educational, cultural, religious) and so on. Age-specific schedules could be constructed to quantify the effluents of each kind of consumption or use. Such schedules would make it possible to deepen our present shallow understanding of the consequences of additional births in a community.

Life would be complicated enough even if there were only one global pyramid of population, environment, economy and culture. But in fact, the Earth is covered with thousands or millions of such pyramids, because populations, environments, economies and cultures vary from place to place, and so do their interactions. Population problems are partly local, partly global.[31] Each local pyramid interacts with many others, often over great distances. The dust of the Sahara brings red sunsets to Miami, Florida[32]; tremors on the Tokyo stock exchange shake Wall Street. Hence the two approaches I suggested—local case studies, and age-specific schedules of inputs and outputs—should be carried out in many different places.

MUTUAL AID

A new quantitative understanding of mutual aid is needed. At the level of an individual, how much is it worth to you, and how much should it be worth to you, to enhance others' welfare so that you assure your own welfare and your descendants' welfare? And what guides you in deciding how much it's worth to you? At the level of social aggregates, when, why and how much does the self-interest of well-off institutions and countries depend on the welfare of other, worse-off or vulnerable individuals, institutions, countries and species? How much of their income or assets should well-off donors invest in the well-being of others for the mutual benefit of donors and recipients? As specific examples, what is the return to rich countries for helping poor countries who ask for assistance in lowering their high rates of population growth? What payoff do rich countries get for helping poor countries get richer?

These questions are not solely of interest to preachers and philosophers. In summarizing the implications of the United Nations Conference on Environment and Development held in Rio de Janeiro in June 1992, Richard N. Gardner of Columbia University wrote: "there are now four overriding national concerns of the American people in events beyond our borders: promoting democratic values and institutions, maintaining an open and growing world economy, building a new system of collective security, and assuring global habitability."[33] Looking at security in health, Joshua Lederberg, a Nobel laureate in medicine and physiology, observed: "The bacteria and viruses know nothing of national sovereignties. . . . As one species, we share a common vulnerability to these scourges. No matter how selfish our motives, we can no longer be indifferent to the suffering of others. The microbe that felled one child in a distant continent yesterday can reach yours today and seed a global pandemic tomorrow."[34]

Some traditional religions justified helping others as a means of earning the favor of divinities. For example, in ancient Babylon the gods promised they would reward piety and charity by providing protection, help in danger, health, comfort, social status, wealth, many children, longevity and happiness.[35]

In the Middle Ages, Moses Maimonides (1135–1204) gave a practical justification for religious commandments "concerned with giving alms, lending, bestowal of gifts, and matters that are connected with this. . . . The reason for all these is manifest, for they are equally useful in turn to all men. For one who is rich today will be poor tomorrow, or his descendants will be poor; whereas one who is poor today will be rich tomorrow, or his son will be rich."[36] The uncertainty of the future requires the rich to attend to the poor out of self-interest.

The English philosopher Thomas Hobbes (1588–1679) explained any appearance of altruism as self-seeking disguised in one form or another. Because undisguised self-seeking would lead to a war of all against all, pure self-interest leads people to a regard for others, Hobbes argued. Once a Christian clergyman saw Hobbes give alms to a beggar. The clergyman asked if Hobbes would have given alms had not Jesus commanded it. Hobbes answered that by giving alms, he relieved both the beggar's distress and his own at seeing the poor man's distress. Hobbes thus provided an egoistic rationale for charity, but he assumed without explanation his own distress at seeing the beggar's distress.[37]

In 1759, in his first book, *The Theory of Moral Sentiments,* Adam Smith assumed sympathy or compassion as the basis of his explanation of morality: "How selfish soever man may be supposed, there are evidently some principles in his nature, which interest him in the fortune of others, and render their happiness necessary to him, though he derives nothing from it except the pleasure of seeing it."[38]

Today, other reasons besides religious and philosophical ones are given for mutual aid: insurance, natural selection and game theory.

Insurance quantifies and rationalizes the argument of Moses Maimonides. It distributes unpredictable risks through a population and reduces the chance of an uncompensated catastrophe for any individual. Each participant can see the actual or potential benefit of participating. In Germany in 1883, Chancellor Otto von Bismarck introduced the first general social insurance scheme. It provided medical care and cash payments during illness for workers in certain types of industry. It was paid for by obligatory contributions from workers and employers. In 1884, the scheme was extended to accident insurance, and in 1889 to pensions for all workers in trade, industry and agriculture starting at the age of 70 years. Bismarck's political motivation was to check socialism and avert revolution by addressing the legitimate grievances of the workers.[39]

Natural selection could lead to apparent altruism as a means of propagating one's genes in related individuals.[40] Altruistic acts by a donor to a genetic relative could be advantageous to the donor, provided the recipient's degree of relatedness to the donor (r) exceeded the cost to the donor (C) divided by the benefit to the recipient (B).[41] This simple model assumes that the donor's specific altruistic behavior toward a relative is under the control of a single gene that obeys the laws of Mendelian genetics, a hotly contested assumption especially in human contexts.

According to this model, the higher the cost to the donor, or the lower the benefit to the recipient, the higher the degree of relatedness between donor and recipient would have to be for the controlling gene to evolve under natural selection. For example, the greatest possible degree of genetic relatedness is that between identical twins; in this case, the value of r is 1. Hence, if altruistic behavior were entirely determined by natural selection (which is highly doubtful), one identical twin should carry out an altruistic act for the other whenever the benefit for the recipient twin exceeds the cost to the donor twin (because then the cost C divided by the benefit B is less than 1). The genetic relatedness r between a parent and child, or between a child and parent, or between two full siblings (siblings with the same father and same mother) is one-half. For a half sibling (a sibling with one shared parent and one different parent), the genetic relatedness r is one-fourth. And so on.

Does this theory of altruism support my charity for refugees in Bangladesh and Somalia? Possibly. A single gift of $1.25, the cost of one subway ride in the city of New York, would affect the number of my genes present in the next generation of humankind practically not at all, so the cost to me would be close to zero. In 1992, roughly two billion people had average annual incomes of $400 per year, or about one dollar per day.[42] If my $1.25 donation delivered one dollar's worth of goods to a famine-stricken child somewhere, the benefit for that child's survival and eventual reproduction might be substantial. So the genetic relatedness r would not have to be very large to justify my making a single small donation on grounds of genetic relatedness.

Is any relatedness remotely plausible? That depends on whether the recipient child and I have common ancestors. One generation back, my parents are two ancestors. Two generations back, my grandparents are four ancestors. Twenty generations back, my ancestors, *if* all distinct, would have been a million ancestors (doubtless they were not all distinct). Thirty generations back, my ancestors, *if* all distinct, would have numbered more than 1,000 million or one billion. If there were five generations per century, then 30 generations would take my ancestors back six centuries, to around A.D. 1400, when there were fewer than half a billion people on the Earth.[43] The calculation just given applies to you and to the child as well as to me. Those ancestors 30 generations back are yours and his or hers as well as mine. Of course, there was much more mating within localized populations than between them, so that individuals within a local population are on the average more related than this global calculation would suggest while individuals from different local populations are somewhat less related than the global calculation indicates. But given the adventures of soldiers, sailors, traveling merchants, slaves and peoples relocated after being conquered in the past, the possibility is strong that you and I are related 30 or 40 or 50 generations back, and that each of us is related to a famine-striken child somewhere.[44] And therefore when in want you are entitled to ask me, and each of us is entitled to ask the other, as the song goes: Brother, can you spare a dime?

On the basis of the amount of mating with people from ethnically distinct groups that I observe in the present generation of my extended family, I suspect that I could be related to Bangladeshi and Somali refugees with a common ancestry far closer than 30 generations back. I can plausibly look on most people in the world today as my likely in-laws a few dozen generations in the future at most. All humankind is literally one family. Of course, before this argument provides a quantitative basis for mutual aid, it will be necessary to put believable numbers in place of the symbols r, B and C and to confirm the assumptions on which the theory rests.

A third justification for mutual aid arises from game theory. Game theory, the mathematical analysis of self-interested strategic behavior, can explain cooperative action as a means of attaining benefits that are inaccessible without cooperation. One explanation is based on an example known as the Prisoner's Dilemma.[45] The Prisoner's Dilemma demonstrates that individuals who independently pursue their own self-interest, utterly without cooperation, may arrive at a result that is not optimal for anyone. It also demonstrates that one party may benefit by paying another to cooperate.

Two prisoners, called Rose and Colin, are arrested and accused of committing a crime jointly. They are interrogated separately. The examiner tells each that if one of them confesses to the crime and the other one denies it, the one who confesses will be rewarded by $1,000 and the one who denies will be fined $2,000. The examiner promises each that if both confess, each will be fined $1,000. The prisoners have left so little evidence at the scene of the crime that if neither confesses neither will be fined anything (a payoff of zero dollars to each).

The names Rose and Colin are mnemonics. When the game is summarized in a table of payoffs to each player, Rose chooses the "row" and Colin chooses the "column." Here is the payoff table:

	Colin confesses	Colin denies
Rose confesses	Rose is fined $1,000. Colin is fined $1,000.	Rose is rewarded with $1,000. Colin is fined $2,000.
Rose denies	Rose is fined $2,000. Colin is rewarded with $1,000.	Rose and Colin receive neither fine nor reward.

What should they do? If Colin confesses, Rose would do better to confess and get the fine of $1,000, rather than deny and get the fine of $2,000. If Colin denies the crime, Rose would do better to confess and get the reward of $1,000, rather than deny and get nothing. Either way, Rose is $1,000 better off if she confesses. By the same argument, whatever action Rose picks, Colin too is better off if he confesses. According to this individualistic reasoning, both Rose and Colin should confess. But if they both confess, they will both be fined $1,000, whereas if they both deny the crime, they will both escape any fines. Clearly, they would be better off making and abiding by a prior agreement to deny the crime than they would be if each independently tried to do as well as possible for herself or himself. In fact, Rose would be better off if she could make and enforce a contract to *pay* Colin not to confess; and vice versa.[46]

A nice game, perhaps, but what does it have to do with international collaboration and foreign aid? Interpret Rose as the industrialized or rich countries, Colin as the developing countries. Interpret denying the crime as cutting back on the consumption of fossil fuels that add carbon dioxide to the atmosphere. Interpret confessing to the crime as continuing to burn fossil fuels at present or even higher levels. If all countries continue to burn fossil fuels (both parties confess), carbon dioxide in the atmosphere will continue its dramatic rise. For the sake of argument, let me posit that the consequence will be global warming and a rise in sea level and all countries will suffer (though, in reality, they will hardly suffer equally: think of low-lying Netherlands and mountainous Nepal). Let me also posit that if the industrialized and developing countries all reduce their consumption of fossil fuels, global warming will be averted.[47] If the developing countries agree to cut back fossil fuel consumption, the threat of global warming recedes temporarily; the industrialized countries feel they can avoid the costs of converting from fossil fuels to other energy sources and are tempted to continue to burn fossil fuels. The same holds if the developing and industrialized countries exchange roles. If both groups of countries yield to temptation and continue to burn fossil fuels, both may suffer the consequences of global warming. If both groups could agree to diminish the use of fossil fuels (both agree to deny the crime), perhaps with assistance ("side payments," in game theory) from the industrialized countries to the developing countries to share the increased costs of developing alternative energy sources, both sides would be better off than if both acted in independent self-interest.

This interpretation of the Prisoner's Dilemma game is not fantasy. At the United Nations Conference on Environment and Development (UNCED) held in 1992 in Rio de Janeiro, William Reilly, the administrator of the United States' Environmental Protection Agency, and Curtis Bohlen, the assistant secretary of state for oceans and international environmental and scientific affairs, saw the potential benefits to the United States of making commitments to higher environmental standards in both developed and developing countries. For developed countries, raising environmental standards in developing countries offered three payoffs: lessening global problems that could be solved by no single party, such as ozone depletion, greenhouse warming and protection of biological diversity; decreasing the handicap on strictly regulated industries in developed countries by increasing the environmental regulation of industries in developing countries; and augmenting the market in developing countries for cleaner technologies and for environmental goods and services that are available in the industrial nations.[48]

The developing countries at Rio wanted higher environmental standards plus foreign aid from the developed countries to assist them in meeting those standards, in preserving biodiversity and in developing economically. Others in the domestic and economic staff of the U.S. White House saw in Rio only political and economic vulnerability. They viewed pressures for increased foreign aid as an unalloyed drawback, as a zero-sum game (what your side gains, our side loses). In the end, the White House view of the Rio conference as a zero-sum game dominated the view of it as a Prisoner's Dilemma.

Thus the interpretation of situations of conflict as Prisoner's Dilemmas cannot be taken for granted. Appropriate action depends on the table of payoffs, and that table must be determined empirically. Before the Prisoner's Dilemma can be used to justify foreign aid from industrialized to developing countries on grounds of the self-interest of industrialized countries, a huge empirical gap must be filled. It must be shown, quantitatively and persuasively, that both industrialized and developing countries would be better off if industrialized countries transferred substantial resources to developing countries as a means of buttressing some agreement than they would be if the industrialized nations provided only humanitarian aid, cosmetic aid or no aid at all.

Another example where developed and developing countries share an interest that could be interpreted as a Prisoner's Dilemma game concerns the effect of rapid population growth on workers' wages.[49] Rapid population growth in developing countries drives down the cost of labor there, other things being equal, and internationally mobile financial capital from abroad is attracted to low-wage workforces with the required level of education and skill.[50] To diminish wage competition from poor countries, workers in the rich countries have a stake in helping poor countries lower their population growth rates by means viewed as desirable in the poor countries. In addition, if developing countries advance faster economically when their population growth rates are lower, then they can more rapidly become markets for the products of the industrialized countries. These arguments, if supported factually, might persuade workers in industrialized countries to provide political support for programs of population assistance to developing countries.[51]

Because it is always difficult to do just what is intended, those who use a theory of mutual aid should be alert for possible pernicious effects of attempts to provide aid. It has been argued that when donor countries provided free surplus grain to African countries, local grain production was driven out of competition. The net result was to increase the recipients' vulnerability to famine. When African countries buy cheap grain on world markets, African farmers may be handicapped because they do not receive the implicit or explicit subsidies for energy, water and soil mining that farmers receive in the major producing countries such as the United States, Canada and Australia.[52]

The United States undertook international aid on an unprecedented scale after World War II. Europe was economically devastated.[53] To avoid a repetition of the mistakes made in Europe after World War I, Secretary of State George C. Marshall and President Harry Truman launched a European Recovery Plan in the spring of 1947. The plan, subsequently known as the Marshall Plan, focused on relieving the bottlenecks that impeded economic recovery: damaged infrastructure, flooded mines and trade barriers. By coordinating actions among all the countries in the region, it also worked to promote the emergence of a regional political framework. Between 1948 and 1951, the United States spent annually close to 2 percent of its gross national product on the Marshall Plan. A similar fraction of the United

States' 1994 gross domestic product of roughly $6.6 trillion would amount to about $130 billion, nearly nine times the $15 billion a year currently spent for all nonmilitary foreign aid and more than 280 times the $352 million the United States gave for all overseas population programs in 1991.

In 1990, for official development assistance, 18 countries of the Organisation for Economic Co-operation and Development (OECD) gave fractions of their respective gross national products ranging from 0.16 percent for Ireland to 1.17 percent for Norway, for an average of 0.36 percent of gross national product.[54] The total was $55.6 billion. In the same year, ten countries of the Organization of Petroleum Exporting Countries (OPEC) gave fractions of their respective gross national products ranging from 0.01 percent for Libya to 3.9 percent for Saudi Arabia, for a total of $6.3 billion.[55]

From the days of Babylon to the days of OECD and OPEC, giving aid to the less well-off has expanded from a direct exchange between persons to a transfer between persons mediated by impersonal insurance schemes, national bureaucracies for taxation and economic development, regional organizations of governments and international agencies. Individual giving has remained alive and important. A persuasive and quantitative rationale for mutual aid based on self-interest remains to be developed.

IMPROVING THE ART OF LIVING

A beautiful quotation from the 1848 *Principles of Political Economy* of the British philosopher John Stuart Mill commends a change of values. You may not agree with all of it. But every part is worthy of serious consideration and, if not assent, serious argument. For perspective, it is useful to know that, at the next censuses after Mill wrote, the combined population of England, Wales and Scotland in 1851 was 21 million; the population of the United States in 1850 was 23 million.[56] The world's population in 1848 was just over one billion, less than one-fifth of its present size.

> There is room in the world, no doubt, and even in old countries, for a great increase of population, supposing the arts of life to go on improving, and capital to increase. But even if innocuous, I confess I see very little reason for desiring it. The density of population necessary to enable mankind to obtain, in the greatest degree, all the advantages both of cooperation and of social intercourse, has, in all the most populous countries, been attained. A population may be too crowded, though all be amply supplied with food and raiment. It is not good for man to be kept perforce at all times in the presence of his species. A world from which solitude is extirpated, is a very poor ideal. Solitude, in the sense of being often alone, is essential to any depth of meditation or of character; and solitude in the presence of natural beauty and grandeur, is the cradle of thoughts and aspirations which are not only good for the individual, but which society could ill do without. Nor is there much satisfaction in contemplating the world with nothing left to the spontaneous activity of nature; with every rood of land brought into cultivation, which is capable of growing food for human beings; every flowery

waste or natural pasture ploughed up, all quadrupeds or birds which are not domesticated for man's use exterminated as his rivals for food, every hedgerow or superfluous tree rooted out, and scarcely a place left where a wild shrub or flower could grow without being eradicated as a weed in the name of improved agriculture. If the earth must lose that great portion of its pleasantness which it owes to things that the unlimited increase of wealth and population would extirpate from it, for the mere purpose of enabling it to support a larger but not a better or a happier population, I sincerely hope, for the sake of posterity, that they will content to be stationary, long before necessity compels them to it.

It is scarcely necessary to remark that a stationary condition of capital and population implies no stationary state of human improvement. There would be as much scope as ever for all kinds of mental culture, and moral and social progress; as much room for improving the Art of Living, and much more likelihood of its being improved, when minds ceased to be engrossed by the art of getting on. Even the industrial arts might be as earnestly and as successfully cultivated, with this sole difference, that instead of serving no purpose but the increase of wealth, industrial improvements would produce their legitimate effect, that of abridging labour. . . . Only when, in addition to just institutions, the increase of mankind shall be under the deliberate guidance of judicious foresight, can the conquests made from the powers of nature by the intellect and energy of scientific discoverers, become the common property of the species, and the means of improving and elevating the universal lot.[57]

———

Conversion Ratios

When the sun never set on the British Empire, English-speaking schoolchildren learned to convert a volume of water to its weight from the jingle "A pint's a pound, the world around." British and other nonstandard measures persist but the metric system is universal in scientific work. In this system, 1 liter of water (a cube 0.1 meter or 3.9 inches on an edge) weighs 1 kilogram (at 4 degrees centigrade). One cubic meter of water weighs exactly 1 tonne.

C. J. Pennycuick's extensive collection of conversion factors for metric and nonmetric systems of measures is extremely useful.[1] Unfortunately, sooner or later the conversion factor you want will not be tabulated in the tables you have handy. At that point, it pays to know how to make the conversion yourself. The procedure is best illustrated by example.

Example: A farmer measures rainwater or irrigation water in acre-feet. How many cubic meters (m^3) or tonnes (thousands of kilograms) of water are there in 1 acre-foot?

The goal is to find the ratio

$$\frac{m^3}{\text{acre-feet}}.$$

Since an acre is an area and a foot is a length, we factor the numerator $m^3 = m^2 \times m$ into a product of an area times a length. Thus

$$\frac{m^3}{\text{acre-feet}} = \left(\frac{m^2}{\text{acre}}\right)\left(\frac{m}{\text{feet}}\right).$$

My table shows 0.4 hectare per acre (actually 0.40469, but that would be useless precision), so I rewrite the equation to use that fact:

$$\frac{m^3}{\text{acre-feet}} = \left(\frac{m^2}{\text{ha}}\right)\left(\frac{\text{ha}}{\text{acre}}\right)\left(\frac{m}{\text{feet}}\right).$$

Since there are 10,000 square meters per hectare (which is a square 100 meters on a side) and 0.3 meter per foot (actually 0.30480), we substitute the numerical value for each ratio on the right and multiply to get the final answer:

$$\frac{m^3}{\text{acre-feet}} = (10,000)(0.4)(0.3) = 1,200.$$

One acre-foot of water contains approximately 1,200 cubic meters or 1,200 tonnes of water.

Example: A farmer reports the yield of his potato field in pounds per acre. How can this be converted to kilograms per hectare?

Proceeding as in the previous example, we start with the goal and rewrite it in manageable pieces:

$$\frac{\text{kg/ha}}{\text{lb/acre}} = \left(\frac{\text{kg}}{\text{lb}}\right)\left(\frac{\text{acre}}{\text{ha}}\right) = (0.45359)(2.4711) = 1.1209.$$

If a farmer gets 1,000 pounds per acre, then he gets 1,121 kilograms per hectare. Roughly speaking, yields measured in kilograms per hectare are just a bit more than yields measured in pounds per acre. This is not surprising because a kilogram is about 2.2 pounds while a hectare is about 2.5 acres, and $2.5/2.2 \approx 1.1$.

Estimates of Past Human Population Sizes (Millions)

year (−means B.C.)	Deevey 1960	McEvedy and Jones 1978	Durand 1977 low	Durand 1977 high	Clark 1977	Biraben 1979	Blaxter 1986[a]	United Nations 1992a	Kremer 1993[b]
−1,000,000	0.125	—	—	—	—	—	—	—	0.1
−300,000	1	—	—	—	—	—	—	—	1
−25,000	3.34	—	—	—	—	—	—	—	3.3
−10,000	—	4.00	—	—	—	—	—	—	4.00
−8000	5.32	—	—	—	—	—	—	—	—
−5000	—	5.0	—	—	—	—	40	—	5.0
−4000	86.5	7	—	—	—	—	—	—	7
−3000	—	14	—	—	—	—	—	—	14
−2000	—	27	—	—	—	—	70[c]	—	27
−1000	—	50	—	—	—	—	100[d]	—	50
−500	—	100	—	—	—	—	—	—	100
−400	—	—	—	—	—	153	162	—	—
−200	—	150	—	—	—	225	231	—	150
1	133	170	270	330	256[e]	252	255	—	170
200	—	190	—	—	—	257	256	—	190
400	—	190	—	—	254[f]	206	206	—	190
500	—	190	—	—	—	207	—	—	—
600	—	200	—	—	237	208	206	—	200
700	—	210	—	—	—	206	207	—	—
800	—	220	—	—	261	224	224	—	220
900	—	240	—	—	—	222	226	—	—
1000	—	265	275	345	280	253	254	—	265
1100	—	320	—	—	—	299	301	—	320
1200	—	360	—	—	384	400	400	—	360
1250	—	—	—	—	—	417	—	—	—
1300	—	360	—	—	—	431	432	—	360
1340	—	—	—	—	378	442	—	—	—
1400	—	350	—	—	—	375	374	—	350
1500	—	425	440	540	427	461	460	—	425
1600	—	545	—	—	498	578	579	—	545
1650	545	545	—	—	516	—	—	—	545
1700	—	610	—	—	641	680	679	—	610
1750	728	720	735	805	731	771	770	—	720
1800	906	900	—	—	890	954	954	—	900
1850	—	1,200	—	—	1,190	1,241	1,241	—	1,200
1875	—	1,325	—	—	—	—	—	—	1,325
1900	1,610	1,625	1,650	1,710	1,668	1,634	1,633	—	1,625
1920	—	—	—	—	—	—	—	—	1,813
1925	—	2,000	—	—	—	—	—	—	—
1930	—	—	—	—	—	—	—	—	1,987
1940	—	—	—	—	—	—	—	—	2,213
1950	2,400	2,500	—	—	—	2,530	2,513	2,516	2,516

APPENDIX 2   *continued*

year (- means B.C.)	Deevey 1960	McEvedy and Jones 1978	Durand 1977 low	Durand 1977 high	Clark 1977	Biraben 1979	Blaxter 1986[a]	United Nations 1992a	Kremer 1993[b]
1955	—	—	—	—	—	—	—	2,752	—
1960	—	—	—	—	—	—	—	3,020	3,019
1965	—	—	—	—	—	—	—	3,336	—
1970	—	—	—	—	—	3,637	—	3,698	3,693
1975	—	3,900	3,950	4,050	—	—	—	4,079	—
1980	—	—	—	—	—	—	4,415	4,448	4,450
1985	—	—	—	—	—	—	—	4,851	—
1990	—	—	—	—	—	—	—	5,292	5,333

[a] Blaxter's estimate "derives from" those of Biraben (1979) and the United Nations (Blaxter 1986, p. 12), but minor ferences from Biraben's figures are not explained.

[b] Kremer's estimate is based on Deevey (1960) up to −25,000, on McEvedy and Jones (1978) from −10,000 to 1900 d on various sources after 1900.

[c] Blaxter's (1986, p. 13) estimate for 1600 B.C. is shown on the line for 2000 B.C.

[d] Blaxter's (1986, p. 13) estimate for 800 B.C. is shown on the line for 1000 B.C.

[e] Clark's (1977, p. 64) estimate for A.D. 14 is shown on the line for A.D. 1.

[f] Clark's (1977, p. 64) estimate for A.D. 350 is shown on the line for A.D. 400.

SOURCES: Deevey (1960); McEvedy and Jones (1978); Durand (1977); Clark (1977); Biraben (1979); Blaxter (1986); nited Nations (1992a); Kremer (1993)

Estimates of How Many People
the Earth Can Support

(in Chronological Order)

billion people and source	methods and limiting factors considered *(quotations are from the source unless otherwise attributed)*
13.4 Leeuwenhoek *(April 25, 1679)[a]*	In a letter from Delft, Holland, to the Royal Society in London, Leeuwenhoek aimed to show that the 150 billion "little animals in the milt of a cod" greatly exceeded the maximum possible number of people on the Earth. Leeuwenhoek estimated that the Earth's surface contained 9,276,218 square miles. (In seventeenth-century Holland, the linear mile was one-fifteenth of a degree of the Earth's circumference, or approximately 7.4 kilometers.) He supposed that one-third of the surface was land, and that two-thirds of the land, or 2,061,382 square miles, was inhabited. He also assumed that Holland and West-Friesland (roughly today's provinces of North- and South-Holland, plus a small portion of North-Brabant) were a rectangle 22 miles long and 7 miles wide. The area of 154 square miles contained an estimated million people, about 120 people per square kilometer. (Holland had no official census in the seventeenth century, but a capitation was levied in 1622.) ". . . if we assume that the inhabited part of the earth is as densely populated as Holland, though it cannot well be so inhabited, the inhabited earth being 13,385 times larger than Holland yields . . . 13,385,000,000 human beings on the earth." (p. 35) Leeuwenhoek's calculation had a very long echo. Ehrlich, Ehrlich and Holdren (1977, p. 717) criticized precisely Leeuwenhoek's argument, possibly without realizing its origin. "The favorite example for showing that the world as a whole is underpopulated (averaging 28 people per square kilometer in 1972) is the prosperous Netherlands, which has 326 people per square kilometer (figures from the United Nations' *Statistical Yearbook* for 1973). This 'Netherlands Fallacy' is an example of what is known in philosophy as the *fallacy of composition*—that what is true for a part must be true for the whole. The Netherlands can support 326 people per square kilometer only because the rest of the world does not. It ranks second in the world behind Denmark in imports of protein per person, a large portion of which, again, is fed to livestock. Much of the Netherlands' food, most of its fiber, and nearly all the metals needed in industry—iron, antimony, bauxite, copper, tin, and so on—are imported. Until the 1970s, when a large natural gas field in the northern part of the country was found and tapped, the Dutch imported nearly half their energy." This criticism invites an analysis of the role of international trade (Chapter 13).
6.3–12.5 King *(1695, p. 2)[a]*	King's manuscript notebook of 1695–1700 was first published in 1973. My extract preserves his spelling, capitalization and punctuation. "The Number of Acres in the World and their proportion by Climates: "1. Between the Equator and 30 Degrees of Latitude both ways - 25.000'000.000 Land Acres . . . at 090 acr. p head, 278'000.000 People "2. From 30 to 55 deg. of Lat. both ways - 16.000'000.000 Land Acres

. . . at 50 acr. p head, 320'000.000 People

"3. From 55 to 70 deg. of Lat. both ways – 4.000'000.000 Land Acres
. . . at 100 acr. p head, 40'000.000 People

"4. From 70 to 90 deg – 3.000'000.000 Land Acres . . . 00.000.000 People [total at present] 48.000'000.000 Land Acres at 78.5 acr. p head, 638'000.000 People.

"Which 4 Tracts of Land If fully Peopled would sustain the following numbers.

No. 1 - . . . at 09 acres p head – 2777'000.000 People

No. 2 - . . . at 5 acres p head – 3200'000.000 People

No. 3 - . . . at 16 acres p head – 250'000.000 People

No. 4 - . . . at 100 acres p head – 30'000.000 People

[total possible] . . . at (above) 8 acr. p head – 6257'000.000 People

"Which is Ten times the Number of People now in being, and it is not possible to maintain more than double that Number or 20 times more than the number of People now in being.

"Neither will it have 10 times the Number of People now in being till A[nn]o Christi 5000 or 5500 which is above 3000 years to come. And if it were possible to Sustain 20 times the Number of People now in being, it could not encrease to that Number till about the year of Christ 10'000, which is above 8000 years to come."

4–6.6
Süssmilch
(1741, pp. 74–75;
my translation of all
quotations)[a]

Süssmilch estimated that the number of people that the Earth could support was much larger than the number then on the Earth (which he overestimated at one billion), or likely to be on the Earth if current growth rates continued for several centuries. He concluded that war and plague were not necessary to limit the human population.

"Solution of the Problem, how many people can live on the Earth

"1.) The entire surface of the Earth contains 9,288,000 German square miles. One third part makes 3,096,000. In French square miles the whole surface is 15,480,000, and a third part of this is 5,160,000. . . .

"2.) The well-known French Marshall Vauban gives all France 28,642 French square miles, as the average of the calculations of Delisle, Nolins, Lefers, Sansons and the French Academy [Projet d'une dixme royale, 1707]. For calculation he takes 30,000 miles. Then he calculates how much grain can grow in the space of a mile. After deducting the houses, gardens, roads, water, heaths etc. he finds 2630 Setiers. Further he supposes that each person annually consumes 3 Setiers, although children, old people, even though they also eat meat and drink wine, cannot consume so much. (Here in this country one calculates, if I am not mistaken, 12 Scheffel for bread, drinks and vegetables.)

"3.) Thus a mile has 876 persons, if one divides the 2630 [Setiers per square mile] by three. But he also figures something for birds and mice, and thus supposes only 850 persons for each mile.

"4.) Now since France contains 30,000 miles, it can support 25,500,000 humans on what it grows there, which number is larger than its present number, as Vauban recalls.

"5.) Now since a French mile can contain and feed 850 persons, it follows that 5,160,000 miles, as one third of the habitable Earth, could hold 4,386 million humans. Q.E.D.

"If one wanted to take half the Earth's surface, one would have 6,579 million. If one wanted to take an average figure between one half and one third, one could put 5,000 million. Surely 4,000 is enough. I am also content if one takes a still smaller number. Meanwhile it would be difficult to find a serious objection against 4,000 million inhabitants of the Earth."

13.9
Süssmilch
(1765, p. 326)[a]

Based on a product of habitable areas and maximal population density, Süssmilch estimated that 13,932 million people can live on the Earth. He also quoted Leeuwenhoek's estimate of 13,385 million, an estimate of 5,472 million based on Vauban's theses and an estimate of 11,500 million based on Thomas Templeman's measure of 375 people per English square mile (*A new survey of the globe:* London, 1729; Süssmilch always spells his name "Templemann").

6.0
Ravenstein
(1891, pp. 29–30)[a]

Ravenstein supposed that fertile lands cover 28.3 million square miles (73.2 million square kilometers) and can support 207 people per square mile (80 per square kilometer), for a total of 5.851 billion people; steppes cover 13.9 million square miles (36 million square kilometers) and can support 10 people per square mile (3.9 per square kilometer), for a total of 139 million people; and deserts cover 4.2 million square miles (10.9 million square kilometers) and can support 1 person per square mile (0.4 per square kilometer), for a total of 4.2 million people. The total of all regions is 5.994 billion people.

8.1
Fircks
(1898, p. 295)[a] and
Wagner *(1923)*[b] via
Penck *(1925, pp. 334–35)*[a]

Fircks (1898, p. 295) estimated the potential population density of the fertile regions as 100 per square kilometer, of the steppes as 20 per square kilometer and of deserts as 5 per square kilometer. Fircks incorrectly converted Ravenstein's estimates of the areas of these regions from square miles to square kilometers and arrived at 9.272 billion people. Using the correctly converted areas shown above and Fircks's estimates of density, I arrive at 8.1 billion.

10.9
Pfaundler
(1902)[b] via Smil
(1994, pp. 255–56)[a]

According to Smil, Pfaundler assumed that traditional agriculture and recycling of organic matter could support 5 people per hectare on the then-existing 2.174 billion hectares of cropland and good grazing land.

2.3–22.4
Ballod
(1912, pp. 99–101)[a]

Ballod estimated the cultivable surface of the Earth at 56 million square kilometers, of which about half, or 28 million square kilometers, would be cultivated at any time. For the U.S.A. "standard of life," 0.9 hectare per person of arable land would be required for food plus 0.3 hectare per person to nourish beasts of burden and grow fibers, for a total land requirement of 1.2 hectares of arable land per person. With this requirement, 2.333 billion people could live on the Earth. Taking 0.5 hectare as the land required for the German standard of life, 5.6 billion could live on the Earth. Taking 0.125 hectare (1,250 square meters) as the requirement for the Japanese standard of life, 22.4 billion could live on the Earth. When horses, oxen and other beasts of burden are replaced by machines, the lands that now grow food for them can grow food for people instead, increasing the maximum supportable populations by 1 / 5 to 1 / 4. The discovery of a large supply of phosphates might permit a further doubling of food supplies; artificial irrigation and drainage could generate additional increases.

132
Knibbs
(1917, p. 455)[a]

"If the earth's . . . land area, excluding the Arctic and Antarctic continents, be assumed to be, say, 33,000,000,000 acres; and if further it is supposed that by some means it is possible to make the whole of this land-area yield an average of as much as 22.8 bushels of food-corn per acre, per annum, the total yield would be only 752,400,000,000 bushels.
"In Australia, and in fact generally, the food-corn consumption is on the average, about equivalent to 5.7 bushels per annum, viz., one-fourth of the amount above assumed, which means that the total pop-

ulation which could be fed with 5.7 bushels of food-corn per annum together with other foods in like proportion, would be only 132,000,000,000."

5.2
East
(1924, p. 69)[a]

Edward M. East was a plant geneticist at the Bussey Institution of Harvard University. ". . . a reasonable maximum for the world's future population is one person for each 2.5 acres on 40 per cent of the land area of the globe. This gives a figure of 5,200 millions, a population which at the present rate of increase would be reached in just a little over a century." East (p. 68) took his estimate that the global population was then doubling in 60 years from the Australian demographer George H. Knibbs.

2
Pearl and Reed
(1924, p. 632)[a]

Raymond Pearl was a professor of biometry and vital statistics at Johns Hopkins University. Pearl and Reed fitted a logistic curve to George H. Knibbs's data on global population size between 1660 and 1914. The fitted curve predicted that world population would eventually approach an upper limit of 2.026 billion, and that the population would first exceed 2 billion just before A.D. 2040.

6–12
Wickens
(1925, p. 9)[a]

"Our present world population is about 1,800 millions, and some inquirers estimate that the maximum attainable is 6,000 millions, while others take a figure nearly double this amount."

7.7–15.9
Penck
(1925, pp. 339–340)[a];
Penck
(1941, p. 11)[a]

Based on the most thickly settled lands in each region, Penck estimated the "average potential population density" and the "highest conceivable population density" of each of 11 climatic zones defined by earlier geographers, then multiplied each density by the area of the corresponding zone and summed over zones to obtain the "probable highest possible number of inhabitats" (7.7 billion) and the "highest conceivable number of inhabitants" (15.9 billion).

6.2
Fischer
(1925, p. 852),[b] via
Penck *(1941, p. 11)*[a]

Fischer applied more extensive statistics to the method of Penck (1925).

5.7
Smith
(1935, p. 41)[a]

Warren D. Smith, a geographer at the University of Oregon, attended Albrecht Penck's seminar on population and carrying capacity at the University of California. Smith used the classification of climates by the German geographer W. Köppen and Penck's formula for a food-limited population, region by region, to estimate a maximum human population of 5.666 billion. "It is of course quite improbable that the world population will ever reach the stupendous total estimated in the above paragraphs. Wars, diseases, the natural curbing of the birth rate with the shifting of civilization from an agricultural to an industrial basis, to say nothing of the operation of birth control and birth selection, which will probably be practised much more in the future than in the past, will tend to keep the population more or less static in many parts of the world, as it is to-day apparently in France."

2.6
Pearl and Gould
(1936)[a]

Pearl and Gould fitted a logistic to Knibbs's collected estimates of world population sizes from 1660 to 1914 with five additional estimates for 1920, 1927, 1930, another for 1930, and 1931. (p. 407) ". . . the asymptotic limit of the current cycle of growth is raised . . . to 2645.5 millions, to be closely approached in the year 2100 A.D. We make no formal prediction that this will represent the ultimate size of the world's human population. . . . But world population is now at a point on its logistic curve such that, unless new and unpredictable forces operate to alter its course, a slowing rate of growth will make itself increasingly manifest with the passage of time. Furthermore . . . the average density of world population is already approaching the point of producing uncomfortable results, under present conditions of living."

13.3
Hollstein *(1937),*[b]
via Penck *(1941,*
p. 11)[a] and Boerman
(1940, pp. 127–29)[a]

Hollstein assumed an average daily food requirement of 2,500 kilocalories per person. For different climatic zones, he considered relief and types of soil and estimated the percentage of land that could be used for agriculture and how many people could be fed per square kilometer of arable land. He estimated that 40 percent of land could be used for the main crops.

5.6–13.3
Boerman *(1940)*[a]

W. E. Boerman, editor of the *Dutch Journal of Economic Geography,* reviewed estimates of others, ranging from Ballod's 1912 estimate of 5.6 billion to Hollstein's 1937 estimate of 13.3 billion.

0.9–2.8
Pearson and Harper
(1945, p. 69)[a]

(p. 68) "Grain represents about three-fourths of man's food" and was taken as the sole constraint on population size in these calculations. As of 1945, Asia produced 269 kilograms of grain per person, Europe 358 kilograms, North America 845 kilograms and the world as a whole 351 kilograms; world population was estimated at 2.17 billion. (p. 69) ". . . there is little opportunity to upgrade the world's food habits in terms of total intake. . . ." Pearson and Harper divided the 1945 total grain production by the 1945 Asiatic, European and North American grain production per person to estimate the number of people grain supplies could support at Asiatic, European and North American standards. The 1945 grain production could feed 2.831 billion people at the Asiatic standard, 2.127 billion at the European standard and 0.902 billion at the North American standard.

7.0–8.6
Mukerjee *(1946,*
pp. 43, 84)[a]

Radhakamal Mukerjee, an economist at the University of Lucknow, India, argued that the key to solving the problems of poverty in southern and eastern Asia was massive emigration to the "empty lands of the world," principally (in Asia) Siberia, Manchuria, parts of what is now Indonesia and the Philippines; Australia and New Zealand; Africa; the United States and Canada; and Argentina and Brazil. He estimated the population capacity of these regions, in addition to their present populations, at 5.0 billion to 6.6 billion people. When this "immigration capacity" is added to his estimated world population (in 1930) of 2.0 billion, the total "population capacity" is apparently 7.0 billion to 8.6 billion.

5
Salter *(1946),*[b] via
Spengler *(1949,*
pp. 65–66)[a]

On 30 December 1946, R. M. Salter spoke to the American Association for the Advancement of Science in Boston under the title "World Soil and Fertilizer Resources in Relation to Food Needs." The Duke University economist Joseph J. Spengler (1949, p. 65) described his estimates as "careful" and reported (p. 66): "Salter's estimate means that at least 5 billion people can be supported at the set of standards assumed for 1960 by the F.A.O. He indicates that enough fertilizer is available for the cultivation of the 3.24 billion acres for five centuries at least."

6.5–10
Fawcett *(1947,*
p. 394)[a]

C. B. Fawcett, a professor of geography at the University of London, estimated that 30 percent of the total land area of the Earth is cultivable. He assumed that human population size was limited by food. He estimated that France had 400 people per square mile (154 per square kilometer) of cultivated land, and British India 600 people per square mile (232 per square kilometer) of cultivated land. At these densities, all the cultivable land in the world could feed roughly 6.5 billion or 10 billion people.

1.8–7.2
Spengler *(1949, p. 163)[a]*

"Given a cultivatable acreage of 4 billions, with nine tenths devoted to food production, and per capita requirements of 0.5–2.0 acres, we get a supportable population of 1.8–7.2 billions. But if, since land and population growth are unevenly divided, we fix this requirement at not less than one acre, we get a maximum of 3.6 billions. This figure may be raised to 4 billion or more, however, on the assumption of adequate improvement in food production and use. . . . Up to this point our discussion has been in terms of technological possibilities. In practice, however, the conversion of these possibilities into realities is conditioned by economic, political, and other circumstances, most of which give promise of reducing the extent to which the technological possibilities will be realized."
(p. 164) "Because fuels and metals are dissipatable and tend in time to be forthcoming only at rising costs, their supply may eventually prove inadequate to support both population growth and the system of living upon which the population insists. In this event fuel and mineral resources rather than food resources will become the limitational factor serving to check population growth. This type of limitation is most likely to be operative in industrial societies."

6–10
Darwin *(1952, pp. 129–30)[a]*

Charles Galton Darwin was the grandson of the evolutionist Charles Robert Darwin. "In view of the fact that it is only the existing vegetable kingdom that can be exploited, I do not believe there will be any revolutionary changes in agriculture but only steady improvements; the improvements will, so to speak, be described by increases in percentages, not by multiples of the present yields. The world will be covered by a population of the same sort of density as is now found in its richer agricultural districts, in countries such as China, India or much of Europe; . . . allowance must be made for differences of climate and of the natural fertility of the soils. . . . the population of the world is never likely to be more than about three to five times its present numbers." Darwin estimated the 1952 population of the Earth at 2 billion, so his upper limits were 6 billion to 10 billion.

50
Brown *(1954, pp. 146–47)[a]*

Food production from existing cultivated land, plus supplemental irrigation of a billion acres (1 acre ≈ 0.4 hectare) now under cultivation, plus 1.3 billion new acres of tropic and northern soils, plus complete irrigation of 200 million acres of desert and near-desert land could increase food production over the current level by a factor of three. Production from these sources plus increased yields from improved plant breeding and selection and foreseeable improvements in agricultural techniques could increase food production over the current level by a factor of six. Production from all these sources, plus a billion acres of algae farms, could increase food production over the current level by a factor of 25. ". . . if food habits were to change sufficiently so that the people of the world were content to derive their main nourishment from the products of algae farms and yeast factories, a world population of 50 billion persons could eventually be supported comfortably from the point of view of nutritional requirements."

3.7–7.7
Brown, Bonner and Weir *(1957, p. 67)[a]*

The low estimate assumed the current European level of productivity of land and the current European type of diet with 3,000 kilocalories per person per day. The high estimate assumed the current Japanese level of productivity of land in Asia, the European level elsewhere;

and the current Asiatic type of diet in Asia, the European type else-where, each at 2,500 kilocalories per person per day.

28
Clark *(1958,
pp. 104–5)*[a]

". . . the world possesses the equivalent of 77 million sq. km. of good temperate agricultural land. We may take as our standard that of the most productive farmers in Europe, the Dutch, who feed 385 people (at Dutch standards of diet, which give them one of the best health records in the world) per sq. km. of farm land, or 365 if we allow for the land required to produce their timber (in the most economic man-ner, in warm climates—pulp requirements can be obtained from sugar cane waste). Applying these standards throughout the world, as they could be with adequate skill and use of fertilizers, we find the world capable of supporting 28 billion people, or ten times its present popu-lation. This leaves us a very ample margin for land which we wish to set aside for recreation or other purposes."

30
Baade *(1960),*[b] via
Norse *(1992, p. 9)*[a]

"F. Baade, . . . assuming that the arable land area was between 2 bil-lion and 3 billion hectares and that average yields could rise to 5 tonnes of cereal equivalent per hectare, estimated the potential carrying capacity at some 30 billion. No consideration was given to whether production could be sustained at this level; to whether all arable land would be used for agriculture; or to the increase in indirect demands for cereals as people switch to higher value but lower calorie-content foods when their income grows." Assuming 3 billion hectares pro-duce 5 tonnes of cereal each and can support 30 billion people is equiv-alent to assuming average annual grain consumption per person is $3 \times 5 / 30 = 0.5$ tonne or 500 kilograms, disregarding seed and spoilage.

16–800
Kleiber *(1961,
pp. 337–41)*[a]

About 0.027 percent of the Earth's mass is carbon. One 70-kilogram man contains about 12 kilograms of carbon. Hence if all the carbon on the Earth were embodied in people (who would have to live by cannibalism alone), the population size could not exceed 10^{20}. Pota-toes sufficient to support one person for a year could be grown on 600 square meters of land, assuming that solar radiation were the only factor to limit plant growth. "In this way the earth could feed 0.8×10^{12} people." To arrive at 800 billion people, Kleiber must have assumed that 48 billion hectares would be planted in potatoes. This would be a challenging exercise, as the ice-free land of the Earth cov-ers only 13.3 billion hectares. Again assuming solar flux as the sole limitation, enough algae to feed a person for a year can be grown on 1 square meter, and enough eggs (allowing for the efficiency of grow-ing feed and converting the feed to animal products) on 30,000 square meters; hence the maximum supportable populations would be 600 times larger, or 480 trillion (for algae alone), and 50 times smaller, or 16 billion (for eggs alone).

10^{16}–10^{18} people,
or 10^7–10^9 billions,
that is, a billion bil-
lions
Fremlin *(1964,
p. 287)*[a]

"If heat removal were the sole limitation, then we could manage about 120 persons per square metre for an outer skin temperature [of struc-tures that cover the Earth] of 1000°C—which represents . . . a world population of 60 000 million million in 890 years' time. 1000°C may be a rather modest figure for the technology of AD 2854 and the pop-ulation could, as far as heat is concerned, be able to double again for each rise of absolute skin temperature of $2^{1/3}$ or 26 per cent. The diffi-culties in raising it much further while keeping all thermodynamic efficiencies high would, however, seem to be formidable. A rise to 2000°C would give us less than three further doublings. We seem, therefore, to have found one possible absolute limit to human population, due to the heat problem, which at the present rate would be reached 800–1000 years from now, with a world population of 10^{16}–10^{18}." The point of the article—written with a very dry humor—is not that such a heat limit is likely ever to be encountered but that, if people are not comfortable with the prospect of such population densities, then they must be willing to *choose* a lower population density at which they would be comfortable.

10
Cépède at al. *(1964, p. 461)*[a]

(p. 343) "The most plausible estimates of the total land surface capable of being cultivated give a figure of 7 billion hectares (17.3 billion acres). Of this, half is actually put to some use. To get an agricultural product out of the rest, enormous efforts, both of human labor and of investment, would be required. . . . What is needed, over and above the reclamation of unused land, is to increase the yield from land already under cultivation, especially in the just developing countries where yields are low." (p. 461) "Let us boldly envisage the prospect of a planet on which ten billion or more human beings shall live better than we live."

30
Schmitt *(1965, p. 652)*[a]

Schmitt (p. 648) analyzed "the possible food production ensuing from the application of conventional practices, or a foreseeable extension of conventional practices." He (p. 652) "estimated, after an examination of possible forces controlling the human population, that 30 billion people ultimately may lead fairly free and enriched lives on this planet. . . . the shortages of food in many areas of the world are caused not so much by the lack of the physical resources for food production, but by economic and sociopolitical factors. Current difficulties arising from dietary habits, traditional cultivation practices, restricted distribution, and other inefficiencies necessitate solutions that are principally socioeconomic in character. I want to stress this point. Socioeconomic restraints control food production before physical factors do, because the potential of *each* major mode—agriculture, silviculture, aquaculture, and microbial culture—in terms of the production of organic matter, is greater than the requirements of three billion people, or even of the 30 billion projected for the future. Yet, food shortages exist."

41
Zierhoffer *(1966)*,[b] via Smil *(1994, p. 256)*[a]

According to Smil, Zierhoffer assumed that 3,350 billion hectares of potentially arable land would produce as much food as Japan's farmland in the early 1960s.

47–157
Clark *(1967; 1977, p. 153)*[a]

"Each person's land requirements for American type food consumption are some 2000 sq. m., or one-fifth of a hectare (half an acre), or 2250 sq. m. including requirement of forest land. If we take world resources of agricultural land at 10.7 billion hectares of standard land equivalent, this could feed, at maximum standards, 47 billion people. To produce 250 kilograms of cereals (i.e. real minimum subsistence requirements) under the most productive conditions, as in Japan, requires 640 sq. m. . . . For people living at Japanese standards of food consumption and Asian standards of timber requirements only 680 sq. m. / person is required, and the world's potential agricultural and forest land could supply the needs of 157 billion people."

79–1,022
De Wit *(1967)*[a]

A computer model, calibrated in the Netherlands, predicted the maximal potential photosynthetic productivity of land, depending on the number of months above 10°C and the angle of elevation of the sun at different latitudes. With no allowance of land for cities and recre-

ation, and assuming optimal soil minerals and water, enough carbohydrates could be grown to furnish an assumed requirement of a
million kilocalories per person per year to 1,022 billion people.
Allowing 750 square meters per person for cities and recreation lowers
the total to 146 billion.

(p. 318) "This figure, 146 billion, may be somewhat too high since
some land is not suitable for urban use, agriculture, or even recreation.
On the other hand, the value may be increased by shifting a part of
the population from highly productive areas in the tropics to more
northern latitudes." Adding to the diet 200 grams of meat per person
per day lowers the maximum population to 126 billion. If land for
non-agricultural purposes is increased to 1,500 square meters per person, the 146 billion figure falls to 79 billion.

1
Hulett *(1970,
p. 161)[a]*

"In all the areas treated [food, wood products and nonrenewable
resources], it appears that of the order of a billion people is the maximum population supportable by the present agricultural and industrial
system (and the present work force) of the world at U.S. levels of
affluence. It would obviously be very difficult to produce food and
raw materials at the present rate with the smaller work force consistent with a world population of about a billion people; therefore, this
number is, if anything, too large to be self-supporting at U.S. affluence levels. As our technology, knowledge, and industrial and
agricultural systems expand so can the optimum population. . . ."

40–60
Austin and Brewer
(1971, p. 28)[a]

Austin and Brewer (1971, pp. 26–28) modified the logistic equation
$dP/dt = rP(K-P)$ to a form that allows the growth rate per person to
increase, but only up to a finite upper limit: $dP/dt
= r(1 - e^{-sP})P(K-P)$. Assuming that the maximum population size is
$K = 50$ billion people (and putting $r = 2 \times 10^{-12}$, $s = 5 \times 10^{-11}$) made the
theoretical curve approximate past population sizes. Based on a sensi-
tivity analysis, "the upper bound $[K]$ likely will lie somewhere
between 40 and 60 billion. . . ." This equation predicted that the maximal absolute increase in population size will occur in 2060, when the
population size reaches 38 billion.

(p. 47) ". . . the predicted upper bound of 50 billion people is based
on the assumption that all necessary developments and full use of the
earth's life-support capabilities can be achieved without major set-
backs. . . . this seems to be over-optimistic, and unless the population
is controlled humanely, the . . . birth rate minus death rate, will be
governed by high death rates."

0.5–1.2
Ehrlich *(1971, p. 8)[a]*

"There are 3.6 billion human beings on the face of the Earth.
According to our best estimates, there are somewhere between three
and seven times more people than this planet can possibly maintain
over a long period of time."

35–40
Mückenhausen
(1973),[b] via Heilig
(1994)[a]

According to Heilig (1994), "Mückenhausen's estimate was based on
a report of the U.S. President's Science Advisory Committee in 1967
which analyzed the world's production capacity of soils." The report
was by Revelle et al. (1967).

100
Lieth *(1973, p. 303)[a]*
and Blaxter *(1986,
p. 90)[a]*

Lieth estimated that, as of 1950, the annual net primary production
for the land vegetation of the Earth was 100 billion tonnes of dry
matter, with an energy content of 426×10^{15} kilocalories. He estimated the energy content of the net primary production of the seas at
261×10^{15} kilocalories. Lieth's sole reference to human population was
(p. 303): "The productivity of vegetation is one major aspect of the

sustained carrying capacity of the earth for man." Without further comment, Blaxter (1986, p. 90) attributed to Lieth the estimate of 100 billion people as the Earth's carrying capacity.

38–48
Revelle *(1974,*
p. 168)[a]

"Omitting the humid Tropics and taking account of the insufficiency of water where it is needed, the total potentially arable land is reduced to 2.5 billion hectares (the present 1.4 billion plus 1.1 billion) and the potential gross cropped area reaches just under 4.1 billion hectares. If 10 percent of this potential gross cropped area were set aside to grow fibers and other nonfood products, and if technology and purchased inputs of production (irrigation water, fertilizer, high-yielding seeds, plant protection, farm tools, farm machinery and farm practices based on scientific knowledge) equivalent to those used in Iowa corn farming were applied to the remainder, a diet based on 4,000 to 5,000 kilocalories of edible plant material could be provided for between 38 and 48 billion people. . . ."

6.7
Buringh et al.
(1975)[b] **and Buringh**
and van Heemst
(1977),[b] **via Hall**
(1980, p. 64)[a] **and**
Norse *(1992, p. 9)[a]*

According Hall (1980, p. 64), Buringh et al. estimated that the present land area is 13,548 million hectares. Of this, 1,406 million hectares (10 percent) were then cultivated. "Potential agricultural land" was 3,419 million hectares (25 percent of land) and "maximum agricultural land" was 2,462 million hectares (18 percent of land); I do not know how these terms were defined. According to Norse (1992, p. 9), using modern agriculture on all "potential agriculture land" and deducting 20 percent from total production for seed and for storage losses, the world could produce net 13,156 million tonnes of grain. Assuming an average grain consumption of 800 kilograms per person per year, this production could feed 16.4 billion people. Using modern agriculture on present agricultural land and again deducting 20 percent from total production for seed and for storage losses, the world could produce net 5,338 million tonnes of grain, sufficient to feed 6.7 billion people. Finally, using labor-oriented agriculture on maximum agricultural land, and assuming only two-thirds of the land is cropped with grains, the world could produce 1,606 million tonnes of grain, sufficient to feed 2 billion people. Hall (1980, p. 64) and Norse (1992, p. 9) agreed in quoting 1,606 million tonnes of grain as the potential production using labor-oriented agriculture on maximum agricultural land. But Hall asserted that this production could support 5.356 billion people, equivalent to 300 kilograms of grain per person per year; Norse asserted that this production could support 2.7 billion people, equivalent to about 600 kilograms of grain per person per year. I calculate that this production could feed 2 billion people if the annual consumption per person were 800 kilograms.

5–7
Whittaker and Lik-
ens *(1975, pp. 317–*
18)[a]

". . . no carrying capacity can be defined independent of technology. Furthermore, at least two concepts should be distinguished: (a) a favorable or optimum population for an industrialized world with a standard of living corresponding, say, to that of Europe 20 years ago, before the recent industrial overgrowth of the West, and (b) a maximum population for a world predominantly nonindustrial. A reasonable estimate for the first of these might be a world population of 1 billion at an American standard of living (Hulett, 1970) or 2 to 3 billion at a more frugal European standard. . . . An agricultural world, in which most human beings are peasants, should be able to support several billion human beings, perhaps 5–7 billion, probably more if the large agricultural population were supported by industry promoting agricultural productivity. . . .The uncertain future role of technology and cost of energy to agriculture makes a much larger estimate of world carrying capacity seem questionable."

40
Revelle *(1976, p. 177)*[a]

"The 3.2 billion arable hectares cover 24 percent of the land area of the earth, about 2.3 times the currently cultivated area and more than three times the area actually harvested in any given year. Of this total .3 billion hectares require irrigation for even one crop. . . . As a result of the uneven distribution of runoff only a third of the land that is potentially arable with irrigation can actually be irrigated (reducing the total potentially arable land to three billion hectares), and the potential increase of the gross cropped area (that is, the sum of potentially arable areas multiplied by the number of four-month-growing-season crops that could be raised in each area) through irrigation development is limited to 1.1 billion hectares. Without irrigation three crops could be grown on .5 billion hectares in the humid Tropics and two crops on .8 billion hectares in subhumid regions. One crop could be grown without irrigation on 1.5 billion hectares. Hence the potential gross cropped area without irrigation is 4.6 billion hectares and with irrigation is 5.7 billion. Of this total, however, 1.5 billion hectares lies in the humid Tropics—where, except for the island of Java and a few other areas with deep, recently weathered soils, no technology is currently available for high-yielding agriculture on a large scale. The potential gross cropped area accessible to relatively high-yielding cultivation with present technology is therefore somewhat more than 4.2 billion hectares. About 10 percent of the gross cropped area would continue to be needed to grow fibers, beverages and other nonfood crops, leaving a total of 3.8 billion gross cropped hectares outside the humid Tropics for human food production in the future. Making the conservative assumption that lower-quality soils and uneven topography would limit the average yields to half those obtained in the U.S. Midwest, 11.4 billion tons of food grains or their equivalent in food energy could be grown on this potential gross cropped area, enough for a minimum diet of 2,500 kilocalories per day for nearly 40 billion people (if pest losses and nonfood uses could be kept to 10 percent of the harvest)."

17
Eyre *(1978, p. 42)*[a] and Blaxter *(1986, p. 90)*[a]

Eyre estimated that human activities reduced the Earth's average annual net primary production aboveground (dry weight) from a potential of just over 78 billion tonnes (p. 31) to a little over 50 billion tonnes by 1975 (p. 42); and that about half the aboveground production returns to the soil in spite of people's best efforts, leaving about 25 billion tonnes for possible human consumption (p. 42). "At the present time, the average person in North America and much of Europe eats the equivalent of one dry-weight [metric] ton per annum. (This is taking account of the fact that much vegetable 'food' is literally wasted at both the manufacturing and domestic stages, and that a very large amount of vegetable material goes into the production of a relatively small quantity of meat. . . .) Apart from this, in Britain each of us consumes almost half a ton dry-weight equivalent of timber in the form of paper, packaging and various other products, and in the USA the per capita consumption is far greater." Taking each gram of plant product as about 4 kilocalories of energy, Eyre's estimated consumption of 1 tonne per person per year is equivalent to 4 million kilocalories per person per year, intermediate between Hulett's high estimate of 7 million kilocalories and several low estimates of 1 million kilocalories or less. Eyre viewed current destruction of all kinds of vegetation, including forests and grasslands, as exceeding replacement, and did not estimate a maximum supportable population. Blaxter (1986, p. 90) attributed to Eyre without comment an upper limit of 17 billion people. I infer that Blaxter used Penck's formula: 17 billion people $\approx$ 50 billion tonnes dry-weight net primary production times 0.5 harvestable fraction divided by 1.5 tonnes annual consumption per person for food, fodder and forest products.

One could equally well attribute to Eyre estimates of 26 billion people potentially supported by the 78 billion tonnes of net primary product in the original landscape, or 7 billion people that could be supported "[i]f the whole of the vegetated land surface—grassland, scrubland and tundra as well as forest—were converted to agricultural usages in the same proportions and at the same levels of productivity as at present, [which] would reduce above-ground mean annual NPP to no more than 20 billion mt [tonnes] . . ." (p. 40).

1,000 Marchetti *(1978,* *pp. iv–v; 1979)*[a]	". . . a very large number of people is assumed, and a technological scenario is designed for a *stationary* system to hold them. . . . The number of people finally chosen, 10^{12}, is intentionally unrealistic, simply to stress the problems to the utmost. . . . it is possible to sustain this number of people without exhausting any basic resource, including environment. . . . from a technological point of view a trillion people can live beautifully on the Earth, for an unlimited time, without exhausting any primary resource and without overloading the environment. . . . most of the physical limits to growth stem from an inappropriate frame of reference." Marchetti proposed to house two-thirds of the population in floating cities on the sea, one-third on the land, in three-dimensional single-roof towns built from abundant elements in the Earth's crust (p. 7): ". . . we visualize 10 percent of the globe built-up, all the rest being left wild. . . ." (If all land including Antarctica, namely 148 million square kilometers, were used to provide habitation for one-third of 10^{12} people, the density would be about 2,250 people per square kilometer, about ten times the 1990 density of the United Kingdom [237 per square kilometer] and about half the 1990 density of Singapore [4,464 per square kilometer]. If one-tenth of the Earth's entire surface [510 million square kilometers, including land and sea] housed 10^{12} people, the density of almost 68,000 per square kilometer would be roughly 15 times the 1990 density of Singapore. Assuring each person gross living space of 100 square meters would require an average of nearly seven stories over the occupied tenth of the Earth's surface; assuring 1,000 square meters per person, or roughly 1 acre for a family of four persons, would require 68-story buildings.) Energy consumption was assumed to be constrained not by supplies, but by the amount of heat that can be radiated into space, after the albedo of the Earth's surface was modified by human habitations. Staple foods would be produced microbiologically from inorganic substrates.
14 Kovda *(1980,* *pp. 4–5)*[a]	". . . modern science, technology, and culture can increase agricultural productivity severalfold on land already developed and on cultivated fields, *provided that social obstacles are removed.* In the opinion of Soviet scientists, currently cultivated soils (15 million square kilometers) could feed a population of 14 billion, under favorable social conditions and with correct scientific and technical use [reference omitted]. Current crop yields for a large part of the planet are inexcusably low."
less than 4.5 Mann *(1981,* *p. 261)*[a]	"The real dreamers are those who assert that we can create a sustainable economy, with a high average standard of living for all, in a healthy environment—with the present world population of 4.5 thousand millions, or even more."

2.0–3.9
Westing *(1981)*[a]

(p. 177) "Two alternative levels of standard of living, and the world populations that will permit their achievement, are estimated below, being referred to as 'affluent' and 'austere'. The first is modelled after the level of an average of the world's 27 richest nations, and the second after that of an average of 43 nations of average wealth. These two groups of nations were delineated purely on the basis of gross national product (GNP) *per caput.*" The 27 rich nations had 1975 GNP per person at least twice the 1975 world average; the 43 nations of average wealth had 1975 GNP per person between twice and one-half of the global average 1975 GNP per person.

(p. 178) "The approach employed for establishing a global carrying-capacity for the human species has been to determine the *per caput* level of utilization of five crucial reusable or renewable resources—total land area, cultivated land area, forest land area, cereals (grain), and wood—at the affluent and austere levels (as defined above), and then to compare these utilization data with the global availability of the respective resources." The technology and politics of 1975 were assumed to govern the global supply of resources, that is, global production in 1975 was taken as fixed.

(p. 178) "Indeed, if the whole world were to be able to live at what is here defined as an affluent standard of living, then the total world population would have to be of the order of two thousand million people by any of the resource standards here employed. . . . On the other hand, an austere standard of living, as here defined, could be attained at a world population of three thousand millions or so—that is, perhaps one-quarter to one-third less than the current level. If the USA alone were used as a model, world population would have to be between 1.5 and three thousand millions, depending upon the resource standards that are considered to be most important."

12
Gates *(1982,*
p. 1044)[a]

"Although man can come close to feeding the present world population, the chances of continuing to do so in the future are diminishing. If the world population ever approaches 12,000,000,000 (in 1971 it was about 3,706,000,000), it is likely that mass starvation will occur in many underdeveloped countries."

7.5
Gilland *(1979; quotation from 1983,*
p. 206)[a]

The limiting factor will be food. "Assuming a per capita requirement of 1 tge [tonne of grain equivalent] per year, the global carrying capacity is 7.5 billion people. . . . Revelle's vision of 40 billion people living on a gross per capita production of 2,500 kcal per day cannot be regarded as anything but a nightmare to be avoided at all costs. A world population of 7.5 billion will be reached in the second decade of the twenty-first century. Recent projections show that population is very unlikely to stabilize at less than 9 billion, and that it may well reach 12 billion. Our assumed dietary allowance of 9,000 kcal cannot be realized as a world average unless population declines after stabilizing." (A daily dietary allowance of 9,000 kilocalories equals an annual allowance of 3.3 million kilocalories. If this is to be obtained from 1 tonne of grain equivalent, then each gram of grain is supposed to yield 3.3 kilocalories.)

4.0–32.8
Higgins et al. *(1983,*
p. 106)[a]

Higgins et al. estimated the physical potential "population supporting capacities" of lands in five regions of the developing world for the years 1975 and 2000: Africa, Southwest Asia, South America, Central America and Southeast Asia. They excluded China and all developed countries. Low, intermediate and high levels of inputs were considered. (p. viii) "Factors limiting attainment of this physical potential, i.e. social, economic and institutional factors, are not included nor are land requirements for non-food crops and demands for diets above the minimum requirement level." To obtain potential population supporting capacities, Higgins et al. divided the country-specific calorie requirements per person (established by the Food and Agricultural Organization) into the rain-fed plus irrigated potential calorie production. Assuming "massive and unrestricted movement of surplus potential food production and labour within and between all five regions," in the year 1975 4.0 billion people could be fed with low inputs and 32.8 billion could be fed with high inputs; in the year 2000 5.6 billion could be fed with low inputs and 33.4 billion with high inputs. If surplus potential food production and labor could move only within countries, with low inputs, 54 of 117 countries studied had too little land to feed their 1975 populations and 64 countries would have too little land to feed the populations projected for the year 2000; "the size of population exceeding the potential [by 2000] is 503 million people" (p. x.).

6.1
Farrell, Sanderson
and Vo *(1984,
p. 19)[a]*

"We believe that *the world possesses the potential to feed a growing population of 6.1 billion people moderately better by the year 2000 than it fed 4.3 billion in 1980.* But we should stress the word *potential.* To do so will require large investments to improve the infrastructure of agriculture, increased investments in research and education to stimulate development and application to productivity-enhancing technologies, public policies to provide greater economic incentives to agricultural producers in many developing countries, and expanded international trade. We estimate that some 85 percent of projected production increases will depend on greater productivity of resources and only 15 percent on expanding the cultivated land base."

300
Hardin *(1986,
pp. 602–3)[a]*

"There is no agreed upon metric to which we can reduce the various goods so that we can compare the level of living of one people with another. There is, however, a useful partial measure, and that is the units of energy used per capita per year in the various countries. . . . On this crude measure, the average inhabitant of the world is about 60 times as well off as an average Ethiopian, while Americans are more than 300 times as well off. If everyone lived on the energy budget of the Ethiopians, the earth might support 60 times the present population, or about 300 billion people. The figure just given is only a crude estimate."

22
Calvin *(1986),[b]* via
Hudson *(1989,
p. 276)[a]*

According to Hudson, Melvin Calvin, in an unpublished letter to David Pimentel, estimated the total energy available for food production as 55 trillion (5.5×10^{13}) kilocalories per day, sufficient to provide 2,500 kilocalories per day to 22 billion people ($5.5 \times 10^{13} / 2,500 = 22 \times 10^9$). To obtain 55 trillion kilocalories per day, Calvin multiplied an assumed 5.5×10^{16} kilocalories per day of total solar energy reaching the Earth by 0.2, the fraction of the Earth's surface assumed to be arable land, multiplied again by 0.001, the assumed photosynthetic efficiency of crops, and multiplied again by 0.5, an assumed maximal possible food production efficiency (Hudson stated that the current estimate of this factor is 0.1). (Unfortunately, the published arithmetic is wrong, probably as a result of a typographical error: $5.5 \times 10^{16} \times 0.2 \times 0.001 \times 0.5 = 5.5 \times 10^{12}$, not 5.5×10^{13}. According to David Pimentel [personal communication, 29 December 1994], the total solar energy should have been 5.5×10^{17} kilocalories per day; in arriving at this figure, Calvin included the Arctic and Antarctic, which increased the area that receives sunlight by more than 30 percent.)

9.8–19.3
Hudson *(1989,
p. 277)[a]*

Based on data from the United States Department of Agriculture for the year 1986, Hudson estimated world grain production at 339 kilograms per person (1.683 billion tonnes divided by 4.96 billion people).

If the total area cultivated for grain in 1986 (710 million hectares) produced the same average grain yield (4.7 tonnes per hectare) as the United States in 1986, and if everyone consumed the same amount of grain as the average person in the U.S., then the world could feed 9.8 billion people. If biotechnology or other advances were able to double average world grain yields to 9.4 tonnes per hectare on a smaller total area (564 million hectares), the world could feed 15.6 billion people at the 1986 U.S. level of consumption. "Finally, if all semi-arable land [700 million hectares] were pressed into emergency service and if yields could be kept high," at 9.4 tonnes per hectare, then 19.3 billion people could be fed at the 1986 U.S. level of consumption.

2.8–5.5
Chen *(1990, p. 3),*[a]
Millman et al.
(1991, p. 2)[a]

The population potentially supported by the 1988 primary food supply on a basic (principally vegetarian) diet was 5.5 billion; on an improved diet (with about 15 percent of calories from animal products) was 3.7 billion; and on a "full-but-healthy diet (about 25 percent of calories from animal products)" was 2.8 billion people. The population potentially supported by the 1989 primary food supply on a basic diet was 5.9 billion; on an improved diet was 3.9 billion; and on a "full-but-healthy" diet was 2.9 billion people. "Of course, more food probably could and would have been produced if more people had had the means to purchase it" (Millman et al. 1991, p. 2). ". . . these estimates . . . assume a total waste factor of 40 percent to account for losses both between harvest and retail and between retail purchase and actual consumption. The global average caloric requirement used, for consistency with previous years' estimates, is derived from the national caloric requirements figures produced by the FAO . . . these requirements figures included an allowance of 10 percent for post-retail loss. The implication is that our estimates are double-counting post-retail loss, and therefore should be viewed as quite conservative indications of how many people could receive a given diet based on total food supply" (Millman et al. 1991, p. 19).

less than 5.3
Raven *(1991,*
p. 265)[a]

"There is no evidence that the world can sustain its present population, much less a larger one."

7.7
Meadows et al.
(1992, p. 201)[a]

"The sustainable society shown in Scenario 10 is one that we believe the world could actually attain, given the knowledge about planetary systems available to us. It has 7.7 billion people, and enough food, consumer goods, and services to support every one of them in material comfort. It is expending considerable effort and employing continually improving technology to protect its land, reduce its pollution, and use its nonrenewable resources with high efficiency. Because its growth slows and eventually stops, its problems are manageable and are being managed. . . . Scenario 10 is not the only sustainable outcome the World3 model can produce. . . . There could be more food and less industrial output or vice versa, more people living with a smaller stream of industrial goods or fewer people living with more."

23.8
Tuckwell and Koz-
iol *(1992, p. 200)*[a]

"If the present logistic regime persists, the world population will double in 47 years and the eventual world population will be 23.8 billion. This will be practically attained by the year 2200. The estimates of the final continental populations are as follows: Africa, 10.57 billion; Asia, 11.08 billion; Commonwealth of Independent States, 320 million; Europe, 556 million; Latin America, 899 million; North America, 336 million; and Oceania, 40 million. . . . In all cases the predictions are much higher than those of the United Nations."

much less than 5.5
Ehrlich et al. *(1993, p. 27)*[a]

"Were society to concentrate its efforts on improving agricultural production and distribution systems worldwide, substantially more food could be grown than is grown today—for a while. It is doubtful, however, whether food security could be achieved indefinitely for a global population of 10 or 12 billion people. Rather, it seems likely that a sustainable population, one comfortably below Earth's nutritional carrying capacity, will number far fewer than today's 5.5 billion people; how many fewer will depend in part on how seriously Earth's carrying capacity will have been degraded in the process of supporting the population overshoot."

12–14
Heilig *(1993, p. iii; 1994)*[a]

"(1) The biophysical maximum carrying capacity of the earth, which is roughly equivalent to its "Net Primary Production' " is reduced by "(2) technical and logistic restrictions [and] limitations, (3) environmental constraints and feedback mechanisms, (4) economic limitations, and (5) socio-cultural conditions. . . . Technology could easily increase the earth's carrying capacity for sustaining a 12 to 14 billion world population if it is applied with ecological care and in the framework of an economically sound and socially-just development policy."

at least 10
Waggoner *(1994, pp. 15, 17)*[a]

(p. 15) ". . . a vegetarian diet for ten billion could be furnished by present agricultural production but . . . production totaling 10,000 [kilocalories per day] for ten billion [people] obviously would exceed the capability of present agriculture on present cropland."

(p. 17) "The present food reaching people could not sustain the ten billion. If the feeding of farm animals were eliminated and people ate all the grains and oilseeds now produced, the ten billion barely could survive on the calories. The protein in all the grains and oilseeds would, however, support them."

For the future, Waggoner envisioned farming on 2.8 billion hectares (roughly twice present cropland) with yields sufficient to feed each of 10 billion people 3,000 to 6,000 kilocalories per day.

(p. 39) "Other things being equal, the fallout from producing the food for ten billion will be diminished as land is saved for Nature by optimizing all factors to produce more tons / hectare."

3
Pimentel et al. *(1994, p. 363)*[a]

(p. 363) "Worldwide, renewable solar energy could be developed to provide 200 quads of sustainable energy per year, while maintaining needed agricultural and forestry production. [A quad is one quadrillion, or 10^{15}, British thermal units or 1,055 petajoules. Thirty quads equal one terawatt-year, or 10^{12} watt-years. For comparison, total worldwide commercial energy production in 1989 was approximately 295 quads, of which a bit over 7 quads was primary electricity from geothermal, wind and hydro sources. World Resources Institute 1992, p. 314, reported 1989 total commercial energy production as 310,972 petajoules, geothermal and wind primary electricity as 141 petajoules, hydroelectricity as 7,539 petajoules. Thus Pimentel et al. assumed less future solar energy than the total currently derived largely from fossil sources, but much more solar energy than is currently used to produce primary electricity.] That combined with active conservation efforts, a satisfactory standard of living would be possible for everyone. However, the human population would have to be much smaller than the present 5.5 billion.

"Based on the estimate that 0.5 ha per capita is necessary for an adequate food supply and assuming a program of soil conservation was implemented, it would be possible to sustain a global population of approximately 3 billion humans. [For comparison, the cropland per person in 1990 was 0.28 hectare; World Resources Institute 1992, p. 274.] With a self-sustaining renewable energy system producing 200 quads of energy per year and providing each person with 5,000 liters of oil equivalents per year (one-half of America's current consumption / yr but an increase for most people in the world), a population of 1 to 2 billion could be supported living in relative prosperity."

10–11
Smil *(1994, pp. 280–81)*[a]

". . . reduction of the irrationalities and inefficiencies of the status quo offers a large and highly cost-effective source of food, both as crops already grown but wasted, and as new harvests that can be produced without increasing existing inputs. Cautious estimates presented in this essay uncover a resource slack equivalent to feeding adequately another 2.5–3 billion people. And equally conservative appraisals of new productive inputs needed to feed yet another 2–2.5 billion people show that we could do so without recourse to revolutionary bioengineering advances. Consequently, it would seem realistic to conclude that the Earth could support a population of 10–11 billion people during the next century. . . .
"Assurance of a globally adequate food supply will obviously . . . have to contain a strong component of what I would label the rich world's self-serving altruism. Except in direst emergencies this should not include any massive food aid, but it will require greatly expanded transfers of efficient farming techniques abroad, as well as the modification of unsustainable diets at home."

11–44
Wetenschappelijke
Raad voor het
Regeringsbeleid
(Scientific Council
for the Dutch Government) *(1994, p. 9)* [a]

Between 11 billion and 44 billion people can be fed, depending on which of four scenarios is accepted as desirable.

---

[a] I checked the original source.
[b] I checked the secondary source.

APPENDIX 4

_____

Verbal Definitions of Human Carrying Capacity
(in Chronological Order)

source	definition
House and Williams (1975, pp. 54–55)	". . . the carrying capacity theme becomes much more complex when applied to the evolution of human activities. It seems clear that rather than defining carrying capacity as a certain level of population or some other point criterion, it must be defined in terms of a rather complicated function or set of functions, which would include a number of regional characteristics and economic parameters and would make explicit the possible trade-offs that are implicit in the definition. This requires a representation of the set of social trade-offs between the citizen's concept of environmental quality and the degree to which that society desires or needs to utilize the production and assimilation capabilities of the natural environment. In examining the critical inter-relationships between human and economic activity, we must be concerned with a number of resource limits and environmental factors that may act as constraints or dampening forces in the dynamic inter-action of population growth, related socio-economic activity, resource base, and environment as an assimilator of waste. . . . "[For] a closed system, carrying capacity would be seen as the ability of a system to produce desired outputs (goods and services) from a given resource base while, at the same time, maintaining desired quality levels. For an open system, the definition would further have to allow for import of both resources and goods and services, and the export of output and residuals. . . . [There are] four relationships that are relevant to the overall measurement of carrying capacity. 1. Resource-production functions: the capacity of available resources to sustain rates of resource use in producing the system output. 2. Resource-residuals functions: the capacity of the environmental media to assimilate wastes and residuals from production and consumption . . . at acceptable quality levels. 3. Infrastructure-congestion functions: the capacity of infrastructure, the distribution and delivery systems, to handle the flow of goods and services and resources. 4. Production-societal functions: the capacity of both resources and production outputs to provide acceptable quality of life levels. "Working from these four relationships, then, human carrying capacity is defined as the level of human activity that a region can sustain at acceptable 'quality of life' levels. "The high degree of interrelation among resources, environmental media, and desired quantity and quality states for human and associated socioeconomic activity underscores the fact that trade-offs must inevitably be made among desired production-consumption levels, resource uses, and a clean, healthy, and pleasant environment. From this perspective, carrying capacity must be interpreted as a variable socially determined within our understanding of economic, social, and environmental values and their relative contribution in maintaining quality of life levels."

Whittaker and Likens *(1975, pp. 314–15)*	"Both the production by the biosphere and man's effects on it bear on what ought to be a guiding question for man's policy in occupying and using the world. This question is the world's carrying capacity for man: the size of the human population that can be supported on a long-term, steady-state basis by the world's resources without detriment to the biosphere or exhaustion of non-renewable resources that are reasonably available. . . . Neither for North America nor for the world can a carrying capacity be defined unless a standard of living and a role of technology are first specified. If the role of technology is large, a time scale for exhaustion of resources may need to be part of the definition; but this time scale itself is (given the uncertainties of substitution and feasible use of low-grade resources) almost indeterminable."
United Nations *(1980, reprinted in Ghosh 1984, p. 74)*	"The carrying capacity, however, is not given exogenously; it is determined endogenously. This implies that development strategies, encompassing interrelated sets of goals and policy measures, can make it possible to have a continuing expansion of carrying capacity."
Simon and Kahn *(1984, p. 45)*	"Because of increases in knowledge, the earth's 'carrying capacity' has been increasing throughout the decades and centuries and millennia to such an extent that the term 'carrying capacity' has by now no useful meaning. These trends strongly suggest a progressive improvement and enrichment of the earth's natural resource base, and of mankind's lot on earth."
Muscat *(1985, p. 20)*	"In sum, the closer a low-income agricultural region or country is to having no trade, only marginal technological improvements available for adoption, no effective institutional base for spreading such improvements as are known and warranted, no vent for surplus [population] in the face of declining marginal returns to incremental arable land, and population growth more rapid than productivity growth, the closer it is to the simple model of a country approaching its carrying capacity ceiling. . . . [T]he key is the speed with which the constraints are pushed back."
Kirchner et al. *(1985, p. 45)*	"The *carrying capacity* of a particular region is the maximum population of a given species that can be supported indefinitely, allowing for seasonal and random changes, without any degradation of the natural resource base that would diminish this maximum population in the future. The concept of carrying capacity is familiar to biologists and wildlife managers, who devised it to express the capacity of natural areas (ecosystems) to support animal life. With modifications, it is also an important measure of the ability of regions to support human populations. Carrying capacity is, therefore, an important concept for the work of development economists, planners, and political decision makers." Kirchner et al. pointed out that it is necessary to allow for seasonal and random changes. Fearnside put this observation to work in 1986.
Thurow *(1986, p. 22)*	"If the world's population had the productivity of the Swiss, the consumption habits of the Chinese, the egalitarian instincts of the Swedes, and the social discipline of the Japanese, then the planet could support many times its current population without privation for anyone. On the other hand, if the world's population had the productivity of Chad, the consumption habits of the United States, the inegalitarian instincts of India, and the social discipline of Argentina, then the planet could not support anywhere near its current numbers."

Thurow's four dimensions are productivity, consumption habits, egalitarianism and social discipline.

Gever et al. *(1986)*

(p. 7) "Human survival, except in the most primitive societies, is now contingent on the ability to obtain energy for our nonliving support systems. The best way to estimate the bounds on what people can and cannot do—that is, the carrying capacity for humans—is to examine the amount of energy available to human populations and the ways in which that energy is used."

(pp. 15–16) "The key to reconciling the use of nonrenewable resources with the concept of carrying capacity lies in the rapid adaptability of humans. We would say that *a population, human or otherwise, is exceeding its carrying capacity if severe hardships and / or population contraction become inevitable.* . . . history is full of examples in which humans adjusted quickly to the absence of a particular resource by finding substitutes and averted substantial hardship.

"In short, simply because we are using certain resources faster than they are replenished does not necessarily mean that we are exceeding our carrying capacity and have doomed ourselves to a population collapse. But, on the other hand, the longer we use resources unsustainably, the closer we come to the edge of our carrying capacity and the more difficult it will be to back away from it."

Hardin
(1986, p. 603)

"When dealing with human beings there is no unique figure for carrying capacity. So when a pronatalist asserts (Revelle 1974) that the world can easily support 40 to 50 billion people—some ten times the present population—he need not be contradicted. . . . The naive question, 'What is the human carrying capacity of the earth?' evokes a reply that is of no human use. No thoughtful person is willing to assume that mere animal survival is acceptable when the animal is *Homo sapiens*. We want to know what the environment will carry in the way of cultural amenities, where the word culture is taken in the anthropological sense to include all of the artifacts of human existence: institutions, buildings, customs, inventions, knowledge. Energy consumption is a crude measure of the involvement of culture. It may not be the best measure possible, but it will do for a first approach. When dealing with human problems, I propose that we abandon the term *carrying capacity* in favor of *cultural carrying capacity* or, more briefly *cultural capacity*. As defined, the cultural capacity of a territory will always be less than its carrying capacity (in the simple animal sense). Cultural capacity is inversely related to the (material) quality of life presumed. Arguments about the proper cultural capacity revolve around our expectations for the quality of life. Given fixed resources and well-defined values, cultural capacity, like its parent carrying capacity, is a conservative concept."

Fearnside *(1986, p. 73)*

"The basic definition of sustainable carrying capacity . . . is: *the maximum number of persons that can be supported in perpetuity on an area, with a given technology and set of consumptive habits, without causing environmental degradation.*"

King
(1987, p. 7)

"In its simplest form, carrying capacity can be expressed as the size of population which may be sustained by a given territory at a given physical standard of living. The concept is, of course, an extension of the biological definition, but when applied to human societies, it becomes infinitely more complex, infinitely more subtle. Not only do cultural, economic and political factors come into play; human societies have the possibility of expanding their carrying capacity through the deliberate selection and pursuit of development options which allow for the enhancement and sustainable use of physical resources while ensuring that economic growth is not surpassed by population growth and the material demands of individuals. It is not, of course, a matter of physical resources alone, for development potential is determined also by a host of other factors: technology, education, agricultural management and land tenure systems, trading opportunities with the outside world, legal and incentive systems or political will."

World Commission on Environment and Development *(1987, p. 8)*

"Humanity has the ability to make development sustainable—to ensure that it meets the needs of the present without compromising the ability of future generations to meet their own needs. The concept of sustainable development does imply limits—not absolute limits but limitations imposed by the present state of technology and social organization on environmental resources and by the ability of the biosphere to absorb the effects of human activities. But technology and social organization can be both managed and improved to make way for a new era of economic growth. The Commission believes that widespread poverty is no longer inevitable."

Srinivasan, in Lee et al. *(1988, p. 13)*

". . . the concept of population-carrying capacity: the maximum population that can be sustained indefinitely into the future."

Demeny *(1988, pp. 215–16)*

"As applied to human populations, the concept of carrying capacity is obviously a slippery one. Man is a toolmaking animal, capable of squeezing out of his environment more than undisturbed nature would provide for his needs. . . . in contrast to the case of animal ecology, the capacity of a given environment to support human populations can expand relatively rapidly. On the other hand, . . . for humans, a physical definition of needs may be irrelevant. Human needs and aspirations are culturally determined. . . ."

Gilbert and Braat *(1991, pp. 3–4)*

"Human carrying capacity may be defined (Unesco and FAO, 1985) as 'the number of people sharing a given area or territory who can, for the foreseeable future, sustain the existing standard of living [through the utilisation of] energy, land, water, skill and organisation'. Quantification of carrying capacity in general is difficult; the given environment is not a constant. Quantification of human carrying capacity is even more difficult because of the interplay between economic and social factors in the human environment and the subjective elements within 'standard of living'."

Davis, in Davis and Bernstam *(1991, pp. 7–8)*

"Obviously, if a country has certain advantages in nonfood trade, it can use these to buy food. A policy of self-sufficiency in food makes no sense for . . . any country that has access to international trade. The Earth is becoming one large trading system; and so the 'carrying capacity' must refer not just to what food could be raised within national borders, but to the total of what could be gained in all ways. . . .
"In short, the notion is false that each region has a carrying capacity that can be calculated and used in making projections and formulating policies. This idea is more applicable to cattle grazing in a pasture than to human beings."

Hillel *(1991, pp. 191–93)*

". . . in international development agencies[, a] term much bandied about . . . is a region's carrying capacity. It is a rather nebulous term, intended to characterize the amount of biological matter an ecosystem—or rather, an agro-ecosystem—can yield for consumption by animals or humans without being degraded. More simply put, it is a measure of how many people and / or animals an area can support on a sustained basis. Obviously, the productive yield obtainable from an area—and hence the number of people deriving their livelihood from it, at whatever standard of life—depends on how the area is being used; it is a function of technology. . . .

"The more intensive forms of utilization also involve inputs of capital, energy, and materials, such as fertilizers and pesticides, that come from outside the region itself but enhance its productivity. It is therefore highly doubtful that any given region can be assigned an intrinsic and objectively quantifiable property called 'carrying capacity.'

". . . the carrying capacity of a region depends on how it is managed, and all that can be said in a given situation is that the particular region is either well-managed or over-exploited under the present mode of utilization which may or may not allow realization of the region's sustainable potential."

Biegman *(1992, p. 9)*

"Because we are talking about human communities and not animal populations there are no direct, clearcut links to be drawn between population and environment. Human culture mediates between man and the environment. Man is continually recreating his natural environment, making the problem all the more complex. The phrase 'the carrying capacity of the environment' has been borrowed from the ecologists to describe the relationship between human communities and their natural environment, but the analogy is limited. If we wish to use this concept to identify and remedy environmental problems at [the] local level, the local technology, social organization, traditional knowledge and skills, and other social and cultural variables will have to be mapped out."

Myers *(1992, pp. 18–19)*

"Carrying capacity can be defined as 'the number of people that the planet can support without irreversibly reducing its capacity to support people in the future'. While this is a global-level definition, it applies at [the] national level too, albeit with many qualifications as concerns international relationships of trade, investment, etc. In fact it is a highly complex affair, reflecting food and energy supplies, ecosystem services, human capital, people's lifestyles, cultural constraints, social institutions, political structures, and above all public policies among many other factors, all of which interact with each other. Particularly important are two points: that carrying capacity is ultimately determined by the component that yields the lowest carrying capacity [Myers here assumes Liebig's law of the minimum]; and that human communities must learn to live off the 'interest' of environmental resources rather than off their 'princip[al]'. . . ."

Meadows et al. *(1992, p. 261)*

"The carrying capacity is the size of population that can be sustained by the environment indefinitely. The concept of carrying capacity was originally defined for relatively simple population / resource systems, such as the number of cattle or sheep that could be maintained on a defined piece of grazing land without degrading the land. For human populations the term 'carrying capacity' is much more complex because of the many kinds of resources people take from the environment, the many kinds of wastes they return, and the great variability in technology, institutions, and lifestyles. Carrying capacity is a dynamic concept. A carrying capacity is not constant; it is always changing with weather and other external changes and with the pressure exerted by the species being carried." (How are the first and last sentences of this definition to be reconciled: "the size of population that can be sustained . . . indefinitely" versus "A carrying capacity is not constant; it is always changing . . ."?)

Miller *(1992, p. 81)*   "Carrying capacity refers to the number of individuals who can be supported in a given land area over the long term without degrading the physical, ecological, cultural and social environment. . . . Although the advent of technology permits humans to exceed natural carrying capacity limits in some respects, the ultimate size of any human population is still constrained by amounts of arable land, potable water, and other resources. The unique limiting factor of energy is also on any modern society's list of required assets. . . .
"Human carrying capacity is not determined exclusively by land, energy and water constraints. Dr. Garrett Hardin of the University of California, Santa Barbara was the first to use the term 'cultural carrying capacity' to explain the role that human choice plays in determining optimum population. The more clean air, fresh water, wilderness, solitude and biodiversity that humans deem necessary, the more population will need to be reduced.
"Increased levels of material consumption ultimately reduce the carrying capacity of any ecosystem. Individual freedom deteriorates as human numbers increase, and social problems . . . become more intractable."

Carrying Capacity   "Carrying capacity refers to the number of individuals who can be
Network *Focus (win-*   supported without degrading the physical, ecological, cultural and
ter 1992, p. 1)   social environment, i.e. without reducing the ability of the environment to sustain the desired quality of life over the long term."

Daily and Ehrlich   (pp. 762–63) "For human beings, the matter [of carrying capacity] is
(1992)   complicated by two factors: substantial individual differences in types and quantities of resources consumed and rapid cultural (including technological) evolution of the types and quantities of resources supplying each unit of consumption. Thus, carrying capacity varies markedly with culture and level of economic development.
"We therefore distinguish between biophysical carrying capacity, the maximal population size that could be sustained biophysically under given technological capabilities, and social carrying capacities, the maxima that could be sustained under various social systems (and, especially, the associated patterns of resource consumption). At any level of technological development, social carrying capacities are necessarily less than biophysical carrying capacity, because the latter implies a human factory-farm lifestyle that would be not only universally undesirable but also unattainable because of inefficiencies inherent in social resource distribution systems [reference omitted]. Human ingenuity has enabled dramatic increases in both biophysical and social carrying capacities for *H. sapiens,* and potential exists for further increases."
(p. 769) ". . . central determinants of social carrying capacity lie in the domain of interactions among resources, among sociopolitical and economic factors, and between biophysical and social constraints. However, the complexity of these interactions makes it unlikely that they will be sufficiently well evaluated in the next several decades to allow firm calculations of any carrying capacity. From a policy perspective, the current great uncertainty in future social carrying capacity is irrelevant because the human population is likely to remain above that carrying capacity for decades at least."

King *(1993, p. 23)*   "The carrying capacity of an ecosystem is the maximum number of a given species that it can support indefinitely without causing environmental degradation. In the case of human populations, 2 important qualifications have to be added: with a given technology and consumption patterns. A population can, however, exceed the carrying capacity of its ecosystem temporarily, but as it does so it consumes its ecosystem's biological resource base, so that the carrying capacity of the ecosystem falls even as the population it supports rises. Since this cannot go on for ever, there comes a time when the ecosystem collapses, so that people either die or migrate. The point at which they do this is their Malthusian ceiling, but they usually start migrating well before they reach it."

Heilig *(1994, p. 255)*   "The carrying capacity of the earth is not a natural constant—it is a dynamic equilibrium, essentially determined by human action."

Postel *(1994, pp. 3–4)*   "Carrying capacity is the largest number of any given species that a habitat can support indefinitely. . . . The earth's capacity to support humans is determined not just by our most basic food requirements but also by our levels of consumption of a whole range of resources, by the amount of waste we generate, by the technologies we choose for our varied activities, and by our success at mobilizing to deal with major threats."

Human Daily Dietary Energy:
Biological Requirements
and Socioeconomic Demand

kilocalories per day[a] and source	comments
3,200 Passmore *(1962, p. 388)*	According to 1957 Food and Agricultural Organization standards, Reference Man "is 25 years of age, healthy and fit for active work. His weight is 65 kg. and he lives in a temperate zone at a mean annual temperature of 10° C. On each working day he is employed eight hours in an occupation which is not sedentary but does not involve more than occasional periods of hard physical labour. He is assumed to require on an average for the entire year 3,200 kcal. / day." Of this total, 1,200 kilocalories are devoted to working (mostly standing), 1,500 kilocalories to non-occupational activities and 500 kilocalories to eight hours of rest in bed at his basal metabolic rate. "The work of a coal miner has never been found to involve an expenditure of more than 4,000 kcal. / day. . . . At the other extreme, sedentary clerks expend about 2,400 kcal. / day."
2,740 De Wit *(1967, p. 317)*	"Each human requires about 1 million kilocalories per year as food."
2,100 Revelle *(1974, p. 163)*	"The average Indian's diet just about meets his physiological requirements of 2,100 kilocalories per day, whereas the food going into the average American's household exceeds his energy requirements by 20 percent."
2,600 Gilland *(1979, p. 25)*	2,600 kilocalories per person per day average for a population.
2,000 Miller *(1980, p. 30)*	"When the energy requirements of whole countries are calculated the differences between rich and poor almost completely disappear because of differences in the structure of the population. . . . Developing countries have young populations with more children who require less, whereas developed countries have more adults. . . . the average energy requirement per head of any population is about 2000 kcal / day or 8.4 MJ / day [megajoules per day] for every man, woman and child."
1,470–1,580 (India), 2,180 (United States) Gates *(1982, p. 1043)*	"Grain consumption in India is about 350 pounds [159.1 kilograms] per person per year, of which 320 pounds [145.5 kilograms] per person per year are eaten directly. In the U.S., 1,700 pounds [772.7 kilograms] per person per year of grain is consumed, but only 200 pounds [90.9 kilograms] per person per year is eaten directly. Most of the grain is fed to cattle and indirectly is consumed by man as meat." If

all Indian grain were rice (3,630 kilocalories per kilogram: Watt and Merrill 1963, p. 52, item 1,871) and were consumed directly by people, the energy supplied would be 1,580 kilocalories per person per day. If one-fifth of the calories fed to animals reached people as animal products, the caloric input would be 1,470 kilocalories per person per day. The aggregate caloric value of 1,700 pounds of wheat per year is 7,400 kilocalories per day. If all U.S. grain were wheat and one-fifth of the calories fed to animals reached people as animal products, the daily caloric input would be 2,180 kilocalories per person.

1.980
Swan *(1983, pp. 416–18)*

In the second round of the National Health and Nutrition Examination Survey, conducted between 1976 and 1980, the United States Department of Health and Human Services examined more than 20,000 non-institutionalized Americans between the ages of 6 months and 74 years at 64 locations in the United States. People were asked to recall what they had eaten in the last 24 hours. Males reported consuming an average 2,381 kilocalories per day. Consumption varied widely: 5 percent of males consumed 976 kilocalories per day or less, half consumed 2,187 kilocalories per day or less and 5 percent consumed more than 4,400 kilocalories per day. Females reported consuming an average 1,579 kilocalories per day; 5 percent consumed 683 kilocalories per day or less, half consumed 1,493 kilocalories per day or less and 5 percent consumed more than 2,889 kilocalories per day. If the population is half male and half female, then the average reported energy consumption was 1,980 kilocalories per day.

2,350
Kates et al. *(1989, p. 12)*

"Estimates of food demand are based on . . . an average 'basic' diet of 2,350 food calories (kcal) per person per day. The latter figure is based on average caloric needs per kilogram of body weight set by the FAO and the World Health Organization (WHO), average body weights by age reported by the FAO, and the present world age distribution based on UN data."

1,884–2,389
James and Schofield
(1990, pp. 30–31)

Average energy requirements for individual countries were computed from the distribution of the national population by age and sex, the average body weight at each age for each sex and the basal metabolic rate and physical activity level based on age and sex. Using the (latest) 1985 Food and Agricultural Organization method and the 1988 FAO data base, James and Schofield calculated average energy requirements (kilocalories per day per person) ranging from 1,884 for Ethiopia and 1,925 for India to 2,382 for Italy and 2,389 for the United States. The median requirement, among the 12 countries presented, was 2,100 kilocalories per day per person.

2,100–2,500
Smil *(1991, p. 593)*

". . . existential food requirements, though individually rather variable (because of age and differences in body weight, basal metabolic rates, and activity levels), are fairly uniform among different populations, clustering for adults between 2.1 and 2.5 megacalories (8.7–10.4 megajoules) and 40 and 50 g of protein a day per capita. . . ."

2,484–3,500
Pimentel and Pimentel *(1991, p. 10)*

In the United States in 1985, 3,500 kilocalories per day per person were "consumed" (produced? purchased? ingested?) and in China in 1986, 2,484 kilocalories per day per person.

1,915–1,990
Li Wenhua in Gilbert and Braat *(1991, p. 142)*

". . . we take 400 kg of crops per person per year as the minimum living standard for food. . . ." If 400 kilograms refers to gross dry weight, and if the edible portion is half of gross dry weight and the crop is wheat, the daily caloric supply is 1,915 kilocalories; if rice,

1,990 kilocalories. But if 400 kilograms refers to grain, the caloric values given should be doubled. The context does not make clear what was intended.

2,050–2,200
Smil *(1994, p. 266)*

For 1990, Smil estimated an average of 2,050 kilocalories per person per day were required to avoid stunting, and 2,200 to avoid stunting and maintain high levels of activity. He estimated that actual food consumption averaged 2,000 kilocalories per person per day.

2,500 (China), 3,600 (United States)
Pimentel et al. *(1994, p. 348)*

These are the foods and feed grains supplied per person. For China, the data are from 1988 to 1991; for the United States, from 1991. The world had 2,667 kilocalories per person per day according to data of the Food and Agricultural Organization from 1989 and 1991.

---

[a]1,000 kilocalories = 4.184 megajoules (million joules) (James and Schofield 1990, p. ix). Rice gives 3,630 kilocalories per kilogram and wheat gives 3,500 kilocalories per kilogram (Watt and Merrill 1963, pp. 52, 66).

APPENDIX 6

Mathematical Cartoons of Human Population Size and Carrying Capacity

> The happiness of a country does not depend, absolutely, upon its poverty or its riches, upon its youth or its age, upon its being thinly or fully inhabited, but upon the rapidity with which it is increasing, upon the degree in which the yearly increase of food approaches to the yearly increase of an unrestricted population.
>
> —THOMAS ROBERT MALTHUS 1798[1]

ADULT ENTERTAINMENT

In the Freudian view of human behavior, basic sexual instincts and impulses are sublimated into other activities that are approved by the culture, including art and science. Mathematicians take an opposite view of what is basic to the human spirit. They have an ironic saying: sex is a sublimation of the mathematical drive. Mathematics *is* a primitive instinct. It is the urge to clarify complexity and to represent it symbolically in a simple form. Mathematics differs from poetry, music, the plastic arts, fiction, religion and other expressions of this urge chiefly in its choice of symbolic medium; but it is, no less than religion and the other arts, a distilled and imaginative view of reality. Using some elementary mathematics, this appendix indulges the primitive instinct to clarify and simplify. The appendix is therefore strictly adult entertainment.

The goal is to show that simple assumptions about the rates of increase of human population size and human carrying capacity can reproduce many phenomena observed in the history, present dynamics and models of human populations. The assumptions that I shall use generalize a simple idea expressed in words two centuries ago by Malthus in the quotation at the beginning of this appendix and echoed in 1988 by the demographer Paul Demeny: "Posed in the simplest terms, the economics of population reduces to a race between two rates of growth: that of population and that of economic output."[2] Economic output includes but generalizes the food supply that concerned Malthus. Human carrying capacity, which incorporates aspects of human well-being not currently measured by economics, includes but generalizes economic output. If, for a given level of well-being, the human carrying capacity grows as fast as or faster than human population size, then the population can continue to grow without diminished well-being. If the human carrying capacity grows more slowly than population size, then either population growth must slow or well-being must suffer, or both.

In 1798, Malthus predicted wrongly that the population growth rate would always promptly win a race against the rate of growth of human carrying capacity. Malthus wrote to oppose the optimism of the Marquis de Condorcet, who saw the human mind as capable of removing all obstacles to human progress. Malthus has been wrong for nearly two centuries because he did not foresee how much people can alter the human carrying capacity of the Earth. Will Malthus continue to be wrong for the next two centuries?

Economists and system modelers have constructed quite a few mathematical models in which population growth drives technological change, which permits further population growth.[3]

I describe here very simple mathematical models for the race between the human population and human carrying capacity. These models make no pretense of detailed realism. They serve only as a playground for ideas.[4] Anyone who likes an intellectual adventure can read this appendix with complete understanding by accepting that the words fairly represent the meaning of the occasional mathematical symbols.

THE LIMIT OF MALTHUS MEETS THE PROGRESS OF CONDORCET

The models come in two major flavors: continuous time and discrete time. In continuous-time models, time is treated as a smoothly changing continuous variable, as time is measured by the average level of sand in an hourglass, without paying attention to the individual grains of sand. Rates of change in continuous-time models are described by derivatives. For example, the rate of population growth or decline dP/dt is the difference (that's what the "d" represents) in population size P per infinitesimally small difference in time t. Similarly, the rate of change in carrying capacity dK/dt is the difference or change in the carrying capacity K per small increment in time t.

In discrete-time models, time is treated as changing abruptly, like the change from one calendar year to the next for income tax purposes. Rates of change in discrete-time models are described by finite differences. For example, $\Delta P(t)$ is defined to mean the difference (that's what the Greek letter delta Δ represents) between the population size P at the next point in time $t+1$ and the population size at the present time t; thus, in mathematical symbols, $\Delta P(t) = P(t+1) - P(t)$ by definition. Similarly for carrying capacity: by definition $\Delta K(t) = K(t+1) - K(t)$. This means that the change in carrying capacity $K(t)$ between t and $t+1$ is $K(t+1) - K(t)$.

For simplicity, consider a single population with no migration in which only the total number of individuals matters. No attention will be paid to the population's age composition, geographical distribution or distribution of well-being. The symbol r will represent a positive constant, such as 0.01 or 0.5, and will be called the Malthusian parameter. Suppose that, at some time t, the population has $P(t)$ individuals and a carrying capacity $K(t)$ (measured in numbers of individuals). In the logistic equation of Verhulst, only the population size $P(t)$ changes in time while the carrying capacity $K(t)$ remains constant. I propose a slight modification in which the carrying capacity $K(t)$ can also change in time:

change in population size during the next time unit $= r \times P(t) \times [K(t) - P(t)]$.

I will call this the equation of Malthus; it is the same as the equation of Verhulst except that the constant carrying capacity K in Verhulst's equation is replaced by the variable carrying capacity $K(t)$ in the equation of Malthus. The "change in population size during the next time unit" becomes the derivative dP/dt in continuous-time models and becomes the finite difference $\Delta P(t)$ in discrete-time models.

To describe changes in the carrying capacity $K(t)$, let us take inspiration from the phrase of former United States president George H. Bush, Jr.: "every human being represents hands to work, and not just another mouth to feed."[5] Additional people clear rocks from fields, build irrigation canals, discover ore deposits and antibiotics and invent steam engines; they also clear-cut primary forests and manufacture polychlorinated biphenyls, chlorofluorocarbons and plutonium. Additional human beings may increase or decrease carrying capacity.

Suppose that the rate of change of carrying capacity is directly proportional to the rate of change in population size. Call the constant of proportionality c in honor of Condorcet, and call this equation the equation of Condorcet:

change in carrying capacity during the next time unit $= c \times$ change in population size during the next time unit.

The "change in carrying capacity during the next time unit" becomes dK/dt in continuous-time models and $\Delta K(t)$ in discrete-time models.

If technological innovations and resource availability affect the change in carrying capacity during the next time unit, the effect is hidden in the parameter c; Condorcet's equation unrealistically assumes that changes in carrying capacity are proportional to changes in population and to nothing else.

Verhulst's logistic equation has two parameters, the Malthusian parameter r and the carrying capacity K. Together the equations of Malthus and Condorcet also have two parameters, the Malthusian parameter r and the Condorcet parameter c.

The Condorcet parameter c can be negative, zero or positive. A negative value of c reflects human activities that destroy carrying capacity, such as wastage of topsoil or use of ozone-destroying aerosols. When c is negative, each additional pair of hands diminishes the Earth's capacity to support people. When c is zero, the change in carrying capacity during the next time unit equals zero, so carrying capacity is constant, exactly as in the logistic equation. Thus Verhulst's model is the special case when $c = 0$. A positive value of c less than 1 means that each additional pair of hands adds to the Earth's carrying capacity, but not quite as much as the accompanying mouth consumes of that carrying capacity. A positive value of c exactly equal to 1 means that each additional pair of hands adds to the Earth's carrying capacity just as much as the accompanying mouth consumes. Finally, if c exceeds 1, each additional pair of hands adds to the Earth's carrying capacity enough for its own wants and something extra as well.

The equation of Condorcet assumes that carrying capacity responds symmetrically to population increases and decreases. That is, if the population increases by one person, then decreases by one person, the carrying capacity comes back exactly to where it was before both changes; likewise if the population loses one person and then gains one person, there is no net effect on the carrying capacity.[6] This assumption is violated if additional people build additional durable infrastructure or make additional scientific or technological discoveries; should the population size then decline, the infrastructure would remain, though it may gradually decay or depreciate.[7] Similarly, if additional people generate additional durable toxins or deplete soil, the effects of those toxins or depletions may persist even after the people go away. Historical memory is embedded in infrastructure, economic capital and many other aspects of culture. In reality, changes in human carrying capacity depend on the past history of human carrying capacity and population size and not just on their present magnitudes. This phenomenon is called hysteresis.

One way to represent the hysteresis of carrying capacity would be to replace the single Condorcet parameter c by two parameters c_{up} and c_{down}, one for increases in population size and the other for decreases in population size. But I don't like gluing feathers on golf balls to make them look like birds; this model is not intended to be realistic at this level of detail. Hence I will not modify the equation of Condorcet to take account of historical effects and will henceforth ignore hysteresis. In any event, the difficulty does not arise in the continuous-time models because, in them, the population cannot change directions: either population size increases, or population size decreases, but it never switches from one to the other.

This basic model is so simple that there should be no risk that anyone will confuse it with reality. Nevertheless, the model displays attributes of complex models that claim more realism. To play with the ideas in this model, you choose values of r and c and see what happens to population size and carrying capacity. The continuous-time and discrete-time versions of this model behave similarly in some respects and differ strikingly in others. I will omit the mathematical details.

CONTINUOUS-TIME MODEL OF MALTHUS AND CONDORCET

When time advances continuously, the changes in population size and carrying capacity are determined by the current population size and carrying capacity with no lags or delays. The equations of Malthus and Condorcet are:

$$\frac{dP(t)}{dt} = r \times P(t) \times [K(t) - P(t)].$$

$$\frac{dK(t)}{dt} = c \times \frac{dP(t)}{dt}.$$

I have found exact formulas to describe how population size and carrying capacity change in time. According to these formulas, population size can change in three distinct ways: logistically, exponentially and superexponentially. Which of these three occurs depends on the value of the Condorcet parameter c.[8]

When c is less than 1, population size changes exactly according to the logistic curve of

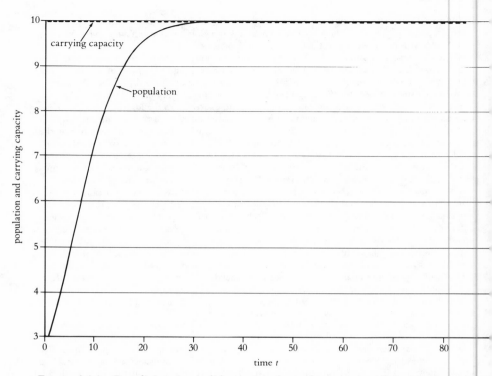

FIGURE A6.1   Population size (solid curve) and carrying capacity (dashed horizontal line at the vertical coordinate 10) according to the equations of Malthus and Condorcet, when additional population has no effect on the carrying capacity (c is zero). Population grows exactly as in Verhulst's logistic equation, and carrying capacity is constant in time as the logistic equation assumes. Parameter values: $r = 0.02$, $c = 0$, $P(0) = 3, K(0) = 10$. SOURCE: original calculations

Verhulst, even though the carrying capacity $K(t)$ will change if c differs from zero. How could the population grow logistically if the carrying capacity is changing? The net effect on population size of changes in the carrying capacity $K(t)$ works out to be equivalent to having a "virtual" constant carrying capacity K'. The virtual carrying capacity K' equals the initial carrying capacity $K(0)$ of the Condorcet equation if and only if c is zero (Figure A6.1). When c is negative, K' is smaller than the initial carrying capacity because the population destroys some of the original endowment of carrying capacity (Figure A6.2). When c is positive (but still less than 1), K' is larger than the initial carrying capacity because the growing population increases the carrying capacity (Figure A6.3). Whether c is negative, zero or positive (and less than 1), if you looked only at the trajectory of population size (without observing the carrying capacity directly), you could not distinguish the curve of population size from an exact solution of Verhulst's logistic equation with a constant carrying capacity K'.

For those who like formulas (blink now if you hate formulas!), the virtual constant carrying capacity is $K' = [K(0) - cP(0)] / (1 - c)$. For example, if I pretend that $c = 0.9$, $P(0) = 3$ and $K(0) = 10$, the formula gives $K' = 73$, and indeed the population size converges toward a final size of 73 even though the initial carrying capacity $K(0)$ was 10 (Figure A6.3). (You may think of the initial population size, 3, as three billion people and the initial carrying capacity, 10, as ten billion people if you are uncomfortable with a population size that changes smoothly through fractional numbers. These made-up

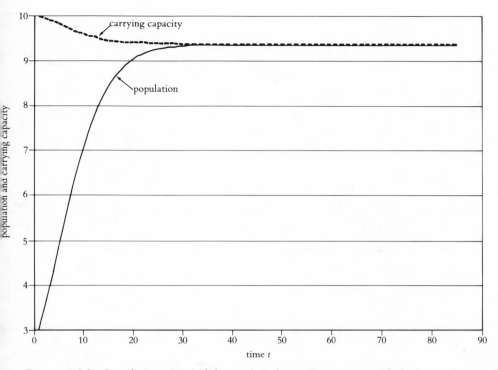

FIGURE A6.2 Population size (solid curve) and carrying capacity (dashed curve) according to the equations of Malthus and Condorcet, when additional population degrades the carrying capacity (c is negative). Parameter values: $r = 0.02$, $c = -0.1$, $P(0) = 3$, $K(0) = 10$. SOURCE: original calculations

numbers are not intended to be remotely realistic in any case.) In this example, $c = 0.9$ means that additional hands replace 90 percent of the carrying capacity that the additional mouths consume, thereby raising the effective carrying capacity K' to 73. The virtual carrying capacity K' does not depend on the Malthusian parameter r at all. For any fixed values of c and $K(0)$, the bigger $P(0)$ is, the smaller K' is: a land almost filled with people offers less opportunity for further population growth and less opportunity for expansion of its carrying capacity than a land with the same initial carrying capacity and fewer people. The closer c is to 1, the bigger K' is.

There is useful news for George H. Bush, Jr., here. If each additional pair of hands adds to the carrying capacity any amount less than the accompanying mouth consumes, the population ultimately faces a fixed finite carrying capacity (which I have called K'). This finite carrying capacity may be larger or smaller than the original carrying capacity, depending on the net balance of the population's constructive and destructive activities, but it is not infinite.

When the Condorcet parameter exactly equals 1, then each increment in carrying capacity exactly equals each increment in population size. The difference between the current carrying capacity and the current population size always exactly equals the initial difference. In this case the population grows exponentially (Figure A6.4). For any finite time, the population size is finite. But if you wait long enough, the hypothetical population will grow larger than any finite size you care to name.

When the Condorcet parameter is greater than 1, the difference between the current carrying capacity and the current population size constantly increases. The population

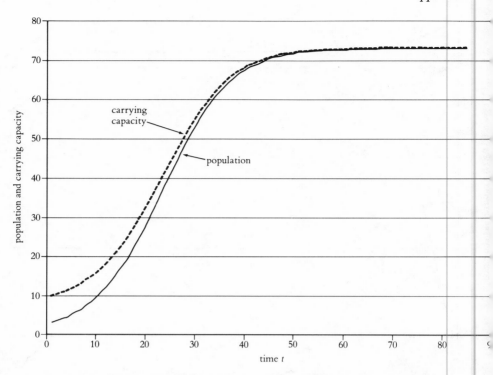

FIGURE A6.3 Population size (solid curve) and carrying capacity (dashed curve) according to the equations of Malthus and Condorcet, when additional population increases the carrying capacity by less than the additional population consumes (c is positive and less than 1). Parameter values: $r = 0.02$, $c = 0.9$, $P(0) = 3$, $K(0) = 10$. SOURCE: original calculations

grows superexponentially because the population growth rate constantly increases (Figure A6.5). This hypothetical population grows as fast as, or faster than, the hypothetical population of the doomsday equation. After some finite time, this hypothetical population explodes to infinity. The time of explosion can be calculated from the parameters c and r and from the initial population size and carrying capacity. In Figure A6.5, the vertical axis is measured in units of 10^{198}. Remember that populations of such size are pure mathematical fiction because there are only 10^{80} charged particles in the universe.[9]

The news for George Bush from this allegorical tale is that to sustain exponential population growth, each additional pair of hands must add to the carrying capacity exactly what each additional mouth consumes. Any smaller addition to carrying capacity leads in time to a finite stationary population; any larger addition to carrying capacity leads to a population explosion in finite time. The resources that are required to make each additional pair of hands productive are not explicit in the model. Resources complementary to labor are represented implicitly by the value of c. When they are available in abundance, c exceeds 1 and the population growth rate accelerates, as observed over the three centuries up to 1965–70. When complementary resources are rare, or possibly even negative in situations of congestion, pollution or overgrazing, c is less than 1 and the population growth rate falls, as observed globally since 1970. I will describe later a simple model of changes in c; for now, keep c constant.

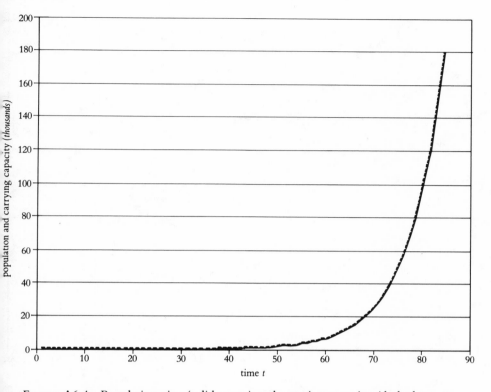

FIGURE A6.4 Population size (solid curve) and carrying capacity (dashed curve, apparently superimposed on the solid curve) according to the equations of Malthus and Condorcet, when additional population increases the carrying capacity by exactly the amount that the additional population consumes. Parameter values: $r = 0.02$, $c = 1$, $P(0) = 3$, $K(0) = 10$. The carrying capacity minus the population size is initially $10 - 3 = 7$ and remains at 7 forever. The population size and carrying capacity both grow exponentially, with exponential growth rate $7 \times 0.02 = 0.14$, equivalent to a population doubling time of just under 5 years. Because the vertical axis is measured in thousands (unlike the previous three graphs), the difference of only 7 between the carrying capacity and the population is too small to see and the two curves (dashed and solid) appear to be superimposed. SOURCE: original calculations

DISCRETE-TIME MODEL OF MALTHUS AND CONDORCET

The discrete-time version of the model of Malthus and Condorcet assumes that time advances in discrete steps. Demographers would routinely interpret each time step as five years, but a year or a decade would do as well. In discrete time, the current population size and current carrying capacity depend on the values of population size and carrying capacity five years (or other time unit) earlier. Time delays or lags are built into the equations. The discrete-time equations of the model are given in the note to Table A6.1.

The equations are most easily solved numerically by starting with assumed values for the population size $P(0)$ and the carrying capacity $K(0)$ at an initial time arbitrarily called time 0. The equations and the assumed parameter values then instruct the computer how to

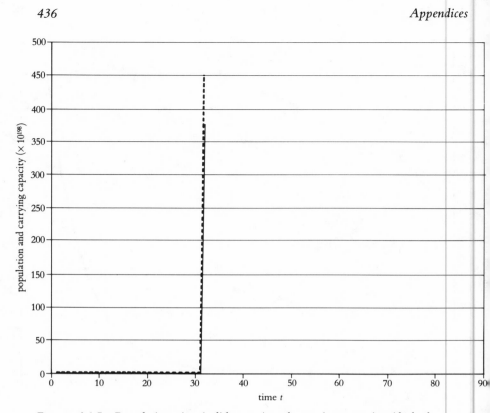

FIGURE A6.5   Population size (solid curve) and carrying capacity (dashed curve, apparently superimposed on the solid curve) according to the equations of Malthus and Condorcet, when additional population increases the carrying capacity by more than the additional population consumes. The population size and carrying capacity become infinite in a finite time (about 31 time units, which may be calculated from the parameter values). The vertical scale is measured in units of 10^{198}. The curves stop because my spreadsheet cannot represent larger numbers. Parameter values: $r = 0.02$, $c = 1.2$, $P(0) = 3$, $K(0) = 10$. SOURCE: original calculations

calculate the values of population size and carrying capacity at time 1. Given values of population size and carrying capacity at time 1, the same equations instruct the computer how to compute the population size and carrying capacity at time 2. The process can be iterated as long as desired.

Solving these equations numerically on a computer raises subtle dangers that are avoided by exact mathematical analysis. Computers rush in where mathematicians fear to tread. One danger is underflow: If two numbers differ by an amount that is smaller than the precision of the computer, and if you ask the computer to subtract one of these numbers from the other, the computer will think the answer is zero. If you then ask the computer to multiply the difference (which it thinks is zero) times any number, even a very large one, it still thinks the result is zero, though the product of a very small number (the true difference) times a large number can be far from zero. A second danger is the cumulation of rounding errors: if each step of a computation introduces a very, very tiny error and the computer repeats the step many times, the error in the result at the end may be far from tiny. When these dangers are avoided, numerical computation is a very useful vehicle for exploration. I will use the computer for exploration here. You can check me on your home

TABLE A6.1   Numerical behavior of the discrete-time equations of Malthus and Condorcet, illustrated by a single example

r	behavior of $K(t)$, $P(t)$[a]
0	constant at $K(0)$, $P(0)$
0.01–0.13	smooth sigmoidal approach to 73, 73
0.14–0.27	damped oscillations to 73, 73
0.28–0.33	period-2 oscillations for large t
0.34	period-4 oscillations for large t
0.35	period-8 oscillations for large t
0.36	period-6 oscillations for large t
0.37–0.38	apparently chaotic
0.39	period-6 oscillations for large t
0.40–0.41	apparently chaotic
0.42–0.50	overshoot and collapse: population size becomes negative

[a] If $P(t)$ is the population size at time $t = 0$, 1, 2, . . . and $K(t)$ is the carrying capacity at time t, the discrete-time equation of Malthus is $P(t+1) = P(t) + rP(t)[(K(t) - P(t)]$. The discrete-time equation of Condorcet is $K(t+1) = K(t) + c[P(t+1) - P(t)]$. Throughout this table, $c = 0.9$, $P(0) = 3$ and $K(0) = 10$. The Malthusian parameter r varies from 0 to 0.50 by increments of 0.01. The accuracy of calculations is approximately 14 decimal digits, but the behavior is described on the basis of 11 or 12 displayed digits. Trajectories are calculated to $t = 700$.

computer, if you are lucky enough to have one, and you can experiment with other parameter values than those reported here.

According to my numerical experimentation with the model equations, when the Condorcet parameter c is greater than or equal to 1, the population size grows superexponentially or exponentially. The qualitative behaviors of the discrete-time and continuous-time versions of the equations are the same.

When the Condorcet parameter c is less than 1, the discrete-time model predicts some strange behavior: the trajectories of the population size and carrying capacity are very sensitive to the value of the Malthusian parameter r.[10] It is easy to see the strange behavior by using a spreadsheet on a personal computer to solve the discrete-time equations of Malthus and Condorcet, taking first $r = 0.01$, then $r = 0.02$, then $r = 0.03$ and so on up to $r = 0.49$, $r = 0.50$, together with fixed values of the Condorcet parameter $c = 0.9$, the initial population size $P(0) = 3$ and the initial carrying capacity $K(0) = 10$.[11]

For low values of the Malthusian parameter r, population size and carrying capacity grow sigmoidally (Figure A6.3), just as in the continuous-time model. For larger values of r, the population size slightly overshoots its eventual stationary level K' and then fluctuates above and below K' with smaller and smaller overshoots and undershoots (Figure A6.6). This behavior is called damped oscillation. The damped oscillation in population size resembles the swinging back and forth, with diminishing amplitude, of a pendulum initially pushed away from its resting position; friction eventually brings the pendulum to rest.

For still larger values of r (0.28 to 0.33), the overshoots and undershoots do not diminish but eventually fall into a regular or periodic oscillation (Figure A6.7), like a frictionless pendulum. At even-numbered time points, the population size returns to one value; at odd-numbered time points, the population size returns to a second value. The carrying capacity behaves in the same way. It takes some time for this so-called period-2 oscillation to become established.

For $r = 0.34$, the variables cycle periodically through four distinct values; for $r = 0.35$, through eight distinct values; and for $r = 0.36$, through six distinct values (Figure A6.8). (This is a good place to illustrate the dangers and difficulties of computation, just so you

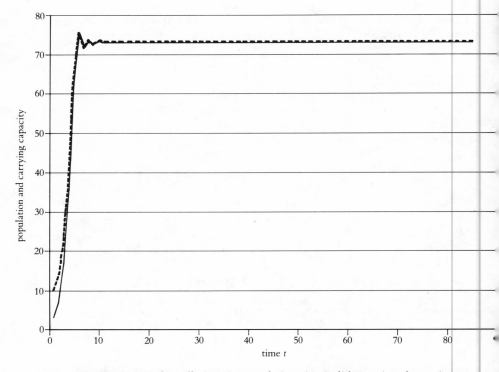

FIGURE A6.6   Damped oscillations in population size (solid curve) and carrying capacity (dashed curve) according to the equations of Malthus and Condorcet. The population size and carrying capacity eventually converge, so that the solid and dashed curves come arbitrarily close together as time increases. Parameter values: r = 0.20, c = 0.9, P(0) = 3, K(0) = 10. SOURCE: original calculations

will not have too much faith in numerical results. Table A6.1 is based on calculations in a spreadsheet called QUATTRO PRO. The arithmetic has about 14 digits of precision, and I described the behavior based on the most significant 11 or 12 digits, for 700 time steps. To avoid rounding errors, I ignored the last few digits. For safety's sake, I programmed all the calculations again in a language called MATLAB 4.1 and examined the results with 16 digits of precision, for 1,000 time steps. The contrasting results are amusing. In MATLAB 4.1, for r = 0.34, the population size and carrying capacity cycle through 8 distinct values instead of 4; for r = 0.35, through 32 values instead of 8; for r = 0.36, through 60 values instead of 6. The greater numerical resolution of MATLAB suggests that the 11-digit precision of QUATTRO PRO conceals fine variations—or is the apparent precision of MATLAB 4.1 meaningless? I conclude only that, to 11 digits of accuracy, the behavior is as I described it.)

For r in the range from 0.37 to 0.41, the population size and carrying capacity are apparently chaotic, fluctuating without apparent periodicity (Figure A6.9). I say "apparently chaotic" rather than asserting "chaotic" because numerical calculation of the values for any finite number of times cannot exclude periodic behavior with a very long cycle time.[12]

Finally, for values of r of 0.42 or larger, the population size eventually far overshoots the carrying capacity and then, at the next time step, falls below zero and heads for negative infinity (Figure A6.10). The most reasonable interpretation of a negative population size is that the population is extinct. This pattern may be called overshoot and collapse.

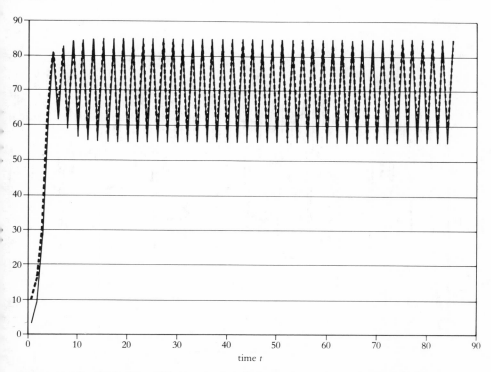

FIGURE A6.7 Period-2 oscillations in population size (solid curve) and carrying capacity (dashed curve) according to the equations of Malthus and Condorcet. Parameter values: $r = 0.30$, $c = 0.9$, $P(0) = 3$, $K(0) = 10$. SOURCE: original calculations

Overall, the larger r is, the wilder the behavior of population size and the carrying capacity.[13] An intuitive feeling for why this might be so can be had by looking closely at the difference equations for the discrete-time model of Malthus and Condorcet, given in the note to Table A6.1. At each time step, the population size $P(t)$ at time t is multiplied by $1 + r[K(t) - P(t)]$. The Malthusian parameter r multiplies (or amplifies) the gap between the carrying capacity and the current population size. The bigger this amplification, the more likely it is that the next population size will overshoot or undershoot the current carrying capacity and the less likely it is that the population size will change smoothly and stably.

The carrying capacity undergoes the same changes in behavior as the population size, when the Condorcet parameter c is a constant less than 1 and the Malthusian parameter r is held at a sequence of values increasing from zero. The larger r is, the more variable the carrying capacity is. Ultimately the carrying capacity becomes unpredictable and then crashes. If the probabilistic view of carrying capacity that Philip Fearnside proposed[14] is extended from individual colonists in the Amazonian rainforest to an entire population, the risk that the current carrying capacity $K(t)$ will fall below any given fixed population size appears to increase, the larger r is. Fearnside's carrying capacity, set by a maximum level of acceptable risk, could thus be interpreted as being smaller, the larger r is.

The exotic behaviors generated by two very simple equations include all those mentioned in *Beyond the Limits*[15] by Meadows et al. (Figure A6.11) and more. Meadows et al. described four modes of population change: steady increase, sigmoidal approach to stationarity, damped oscillation and overshoot and collapse. Beneath. Figure A6.11, Meadows et al. wrote:

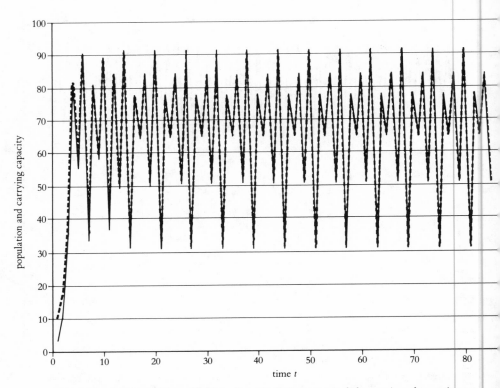

FIGURE A6.8   Period-6 oscillations in population size (solid curve) and carrying capacity (dashed curve) according to the equations of Malthus and Condorcet. Parameter values: $r = 0.36$, $c = 0.9$, $P(0) = 3$, $K(0) = 10$. SOURCE: original calculations

> Computer modelers, if they are not to produce impenetrable thickets, . . . cannot put into their models all they know; they have to put in only what is relevant for their purpose. The art of modeling, like the arts of poetry writing or architecture or engineering design, is to include just what is necessary to achieve the purpose, and no more. That is easy to say and hard to do.
>   Therefore to understand a model and judge its "validity," one needs to understand its purpose. The purpose—the *only* purpose—of World3 is to understand the possible modes of approach of the human economy to the carrying capacity of the planet. It is for that purpose *only* that we believe the model is "valid."[16]

Comparing the Malthus-Condorcet bestiary with Figure A6.11 suggests that the World3 and World3/91 models of Meadows et al. contain much more than "just what is necessary to achieve the purpose" stated. The extras make it difficult to see exactly which features of World3 determine how the model behaves. The lack of intellectual transparency is the chief shortcoming of the World3 system model, in light of the stated goal. That World3 lacks realism, many critics have correctly observed; but Meadows et al. disavow realism (at least in the text quoted) as a goal of World3.

In summary thus far, the Malthusian race between the increase of population size and the increase of human carrying capacity can have many outcomes. In continuous time, when population and carrying capacity affect each other's growth rates without lags or delays, population can grow logistically, exponentially or superexponentially. In discrete time with lags in responses, additional modes of behavior are possible: damped oscillations, periodic oscilla-

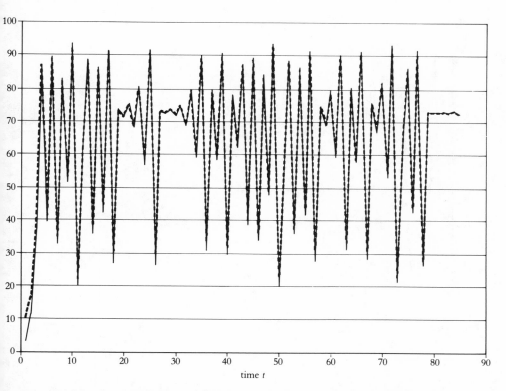

FIGURE A6.9   Apparently chaotic fluctuations in population size (solid curve) and carrying capacity (dashed curve) according to the equations of Malthus and Condorcet. Parameter values: r = 0.38, c = 0.9, P(0) = 3, K(0) = 10. SOURCE: original calculations

tions, chaos and overshoot and collapse. In the simple equations of Malthus and Condorcet proposed here, these modes of behavior depend in a simple way on the Condorcet parameter *c* and the Malthusian parameter *r*.

The equations of Malthus and Condorcet can easily be extended to describe two, three or any number of regional populations that interact demographically through migration as well as by influencing one another's carrying capacity. More modes of behavior then appear, but I will spare you the details.

Malthus and Condorcet Meet John Stuart Mill

The equation of Condorcet assumes that the rate of increase of carrying capacity is always the *same* multiple of the rate of increase of population. That multiple is the fixed Condorcet parameter *c*. A better model would replace the constant *c* by a variable multiplier $c(t)$ which depends on time *t*. If the increment to carrying capacity that an additional person can contribute depends on the resources available to make her or his hands productive, and if these resources must be shared among more people as the population increases, then perhaps $c(t)$ would decline as population size increases. As one of many simple possibilities, suppose for example that there is a finite positive constant *L* such that

$$c(t) = \frac{L}{P(t)}.$$

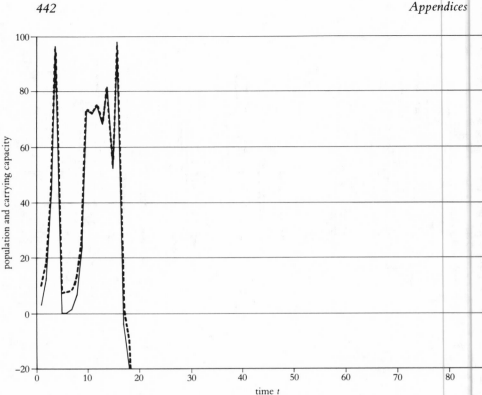

FIGURE A6.10   Overshoot and collapse in population size (solid curve) and carrying capacity (dashed curve) according to the equations of Malthus and Condorcet. Parameter values: $r = 0.42$, $c = 0.9$, $P(0) = 3$, $K(0) = 10$. SOURCE: original calculations

I propose to call this the equation of Mill, after the British philosopher John Stuart Mill who foresaw a stationary population as both inevitable and desirable; L is the Mill parameter. This equation is decidedly optimistic, because $c(t)$ is always positive no matter how big $P(t)$ is: with this assumption, a large population never degrades the carrying capacity, but merely decreases the effectiveness of additional population in increasing the carrying capacity. Other formulas for $c(t)$, such as $L - P(t)$, could be chosen that would allow $c(t)$ to become negative. Let us persist with $c(t) = L / P(t)$.

Assume further that L is bigger than $P(0)$, so that $c(0) = L/P(0)$ is initially bigger than 1. The population initially grows superexponentially. As $P(t)$ increases past L, $c(t)$ passes through the value of 1 and the population experiences a brief instant of exponential growth. Then $c(t)$ continues to fall to values below 1, and the population size begins, and never stops, sigmoidal growth. The sigmoid looks like a logistic curve increasingly compressed downward as population size increases.

Replacing the constant Condorcet parameter c in the equation of Condorcet by the expression $L / P(t)$ from the equation of Mill gives the Condorcet-Mill equation:

change in carrying capacity during the next time unit
$= [L/P(t)] \times$ change in population size during the next time unit.

Together, the equations of Malthus and Condorcet-Mill have two constant parameters, r and L. In the continuous-time version of this model, the population size rises to approach one and only one stationary level.[17] The stationary level is independent of the Malthusian

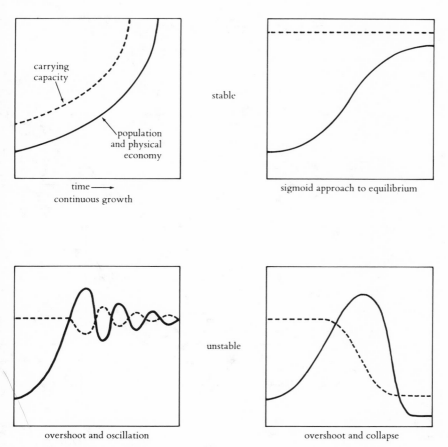

FIGURE A6.11   Original title: "Possible modes of approach of a population to its carrying capacity." In these four charts, time, measured on the horizontal axis, increases from left to right. Carrying capacity (dashed curve) and a combination of population size and the physical economy (solid curve) are measured on the vertical axis; both increase upward. Counterclockwise from the chart in the upper right corner, the four charts represent, respectively, logistic growth (as in Figure A6.1); exponential or superexponential growth (as in Figure A6.4 and Figure A6.5); damped oscillations (as in Figure A6.6); and overshoot and collapse (as in Figure A6.10). SOURCE: Meadows et al. (1992, p. 108, Fig. 4-2)

parameter r. The bigger the initial carrying capacity $K(0)$ and the bigger the Mill parameter L, the bigger the stationary level is, other things being equal.

As in the model of Malthus and Condorcet, here also the bigger the initial population size $P(0)$, the smaller that stationary level is, other things being equal. If this seems surprising, remember that the variable Condorcet parameter in this model is $c(t) = L / P(t)$. When the initial population $P(0)$ is bigger and L is unchanged, the initial $c(0)$ is smaller; so the carrying capacity grows at a slower rate, for each increment in population size, and therefore the population grows less.

To illustrate the initially superexponential but ultimately sigmoidal growth of population in this model, I use a logarithmic scale for population size. At first the graph of population

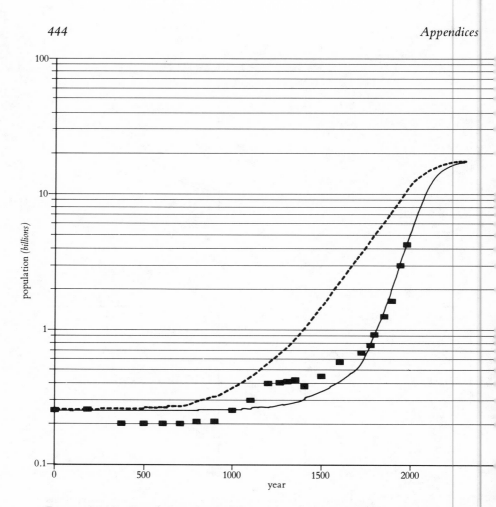

FIGURE A6.12 Population size (solid curve) and carrying capacity (dashed curve) according to the equations of Malthus and Condorcet-Mill. The population size and carrying capacity grow superexponentially at first, then sigmoidally. Solid symbols represent estimated population size. SOURCE: Cohen (1995)

size curves convexly upward, showing that the relative population growth rate is increasing (Figure A6.12). Then the curve quickly levels off and approaches its ultimate stationary level. The qualitative similarity between Figure A6.12 (up to the point where the population growth rate begins to level off) and the graph of world population history (Figure 5.3) is entirely intentional. With the chosen parameters and initial conditions of these equations, the calculated graph of a hypothetical population over 2,000 years starts from a quarter billion people and ends at nearly six billion people and looks very much like the graph of world population history.[18] However, the similarity does not suggest that the equations of Malthus and Condorcet-Mill represent "the truth." Whatever truth this model embodies is purely at the level of allegory.

MORALS OF THE STORY

What do these models suggest about the measurement of the Earth's human carrying capacity? First, at any given time, it make sense to think of a *current* but changing human carrying capacity defined by the *current* state of technology, social, political and economic institutions, styles of life and physical and biological environment. Second, the recent historical record of superexponential population growth, accompanied by an immense improvement in average well-being, is *logically* consistent with a variety of alternative futures: continued expansion of population and carrying capacity (a Condorcet parameter forever greater than 1), or a rapid sigmoidal tapering off of the growth in population size and carrying capacity, or oscillations (damped or periodic), or chaotic fluctuations, or overshoot and collapse. Logic alone will not choose among the alternatives. Third, to believe that no ceiling to population size or carrying capacity is in prospect you have to believe that nothing will stop a sufficient proportion of additional people from increasing the Earth's carrying capacity by more than, or at least as much as, they consume.

Notes

1: BETWEEN CHOICES AND CONSTRAINTS

1. Tablet I, lines 352–60, in Kilmer 1972, p. 166.
2. Leichty 1971, p. 26.
3. Kilmer 1972, p. 176.
4. Meadows et al. 1972, p. 31; Hardin 1964, p. 22. According to W. T. de Bary (personal communication, 14 June 1995), the date for Han Fei-Tzu should be the third century B.C., not the fifth.
5. Holland 1993, pp. 328–29.
6. Pickering and Chatto 1992, item 22.
7. Saether 1993, p. 511.
8. Karplus 1992, p. 228.
9. McEvedy and Jones 1978, p. 344.
10. Weiss et al. 1993, p. 1002.
11. Demeny 1991, p. 410; Meadows et al. 1992.
12. World Health Organization Commission on Health and Environment 1992, p. 118.
13. Berger 1992.
14. A meter is about 9 percent longer than a yard.
15. Chapter 1 of Paul Ehrlich's famous 1968 book, *The Population Bomb,* opens with his account of passing through a Delhi slum one steaming, fetid evening. "The streets seemed alive with people. People eating, people washing, people sleeping. People visiting, arguing, and screaming. People thrusting their hands through the taxi window, begging. People defecating and urinating. People clinging to buses. People herding animals. People, people, people, people. . . . Would we ever get to our hotel? All three of us were, frankly, frightened. . . . since that night I've known the *feel* of overpopulation." Ehrlich 1968, pp. 15–16.
16. Julian Simon, an economist at the University of Maryland, wrote: "India is poor and underdeveloped for many reasons, and it might be even more so if it had a smaller population." Simon 1990, pp. 169–70. As a historical matter, India *was* poorer, as economists measure poverty, when its population was smaller. But the operative question here is whether India would have been poorer in 1990 if its population had grown more slowly in the decades before 1990. Demographic history does not answer that question.
17. I use *fertility* to refer to the actual number of children born, and *fecundity* to refer to the biological potential for bearing children. Thus, well-fed, disease-free, educated women may have high fecundity (high biological capacity to have children) and low fertility (few actual children). A population cannot combine low fecundity and high fertility. The words "fertility" and "fecundity" are used differently in different fields of science. My usage is standard in demography.
18. Sensitivity analysis has nothing to do with sensitivity training or other group psychotherapies. Sensitivity analysis is techno-nerdy, not touchy-feely.
19. The average annual world population growth rate over the last 10,000 years, around 0.07 percent per year, has been far higher than in this hypothetical example.
20. United Nations 1992a.
21. Let me dispense once and for all with extraterrestrial emigration. To achieve a reduction in the global population growth rate from, say, 1.6 percent to 1.5 percent would currently require the departure of 0.001×5.7 billion $= 5.7$ million astronauts in the first year and increasing numbers in each later year. To export this number of people would bankrupt the remaining Earthlings and would still leave a population that doubled every 46 years. Demographically speaking, space is not the place.

22. Erikson 1963, p. 419.
23. Dubos 1971, p. xi.
24. World Bank 1992, p. 2.
25. Johnson 1991, p. 393. Of these major religious groups, which has the highest average completed family size? Not the Roman Catholics, but the Muslims, with roughly six children per woman; Ehrlich and Ehrlich 1990, p. 212.
26. In continental European equivalents, this number is the milliard. The continental European billion means a million million, or 1,000,000,000,000.
27. Johnson 1991, p. 785.
28. Population Reference Bureau 1992.
29. Barringer 1992.
30. Central Intelligence Agency 1991, p. 142.
31. World Bank 1992, p. 218.

2: Four Evolutions in Population Growth

1. Simply because 63 years × 90 million per year = 5.67 billion.
2. The decimal fraction 0.016 and the percentage 1.6 percent are exactly equivalent; the choice is strictly a matter of convenience.
3. To check this calculation and other calculations involving exponents, you'll need a scientific calculator or a working knowledge of logarithms. Check that $2 \times 1.016^{1.371}$ is approximately 5.65 billion. Many demographers would estimate the consequences of a 1.6 percent growth rate using the formula $2 \times e^{0.016 \times 1.371}$, where $e \approx 2.718$ is the base of the natural logarithms, to get 6.7 billion. When this formula is used, about 1,361 years are required for a population of two people to grow to 5.7 billion, if the population increases steadily at a rate of 0.016 per year.
4. Gould 1992, p. 181.
5. *Encyclopaedia Britannica* 1989, 15th ed., 16:706.
6. Check this, using your calculator.
7. Davies 1982, p. 82.
8. Cannan 1895, p. 507, made this argument a century ago to show that the population growth rate of England in the decade 1881–91 could not have been sustained 14 centuries into the past and could not be sustained three centuries into the future. The same argument has been made many times for world population; for example, by Knibbs 1917 and Hauser 1979, p. 4.
9. The formula for doubling time follows from the equation of exponential growth:

$$\text{population after } t \text{ years} = \text{initial population} \times (1 + \text{relative change})^t.$$

We want to know the number of years t when the population after t years is twice the initial population. The trick is to set the population after t years, which I call the "final population," equal to two times the initial population,

$$\text{final population} = 2 \times \text{initial population} = \text{initial population} \times (1 + \text{relative change})^t,$$

and divide both sides of the equation by the initial population:

$$2 = (1 + \text{relative change})^t.$$

For each value of relative change, numerical experimentation with a calculator can be used to find the number t of years in which the population doubles.

People who remember logarithms from high school can take the natural logarithm, abbreviated ln, of both sides of the equation $2 = (1 + \text{relative change})^t$ to get the exact equation $\ln 2 = t \times \ln(1 + \text{relative change})$. Now approximate both sides of this equation: $\ln 2 \approx 0.693$ and, for relative changes of only a few percent per year, $\ln(1 + \text{relative change}) \approx \text{relative change}$ (as a decimal fraction). Thus, $0.693 \approx t \times \text{relative change}$. Multiplying both sides of this equation by 100 converts it to percentages, giving finally: the doubling time $t \approx 69.3$/relative change (in percent).

10. Hassan 1981.

11. Alterman 1969, pp. 18, 19, 27. Hollingsworth 1969, p. 65, reported that the Chinese conducted the first censuses in the second millennium B.C.

12. Coale 1974, p. 41.

13. Van de Walle and Knodel 1980, p. 7.

14. Coale 1974, p. 41.

15. Durand 1977.

16. Deevey 1960.

17. Rogers and Harpending 1993; Harpending et al. 1993; Gibbons 1993.

18. Cipolla 1974, pp. 33–34.

19. Hardesty 1977, p. 210.

3: PEOPLE CONTROL THE GROWTH OF NONHUMAN POPULATIONS

1. Press and Siever 1986, pp. 353–55.

2. Margulis and Fester 1991, p. 9; Keeton, Gould and Gould 1993, pp. 551–57.

3. Margulis and Fester 1991.

4. Margulis and Cohen 1994.

5. Wilson 1971, pp. 349–425.

6. Ibid., pp. 104, 119.

7. Ibid., pp. 391–400.

8. Ibid., p. 424.

9. In Hirschoff and Kotler 1989, pp. 115–16.

10. Ibid., p. 116.

11. Smith 1975.

12. McNeill 1967, p. 10.

13. Ibid., p. 1.

14. Ibid., p. 9.

15. Smith 1991 argued that native North Americans domesticated local plants before maize was introduced from the south; also see Wilford 1992.

16. Rita Wright, Department of Anthropology, New York University, personal communication, 18 May 1994.

17. McNeill 1967, p. 10.

18. Ibid., pp. 22–23.

19. Hillel 1991, p. 75.

20. McNeill 1963, 1967; Cipolla 1974, pp. 18–27.

21. Coale 1974, pp. 47–48.

22. Livi-Bacci 1992, pp. 90–94.

23. Boserup 1965; Cohen 1977.

24. Cole et al. 1973, p. 159; Petersen 1979; Mann 1993, p. 49. Adam Smith, who predated Malthus, held a chair of philosophy.

25. Boserup 1965, 1981; Petersen 1979, p. 40; Simon and Kahn 1984; Simon 1990. Of course, even without population growth, increasing expectations or wants can also stimulate technological innovation.

26. Blaxter 1986, p. 102.

27. Carrying Capacity Network 1992, p. 57.

28. Lee 1986, p. 96.

29. Ibid., p. 128.

30. Tuchman 1978, p. xiii.

31. Biraben 1979.

32. McEvedy and Jones 1978.

33. Hollingsworth 1969.

34. Population Reference Bureau 1990.

35. Whitmore et al. 1990, p. 31. The estimates of Whitmore et al. and Hollingsworth appear to refer to the same territory because the estimated population for 1966 in both estimates is 30

million people. McEvedy and Jones 1978 estimated population fluctuations for Egypt that were, like those of Whitmore et al., more restrained than those of Hollingsworth.

36. Wrigley 1969, p. 78, Figure 3.3.

37. Wrigley 1969, p. 78.

38. Livi-Bacci 1992, p. 6.

39. Hammel and Howell 1987, p. 142.

40. So that you'll know the jargon if you see it elsewhere, these two types are named "r-selected" and "K-selected," in honor of the symbols r and K that are often used in writing the logistic equation. I won't use that jargon again, but you'll see r and K in the logistic equation later. Recent biological evidence bearing on this theory has been collected and analyzed by Pimm 1991, pp. 39–58.

41. Livi-Bacci 1992, p. 4.

42. Bonner 1965, p. 17.

43. Crosby 1972, p. 165.

44. Crosby 1972, 1986; McNeill 1967, p. 293; Coale 1974; McKeown 1976; Thomas 1985; Livi-Bacci 1991.

45. Sauer 1969, p. 167.

46. Crosby 1972, p. 170.

47. Ibid., pp. 171–74.

48. McNeill 1967, p. 293.

49. Durand 1977, p. 288.

50. Thomas 1985, p. 40.

51. McNeill 1967, p. 293. Durand 1977, p. 279, reported no significant increase in the population of tropical Africa before the beginning of the nineteenth century.

52. Durand 1977, p. 288.

53. McKeown 1976.

54. McNeill 1990, pp. 4–5.

55. Coale 1974, pp. 48–49; Livi-Bacci 1992, pp. 68–73; see Fogel 1994 for recent data.

56. Livi-Bacci 1991, pp. 107–10; Livi-Bacci 1992, p. 72.

57. Dyson and Murphy 1985. Rising fertility accounted for more than half of the increases in population growth rates in some recent Latin American countries, but typically a bit less than half.

58. Wrigley and Schofield 1981.

59. McNeill 1967, p. 295.

4: People Control the Growth of Human Populations

1. Coale 1974, p. 48.

2. Mayer 1964, pp. 833–34.

3. Livi-Bacci 1992, p. 147.

4. Coale and Hoover 1958, pp. 29–30.

5. Reddaway 1939; Teitelbaum and Winter 1985.

6. United Nations 1953, pp. 161–62. Full citations to Clark 1949 and Notestein 1950 are given here.

7. Spengler 1949, p. 71.

8. United Nations 1992a.

9. Notestein projected the populations of individual regions using the cohort-component method, then summed them. Essentially this procedure is followed by the United Nations today.

10. Quoted in United Nations 1953, p. 161.

11. Coale 1973, pp. 67–68.

12. McKeown 1976.

13. The effectiveness of some of these drugs has since faltered as the microbes have evolved resistance to them. Earnest and Sbarbaro 1993; Caldwell 1992.

14. Dorn 1962.

15. Population Reference Bureau 1992.

16. Technically, this defines the *period* life expectancy, not the *cohort* life expectancy.

17. Coale 1973, p. 68.

18. Livi-Bacci 1992, p. 156.

19. Coale 1974, p. 51.

20. Coale 1973, p. 68.

21. Farrell, Sanderson and Vo 1984, p. 2.

22. World Resources Institute 1992, p. 272.

23. Farrell, Sanderson and Vo 1984, pp. 2–3.

24. United Nations Development Program 1992, p. 36. The report does not explicitly say whether the countries that fell in the top and bottom groups changed as time passed.

25. United Nations Development Program 1992, p. 35. These may be comparisons between different sets of countries in 1960 and 1989.

26. This ratio differed from the ratio of 59 to 1 quoted earlier because only 41 countries are considered here, rather than 160 earlier, and here the year is 1988, not 1989.

27. United Nations Development Program 1992, pp. 34–35.

28. According to 1994 World Bank estimates as presented by Demeny 1994, p. 17.

29. World Resources Institute 1994, p. 296.

30. Ibid., p. 262.

31. Ibid., p. 108.

32. Horiuchi 1992.

33. Ibid., p. 761.

34. Hassan 1981, pp. 154–55.

35. Van de Walle and Knodel 1980, p. 29.

36. Ibid., p. 29. According to van de Walle and Knodel, the English nobility still gave no evidence of fertility control by the middle of the nineteenth century. Johannson 1991, p. 393, on the contrary, cited genealogical data of high quality from Britain that "indicate that titled families, whose politically active male members officially controlled government policy, had already begun to reduce their marital fertility by the late eighteenth century."

37. Quoted by van de Walle and Knodel 1980, p. 30.

38. McNeill 1990, p. 12, proposed that fertility fell because, after the French Revolution, "so many soldiers returned to rural society after years of exposure to army prostitutes and their ways of preventing unwanted births. . . . the revolutionary upheaval solved the problem of too many surplus youths by reducing that surplus violently at first and through changed sexual behavior in the long run." The only trouble with this explanation is that French fertility clearly fell among aristocrats and peasants before the Revolution that McNeill invoked to explain the fall.

39. Coitus interruptus was widely known and practiced long before the seventeenth century. The biblical story of Onan attests to the age of the practice, and the euphemisms for it found in many languages attest to widespread knowledge.

The prize for the best collection of euphemisms for coitus interruptus goes to Gigi Santow, a demographer at the Australian National University, Canberra. According to Santow 1995, rabbinical scholars called the sin of Onan "threshing inside and winnowing outside." A cleric from the fifteenth century condemned the husband "who works the earth, and then throws the seed upon stone." In the sixteenth century, a chevalier "ground very well in his lady's mill without spilling any water." In the seventeenth century, a husband "threshed only at the barn door." In the eighteenth century, a definition of coitus interruptus is "to make a coffee house of a woman's **** [sic], to go in and out and spend nothing"; a verse suggested "watering the lawn without wetting the earth" and "leaving the dance before it's over." In Émile Zola's nineteenth-century novel *La Terre* (*The Earth*), peasants, "like the miller, emptied the cart at the door of the mill." Sicilians reportedly still say that if nothing is put in the pan, nothing will cook; Muslims in southern Thailand "eat in the kitchen and spit it out on the porch." The spiritual Dutch "leave the church before the singing."

These examples are a mere sample. Coitus interruptus remains important in the twentieth century; Santow 1993.

40. Van de Walle and Knodel 1980, p. 30.

41. Coale and Watkins 1986, p. 38.

42. Van de Walle and Knodel 1980, p. 30.

43. McLaren 1992, p. 85.

44. Van de Walle and Knodel 1980, p. 30.

45. Cited in Coale 1973, p. 62.

46. Van de Walle and Knodel 1980, p. 34.

47. Ibid., p. 31.

48. Ibid., pp. 31–33.

49. Coale 1973, p. 62.

50. Cook and Repetto 1982, p. 128.

51. Coale 1973, p. 61.

52. Van de Walle and Knodel 1980, p. 33.

53. Ibid., p. 34.

54. Ibid., p. 36.

55. This slogan apparently originated at the 1974 World Population Conference in Bucharest.

56. Livi-Bacci 1992, pp. 66–67. The same pattern appeared in estimates of Biraben 1979, p. 16, for Japan during these centuries, though his numbers differed slightly. Biraben estimated rapid population growth in the seventeenth century, from 11 million to 25 million, followed by a population size nearly constant at 25 million from 1700 to 1800. McEvedy and Jones 1978 estimated a larger Japanese population in 1600, but the same pattern of virtually no growth between 1720 and 1830.

57. Livi-Bacci 1992, pp. 66–67.

58. Coale 1973, p. 64.

59. Van de Walle and Knodel 1980, p. 33.

60. Kabeer 1990, p. 3.

61. Horiuchi 1992, p. 763.

62. King 1993, p. 24.

63. Ibid., p. 24.

64. Horiuchi 1992.

65. Coale et al. 1991, p. 390.

66. Johansson 1991 argued that "implicit" or "net" governmental policy—every policy that affected childbearing—determined the fertility evolution in every western European country.

67. Horiuchi 1992, p. 765.

68. Haub 1993, p. 2.

69. Handwerker 1986, p. 3: ". . . fertility transition in the contemporary world comes about when personal material well-being is determined less by personal relationships than by formal education and skill training. This transformation occurs when changes in opportunity structure and the labor market increasingly reward educationally-acquired skills and perspectives, for these changes have the effect of sharply limiting or eliminating the expected intergenerational income flows both from children, and from the social relationships created by or through the use of children."

70. Charles F. Westoff, personal communication, 21 March 1994.

71. Faye Duchin, personal communication, 16 May 1994.

72. Robinson 1992.

73. Caldwell et al. 1992, p. 211.

74. Ibid., pp. 212–13.

75. Robinson 1992, pp. 446–47.

76. Charles F. Westoff, personal communication, 21 March 1994, based on a preliminary report of the Demographic and Health Surveys.

77. Robinson 1992, p. 450.

78. Ibid., p. 457.

79. Charles F. Westoff, personal communication, 21 March 1994.

80. Robinson 1992, p. 457.

81. Caldwell et al. 1992, p. 219.

82. Mukerjee 1946, p. 94.

83. Belshaw 1947.

84. United Nations 1953, p. 185.

85. Madhavan 1985.

86. In 1973, George H. Bush, Jr., then United States representative to the United Nations, told the story in his foreword to Piotrow 1973, p. vii. It is tempting to speculate that his father's experience, which "came with a jolt" to George Jr., influenced George Jr. later, as a

presidential candidate, to recant his youthful support for population programs in the face of conservative opposition to them; Mathews 1990.

87. Piotrow 1973, p. x.
88. Ibid., p. 16.
89. Ibid., p. viii.
90. Bongaarts 1994; Piotrow 1973, p. 13.
91. Piotrow 1973 told the complex story of the political response in the United States in detail.
92. Ehrlich 1968, p. 69.
93. Van de Walle 1992.
94. United Nations Fund for Population Activities 1993a, p. 18.
95. Heer 1968, pp. 58–63.
96. Jolly 1993, p. 32.
97. United Nations Fund for Population Activities 1993a, p. 9.
98. Pritchett 1994, pp. 2–3.
99. Thomas 1991, p. 395, concluded that "it can be argued that the causal relationship between women's education and fertility is unproven. . . ."
100. Isiugo-Abanihe 1994.
101. E.g., Cassen et al. 1994.
102. Gertler and Molyneaux 1994.
103. Ibid., p. 60.
104. Robey, Rutstein and Morris 1993, p. 65.
105. Ibid., p. 65.
106. Smith 1776, book III, chap. iv, paragraph 17: "A revolution of the greatest importance to the public happiness, was in this manner brought about by two different orders of people, who had not the least intention to serve the public." Schelling 1978 gives many contemporary examples.
107. Hardin 1985, p. 59.

5: HUMAN POPULATION HISTORY IN NUMBERS AND GRAPHS

1. McNeill 1967, p. 1.
2. To estimate how many people the Earth held in prehistoric times, Deevey 1960, p. 196, assumed a density of people per square kilometer and multiplied by an assumed area populated. If people covered Africa at an average density of 0.00425 per square kilometer a million years ago, there would have been 125,000 of them. If people covered Africa, Europe and Asia at a density of 0.012 per square kilometer 300,000 years ago in the Middle Paleolithic, there would have been a million of them. Birdsell 1981, p. 393, favored higher estimates: 400,000 individuals three million years ago and a million persons 500,000 years ago. Comparing the estimates of Deevey and Birdsell suggests that neither should claim much precision. Such large numbers of individuals are the result of very successful human propagation; they could not describe a breeding group in which humans originated.
3. Schick and Toth 1993.
4. McEvedy and Jones 1978.
5. Hassan 1981, p. 196, Fig. 12.1.
6. Pressat 1970, p. 10.
7. Cipolla 1974, p. 112.
8. Birdsell 1981, p. 393.
9. McEvedy and Jones 1978.
10. Biraben 1979, p. 16.
11. Hauser 1979, p. 3.
12. Durand 1977, p. 278.
13. Cipolla 1974, p. 113. Deevey 1960, p. 196, estimated world population in 1750 at 728 million. Biraben 1979, p. 16, estimated 771 million. Wrigley 1969, p. 205, estimated 791 million. These estimates assert more precision than the available evidence justifies, because the estimates are given to the nearest million but differ by as much as 63 million. Durand 1977, p. 259, estimated a range from 735 to 805 million.

14. United Nations 1992a, p. 14.
15. Cipolla 1974, p. 113.
16. For 1850 to 1900, Coale 1974, p. 43, estimated 1.3 billion to 1.7 billion, with an average population growth rate just over 0.5 percent per year.
17. Coale 1974, p. 41.
18. Anderson and May 1991, pp. 653 ff.
19. Blaxter 1986, p. 11.
20. Cannan 1895, p. 506.
21. Henry and Gutierrez 1977.
22. The logistic equation is sometimes written in other, equivalent ways.
23. The population might exceed its carrying capacity as a result of prior immigration, or because the carrying capacity has just been reduced as a result of pollution or climatic change. Both of these possibilities fall outside the scope of the logistic model, which excludes migration and assumes a constant carrying capacity.
24. People who are offended by strong language should skip this note. I am going to use the strongest language I know, apart from poetry, which is mathematics. In fact, its terseness, immense analogical power and frequent difficulty make mathematics the poetry of the sciences. If you haven't read some mathematics or some poetry lately, you're not having as much fun in life as you could be. A mathematical expression of the logistic equation is

$$dP/dt = rP(K - P), \quad t \geq 0, \quad K > P_0 > 0, \quad r > 0,$$

where P_0 is the population size when t is 0. The solution of this differential equation is $P(t) = 1 / [e^{-rKt}(1/P_0 - 1/K) + 1/K]$, $t \geq 0$. No surprises here for anyone who survived a course in calculus. Calculus escapees can think of dP/dt as the difference in population size P for each difference in time t. Now you can relax: no more strong language for a long time to come!
25. Yule 1925, p. 41, reviewed Verhulst's memoirs in detail. Smith and Keyfitz 1977, pp. 333–39, translated Verhulst's 1838 paper into English.
26. Lowell J. Reed 1936, p. 162, a biostatistician at Johns Hopkins University who was a great enthusiast of the use of the logistic curve for population projection, commented on Verhulst's projections: "His numerical results naturally have little value since his period of observation was so short."
27. Pearl and Reed 1920.
28. Johnson 1991, p. 796, gives the land area of the United States as 864,746 square miles in 1790 and 2,969,565 square miles in 1910, an increase by a factor of 3.4.
29. Wolfe 1927, p. 559.
30. Pearl and Reed 1924.
31. Ibid., p. 585.
32. Ibid., p. 586.
33. Ibid., p. 632.
34. Hart 1945.
35. Chou et al. 1977, p. 7.
36. Tuckwell and Koziol 1992, p. 200.
37. Monro 1993.
38. Lotka 1925, pp. 69–71.
39. Wolfe 1927; Cole et al. 1973, pp. 159–74.
40. The "discrete-time" logistic equation is $P(t+1) - P(t) = rP(t) \times [K - P(t)]$.
41. Myrberg 1962; May 1974, 1975, 1986; Hastings et al. 1993.
42. Von Foerster et al. 1960; see also the correspondence in von Foerster et al. 1961, 1962; and Serrin 1975.
43. Pulliam and Haddad 1994, p. 145.
44. Dorn 1962, in Cox 1969, p. 264.
45. Umpleby 1990.
46. Lee 1988 derived a model in which population size is a sum of exponentials. His model rests on assumptions about the interactions between technological progress and population growth. In his model, with his parameter estimates, one exponential is increasing and the other exponential is decreasing. In the simple model suggested here, both exponentials are increasing.

47. McEvedy and Jones 1978.
48. Lee 1992, p. 1547.

6: THE UNIQUENESS OF THE PRESENT RELATIVE TO THE PAST

1. Torrey et al. 1987, p. 4; United States Bureau of the Census 1991, 1992.
2. United Nations 1992c, p. 12.
3. United States Bureau of the Census 1992, p. 10.
4. Torrey et al. 1987, p. 21.
5. United States Bureau of the Census 1992, p. 4.
6. Torrey et al. 1987, p. v.
7. Cipolla 1974, pp. 42–66.
8. Where do such numbers come from? The maximum amount of work per unit of time (power) that an ordinary man can sustain without incurring an oxygen deficit has been estimated at 12 times his basal metabolic rate (Blaxter 1989, p. 177). Pulling a rickshaw with a typical load of 180 kilograms consumes energy at 10.4 times the basal metabolic rate; pedaling a rickshaw with a passenger requires 8.5 times the basal metabolic rate (James and Schofield 1990, pp. 134, 137). The basal metabolic rate of an adult man ranges from 4.8 to 8.5 megajoules per day, depending on his age and height (Blaxter 1989, p. 144). For early and pre-industrial man, a height of 1.5 meters, a weight of 50 kilograms and a basal metabolic rate of six megajoules per day ≈ 70 watts seem plausible. The maximal sustainable power would be $12 \times 6 = 72$ megajoules per day ≈ 840 watts, about one horsepower (Pennycuick 1988, p. 30). A more realistic calculation would suppose that a man is unlikely to be able to consume more than 5,000 kilocalories per day, on average. If all of that energy were converted into useful work, ignoring basal metabolism, the sustainable power output would be about 240 watts or one-third horsepower.
9. Cipolla 1974, p. 48.
10. Ibid., p. 51.
11. Ibid., p. 55.
12. Since there are roughly 8,766 hours per year, one megawatt-hour per year per person corresponds to a constant power supply of 114 watts. At about 1.6 times the basal metabolic rate (70 watts) of a hypothetical pre-industrial standard person weighing 50 kilograms, 114 watts would permit that person to do light work, such as office clerical work (your typical businessman, lawyer or university professor) or housekeeping in an affluent society.
13. World Bank 1992.
14. Harte 1988, p. 242.
15. Livi-Bacci 1992, p. 28.
16. Gever et al. 1986, pp. 17, 19. The balance came from nuclear, hydroelectric, solar, geothermal and wind sources.
17. World Bank 1992, pp. 226–27.
18. Chandler and Fox 1974. How to measure the spatial concentration of people is not entirely obvious. If, in one region, large families live in single-room huts that are widely separated, while in another region small families live in multi-room homes on neighboring plots of a hectare (2.5 acres) or so, the average number of people per square kilometer may be the same in both regions but the extent of contacts within families may be higher in the first and the extent of contacts, or at least sitings, between families may be higher in the second.
19. Hauser 1971.
20. Rita Wright, personal communication, 18 May 1994.
21. McNeill 1967, p. 401.
22. United Nations 1992b, pp. 185–88.
23. Ibid., p. 226.
24. United Nations Population Division 1992, p. 5; World Resources Institute 1994, p. 286.
25. United Nations Population Division 1992, p. 6. The United States Bureau of the Census 1992, p. 40, estimated that 2.4 billion people, 45 percent of world population, were urban in the early 1990s.
26. United States Bureau of the Census 1992.
27. World Resources Institute, 1992 data diskette.
28. Hauser 1971, pp. 19, 21.

29. Rubin-Kurtzman et al. 1993.

30. Check: if the average growth rate is 0.069 percent per year, then the doubling time is 69 / 0.069 = 1,000 years. If the average growth rate exceeded 0.069 percent per year, the doubling time would be shorter.

31. Check that $(1.016)^{436} = 1,013$.

7: Projection Methods: The Hazy Crystal Ball

1. Cannan 1895, pp. 505–6.

2. *Economist* 1990a.

3. Horiuchi 1992.

4. United Nations 1991b, p. 10.

5. Wolfe 1927, pp. 578–79; Dorn 1962, in Cox 1969, p. 263.

6. Brass 1979, p. 100.

7. Population Reference Bureau 1990.

8. Hajnal 1957.

9. Cannan 1895 did not distinguish between the sexes at all.

10. Frejka 1973, pp. 36–37.

11. Rogers 1968.

12. Frejka 1973, p. 37.

13. United Nations 1992a, p. 13.

14. United Nations 1991b.

15. United Nations 1992a, p. 13.

16. Haub 1994.

17. Gilland 1979, 1983.

18. Frejka 1973, p. 55. For small regions, birth rates often matter less than rates of migration, which are even more unpredictable.

19. Westoff 1993.

20. Charles F. Westoff, "Fertility forecasts," memorandum dated 8 April 1994, personal communication. Tan and Tey 1994, p. 222, matched the 1984 Malaysian Population and Family Survey with birth registration records for 1985–87. They found that "stated fertility intention provides fairly accurate forecasts of fertility behavior in the subsequent period. In other words, whether a woman has another child is predicted closely by whether she wanted an additional child."

21. Keyfitz 1968; Inaba 1989.

22. Alho 1990; Ahlburg and Land 1992; Lee and Tuljapurkar 1994.

23. Sanderson 1995.

24. A tonne is a metric ton, that is, 1,000 kilograms or roughly 2,200 pounds, almost the same as the British long ton.

25. In Kotler 1990, pp. 175–77.

26. Population Reference Bureau 1992.

27. Forrester 1971; Randers and Meadows 1972; Meadows et al. 1972; Cole et al. 1973; Mesarovic and Pestel 1974; a review by van de Walle 1975; House and Williams 1975; Gever et al. 1986; Gilbert and Braat 1991; Meadows et al. 1992.

28. Meadows et al. 1992.

29. Meadows et al. 1972.

30. Forrester 1971.

31. Meadows et al. 1972 (1974 ed., p. 149), italics in original.

32. E.g., Kaysen 1972; Cole et al. 1973; Nordhaus 1973; Berlinski 1976; Ehrlich, Ehrlich and Holdren 1977, pp. 730–33.

33. Berlinski 1976, p. xi.

34. Srinivasan 1987, p. 4.

35. Davis, in Davis and Bernstam 1991, pp. 11–12. For the controversy over the 1992 reprise by Meadows et al., see Lippman 1992.

36. Forrester 1971.

37. Meadows et al. 1972.

38. Cole et al. 1973.

39. Ibid., pp. 125–34.
40. Hayes 1993 reported his independent experiments with the computer model of *Beyond the Limits*.
41. Forrester 1971, p. 19.
42. Ibid., p. 46.
43. Ibid., p. 46.
44. Cole et al. 1973, pp. 43–55.
45. Ibid., p. 54.
46. Meadows et al. 1992, pp. 240–41.
47. Ibid., pp. 247–49.
48. See any issue of *Population Index,* the journal that prints abstracts of scholarly articles on demography.
49. Nordhaus 1973, p. 1157, italics in original.
50. Ibid., p. 1158.
51. Kaysen 1972, p. 665, observed that from an economic perspective, a "major flaw . . . lies in the total absence of adjustment mechanisms of any kind in the model [in *The Limits to Growth*]. . . . Especially in the workings of the economy, adjustment mechanisms play a crucial role. The most important of these is price: as a resource becomes scarce, the consequent rise in price leads to savings in use, to efforts to increase supply, and to technical innovation to offset the scarcity. . . . [D]ynamic models structurally similar to those employed in 'Limits,' that characteristically display various forms of unstable behavior in the absence of prices as variables, are stabilized by the incorporation of prices and normal responses to price changes." Also see Nordhaus 1993.
52. Cole et al. 1973.
53. Harvey Simmons, in Cole et al. 1973, p. 202.
54. Meadows et al. 1992, pp. 108–10.
55. Meadows et al. 1972 (1974 ed., p. 29).
56. Meadows et al. 1992, pp. xv–xvi.
57. Arthur and McNicoll 1975, p. 261.
58. House and Williams 1975.
59. Gever et al. 1986.
60. Lutz and Baguant 1992, p. 61.
61. Lutz and Baguant 1992; Lutz 1993; Lutz 1994. This work followed the earlier modeling of Mauritius by Malcolm Slesser and Janet King, a husband-and-wife team then at the Centre for Human Ecology of Edinburgh University, some of it in collaboration with Baguant; e.g., Baguant and Slesser, in Gilbert and Braat 1991, pp. 95–125; Slesser and King 1988.
62. Lutz and Baguant 1992, p. 74.
63. Lutz 1993, p. 9.
64. Lutz and Baguant 1992, p. 74.
65. Frejka 1978.
66. Blaxter 1986, p. 26.
67. Grummer-Strawn and Espenshade 1991.
68. Dorn 1950, 1962; Hajnal 1954, 1957; Myers 1954; Shryock 1954; Grauman 1967; Törnqvist 1967; Keyfitz 1982a (especially chap. 13 on "The Limits of Population Forecasting"), 1982b; Demeny 1988, pp. 232–35.
69. Henry and Gutierrez 1977; Cohen 1986, p. 122.
70. Keyfitz 1982a, p. 184.
71. Lee and Tuljapurkar 1994; Sanderson 1995.

8: Scenarios of Future Population

1. Huxley 1950 (1993, p. 614).
2. United Nations 1992a, p. vii.
3. Ibid., p. 31.
4. Ibid., p. 22.
5. The average number of children per woman required for replacement depends on the death rates. If higher death rates had been assumed at ages before the end of reproduction, then

the replacement-level total fertility rate would have been higher than 2.06 children per woman. If lower death rates had been assumed at ages before the end of reproduction, then the replacement-level total fertility rate would have been lower than 2.06 children per woman.

6. This scenario does not give a lower bound on future population growth because fertility is assumed to rise to replacement level in areas where it is presently below replacement, and because death rates are assumed to fall. Assuming current mortality and no rises in fertility would have given a lower projection.

7. Bongaarts 1994.

8. United Nations 1992a, p. 8.

9. Ibid., p. 34.

10. United Nations 1991b, p. 2.

11. Population Reference Bureau 1992.

12. Ibid.

13. Seckler 1994.

14. Population Reference Bureau 1993.

15. Lee and Tuljapurkar 1994.

16. E.g., Lee and Tuljapurkar 1994.

17. United Nations 1992a.

18. United Nations 1993, pp. 284–85.

19. United Nations 1992a, p. viii.

20. McNicoll 1992, pp. 334–35.

21. World Bank 1992, p. 26.

22. Frejka 1973.

23. United Nations 1992a.

24. Gilland 1979, p. 19.

25. Dorn 1962.

26. Dorn 1962, in Cox 1969, pp. 273–74.

27. Poor European tenants would have been aware of their landlord's wealth if he or she lived with them on the land, but not if in a remote city. The late-nineteenth-century rumors in eastern Europe that the streets of America were paved with gold were poor analogues of today's electronic images.

28. Dorn 1962.

29. Van de Walle and Knodel 1980, p. 37.

30. Ibid., p. 37.

31. King 1993, p. 23.

32. Thomas 1993, pp. 358–59.

33. King 1993, p. 24.

34. Cassen 1994, pp. 13, 26.

35. Kirk 1967, in Cox 1969, pp. 297–98.

36. Kirk 1967.

37. Van de Walle 1992.

38. Kirk 1967.

39. Ibid.

40. United Nations Fund for Population Activities 1993b, p. 1.

41. Van de Walle and Knodel 1980, pp. 37–38.

42. United Nations 1987, p. 382.

43. United Nations Fund for Population Activities 1993b, p. 1.

9: WHAT DO WE KNOW FOR SURE ABOUT THE FUTURE OF GLOBAL POPULATION?

1. Dorn 1962, in Cox 1969, p. 274.

2. United Nations 1992a.

3. Coale 1970, in Reining and Tinker 1975, p. 116.

4. United Nations 1992a.

5. Meadows et al. 1972, p. 21.

6. Gever et al. 1986 (1991, p. 15).

7. Science Summit 1994, pp. 7–8.

8. Population Reference Bureau 1992.

9. In Niger in 1992, life expectancy for men was 43 years, for women 46 years; in Ethiopia, 46 and 48 years—less than the 50 years predicted from the 2 percent death rate for a stationary population. Why? In Niger and Ethiopia, the death rates were lower than the reciprocal of the life expectancy because both populations had a higher fraction of young people than would be present in a stationary population with the same age-specific death rates. Both populations had a higher fraction of young people than a stationary population because both populations were growing.

10. Boulding 1964, p. 127.

11. United Nations 1992a. Also see United States Bureau of the Census 1992.

10: EIGHT ESTIMATES OF HUMAN CARRYING CAPACITY

1. Dorn 1962, in Cox 1969, p. 262.

2. McNeill 1963, p. 730.

3. Ibid., p. 731; Crosby 1972, 1986.

4. Ravenstein 1891, p. 27.

5. Ibid., p. 28.

6. Ibid., p. 28.

7. Ibid., p. 28.

8. Ibid., pp. 28–29.

9. Ibid., p. 29.

10. Ibid., p. 29.

11. Ibid., p. 30.

12. Ibid., p. 31.

13. Ibid., p. 31.

Ravenstein's assertion here (and in his table, which I have reproduced in Table 10.1) that "1468 millions . . . now dwell upon the earth" is mistaken. (I thank the Honorable Danny J. Boggs for pointing out this mistake.) If his estimates of the 1890 population of each continent are summed, the total excluding the polar regions is not 1,467,600,000 as he asserts but 1,487,600,000. (Check with your calculator.) Taking as given his estimates of each continent's population size and of the decadal rate of increase, region by region, I calculated the population expected in 1900. The sum of the regional figures for 1900 (excluding the polar regions) is 1,609,109,400, an increase of more than 9.6 percent over 1,468 million (Ravenstein's mistaken figure for 1890) but an increase of 8.2 percent over 1,488 million (the correct total). Ravenstein must have computed the 8 percent decadal growth rate for the whole world based on the correct total for 1890 and then miscopied the total when he composed the table and text based on it.

A second puzzle is that, according to my calculator, 182 years of growth at Ravenstein's 8 percent per decade starting from the incorrect 1,468 million gives 5,957 million people, and 182 years of growth at 8 percent per decade starting from the correct 1,488 million gives about 6,038 million, neither of which matches Ravenstein's figure of 5,977 million. Ravenstein's 3,426 million in the year 2000 is exactly the result of ten decades of growth at 8 percent per decade applied to his figure of 1,587 million for the year 1900, so he evidently intended to continue the global population growth rate into the future.

Of course, the differences between Ravenstein's calculations and mine are minuscule compared to the uncertainty of the estimates. The errors show only that it is easier to do arithmetic these days, not that it is easier to make correct predictions.

14. Ravenstein 1891, p. 33. Marshall's concern about fuel shortages may have arisen from the influential book of William Stanley Jevons (1835–1882) entitled *The Coal Question* (first published in 1865, with later editions).

15. Biraben 1979.

16. Rounded to the nearest million, Biraben's estimates (with Ravenstein's estimates in parentheses) were: Europe, 422 (413); Asia, 903 (901); Africa, 138 (140); Australasia, 6 (6); all the Americas, 165 (149).

17. The German scholar Arthur Freiherr von Fircks (1898, p. 295) estimated the potential

population density of the fertile regions as 100 per square kilometer (instead of Ravenstein's 80), of the steppes as 20 per square kilometer (instead of Ravenstein's 4) and of deserts as 5 per square kilometer (instead of Ravenstein's 0.4). Fircks converted Ravenstein's estimates of the areas of these regions from square miles to square kilometers; all three of his conversions are incorrect and each uses a different apparent conversion factor. Using Fircks's incorrect figures for the areas of these regions, I arrived at 9.272 billion people, exactly the figure Fircks obtained. Using the correctly converted areas and Fircks's estimates of denstiy, I arrived at 8.1 billion. According to Albrecht Penck (1925, pp. 334–35), a professor of geography at the University of Berlin who lectured and was widely known in the United States (Smith 1935, p. 34), the geographer Hermann Wagner obtained 7.8 billion people from the same assumptions, claiming to correct an arithmetic error of Fircks. If my arithmetic is right, Wagner's correction is in error. Incidentally, Penck (1925, pp. 334–35) mistakenly reported that Fircks (1898, p. 295) estimated the potential population density of the steppes as 50 per square kilometer instead of Fircks's actual estimate of 20 per square kilometer.

18. Penck 1925, p. 331. All quotations in English from Penck are my translations.

19. Ibid., p. 332.

20. Ibid., p. 333.

21. Ibid., p. 334.

22. Ibid., p. 336.

23. Ibid., p. 336.

24. Ibid., p. 339. Penck's arithmetic is puzzling. Based on his estimates of area (column I) and of the maximal possible population density (column II), I calculated the product (column A on the right), which should correspond to the highest conceivable number of inhabitants (column III). There are enough agreements between columns III and A to show that Penck intended to compute the product. There are four discrepancies. One of them (that for climate 6) is trivial. The other three arise from Penck's use of the population density of the "most thickly settled lands" (West Java for climate 1, Region of the Don for climate 3, Egypt for climate 4) in place of his "assumed maximum population density" (column II). Based on his assumptions in columns I and II, the highest conceivable number of inhabitants, according to column A, should, be 15,634 million, and the average population density in this case should be 105 people per square kilometer. Penck's computation of column V as the product of columns I and IV is correct.

25. Penck 1925, p. 342.

26. E.g., De Wit 1967; Revelle 1974, 1976.

27. A rough estimate used, for example, by De Wit 1967, p. 319.

28. Kates et al. 1989, p. 12.

29. Penck 1925, p. 334.

30. Penck 1941, p. 32.

31. De Wit 1967, p. 315.

32. Odum 1971, p. 48.

33. De Wit 1967, p. 317.

34. Ibid., p. 317.

35. Ibid., p. 318. Check that 2.75×10^{10} square meters / 37×10^6 people = 743 square meters per person.

36. De Wit 1967, p. 318.

37. Check: If all food came from the sea, then all land could be used for "urban and recreational needs" (at 750 square meters per person). The total land surface is 131×10^8 hectares, so 131×10^{12} square meters / 750 square meters = 174.7 billion people.

38. De Wit 1967, pp. 318–20.

39. Ibid., pp. 319–20.

40. Ibid., p. 320.

41. Higgins et al. 1983.

42. Revelle 1976, p. 167.

43. Ibid., p. 174.

44. Odum 1971, p. 44.

45. Schlesinger 1991, pp. 121, 267; Lieth 1973, p. 309.

46. Bugbee and Monje 1992, p. 494.

47. Ibid., p. 500.

48. Check: 1.67×10^{10} hectares $= 10^{12}$ tonnes total / 60 tonnes per hectare.
49. Hulett 1970, p. 160.
50. Ibid., p. 160.
51. Ibid., p. 160.
52. Schmitt 1965.
53. Here is Penck's (1925) formula again: $P = 8.4 \times 10^{15}$ / $(7 \times 10^6) = 1.2 \times 10^9$, with the individual's requirement for food, the denominator, estimated from United States consumption in 1966.
54. Hulett 1970, p. 160.
55. Ibid., p. 161.
56. Ibid., p. 161.
57. De Wit 1967, p. 319.
58. "Chickens and cows eat about 4.5 calories of plant material per calorie contained in the eggs and milk they produce. Most of the plant calories eaten by domestic animals in the U.S. could also be eaten by human beings, so that Americans actually use, directly or indirectly, close to 10,000 kilocalories of humanly edible plant products per person per day." Revelle 1974, p. 164. The equivalent of 10,000 kilocalories per person per day is roughly 3.7 million kilocalories per person per year, little more than half of Hulett's estimate of 7 million kilocalories per American per year.
59. "Based on the proportions of the different kinds of animal-based foods in the average U.S. diet, each kcal of animal-based food requires about 16 kcal . . . of crops to produce." Gever et al. 1986, p. 28.
60. Hulett 1970, p. 160.
61. James and Schofield 1990, p. 53.
62. Quoted by Revelle and Frisch 1967, p. 46.
63. Miller 1980, pp. 25, 30.
64. World Resources Institute 1994, p. 108.
65. United States Bureau of the Census 1974, p. 614.
66. Pearson and Harper 1945, pp. 68–69.
67. Westing 1981.
68. E.g., Revelle et al. 1967; Goldsmith et al. 1967.
69. Revelle 1974.
70. Revelle 1976.
71. Ibid., p. 177.
72. Ibid., p. 177.
73. Ibid., p. 168.
74. Revelle (1974, p. 167) estimated that "The average harvest of corn in Iowa is about 100 bushels per acre, or 6.4 tons per hectare. . . ."
75. Revelle 1976, p. 177. Revelle must have assumed 3.56 kilocalories per gram of harvested grain. (Check me, please!)
76. Revelle 1976, p. 168.
77. Ibid., p. 178.
78. Ibid., p. 172.
79. Ibid., p. 170.
80. World Resources Institute 1992, p. 94; World Resources Institute 1994, p. 292.
81. World Resources Institute 1992, p. 95.
82. Blaxter 1986, p. 66.
83. World Resources Institute 1994, p. 294.
84. World Resources Institute 1992, p. 96.
85. World Resources Institute 1994, p. 292.
86. Ibid., p. 294.
87. World Resources Institute 1992, p. 98.
88. Ehrlich, Ehrlich and Daily 1993, p. 28, citing a "Statement of Catholic Bishops, reported in *The Washington Post,* 19 November 1988."
89. Ibid., pp. 21–22, citation omitted.
90. Clark 1958, pp. 104–5.
91. Clark 1977, pp. 142–44; the 1977 second edition differs from the first by the addition of a final chapter. Of the total 7.68 billion "standard land" hectares, 2.039 billion are twice-

counted tropical areas capable of growing two crops per year. The actual physical area of these zones must be 1.02 billion hectares (half of 2.04 billion). If each tropical hectare used to grow grass and fodder crops could yield as much as five temperate hectares, the previous 7.68 billion hectares total would be increased by $3 \times 1.02 = 3.06$ billion "standard land" hectares to get 10.7 billion hectares. Since the cold areas vary in their productivity, it is not possible to infer the actual physical area of the cold lands that Clark included in his estimates of total standard farmland.

92. Clark 1977, pp. 151–52.
93. Ibid., p. 151.
94. Ibid., p. 150.
95. Ibid., p. 153.
96. Ibid., p. 128.
97. Ibid., p. 130.
98. Ibid., p. 153. Clark's arithmetic about subsistence land requirements was mistaken. If the yield of bamboo is 20 cubic meters per hectare per year and the subsistence requirement is 1/6 cubic meter per person per year, as Clark assumed, the required area is 1/120 hectare or about 83 square meters per person per year. Added to the assumed requirement of 640 square meters for food, the total requirement for land would be 723 square meters per person (not 680 square meters as Clark asserted). Assuming potential agricultural land of 10.7 billion hectares would give a maximum population of 148 billion people. Clark's widely quoted figure of 157 billion is 9 billion too high as a result of a minor arithmetic error.
99. Clark 1977, p. 153.
100. Check: 47.6 billion people equals $10.7 \times 10^9 \times 10^4$ square meters of agricultural land divided by 2,250 square meters of land per person.
101. Clark 1958.
102. Clark's estimate that 20 cubic meters of wood could be produced per hectare per year may be attainable locally under the most favorable conditions. For example, an Arkansas loblolly-shortleaf pine farm under intensive management produced two cords of pulpwood per acre per year (Allen and Sharpe 1960, p. 72). As one cord is 128 cubic feet whereas one cubic meter is 35.32 cubic feet, two cords per acre per year equals 17.9 cubic meters per hectare per year (check me!), not far below Clark's assumed yield.
103. World Resources Institute 1992, pp. 288–89.
104. Spears and Ayensu 1985, p. 313.
105. Basia Zaba, personal communication, 20 May 1994.
106. Hall 1980, p. 75.
107. Li 1991, pp. 256–57.
108. Kirchner et al. 1985, p. 67.
109. Ibid., p. 84.
110. Higgins et al. 1983, p. 5.
111. Ibid., p. 5.
112. Higgins et al. 1983.
113. Ibid., p. viii.
114. Ibid., p. 26.
115. Ibid., pp. 20, 25.
116. Higgins et al. 1983 do not give figures. I quote from James and Schofield 1990, p. 31, who used FAO's 1973 method with FAO's 1973 data base. For the same countries, requirements are usually, but not always, lower when FAO's 1985 method is used with FAO's 1988 data base (in kilocalories per person per day): 1,925 for India, 1,994 for Thailand, 2,142 for Chile and 2,308 for Turkey. (Turkey's requirement increased.)
117. Higgins et al. 1983, p. 11.
118. World Resources Institute 1992, p. 98.
119. As reported by Higgins et al. 1983.
120. United Nations 1993, pp. 154–57. Because the 1992 United Nations groupings of countries differed from the groupings Higgins et al. used, I summed the United Nations' projected populations of individual countries according to the regional groupings of Higgins et al.
121. Higgins et al. 1983; United Nations 1993.
122. Higgins et al. 1983, p. 17.

123. Not a calculation reported by Higgins et al. 1983.
124. Higgins et al. 1983, p. vii.
125. Ibid., pp. 55–56.
126. For some reason, Higgins et al. 1983, p. 56, assert that Western Sahara and Cape Verde would require less than 0.1 percent of Guinea's surplus potential food production; check that 0.4 / 170.2 = 0.002.
127. Higgins et al. 1983, p. 57.
128. Fearnside 1990, p. 193.
129. Ibid., p. 193.
130. Ibid., pp. 193–94.
131. Murdoch 1990, pp. 3–4.
132. Srinivasan 1987, p. 6; reprinted in Lee et al. 1988.
133. Srinivasan 1987, p. 17.
134. E.g., Kates et al. 1988, 1989; Chen 1990; Millman et al. 1991.
135. Millman et al. 1991, p. 2.
136. They took this conversion factor from Blaxter, 1986.
137. Kates et al. 1989, p. 12. Check the last bit of arithmetic: The basic diet of 2,350 kilocalories per day was assumed to be vegetarian. The improved diet contained the same total calories, but 90 percent (or 2,115 kilocalories) was vegetarian and the remaining 10 percent (235 kilocalories) required $1,410 = 6 \times 235$ of primary food supply as animal feeds, so the total primary food requirement was $3,525 = 2,115 + 1,410$ kilocalories per day, which is 1.5 times the calories of primary food required by the basic diet. The calculation for the "full-but-healthy" diet with 20 percent of calories from animal products proceeded similarly.
138. Millman et al. 1991, p. 19.
139. Millman et al. 1991.
140. Hulett 1970.
141. Ibid., p. 160.
142. Millman et al. 1991. I calculated this quantity as 5.5×10^9 (people in the world) × 2,350 (kilocalories per person per day) × 365.25 (days per year) / 0.6 the denominator of 0.6 is required to adjust for the assumed 40 percent loss between growth and consumption.

11: ESTIMATES OF HUMAN CARRYING CAPACITY: A SURVEY OF FOUR CENTURIES

1. Pearl and Reed 1924, p. 632.
2. Brown 1954; Brown, Bonner and Weir 1957; Clark 1958; Cépède et al. 1964; Schmitt 1965; Lieth 1973; Blaxter 1986; Buringh et al. 1975; Buringh and van Heemst 1977; Higgins et al. 1983; Chen et al. 1990; Millman et al. 1991; Brown and Kane 1994.
3. Hulett 1970, p. 160.
4. Millman et al. 1991.
5. This is 7.9×10^{15} kilocalories per year divided by 7×10^6 kilocalories per person per year.
6. Daily and Ehrlich 1992, pp. 762–63.
7. World Resources Institute 1992, p. 273.
8. Ibid., p. 274.
9. Hayes 1993, p. 515.
10. Quoted by Gardner 1992, p. 52.
11. Pulliam and Haddad 1994, p. 144.
12. Brigham 1909, pp. 209–10.
13. Ibid., pp. 211–15.
14. Brown 1954, pp. 116–17.
15. Pimentel and Pimentel 1991, p. 13.
16. Pimentel et al. 1994, pp. 362–63.
17. Miller 1992, p. 81.
18. Song and Yu 1988, p. 248; see also pp. 239–49.
19. In addition to Song and Yu 1988, see also Song 1982; Song and Yu 1985; Adlakha and Banister 1993.
20. I rely on Australian Government 1975. However, that report mistakenly asserts in two

places (pp. 183, 191) that the Commonwealth Statistician G. H. Knibbs estimated a maximum population for Australia of 132 million people. A more careful reading of Knibbs (1917, p. 455) shows that he estimated a maximum population of 132 *billion* for the world as a whole.

21. Wickens 1925, p. 9.

22. Australian Government 1975, p. 712.

23. Scott 1994; Parliament of the Commonwealth of Australia 1994.

24. Hardesty 1977, pp. 195–211; Fearnside 1986, pp. 61–92.

25. Andreae 1991, p. 268.

26. Hardesty 1977, p. 201; Fearnside 1986, p. 75.

27. Fearnside 1986, p. 70.

28. Ibid., p. 79.

29. Ibid., p. 126.

30. Specifically, Fearnside 1986, p. 136, calculated "sustainable probabilities of colonist failure . . . as the proportion of the total number of colonist-years in the last ten years of . . . 25-year-long simulations in which failures occurred by each criterion."

31. Fearnside 1986, p. 122.

32. Cook and Repetto 1982.

33. Fearnside 1986, p. 137.

34. Ibid., pp. 144–45.

35. Ibid., p. 81.

36. Ibid., p. 84.

37. Ibid., p. 85.

38. Australian Government 1975, p. 713.

39. Ibid., p. 719.

40. E.g., World Bank 1984; Myers 1991a (and the review by Thomas 1992), 1992; Carrying Capacity Network 1992; Meadows et al. 1992.

41. Whittaker and Likens 1975.

42. Muscat 1985.

43. Davis and Bernstam 1991.

44. E.g., United Nations 1980; Simon and Kahn 1984.

45. E.g., House and Williams 1975; Thurow 1986; Gever et al. 1986; Gilbert and Braat 1991; Heilig 1994.

46. Blaxter 1986, pp. 91–92.

47. Mayer 1964, p. 843.

48. As emphasized by Hardin 1986, 1993.

49. Brown 1954, pp. 146–47.

50. Brown, Bonner and Weir 1957, p. 67.

51. Brown 1954, p. 146.

52. Ibid., pp. 146–47.

53. Brown, Bonner and Weir 1957, p. 77.

54. In Hirschoff and Kotler 1989, pp. 114–15.

12:   CARRYING CAPACITY IN ECOLOGY AND APPLIED ECOLOGY

1. Dorn 1962, in Cox 1969, p. 274.

2. Pulliam and Haddad 1994, pp. 141–42, suggested that the 1953 first edition of Eugene P. Odum's textbook *Fundamentals of Ecology* popularized this definition of carrying capacity. As the logistic equation was invented more than a century before 1953 and had been promoted enthusiastically by Raymond Pearl since 1920, it could also be that Odum's text recognized, rather than shaped, a common definition of carrying capacity.

3. Ricklefs 1990, p. 803. Also see Wilson and Bossert 1971, p. 18.

4. One way to derive the logistic equation is to suppose that the birth rate per individual is a decreasing linear (straight-line) function of the population size and that the death rate per individual is an increasing linear function of the population size.

5. E.g., Begon et al. 1990, pp. 203–5, 847.

6. E.g. Gever et al. 1986, p. 4.

7. Liebig 1855; Blackman 1905; Baker 1950, pp. 128–29; DeAngelis 1992, pp. 38–45, 228.

8. Baker 1950, pp. 128–29.

9. Smil 1991, pp. 586, 597.

10. Baker 1950, pp. 128–29.

11. Blackman 1905, p. 289 (italics in original).

12. DeAngelis 1992, p. 41.

13. Pomeroy 1974, p. 7.

14. Schindler 1977.

15. Pomeroy 1974, p. 7.

16. By contrast, the concentrations of the major ions of seawater vary much less from place to place. Redfield's remarkable 1934 paper was reprinted by Pomeroy 1974; for the current state of play see Chisholm 1992.

17. DeAngelis 1992, p. 39; Sayles 1992, p. 72.

18. Miller et al. 1991; Chisholm 1992, pp. 43–46.

19. Martin and Fitzwater 1988.

20. Kunzig 1994, p. 35.

21. Blackman 1905, pp. 289, 293.

22. DeAngelis 1992.

23. Smil 1991, pp. 586, 597.

24. DeAngelis 1992, p. 228.

25. Holdren and Ehrlich 1974.

26. DeAngelis 1992, p. 43.

27. Pomeroy 1992.

28. DeAngelis 1992, p. 44.

29. Meadows et al. 1972, according to Cole et al. 1973, p. 76.

30. Liebig and the French economist Marie Esprit Léon Walras (1834–1910) lived only 35 years apart. The appearance of Liebig's law in Walras's production function may not reflect an independent discovery.

31. Meadows et al. 1992.

32. Meadows et al. 1972 (1974), 1992.

33. Keeton, Gould and Gould 1993, pp. 473–87.

34. Zaba and Scoones 1994; Dhondt 1988.

35. The species was *Rangifer tarandus*. See Pulliam and Haddad 1994, p. 141.

36. Clark 1990.

37. To avoid complications, assume that the animals consume the plants but do not contribute to the growth of the plants by fertilizing them (as cattle fertilize a pasture) or by protecting them (as some ants and wasps protect plants they dwell on from plant pests).

38. Clark 1990, p. 58.

39. Ibid., pp. 62–63.

40. Ibid., pp. 60–61.

41. Zaba and Scoones 1994, p. 203.

42. Clark 1990, p. 24.

43. Pearce and Warford 1993, pp. 244–45.

44. Hardin 1968.

45. Following Clark 1990, pp. 24–36.

46. Clark 1990.

47. "Bionomics" is another word for ecology. Here "bionomic" may be used to suggest a splice of biological with economic.

48. Clark 1990, p. 27.

49. Hardin 1968.

50. Danny J. Boggs, personal communication, 2 September 1994.

51. Cassen 1993, p. 16.

52. Muscat 1985, p. 20.

53. Myers 1991b.

54. Economists recognized this clearly decades ago. Sorenson 1971, p. 117: "The basic economic explanation for excessive population growth is that individual decisions concerning size of family do not take account of the total cost to society of additional children. . . . The problem is that significant external costs are not included in the family's estimate of the supply cost of an additional birth. Externalities such as the increased cost of education, public health,

466   *Notes (pp. 258–270)*

police services, and highways readily come to mind. But more important external costs arise from the environmental blight that follows population growth: pollution of the air and water, disappearance of undeveloped land, over-crowding of recreation sites, and the reduction of space and of privacy."

55. Lee 1991, pp. 315–17. For further analysis of externalities and population, see Nerlove et al. 1987; the chapter by Robert J. Willis in Johnson and Lee 1987, pp. 661–702; Lee and Miller 1990.

56. Cassen 1993, p. 15. Economists distinguish pecuniary externalities, which are mediated by markets, from technical externalities, in which costs and benefits of actions do not pass through any markets. Cassen's example of high birth rates depressing wages for all workers is a pecuniary externality, because what workers lose through lower wages, factory owners gain in profits, according to pure economic theory (neglecting the effects of poorer health on the workers' productivity, for example). Lee's example of population growth diminishing each person's right to visit Yosemite National Park is a technical externality. If properly organized, workers could pay other workers, from the wages they would otherwise lose, not to have enough children to depress wages; or a government could redistribute the factory owners' increased profits to the workers by means of taxation (neglecting the cost of the transactions and the likely social impediments). But there is no market through which I can pay you to keep away from my favorite public wild place.

57. Leichty 1971; Kilmer 1972.

58. Potter and Potter 1990; Greenhalgh 1993; Greenhalgh et al. 1994.

59. Simon 1990.

60. Daly and Cobb 1989, p. 2.

61. O'Neill 1993, p. 46.

62. Ibid., p. 50.

13: HUMAN CHOICES

1. In Davis and Bernstam 1991, p. 7.

2. World Commission on Environment and Development 1987.

3. Schell 1993, pp. 12–13.

4. One exception is the probabilistic estimate of human carrying capacity in the Brazilian Amazon by Fearnside 1986.

5. Ausubel 1989; Ausubel and Sladovich 1989; Allenby 1992a, 1992b, 1993; Graedel and Allenby 1994.

6. Nordhaus 1993; World Resources Institute 1994, p. 262.

7. Wilson 1992.

8. Daily and Ehrlich 1992, p. 4; references omitted.

9. Simon and Kahn 1984, p. 45. Julian Simon restated his views in a debate with Norman Myers: Myers and Simon 1994.

10. Benedick 1991, p. 201.

11. Gardner 1992, p. 30.

12. Ibid., p. 19.

13. Adams 1965; Hardesty 1977, p. 204.

14. Dahl and Tufte 1973, p. 20.

15. Olson 1965.

16. Dahl and Tufte 1973, p. 108.

17. Ibid., p. 113.

18. Ibid., p. 116.

19. Ibid., p. 122.

20. Ibid., p. 128.

21. Ibid., p. 135.

22. Parsons 1971.

23. Diaz-Briquets 1986.

24. Daly and Cobb 1989, pp. 51–52.

25. Choucri 1974, 1984; Homer-Dixon 1994b.

26. Romm 1993.

27. Quoted in Romm 1993, p. 5.

28. As quoted in Romm 1993, p. 6.

29. Romm 1993, pp. 25–29.

30. Bloom and Brender 1993, p. 20. "Value added" is presumably defined in terms of market prices.

31. The example is given by Bloom and Brender 1993, p. 15, but can be traced at least to Ricardo and probably farther back.

32. Capital may be more or less mobile than labor. If the language and culture of country A differ from those of country B, the mules (or machinery, or money) of country B may be far more acceptable in country A than the people of country A would be in country B. If the resource is mineral deposits or natural spectacles (like the Grand Canyon of the United States or Angel Falls of Venezuela), it may not be mobile at all. Consequently, the possibility and benefits of integration may not be as symmetric between countries as simple theories sometimes assume.

33. Livi-Bacci 1992, p. 135.

34. Bloom and Brender 1993, p. 3.

35. Daly 1993.

36. Daly 1993, p. 52.

37. Bhagwati 1993; Daly 1993.

38. Daly and Cobb 1989, p. 11.

39. Wilkinson 1992, pp. 165–66; Marmot 1994, pp. 204–5. Wilkinson defined net cash income as gross original income plus public and private transfers minus direct (payroll and income) taxes.

40. Dymond 1992, p. 62.

41. Algebra aficionados: prove that if $0 < f < 1/2$, then $2[1 / (1-f) - 1] < 1 / (1-2f) - 1$ and explain to someone in your family how this algebraic inequality represents the words "a doubling of the recovery rate more than doubles the gain in use per primary unit."

42. *Economist* 1992, p. 80.

43. Rogers 1985, p. 268; Gleick 1993, p. 410 gives other estimates.

44. Allenby 1992b, p. 49.

45. Ibid., pp. 49–50.

46. Bloom and Brender 1993, pp. 21–22.

47. Ibid., p. 14.

48. Commission for the Study of International Migration and Cooperative Economic Development 1990, p. xiv.

49. Weiner 1992.

50. Potter and Potter 1990.

51. Demeny 1991, p. 416.

52. Ehrlich and Ehrlich 1981; Woodwell 1985; Wilson 1988, 1992; Zavarin 1991.

53. E.g. Smith 1993; Pearce and Warford 1993.

54. World Commission on Environment and Development 1987, p. 8.

55. Duchin and Lange 1994, p. 254.

56. Ibid., p. 258.

57. Ibid., pp. 259–60.

58. Ibid., p. 262.

59. Gardner 1992, pp. 29–30.

60. World Bank 1992, p. iii.

61. Gardner 1992, pp. 30–31.

62. Gever et al. 1986, pp. 13–14.

63. Meadows et al. 1972, p. 69.

64. Ibid., p. 64.

65. E.g., Bartlett 1978; Meadows et al. 1972.

66. Bartlett 1978 (1992, p. 28).

67. Meadows et al. 1972.

68. Bartlett 1978.

69. Meadows et al. 1972, p. 64. Calculus aficionados: derive the formula for the exponential index. Extra credit: prove that for any positive annual growth rate of consumption, the exponential index is less than the static reserve index.

70. Meadows et al. 1972, Table 4. See commentaries of Hayes 1993, p. 514, and Robert N. Stavins following Nordhaus 1993, p. 45.

71. Robert N. Stavins, in commentary following Nordhaus 1993, pp. 44–45.

72. Ibid., p. 48.

73. Hardesty 1977, p. 199.

74. Revelle 1976.

75. In economics, a measure of the well-being of a population is called a "social welfare function." Choosing a social welfare function to compare the desirability of alternative possible future populations, some members of which already exist and others of which may or may not be born, is a nightmare for theoretical economists, such as Partha Dasgupta, in Johnson and Gale 1987, pp. 631–59; Nerlove et al. 1987.

76. Nerlove et al. 1987, pp. 4–5; Wonnacott 1992.

77. I do not know the original source. Thomas K. Burch, personal communication, 12 September 1993, sent me a mailing of Save the Children–Canada with this quotation.

78. Cassen 1993, p. 13.

79. A very similar problem of choosing a measure to decide what constitutes the best strategy arises in the theory of games against nature (Straffin 1993, pp. 56–61). When you play a game against nature, you choose one action from a set of possible actions, and you receive a payoff that depends on your action and on the state of nature, which is revealed to you *after* you choose your action. In 1812, Pierre-Simon de Laplace recommended that you choose an action with the highest average payoff, where the average is computed over all the possible states of nature, weighted equally. In 1950, Abraham Wald, a founder of modern statistical decision theory, recommended that you choose an action with the largest minimum payoff; again, the minimum is computed over all the possible states of nature. The economist Leonid Hurwicz recommended that you choose according to a weighted average between the worst possible outcome and the best possible outcome, the relative weights depending on your optimism. The statistician L. J. Savage in 1954 recommended that you act so as to minimize your maximum regret, where your regret is the difference between what you'll actually get from a choice you made and the best you could have done if you had known the real state of nature. Straffin gave a simple example of a game against nature in which these four recommendations lead you to choose four different actions. John Milnor showed in 1954 that no choice of a measure can have every property you might think desirable.

To make the analogy between a game against nature and the choice among alternative possible populations, let each choice in the game against nature correspond to one possible population; let each state of nature correspond to one person in that population (perhaps that person is you: there, but for the grace of God, go I); and let the payoff be the calories that person gets. In this analogy, the number of possible states of nature depends on the population chosen.

80. Rogers 1985, p. 257.

81. Morrison and Boyd 1959, pp. 678–80.

82. Ibid., pp. 798–99.

83. Darwin 1952, p. 78.

84. Miller 1980, p. 38.

85. Hammel and Howell 1987, p. 141.

86. Gever et al. 1986, p. 217.

87. Bloom and Brender 1993, p. 8.

88. Ibid., pp. 8–9.

89. Blaxter 1986, pp. 96–97.

90. World Health Organization Commission on Health and Environment 1992, p. xxx.

91. Goodkind 1992, 1993.

92. Sander 1992, p. 478.

93. Rausky 1983.

94. Johnson 1991, p. 393.

95. Population Reference Bureau 1993.

96. Williams and Zimmer 1990.

97. Sander 1992, p. 489.

98. *Popline* 1992, p. 1. Maguire and Maguire 1983 describe the diverse Catholic views on abortion.

99. Daly and Cobb 1989, p. 6.

100. Gardner 1992, p. 6.
101. At Harvard Commencement June 1992; in Anonymous 1992, p. 48.
102. Gore 1992, p. 316.
103. Cowell 1994.
104. Johnson 1991, p. 393.
105. Ehrlich and Ehrlich 1990, p. 212.
106. *Economist* 1990b, p. 4. Accept these statistics with caution. The United Nations 1992b, p. 357, reported an infant mortality rate of 7.1 percent for 1988, the latest available year. Remember the Law of Information!
107. Omran 1992.
108. *Economist* 1990b, p. 5.
109. Kirk 1967; Omran 1992.
110. Livi-Bacci 1992, pp. 158–59.
111. Karplus 1992, p. 288.
112. Murdoch 1990, p. 7.
113. Keyfitz 1991, p. 16.
114. Shrader-Frechette 1985.
115. Ibid., p. 101.
116. Sen 1992; Young 1994.
117. Abernethy 1991, pp. 323–24.
118. Blaxter 1986, p. 101.
119. Zaba 1993, pp. 401–2.
120. Hardin 1993.
121. Muscat 1985, pp. 33–34.
122. Shrader-Frechette 1985, p. 109.
123. Coale 1973, p. 64.
124. Quoted by Sorenson 1971, p. 119.
125. Muscat 1985, pp. 35–36.
126. Ibid., p. 36.
127. Gore 1992, p. 277.
128. Biegman 1992, p. 6.
129. Dobb 1992, p. 46.
130. Calabresi and Bobbitt 1978.
131. Potter and Potter 1990, chap. 11.
132. Greenhalgh 1993, pp. 219–20.
133. King 1993, p. 26.
134. World Health Organization Commission on Health and Environment 1992, p. 4; reference omitted.
135. Ibid., p. 14; Low 1992.

14: Water: A Case Study of Natural Constraints

1. Qutub 1993, p. 25.
2. Skinner 1969, p. 130.
3. Postel 1992; Gleick 1993.
4. Altmann and Altmann 1970.
5. Birdsell 1953, p. 182, showed that if Y is the tribal area and X is the mean annual rainfall, then it is possible to find numbers a and b such that, to a good approximation, $Y \approx aX^b$. Approximating the population P as a constant, Birdsell inferred that the population density $D = P / Y$ is $D \approx (P / a)X^{-b}$. For 123 tribes in his "basic" series, Birdsell estimated $a = 7,112.8$ and $b = -1.58451$ when X is measured in inches per year and Y is measured in hundreds of square miles. What a bizarre mixture of units! When X is measured in meters and Y is measured in square meters, I find $Y \approx aX^b$ with $a = 5.467 \times 10^9$ and $b = -1.58451$. Do not believe the four or five digits of apparent precision in these estimates. Birdsell's "basic" series of 123 tribes is a highly selected subset of the available collection of 409 aboriginal tribes; even for the basic series, mean annual rainfall accounts for about 65 percent of the variation in tribal area. Other factors besides rainfall evidently influence tribal area and, by inference, population density. See also Hardesty 1977, p. 197.

6. Postel 1992.

7. One cubic kilometer equals one billion cubic meters or 810,000 acre-feet.

8. Shiklomanov, in Gleick 1993, p. 13; Rogers 1985. Engelman and LeRoy 1993, p. 9, give figures very similar to those of Shiklomanov, in Gleick 1993.

9. Rogers 1985, p. 262.

10. Hillel 1991, p. 31.

11. Gleick 1993, p. 121.

12. Shiklomanov, in Gleick 1993, p. 15.

13. Press and Siever 1986, p. 154.

14. World Resources Institute 1992, p. 160; L'vovich was quoted by Rogers 1985, p. 260, and by Gleick 1993, p. 121.

15. Engelman and LeRoy 1993, p. 11.

16. Shiklomanov, in Gleick 1993, p. 15, estimated 47,000 cubic kilometers of runoff water per year.

17. Downes 1964.

18. Check: 2,000 cubic kilometers (river volume) times 20.5 turnovers per year equals 41,000 cubic kilometers per year of freshwater runoff and infiltration.

19. World Resources Institute 1992, p. 160.

20. Ambroggi, quoted by Rogers 1985, p. 261.

21. E.g., World Resources Institute 1992, p. 160.

22. Engelman and LeRoy 1993, p. 11, gave the range 9,000 to 14,000 cubic kilometers per year, but there is no unanimity in experts' estimates.

23. Press and Siever 1986, p. 157.

24. World Resources Institute 1992, p. 160.

25. Rogers 1985, p. 259.

26. Press and Siever 1986, p. 160.

27. World Resources Institute 1992, p. 171.

28. Ibid., p. 163; Postel 1992, p. 78.

29. Engelman and LeRoy 1993, p. 44. Because of uncertainty in some of the underlying data, different sources (Gleick 1993; Engelman and LeRoy 1993, pp. 50–54; World Resources Institute 1990, pp. 254–55, 330–31) estimated renewable water supplies and populations differently. According to Engelman and LeRoy (1993, p. 44), Gleick combined internal renewable water resources plus inflow from rivers where that information is known; for comparability, I added together the World Resources Institute's estimates of annual internal renewable water resources plus annual river flows from other countries. For Saudi Arabia and Yemen, the estimates of freshwater supplies per person per year in Engelman and LeRoy 1993 (306 and 445 cubic meters, respectively) were twice the estimates by the World Resources Institute (156 and 238 cubic meters, respectively). For Singapore, the estimates from both sources were very close (221 cubic meters versus 222 cubic meters). Different sources of data agreed relatively well for most countries.

30. World Resources Institute 1992, pp. 236–37.

31. Ibid., p. 328.

32. Kates et al. 1990, p. 1.

33. Falkenmark 1992, pp. 34–35.

34. Shiklomanov, in Gleick 1993, p. 16.

35. Qutub 1993, pp. 24–25.

36. World Resources Institute 1992, p. 160.

37. Rogers 1985, p. 294. Such estimates must be based on limited data supplemented at least in part by statistical models of stream flows, since it is unlikely that a century of streamflow data would be available for many of the world's dry countries.

38. Hillel 1991, p. 111.

39. Scarborough 1992.

40. World Resources Institute 1992, p. 160, gave 3,000 cubic kilometers; Shiklomanov 1993, p. 14, gave 5,000 cubic kilometers.

41. World Resources Institute 1992.

42. Engelman and LeRoy 1993, p. 27.

43. White 1984, p. 256.

44. Engelman and LeRoy 1993, p. 12.

45. Bradley 1962.

46. World Resources Institute 1992, p. 169.

47. Ibid., p. 161. These figures are global averages based on current practices. They should not be viewed as constants of nature. For example, if drip irrigation to the roots of plants were used instead of current wasteful practices, much less of the water withdrawn for agriculture would return to streams.

48. World Resources Institute 1992, p. 328.

49. Check: $1 / (1 - 0.4183) = 1.7$, which means a 70 percent increase.

50. Rogers 1985, p. 261.

51. Postel 1992.

52. World Resources Institute 1992, p. 159.

53. World Health Organization Commission on Health and Environment 1992, p. xix.

54. Cannon and Hopps 1971.

55. Falkenmark 1992, p. 46.

56. Fair et al. 1966, pp. 5–13, Table 5-5, estimated that, of 208 cubic meters per year per person of fresh water delivered to towns and cities in North America in 1966, 69 cubic meters per year per person went for domestic use. Miller 1982, p. 365, estimated that 84 cubic meters per year per person were used domestically in the United States in 1980.

57. Rogers 1985, pp. 257, 265–66.

58. Ibid., p. 264.

59. Muller 1974, p. 214; Bradley 1962.

60. Bradley 1962.

61. Penning de Vries et al. 1989.

62. Qutub 1993, p. 25.

63. Rogers 1985, p. 257.

64. Ibid., p. 257.

65. By L'vovich, quoted by Rogers 1985, p. 291.

66. Watt and Merrill 1963, p. 120; Kates et al. 1989, p. 12.

67. Watt and Merrill 1963, p. 77.

68. Fogel 1994, p. 377.

69. James and Schofield 1990.

70. As assumed by Kates et al. 1989.

71. Bradley 1962.

72. De Wit 1967; Revelle 1974, p. 164; Holmes, in Blaxter 1980; Kates et al. 1989.

73. Postel 1992, p. 190.

74. Watt and Merrill 1963, p. 12, item 267.

75. World Resources Institute 1994, p. 294.

76. Revelle 1974, pp. 163–64. We can reconstruct Revelle's estimate by supposing that Americans buy at the store (but do not necessarily consume) a diet with 3,100 kilocalories per day, of which 25 percent (775 kilocalories per day) derives from animals that convert ten kilocalories of plant food to one kilocalorie of animal food. Then $0.75 \times 3,100 + 0.25 \times 3,100 \times 10 = 10,075$ kilocalories per day. This calculation (in units of kilocalories) is similar to the calculation (in units of cubic meters) of the annual water requirement for each 1,000 kilocalories of diet. In countries where meat animals graze or forage instead of consuming feed grains, Revelle's assumption that the diets of domestic animals could also be eaten by humans would not apply.

77. World Resources Institute 1992, p. 329.

78. Ibid., p. 328.

79. Falkenmark 1991, p. 84; Falkenmark 1992, p. 47; see also Engelman and LeRoy 1993.

80. Falkenmark 1991, p. 86.

81. World Resources Institute 1992, p. 328.

82. Engelman and LeRoy 1993; United Nations 1993.

83. Falkenmark 1992, p. 46; italics in original.

84. Spears and Ayensu 1985.

85. Engelman and LeRoy 1993, p. 24.

86. Daily and Ehrlich 1992; Ehrlich and Ehrlich 1990, p. 291; Ehrlich, Ehrlich and Daily 1993; Myers 1983, 1991a, 1991b, 1992, p. 18.

87. Rogers 1985, p. 265.

88. World Health Organization Commission on Health and Environment 1992, p. xix.

89. Robert F. Chandler, Jr., in Kotler 1990, p. 178.

90. Other forms of food production, such as the growth of fish in brackish ponds, are not considered here.

91. The World Resources Institute 1992, p. 328, actually gave the figure 40,673 cubic kilometers, but the apparent precision was entirely spurious.

92. Clark 1977.

93. De Wit 1967.

94. United Nations 1992a.

95. Malin Falkenmark, personal communication, 15 February 1994.

96. White 1984, p. 263.

97. Gleick 1993, pp. 394–96.

98. World Resources Institute 1992, p. 236.

99. Engelman and LeRoy 1993, p. 35.

100. Bernstam 1991, p. 334.

101. Sorenson 1971, p. 116.

102. Nordhaus 1993, pp. 34–35.

103. Cassen 1993, p. 15.

104. Gleick 1993, pp. 67–79.

105. Engelman and LeRoy 1993, p. 13.

106. World Bank 1992, p. 36.

107. Postel 1994, p. 14.

108. Farrell et al. 1984, p. 15.

109. Gleick 1993, pp. 67–79.

110. Ibid., p. 396. Austin and Brewer 1971, p. 38, estimated 70 percent in 1970. Another large fraction of water use (estimated at 20 percent in 1970) is for other cooling.

111. Rogers 1985, p. 269.

112. World Resources Institute 1992, pp. 330–31.

113. Postel 1992.

114. World Bank 1992, p. 36; Fair et al. 1966, pp. 5–13, Table 5-5.

115. Bugbee and Monje 1992, p. 494.

116. Falkenmark 1992, p. 50.

117. According to a 1984 report cited by Smil 1991, p. 589.

118. 25 milligrams of nitrate NO_3 per liter of water.

119. Bernstam 1991, p. 352.

120. Ehrlich and Ehrlich 1990, p. 94; Hillel 1991.

121. Hillel 1991.

122. White 1984, p. 261.

123. Muller-Schwarze 1992.

124. Myers 1991b, pp. 245–46.

125. Blaikie and Brookfield 1987, pp. 37–48.

126. Homer-Dixon 1992, p. 35.

127. This is an oversimplified account of a very complex situation; Blaikie and Brookfield 1987 give a more detailed picture.

128. Goldberg 1991, p. 222.

129. Parry 1990.

130. Blaxter 1986, p. 68.

131. Gleick 1992; Kolars 1992; Lowi 1993; Aftandilian 1993, p. 2.

132. Postel 1992, p. 189.

133. White 1984, p. 263.

134. Mohamed A. Nour, in Hirschoff and Kotler 1989, p. 49.

135. World Health Organization Commission on Health and Environment 1992, pp. xxv–xxvi.

136. Kelley 1988, p. 1715.

137. A population also changes by chronological aging, which time alone controls.

138. Weiss et al. 1993, p. 1002.

139. Döös 1994, p. 130.

140. World Resources Institute 1992, p. 164. Prices from a 1984 United Nations publication quoted by Gleick 1993, p. 429, are higher.

141. World Resources Institute 1992, p. 164; Gleick 1993, p. 69.

142. Browne 1993a, 1993b.

143. World Resources Institute 1992, pp. 22–23.

144. MacDonald 1982, p. 229.

145. Kihlberg 1972.

146. Chou et al. 1977, p. 44, quote an earlier estimate that half a square mile of land could grow enough single-celled protein to feed 350 million people. Check my conversion!

147. Rogers 1985, pp. 260–61, estimated oceanic precipitation at 411,600 cubic kilometers and global precipitation at 525,100 cubic kilometers (78 percent on the ocean). Shiklomanov, in Gleick 1993, p. 15, estimated oceanic precipitation at 458,000 cubic kilometers and global precipitation at 577,000 cubic kilometers (79 percent on the ocean).

15: NATURAL CONSTRAINTS AND TIME

1. The bibliography at the end of this book lists many detailed studies of natural constraints. Demeny (1988) gave a brief overview; detailed surveys from widely divergent perspectives have been written by Eyre (1978) and edited by Simon and Kahn (1984), Repetto (1985), Davis and Bernstam (1991) and Brown et al. (1994b and prior years). Additional useful overviews are listed at the beginning of the bibliography.

2. Biegman 1992, p. 6.

3. Daily and Ehrlich 1992, p. 764.

4. Smil 1991.

5. Two (for the first dichotomy) times two (for the second dichotomy) times two (for the third dichotomy) equals eight.

6. Homer-Dixon 1992, pp. 4–7.

7. Dorn 1962.

8. World Resources Institute 1994, p. 308.

9. Gever et al. 1986, p. 20. In fact, pumping leaves about two-thirds of the hydrocarbons in the ground (Hatten S. Yoder, Jr., Carnegie Institution of Washington, personal communication, 4 April 1994).

10. Browne 1993a, p. C12.

11. Browne 1993b, p. A33.

12. Weaver 1981, p. 2.

13. Postel 1994, p. 13.

14. Holmes 1993; see also Borlaug 1983; Kotler 1990, especially chap. 9 by Robert F. Chandler.

15. Holmes 1993; Smil 1994.

16. Borlaug 1983, p. 692.

17. Schell 1993, p. 10.

18. Gever et al. 1986, p. 108.

19. Ibid., p. 109.

20. Vogely 1985, p. 458.

21. Gever et al. 1986.

22. Vogely 1985, p. 457.

23. Holdren and Ehrlich 1974; Ehrlich, Ehrlich and Holdren 1977.

24. Yoder 1982, pp. 231–32.

25. Ibid., p. 241.

26. Ibid., p. 230.

27. Wilson 1984, p. 121.

28. Ehrlich and Ehrlich 1981; Myers 1983, 1991b, 1992; Raven 1991, 1994; Wilson 1984, 1988, 1992; Woodwell 1985.

29. Margulis and Fester 1991.

30. I will not venture a definition of an asexually reproducing species, because I would be bound to get into trouble with any definition. May 1990, p. 301, reviewed the still-evolving answers to the question of what a species is.

31. May 1994, p. 105.

32. Raven 1994.

33. Wilson 1992, p. 280.

34. May 1990, p. 293.

35. Wilson 1988, p. 280; Raup 1991, p. 108; May, Lawton and Stork 1995, pp. 2–3.

36. Rowley 1993, p. 3.

37. Wilson 1992, p. 280.

38. May, Lawton and Stork 1995, p. 21, estimated that current trends imply extinction rates at least 10,000 times faster than those seen in the prehuman fossil record.

39. Ehrlich and Ehrlich 1981 gave detailed answers to both questions. World Resources Institute 1994, p. 149.

40. Harrison 1993, p. 8; Pearce and Warford 1993, pp. 165–68.

41. Harrison 1993, p. 9.

42. Ibid., p. 9.

43. United Nations 1993, p. 148.

44. Harrison 1993, p. 9.

45. In Simon and Kahn 1984, pp. 171–83.

46. Zavarin 1991; Lovejoy 1994.

47. Ehrlich and Ehrlich 1981.

48. Merson 1993, p. 1266.

49. United Nations 1991a, p. 2.

50. Cockburn 1963; Burnet and White 1972; McNeill 1976; Crosby 1972, 1986; Lederberg 1988; Anderson and May 1991; Weller 1993; Morse 1993.

51. McKeown 1988, p. 27.

52. Anderson and May 1991, pp. 655–56, estimated a reduction of 95 percent or more. Keep the Law of Information in mind.

53. United Nations 1993, p. 53. The World Health Organization's Global Program on AIDS estimated there were 13 million infected adults and 1 million infected children by the middle of 1993, for a total of 14 million. Eight million were in sub-Saharan Africa; Way and Stanecki 1994, pp. 47–51.

54. World Health Organization Commission on Health and Environment 1992, p. 118.

55. Ibid., p. 119.

56. Caldwell 1992, p. 60; World Health Organization Commission on Health and Environment 1992, p. 1.

57. United Nations 1991a, pp. 5–14.

58. The surveys detected antibodies against HIV in people's blood serum.

59. United Nations 1991a, p. 6; references omitted.

60. United Nations 1991a, p. 51.

61. Ibid., pp. 53–54.

62. Ibid., pp. 52–53.

63. Ibid., p. 2.

64. United Nations 1993.

65. United Nations 1991a.

66. United Nations 1994.

67. United Nations 1993, p. 56.

68. Ibid., p. 55.

69. Ibid., p. 57.

70. Ibid., p. 60. The doubling times implied by the population growth rates at the *end* of the projection period are longer than those calculated at the *beginning* of the projection period because population growth slowed during the course of the projection period, with or without AIDS.

71. United Nations 1993, p. 57.

72. United Nations 1993.

73. Garnett and Anderson 1993, p. 19.

74. Way and Stanecki 1994, p. 60.

75. Ibid., p. 64.

76. Garnett and Anderson 1993, p. 19; United Nations 1993; Way and Stanecki 1994.

77. United Nations 1993, p. 54.

78. Weller 1993, p. 32.

79. Way and Stanecki 1994, p. 61.

80. Burnet and White 1972, p. 263.

81. Lederberg 1988.
82. Holdren and Ehrlich 1974.
83. Blaxter 1986, p. 27.
84. National Academy of Sciences 1971.
85. National Research Council 1986; see the review symposium on this report in *Population and Development Review* 12(3):563–85. My summary derives from United Nations Fund for Population Activities 1993b and MacKellar 1994, p. 184.
86. United Nations Fund for Population Activities 1993b, p. 88.
87. Ibid., p. 93.
88. The argument on this issue is extensive and complex: Coale and Hoover 1958; Kelley 1988; Johnson and Lee 1987; Coleman and Schofield 1986; Lee et al. 1988; Simon 1990; National Academy of Sciences 1971; World Bank 1984; National Research Council 1986; Daly and Cobb 1989; United Nations Fund for Population Activities 1993b; Cassen et al. 1994.
89. Thurow 1986, p. 29.
90. Kelley 1988, p. 1715.
91. Cassen et al. 1994, pp. 4, 17–18.
92. Population Reference Bureau 1992. Steshenko 1993 also reported a decline in the Ukraine.
93. Hoyle 1963, on p. 554 of 1986 reprint.
94. Ibid., on p. 555 of 1986 reprint.
95. Homer-Dixon 1992, pp. 3, 14–15. Homer-Dixon 1994a is a later revision of this manuscript.
96. Homer-Dixon 1992, p. 38.

16: HUMAN CARRYING CAPACITY: AN OVERVIEW

1. In Repetto 1985, p. 48.
2. Bahn and Flenley 1992, on whom I largely rely. Diamond 1992, pp. 329–31, gives a concise summary and commentary.
3. Hillel 1991; Demeny 1991; Diamond 1992; Weiss et al. 1993.
4. Bahn and Flenley 1992, pp. 22, 26.
5. Ibid., pp. 80–81.
6. Ibid., p. 12.
7. Ibid., pp. 8, 113.
8. Ibid., p. 176.
9. Ibid., p. 178.
10. Ibid., p. 165.
11. Ibid., p. 164.
12. Ibid., p. 165.
13. Ibid., p. 186.
14. Ibid., pp. 178–80.
15. Ibid., p. 213.
16. Ibid., p. 213.
17. Ibid., pp. 211–12.
18. Ibid., pp. 212–13.
19. Some of my ideas here are close to those of House and Williams 1975, pp. 54–55.
20. Kelley 1988, p. 1686.
21. Spengler 1968; Taylor 1970; Singer 1971.
22. Hillel 1991, pp. 59–62.
23. Even today's subsistence farmers are linked to global dynamics: "The proportion of land used for cash cropping, the proportion of land used for subsistence crops, weather patterns, market forces—all of these and others interact to determine how many people with a given technology can be supported by the habitat. One thing is certain: Carrying capacity is dynamic, changing with changes in a multitude of other factors. It is not the static concept suggested by the logistic population growth curve and by most people who have used it." Hardesty 1977, pp. 205–6.
24. In 1968, the sociologist Amitai Etzioni of Columbia University envisioned what he

called "the active society" as one that is self-conscious, knowing and responsive, committed to its goals and with power to reset its internal social codes in order to achieve its goals. The active society can plan its future with full participation of all its members and can organize conflicts to make them more productive than at present. Etzioni's vision is an example of a dynamic, self-regulating and ever-changing society. Some such society—not necessarily Etzioni's, but certainly an adaptive one—seems necessary to sustain humankind's forward fall.

17: ENTERING THE ZONE

1. Dorn 1962, in Cox 1969, p. 275.
2. According to the Honorable Danny J. Boggs (personal communication, 28 December 1994), this phrase appears in 71 United States federal cases; the variant form "Justice deferred is justice denied" occurs in one.
3. Victor Fuchs, in Singer 1971.
4. Ausubel 1993, p. 17.
5. E.g., Carlson and Bernstam 1991.
6. Dennis A. Ahlburg in Cassen et al. 1994, p. 35.
7. Cassen et al. 1994, p. 23.
8. Gore 1992, pp. 305–7.
9. Ibid., pp. 313–14.
10. E.g., Mauldin and Ross 1991.
11. Bongaarts 1994, p. 774.
12. Ibid., p. 775.
13. Ibid., p. 773. The United Nations Fund for Population Activities 1993b, p. 1, estimated that at least 120 million couples worldwide want to limit the number of their children or space childbearing, but lack access to adequate family-planning services. Bongaarts's estimate of 100 million women with an unmet demand for family planning applied only to developing countries outside of China.
14. Bongaarts 1994, p. 774.
15. Ibid., p. 774.
16. Ibid., p. 774.
17. Ibid., p. 774.
18. Population Council 1994, p. 2.
19. Ibid., pp. 7–13.
20. Science Summit 1994.
21. African Academy of Sciences 1994.
22. United Nations Fund for Population Activities 1993a.
23. Passell 1994.
24. Westoff 1994; Chesler 1994.
25. Pritchett 1994, p. 3.

18: LOOKING BEYOND THE NEXT HILL: SOME SUGGESTIONS

1. Muscat 1985, pp. 33–34.
2. Equality is a complicated notion. Sen 1992; Young 1994.
3. Gerhard Heilig, personal communication, 12 May 1994.
4. Putnam 1993, pp. 35–36. Putnam referred to such instruments of social integration as "social capital," but this term has traditionally been used in economics to refer to capital that produces nonmarketed goods and services, such as defense equipment, schools and hospitals.
5. Repetto et al. 1989; Smith 1993.
6. Daly and Cobb 1989, pp. 62–84; Repetto et al. 1989. The gross domestic product is sometimes used instead of the gross national product; the difference does not affect the argument here.
7. United Nations Development Program 1992, pp. 91–96.
8. Hillel 1991, pp. 255–56.
9. Gleick 1993, p. 69.

10. Glantz and Ausubel 1984; Glantz 1990; Hillel 1991, p. 232; Postel 1992; Gleick 1993.

11. Hillel 1991, pp. 166–68.

12. Cornell 1988.

13. Putnam 1993, p. 39.

14. Hillel 1991, p. 271.

15. Fearnside 1986, p. 151.

16. Turner et al. 1990, p. 241.

17. Livi-Bacci 1992, p. 158. The values of GNP per person are World Bank estimates for 1988; the values of life expectancy are United Nations estimates for 1985–90.

18. Livi-Bacci 1992, pp. 158–59.

19. Wilkinson 1992; World Health Organization Commission on Health and Environment 1992, p. 11; Marmot 1994.

20. Revelle 1974, p. 169.

21. Derived from an earlier, simpler equation of Holdren and Ehrlich 1974.

22. World Bank 1992, p. 39, Fig. 1.4.

23. United Nations Population Division 1992, p. 21.

24. This pyramidal concept (Cohen 1992) is very similar to a pyramidal concept published independently by Ekins et al. 1992, p. 41. The four vertices of the pyramid of Ekins et al. are society (analogous to "population" in my pyramid), ecology (analogous to "environment" in mine), economy (same) and ethics (included in "culture" in my pyramid; my "culture" includes some features that Ekins et al. would group with "society").

I claim no priority for realizing that population, economy, environment and culture all interact. House and Williams 1975, p. 55, wrote: "carrying capacity must be interpreted as a variable socially determined within our understanding of economic, social, and environmental values and their relative contribution in maintaining quality of life levels." Keynes 1983, p. 364, wrote of human population regulation as "an area where economics, sociology, ethics and biology interact in such an appallingly difficult fashion." Daily and Ehrlich 1992, p. 769, wrote: ". . . central determinants of social carrying capacity lie in the domain of interactions among resources, among sociopolitical and economic factors, and between biophysical and social constraints." Cassen 1993, p. 13, wrote: ". . . it is not population alone, but the relations between population and income growth and technological and policy choices, which have to be understood if the 'population problem' is to be seen in true perspective."

All these quotations recognize that human existence and well-being are multidimensional, not to be measured by a single yardstick, and that among the major dimensions are economics; the population and society; culture and values; and the natural world.

25. Arthur and McNicoll 1975; Sanderson 1980; Blanchet 1991.

26. Davis, in Davis and Bernstam 1991, p. 1.

27. Hammel 1990; Hammel and Howell 1987.

28. Perrings 1987; Daly and Cobb 1989; Clark 1990; Pearce and Turner 1990; Daly, in Davis and Bernstam 1991; Cropper and Oates 1992; Duchin and Lange 1994; Pearce and Warford 1993.

29. Keyfitz 1991, p. 16.

30. United Nations Population Division 1992, p. 14.

31. Dorn 1962.

32. Simons 1992.

33. Gardner 1992, p. 47.

34. Lederberg 1988.

35. Roux 1964, p. 90.

36. Maimonides 1963, p. 536 (book III, chap. 35).

37. MacIntyre 1967.

38. Smith 1759, p. 1.

39. "Social welfare," Encyclopaedia Britannica 1989, 15th ed., 27:428–29.

40. This line of argument, now called sociobiological, began with the great British population geneticist J. B. S. Haldane and continued with William D. Hamilton, Edward O. Wilson, Robert Trivers and others; see Trivers 1985. Beneath this theory lies Darwin's theory of evolution of natural selection. That Darwin was inspired to formulate this theory by reading Malthus has been meticulously documented by Keynes 1983.

41. That is, when $r > C / B$. Trivers 1985, p. 45; Singer 1981. The relatedness r here has

nothing to do with the Malthusian parameter r in the logistic equation; it is only an accident that the same letter is used.

The relatedness r is the probability that both the donor and the recipient have a copy of a hypothetical altruistic gene by direct descent from a common ancestor. This probability can be calculated by the laws of Mendelian genetics. The cost of altruism to the donor C is measured as the average reduction in the number of copies of the altruistic gene in the donor's offspring in the next generation. The benefit of altruism to the recipient B is measured as the average increase in the number of copies of the altruistic gene in the recipient's offspring in the next generation. Because B and C are measured in the same units (number of copies of the altruistic gene in the next generation), the ratio C / B is a pure number and can be compared with the pure number r.

42. World Bank estimates quoted by Demeny 1994.

43. If there were fewer than five generations per century, then 30 generations ago was before A.D. 1400 and there were still fewer people on the Earth.

44. Shoumatoff 1985.

45. Singer 1981, pp. 45–49; Axelrod 1984. Straffin 1993, p. 73, called the Prisoner's Dilemma "the most widely studied and used game in social science."

46. As each player would be better off paying all but one dollar of the potential gain to the other, a great variety of outcomes is possible.

47. For one view of the evidence, see Schneider 1989, Revkin 1992 and Stevens 1992; for an opposite view, see Ray 1992. Bongaarts 1992 and Birdsall 1992 discussed demographic aspects of global warming. Birdsall argued that one of the most cost-effective approaches to reducing carbon emissions that is open to developed countries is to pay developing countries to educate girls and promote family planning.

48. Gardner 1992, pp. 9–10.

49. Cassen 1993.

50. Rapid population growth will not necessarily drive down the cost of labor in the presence of economic and political reforms, for example; but rapid population growth probably does make wages rise more slowly than they would without population growth, even in the presence of economic and political reforms.

51. It might seem plausible to argue conversely that, all else being equal, consumers in rich countries who want to buy products as cheaply as possible from developing countries have no incentive to discourage rapid population growth in poor countries, if they are unconcerned about the possible effects on their own jobs. But the hypothesis, "all else being equal," will be false in many poor countries and the would-be conclusion mistaken. Slower population growth in poor countries is likely to have pervasive benefits initially for them and ultimately for all countries.

52. Hillel 1991, p. 212.

53. Gore 1992, pp. 296–304.

54. World Bank 1992, p. 254.

55. Ibid., p. 255.

56. Mitchell 1978, p. 8; Johnson 1991, p. 796.

57. Mill 1848, book IV, chap. VI, pp. 756–57.

Appendix 1

1. Pennycuick 1988.

Appendix 6

1. Malthus 1798, chap. VII; 1960 ed., p. 51.

2. Demeny 1988, p. 232.

3. E.g., among recent economists, Pryor and Maurer 1982; Lee 1986, 1988, 1992, 1993; Kremer 1993. Among the system modelers, House and Williams 1975; Meadows et al. 1992.

4. A nice phrase of Cole et al. 1973, p. 24.

5. Carrying Capacity Network 1992, p. 57.

6. I thank Adam E. Cohen for pointing this out, 6 August 1993.

7. Van de Walle 1975, p. 1078, made the same point in reviewing the World3 model of Meadows et al.: ". . . a decline of industrial output per capita would not bring fertility and mortality all the way back to where it [they] had been brought from by the equivalent rise of that output. Many things that took time in the learning cannot be unlearned: the germ theory of disease, vaccination, and the technology of contraception, for example, could continue to be used by a population with a much reduced access to resources and to capital."

8. Let $K(0)$ be the initial carrying capacity at a starting time $t=0$, and let $P(0)$ be the initial population size at that time. Assume that $K(0) > P(0) > 0$, so that the population starts with carrying capacity to spare. The Malthusian parameter r will be assumed to be a positive constant real number. The solution for $P(t)$ takes different forms, depending on whether (i) $c < 1$, (ii) $c = 1$ or (iii) $c > 1$.

Case (i): $c < 1$. Since $K(0) > P(0) > cP(0)$,

$$(\star) \qquad P(t) = \cfrac{1}{\left[\cfrac{1}{P(0)} + \cfrac{c-1}{K(0) - cP(0)}\right] e^{-r[K(0) - cP(0)]t} - \cfrac{c-1}{K(0) - cP(0)}}$$

The solution $P(t)$ is a logistic curve with the "virtual" Malthusian parameter $r' = r(1-c) > 0$ and the constant "virtual" carrying capacity $K' = [K(0) - cP(0)] / (1-c)$. [The special case $c = 0$ reproduces Verhulst's equation with $r' = r$ and $K' = K(0)$.] The carrying capacity behaves as an affine transformation of a logistic curve, that is, $K(t)$ is logistic in shape after possible shifting by $K(0) - cP(0)$ and rescaling by c. $K' >$, $=$ or $< K(0)$ according to whether $1 > c > 0$, $c = 0$ or $0 > c$.

Case (ii): $c = 1$. Then $P(t)$ grows exponentially with "virtual" Malthusian parameter $r[K(0) - P(0)]$.

Case (iii): $c > 1$. For some finite time T $(0 < T < \infty)$, the population size approaches infinity: $\lim_{t \uparrow T} P = \infty$. The exact trajectory of $P(t)$ has a different form depending on whether $K(0) - cP(0) \neq 0$ or $K(0) - cP(0) = 0$. When $K(0) - cP(0) \neq 0$, the equation above marked $(\star)$ again describes $P(t)$; in this case, the denominator falls to zero and hence the population size reaches infinity when t rises to

$$T = \frac{1}{r[K(0) - cP(0)]} \log \left\{ \left[\frac{1}{P(0)} + \frac{c-1}{K(0) - cP(0)} \right] \Big/ \left[\frac{c-1}{K(0) - cP(0)} \right] \right\}.$$

When $K(0) - cP(0) = 0$, then the population size follows the trajectory

$$P(t) = \frac{P(0)}{1 - r(c-1)P(0)t},$$

which is the solution of the "doomsday equation." The population size reaches infinity when the time t rises to

$$T = \frac{1}{r(c-1)P(0)}.$$

Try proving these assertions yourself.

9. Davies 1982, p. 82.

10. One factor that contributes to the strange behavior is the assumption, pointed out above, that increases and decreases of population size lead to changes in carrying capacity of equal magnitude but opposite sign. However, making the equation of Condorcet more realistic as suggested would not make the strange behavior disappear.

11. For values of r between exact multiples of 0.01, there may be other behaviors.

12. My computer, and yours, can represent only a finite number of different numbers. Therefore it is inevitable that any very, very long trajectory of any deterministic system of equations would begin to repeat itself eventually. Computer solution of equations cannot tell you the exact behavior of the solution, but it does usually suggest the general behavior very effectively.

13. By mathematics very similar to that I used to reduce the continuous-time model of

Malthus and Condorcet to a single (Verhulst) logistic equation, the discrete-time model of Malthus and Condorcet may be reduced to a single discrete-time logistic equation (Ignacio Barradas, personal communication, 15 August 1994). I will omit the details here. The discrete-time logistic equation has been proved mathematically to display all the behaviors described for the discrete-time model of Malthus and Condorcet, originally by Myrberg 1962; see also May 1974, 1975, 1986; May and Oster 1976; May and Seger 1986; Hastings et al. 1993.

14. Fearnside 1986.

15. Meadows et al. 1992, p. 108.

16. Ibid., pp. 108–9; emphasis in original.

17. This much can be proved mathematically. However, it is not possible to write the ultimate stationary level explicitly using elementary mathematical functions.

18. Cohen 1995.

Bibliography

SELECTED REFERENCES

Sources are identified by a combination of the last name of the author or authors and the year of publication. Full citations are given in the references that follow. For example, "Greenhalgh et al. 1994" refers to the article by Susan Greenhalgh, Chuzhu Zhu and Nan Li published in 1994. When the same author(s) published more than one publication in the same year, the year is followed by an identifying letter, for example, 1991a, 1991b.

Some good books on population and topics related to this book

Acsádi and Nemeskéri 1970
Bahn and Flenley 1992
Blaxter 1980, 1986
Bury 1932
Cassen et al. 1994
Cipolla 1974
Clark 1990
Coale and Hoover 1958
Coale and Watkins 1986
Coleman and Schofield 1986
Crosby 1986
Dahl and Tufte 1973
Davis and Bernstam 1991
Diamond 1992
Gleick 1993
Harte 1988
Hauser 1979
Hillel 1991
Karplus 1992

Keyfitz 1968, 1982a
Kleiber 1961
Lieth and Whittaker 1975
Livi-Bacci 1992
McNeill 1967
Menken 1986
Odum 1971
Parsons 1971
Pearce and Turner 1990
Postel 1992
Reining and Tinker 1975
Repetto 1985, 1986
Smil 1987
Teitelbaum and Winter 1985, 1988
Turner et al. 1990
United Nations 1953
United States Department of Agriculture 1981
World Bank 1984, 1992

Useful compendiums of data

Brown et al. 1993, 1994a
Central Intelligence Agency 1991, 1992
Economist 1990a, 1992
Gleick 1993
Harte 1988 (Appendix)
Johnson 1991
McEvedy and Jones 1978
Mitchell 1978, 1992, 1993

Organisation for Economic Co-operation and Development 1991
Pennycuick 1988
Population Reference Bureau 1990–94
United Nations 1992b, 1992c, 1993
United Nations Development Program 1992
Watt and Merrill 1963
World Bank 1992
World Resources Institute 1992, 1994

REFERENCES

Abernethy, V. 1991. Comment: The "one world" thesis as an obstacle to environmental preservation. In *Resources, environment, and population: Present knowledge, future options,* ed.

Kingsley Davis and Mikhail S. Bernstam. New York: Oxford University Press. Supplement to vol. 16, 1990, of *Population and Development Review*, pp. 323–28.

Acsádi, G., and J. Nemeskéri. 1970. *History of human life span and mortality*. Budapest: Akadémiai Kiadó.

Adams, Robert McC. 1965. *Land behind Baghdad: A history of settlement on the Diyala plains*. Chicago: University of Chicago Press.

Adlakha, Arjun, and Judith Banister. 1993. Demographic perspectives on China and India. Paper presented at the General Conference of the International Union for the Scientific Study of Population (IUSSP) in Montreal, August 31.

African Academy of Sciences. 1994. Statement by the African Academy of Sciences at the Population Summit. Reprinted in *Population and Development Review* 20, no. 1 (March): 238–39.

Aftandilian, Gregory. 1993. *Political change in the Arab world*. A report on the deliberations of a Meetings Program conference, 24 April 1992. New York: Council on Foreign Relations.

Ahlburg, Dennis A., and Kenneth C. Land, eds. 1992. Population forecasting: Special issue. *International Journal of Forecasting* 8, no. 3: 289–542.

Alho, Juha M. 1990. Stochastic methods in population forecasting. *International Journal of Forecasting* 6:521–30.

Allen, Shirley Walter, and Grant William Sharpe. 1960. *An introduction to American forestry*. 3d ed. New York: McGraw-Hill.

Allenby, Braden R. 1992a. Achieving sustainable development through industrial ecology. *International Environmental Affairs* 4, no. 1 (winter): 56–68.

———. 1992b. Industrial ecology: The materials scientist in an environmentally constrained world. *Materials Research Society Bulletin* 17, no. 3 (March):46–51.

———. 1993. Supporting environmental quality: Developing an infrastructure for design. *Total Quality Environmental Management*, spring: 303–8.

Alterman, H. 1969. *Counting people: The census in history*. New York: Harcourt, Brace & World.

Altmann, Stuart A., and Jeanne Altmann. 1970. *Baboon ecology: African field research*. Basel / New York: S. Karger.

Anderson, Roy M., and Robert M. May. 1991. *Infectious diseases of humans: Dynamics and control*. Oxford: Oxford University Press.

Andreae, M. O. 1991. Biomass burning in the tropics: Impact on environmental quality and global climate. In *Resources, environment, and population: Present knowledge, future options*, ed. Kingsley Davis and Mikhail S. Bernstam. New York: Oxford University Press. Supplement to vol. 16, 1990, of *Population and Development Review*, pp. 268–69.

Anonymous. 1992. A happy observance. *Harvard Magazine*, July–August: 47–48.

Arthur, W. Brian, and Geoffrey McNicoll. 1975. Large-scale simulation models in population and development: What use to planners? *Population and Development Review* 1:251–65.

Austin, Arthur L., and John W. Brewer. 1971. World population growth and related technical problems. *Technological Forecasting and Social Change* 3, no. 1:23–49. Reprinted from *IEEE Spectrum* 7, no. 12 (December 1970).

Australian Government. 1975. *Population and Australia: A demographic analysis and projection*, vol. 1. Canberra: Australian Government Publishing Service.

Ausubel, Jesse H. 1989. Regularities in technological development: An environmental view. In *Technology and environment*, ed. J. H. Ausubel and H. E. Sladovich. Washington, D.C.: National Academy Press, pp. 70–91.

———. 1993. 2020 vision. *The Sciences (New York Academy of Sciences)* 33, no. 6 (November–December):14–19.

Ausubel, Jesse H., and H. E. Sladovich, eds. 1989. *Technology and environment*. Washington, D.C.: National Academy Press.

Axelrod, Robert. 1984. *The evolution of cooperation*. New York: Basic Books.

Baade, Fritz. 1960. *Der Wettlauf zum Jahre 2000; unsere Zukunft: ein Paradies oder die Selbstvernichtung der Menschheit*. 2. Aufl. Oldenburg, Germany: G. Stalling. English translation by Ernst Pawel: *The race to the year 2000; our future: A paradise or the suicide of mankind*. Garden City, N.Y.: Doubleday, 1962.

Bahn, Paul G., and John Flenley. 1992. *Easter Island, Earth Island*. New York: Thames and Hudson.

Baker, Frederick S. 1950. *Principles of silviculture.* New York: McGraw-Hill.

Ballod, Karl. 1912. Wieviel Menschen kann die Erde ernähren? *Schmollers Jahrbuch für Gesetzgebung, Verwaltung und Volkswirtschaft* 36, no. 2:81–102.

Barringer, Felicity. 1992. U.S. population passes 256 million, Bureau says. *New York Times* (30 December), p. A12.

Bartlett, Albert A. 1978. Forgotten fundamentals of the energy crisis. *American Journal of Physics* 46, no. 9:876–88. Reprinted in *Carrying Capacity Network Focus,* Winter 1992:26–40.

Begon, Michael, John L. Harper and Colin R. Townsend. 1990. *Ecology: Individuals, populations and communities.* 2d ed. Boston / Oxford: Blackwell Scientific Publications.

Belshaw, H. 1947. Review article: Races, lands and foods. *Pacific Affairs* 20, no. 1:71–80.

Benedick, Richard E. 1991. Comment: Environmental risk and policy response. In *Resources, environment, and population: Present knowledge, future options,* ed. Kingsley Davis and Mikhail S. Bernstam. New York: Oxford University Press. Supplement to vol. 16, 1990, of *Population and Development Review,* pp. 201–4.

Berger, John. 1992. The Hackensack River Meadowlands. In Water Science and Technology Board, Commission on Geosciences, Environment, and Resources, National Research Council, *Restoration of aquatic ecosystems: Science, technology, and public policy.* Washington, D.C.: National Academy Press, pp. 510–18.

Berlinski, D. 1976. *On systems analysis: An essay concerning the limitations of some mathematical methods in the social, political, and biological sciences.* Cambridge: MIT Press.

Bernstam, M. S. 1991. The wealth of nations and the environment. In *Resources, environment, and population: Present knowledge, future options,* ed. Kingsley Davis and Mikhail S. Bernstam. New York: Oxford University Press. Supplement to vol. 16, 1990, of *Population and Development Review,* pp. 333–407.

Bhagwati, Jagdish. 1993. The case for free trade. *Scientific American* 269, no. 5 (November):42–49.

Biegman, N. H. 1992. Population, environment, and development: Government's view. In *Population, environment and development,* ed. Evert van Imhoff, Ellen Themmen and Frans Willekins, pp. 5–14. Amsterdam, Netherlands / Berwyn, Penn.: Swets and Zeitlinger.

Biraben, Jean-Noël. 1979. Essai sur l'évolution du nombre des hommes. *Population (Paris)* 34, no. 1:13–25.

Birdsall, Nancy. 1992. *Another look at population and global warming.* World Bank Country Economics Department, WPS 1020, November. Washington, D.C.: World Bank.

Birdsell, Joseph B. 1953. Some environmental and cultural factors influencing the structuring of Australian aboriginal populations. *American Naturalist* 87:171–207.

———. 1981. *Human evolution: An introduction to the new physical anthropology.* 3d ed. Boston: Houghton Mifflin.

Blackman, F. F. 1905. Optima and limiting factors. *Annals of Botany* 19, no. 74 (April):281–95.

Blaikie, Piers, and Harold Brookfield. 1987. *Land degradation and society.* London / New York: Methuen.

Blanchet, Didier. 1991. *Modélisation démo-economique: conséquences économiques des évolutions démographiques.* INED Cahier 130. Paris: Presses Universitaires de France.

Blaxter, Kenneth. 1986. *People, food and resources.* Cambridge, U.K. / New York / Melbourne: Cambridge University Press.

———. 1989. *Energy metabolism in animals and man.* Cambridge, U.K.: Cambridge University Press.

Blaxter, Kenneth, ed. 1980. *Food chains and human nutrition.* Barking, Essex, England: Applied Science Publishers.

Bloom, David E. and Adi Brender. 1993. Labor and the emerging world economy. *Population Bulletin* 48, no. 2:1–39.

Boerman, W. E. 1940. De voedselcapaciteit der aarde en de toekomstige wereldbevolking. *Tijdschrift voor Economische Geographie (Dutch Journal of Economic Geography)* 31, no. 5 (May):121–32. In Dutch, with English summary.

Bongaarts, John. 1992. Population growth and global warming. *Population and Development Review* 18, no. 2 (June):299–319.

———. 1994. Population policy options in the developing world. *Science* 263 (11 February):771–76.

Bonner, John T. 1965. *Size and cycle: An essay on the structure of biology.* Princeton: Princeton University Press.

Borlaug, Norman E. 1983. Contributions of conventional plant breeding to food production. *Science* 219, no. 4,585 (11 February):689–93.

Boserup, Ester. 1965 (1974). *The conditions of agricultural growth.* Chicago: Aldine.

———. 1981. *Population and technological change: A study of long-term trends.* Chicago: University of Chicago Press.

Boulding, Kenneth E. 1964. *The meaning of the twentieth century: The great transition.* Vol. 34 of *World perspectives,* ed. R. N. Anshen. New York: Harper and Row.

Bradley, Charles C. 1962. Human water needs and water use in America. *Science* 138, no. 3539 (26 October 1962):489–91. Reprinted in Cox 1969.

Brass, W. 1979. Note on how to improve the United Nations population projections. In *Prospects of population, methodology and assumptions.* New York: United Nations.

Brigham, Albert P. 1909. Capacity of the United States for population. *Popular Science Monthly* 75, no. 14 (September):209–20.

Brown, Harrison. 1954. *The challenge of man's future: An inquiry concerning the condition of man during the years that lie ahead.* New York: Viking.

Brown, Harrison, James Bonner and John Weir. 1957. *The next hundred years: Man's natural and technological resources.* New York: Viking.

Brown, Lester R., and Hal Kane. 1994. *Full house: Reassessing the earth's population carrying capacity.* New York: W. W. Norton.

Brown, Lester R., Hal Kane and Ed Ayres. 1993. *Vital signs: The trends that are shaping our future.* New York: W. W. Norton.

———. 1994a. *Vital signs: The trends that are shaping our future.* New York: W. W. Norton.

Brown, Lester R., and 11 others. 1994b. *State of the world 1994.* New York: W. W. Norton.

Browne, Malcolm W. 1993a. High-power fuel for fusion energy. *New York Times* (7 December), pp. C1–C12.

———. 1993b. Scientists at Princeton produce world's largest fusion reaction. *New York Times* 10 December, pp. A1–A33.

Bugbee, Bruce, and Oscar Monje. 1992. The limits of crop productivity. *BioScience* 42, no. 7 (July / August):494–502.

Buringh, P., and H. D. J. van Heemst. 1977. *An estimation of world food production based on labour-oriented agriculture.* Wageningen, Netherlands: Agricultural Press.

Buringh, P., H. D. J. van Heemst and G. J. Staring. 1975. *Computation of the absolute maximum food production of the world.* Wageningen, Netherlands: Agricultural Press.

Burnet, Sir Macfarlane, and David O. White. 1972. *Natural history of infectious disease.* 4th ed. Cambridge, U.K.: Cambridge University Press.

Bury, J. B. 1932. *The idea of progress: An inquiry into its origin and growth.* London: Macmillan. Reprint, New York: Dover, 1955.

Calabresi, Guido, and Philip Bobbitt. 1978. *Tragic choices.* New York: W. W. Norton.

Caldwell, John C., I. O. Orubuloye and Pat Caldwell. 1992. Fertility decline in Africa: A new type of transition? *Population and Development Review* 18, no. 2 (June):211–42.

Caldwell, Mark. 1992. Resurrection of a killer. *Discover* (December): 57–64.

Calvin, Melvin. 1986. Letter to David Pimentel, 18 December. Cited in Hudson 1989, pp. 276, 298.

Cannan, Edwin. 1895. The probability of a cessation of the growth of population in England and Wales during the next century. *Economic Journal* 5, no. 20 (December):505–15.

Cannon, Helen L., and Howard C. Hopps, eds. 1971. *Environmental geochemistry in health and disease: American Association for the Advancement of Science Symposium, Dallas, Texas, December 1968.* Boulder, Color.: Geological Society of America, memoir 123.

Carlson, Elwood, and Mikhail S. Bernstam. 1991. Population and resources under the socialist economic system. In *Resources, environment, and population: Present knowledge, future options,* ed. Kingsley Davis and Mikhail S. Bernstam. New York: Oxford University Press. Supplement to vol. 16, 1990, of *Population and Development Review,* pp. 374–407.

Carrying Capacity Network. 1992. In and out of focus. *Focus: Carrying Capacity Selections* 1, no. 2 (winter):57. Washington, D.C.: Carrying Capacity Network.

Cassen, Robert H. 1993. Economic implications of demographic change. *Transactions of the Royal Society of Tropical Medicine and Hygiene* 87(supplement 1):13–18.

Cassen, Robert, and 15 contributors. 1994. *Population and development: Old debates, new conclusions*. New Brunswick, N.J. / Oxford, U.K.: Transaction Publishers.

Central Intelligence Agency. 1991. *World factbook 1991*. Washington, D.C.: Central Intelligence Agency.

————. 1992. *World factbook 1992*. Washington, D.C.: Central Intelligence Agency.

Cépède, Michel, François Houtart and Linus Grond. 1964. *Population and food*. New York: Sheed and Ward.

Chandler, T., and G. Fox. 1974. *3000 years of urban growth*. New York: Academic Press.

Chen, Robert S., ed. with William H. Bender, Robert W. Kates, Ellen Messer and Sara R. Millman. 1990. *The hunger report: 1990*. HR-90-1. Alan Shawn Feinstein World Hunger Program, Brown University, June.

Chesler, Ellen. 1994. No, the first priority is: Stop coercing women. *New York Times Magazine* (6 February), pp. 31, 33.

Chisholm, Sallie W. 1992. What limits phytoplankton growth? *Oceanus* 35, no. 3 (Fall): 36–46.

Chou, Marylin, David P. Harmon, Jr., Herman Kahn and Sylvan H. Wittwer. 1977. *World food prospects and agricultural potential*. New York / London: Praeger.

Choucri, Nazli. 1974. *Population dynamics and international violence: Propositions, insights, and evidence*. Lexington, Mass.: Lexington Books.

————, ed. 1984. *Multidisciplinary perspectives on population and conflict*. Syracuse, N.Y.: Syracuse University Press.

Cipolla, Carlo M. 1974. *The economic history of world population*. 6th ed. Harmondsworth, England / Baltimore: Penguin.

Clark, Colin. 1958. World population. *Nature* 181 (3 May): 1235–1236. Reprinted in Wayne Y. Davis, ed., *Readings in human population ecology*. Englewood Cliffs, N.J.: Prentice-Hall, 1971, pp. 101–6.

————. 1977. *Population growth and land use*. 2d ed. (1st ed. 1967). London: Macmillan.

Clark, Colin W. 1990. *Mathematical bioeconomics: The optimal management of renewable resources*. 2d ed. New York: Wiley.

Coale, Ansley J. 1970. Man and his environment. *Science* 170: 132–36. Pp. 114–18 in Reining and Tinker 1975.

————. 1973. The demographic transition reconsidered. *International Population Conference (Liège)* 1: 53–72. International Union for the Scientific Study of Population, Liège.

————. 1974. The history of the human population. *Scientific American* 231 (September): 41–51.

Coale, Ansley J., and Edgar M. Hoover. 1958. *Population growth and economic development in low-income countries: A case study of India's prospects*. Princeton: Princeton University Press.

Coale, Ansley J., and Susan C. Watkins, eds. 1986. *The decline of fertility in Europe: Revised proceedings of a conference on the Princeton European Fertility Project*. Princeton: Princeton University Press.

Coale, Ansley J., Feng Wang, Nancy E. Riley and Lin Fu De. 1991. Recent trends in fertility and nuptiality in China. *Science* 251 (25 January):389–93.

Cockburn, Aidan. 1963. *The evolution and eradication of infectious diseases*. Baltimore: Johns Hopkins University Press.

Cohen, Joel E. 1986. Population forecasts and confidence intervals for Sweden: A comparison of model-based and empirical approaches. *Demography* 23, no. 1 (February):105–26.

————. 1992. How many people can Earth hold? *Discover* 13, no. 11 (November):114–19.

————. 1995. Population growth and the Earth's human carrying capacity. *Science* (21 July).

Cohen, Mark N. 1977. *The food crisis in prehistory: Overpopulation and the origin of agriculture*. New Haven: Yale University Press.

Cole, H. S. D., Christopher Freeman, Marie Jahoda and K. L. R. Pavitt, eds. 1973. *Models of doom: A critique of "The limits to growth," with a reply by the authors of "The limits to growth."* New York: Universe Books.

Coleman, David, and Roger Schofield, eds. 1986. *The state of population theory: Forward from Malthus*. Oxford / New York: Basil Blackwell.

Commission for the Study of International Migration and Cooperative Economic Development. 1990. *Unauthorized migration: An economic development response*. Washington, D.C.: The Commission.

Cook, Maria S. L., and Robert Repetto. 1982. The relevance of the developing countries to demographic transition theory: Further lessons from the Hungarian experience. *Population Studies* 36, no. 1:105–28.

Cornell, Laurel L. 1988. Taking reproduction seriously: Marxism and the "modern family" in China and Japan. In *Social structures and human lives,* ed. Matilda White Riley. Newbury Park, Calif.: Sage Publications.

Cowell, Alan. 1994. Scientists linked to the Vatican call for population curbs. *New York Times* (16 June), p. A6.

Cox, George W., ed. 1969. *Readings in conservation ecology.* New York: Appleton-Century-Crofts.

Cropper, Maureen L., and Wallace E. Oates. 1992. Environmental economics: A survey. *Journal of Economic Literature* 30 (June):675–740.

Crosby, Alfred W. 1972. *The Columbian exchange: Biological and cultural consequences of 1492.* Westport, Conn.: Greenwood Press.

———. 1986. *Ecological imperialism: The biological expansion of Europe, 900–1900.* Cambridge, U.K.: Cambridge University Press.

Dahl, Robert A., and E. R. Tufte. 1973. *Size and democracy.* Stanford, Calif.: Stanford University Press.

Daily, Gretchen C., and Paul R. Ehrlich. 1992. Population, sustainability, and Earth's carrying capacity. *BioScience* 42, no. 10 (November):761–71.

Daly, Herman E. 1993. The perils of free trade. *Scientific American* 269, no. 5 (November):50–57.

Daly, Herman E., and J. B. Cobb. 1989. *For the common good: Redirecting the economy toward community, the environment, and a sustainable future.* Boston: Beacon Press.

Darwin, Charles Galton. 1952. *The next million years.* London: Hart-Davis. Reprint, Westport, Conn.: Greenwood Press, 1973. Paperback, Garden City, N.Y.: Dolphin Books, Doubleday.

Davies, P. C. W. 1982. *The accidental universe.* Cambridge, U.K.: Cambridge University Press.

Davis, Kingsley, and Mikhail S. Bernstam, eds. 1991. *Resources, environment, and population: Present knowledge, future options.* Supplement to vol. 16 of *Population and Development Review,* 1990. New York: Population Council, and New York / Oxford: Oxford University Press.

DeAngelis, Donald L. 1992. *Dynamics of nutrient cycling and food webs.* London: Chapman and Hall.

Deevey, Edward S., Jr. 1960. The human population. *Scientific American* 203, no. 9 (September):195–204.

Demeny, Paul. 1988. Demography and the limits to growth. In *Population and resources in Western intellectual traditions,* ed. Michael S. Teitelbaum and Jay M. Winter. Supplement to vol. 14 of *Population and Development Review* (winter), pp. 213–44.

———. 1991. Tradeoffs between human numbers and material standards of living. In *Resources, environment, and population: Present knowledge, future options,* ed. Kingsley Davis and Mikhail S. Bernstam. New York: Oxford University Press. Supplement to vol. 16, 1990, of *Population and Development Review,* pp. 408–21.

———. 1994. *Population and development: International Conference on Population and Development 1994.* Liège: International Union for the Scientific Study of Population.

De Wit, C. T. 1967. Photosynthesis: Its relationship to overpopulation. In *Harvesting the sun: Photosynthesis in plant life,* ed. A. San Pietro, Frances A. Greer and T. J. Army. New York: Academic Press, pp. 315–20.

Dhondt, André A. 1988. Carrying capacity: A confusing concept. *Acta Oecologica / Oecologia Generalis* 9, no. 4:337–46.

Diamond, Jared M. 1992. *The third chimpanzee: The evolution and future of the human animal.* New York: Harper Collins.

Diaz-Briquets, Sergio. 1986. *Conflict in Central America: The demographic dimension.* Population Trends and Public Policy No. 10 (February). Washington, D.C.: Population Reference Bureau.

Dobb, Edwin. 1992. Cultivating nature. *The Sciences (New York Academy of Sciences),* January / February:44–50.

Döös, Bo R. 1994. Environmental degradation, global food production, and risk for large-scale migrations. *Ambio* 23, no. 2:124–30.

Dorn, Harold F. 1950. Pitfalls in population forecasts and projections. *Journal of the American Statistical Association* 45, no. 251 (September):311–34.

———. 1962. World population growth: An international dilemma. *Science* 135, no. 3,500 (26 January 1962):283–90. Reprinted in Cox 1969.

Downes, R. G. 1964. The water balance and land-use. In *Water resources, use and management.* Melbourne: Melbourne University Press, pp. 329–41. Reprinted in Cox 1969.

Dubos, René. 1971. Foreword to Noël Hinrichs, ed., *Population, environment and people.* New York: McGraw-Hill.

Duchin, Faye, and Glenn-Marie Lange. 1994. Strategies for environmentally sound economic development. In *Investing in natural capital: The ecological economics approach to sustainability,* ed. A. M. Jansson, J. Hammer, C. Folke and R. Costanza. Washington, D.C.: Island Press, pp. 250–65.

Durand, John. 1977. Historical estimates of world population: An evaluation. *Population and Development Review* 3, no. 3:253–96.

Dymond, Jack. 1992. Particles in the oceans. *Oceanus* 35, no. 1:60–67.

Dyson, Tim, and Mike Murphy. 1985. The onset of fertility transition. *Population and Development Review* 11, no. 3:399–440.

Earnest, Mark, and John A. Sbarbaro. 1993. A plague returns: TB is back, the grim harvest of decades of complacency. *The Sciences (New York Academy of Sciences),* September / October: 14–19.

East, Edward M. 1923. *Mankind at the crossroads.* New York / London: Scribner's. 1924 issue reprinted in 1977 by Arno Press, New York.

Economist. 1990a. *Book of vital world statistics.* Introduction by Robert J. Samuelson. New York: Times Books.

———. 1990b. Survey of the Arab world—Pop: Think of a problem then multiply. *Economist,* 12 May:4–7.

———. 1992. *Pocket world in figures, 1993 ed.* London: The Economist Books.

Ehrlich, Paul R. 1968. *The population bomb.* New York: Ballantine Books.

———. 1971. The population crisis: Where we stand. In *Population, environment and people,* ed. Noël Hinrichs. New York: McGraw-Hill, pp. 8–16.

Ehrlich, Paul R., and Anne H. Ehrlich. 1981. *Extinction: The causes and consequences of the disappearance of species.* New York: Random House.

———. 1990. *The population explosion.* New York: Simon and Schuster.

Ehrlich, Paul R., Anne H. Ehrlich and Gretchen C. Daily. 1993. Food security, population, and environment. *Population and Development Review* 19, no. 1: 1–32.

Ehrlich, Paul R., Anne H. Ehrlich and John P. Holdren. 1977. *Ecoscience: Population, resources, environment.* San Francisco: W. H. Freeman.

Ekins, Paul, Mayer Hillman and Robert Hutchison. 1992. *Wealth beyond measure: An atlas of new economics.* London: Gaia Books. Also published as *The Gaia atlas of green economics.* New York: Anchor Books.

Engelman, Robert, and Pamela LeRoy. 1993. *Sustaining water: Population and the future of renewable water supplies.* Washington, D.C.: Population and Environment Program, Population Action International.

Erikson, Erik H. 1963. *Childhood and society.* 2d ed. New York: W. W. Norton.

Etzioni, Amitai. 1968. *The active society: A theory of societal and political processes.* London: Collier-Macmillan; New York: Free Press.

Europa. 1992. *Europa world year book.* London: Europa Publications.

Eyre, S. R. 1978. *The real wealth of nations.* New York: St. Martin's Press; London: Edward Arnold.

Fair, Gordon M., John C. Geyer and Daniel A. Okun. 1966. *Water and wastewater engineering.* Vol. 1, *Water supply and wastewater removal.* New York: John Wiley.

Falkenmark, Malin. 1991. Rapid population growth and water scarcity: The predicament of tomorrow's Africa. In *Resources, environment, and population: Present knowledge, future options,* ed. Kingsley Davis and Mikhail S. Bernstam. New York: Oxford University Press. Supplement to vol. 16, 1990, of *Population and Development Review,* pp. 81–94.

———. 1992. A water perspective on population, environment, and development. In *Population, environment and development,* ed. Evert van Imhoff, Ellen Themmen and Frans Willekens. Amsterdam, Netherlands / Berwyn, Penn.: Swets and Zeitlinger, pp. 33–56.

Farrell, Kenneth R., Fred H. Sanderson and Trang T. Vo. 1984. U.S. food and fiber—abundance or austerity? *Resources* no. 76 (spring), pp. 2–20. Washington, D.C.: Resources for the Future.

Fawcett, C. B. 1947. The numbers and distribution of mankind. *Scientific Monthly (U.S.A.)* 64, no. 5 (May):389–96.

Fearnside, Philip M. 1986. *Human carrying capacity of the Brazilian rainforest.* New York: Columbia University Press.

———. 1990. Estimation of human carrying capacity in rainforest areas. *Trends in Ecology and Evolution* 5, no. 6:192–96.

Fircks, Arthur Freiherr von. 1898. *Bevölkerungslehre und Bevölkerungspolitik.* Leipzig: Verlag von C. L. Hirschfeld.

Fischer, Alois. 1925. Zur Frage der Tragfähigkeit des Lebensraumes. *Zeitschrift für Geopolitik:* 762, 844, 852.

Fogel, Robert W. 1994. Economic growth, population theory, and physiology: The bearing of long-term processes on the making of economic policy. *American Economic Review* 84, no. 3 (June):369–95.

Forrester, Jay W. 1971. *World dynamics.* Cambridge, Mass.: Wright-Allen Press.

Franklin, Benjamin. 1755. *Observations Concerning the Increase of Mankind, Peopling of Countries, &c.* Boston: S. Kneeland.

Frejka, Tomas. 1973. *The future of population growth: Alternative paths to equilibrium.* New York: John Wiley.

———. 1978. Future population growth. In *Handbook of futures research,* ed. Jib Fowles. Westport, Conn.: Greenwood Press. Also issued May 1977 as a Working Paper of the Center for Policy Studies, New York: Population Council.

———. 1981. World population projections: A concise history. Working Paper 66 (March), Center for Policy Studies, New York: Population Council. Presented at the General Conference of the International Union for the Scientific Study of Population, Manila, December 1981.

Fremlin, J. H. 1964. How many people can the world support? *New Scientist* 24, no. 415 (29 October):285–87.

Gardner, Richard N. 1992. *Negotiating survival: Four priorities after Rio.* New York: Council on Foreign Relations Press.

Garnett, Geoff P., and Roy M. Anderson. 1993. No reason for complacency about the potential demographic impact of AIDS in Africa. *Transactions of the Royal Society of Tropical Medicine and Hygiene* 87(supplement 1):19–22.

Gates, David M. 1982. Biosphere. *Encyclopædia Britannica.* 15th ed. 2:1037–44.

Gertler, Paul J., and John W. Molyneaux. 1994. How economic development and family planning programs combined to reduce Indonesian fertility. *Demography* 31, no. 1:33–63.

Gever, John, Robert Kaufmann, David Skole and Charles Vörösmarty. 1986. *Beyond oil: The threat to food and fuel in the coming decades.* Cambridge, Mass.: Ballinger. 3d ed. with new prologue and introduction, Niwot: University Press of Colorado, 1991.

Ghosh, Pradip K., ed. 1984. *Population, environment and resources, and Third World development.* International Development Resource Books, vol. 5. Westport, Conn.: Greenwood Press.

Gibbons, Ann. 1993. Pleistocene population explosions. *Science* 262 (1 October):27–28.

Gilbert, A. J., and L. C. Braat, eds. 1991. *Modelling for population and sustainable development.* London / New York: Routledge.

Gilland, B. 1979. *The next seventy years: Population, food and resources.* Tunbridge Wells, Kent, U.K.: Abacus Press (available from ISBS, Inc., P.O. Box 555, Forest Grove, OR 97116).

———. 1983. Considerations on world population and food supply. *Population and Development Review* 9, no. 2:203–11.

Glantz, Michael H. 1990. Running on empty: Irrigation is depleting a vast reservoir under the American great plains. *The Sciences (New York Academy of Sciences)* 30, no. 6 (November / December):16–20.

Glantz, Michael H., and Jesse H. Ausubel. 1984. The Ogallala aquifer and carbon dioxide: Comparison and convergence. *Environmental Conservation* 11:123–31.

Gleick, Peter H. 1992. Water and conflict. Project on Environmental Change and Acute Conflict, Occasional Paper Series No. 1, September 1992, pp. 3–27. Cambridge, Mass.: American Academy of Arts and Sciences. Published as Water and conflict: Fresh water resources and international security. *International Security* 18, no. 1 (summer 1993):79.

———, ed. 1993. *Water in crisis: A guide to the world's fresh water resources*. New York / Oxford: Oxford University Press.

Goldberg, Edward D. 1991. Ocean space: Use and protection. In *Resources, environment, and population: Present knowledge, future options*, ed. Kingsley Davis and Mikhail S. Bernstam. New York: Oxford University Press. Supplement to vol. 16, 1990, of *Population and Development Review*, pp. 221–34.

Goldsmith, Grace A., Roger Revelle, Calvin L. Beale, James W. Brackett, R. W. Engel, Willis A. Gortner, Ogden C. Johnson, Trienah Meyers, Max Milner and Robert E. Shank. 1967. Population and nutritional demands. In *The world food problem, report of the Panel on the World Food Supply*, vol. II. A Report of the President's Science Advisory Committee, the White House, May 1967, pp. 1–135. Harvard University, Center for Population Studies, Contribution No. 31.

Goodkind, Daniel M. 1992. Motivating ethnic fertility values: A regional study of the Dragon Year baby boom among the Chinese in peninsular Malaysia, 1976 and 1988. Working Paper in Demography 37, Research School of Social Sciences, Canberra: Australian National University.

———. 1993. New zodiacal influences on Chinese family formation: Taiwan, 1976. *Demography* 30, no. 2 (May):127–42.

Gore, Al. 1992. *Earth in the balance: Ecology and the human spirit*. New York: Houghton Mifflin.

Gould, Stephen Jay. 1992. *Eight little piggies: Reflections in natural history*. New York: W. W. Norton.

Graedel, T. E., and B. R. Allenby. 1994. *Industrial ecology*. Englewood Cliffs, N.J.: Prentice-Hall.

Grauman, John V. 1967. Success and failure in population forecasts of the 1950's: A general appraisal. In *Proceedings of the World Population Conference, Belgrade, August–September 1965*, vol. 3. New York: United Nations, Department of Economic and Social Affairs, pp. 10–14.

Graunt, John. 1662. *Natural and Political Observations Mentioned in a following Index, and made upon the Bills of Mortality. With reference to the Government, Religion, Trade, Growth, Ayre, Diseases, and the several Changes of the said City*. London.

Greenhalgh, Susan. 1993. The peasantization of the one-child policy in Shaanxi. In *Chinese families in the post-Mao era*, ed. Deborah David and Stevan Harrell. Berkeley: University of California Press, pp. 219–50.

Greenhalgh, Susan, Chuzhu Zhu and Nan Li. 1994. Restraining population growth in three Chinese villages: 1988–93. *Population and Development Review* 20, no. 2:365–95.

Grummer-Strawn, Laurence, and Thomas J. Espenshade. 1991. Evaluating the accuracy of U.S. population projection models. In *Improving information for social policy decisions: The uses of microsimulation modeling*, vol. 2, ed. Constance F. Citro and Eric A. Hanushek. Washington, D.C.: National Research Council, pp. 305–29.

Hajnal, John. 1954. The prospect for population forecasts. In *Proceedings of the World Population Conference, Rome, August–September, Meeting No. 13*, vol. 3 (E/CONF.13/415). New York: United Nations, pp. 43–51.

———. 1957. Mathematical models in demography. *Cold Spring Harbor Symposia in Quantitative Biology* 22:97–103.

Hall, D. O. 1980. World production of organic matter. In *Food chains and human nutrition*, ed. Kenneth Blaxter. London: Applied Science Publishers, pp. 51–87.

Hammel, E. A. 1990. A theory of culture for demography. *Population and Development Review* 16, no. 3:455–85.

Hammel, Eugene A., and Nancy Howell. 1987. Research in population and culture: An evolutionary framework. *Current Anthropology* 28, no. 2:141–60.

Handwerker, W. Penn. 1986. *Culture and reproduction: An anthropological critique of demographic transition theory*. Boulder/London: Westview Press.

Hardesty, Donald L. 1977. *Ecological anthropology*. New York: John Wiley.

Hardin, Garrett. 1968. The tragedy of the commons. *Science* 162:1243–48. Pp. 11–16 in Reining and Tinker 1975.

———. 1985. *Filters against folly: How to survive despite economists, ecologists, and the merely eloquent*. New York: Viking Penguin.

———. 1986. Cultural carrying capacity: A biological approach to human problems. *BioScience* 36, no. 9:599–606.

———. 1993. *Living within limits: Ecology, economics, and population taboos.* New York/Oxford: Oxford University Press.

———, ed. 1964. *Population, evolution, and birth control: A collage of controversial readings.* San Francisco: W. H. Freeman.

Harpending, Henry C., Stephen T. Sherry, Alan R. Rogers, and Mark Stoneking. 1993. The genetic structure of ancient human populations. *Current Anthropology* 34, no. 4 (August):483–96.

Harris, Sidney. 1992. *Chalk up another one: The best of Sidney Harris.* Washington, D.C.: AAAS Press.

Harrison, Paul. 1993. Wildlife and people: Scrambling for space. *People and the Planet* 2, no. 3:6–9.

Hart, Hornell. 1945. Logistic social trends. *American Journal of Sociology* 50, no. 5 (March):337–52.

Harte, John. 1988. *Consider a spherical cow: A course in environmental problem solving.* Mill Valley, Calif.: University Science Books.

Hassan, Fekri A. 1981. *Demographic archaeology.* New York/London: Academic Press.

Hastings, Alan, Carole L. Hom, Stephen Ellner, Peter Turchin and H. Charles J. Godfray. 1993. Chaos in ecology: Is Mother Nature a strange attractor? *Annual Review of Ecology and Systematics* 24:1–33.

Haub, Carl. 1993. China's fertility drop lowers world growth rate. *Population Today* 21, no. 6 (June):1–2.

———. 1994. Russia's new revolution: A demographic baby bust. *Population Today* 22, no. 4 (April):1–2.

Hauser, P. M. 1971. On population and environmental policy and problems. In *Population, environment and people,* ed. Noël Hinrichs. New York: McGraw-Hill, pp. 17–34.

———, ed. 1979. *World population and development: Challenges and prospects.* Syracuse, N.Y.: Syracuse University Press.

Hayes, Brian. 1993. Balanced on a pencil point. *American Scientist* 81 (November–December):510–16.

Heer, David M. 1968. *Society and population.* Englewood Cliffs, N.J.: Prentice-Hall.

Heilig, Gerhard K. 1993. How many people can be fed on earth? Working Paper WP-93–40 (August). Laxenburg, Austria: International Institute for Applied Systems Analysis.

———. 1994. How many people can be fed on earth? In *The future of world population: What can we assume today,* ed. Wolfgang Lutz. London: Earthscan, pp. 207–61.

Henry, Louis, and H. Gutierrez. 1977. Qualité des prévisions démographiques à court terme. Étude de l'extrapolation de la population totale des départements et villes de France, 1821–1975. *Population (Paris)* 32, no. 3:625–47.

Higgins, G. M., A. H. Kassam, L. Naiken, G. Fischer and M. M. Shah. 1983. Potential population supporting capacities of lands in the developing world: Technical report of project INT/75/P13, "Land resources for populations of the future," FPA/INT/513. Rome: Food and Agricultural Organization of the United Nations.

Hillel, Daniel. 1991. *Out of the earth: Civilization and the life of the soil.* Berkeley/Los Angeles: University of California Press.

Hirschoff, P. M., and N. G. Kotler, eds. 1989. *Completing the food chain: Strategies for combating hunger and malnutrition.* Washington, D.C.: Smithsonian Institution Press.

Holdren, John P., and Paul R. Ehrlich. 1974. Human population and the global environment. *American Scientist* 62 (May–June):282–92.

Holland, Bart K. 1993. A view of population growth circa A.D. 200. *Population and Development Review* 19, no. 2:328–29.

Hollingsworth, T. H. 1969. *Historical demography.* London: The Sources of History Ltd. & Hodder and Stoughton Ltd.

Holmes, Bob. 1993. A new study finds there's life left in the green revolution. *Science* 261 (17 September):1517.

Homer-Dixon, Thomas F. 1992. Malthus in the real world: Environmental scarcity and the ingenuity gap in developing countries. Unpublished manuscript, November.

———. 1994a. The ingenuity gap: Can poor countries adapt to resource scarcity? Unpublished manuscript.

———. 1994b. Environmental scarcities and violent conflict: Evidence from cases. *International Security* 19, no. 1 (summer):5–40.

Horiuchi, Shiro. 1992. Stagnation in the decline of the world population growth rate during the 1980s. *Science* 257:761–65.

House, Peter W., and Edward R. Williams. 1975. *The carrying capacity of a nation: Growth and the quality of life.* Lexington, Mass.: Lexington Books (D. C. Heath).

Hoyle, Fred. 1963. A contradiction in the argument of Malthus. The 1962–63 St. John's College Cambridge Lecture at the University of Hull, 17 May 1963. University of Hull Publications, Hull, England. Reprinted in *Population and Development Review* 12, no. 3 (1986):548–62.

Hudson, William J. 1989. Population, food, and the economy of nations. In *Food and natural resources,* ed. David Pimentel and Carl W. Hall. San Diego, Calif.: Academic Press, pp. 275–99.

Hulett, H. R. 1970. Optimum world population. *BioScience* 20 (1 February):160–61. Reprinted in *Readings in human population ecology,* ed. Wayne Y. Davis. Englewood Cliffs, N.J.: Prentice-Hall, 1971, pp. 172–73.

Huxley, Julian. 1950 (1993). Population and human destiny. *Harper's Magazine* (September 1950). Reprinted in *Population and Development Review* 19, no. 3:607–20.

Inaba, Hisashi. 1989. Functional analytic approach to age-structured population dynamics. Doctoral dissertation, University of Leiden, Netherlands.

Isiugo-Abanihe, Uche C. 1994. Reproductive motivation and family-size preferences among Nigerian men. *Studies in Family Planning* 25, no. 3 (May–June):149.

James, W. P. T., and E. C. Schofield. 1990. *Human energy requirements: A manual for planners and nutritionists.* Oxford: Oxford University Press.

Jevons, William Stanley. 1965. *The coal question.* 3d rev. ed. New York: A. M. Kelley (1st ed. 1865; 2d ed. 1866).

Johansson, S. Ryan. 1991. "Implicit" policy and fertility during development. *Population and Development Review* 17, no. 3 (September):377–414.

Johnson, D. Gale, and Ronald Demos Lee, eds. 1987. *Population growth and economic development: Issues and evidence.* Madison: University of Wisconsin Press.

Johnson, Otto, ed. 1991. *Information please almanac atlas and yearbook 1992.* 45th ed. Boston/New York: Houghton Mifflin.

Jolly, Richard. 1993. UNICEF policy and perspectives: Child survival, population growth, environment and development. *Transactions of the Royal Society of Tropical Medicine and Hygiene* 87(supplement 1):32–35.

Kabeer, Naila. 1990. The economic, social, political and environmental implications of population growth in the developing world. Ditchley Foundation Conference Report D90/11, 21–23 September 1990. Oxfordshire, England: Ditchley Foundation.

Karplus, Walter J. 1992. *The heavens are falling: The scientific prediction of catastrophes in our time.* New York/London: Plenum Press.

Kates, R. W., R. S. Chen, T. E. Downing, J. X. Kasperson, E. Messer and S. R. Millman. 1988. *The hunger report: 1988.* Alan Shawn Feinstein World Hunger Program, Brown University, August.

——. 1989. *The hunger report: Update 1989.* HR-89-1. Alan Shawn Feinstein World Hunger Program, Brown University, March.

Kates, Robert W., B. L. Turner and William C. Clark. 1990. The great transformation. In *The earth as transformed by human action: Global and regional changes in the biosphere over the past 300 years,* ed. B. L. Turner, W. C. Clark, R. W. Kates, J. F. Richards, J. T. Mathews and W. B. Meyer. Cambridge, U.K.: Cambridge University Press with Clark University, pp. 1–17.

Kaysen, Carl. 1972. The computer that printed out W*O*L*F*. *Foreign Affairs* 50, no. 4 (July): 660–68.

Keeton, William T., James L. Gould and Carol Grant Gould. 1993. *Biological science.* 5th ed. New York: W. W. Norton.

Kelley, Allen C. 1988. Economic consequences of population change in the Third World. *Journal of Economic Literature* 26:1685–1728.

Keyfitz, Nathan. 1968. *Introduction to the mathematics of population.* Reading, Mass.: Addison-Wesley.

——. 1982a. *Population change and social policy.* Cambridge, Mass.: Abt Books.

——. 1982b. Can knowledge improve forecasts? *Population and Development Review* 8, no. 4:729–51.

———. 1991. Population and development within the ecosphere: One view of the literature. *Population Index* 57, no. 1:5–22.

Keynes, Richard D. 1983. Malthus and biological equilibria. In *Malthus past and present*, ed. J. Dupâquier, A. Fauve-Chamoux and E. Grebenik. London/New York: Academic Press, pp. 359–64.

Kihlberg, Reinhold. 1972. The microbe as a source of food. *Annual Review of Microbiology* 26:427–66.

Kilmer, Anne D. 1972. The Mesopotamian concept of overpopulation and its solution as reflected in the mythology. *Orientalia* 41:160–76 (N. S.)

King, Gregory. 1695–1700 (published 1973). Seventeenth-century manuscript book of Gregory King. In *The earliest classics: Graunt and King*. With an introduction by Peter Laslett. Westmead, Farnborough, Hants, England: Gregg International Publishers.

King, Jane. 1987. *Beyond economic choice: Population and sustainable development: The application of a resource accounting method to long term development planning in the context of population, resources and the environment*. Edinburgh, Scotland: UNESCO and the University of Edinburgh.

King, Maurice. 1993. Demographic entrapment. *Transactions of the Royal Society of Tropical Medicine and Hygiene* 87(supplement 1):23–28.

Kirchner, James W., George Ledec, Robert J. A. Goodland and Janet M. Drake. 1985. Carrying capacity, population growth, and sustainable development. In *Rapid population growth and human carrying capacity: Two perspectives*, ed. Dennis J. Mahar. World Bank Staff Working Papers Number 690, Population and Development Series Number 15. Washington, D.C.: World Bank, pp. 40–89.

Kirk, Dudley. 1967. Prospects for reducing natality in the underdeveloped world. *Annals of the American Academy of Political and Social Science* 369:48–60. Reprinted in Cox 1969.

Kleiber, Max. 1961. *The fire of life: An introduction to animal energetics*. New York: John Wiley.

Knibbs, G. H. 1917. The mathematical theory of population, of its character and fluctuations, and of the factors which influence them, being an examination of the general scheme of statistical representation, with deductions of necessary formulae; the whole being applied to the data of the Australian Census of 1911, and to the elucidation of Australian population statistics generally. Appendix A. Vol. 1. Census of the Commonwealth of Australia. Published under instructions from the Minister of State for Home and Territories, Melbourne. Melbourne: McCarron, Bird & Co.

Kolars, John. 1992. Trickle of hope: Negotiating water rights is critical to peace in the Middle East. *The Sciences (New York Academy of Sciences)* 32, no. 6 (November/December):16–21.

Kotler, N. G., ed. 1990. *Sharing innovation: Global perspectives on food, agriculture, and rural development*. Washington, D.C.: Smithsonian Institution Press.

Kovda, Victor A. (Viktor Abramovich). 1980. Land aridization and drought control. (English translation of: Aridizatsiia sushi i bor'ba s zasukhoi.) Boulder, Colo.: Westview Press.

Kremer, Michael. 1993. Population growth and technological change: One million B.C. to 1990. *Quarterly Journal of Economics* 108, no. 3 (August):681–716.

Kunzig, Robert. 1994. The iron man's revenge. *Discover* 15, no. 6 (June):32–35.

Lederberg, Joshua. 1988. Medical science, infectious disease, and the unity of humankind. *Journal of the American Medical Association* 260, no. 5:684–85.

Lee, Ronald D. 1986. Malthus and Boserup: A dynamic synthesis. In *The state of population theory: Forward from Malthus*, ed. David Coleman and Roger Schofield. Oxford/New York: Basil Blackwell, pp. 96–130.

———. 1988. Induced population growth and induced technological progress: Their interaction in the accelerating stage. *Mathematical Population Studies* 1, no. 3:265–88.

———. 1991. Comment: The second tragedy of the commons. In *Resources, environment, and population: Present knowledge, future options*, ed. Kingsley Davis and Mikhail S. Bernstam. New York: Oxford University Press. Supplement to vol. 16, 1990, of *Population and Development Review*, pp. 315–22.

———. 1992. Croissance démographique, progrès et pauvreté. *Population (Paris)* 47, no. 6 (November–December):1533–54. English translation in manuscript (1992): Population growth, resource constraints, and technical progress.

———. 1993. Accidental and systematic change in population history: homeostasis in a stochastic setting. *Exploration in Economic History* 30:1–30.

Lee, Ronald D., and Tim Miller. 1990. Population policy and externalities to childbearing. *Annals of the American Academy of Political and Social Science* 510 (July):17–32.

Lee, Ronald D., and Shripad Tuljapurkar. 1994. Stochastic population forecasts for the U.S.: Beyond high, medium and low. *Journal of the American Statistical Association* 89, no. 428 (December):1175–89.

Lee, Ronald D., W. Brian Arthur, Allen C. Kelley, Gerry Rodgers and T. N. Srinivasan, eds. 1988. *Population, food and rural development*. New York: Clarendon Press/Oxford University Press.

Leeuwenhoek, Antoni van. 1679 (1948). *The collected letters*, vol. 3. Amsterdam: Swets and Zeitlinger, Letter 43, 25 April 1679, to Nehemias Grew, Secretary of the Royal Society, pp. 4–35.

Leichty, Erle. 1971. Demons and population control. *Expedition* 13, no. 2 (winter):22–26. University Museum of the University of Pennsylvania (Philadelphia).

Li, Jing-Neng. 1991. Comment: Population effects on deforestation and soil erosion in China. In *Resources, environment, and population: Present knowledge, future options*, ed. Kingsley Davis and Mikhail S. Bernstam. New York: Oxford University Press. Supplement to vol. 16, 1990, of *Population and Development Review*, pp. 254–58.

Liebig, Justus Freiherr von. 1855. *Principles of agricultural chemistry: With special reference to the late researches made in England*. New York: John Wiley. German edition: *Die Grundsätze der Agriculturchemie*. Braunschweig: F. Vieweg und Sohn.

Lieth, Helmut. 1973. Primary production: Terrestrial ecosystems. *Human Ecology* 1, no. 4:303–32.

Lieth, Helmut, and Robert H. Whittaker, eds. 1975. *Primary productivity of the biosphere*. New York: Springer-Verlag.

Lippman, T. W. 1992. Report warns of environmental crisis. *Washington Post*, 14 April, p. A8.

Livi-Bacci, Massimo. 1991. *Population and nutrition: Essay on the demographic history of Europe*. Cambridge: Cambridge University Press.

———. 1992. *A concise history of world population*. Trans. Carl Ipsen. Cambridge, Mass./ Oxford, U.K.: Blackwell.

Lotka, Alfred J. 1925. *Elements of physical biology*. Baltimore: Williams and Wilkins. Reprint, *Elements of mathematical biology*, New York: Dover, 1956.

Lovejoy, Thomas E. 1994. People and biodiversity. *Nature Conservancy* 44, no. 1:29–33.

Low, Patrick, ed. 1992. *International trade and the environment*. Washington, D.C.: World Bank, World Bank Discussion Paper 159.

Lowi, Miriam R. 1993. West bank water resources and the resolution of conflict in the Middle East. Project on Environmental Change and Acute Conflict, Occasional Paper Series No. 1, September 1992, pp. 29–60. Cambridge, Mass.: American Academy of Arts and Sciences. Published as: Bridging the divide: Transboundary resource disputes and the case of West Bank water. *International Security* 18, no. 1 (summer 1993):113.

Lutz, Wolfgang. 1993. Population-development-environment: An attempt to set some basic parameters for analysis. Paper presented at the Population Association of America annual meeting, Cincinnati, Ohio, 1–3 April.

———, ed. 1994. *Population-development-environment: Understanding their interactions in Mauritius*. Heidelberg: Springer-Verlag. Chap. 18 reprinted as: *Population-development-environment: Lessons from Mauritius in the global context and philosophy of the PDE approach*. Laxenburg, Austria: International Institute for Applied Systems Analysis.

Lutz, Wolfgang, and Jawaharlall Baguant. 1992. Population and sustainable development: A case study of Mauritius. In *Population, environment and development*, ed. Evert van Imhoff, Ellen Themmen and Frans Willekens. Amsterdam, Netherlands/Berwyn, Penn.: Swets and Zeitlinger, pp. 57–82.

MacArthur Foundation, John D. and Catherine T. 1992. *Report on activities*. Chicago: The Foundation.

MacDonald, G. J., ed. 1982. *The long-term impacts of increasing atmospheric carbon dioxide levels*. Cambridge, Mass.: Ballinger.

MacIntyre, Alasdair. 1967. Egoism and altruism. *Encyclopedia of Philosophy* 2:462–66.

MacKellar, F. Landis. 1994. Population and development: Assessment before the 1994 conference. *Development Policy Review* 12, no. 2 (June):165–91.

Madhavan, M. C. 1985. Indian emigrants: Numbers, characteristics, and economic impact. *Population and Development Review* 11, no. 3: 457–81.

Maguire, Marjorie R., and Daniel C. Maguire. 1983. *Abortion: A guide to making ethical choices.* Washington, D.C.: Catholics for a Free Choice.

Maimonides, Moses. 1963. *The guide of the perplexed.* Trans. Shlomo Pines. Chicago: University of Chicago Press.

Malthus, Thomas Robert. 1798 (1960). *An Essay on the Principle of Population, as It Affects the Future Improvement of Society. With remarks on the speculations of Mr. Godwin, M. Condorcet, and other writers.* Complete 1st ed. and partial 7th ed. (1872) reprinted in *On population,* ed. Gertrude Himmelfarb. New York: Modern Library.

Mann, Charles C. 1993. How many is too many? *Atlantic Monthly,* February:47–67.

Mann, Donald W. 1981. Fewer people for a better world: A plea for negative population growth. *Environmental Conservation* 8, no. 4:260–61.

Marchetti, C. 1979. 10^{12}: A check on the Earth-carrying capacity for man. *Energy* 4:1107–17. London: Pergamon Press. Originally issued in 1978 as: On 10^{12}: A check on Earth carrying capacity for man. Research Report RR-78-7 (May). Laxenburg, Austria: International Institute for Applied Systems Analysis.

Margulis, Lynn, and Joel E. Cohen. 1994. Combinatorial generation of taxonomic diversity: Implication of symbiogenesis for the Proterozoic fossil record. In *Early life on Earth: Nobel symposium 84,* ed. Stefan Bengtson. New York: Columbia University Press, pp. 327–33.

Margulis, Lynn, and R. Fester, eds. 1991. *Symbiosis as a source of evolutionary innovation: Speciation and morphogenesis.* Cambridge: MIT Press.

Marmot, Michael G. 1994. Social differentials in health within and between populations. *Daedalus* 123, no. 4 (fall):197–216.

Martin, John H. 1990. Glacial-interglacial CO_2 change: The iron hypothesis. *Paleoceanography* 5:1–13.

Martin, John H., and S. E. Fitzwater. 1988. Iron deficiency limits phytoplankton growth in the north-east Pacific subarctic. *Nature* 331:341–43.

Mathews, Jessica. 1990. World population: As the president turns. *Washington Post* (1 November), op-ed page.

Mauldin, W. Parker, and John A. Ross. 1991. Family planning programs: Efforts and results, 1982–89. *Studies in Family Planning* 22, no. 6:350–67.

May, Robert M. 1974. Biological populations with nonoverlapping generations: Stable points, stable cycles, and chaos. *Science* 186 (15 November):645–47.

———. 1975. Biological populations obeying difference equations: Stable points, stable cycles and chaos. *Journal of Theoretical Biology* 51:511–24.

———. 1986. The search for patterns in the balance of nature: Advances and retreats. *Ecology* 67, no. 5:1115–26.

———. 1990. How many species? *Philosophical Transactions of the Royal Society of London B* 330:293–304.

———. 1994. Biological diversity: Differences between land and sea. *Philosophical Transactions of the Royal Society of London B* 343:104–11.

May, Robert M., and George F. Oster. 1976. Bifurcations and dynamic complexity in simple ecological models. *American Naturalist* 110:573–99.

May, Robert M., and Jon Seger. 1986. Ideas in ecology. *American Scientist* 74 (May–June):256–67.

May, Robert M., John H. Lawton and Nigel E. Stork. 1995. Assessing extinction rates. In *Extinction rates,* ed. John H. Lawton and Robert M. May. Oxford: Oxford university Press.

Mayer, Jean. 1964. Food and population: The wrong problem? *Daedalus* 93, no. 3 (Summer):830–44.

McEvedy, Colin, and Richard Jones. 1978. *Atlas of world population history.* New York: Viking Penguin.

McKeown, Thomas. 1976. *The modern rise of population.* New York: Academic Press; London: E. Arnold.

———. 1988. *The origins of human disease.* Oxford: Basil Blackwell.

McLaren, Angus. 1992. The sexual politics of reproduction in Britain. In *The European experience of declining fertility, 1850–1970: The quiet revolution,* ed. John R. Gillis, Louise A. Tilly and David Levine. Cambridge, Mass./Oxford, U.K.: Blackwell, pp. 85–100.

McNeill, William H. 1963. *The rise of the West: A history of the human community.* Chicago: University of Chicago Press.

———. 1967. *A world history.* New York/London: Oxford University Press.

———. 1976. *Plagues and peoples.* Oxford, U.K.: Blackwell; New York: Anchor Books, Doubleday.

———. 1990. *Population and politics since 1750.* Charlottesville/London: University Press of Virginia.

McNicoll, Geoffrey. 1992. The United Nations' long-range population projections. *Population and Development Review* 18, no. 2:333–40.

Meadows, Donella H., Dennis L. Meadows, Jørgen Randers. and William W. Behrens III. 1972. *The limits to growth: A report for the Club of Rome's Project on the Predicament of Mankind.* 2d ed., 1974. New York: Signet, New American Library.

Meadows, Donella H., Dennis L. Meadows and Jørgen Randers. 1992. *Beyond the limits: Global collapse or a sustainable future.* London: Earthscan Publications.

Menken, J., ed. 1986. *World population and U.S. policy: The choices ahead.* New York: W. W. Norton.

Merson, Michael H. 1993. Slowing the spread of HIV: Agenda for the 1990s. *Science* 260 (28 May):1266–68.

Mesarovic, M., and E. Pestel. 1974. *Mankind at the turning point: The second report to the Club of Rome.* New York: E. P. Dutton and Reader's Digest Press.

Mill, John Stuart. 1848 (1965). *Principles of political economy with some of their applications to social philosophy,* ed. V. W. Bladen and J. M. Robson. Toronto: University of Toronto Press; London: Routledge and Kegan Paul, 2 vols.

Miller, Charles B., Bruce W. Frost, Patricia A. Wheeler, Michael R. Landry, Nicholas Welschmeyer and Thomas M. Powell. 1991. Ecological dynamics in the subarctic Pacific, a possibly iron-limited ecosystem. *Limnology and Oceanography* 36, no. 8:1600–15.

Miller, D. S. 1980. Man's demand for energy. In *Food chains and human nutrition,* ed. Kenneth Blaxter. London: Applied Science Publishers, pp. 23–49.

Miller, G. Tyler. 1982. *Living in the environment.* 3d ed. Belmont, Calif.: Wadsworth Publishing.

Miller, Monique. 1992. Has the United States exceeded its carrying capacity? *Wild Earth,* fall: 18.

Millman, S. R., R. S. Chen, J. Emlen, V. Haarmann, J. X. Kasperson and E. Messer. 1991. *The hunger report: Update 1991.* HR-91-1. Alan Shawn Feinstein World Hunger Program, Brown University, April.

Mitchell, B. R. 1978. *European historical statistics 1750–1970.* Abridged ed. London: Macmillan; New York: Columbia University Press.

———. 1992. *International historical statistics: Europe 1750–1988.* 3d ed. New York: Stockton Press.

———. 1993. *International historical statistics: The Americas 1750–1988.* New York: Stockton Press.

Moen, Aaron N. 1973. *Wildlife ecology: An analytical approach.* San Francisco: W. H. Freeman.

Monro, John M. 1993. World population forecasts. *Nature* 363 (20 May):215–16.

Morrison, Robert T., and Robert N. Boyd. 1959. *Organic chemistry.* Boston: Allyn and Bacon.

Morse, Stephen S., ed. 1993. *Emerging viruses.* New York: Oxford University Press.

Mückenhausen, E. 1973. *Die Produktionskapazität der Böden der Erde.* Germany: Rheinisch-Westfälische Akademie der Wissenschafter, Vorträge N234.

Mukerjee, Radhakamal. 1946. *Races, lands, and food: A program for world subsistence.* New York: Dryden Press.

Muller, Walter H. 1974. *Botany: A functional approach.* 3d ed. New York: Macmillan.

Muller-Schwarze, Dietland. 1992. Beaver waterworks. *Natural History,* May: 52.

Murdoch, William. 1990. World hunger and population. In *Agroecology,* ed. C. Ronald Carroll, John H. Vandermeer and Peter Rosset. New York: McGraw-Hill, pp. 3–20.

Muscat, Robert. 1985. Carrying capacity and rapid population growth: Definition, cases, and consequences. In *Rapid population growth and human carrying capacity: Two perspectives,* ed. Dennis J. Mahar. World Bank Staff Working Papers Number 690, Population and Development Series Number 15. Washington, D.C.: World Bank, pp. 1–39.

Myers, Norman. 1983. *A wealth of wild species: Storehouse for human welfare.* Boulder, Colo.: Westview Press.

————. 1991a. *Population, resources and the environment: The critical challenges.* New York: United Nations Fund for Population Activities.

————. 1991b. The world's forests and human populations: The environmental interconnections. In *Resources, environment, and population: Present knowledge, future options,* ed. Kingsley Davis and Mikhail S. Bernstam. New York: Oxford University Press. Supplement to vol. 16, 1990, of *Population and Development Review,* pp. 237–51.

————. 1992. Population/environment linkages: Discontinuities ahead? In *Population, environment and development,* ed. Evert van Imhoff, Ellen Themmen and Frans Willekens. Amsterdam, Netherlands/Berwyn, Penn.: Swets and Zeitlinger, pp. 15–31.

Myers, Norman, and Julian L. Simon. 1994. *Scarcity or abundance? A debate on the environment.* New York: W. W. Norton.

Myers, Robert J. 1954. Comparison of population projections with actual data. *Proceedings of the World Population Conference, Rome, August–September, Meeting No. 13* 3:101–10; E/CONF.13/415. New York: United Nations.

Myrberg, P. J. 1962. Sur l'itération des polynomes réels quadratiques. *Journal de Mathématiques Pures et Appliqués,* Series 9, 41:339–51.

National Academy of Sciences (Office of the Foreign Secretary). 1971. *Rapid population growth: Consequences and policy implications.* 2 vols. Baltimore: Johns Hopkins Press.

National Research Council. 1986. *Population growth and economic development: Policy questions.* Working Group on Population Growth and Economic Development. Committee on Population. Commission on Behavioral and Social Sciences and Education. Washington, D.C.: National Academy Press.

Nerlove, Marc. Assaf Razin and Efraim Sadka. 1987. *Household and economy: Welfare economics of endogenous fertility.* Boston: Academic Press.

New York State Department of Health. 1993. *Health advisories: Chemicals in sportfish and game, 1993–1994.* Albany, New York: Center for Environmental Health, Department of Health, State of New York.

Nordhaus, William D. 1973. World dynamics: Measurement without data. *Economic Journal* 83, no. 332 (December):1156–83. Cowles Foundation Paper No. 399, Yale University, 1974.

————. 1993. Lethal model 2: The limits to growth revisited. Brookings Papers on Economic Activity 2, 1992. Cowles Foundation Paper no. 831. New Haven: Cowles Foundation for Research in Economics at Yale University.

Norse, David. 1992. A new strategy for feeding a crowded planet. *Environment* 34, no. 5:6–39.

Nour, M. A. 1989. Food security and nutrition in the Arab world. In *Completing the food chain,* ed. P. M. Hirschoff and N. G. Kotler. Washington, D.C.: Smithsonian Institution Press, pp. 44–53.

Odum, Eugene P. 1971. *Fundamentals of ecology.* 3d ed. Philadelphia: W. B. Saunders.

Office for Population Censuses and Surveys. 1993. Final mid-1991 population estimates for England and Wales and constituent local and health authorities, based on 1991 census results. OPCS Monitor, PP1 93/1. London.

Olson, Mancur, Jr. 1965. *The logic of collective action: Public goods and the theory of groups.* Cambridge: Harvard University Press.

Omran, Abdel R. 1992. *Family planning in the legacy of Islam.* London/New York: Routledge.

O'Neill, John. 1993. Future generations: Present harms. *Philosophy* 68, no. 263:35–52.

Organisation for Economic Co-operation and Development. 1991. *Environmental indicators.* Paris: OECD.

Orwell, George. 1968. *Collected essays, journalism and letters,* ed. Sonia Orwell and Ian Angus. New York: Harcourt, Brace and World, 4 vols.

Parliament of the Commonwealth of Australia. 1994. *Australia's Population 'Carrying Capacity': One Nation—Two Ecologies.* Canberra: Australian Government Publishing Service.

Parry, Martin. 1990. *Climate change and world agriculture.* London: Earthscan (with IIASA and UNEP).

Parsons, Jack. 1971. *Population versus liberty.* London: Pemberton Books.

Passell, Peter. 1994. Controlling world population growth: Where to put the money. *New York Times* (21 April), p. D2.

Passmore, R. 1962. Estimation of food requirements. *Journal of the Royal Statistical Society Series A* 125, no. 3:387–98.

Pearce, David W., and R. Kerry Turner. 1990. *Economics of natural resources and the environment.* Baltimore: Johns Hopkins University Press.

Pearce, David W., and Jeremy J. Warford. 1993. *World without end: Economics, environment, and sustainable development.* New York: Oxford University Press; published for the World Bank.

Pearl, Raymond. 1924. *Studies in human biology.* Baltimore: Williams and Wilkins.

Pearl, Raymond, and Sophia Gould. 1936. World population growth. *Human Biology* 8, no. 3:399–419.

Pearl, Raymond, and Lowell J. Reed. 1920. On the rate of growth of the population of the United States since 1790 and its mathematical representation. *Proceedings of the National Academy of Sciences* 6 (June):275–88.

Pearl, Raymond, and Lowell J. Reed. 1924. The growth of human population. In *Studies in human biology,* ed. Raymond Pearl. Baltimore: Williams and Wilkins, pp. 584–637.

Pearson, Frank A., and Floyd A. Harper. 1945. *The world's hunger.* Ithaca, N.Y.: Cornell University Press.

Penck, Albrecht. 1925. Das Hauptproblem der physischen Anthropogeographie. *Zeitschrift für Geopolitik* 2:330–48. (Reprinted from *Sitzungsberichte der Preußischen Akademie der Wissenschaften* 22:242–57, 1924.)

———. 1941. Die Tragfähigkeit der Erde. In *Lebensraumfragen europäischer Völker,* ed. K. H. Dietzel, O. Schmieder and H. Schmitthenner. Band I: Europa. Leipzig: Verlag von Quelle & Meyer, pp. 10–32.

Penning de Vries, F. W. T., D. M. Jansen, H. F. M. Ten Berge and A. Bakema. 1989. *Simulation of ecophysiological processes of growth in several annual crops.* Wageningen, Netherlands: Pudoc. 271 pp.

Pennycuick, C. J. 1988. *Conversion factors: SI units and many others.* Chicago: University of Chicago Press.

Perrings, C. 1987. *Economy and environment.* New York: Cambridge University Press.

Petersen, William. 1979. *Malthus.* Cambridge: Harvard University Press.

Pfaundler, L. 1902. Die Weltwirtschaft im Lichte der Physik. *Deutsche Revue* 22, no. 2:29–38, 171–82.

Pickering and Chatto. 1992. Science, Catalogue 696. Pickering and Chatto (rare-book sellers), 17 Pall Mall, London, U.K.

Pimentel, David, and Marcia Pimentel. 1991. Land, energy and water: The constraints governing ideal U.S. population size. *Focus: Carrying Capacity Selections* 1, no. 1 (spring):9–14.

Pimentel, David, Rebecca Harman, Matthew Pacenza, Jason Pecarsky and Marcia Pimentel. 1994. Natural resources and an optimum human population. *Population and Environment: A Journal of Interdisciplinary Studies* 15, no. 5 (May):347–69.

Pimm, Stuart L. 1991. *The balance of nature? Ecological issues in the conservation of species and communities.* Chicago: University of Chicago Press.

Piotrow, Phyllis T. 1973. *World population crisis: The United States response.* Foreword by George H. Bush, Jr. New York: Praeger.

Pomeroy, Lawrence R. 1992. The microbial food web. *Oceanus* 35, no. 3:28–35.

———, ed. 1974. *Cycles of essential elements.* Benchmark Papers in Ecology. Stroudsburg, Penn.: Dowden, Hutchinson and Ross.

Popline. 1992. Catholics polled on birth control. *Popline,* November–December: 1.

Population Council. 1994. *Population growth and our caring capacity.* Population Council Issues Papers. New York: Population Council.

Population Reference Bureau. 1990–94. *World population data sheet* (annual). Washington, D.C.: Population Reference Bureau.

Postel, Sandra. 1992. *Last oasis: Facing water scarcity.* New York: W. W. Norton.

———. 1994. Carrying capacity: Earth's bottom line. In *State of the world 1994,* ed. Lester R. Brown et al. New York: W. W. Norton, pp. 3–21.

Potter, Sulamith H., and Jack M. Potter. 1990. *China's peasants: The anthropology of a revolution.* Cambridge, U.K.: Cambridge University Press.

Press, Frank, and Raymond Siever. 1986. *Earth.* 4th ed. New York: W. H. Freeman.

Pressat, R. 1970. *Population.* London: C. A. Watts; Baltimore: Penguin.

Pritchett, Lant H. 1994. Desired fertility and the impact of population policies. *Population and Development Review* 20, no. 1 (March): 1–55.

Pryor, F. L., and S. B. Maurer. 1982. On induced economic change in precapitalist societies. *Journal of Development Economics* 10:325–53.

Pulliam, H. Ronald, and Nick M. Haddad. 1994. Human population growth and the carrying capacity concept. *Bulletin of the Ecological Society of America* 75 (September):141–57.

Putnam, Robert D. 1993. The prosperous community: Social capital and public life. *The American Prospect* 13 (spring):35–42.

Qutub, Syed Ayub. 1993. Pakistan on collision course. *People and the Planet* 2, no. 2:24–25 (UNFPA, IPPF, IUCN, London).

Randers, Jørgen, and Donella Meadows. 1972. The carrying capacity of the globe. *Sloan Management Review* 15, no. 2 (winter):11–17.

Raup, David M. 1991. *Extinction: Bad genes or bad luck?* New York: W. W. Norton.

Rausky, F. 1983. Malthusianism and the secularization of Jewish thought: Towards an historical psychology of the religious mentality. In *Malthus past and present,* ed. J. Dupâquier, A. Fauve-Chamoux and E. Grebenik. London / New York: Academic Press, pp. 183–93.

Raven, Peter H. 1991. Winners and losers in the twentieth-century struggle to survive. In *Resources, environment, and population: Present knowledge, future options,* ed. Kingsley Davis and Mikhail S. Bernstam. New York: Oxford University Press. Supplement to vol. 16, 1990, of *Population and Development Review,* pp. 259–67.

———. 1994. Defining biodiversity. *Nature Conservancy* 44, no. 1 (January / February): 11–15.

Ravenstein, E. G. 1891. Lands of the globe still available for European settlement. *Proceedings of the Royal Geographical Society* 13:27–35.

Ray, Dixie Lee. 1992. Are the global threats real? Scientific facts vs. environmental myths. *Priorities,* spring: 6–10.

Reddaway, W. B. 1939. *The economics of a declining population.* London: George Allen and Unwin.

Reed, Lowell J. 1936. Population growth and forecasts. *Annals of the American Academy of Political and Social Science,* November: 159–66.

Reining, P., and I. Tinker, eds. 1975. *Population: Dynamics, ethics and policy.* Washington, D.C.: American Association for the Advancement of Science.

Repetto, Robert. 1986. *World enough and time: Successful strategies for resource management.* New Haven: Yale University Press.

———, ed. 1985. *The global possible: Resources, development, and the new century.* New Haven: Yale University Press.

Repetto, Robert, William Magrath, Michael Wells, Christine Beer and Fabrizio Rossini. 1989. *Wasting assets: Natural resources in the national income accounts.* Washington, D.C.: World Resources Institute.

Revelle, Roger. 1974. Food and population. *Scientific American* 231 (September): 161–70.

———. 1976. The resources available for agriculture. *Scientific American* 235, no. 3 (September): 165–78.

Revelle, Roger, and Rose Frisch. 1967. Distribution of food supplies by level of income. In *The world food problem,* Report of the Panel on the World Food Supply, vol. III. A Report of the President's Science Advisory Committee, the White House, September 1967, pp. 43–54. Contribution No. 35. Cambridge: Center for Population Studies, Harvard University.

Revelle, Roger, N. C. Brady, A. L. Brown, R. M. Hagan, A. C. Orvedal, D. F. Peterson, M. B. Russell, W. Thorne and J. van Schilfgaarde. 1967. Water and land. In *The world food problem,* Report of the Panel on the World Food Supply, vol. II. A Report of the President's Science Advisory Committee, the White House, May 1967, pp. 405–69. Contribution No. 32. Cambridge: Center for Population Studies, Harvard University.

Revkin, Andrew. 1992. *Global warming: Understanding the forecast.* New York: Abbeville Press.

Ricklefs, Robert E. 1990. *Ecology.* 3d ed. New York: W. H. Freeman.

Robey, Bryant, Shea O. Rutstein and Leo Morris. 1993. The fertility decline in developing countries. *Scientific American,* December: 60–67.

Robinson, Warren C. 1992. Kenya enters the fertility transition. *Population Studies* 46:445–57.

Rogers, Alan R., and Henry Harpending. 1993. Population growth makes waves in the distribution of pairwise genetic differences. *Molecular Biology and Evolution* 9, no. 1 (1 May): 552.

Rogers, Andrei. 1968. *Matrix analysis of interregional population growth and distribution.* Berkeley: University of California Press.

Rogers, Peter P. 1985. Fresh water. In *The global possible: Resources, development, and the new century,* ed. Robert Repetto. New Haven: Yale University Press, pp. 255–98.

Romm, Joseph J. 1993. *Defining national security: The nonmilitary aspects.* New York: Council on Foreign Relations Press.

Roux, Georges. 1964. *Ancient Iraq.* London: George Allen and Unwin; Cleveland / New York: World Publishing.

Rowley, John. 1993. Beyond the butterfly. *People and the Planet* special issue on "Wildlife and people" 2, no. 3:3.

Royal Society of London and the United States National Academy of Sciences. 1992. Population growth, resource consumption, and a sustainable world. Statement released Thursday, 27 February 1992, published in *Science* 255 (13 March): 1358.

Rubin-Kurtzman, Jane R., Roberto Ham-Chande, Maurice D. Van Arsdol and Qian Wei Wang. 1993. Demographic and economic interactions in trans-border cities: The southern California–Baja California urban system. Annual meeting of the Population Association of America, Cincinnati, Ohio, 1–4 April.

Saether, Arild. 1993. Otto Diederich Lütken—40 years before Malthus? *Population Studies* 47, no. 3:511–517.

Sander, William. 1992. Catholicism and the economics of fertility. *Population Studies* 46:477–89.

Sanderson, Warren C. 1980. Economic-demographic simulation models: A review of their usefulness for policy analysis. *IIASA Reports* 1, no. 2:433–542, Research Report RR-80-14, May.

———. 1995. Predictability, complexity, and catastrophe in a collapsible model of population, development, and environmental interactions. *Mathematical Population Studies* 5, no. 2: in press.

Santow, Gigi. 1993. *Coitus interruptus* in the twentieth century. *Population and Development Review* 19:767–92.

———. 1995. *Coitus interruptus* and the control of natural fertility. *Population Studies* 49, no. 1: 19–43.

Sauer, C. O. 1969. *Agricultural origins and dispersals: The domestication of animals and foodstuffs.* 2d ed. Cambridge: MIT Press.

Sayles, Fred L. 1992. Biogeochemical processes on the seafloor. *Oceanus* 35, no. 1 (spring): 68–75.

Scarborough, Vernon L. 1992. Flow of power: Water reservoirs controlled the rise and fall of the ancient Maya. *The Sciences (New York Academy of Science)* 31, no. 2 (March / April): 38–43.

Schell, Jozef St. 1993. Plant biotechnology: A powerful tool to use plant resources and to improve the environmental impact of agriculture. *AvH-Magazin* (Alexander von Humboldt Stiftung Mitteilungen) 61 (July): 9–16.

Schelling, Thomas C. 1978. *Micromotives and macrobehavior.* New York: W. W. Norton.

Schick, Kathy D., and Nicholas Toth. 1993. *Making silent stones speak: Human evolution and the dawn of technology.* New York: Simon and Schuster.

Schindler, D. W. 1977. Evolution of phosphorus limitation in lakes. *Science* 195:260–62.

Schlesinger, William H. 1991. *Biogeochemistry: An analysis of global change.* San Diego / London: Academic Press.

Schmitt, Walter R. 1965. The planetary food potential. *Annals of the New York Academy of Sciences* 118, no. 17:645–718.

Schneider, S. H. 1989. *Global warming: Are we entering the greenhouse century?* San Francisco: Sierra Club Books.

Science Summit. 1994. *Population summit of the world's scientific academies.* Washington, D.C.: National Academy of Sciences. Reprinted in *Population and Development Review* 20, no. 1:233–38.

Scott, Keith. 1994. Population issue must be faced. *Canberra Times,* Australia (7 May), p. 7.

Seckler, David. 1994. Trends in world food needs: Toward zero growth in the 21st century. Arlington, Va.: Winrock International Institute for Agricultural Development, Center for Economic Policy Studies Discussion Paper No. 18.

Sen, Amartya. 1992. *Inequality reexamined.* Cambridge: Harvard University Press.

Serrin, James. 1975. Is "doomsday" on target? *Science* 189:86–88.

Shoumatoff, Alex. 1985. *The mountain of names: A history of the human family.* New York: Simon and Schuster.

Shrader-Frechette, Kristin. 1985. Environmental ethics and global imperatives. In *The global possible: Resources, development, and the new century,* ed. Robert Repetto. New Haven: Yale University Press, pp. 97–127.

Shryock, Henry S., Jr. 1954. Accuracy of population projections for the United States. *Estadística, Journal of the Inter-American Statistical Institute* 12, no. 45 (December): 587–98.

Simon, Julian L. 1990. *Population matters: People, resources, environment, and immigration.* New Brunswick, N.J. / London: Transaction.

Simon, Julian L., and Herman Kahn, eds. 1984. *The resourceful Earth: A response to global 2000.* Oxford: Basil Blackwell.

Simons, Marlise. 1992. Winds sweep African soil to feed lands far away. *New York Times* (29 October), pp. A1, A16.

Singer, Peter. 1981. *The expanding circle: Ethics and sociobiology.* New York: Farrar, Straus and Giroux.

Singer, S. Fred, ed. 1971. *Is there an optimum level of population?* New York: McGraw-Hill.

Skinner, B. J. 1969. *Earth resources.* Englewood Cliffs, N.J.: Prentice-Hall.

Slesser, Malcolm, and Janet King. 1988. Resource accounting: An application to development planning. *World Development* 16, no. 2:293–303.

Smil, Vaclav. 1987. *Energy, food, environment: Realities, myths, options.* Oxford: Clarendon Press.

———. 1991. Population growth and nitrogen: An exploration of a critical existential link. *Population and Development Review* 17, no. 4:569–601.

———. 1994. How many people can the Earth feed? *Population and Development Review* 20, no. 2 (June): 255–92.

Smith, Adam. 1759. *The theory of moral sentiments,* ed. D. D. Raphael and A. L. Macfie. New York: Oxford University Press, 1976; reprint, Indianapolis: Liberty Press, 1982.

———. 1776 (1937). *An inquiry into the nature and causes of the wealth of nations.* New York: Modern Library.

Smith, Bruce D. 1991. Harvest of prehistory: Ancient seeds yield insight into early American agriculture. *The Sciences (New York Academy of Sciences)* 31, no. 3 (May / June): 30–35.

Smith, David, and Nathan Keyfitz. 1977. *Mathematical demography: Selected papers.* Berlin / Heidelberg / New York: Springer-Verlag.

Smith, V. Kerry. 1993. *Valuing natural assets: The economics of natural resource damage assessment.* Washington, D.C.: Resources for the Future.

Smith, V. L. 1975. The primitive hunter culture, Pleistocene extinction, and the rise of agriculture. *Journal of Political Economy* 83, no. 4:727–55.

Smith, Warren D. 1935. World population. *Scientific Monthly (U.S.A.)* 40, no. 1 (January):33–43.

Song, J. 1982. Some developments in mathematical demography and their application to the People's Republic of China. *Theoretical Population Biology* 22, no. 3 (December):382–91.

Song, J., and J. Yu. 1985. *Population control.* Beijing: Science Publishers.

———. 1988. *Population system control.* Beijing: China Academic Publishers; Berlin / Heidelberg: Springer-Verlag.

Sorenson, Philip E. 1971. Optimum population and economic externalities. In *Population, environment and people,* ed. Noël Hinrichs. New York: McGraw-Hill, pp. 113–21.

Spears, John, and Edward S. Ayensu. 1985. Fresh water. In *The global possible: Resources, development, and the new century,* ed. Robert Repetto. New Haven: Yale University Press, pp. 299–335.

Spengler, Joseph J. 1949. The world's hunger—Malthus, 1948. *Proceedings of the Academy of Political Science* 23, no. 2:149–67.

———. 1968. Optimum population theory. In *International Encyclopedia of the Social Sciences* 12:358–62. New York: Macmillan and Free Press.

Srinivasan, T. N. 1987. Population and food. In *Population growth and economic development: Issues and evidence,* ed. D. Gale Johnson and Ronald Demos Lee. Madison: University of Wisconsin Press, pp. 3–26.

Steshenko, Valentina. 1993. Population crisis in Ukraine: Contemporary situation and prospects. Paper presented at the General Population Conference, IUSSP, Montreal, Canada, 24 August–1 September.

Stevens, W. K. 1992. Estimates of warming gain more precision and warn of disaster. *New York Times* (15 December), pp. C1–C9.

Straffin, Philip D. 1993. *Game theory and strategy.* Washington, D.C.: Mathematical Association of America.

Süssmilch, Johann Peter. 1741. *Die göttliche Ordnung in den Veränderungen des menschlichen Geschlechts, aus der Geburt, Tod und Fortpflanzung desselben. . . . Nebst einer Vorrede Herrn Christian Wolffens. (The divine order in the changes of the human species, from the birth, death and reproduction thereof. . . . With a foreword by Mr. Christian Wolff.)* Berlin: J. C. Spener.

———. 1765. *Die göttliche Ordnung in den Veränderungen des menschlichen Geschlechts, aus der Geburt, dem Tode und der Fortpflanzung desselben. Erster Theil, Dritte verbesserte Ausgabe.* (The divine order in the changes of the human species, from the birth, death and reproduction thereof. Part one, third improved edition.) Berlin: Verlag der Buchhandlung der Realschule.

Swan, Patricia B. 1983. Food consumption by individuals in the United States: Two major surveys. *Annual Review of Nutrition* 3:413–32.

Tan, Poo Chang, and Nai Peng Tey. 1994. Do fertility intentions predict subsequent behavior? Evidence from peninsular Malaysia. *Studies in Family Planning* 25, no. 4 (July–August):222–31.

Taylor, L. R., ed. 1970. *The optimum population for Britain: Proceedings of a symposium held at the Royal Geographical Society, London, on 25 and 26 September 1969.* London / New York: Academic Press.

Teitelbaum, Michael S., and Jay M. Winter. 1985. *The fear of population decline.* Orlando, Fla.: Academic Press.

———, eds. 1988. *Population and resources in Western intellectual traditions.* Supplement to vol. 14 (winter) of *Population and Development Review.*

Thomas, Hugh. 1985. The historical context. In *The global possible: Resources, development, and the new century,* ed. Robert Repetto. New Haven: Yale University Press, pp. 33–46.

Thomas, Neil. 1991. Land, fertility, and the population establishment. *Population Studies* 45:379–97.

———. 1992. Review of Norman Myers's *Population, resources and the environment: The critical challenges. Population Studies* 46, no. 3:559–60.

———. 1993. Economic security, culture and fertility: A reply to Cleland. *Population Studies* 47:353–59.

Thurow, Lester C. 1986. Why the ultimate size of the world's population doesn't matter. *Technology Review,* August / September: 22, 29.

Törnqvist, Leo. 1967. The post-war population development of Finland compared with predictions made after the war. Vol. 3 of *Proceedings of the World Population Conference, August–September 1965, Belgrade.* New York: United Nations, Department of Economic and Social Affairs, pp. 44–46.

Torrey, Barbara Boyle, Kevin Kinsella and Cynthia M. Taeuber. 1987. *An aging world.* Washington, D.C.: United States Bureau of the Census, International Population Reports Series P-95, no. 78.

Trivers, Robert. 1985. *Social evolution.* Menlo Park, Calif.: Benjamin / Cummings.

Tuchman, Barbara. 1978. *A distant mirror: The calamitous 14th century.* New York: Alfred A. Knopf.

Tuckwell, Henry C., and James A. Koziol. 1992. World population. *Nature* 359 (17 September): 200.

Turner, B. L., W. C. Clark, R. W. Kates, J. F. Richards, J. T. Mathews and W. B. Meyer, eds. 1990. *The Earth as transformed by human action: Global and regional changes in the biosphere over the past 300 years.* Cambridge, U.K.: Cambridge University Press with Clark University.

Umpleby, Stuart A. 1990. The scientific revolution in demography. *Population and Environment* 11, no. 3:159–74.

United Nations. 1953. *The determinants and consequences of population trends.* New York: United Nations; ST / SOA / Ser. A / 17.

————. Department of Economic and Social Affairs. 1980. Some issues arising from interrelations between resources, environment, population and development. In *Resources, environment, population and development*. New York: United Nations Publications, pp. 47–57. Reprinted in Ghosh 1984.

————. 1987. *Fertility behaviour in the context of development: Evidence from the World Fertility Survey*. New York: United Nations; Population Studies, no. 100; ST / ESA / SER.A / 100.

————. Department of International Economic and Social Affairs, and World Health Organization, Global Program on AIDS (UN / WHO). 1991a. *The AIDS epidemic and its demographic consequences*. New York: United Nations, ST / ESA / SER.A / 119.

————. Department of International Economic and Social Affairs. 1991b. *World population prospects 1990*. New York: United Nations, ST / ESA / SER.A / 120.

————. Department of International Economic and Social Affairs. 1992a. *Long-range world population projections: Two centuries of population growth, 1950–2150*. New York: United Nations, ST / ESA / SER.A / 125.

————. Department of International Economic and Social Affairs. 1992b. *Demographic yearbook 1990*. 42d ed. New York: United Nations, ST / ESA / STAT / SER.R / 20.

————. Department of International Economic and Social Affairs. 1992c. *World population monitoring 1991, with special emphasis on age structure*. New York: United Nations, ST / ESA / SER.A / 126.

————. Department for Economic and Social Information and Policy Analysis. 1993. *World population prospects: The 1992 revision*. New York: United Nations, ST / ESA / SER.A / 135.

————. Department for Economic and Social Information and Policy Analysis. 1994. *AIDS and the demography of Africa*. New York: United Nations, ST / ESA / SER.A / 137.

United Nations Development Program. 1992. *Human development report 1992*. New York / Oxford: Oxford University Press.

United Nations Fund for Population Activities. 1993a. *Population issues: Briefing kit 1993*. New York: United Nations Fund for Population Activities.

————. 1993b. *Population growth and economic development: Report on the consultative meeting of economists convened by the United Nations Population Fund, 28–29 September 1992, New York*. New York: United Populations Fund.

United Nations International Conference on Population and Development. 1994. *Programme of Action of the United Nations International Conference on Population and Development*, September 19.

United Nations Population Division. 1992. *Population newsletter*, December. New York: United Nations, Department of Economic and Social Development.

United States Bureau of the Census. 1974. *Statistical abstract of the United States: 1974*. 95th ed. Washington, D.C.: United States Government Printing Office.

————. 1991. *Global aging*. Washington, D.C.: Department of Commerce, Economics and Statistics Administration.

————. 1992. *An aging world II*, by Kevin Kinsella and Cynthia M. Taeuber. Washington, D.C.: United States Government Printing Office, International Population Reports, P25, 92–3.

United States Department of Agriculture. 1981. Will there be enough food? In *1981 yearbook of agriculture*.

van de Walle, Etienne. 1975. Foundations of the model of doom. Book review of *Dynamics of growth in a finite world*, by Dennis L. Meadows et al. (1974). *Science* 189:1077–78.

————. 1983. Malthus today. In *Malthus past and present*, ed. J. Dupâquier, A. Fauve-Chamoux and E. Grebenik. London / New York: Academic Press, pp. 233–45.

————. 1992. Fertility transition, conscious choice, and numeracy. *Demography* 29, no. 4 (November): 487–502.

van de Walle, Etienne, and John Knodel. 1980. Europe's fertility transition: New evidence and lessons for today's developing world. *Population Bulletin* 34, no. 6:1–43.

Vogely, William A. 1985. Nonfuel minerals and the world economy. In *The global possible: Resources, development, and the new century*, ed. Robert Repetto. New Haven: Yale University Press, pp. 457–73.

von Foerster, Heinz, Patricia M. Mora and Lawrence W. Amiot. 1960. Doomsday: Friday, 13 November, A.D. 2026. *Science* 132 (4 November): 1291–95.

————. 1961. Doomsday. *Science* 133 (24 March): 936–46 and 133 (16 June): 1931–37.

————. 1962. "Projections" versus "forecasts" in human population studies. *Science* 136 (13 April): 173–74.

Waggoner, Paul E. 1994. *How much land can ten billion people spare for nature?* Ames, Iowa: Council for Agricultural Science and Technology, Task Force Report No. 121, February.

Watt, B. K., and A. L. Merrill. 1963. *Composition of foods: Raw, processed, prepared.* Washington, D.C.: United States Department of Agriculture, Agriculture Handbook 8.

Way, Peter O., and Karen A. Stanecki. 1994. Special chapter on HIV / AIDS. In *World population profile: 1994.* United States Bureau of the Census, Report WP / 94. Washington, D.C.: United States Government Printing Office.

Weaver, Kenneth F. 1981. *Our energy predicament: America's thirst for imported oil.* Washington, D.C.: National Geographic Society, Special Report.

Weiner, Myron. 1992. The moral implications of international population movements. *Bulletin of the American Academy of Arts and Sciences* 46, no. 3 (December): 7–16.

Weiss, H., M.-A. Courty, W. Wetterstrom, F. Guichard, L. Senior, R. Meadow and A. Curnow. 1993. The genesis and collapse of third millennium north Mesopotamian civilization. *Science* 261 (20 August): 995–1004.

Weller, Thomas H. 1993. Can control of infectious diseases be sustained? *Hospital Practice,* 30 October: 32–34.

Westing, Arthur H. 1981. A world in balance. *Environmental Conservation* 8, no. 3 (autumn): 177–83.

Westoff, Charles F. 1993. Reproductive preferences and future fertility in developing countries. Paper presented at the Population Association of America annual meeting, April, Cincinnati, Ohio.

————. 1994. What's the world's priority task? Finally, control population. *New York Times Magazine* (6 February), pp. 30, 32.

Wetenschappelijke Raad voor het Regeringsbeleid (Scientific Council for the Dutch Government). 1994. Duurzame risicos: een blijvend gegeven (Sustainable risks: An enduring given). Den Haag, Netherlands: Sdu Uitgeverij Plantijnstraat.

White, Gilbert F. 1984. Water resource adequacy: Illusion and reality. In *The resourceful Earth: A response to global 2000,* ed. Julian L. Simon and Herman Kahn. Oxford: Basil Blackwell, pp. 250–66.

Whitmore, Thomas M., B. L. Turner II, Douglas L. Johnson, Robert W. Kates and Thomas R. Gottschang. 1990. Long-term population change. In *The Earth as transformed by human action: Global and regional changes in the biosphere over the past 300 years,* ed. B. L. Turner, W. C. Clark, R. W. Kates, J. F. Richards, J. T. Mathews and W. B. Meyer. Cambridge, U.K.: Cambridge University Press with Clark University, pp. 25–39.

Whittaker, Robert H., and Gene E. Likens. 1975. The biosphere and man. In *Primary productivity of the biosphere.* ed. Helmut Lieth and Robert H. Whittaker. New York: Springer-Verlag, pp. 305–28.

Wickens, C. H. 1925. Australian population: Its nature and growth. *Economic Record* 1, no. 1:1–16.

Wilford, John N. 1992. Clues to food crops are found in Africa. *New York Times* (27 October), p. C2.

Wilkinson, R. G. 1992. Income distribution and life expectancy. *British Medical Journal* 304: (18 January): 165–68.

Williams, Linda B., and Basil G. Zimmer. 1990. The changing influence of religion on U.S. fertility: Evidence from Rhode Island. *Demography* 27, no. 3:475–81.

Wilson, Edward O. 1971. *The insect societies.* Cambridge: Harvard Univesity Press.

————. 1984. *Biophilia.* Cambridge: Harvard University Press.

————. 1992. *The diversity of life.* Cambridge: Harvard University Press.

————, ed. 1988. *Biodiversity.* Washington, D.C.: National Academy Press.

Wilson, Edward O., and William H. Bossert. 1971. *A primer of population biology.* Stamford, Conn.: Sinauer Associates.

Wolfe, A. B. 1927. Is there a biological law of human population growth? *Quarterly Journal of Economics* 41 (August): 557–94.

Wonnacott, Thomas H. 1992. Some ethical tensions among people, animals, and growing numbers. Paper 38.12 in the symposium "Population pressure and environment," 22nd

General Population Conference, International Union for the Scientific Study of Population, Montréal, Canada. University of Western Ontario, London, Ontario, Canada.

Woodwell, George M. 1985. On the limits of nature. In *The global possible: Resources, development, and the new century,* ed. Robert Repetto. New Haven: Yale University Press, pp. 47–65.

World Bank. 1984. *World development report 1984.* New York / Oxford: Oxford University Press.

———. 1992. *World development report 1992: Development and the environment.* New York / Oxford: Oxford University Press.

World Commission on Environment and Development. 1987. *Our common future.* New York: Oxford University Press.

World Health Organization Commission on Health and Environment. 1992. *Our planet, our health.* Geneva: World Health Organization..

World Resources Institute. 1990. *World resources 1990–91.* New York / Oxford: Oxford University Press.

———. 1992. *World resources 1992–93.* New York / Oxford: Oxford University Press.

———. 1994. *World resources 1994–95.* New York / Oxford: Oxford University Press.

Wrigley, E. A. 1969. *Population and history.* New York / Toronto: McGraw-Hill.

Wrigley, E. A., and R. S. Schofield. 1981. *The population history of England, 1541–1871.* London: Edward Arnold.

Yoder, Hatten S. 1982. Strategic minerals: A critical research need and opportunity. *Proceedings of the American Philosophical Society* 126, no. 3:229–41.

Young, H. Peyton. 1994. *Equity in theory and practice.* Princeton: Princeton University Press.

Yule, G. Udny. 1925. The growth of population and the factors which control it. *Journal of the Royal Statistical Society* 88 (January): 1–58.

Zaba, Basia. 1993. Limits of growth. Book reviews of *Living within limits: Ecology, economics, and population taboos,* by Garrett Hardin (Oxford University Press), and *Population politics: The choices that shape our future,* by Virginia Abernethy (Plenum). *Nature* 365 (30 September):401–2.

———. 1994. The demographic impact of AIDS: Some stable population simulation results. London: London School of Hygiene and Tropical Medicine, Centre for Population Studies Research papers, CPS 94-2.

Zaba, Basia, and Ian Scoones. 1994. Is carrying capacity a useful concept to apply to human populations? In *Environment and population change,* ed. Basia Zaba and John Clarke. Liège: Ordina Editions, pp. 197–219.

Zavarin, Eugene. 1991. Comment: On the medicinal value of tropical ecosystems. In *Resources, environment, and population: Present knowledge, future options,* ed. Kingsley Davis and Mikhail S. Bernstam. New York: Oxford University Press. Supplement to vol. 16, 1990, of *Population and Development Review,* pp. 252–53.

Zierhoffer, A. 1966. Luzne uwagi na temat pojemnosci ludnosciowej kuli ziemskiej na przykladzie Japonii. (Unrestricted thoughts about the global carrying capacity using the example of Japan.) *Czasopismo Geograficzne* 37:119–28.

Acknowledgments

This book contains many alleged facts and quotations from other sources. I have made strenuous efforts to check facts and quotations against sources, but surely I have made errors. In some quotations, I have altered capitalization, treated "%" as interchangeable with "percent" and have expanded some abbreviations, for example, replacing "UN" by "United Nations." Please inform me through the publisher of any error of fact or quotation (apart from minor typographical deviations like those just indicated).

My employer throughout my writing of this book has been Rockefeller University. I am very grateful for the freedom and support to think and write about the questions raised here. Much of the work for this book was done on the flank of High Point, West Shokan, New York, through the generous hospitality of Mr. and Mrs. William T. Golden. Portions of this book were written with the support of an Edward Goldberg Visiting Professorship in the Faculty of Industrial Engineering and Management of the Technion (Israel Institute of Technology), Haifa, Israel, by invitation of Dean Uriel G. Rothblum. I lectured on parts of the book as a Phi Beta Kappa Visiting Scholar, 1992–93, and as an invited guest at the American Philosophical Society, Philadelphia, 11 November 1993. I thank my patient auditors for helpful comments and questions. The original research in Appendix 6 summarized here was partially supported by U.S. National Science Foundation Grant BSR92-07293 to Rockefeller University.

I thank Gerri Lindner for preparing notes in machine-readable form and other secretarial and administrative help; John Wilson for securing many interlibrary loans through the Rockefeller University Library; Paul Demeny and H. Neil Zimmerman for permission to use the library of the Population Council, New York; the reference staff of the library of the American Museum of Natural History for assistance; Joseph Wisnovsky, my editor at W. W. Norton, for patient listening and sage advice; and Debra Makay of W. W. Norton for meticulous manuscript editing.

A number of friends devoted extraordinary amounts of time, care and thought to improving the manuscript. For valuable criticisms, suggestions and comments on parts or all of the manuscript in various drafts, I am very grateful to: Paul Bahn, Hull, England; the Honorable Danny J. Boggs, U.S. Court of Appeals; Sallie W. Chisholm, Massachusetts Institute of Technology; Ansley J. Coale, Princeton University; Audrey J. Cohen, Baruch College of the City University of New York; Peter E. de Jánosi, International Institute for Applied Systems Analysis; Faye Duchin, New York University; Malin Falkenmark, Swedish Natural Science Research Council, Stockholm; Peter H. Gleick, Pacific Institute for Studies in Development, Environment, and Security, Oakland, California; Sibyl R. Golden, Postcards Inc., New York; William T. Golden, New York; Gerhard K. Heilig, International Institute for Applied Systems Analysis; Shiro Horiuchi, Rockefeller University; Donald Lamm, W. W. Norton & Co.; Ronald D. Lee, University of California, Berkeley; Pamela LeRoy, Population Action International, Washington; Massimo Livi-Bacci, Università degli Studi di Firenze, Italy; W. Parker Mauldin, Population Council; Robert M. May, Oxford University; Lawrence A. Mayer, New York; Lawrence Pomeroy, University of Georgia; Michiko Shimoda, Towa Kagaku Co., Ltd., Hiroshima, Japan; Eric Siggia, Cornell University; Neil Thomas, University of Wales College of Cardiff; Charles Westoff, Princeton University; Rita Wright, New York University; Hatten S. Yoder, Jr., Carnegie Institution of Washington; and Basia Zaba, London School of Hygiene and Tropical Medicine.

For helpful references and documents, I thank many of the readers just listed, plus: Braden R. Allenby, AT&T; Jesse Ausubel, Rockefeller University; Leon Blaustein, Haifa University; John Bongaarts, Population Council; Thomas K. Burch, University of Western Ontario; Hal Caswell, Woods Hole Oceanographic Institution; Nazli Choucri, Massachusetts Institute of Technology; Stephen R. Coffee, Carrying Capacity Network; Laurel L. Cornell, Indiana University; Pieter D. de Jong, Research Institute for Plant Protection, Wageningen, the Netherlands; Paul Demeny, Population Council; Jared M. Diamond, University of California at Los Angeles; Klaus Dietz, Eberhard-Karls-Universität, Tübingen; Paul R. Ehrlich, Stanford University; Barbara Finberg, Carnegie Corporation of New York; Bruce W. Frost, University of Washington; Neva R. Goodwin, Tufts University; Susan Greenhalgh, Population Council; John Hajnal, London School of Economics and Political Science; Michael D. Intriligator, University of California, Los Angeles; Carole L. Jolly, Committee on Population, National Research Council; Carl Kaysen, Massachusetts Institute of Technology; John Klingenstein, Esther A. and Joseph Klingenstein Fund; Saul Kripke, Princeton University; Mack Lipkin, Jr., New York University; Marc Mangel, University of California, Davis; C. Marchetti, International Institute for Applied Systems Analysis; David Pimentel, Cornell University; the Population Reference Bureau, Washington, D.C.; Norman B. Ryder, Princeton University; Gigi Santow, Australian National University; David Seckler, Winrock International Institute for Agricultural Development; Sheldon J. Segal, Rockefeller Foundation; André Shleifer, Harvard University; Burton H. Singer, Princeton University; Åke Sjöberg, University of Pennsylvania; Robert Socolow, Princeton University; Louise A. Tilly, New School for Social Research; the Press Office of the United Kingdom Mission to the United Nations, New York; and Stephen J. Vicchio, College of Notre Dame of Maryland.

For patience during numberless soliloquies by me on the ideas and progress of this book, and for helpful comments from time to time, I thank Audrey, Zoe and Adam Cohen. For sympathy from one who has been there, I thank George Orwell, who wrote in 1946: "Writing a book is a horrible, exhausting struggle, like a long bout of some painful illness. One would never undertake such a thing if one were not driven on by some demon whom one can neither resist nor understand."

Index

Page numbers in *italics* indicate figures. Those in **boldface** refer to tables.

3 1/99